SOCIAL-STUDIES
INSTRUCTION
IN THE
ELEMENTARY
SCHOOL

SOCIAL-STUDIES INSTRUCTION IN THE ELEMENTARY SCHOOL

RICHARD E. SERVEY

San Diego State College

L B 1584

S 49

95071

CHANDLER PUBLISHING COMPANY

124 Spear Street

San Francisco, California 94105

Science Research Associates, Inc., 259 East Erie Street, Chicago, Illinois 60611   S R A

Distributors   A Subsidiary of IBM

CONTENTS

PREFACE

Social-studies instruction is both a freedom and a discipline. As a discipline, it demands that the teacher develop and use effective procedures that provide children with learnings necessary to citizenship. As a freedom, it offers a wide variety of procedures from which each teacher may select and structure his practice. The purpose of this book is to present an array of procedures from which the teacher, either neophyte or veteran, may select and build a structure of practice meaningful to him and effective with children.

The procedures offered in the book are organized under the assumption that thinking skills are the basic skills of social studies, and that the other skills associated with social studies, such as reading, map-and-globe skills, group-work skills, and the like, are supportive to thinking skills.

The first eight chapters of the book present an overview of social-studies instruction and objectives and a discussion of how teachers plan and work to select and reach objectives. The next six chapters identify the problems associated with social-studies instruction—improving investigative, expressive, and group-work skills, dealing with controversial issues, and providing for individual differences—and ways of coping with them. The final chapter of the book offers suggestions on evaluating social-studies instruction. A selective bibliography and exercises at the end of each chapter, as well as several units in the appendix of the book, serve as guides for further study and exploration.

The author acknowledges a deep indebtedness to those who prepared him for the task of writing the book: the late Mrs. Frances Grinnell, Supervisor of Fifth and Sixth Grades, Los Angeles City Schools; Dr. Robert A. Naslund, University of Southern California; Dr. Francis A. Ballantine, Dr. Peter C. Gega, and Dr. Joseph Rodney, San Diego State College. Each has provided a unique impetus leading to the writing of the book.

For permission to use excerpts from district curriculum publications, the author expresses his gratitude to the following school districts: El Paso Public Schools; Pasadena City Schools; Prince George's County Schools, Maryland; and San Diego City Schools.

Special appreciation for receptiveness to ideas and interpretation of them in a practical way goes to the classroom supervisors in the Campus Laboratory School, San Diego State College: Mrs. Pauline Givens, Mrs. Patricia Hill, Mrs. Aileen Birch, Miss Corinne Klann, Mr. Bill Moore, and Miss Jane Reel; and to Mr. Sy Finley, photographer.

The author is deeply grateful to his wife, Mrs. Bette Servey, for her help in preparing the manuscript and her constant encouragement.

SOCIAL-STUDIES
INSTRUCTION
IN THE
ELEMENTARY
SCHOOL

1

Elementary Social Studies Today

In the course of a year, any one of us may read or hear that:

A large Asiatic nation is suffering from crop failure.
An emerging nation in Africa is having difficulty establishing a stable government.
The economy of a European nation is faltering.
Management and labor cannot arrive at agreement on wages and benefits for workers.

Frequently we read or hear about actions being taken:

Our government appropriates a large sum of money for foreign aid.
A man is executed for having committed a serious crime.
Border troops fire upon each other.
A group of workers strike against their employers.
Some people demonstrate against the removal of a historic monument to provide space for a multistoried business building.

Most of us react when we hear or read about such conditions and actions. Depending upon our commitment to the people involved or to certain modes of action, we express feelings and opinions and occasionally are moved toward some sort of action. These feelings, opinions, and actions may be supported by rich funds of knowledge or deeply felt values or both.

No matter how, to what degree, or in what direction we react, our reactions are determined somewhat by our social education. From the moment of birth, each of us has been introduced informally to the ways of society and encouraged to make them individually his own. We have been taught by our parents and siblings, friends and the members of groups to which we have belonged, and those with whom we've carried on any transaction. Newspaper and magazine editors and television producers have influenced us, too. Our informal curriculum content has been restricted largely to ways of conducting ourselves before and with other persons, how we should feel toward others, and how to tell "good" persons from "bad." We have learned through imitation, suggestion, experimentation, and firmly given directions. As a result, we have certain beliefs, attitudes, and preferred patterns of action about ourselves and other individuals in our society. These color our reactions to every human condition and action that we hear or read about.

The formal aspect of social education in our society begins the moment we enter school. A certain part of the school day is devoted to social studies, in which we learn about people in other times and places, their problems, and their ways of coping with these problems. Our teachers are specialists trained to guide us in our contact with other people who exist at various distances from us—at economic, political, social, and cultural distance, as well as temporal and spatial distance. We learn through the study of the community, both as a unique place and as a replica of other communities, and through the study of information-laden sources—books, films, filmstrips, maps, charts, diagrams, pictures, and available realia. Our learning contributes richly to our reactions to the conditions in which people find themselves and to the actions of these people as they work to establish and maintain a stable government, maintain a level of economic welfare, and assure the perpetuation of a way of life.

In short, then, social education molds our behavior toward others in particular ways. The informal aspect of social education is pervasive, amenable only to slow change after harsh testing of innovations. The formal aspect of social education, much of which is contained within social-studies programs in the school, is specialized and organized. The formal aspect is much more amenable to change and is, in fact, innovation-seeking.

Our concern in this book is with social studies, particularly social studies in the American elementary school. A brief review of the innovations in social studies will serve to clarify some of the currently unresolved issues related to content, teaching methods, and desired outcomes.

Reference will be made occasionally to the *social-studies function* —the molding of children's behavior toward themselves and toward others and the actions of others, at various distances from them, through a program of study at school.

INNOVATIONS IN SOCIAL STUDIES

Innovations characterized the development of elementary education in early New England. In seventeenth-century England, very little provision was made for educating children of elementary age; in the same century in New England strong provisions were made. Reading and Bible study were the most important subjects. The term *social studies* was not used in those early days, but the social-studies function was served through Bible study. Course content was the Bible; the method of learning was through memorizing catechism, reading the Bible, and listening to preaching. The desired outcome of this religion-centered innovation was a God-fearing, moral, industrious individual whose salvation was assured.

The next innovation occurred during the early nineteenth century. The growing need for clerical workers and record keepers in commercial enterprises placed the emphasis in the elementary school on language skills and arithmetic. However, the social-studies function was served through some formal teaching of good behavior and manners and morals as school subjects. In some schools, aspects of physical geography were taught, perhaps more to assure the correct spelling of far-off places and a better understanding of shipping distance than to acquaint children with people and places miles from them. The content of the manners-and-morals curriculum was largely the graces of well-mannered, morally correct persons. Students were taught through exhortation, activities which encouraged thought about the graces, and continually evaluated practice. The desired outcome of this manners-morals-centered curriculum was a genteel, God-fearing, moral, industrious individual who could meet the public.

During the nineteenth century, a major innovation, the teaching of geography and history as a way of guiding children toward an understanding of physical environment and people, was developed and accepted as standard. By 1900 most schools included United States history, geography of the immediate region, and more extensive geography in their elementary curriculum. Study in these subjects usually did not begin before grade four or its equivalent. Instruction was tied closely to textbooks. Reading, oral recitation, and map drawing were common learning activities. The desired outcome of this history-geography-centered curriculum was a loyal American citizen, somewhat knowledgeable in the history of his nation, in his geographical environment, and in the geographical wonders across the seas.

The term *social studies* entered the professional literature toward the close of the century.

The first quarter of the twentieth century was marked by an individual- or child-centered innovation in the social-studies function. Attention was focused on the individual child, what he is, and how he develops. Behavioral change would be due to his commitment to his physical and social environment, a commitment reflected in his interests. Through his interests, the teacher could guide him in exploring his environment. His experience would bring him to the understandings, attitudes, and patterns of behavior necessary for his survival as an individual and for the survival of his society and mankind generally. His emerging interests would be the content of social studies; he would learn through experiences, many of them self-chosen. The outcome was to be a reasonably well-adjusted individual capable of looking out for himself and contributing to the welfare of society.

By the 1920's, *social studies* had become a commonly accepted term.

The economic depression during the 1930's appeared to engender a society-centered innovation which placed the social-studies emphasis on the need for every individual to know about social problems and how to deal with them. The problems were to be community-oriented at various levels of community—local, state, national, and international. Through the study of these problems, children would not only come to know about themselves and others, and problems due to conditions and actions of others, but would also learn the group skills necessary to action. Curriculum content would be problems; learning would come through working on problems in groups; the outcome would be an effective, contributing member of society.

THE SOCIAL-STUDIES MOSAIC

Some innovations were replaced; others remained part of the field of social studies. The religion-centered and manners-morals innovations were for the most part replaced by the geography-history innovation, which became standard. The individual- or child-centered innovation continues to vie with the geography-history-centered standard as well as the later society-centered innovation. Thus many unresolved issues exist in elementary social studies today.

The issues have been partially resolved by a fitting together of both standard elements and innovations, as reflected in most current social-studies programs. Content labels have been drawn from the geography-history standard, particularly in content listings for grades four through eight or nine. A representative set of general listings for these grades includes

Grade 4: Geography and history of the state
Grade 5: Geography and history of the nation
Grade 6: Geography and history of the hemisphere
Grade 7: World history
Grade 8: United States history
Grade 9: Global geography.

Reliance on basic textbooks and the practice of measuring learnings through gauging factual retention has also come from the geography-history standard.

From the individual- or child-centered innovation have come contributions to the way of listing content. As can be noted in the above set of listings, a "widening horizons" idea has been used as a structure of organization, that is, the nation is a wider area than the state, the hemisphere is wider than the nation, and so on. This innovation has also provided listings for the early grades:

Kindergarten: Home and school
Grade 1: Community helpers
Grade 2: Processes in the community
Grade 3: Our community.

Here the "widening horizons" suggest somewhat more clearly that the program parallels the child's ability to perceive more and more as he grows and develops.

Another contribution from the individual- or child-centered innovation has been the heavy emphasis on interesting learning activities for children, particularly in the early grades. Children are encouraged to build many different kinds of constructions, to express through many media, and to become involved with roleplaying.

Although strong support for highly structured preplanning by teachers is not part of this innovation, unit construction by teachers as a means of guiding instruction has been encouraged. However, the emphasis is on plans for activities.

The society-centered innovation has contributed an emphasis on group activity as a means of learning.

This mosaic drawn from standard elements and innovations represents the results of continuing effort by educators to make the social-studies function more effective in guiding children toward more adequate ways of reacting to the conditions and actions of others. Although teaching practices have tended to stabilize around the mosaic, it is a difficult structure to manage with any semblance of balance. Teachers may concentrate on guiding children into interesting activities to the detriment of any substantive learning, or involve the children in so much factual learning that interest in social studies is lost. Or teachers may guide children into so much group activity that concern for what they do as individuals is lost.

The mosaic, particularly the emphasis on geography and history, is difficult to justify. A cultural geographer's interpretation of the human use of natural resources is all but meaningless if he does not have a good working knowledge of economics, political science, and anthropology. Much the same is necessary for the historian as he interprets an era in time; he must also have a background in sociology and psychology. Why, then, should children be guided into geographical and historical studies of people without preparation from the other social sciences?

Another aspect of the mosaic difficult to justify is the nature of learning activities. On one hand, a heavy emphasis is placed on reading for information and retention of it, and on the other hand, interesting "fun" activities are emphasized. How does this combination of activities bring children to understandings, attitudes, and patterns of actions necessary for reaction to the conditions and actions of others?

Some social-studies educators find these questions so unanswerable that they would gladly scrap the mosaic for the first reasonably acceptable innovation that comes along. Others are somewhat more cautious. The mosaic does contain some useful practices, supported by knowledge of children and how they grow and learn. Teachers are reasonably secure in applying those teachable and demonstrable practices to students preparing for careers in professional education. The mosaic also contains some useful materials developed for the use of children and teachers. Some social-studies educators look more favorably upon discarding pieces of the mosaic, replacing them with others, and fitting both the old and the new pieces into a new structure.

Two innovations appear promising as sources of new elements to be fitted into the mosaic. One of these, in the making since about 1950, involves organization of social-studies content around "big ideas," that is, around the significant generalizations basic to the social-science disciplines of economics, political science, anthropology, sociology, psychology, and social psychology. Physical geography and philosophy are sometimes included as disciplines closely related in some ways to the social sciences. Cultural geography and history are frequently regarded as social sciences of descriptive synthesis, in which the "big ideas" from all the others are somewhat verifiable as seen in application. Currently teaching and learning materials are reflecting this new structure of content, which is replacing the older elements of geography and history.

The other innovation, closely related to problem solving as a means of acquiring social-studies learnings but with a different emphasis, is the introduction and wider use of "thinking" ways of learning in social studies. No fundamental agreement exists as to how to incorporate this innovation or the amount of emphasis to be given to thinking ways as a way of learning. Ideas of how to use it are many and varied; opinions about the matter of emphasis range from converting the elementary social-studies program to a program in critical thinking to placing emphasis on thinking ways only when most appropriate. This variety of ideas currently being offered and reviewed in the professional literature about thinking activities seems to indicate a new element to be given a place in the mosaic, although the place is not clear.

As far as I am concerned, the most feasible step at this moment is the rearrangement of the mosaic of elementary social-studies education. The new element to replace history and geography in the expression of content is a structure of "big ideas" or generalizations basic to the social sciences. The new element to be added is thinking activity as a means of learning. The precise ways in which these elements are to be placed in the mosaic will be guided by a deep concern for children as they are and as they can be, and for what teachers can do within the limitations of time, energy, and materials. The anticipated outcome of this new mosaic is children aware of their multidimensional social environment to the extent that they recognize their commitment within it and are disposed to arrive at and act upon decisions related to the commitment.

Exercises for Further Understanding

1. Consult *The Encyclopedia of Educational Research,* and the most recent yearbooks relating to elementary social studies published by the National Society for the Study of Education and the National Council for Social Studies, for definitions of social studies. Compare these definitions with the one given in this chapter. Which do you feel to be the most compatible with your beliefs and attitudes about social studies?

2. During an informal discussion session, bring up elementary social studies as a topic. Encourage the participants to arrive at a definition of social studies as based on their own experience in elementary and secondary school. Listen for a variety of responses. Try to identify areas of agreement among the participants.

3. Interview informally several elementary-school pupils from various grades to learn what these children believe social studies to be. Encourage them to discuss the subject matter and activities associated with social studies in their classroom.

4. There was a time in the United States when studies in geography, history, and civics were quite adequate to social-studies instruction. Make an estimate as to when this era existed and prepare a list of reasons for the adequacy of such a program. As you prepare your list of reasons, consider such factors as the development of communication and transportation and economic structure of the nation at the time.

5. Christ and Socrates as teachers were deeply interested in improving human behavior particularly as it is related to universal citizenship. Christ was adept at the use of the parable as an instructional device, and Socrates was a master at conducting a probing discussion. Both were very effective. One of the secrets of their effectiveness was their concern

for the learner. Try to discover this concern by reading the parable of the Good Samaritan (Luke 10: 30-37) and Book I of Plato's *Republic*.

Consider briefly the communicative aspect of the parable as used by Christ and the discussion as conducted by Socrates. How does each prompt inquiry? Do they both have current applications? Why or why not?

Selected References

Cartwright, William, "The Future of the Social Studies." *Social Education,* 30:79-82 (February 1966).

Dunfee, Maxine, and Helen Sagl, *Social Studies through Problem Solving,* Chap. 1, "Exploring Foundations of Social Studies." New York: Holt, Rinehart and Winston, Inc., 1966.

Educational Policies Commission, *The Central Purpose of American Education.* Washington, D.C.: National Education Association, 1961.

Foshay, Arthur W., "A Modest Proposal." *Educational Leadership,* 18:506-516, (May 1961).

Fiorino, John A., "Why Social Studies." *Elementary School Journal,* 66:229-233, (February 1966).

Gross, Richard E., and William V. Badger, "Social Studies." *Encyclopedia of Educational Research,* 3d ed. New York: The Macmillan Company, 1960.

Hanna, Lavone A., Gladys L. Potter, and Neva Hagaman, *Unit Teaching in the Elementary School,* Chap. 1, "The Relationship of Social Change to Unit Teaching." Rinehart and Company, Inc., 1955.

Hill, Wilhelmina, *Social Studies in the Elementary School Program.* U.S. Office of Education, Washington, D.C.: Government Printing Office, 1960.

Joyce, Bruce R., *Strategies for Elementary Social Science Education,* Chap. 1, "The Purpose of Social Science Education." Chicago: Science Research Associates, Inc., 1965.

Miehl, Alice, and Peggy Brogan, *More Than Social Studies,* Chap. 1, "The Discipline of Democracy;" Chap. 2, "Social Learning in a Democracy;" and Chap. 3, "Democratic Socialization in Childhood." Englewood Cliffs, N.J.: Prentice-Hall, Inc., 1957.

Muessig, Raymond, "The 'Why' of Social Studies, or the Story of the Wise Young Owl." *Social Studies,* 50:44-49 (February 1959).

Preston, Ralph C. "The Social Studies: Nature, Purpose, and Signs of Change." *National Elementary Principal,* 42:8-13 (April 1963).

Sowards, G. Wesley, and Mary-Margaret Scobey, *The Changing Curriculum and the Elementary Teacher,* Chap. 7, "General Curriculum Patterns: Designing the Curriculum;" and Chap. 13, "Exploring the Social Environment." Belmont, Calif.: Wadsworth Publishing Company, 1961.

Zinsmaster, Wanna, "Man Stands Confronted: An Approach to Teaching Social Studies." *Social Studies,* 57:117-124 (March 1966).

2

Elementary Social-Studies
Objectives

In the previous chapter, elementary social studies was identified as the formal aspect of social education, serving two closely related purposes: (1) to guide children toward understandings about people at various distances from them, the conditions in which people find themselves, and the ways used to cope with problems; and (2) to guide children in developing ways of reacting to people, conditions, and actions to assure the survival and growth of themselves as individuals, of their society, and of the total society of man. As a social-studies teacher works with children to accomplish these purposes, he contributes toward the basic objective of social studies, that is, the development of the citizen now living and likely to continue living in the American democratic society.

Implicit within the term *citizen,* as used here, is a definition of the individual who recognizes and acts upon his responsibility to himself and to others, regardless of their social, economic, political, or cultural distance from him. The inclusion of the word *citizen* within the basic objective serves to pinpoint the complexity of social studies. One way to deal with the complex basic objective is to subject it to close scrutiny to determine what it involves. The results of such scrutiny are expressed in further objectives, all in some way supportive of the basic objective. These supportive objectives vary in type and function, and may be classified as eloquent objectives, delimiting objectives, and teaching objectives.

ELOQUENT OBJECTIVES

Frequently, somewhere near the beginning of a social-studies curriculum document such as a guide or a course of study, a statement of objectives appears. The statement, usually no longer than a page or two, represents a spelling out in general terms of the basic objective of social studies, that is, the development of the citizen. The statement will probably be expressed in lofty language with a rich emotional appeal. The following statement appearing in a San Diego City Schools social-studies guide is a good example:

The major goals of social studies reflect the values and ideals of American citizenship, as well as the knowledge and skills needed for successful living in a democratic society. Objectives with special significance for San Diego's program of social studies are the following:

Demonstrating loyalty to American ideals.
Appreciating our national heritage.
Showing concern for others and respect for human dignity.
Appreciating individual worth and the moral and spiritual qualities valued by our society.
Developing an appreciation of the rights and responsibilities of the individual in a democratic society.
Learning to respect the patriotic contributions of people and institutions to the American way of life.
Understanding the basic principles on which our nation was founded.
Acquiring the necessary knowledge which enables the individual to understand his relationship to the community, the state, the nation, and the world.
Learning how certain aspects of the natural environment affect man and how man in turn modifies the environment.
Developing an awareness of the basic means by which man provides for food, clothing, shelter, and other necessities.
Understanding the significance of the changing times and how the lives of people are thus affected.

Locating, reading, organizing, and summarizing content material.
Comprehending and interpreting factual materials.
Recording and reporting information.
Learning to work with others.
Communicating ideas effectively to others.
Thinking critically and creatively and solving problems in an organized fashion.
Using maps, globes, and other graphical materials to increase understandings.[1]

The above statement of objectives has two bases in eloquence. The use of such terms as *democratic society, national heritage, human dignity,* and *American way of life* evokes certain warm, positive attitudes. The other base in eloquence is the totality of the areas of concern to which the reader responds by sensing the magnitude and the seriousness of the task of the social-studies teacher. He is inspired with pride at being included in such a significant venture and with humility in facing such an awesome task. Because the objectives stated above do evoke such feelings, they may functionally be termed *eloquent objectives.*

Eloquent objectives serve little or no useful purpose for the social-studies teacher in his day-to-day, week-to-week, month-to-month teaching of social studies. However, if ever he needs to find an economical statement of the scope of his district's social-studies program—that is, what the program includes in its entirety in understandings, skills, and attitudes—a glance at the eloquent objectives will give him the desired information.

DELIMITING OBJECTIVES

A section of a social-studies guide is devoted to precise listings of the subject matter and skills that the teacher at each grade level is supposed to teach. Since the assumption of mastery is implicit in each, the listings themselves may be regarded as objectives. Functionally, they are *delimiting objectives,* for they give each teacher a set of learnings for the grade which he teaches. This specification of learnings does not expressly forbid the teacher to teach material other than what is listed, but it does strongly suggest that he cover all that is listed.

A positive way for a social-studies teacher to regard delimiting

[1]*Social Studies Grade One,* San Diego City Schools, San Diego, California, 1961, pp. 3-4. *Used by permission.*

objectives is to look upon them as decisions reached by policy-making bodies concerned about what children learn. Frequently, a straight-line relationship exists between an education law passed by a state legislature; decisions made by a state curriculum commission or committee, by a committee of administrators and teachers in a school district, and by the local board of education; and an entry in the district social-studies guide or course of study. Each body, with the exception of the local board, interprets more fully and thus makes more specific the decision reached by the previous body. The strength and wisdom of each body lends validity to the listing in the guide.

Delimiting objectives are useful to social-studies teachers in several ways. School districts attempt to implement the objectives by providing the teaching and learning materials necessary for their accomplishment. The teacher is not given the task of devising or seeking out his own materials. The delimiting objectives are articulated in such a way that children are guided into relatively new knowledge each year. One year provides background for the next. Thus the teacher is assured that children are to a certain extent ready for what is to be studied and will find it new enough to be interesting. The delimiting objectives also indicate to the teacher the areas into which he must probe more deeply to prepare himself more adequately for guiding children.

A variety of ways is used for expressing delimiting objectives. They are occasionally expressed as purposes:

Specific purposes of the unit, *Transportation in the Immediate Community*, in first and second grades are to

Increase the child's understanding and appreciation for the important part transportation plays in his life and in the functioning of his community.

Help him understand that many types of transportation and the services of many people are required to move people and materials.

Help him understand that transportation links cities and towns together.

Help him understand the necessity of rules and regulations.

Lead him to see that many people, including himself, have an obligation towards safe travel.

Build a background of knowledge of the various services rendered to his community by its transportation facilities.

Develop some beginning geographic understandings.[2]

[2]*Education for Responsible Freedom, Our American Heritage, First Grade* (Pasadena City Schools, Division of Instructional Services, Pasadena, Calif., 1963), p. 29. *Used by permission.*

The delimiting objectives may be expressed in greater detail as anticipated outcomes in terms of pupil behavior and in terms of generalizations, exemplified in the following excerpt from a social-studies guide:

ANTICIPATED OUTCOMES IN TERMS
OF PUPIL BEHAVIOR

a. **Understandings.** As a result of the activities in this unit, the pupil increasingly understands that:

(1) The earth is a large sphere on which there are land masses and water.

(2) The equator is an imaginary line around the surface of the earth halfway between the poles.

(3) Through the center of the earth there is an imaginary line called the axis which comes out at two places called poles, the North Pole and the South Pole.

(4) Areas near the equator are usually hot.

(5) Areas near the poles are usually cold.

(6) *North* always means toward the North Pole; *south* always means toward the South Pole; *up* always means away from the center of the earth; *down* means toward the center of the earth.

(7) El Paso's location in relation to the equator and to the North Pole helps determine its climate.

(8) The mild climate of El Paso makes it possible to wear lightweight clothing much of the year.

(9) Outdoor activities are enjoyed throughout the year in El Paso.

(10) The scarcity of rainfall limits growth of vegetation in El Paso.

(11) Water from the Rio Grande has been directed into farm areas.

(12) The hot dry climate of El Paso limits the production of food crops and other basic commodities.

(13) A globe is a small model of the earth and gives the truest picture of the world.

(14) A map is an enlarged flat drawing of the globe or of a part of it.

(15) Map legends and symbols tell how to read a map.

(16) Specific types of maps are used for different purposes.

(17) The rotation of the earth on its axis causes day and night.

(18) Seasons are determined by the slant of the earth's axis together with the earth's revolution around the sun.

(19) Areas near the base of mountains are warmer than those nearer the top.

(20) Winds lose their moisture when they reach the colder regions at the tops of mountains.

(21) Mountains tend to take moisture from the winds and cause the valleys beyond to be dry.

(22) Ancient beliefs about the earth were based on limited travel and super-stition.

(23) More accurate information has been brought about as a result of in-creased travel and exploration.

b. **Value patterns.** As a result of participation in this unit, the pupil increasingly appreciates:

(1) The wonders of the orderly universe.

(2) The courage and vision of men who ventured into the unknown to explore and record uncharted areas of the earth.

(3) The influence that climate and environment exert over way of life.

(4) Man's ability to adapt to and control his environment to some extent.

(5) The use of maps and globes as tools for greater comprehension of the world in which man lives.

(6) The unlimited opportunities of the present generation to add to man's knowledge of his surroundings, including space.

c. **Skills and abilities.** The skills and abilities shown herein may be summarized as facility in logical reasoning, abstract thinking, organization, discriminating judgment, creative writing and reporting, and the ability to engage profitably and purposefully in group work. Actually, a complete list of the sorts of research skills sought might well run into a half-hundred state-ments. For purpose of brevity, however, each unit is so constructed and organized that the pupil should increasingly:

(1) Read adequately with understanding and enjoyment.

(2) Analyze problems into component and meaningful parts.

(3) Develop diligence in defining and investigating problems.

(4) Utilize the library, the community, and visual resources to further the solving of problems.

(5) Become more skillful in differentiating between materials for scanning and those that require careful study.

(6) Use dictionaries, encyclopedias, magazines, newspapers, and books with facility and intelligence.

(7) Interpret maps, graphs, diagrams, and pictures.

(8) Critically evaluate sources of information as to documentation, edi-torialization, fiction, and fact.

(9) Gather and organize facts for a specific purpose.

(10) Take notes and prepare meaningful outlines and bibliographies.

(11) Learn to find and interpret and put into his own words information from various sources about the same subject.

(12) Draw conclusions from facts and ideas.

(13) Summarize and organize data.

(14) Appreciate completeness in reporting.

(15) Distinguish between fact and supposition.

(16) Make logical and intelligent oral and written reports.

(17) Learn to speak in a clear, concise, and forceful manner.

(18) Learn the advantages of illustrated presentation.

(19) Become aware of the importance of clarity in communication.

(20) Express himself clearly and concisely without antagonizing others.

(21) Work effectively and advantageously with both small and large groups.

(22) Budget his time wisely.

(23) Interpret cause-and-effect relationships in dealing with the facts of past history.

(24) Improve his ability to correlate, evaluate, and form discriminative judgment concerning what he sees, hears, and reads.

(25) Evaluate his own work and his efforts toward positive improvement.

ANTICIPATED OUTCOMES IN TERMS OF GENERALIZATIONS

a. Accurate information has enabled man to chart the earth and describe it in exact terms.

b. Climate is determined by location on the earth and by the natural features of the land.

c. Climate determines the weight of the clothing that people wear and many of their activities.

d. Man has learned to irrigate dry lands of the earth and make them productive.

e. Maps and globes picture actual places and things.

f. The movements of the earth cause night and day and bring about seasons.

g. Mountains help determine rainfall.

h. Explorations have given new and accurate information which has replaced many old superstitions and beliefs about the earth.

i. As man learns more about his surroundings, the desire for further knowledge grows.[3]

Sometimes the delimiting objectives are expressed as a theme, a problem suggestion, and related basic understandings stated as generalizations, as illustrated in the excerpt below:

Theme for the Year: Learning about Our World

Problem: How does environment (physical features, natural resources, and climate) affect man's way of living and what does he do about it?

[3]*Social Studies Guide for Teachers, Grade 4* (El Paso, Texas: El Paso Public Schools), pp. xi-xii, Items 3-5. *Used by permission.*

Basic Understandings:

People everywhere have the same basic needs—food, clothing, and shelter.

People work and use the world's resources to satisfy these basic needs.

People around the world have different ways of living due to varying kinds of climate, physical features, and natural resources.

People make adaptations to their environment and changing conditions; they may change certain aspects of their environment when desirable or necessary.

Natural resources must be used wisely and conserved for future generations.[4]

The above examples represent only a few of the ways in which delimiting objectives may be expressed. However expressed, they provide guidelines for the teacher as he works to develop teaching objectives.

TEACHING OBJECTIVES

It was pointed out previously that the delimiting objectives represent the decisions made by educational policy-making bodies to assure that children acquire needed learnings. Teaching objectives represent the decisions made by the teacher for the same purpose. Though specificity in delimiting objectives tends to increase as they pass down through the hierarchy of policy-making bodies, by far the greatest specificity of objectives occurs when the teacher converts delimiting objectives to *teaching objectives.*

To understand better this greater specificity, let us examine briefly the ways in which the social-studies teacher must think as he responds to delimiting objectives and converts them to teaching objectives. Not all teachers think alike. When they see a list of delimiting objectives, some teachers will immediately think about the intellectual abilities of the pupils they are to teach; others will consider their pupils' total experiential background and environment of first concern. Some will give first consideration to how the subject matter is to be structured, while others will think in terms of the materials available for use with children and of activities interesting to children. No brief can be made for the superiority of any one of these points of departure over any other. Where the teacher starts his thinking does not make much difference; it is important only that his thinking touch deeply in all these areas.

[4]*Social Studies—Science, Intermediate Program* (Upper Marlboro, Maryland: Board of Education of Prince George's County), p. 21. *Used by permission.*

Suppose that a teacher of fourth grade has for the first time the responsibility of converting the following objectives to teaching objectives:

The state of _____ has a unique geography.

The geography of _____ influences the life of its people economically, politically, and culturally.

The people of _____ work to maintain and improve economic, political, and cultural conditions in their state.

At some time the teacher is going to have to consider the facts and ideas that support these simple generalizations. In his thinking he will seek definitive statements that will serve as answers to the following cognitive aspects about a state's geography:

What is a state as differentiated from a city, county, or nation?

What is a state among states?

What is a state as a geographic entity?

What is a state as an economic entity?

What is a state as a political entity?

What is a state as a cultural entity?

He will seek also statements reflecting the relationship between that state and its functions, its people, and its geography as answers to the following questions about the cognitive aspects of a state:

How is a state limited by its geography?

How is the potential of a state dependent upon its geography?

How does the geography of a state link its economy with that of other states? Its political organization with that of other states? Its cultural attributes with those of other states?

How does the geography of a state influence the economic roles and economic organization of its people? The political roles and governmental organization of its people? The culture and cultural accomplishments of its people?

How does the geography of a state serve to relate its people economically, politically, and culturally with the nation and the rest of the world?

The questions above deal with objective ideas. The teacher must also give some thought to the feelings, attitudes, and values that an active, contributing member of the state community should have. These subjective ideas exist within individuals. In his thinking the teacher considers subjective, attitudinal reactions to the cognitive aspects suggested above. The questions to which he seeks answers are:

How should an individual regard his state as a geographical complex?
How should he feel about its potential and its limitations?
How should he feel about its economic organization? The choice of economic roles offered him? Its place among the other states as a contributor to the national economy? Its place as a contributor to the world economy?
How should an individual feel about the governmental structure of his state? The choice of political roles offered him? The state's political role with the rest of the states in the national government? Its governmental relations with the national government?
How should an individual feel about the level of culture generally accorded his state? About his place within its culture?
How should an individual feel about changes in the state's economy, its government, and its culture?

Another set of subjective ideas with which the teacher must concern himself is that relating to the actions which individuals may make in response to certain conditions, including the actions of others. In many ways an individual's actions are influenced by what he knows about things and how he feels about them. Thinking about the cognitive aspects and the attitudinal aspects as factors related to patterns and directions of action, the teacher tries to develop answers to the following:

What does an individual do about his use of natural resources to assure a sufficiency of them for himself and those to come after him? What does he do when he discovers a conflict between his personal interest and that of the other people in his state?
What does an individual do to maintain the economy of his state? What does he do when the economy of his state is faltering? When it is working successfully? What does he do when an act threatens the economy of his state and his own economic security? What does he do when his own economic interest runs counter to that of the other people of the state?
What does an individual do to maintain a public authority at the state level to look after the interests of the state as well as his own? What does he do when a governmental body performs an act beneficial to his interests? When it performs an act contrary to his interests?
What does an individual do to support the culture of his state? What does he do when the culture of the state is praised? When it is made the subject of jokes good or bad? What does he do when maintaining the culture of his state conflicts with what he personally wants to do?

When the teacher has completed this phase of his thinking, he has in mind an array of general possibilities for objectives to be used in teaching children about the state in which they live. He could just as well use these for a class of adults. The next phase in his thinking brings him to a consideration of the teaching objectives most appropriate for his pupils in terms of their background, needs, and abilities.

At some time, the teacher is going to have to project himself into the group-mind of a particular classroom of nine-year-olds. Although developmental psychology provides the teacher with some basic clues to the nine-year-old and his ways of thinking and behaving, it cannot provide him with all that he needs to know for an accurate projection into the group-mind of a particular classroom of nine-year-olds who have lived in a certain place under certain conditions of learning and experience for a period of time. He seeks out the necessary information by consulting the children's school records, by conversing with their former teachers, and by studying the immediate community. When he has this information in hand, he seeks answers to the following:

What idea or ideas and what feelings do my pupils have about the state as a geographical entity? As an economic entity? As a political entity? As a cultural entity? As an entity unto itself?

What idea or ideas and what feelings do they have about the geographic limitations and potential of the state and how these affect the state's economic, political, and cultural relationships with other states?

What idea or ideas and what feelings do they have about how the geography of the state affects the economic roles and organization of the people of the state? The political roles and governmental roles of the people of the state? The culture and cultural accomplishments of the people of the state?

What idea or ideas and what feelings do they have about the economic, political, and cultural relationships that obtain between them, their state, the nation as a whole, and the world?

Do they know, as individuals and members of groups, how to arrive at decisions about the use of natural resources and about maintaining and improving economic welfare, how to maintain and improve public authority, and how to support the culture and cultural accomplishments of the state?

Do they know how to act upon decisions and how to evaluate their actions?

The teacher will have to consider at some time the point in growth that his pupils have reached as students, that is, growth in independence in the ability to seek out and respond to problems, to develop designs for inquiry, to gather and process information prompted by inquiry, to synthesize facts and ideas into "big ideas" or generalizations, and to seek out applications of "big ideas." Much of the children's investigating and learning comes through contact with a reality represented in symbols. It is essential that they have the skills to interpret symbols. The teacher consults the pupils' former teachers and examines school records to seek at least partial answers to the following:

Will the children become easily involved in discussion? Can they occasionally carry on independent discussions?

Can the children develop reasonable statements to explain various sorts of conditions or phenomena? Can they develop pertinent questions to serve as guides in investigating matters at issue?

How sophisticated are the children's observation and listening skills? Can they conduct simple interviews?

How well do the children read? Can they use the usual verbal materials effectively? How well can they read pictures, cartoons, diagrams, maps, and graphs suitable to their grade level? Can they find their way in reference materials?

How well do they do in pulling facts together and arriving at supporting ideas and "big ideas"?

How willing are they to project themselves in roleplaying and creative interpretations to discover attitudes and patterns of action?

How much independent responsibility can they assume in hypothesizing, developing questions, finding the answers to questions, and relating their findings to hypotheses?

How well do they go about seeking applications of their learnings?

The children must know the skills of dealing with symbols to make contact with much of the reality which they study. It is just as essential that they know how to use symbols to express what they have learned and to present the applications they have found. For this reason, the teacher, as he works to determine teaching objectives, must look into the children's effectiveness in using various media for expression. Consulting the children's former teachers, he arrives at a limited assessment about the following:

How effective are the children in the general use of language as a means of expression? In developing oral and written reports? In creative writing?

Are they able to plan and make simple constructions?

Can they develop simple maps, charts, graphs, and cartoons for expressing ideas precisely?

How well can they use paint and clay for expressing ideas?

To a certain extent, teaching objectives are influenced by the instructional materials and devices available. It does little good to encourage children to investigate outdated or poorly prepared materials. Rigidly scheduled projectors, films, and filmstrips are sometimes next to useless. Inadequate provisions for field trips can make community studies sterile and lifeless. For these reasons, the teacher who is developing teaching objectives must consider these questions:

What teaching materials and devices are available to me? How recent and well-prepared are the materials? How available are the teaching materials and devices to me?
What can I develop myself as a means of assuring children of an understandable contact with the reality they are to study?

The preceding welter of questions has no complete answers. The teacher of elementary social studies must formulate the best answers he can based on available data in order to decide what his teaching objectives are to be. To be sure, answers to the above questions will be much more complete after he spends several weeks with his pupils, and he may delay making firm decisions until he has had such direct contact. However, this period is of greater value when seen in the light of specific teaching objectives selected beforehand; therefore, some preselection is necessary. Whatever the preselection of teaching objectives may be, it is held subject to modification after the teacher has become better acquainted with his pupils.

Let us consider briefly the situations in which two teachers find themselves. Both teachers are to have assignments in fourth grade in the same state. As specified by the state legislature and the state curriculum commission, both are to convert the same delimiting objectives (similar to those on page 18). Both have been teaching for the same number of years, and both are considered competent. At this point the similarities between the two situations end.

One teacher, Mr. Denton, works in a school located in an area which reflects many disadvantages. Occupational opportunities are restricted largely to coal mining and subsistence farming. Most of the children have never traveled beyond the area other than to the county seat some twenty miles away. There is no library in the immediate vicinity. A few homes in the area contain television sets, most have radios, and almost every family subscribes to a weekly newspaper which arrives by mail from the county seat. The school building itself, the most modern and best-kept edifice in the area, reflects austerity in the provisions made for the education of children in grades one through eight—no library, small classrooms skimpily furnished, and few instructional materials and devices.

The other teacher, Mr. Allen, works in a large school in the state capital. The school is situated in the "better" part of the city where professional people and large-business owners and managers live. Most of the children have traveled extensively throughout the state, many have at least made an extended trip across the nation and back, and a few have been to Europe. Nearly every home is equipped with television, radios, and hi-fidelity phonographs, and almost every family subscribes to the large daily newspaper and several magazines, including at least one weekly news magazine. The school building, although it does not match in any way the architectural quality of the homes surrounding it, has been made to fit into the neighborhood through careful landscaping and maintenance. It is well-equipped to provide adequately for the elementary instructional needs of children in kindergarten through grade six. It contains a library well stocked with reference materials. Each classroom is large enough to accommodate many activities other than reading, and is provided with furniture that can be moved about easily. A good supply of instructional materials and devices is available either in each classroom or in a central supply center.

Both Mr. Denton and Mr. Allen, experienced in teaching other grades, are faced for the first time with the task of converting delimiting objectives into teaching objectives in social studies for a fourth grade. Each consults the guide provided him and begins to arrive at answers to the myriad of questions necessary to the determination of teaching objectives.

After a period of thought about what his fourth-grade pupils are likely to know and what they need to know, Mr. Denton lists the following as teaching objectives:

Our community has its own particular geography.

Like our community, our state has its own geography.

Because of its geography, our community is somewhat limited in the kinds of work it can offer its people and the kinds of products that it can produce.

Like our community's geography, our state's geography somewhat limits the kinds of work its people can do and the kinds of products it can produce.

Our community is related to other parts of the state because of the kinds of products it produces.

Our community's products link us with the state, and through the state to the nation and the whole world.

People within a community work to improve its economy or seek improved conditions in another community.

Groups within a state work to improve the uses of natural resources and to attract new industries.

The improvement of our community represents cooperation with other groups working at the state level.

Our community, in spite of its difficulties, is a good place in which to live; it is worth improving.

Our state can help us to improve it.

Through group planning and work, we can make improvements.

Mr. Denton's reasons for selecting these teaching objectives are:

It is likely that my pupils regard their state as a nebulous something-or-other within which they live. It is bigger than the immediate community and bigger than the county seat. It contains these as well as some other places just like them. Although these children spent some time at community study last year, their ideas about it do not include an economic geographic unit. Therefore, I intend to guide them first into a study of the community to acquire these ideas, which will serve as a foundation for the study of the state.

My pupils' feeling about the state are almost nonexistent. They have little or no idea of what they can do to maintain or improve conditions. Therefore, it is necessary for me to guide them in seeing how they, their community, and their state are tied together in an interrelationship of responsibility and action.

I know that my objectives omit emphasis on government and culture. I have omitted them for these reasons: (1) it seems to me that many ideas about government and culture are too abstract for my pupils; (2) the children need more than anything else an understanding of economics ideas as related to geography; and (3) if I guide my children in a study of the community for foundational ideas, there will be little time for considering anything other than ideas about geography and economics.

Now we shift our attention to Mr. Allen who performs the same task. Mr. Allen's thinking about what his pupils know, feel, and know how to do is reflected in the following:

Our state is located within a geographical region having its own particular characteristics.

Our state is marked off within the region by boundary lines separating it from other states.

Our state is subdivided into other regions lying within its boundary lines.

The natural resources of each region within the state determine to a certain extent the work of the people and the goods produced.

The location of each region with respect to other regions and their characteristics determines to a certain extent the work of the people and the goods produced.

The goods and services produced in each region vary.

No region can produce all the goods and services that it needs; therefore, it is interdependent for these with other regions, other states, and other countries.

Each region, because of its geography, offers different forms of recreation.

The people in one region may depend on other regions for recreation.

Our family, our city, and our county are sources of authority within the state.

Our state as marked off within boundary lines is a political unit within which people govern themselves through elected officers to whom they give certain responsibilities.

Our state government works to solve problems which individuals or separate groups of people within the state cannot solve for themselves.

The problems which our state government works with include problems in conserving natural resources, problems in transportation, problems in education, problems in law enforcement, and problems in providing public utilities.

Our state is known throughout the nation for its scenic beauty.

Our state offers many opportunities for highly skilled workers, but it must seek opportunities for its less skilled workers.

Our state produces goods of vital importance in the support of industry in other states.

Our state government works toward the solution of problems of concern to all the people.

Each of us must do what he can to preserve our state's scenic beauty and its natural resources.

Each of us must give some thought to our future and to the future of our state.

Each of us must be concerned about our state's problems and how they are being treated.

Through individual and group action we can contribute toward the solution of problems.

Mr. Allen gives these reasons for choices of teaching objectives related to his pupils' knowledge, attitudes, and patterns and ways of action:

Most of my pupils have at least a limited sense of what is meant by "state" as a geographic and political entity. Not many class discussions devoted to pooling knowledge will be required to establish these ideas more firmly. However, these ideas will need to be enlarged upon more fully to promote a deeper understanding of *region* and *location* as factors which influence the ways that people live within the state.

I think that the most abstract area of ideas for my pupils will be governmental structure and relationships within the state. For this reason I have included among my teaching objectives an examination of the basis of authority. An election will occur during the fall, and this will be an aid in guiding the children toward a better understanding of the state as a political entity and the relationship between the people and the government.

My pupils exist within affluent circumstances. They need to develop a concern for others in less affluent circumstances and for the problems existing within the state. Since there is a likelihood that their parents are, and that they some day will be, strongly involved in the solution of these problems, they need a background in how people work to solve problems having a bearing on their general welfare.

I have not made many provisions for teaching the children about cultural interdependency within the state. This will receive emphasis in the study of the history of the state later in the year.

As can be seen in the above examples, teachers select different kinds of teaching objectives. Some of the differences are due largely to the different needs of the two groups of children. There may be some errors. Mr. Denton's pupils may know more than he thinks; Mr. Allen's pupils may not be as knowledgeable as he expects them to be. Only after a few weeks with his pupils will either teacher really know their capabilities. But at least at this point each teacher has something definite within which directions and purposes related to children's understandings, attitudes, and ways and patterns of action can be found.

Both of these teachers must now consider teaching objectives related to the skills through which the study of social studies is accomplished. The following is Mr. Denton's list of objectives as he sees them:

To encourage willingness to become involved in an open-minded discussion.
To introduce the skills involved during a group discussion to clarify and complete a group task; to encourage the application of these skills whenever practicable.
To introduce and provide practice in the skills of establishing a point about which to inquire.

To introduce and encourage the skill of staying on the point of a discussion.

To introduce the observation and listening skills necessary to develop a point in question; to provide practice in these skills whenever practicable.

To introduce and provide practice in the skills necessary to acquiring information from pictures, diagrams, charts, maps, cartoons, and printed materials.

To introduce and provide practice in the skills involved in pulling information together to establish a new point or to strengthen a point already established.

To encourage the use of introspective skills to make discoveries about attitudes and patterns of action.

To encourage the development of projective skills for the expression of within-self-discovered attitudes and patterns of behavior.

To introduce and provide practice in the skills of verifying and extending the ideas learned.

And here is Mr. Denton's rationale for the above choices:

My pupils have had very little experience with these skills. During the past year the greatest emphasis in their instruction has been in the fundamentals of reading, language expression, and arithmetic. Their social-studies instruction has been restricted for the most part to individual craft activities. I shall have to introduce the skills of social studies and plan to emphasize the thinking, observing, listening, and discussing skills.

Mr. Allen's list of teaching objectives in this area does not differ greatly from Mr. Denton's list. The basic difference lies in the teachers' assessments of what the children can do. These basic differences are apparent in the two entries taken from Mr. Allen's list:

To improve the children's ability to conduct open-ended discussions.

To improve the children's ability to use discussion to clarify and complete a group task.

A considerable difference exists between *introducing* and *improving* skills. Mr. Allen's reasons for choosing these teaching objectives are as follows:

My pupils were given a strong introduction to the thinking, observing, listening, and discussing skills in second grade. During the last year they were encouraged to use these skills as often as possible. All that I can do at this point is to guide the children toward growth in these skills as they work with increasingly complex ideas and more abstract sources of information. Helping them to learn their way through reference books will most likely receive the greatest emphasis in this area.

In this instance, the teaching areas are identical as far as the two teachers are concerned. However, the nature of the objectives are differentiated on the basis of children's needs. This difference will also be somewhat apparent in teaching objectives concerning expressive skills in social studies.

Mr. Denton's listing of teaching objectives in this area includes:

To introduce and provide practice whenever practicable in the skills of preparing and presenting oral and written reports.

To encourage the use of social-studies understandings in writing stories, plays, and poems.

To encourage the improvement of construction skills through use in expressing social-studies learning.

To introduce and provide practice whenever practicable in the skills needed for group construction.

To introduce and provide practice whenever practicable in the skills of making maps and illustrative charts.

To encourage the improvement of art skills through use in social studies for expressing learnings.

Mr. Denton presents the following reasons for choices of teaching objectives in this area:

In third grade, my pupils had considerable experience in expressing ideas in individual constructions, paintings, and clay models. Their experience in creative language has been extensive. I shall have to encourage them to make more precise use of these skills. Group construction, map making, chart making, and reporting skills will have to be introduced. As the year progresses I shall expect the children to make simple applications of these skills whenever needed.

Mr. Allen's teaching objectives in this area are little different from Mr. Denton's as can be seen in the following sampling from his list:

To improve and extend children's reporting skills.

To encourage further growth in the use of individual and group construction skills to express understandings about social studies.

Mr. Allen explains his choice of teaching objectives in this way:

My pupils have been introduced to these skills and have had many opportunities to apply them. I shall have to check individual ability in each of
the skills and do some reteaching before guiding the children toward further
sophistication. Considerable emphasis will have to be placed on reporting
skills.

As Mr. Denton and Mr. Allen have been listing these teaching
objectives, either as mental notes or on paper, they have been in some
ways limited and in some ways encouraged by their knowledge about
the quality and abundance of materials and resources available to them.

Mr. Denton's catalog of materials and resources includes:

In the classroom:
   3 wall maps (political-physical: state, nation, and world), fairly new.
   1 16-inch globe, very much outdated.
   1 set of basic social-studies textbooks, one per child.
   1 package of 100 outline maps of the state.

In the school:
   1 encyclopedia, to be shared with four other classrooms.
   1 motion-picture projector, to be shared with all the other classrooms in
      the school.
   1 filmstrip and slide projector, to be shared with half the classrooms in the
      school.
   2 trips per month by bus to various places within the immediate county.
   2 trips per year by bus to the county seat.

In the education center at the county seat:
   1 set of eight textbooks to be used with faster learners.
   3 suitable, although somewhat dated, films.
   5 suitable filmstrips.
   1 map of the county.

Personal teaching aids:
   40 automobile maps of the state and the region.
   100 photographic slides made during a recent tour of the state.
   Plans for making more photographic slides with emphasis on the capital.
   1 slide projector.
   2 hand viewers.
   50 picture postal cards showing scenes of places within the state.
   A functional skill in drawing.

The following is what Mr. Allen has available to him for instructional purposes:

In the classroom:
   5 wall maps (political-physical: state, nation, and world; physical: state
      and nation), up-to-date.
   1 project map of the state, on which the children can draw lines with chalk.
   1 16-inch globe, up-to-date.
   1 set of basic social-studies textbooks, one per child.
   1 set of supplemental textbooks, one per three children.
   1 set of eight supplemental textbooks for slower learners.
   1 set of eight supplemental textbooks for faster learners.
   1 state almanac.
   1 encyclopedia.
   A bookcase containing several atlases, almanacs, and a collection of books
      about the state.

In the school:
   1 motion-picture projector, to be shared with five other classrooms.
   1 filmstrip and slide projector, to be shared with three other classrooms.
   1 tape recorder, to be shared with six other classrooms.
   2 trips per year by bus to selected areas within the city.
   2 packages of outline maps of the state, each package containing 100 maps.
   A library containing more reference materials.

In the city education center:
   1 relief map of the state, available for one week during the year.
   4 suitable films.
   6 suitable filmstrips.
   8 picture series about industries within the state.
   A list of resource persons acquainted with various problems within the state.

Personal teaching aids:
   A picture file containing a section devoted to the state.
   A file of newspaper clippings about problems in the state (gathered during
      the past two years).
   200 feet of 8-millimeter motion-picture film showing scenic places within
      the state.
   1 home-movie projector.

   As we review these lists of materials and resources (no claim is
made here for the representativeness of the lists for schools, city school
districts, or county school districts) and review the teaching objectives
as listed by each teacher, it becomes apparent that the availability of
instructional materials and devices can and does influence the develop-

ment of teaching objectives. Of particular significance are the personal teaching aids, for it is these that often determine whether the teacher can choose a particular teaching objective.

SUMMARY

We have briefly previewed social-studies objectives—the eloquent objectives which inspire us, the delimiting objectives which specify generally what we are to teach, and the teaching objectives which express more precisely the understandings, skills, and attitudes toward which we guide children. When the delimiting objectives have been converted to teaching objectives, much remains to be done. Many other decisions about teaching must be made. The remainder of this book deals with the problems and practices involved in making those decisions.

Exercises for Further Understanding

1. Obtain a copy of the social-studies course of study or guide at your grade level in the district where you intend to teach and examine carefully the objectives listed in it. Analyze your own feelings as you read the eloquent objectives. Note the detail in which the delimiting objectives are expressed.

2. Examine several social-studies courses of study or guides—one prepared at the state level, one at the county level, and one at the district level—to determine differences in the statements of the various objectives. Which statements of objectives tend to parallel each other? Which tend to differ?

3. At the curriculum library in your college or university, obtain social-studies courses of study or guides from cities located in various parts of the country. Examine these for differences in delimiting objectives. Develop a reason or two for the existence of such differences.

4. In the recent past there have been suggestions from various quarters to the effect that the delimiting objectives of social studies be standardized throughout the nation. What do you think about this? What would be the advantages of such a move? The disadvantages? How would such a move work against the accomplishment of the major

objective of social studies? In what way would it facilitate reaching this objective?

5. Suppose that you were given the task of writing the statement of eloquent objectives for a district. You are limited to two hundred words and you are not to repeat yourself. What would you write?

6. Analyze the two expressions of delimiting objectives shown below to determine which is broader. Substantiate your choice by listing the general areas of study that would be included within each. You will most likely need to consult a good textbook in United States history.

(a) The Westward Movement.
(b) The economic motivation of the American people pushes the western frontier to the Pacific Ocean.

Selected References

Engle, Shirley H., "Objectives of the Social Studies," in Byron G. Massialas and Frederick R. Smith, eds., *New Challenges in the Social Studies*. Belmont, Calif.: Wadsworth Publishing Company, 1965, pp. 1-19.

Fisher, Robert, "Social Studies Objectives for Primary Grades." *Social Education*, 30:534-536 (December 1965).

Gross, Richard E., and Glen F. Ovard, "A Review of Aims and Objectives in Social Education." *Social Studies*, 51:170-174 (October 1960).

Jarolimek, John, *Social Studies in Elementary Education*, 2d ed., Chap. 1, "Social Studies in the Elementary Curriculum." New York: The Macmillan Company, 1963.

Michaelis, John U., "Introduction." *Social Studies in Elementary Schools*, pp. 1-16. Thirty-Second Yearbook of the National Council for the Social Studies, Washington, D.C.: National Education Association, 1960.

_____, *Social Studies for Children in a Democracy*, 3d ed., Chap. 1, "Definition, Purposes, and Trends." Englewood Cliffs, N.J.: Prentice-Hall, Inc., 1963.

Patterson, Franklin, ed., *Citizenship and a Free Society: Education for the Future*. Thirtieth Yearbook of the National Council for the Social Studies, Washington, D.C.: National Education Association, 1960.

Preston, Ralph C., *Teaching Social Studies in the Elementary School*, Chap. 2, "Objectives of Social Studies." New York: Rinehart and Company, Inc., 1958.

Quillen, I. James, "Desirable Objectives for the Lower Elementary School," *Social Education for Young Children in the Kindergarten and Primary Grades*, pp. 21-31. Curriculum Series, No. 4, National Council for the Social Studies, Washington, D.C.: National Education Association, 1946.

Reynolds, Robert W., *et al.*, *Guiding Children through the Social Studies*, Chap. 1, "Reasons for Teaching the Social Studies." Washington, D.C.: National Education Association, 1964.

"The Role of the Social Studies." *Social Education*, 27:315-318ff (October 1962).

Taba, Hilda, *Curriculum Development: Theory and Practice*, Chap. 14, "The Types of Behavioral Objectives." New York: Harcourt, Brace & World, Inc., 1962.

3

Acquiring Background for
Teaching Social Studies

After a brief glimpse of the social-studies teacher developing teaching objectives, we turn our attention to the problems he must cope with before and during his work with objectives. One problem is that of acquiring the social-science background necessary for guiding children in social studies. The purpose of this chapter is to present a brief introduction to the social sciences and to suggest ways in which a teacher may acquire the needed background.

THE SOCIAL SCIENCES AS A TOTAL AREA

The social sciences encompass the study of man and his functions in time and space. Those generally considered to be of particular significance to elementary social studies include cultural geography, history, economics, political science, anthropology, sociology, psychology, and social psychology. Each discipline focuses its attention on some aspect of man and his activities from its own particular point of view;

thus the social sciences as a total area make a fascinating complex of overlapping and divergent ideas.

The social-studies teacher has to find his way in and around this complex of ideas as he prepares to organize a unit. As he studies, he will need to delve into one social science or another to determine the meaning of a "big idea" and to understand and know the ideas and facts that support it. Sooner or later he discovers the reasons for overlap and divergency; this discovery makes his way somewhat easier.

The overlap of ideas in the social sciences is due largely to several conditions. The first and most obvious is that man is the central concept of all the social sciences. Although man and his activities have many facets, predominant aspects are likely to be closely examined by all the social sciences. The findings may differ somewhat, but the similarity of findings will be close enough to overlap. All the social sciences are somewhat concerned with natural and human resources, level of technological development of a people, and the motivation of individuals and groups. A more specific common concern is *division of labor*, an aspect of human organization examined by economics, sociology, anthropology, and cultural geography.

The second condition which reflects an overlap occurs in the extended development of ideas in some of the social sciences. For example, the cultural geographer may hold geography to be his area of emphasis, but he finds it necessary to branch into history, culture, economics, and political science to describe fully a selected region. The political scientist may be dealing primarily with political behavior, but to describe completely his area of scrutiny, he may have to deal with ideas which are primarily the province of sociology, social psychology, anthropology, and economics.

The third condition which contributes toward overlap of ideas is similarity in the ways of gathering data and expressing findings in social-science research. The case study and the survey are favored ways of investigating phenomena in most of the social sciences; the use of statistical method for expressing findings precisely tends to be favored by many social scientists.

Sometimes the overlap is so great that the student may not be able to identify with any exactitude whether he is dealing with one social science or another.

The divergency of ideas among and within the various social sciences is largely accountable to the way in which social scientists regard the generalizations or "big ideas" around which their disciplines are organized. These ideas are regarded as tentative, that is, subject to modification through extended thinking and research. This attitude has given rise to several conditions which prevail within the total area and contribute toward divergency of ideas in the social sciences. The first of these conditions is an aura of competition in which social scientists in one discipline vie with those in others to establish their own view of man and his activities as predominant. For example, some economists tend to believe that man's economic life and his ways of solving economic problems are central to his existence, and that other forces that impinge upon him are to be regarded as important but somewhat secondary.

The second condition is controversiality within each of the various social sciences. Some social scientists in each of the disciplines focus their efforts on erecting theoretical constructs about man and his activities. Based on a central assumption or set of assumptions, or on a basic interpretation of reality, these constructs do not agree. For example, some political scientists may hold firmly to a theoretical construct which maintains that government exists to provide only those services which individuals cannot, or cannot as well, provide for themselves; others may hold as firmly to a construct supporting a more paternalistic function of government.

The third condition contributing to divergency among the social sciences as a total area is a continual striving for precision in language. This precision steers clear of language invention and emphasizes precise use of terms already a common part of language. To most of us, for example, to sell is to exchange goods for money; to some economists it means to create a demand. When many of us think of culture, our thoughts gravitate toward appreciation of the fine arts; an anthropologist has in mind a total complex of beliefs, values, and practices which a people has developed for effective living. To many of us, a group is synonymous with set, flock, herd, bunch, or the like; the sociologist thinks of a human group having a structure and a purpose.

A sense of the overlap and divergency within the social sciences serves as an aid to the teacher as he decides on the content to be treated in a unit. An appreciation of the divergency is particularly helpful, for through it he can determine the extent of overlap, choose the precise items of language appropriate to the unit, and make provisions for children to learn the terms. Because of the controversiality within each of the social sciences and the competitive aspect among them in establishing a predominant position, he will have to run the risk of displeasing some social scientists in his choices. Perhaps his only adequate defense is an objective attitude which appreciates the products of controversy and the contributions made by all the social sciences toward a more complete understanding of man.

STRUCTURES OF THE SOCIAL SCIENCES

One of the controversies within the social sciences strikes deeply into the foundation of each science. It relates to the structure of each as an area of knowledge and to the method used to extend that knowledge. Some social scientists believe that a social science is a system or model of abstract thought logically erected and extendable through further thought and research. Others believe that a social science is essentially processive, that is, an area of knowledge being gradually extended through careful observation and description. The modern elementary social-studies teacher is caught up in this controversy. His view of the controversy and where he places himself within it will influence his choice of content, the way he visualizes and expresses it, and the strategy he will follow in teaching it.

One way to examine this controversy is to examine two theoretical structures of the social sciences as a whole, one which presents these sciences as systems of interrelated thought and the other which tends to be processive in the study of the behavior of man. In the first structure, the earth's resources serve as a base.

If the earth's resources are used as a structural base, all the social sciences are interpreted as being tangent in some way to the natural and physical sciences. Therefore, a complete understanding of any social science depends upon an understanding of scientific facts and principles from such sciences as geology, physical geography, biology, botany, zoology, chemistry, and physics. Scientists in these fields of knowledge attempt to define, with ever-increasing precision, the earth's resources in terms of composition, natural state, location, and abundance; they strive to arrive at principles more reliable in predicting the action of forces which operate on the various materials that comprise the earth's resources. The primary purpose of scientists in the natural and physical sciences is to extend and particularize their fields of knowledge. From time to time, however, they direct their efforts toward applying their knowledge to the solution of human problems dealing with the use of materials and forces. As a result of these efforts they discover facts and arrive at principles useful to social scientists.

The social scientists accept as their primary purpose the extension and particularization of facts and principles about the earth's resources in terms of man's uses of them and the problems arising from his attempts to use them to accomplish his own ends—survival and prosperity. Some social scientists address themselves to the scientific problem of defining the patterns of use. Anthropologists, for example, study societies of the past and present to discover precisely how man everywhere uses and has used the earth's resources to provide himself with food, clothing, and shelter, and to maintain a way of living. Man develops artifacts, practices, and beliefs which reflect not only patterns of use but patterns of control as well. Some societies apply patterns of passive control of the earth's resources. They use whatever is about them in a more or less natural state. Others apply patterns of active control in which they develop intricate systems for producing and using energy to convert materials into many useful articles. As far as the anthropologist is concerned, no pattern of use or pattern of control is superior to any other. Determining the superiority of patterns is left to other social scientists.

The other social scientists tend to focus their scrutiny on particular patterns of control. The psychologist examines the patterns of control related to individual self-direction; the sociologist centers his attention on the patterns of control involving the use of groups; the social psychologist takes a careful look at the patterns of control as they relate to the individual as a member of a group. The political scientist analyzes patterns of control among individuals and political groups as they attempt to establish and maintain a public authority. The economist examines patterns of control related to the production, distribution, and consumption of goods and services.

These social scientists are also concerned with patterns of uses. They define them in ways particular to their areas of emphasis. For example, the psychologist interprets uses of the earth's resources in terms of his definitions of primary drives, and the economist views them as factors in production, distribution, and consumption of goods. But the basic concern of most social scientists is the problems which human beings have in controlling their physical, social, and personal environment for their betterment and survival. They discover facts and arrive at principles helpful to man in his problems of control of environment.

The social sciences share a similarity in their methods of work. To a certain extent, all have difficulty in abstracting scientific universes with which to experiment. All must rely heavily on careful observation and interview techniques to gather facts. Statistical analysis and expression of data tend to be crude. Verification of findings tends to be historical-geographical, or analysis of what has occurred in other times and places; historical, or analysis of what has occurred in the light of most recent developments, or geographical, analysis of phenomena in other places.

Regardless of the limitations of social-science research, the social scientists have arrived at important basic principles useful to man in his approach to problems of control of environment. These principles always deal with either of two concepts, dependency (man's dependence on the earth's resources) or interdependency (man's interdependence with other men in the use of the earth's resources), to promote life and to maintain a way of living. And if a man knows and understands these principles to the extent that they are regulative of his attitudes and actions, he will both survive and prosper.

A structure of the social sciences based on the earth's resources is presented below, with a more brief expression in Figure 1.

DEPENDENCY APPROACH TO THE SOCIAL SCIENCES BY REFERENCE TO THE EARTH'S RESOURCES

First-Level Concepts: The Earth's Resources

Materials (defined in terms of composition, natural state, location, and abundance)

Forces (defined in terms of characteristics, causes, and effects)

[Study will deal with facts and principles significant to geology, geography, biology, zoology, botany, physics, chemistry, and the like.]

Second-Level Concepts: The Social Sciences

Patterns of Use (consumption to promote life—food, clothing, and shelter; consumption to maintain a way of living—communication, transportation, education, religion, and art)

Patterns of Control (passive control—conservation, allocation, distribution, and rules of property; active control—fuel and power conversion, conversion from raw materials to useful products)

[Study will deal with facts and principles significant to anthropology, economics, political science, sociology, psychology, and the like.]

Third-Level Concepts: Generalizations

Generalizations about man's dependency on the earth's resources and his interdependency in their use

[Study will deal with ideas significant to social studies.]

Verification: Criticizing and Testing the Generalizations

1. As related to other peoples
2. As related to other places
3. As related to other times
4. As related to recent developments

Attitudes and Patterns of Action

Out of verification and discussion come the ability to have and express attitudes, viewpoints, and opinions and to plan actions to express them.

Not all social scientists and social-studies specialists would whole-heartedly accept a structure of the social sciences based upon the earth's resources. It appears to give too much emphasis to economics as a social science, thus suggesting a hierarchy of the social sciences with economics at the apex. This structure would meet with the approval of some economists, but would alienate others. Some social scientists in other disciplines might assert that their discipline should stand at the top of the hierarchy; others would not object to the structure. In interpreting the structure, their way of thinking would place their particular science in the predominant position.

FIGURE 1. A STRUCTURE OF THE SOCIAL SCIENCES BY REFERENCE TO THE EARTH'S RESOURCES. THIS STRUCTURE HAS BEEN ELABORATED IN THE TEXT.

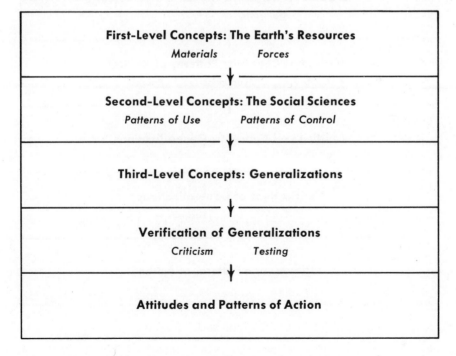

First-Level Concepts: The Earth's Resources
Materials   *Forces*

Second-Level Concepts: The Social Sciences
Patterns of Use   *Patterns of Control*

Third-Level Concepts: Generalizations

Verification of Generalizations
Criticism   *Testing*

Attitudes and Patterns of Action

Now let us examine another structure (Figure 2), one based on human resources. At the very outset it centers on man and his nature. It strongly suggests the observation of process.

INTERDEPENDENCY APPROACH TO THE SOCIAL SCIENCES BY REFERENCE TO HUMAN RESOURCES

First-Level Concepts: Human Resources

Forces (physiological needs, such as nutrition, activity, and the like; psychological needs as related to awareness of self, intrapersonal relationships, and the like; sociological needs, particularly the need for group contact; sociopsychological needs: security, recognition, belonging, affection, and new experience)

FIGURE 2. A STRUCTURE OF THE SOCIAL SCIENCES BY REFERENCE TO HUMAN RESOURCES. THIS STRUCTURE HAS BEEN ELABORATED IN THE TEXT.

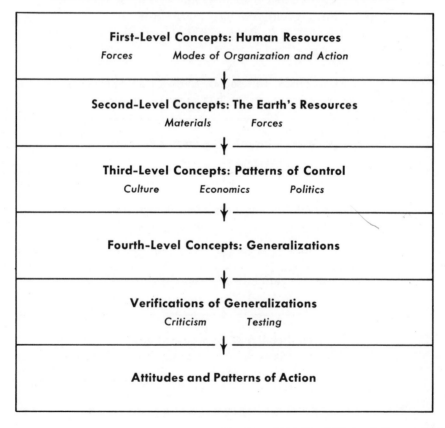

First-Level Concepts: Human Resources

Forces   *Modes of Organization and Action*

Second-Level Concepts: The Earth's Resources

Materials   *Forces*

Third-Level Concepts: Patterns of Control

Culture   *Economics*   *Politics*

Fourth-Level Concepts: Generalizations

Verifications of Generalizations

Criticism   *Testing*

Attitudes and Patterns of Action

Modes of Organization and Action (sociological: association, dissociation, stratification, cooperation, accommodation, competition, conflict, and assimilation; cultural: the mores, as related to kinship, marriage, property, law, commerce, religion, education, and the like; individual: as determined by life experience)

[Study will deal with facts and principles significant to human physiology, psychology, sociology, social psychology, anthropology, and the like.]

Second-Level Concepts: The Earth's Resources

Materials (defined in terms of composition, natural state, location, and abundance)

Forces (defined in terms of characteristics, causes, and effects)

[Study will deal with facts and principles significant to the various sciences.]

Third-Level Concepts: Patterns of Control

Culture (ways of establishing, maintaining, and improving ways of life)

Economics (ways of establishing, maintaining, and improving economic welfare)

Politics (ways of establishing, maintaining, and improving public authority)

[Study will deal with facts and principles significant to anthropology, economics, and political science]

Fourth-Level Concepts: Generalizations

Generalizations about man's dependency and interdependency

Verification: Criticizing and Testing the Generalizations

1. As related to other peoples
2. As related to other places
3. As related to other times
4. As related to recent developments

Attitudes and Patterns of Action

Out of verification and discussion come the ability to have and express attitudes, viewpoints, and opinions and to plan actions to express them.

To define human resources is to define man dynamically in terms of the various functional systems within which he lives. The first and most basic of all these systems is his physiological system. It functions in terms of physiological needs—needs for nutrition, activity, respiration, circulation, and digestion. The state of this system and how well it works influence man's psychological system, which functions in terms of intrapersonal needs related to his awareness of self within a total environment. These needs and the extent of their impingement upon him change in accord with experience. Beyond the self lies another system, the sociological system, in which man, an integrated system, becomes a part of another integrated system. He is involved in reacting to and exerting action within such social forces as association, dissociation, stratification, cooperation, accommodation, competition, conflict, and assimilation. And for a moment one may regard man as an individual caught up in the sway of social forces that are affecting him as he reacts to his sociopsychological needs—needs for security, recognition, belonging, affection, and new experience. To a very large extent man's choice of ways to react is determined by his cultural system, which accepts only certain modes of social organization and action and certain ways of believing. In short, all human needs and all human forces comprise human resources. The study of these needs and forces is the particular province of physiology, psychology, sociology, social psychology, and anthropology. All but physiology are social sciences.

However, if a human being were aware of himself as a human resource as defined by psychology, sociology, and anthropology, his knowledge would not be adequate to the task of knowing and using the world about him. He must know something about the earth's resources. The natural and physical sciences such as physical geography, geology, botany, chemistry, and the like provide him with the necessary facts and principles. The combination of what he knows about himself as a human resource, about the earth's resources, and about other men as human resources is provided by the social sciences of psychology, sociology, social psychology, anthropology, economics, and political science as they deal with patterns of control related to personal, social, cultural, economic, and political problems. Such knowledge results in the formulation of principles (including attitudes and patterns of behavior) which, if totally known, help him to survive and prosper.

This structure of the social sciences based on human resources, brief and somewhat oversimplified, still serves to place man and his activities as central to the social sciences. Some social scientists believe that if man and his activities are so central, then the study of man focuses precisely on them.

A BRIEF SURVEY OF THE SOCIAL SCIENCES

To this point, it has been established that to acquire background (1) the social-studies teacher needs to be aware of the overlapping and divergency of ideas in the social sciences, and (2) he needs to ascertain what he believes the structure of the social sciences to be. These ideas suggest that acquiring background in the social sciences is less a matter of passive saturation and absorption of facts and ideas than of self-study and anticipation of choices and decisions. To heighten the anticipation of these, a brief survey of each of the various social sciences is presented in this section.

Because of space limitations it is possible to present only the briefest review of each of the disciplines, and impossible to present different points of view within each discipline. However, since the stated purpose is to prepare for the acquisition of background rather than to transmit background directly, these surveys should serve adequately.

HISTORY

History is often considered a discipline in the humanities rather than a social science. In the humanities, its content is the vast panorama of human experience pieced together from the artifacts and records of the past, arranged in chronological order dating from the earliest times to the present. Such history evokes awe, like the night sky demarcated by shadowed horizons and pinpoints of light from varidistanced stars, some of which have long since died. In history, shadows mark the limits of the perceptive powers of man; the pinpoints of light are the deeds of men and the accomplishments of civilizations. History is a source of pride and humility; as a source of wisdom, it shares a place with philosophy and literature.

As a social science, history is basically a method in the study of the development of institutions and the problems within them which arise as a function of changes in political control, economic structure, technological advancement, social organization, and cultural interaction. In its simplest expressive form, history records something fairly discrete. For example, a history of communication, or of manufacturing, tends to give a chronological picture of the development of communication or manufacturing. The important contributors and contributions are presented in terms of time from the earliest known beginnings to the present. History establishes a particular trend or complex of related trends and certain predictions can be made.

When history deals with people and civilizations, it synthesizes several trends. Social, cultural, economic, and political trends are treated as a huge complex of contributions and events. Frequently a historian who deals with so many trends must struggle not to accept one, such as the political, as being the only trend significant in the lives of people. He must exercise great care in establishing trends and following their progress honestly. Much of his work involves seeking original sources, such as records maintained during the period studied and documents written by observers living then. Realizing the limitations of his data, he makes only those assessments which can be fully supported, or makes assessments in which limitations are duly noted.

Aspects of history as a social science are suitable for elementary social studies. Children need to know history as a way of representing truth in time, as a way of learning about change and the factors that contribute to change, and as a way of determining a pattern and direction of action in the solution of a problem. Children should be guided toward demanding authenticity to the extent that they are able.

It is particularly important for the teacher to remember that history often tends to be an area of synthesis rather than the study of a discrete trend. Children must be guided toward looking at various trends rather than just one. More important still, children need to sense that history is the record of an entity. The entity should be identified before historical study begins. Before children begin to study a topic such as the history of communication, they need to know what is meant by *communication* as a process. If they are expected to study political, economic, social, and cultural trends, their study should begin with some knowledge of what is meant by *public authority, economic structure, social organization,* and *culture.*

GEOGRAPHY

Geography as an area of study encompasses both science and social science. As a science, geography is usually referred to as physical geography. It includes the definitive study of the following factors as they operate in the various regions of the world: (1) location on the globe in relation to the location of other geographical regions and political divisions; (2) topography—the lay of the land and its manifestation of richness in terms of soil, minerals, wildlife, and vegetation; (3) climate—its causes, and its manifestations in terms of temperature, precipitation, winds, and seasons; (4) the interrelationships among location, topography, and climate; and (5) the general influence of these factors on the life of man.

As a social science, geography is usually referred to as cultural geography, or as a more specific aspect such as economic or industrial geography. Basically, it is a study of patterns of application of physical geography principles in terms of the utility of geographical factors in the life of man in specific regions. The student of cultural geography usually is guided toward a review of physical geography, utility patterns, the relationship between geographical factors and utility, and the significance of these in terms of world economy, political structure, and the structure of world culture.

The student of cultural geography must always be on guard against one weakness. He may tend to regard geographical factors as the determiners of life everywhere. He may forget that cultural interaction often affects the ways in which geographical factors are used, that the level of technological development contributes to the use of natural resources, and that political and economic stability often have much to do with the efficiency with which geographical factors are used.

When the study of physical geography guides towards aesthetic and economic appreciation of the factors of geography and related patterns of behavior, it becomes a study in conservation. Patterns of behavior are related to preservation, wise use, and preparation for the future by planning and discovering new uses of resources.

For the elementary social-studies teacher, the study of geography is usually cultural geography which depends so much on ideas from physical geography, history, economics, political science, and anthropology for its fullest contribution to the understanding of man. Whenever a unit is basically geographical in nature, it is usually necessary for the teacher to guide children into the study of physical geography to the extent that the children can understand it. Often children will have to be taught something about cultural, political, and economic factors which influence patterns of use of geographical factors. A simple frame of reference is frequently required: location, topography, and climate of the area studied, basic occupations, general standard of living, government, products for home use and products for export, value of products, contributions of the area to the world market.

The social-studies teacher also regards geography as an area of extension. Children are helped to see that geography is a way of representing truth in space in terms of the surface of the earth. They may verify basic learnings in geography by taking a quick glimpse at some other region or political division, or they may set out to verify important social-studies generalizations by making comparisons between two areas. Children need to know that one way of becoming better acquainted with peoples around the earth and their problems is to study the geography of the regions the peoples inhabit.

ECONOMICS

As an area of study, economics tends to be both an analytical philosophy and a social science.

As an analytical philosophy, the area of scrutiny is restricted to that part of the universe which deals with economic reality, particularly the activity of man as he copes with his environment to solve economic problems. It is assumed that the essential nature of man is that of producer and consumer of goods and services. It is assumed further that man is an intelligent being who strives continually not only to maintain a level of economic welfare, but to raise it as well. Within these assumptions, thinkers in economics have logically constructed philosophies of economics characterized by abstract definitions and principles which assure survival and prosperity.

As a social science, economics is that area of investigation in which social scientists seek to extend man's knowledge about his economic life so that he may control it. They attempt to define clearly such terms as utility, goods and services, wealth, production, factors of production, consumption, income and its distribution, value, and price. Within their definitions, they derive principles useful to man in coping with his economic problems. In their research, they rely heavily on historical investigation, careful deductive reasoning, and statistical analysis and expression of data.

For the elementary social-studies teacher, economics is studied as a social science, generally in its definitive aspects. In the primary grades, children learn about the division of labor in the production of community services such as police protection, protection from fire, mail delivery, and the like and in the various processes involved in the production, distribution, and consumption of goods useful to everyone. They may be guided into the study of such processes as farming, manufacturing, mining, and the like, depending on the kind of community in which they live. Often the study of the division of labor is only one aspect of a unit about the policeman, the fireman, the farmer, or the like.

Basic economics units usually are constructed around such topics as *saving* or *wise spending*.

In the later grades, the social-studies teacher may teach economics ideas either as supportive or basic. In almost every unit dealing with a geographical region, the children learn basic economics ideas to extend their knowledge about life in the area. Basic economics ideas are also presented in the study of historical eras. If the teacher wishes to guide his pupils into units basically economics in nature, he may build units around the study of "big ideas" about the following: factors of production, distribution, and price; factors of production and distribution as the dominant influence in the life of a people living during a particular era.

As the social-studies teacher guides his pupils in the discussion of economic ideas, he should expect controversy to arise. He must be prepared to guide his pupils in treating controversy.

POLITICAL SCIENCE

Like economics, political science, as an area of study, tends to be both an analytical philosophy and a social science.

As an analytical philosophy, its area of philosophical inquiry is restricted to that part of the universe which deals with political reality and the nature of man as a political entity. It is assumed that man is part of a political body, the basis for the organization of which is the establishment and maintenance of a public authority. Through the exercise of this authority, man governs and is governed and expresses himself to other political bodies. The political philosopher works to construct a logically organized political universe in terms of definitions and principles. Not all political philosophers agree on what political reality is or should be. Some feel that man as an individual is the primary factor. Since his interests and freedom are of first concern, the solution of all political problems should be in some way formulated to protect man's individual interests and freedom. Others feel that the state is of primary concern; therefore, the solution of all political problems should give first consideration to the welfare of the state. Between these extremes are various gradations of opinions as to what the relationship is between individual man and the political body. Some of the terms frequently used are absolute monarchy, constitutional monarchy, democracy, dictatorship, and oligarchy. Controversy often arises about the definition of these terms and about which is best for a political body.

As a social science, political science is that area of investigation in which social scientists seek to extend man's knowledge about how to establish and maintain public authority in modern, complex societies. They study carefully the institution of government and the structure of constitutions. They place particular emphasis on investigating the relations between the governors and the governed. In the midst of the process of government itself, they probe constantly to determine public opinions about current issues in government, voting patterns, and executive, judicial, and legislative trends. They make rigorous use of historical method, interviews, and statistical analysis and expression of data.

For the elementary social-studies teacher, political science is basically a social science dealing generally with government in a democracy. Most of the teacher's efforts are directed toward the definitive aspects of government in a democracy so that children may understand the complex of government within which they live. Learning may be acquired directly or indirectly. In the primary grades the pupils learn political-science ideas indirectly, that is, they learn them as related to other ideas. For example, the primary child may be learning about the family, the school, or the policeman, and he learns, among other things, that there are different aspects of authority within the family, at school, and in the community. In the later grades, children acquire political-science ideas both directly and indirectly. In learning the ideas directly, they are guided toward learning about government, what it is basically, its ramifications at various levels (local, state, national, international), and the historical development of national government. They learn political-science ideas indirectly as they find out about the governments of other countries in the present and in the past.

The teacher must expect controversy to arise as he guides his pupils in the study of political ideas. Actually, if he uses sound judgment, he may guide his pupils into the study of political ideas by guiding them into an examination of controversy.

ANTHROPOLOGY

As an area of study, anthropology is a social science which rigorously attempts to define man realistically and scientifically. The social scientists working in the area of anthropology strive to learn how man has come to be what he is as a species. They study the structure of the institutions developed by man as reflected in his artifacts, his behaviors, his beliefs, and values. The more they can learn of his institutions, the more clearly they can define men as reflected in his culture. At times they seek to know why culture is the way it is, to know its significant innovations and their sources. Are the innovations crystallized expressions of the unique culture, or are they borrowed from neighboring or visiting cultures? Anthropologists have no concern for what man should be, only for what he is. To discover this, they observe and record carefully, interview perceptively, and examine in detail artifacts obtained in many ways. The purpose of their investigation is to construct a mirror that accurately reflects man so that he may recognize and know himself wherever he may be. When man can understand himself in terms of his culture, the members of his own culture cannot be alien to him, nor can the members of any other culture.

For the elementary social-studies teacher, anthropology is a social science which may be taught directly or indirectly. In the elementary grades, direct instruction involves the study of primitive cultures, particularly as it relates to satisfying basic human needs, to family life, and to education. Direct study may involve the immediate family in which the practices of biological kinship within a culture are studied, or the neighborhood and school in which certain practices in social kinship are scrutinized and structured. In the later grades, pupils may be guided toward studying their own culture, particularly the institutions of law, property, education, and religion; they may study a modern culture outside their immediate culture to discover its institutions and their structure. Often they will profit from making a comparative study of two primitive cultures.

Anthropology contains ideas which may be taught indirectly as other topics are being studied. In the primary grades, whenever a worker, a process, or an institution has been studied, the pupils may be guided toward investigating quickly to find how the same worker, process, or institution is reflected in another culture. In the later grades, the pupils are guided to learn specifically how culture functions as a force in the lives of people—how it contributes to the solution of the political, economic, and social problems of a people.

PSYCHOLOGY

Psychology, a science familiar to most teachers, deals with the behavior of man as an individual. One of the unique aspects of the teaching profession is that it is dedicated to guiding children from one positive point to another in their growth in effective behavior. Educational psychology is that branch of the science which treats specifically of the problems involved in bringing about changes of behavior in the various areas of knowledge taught in school. It is closely allied to the basic science of psychology which places its focus on man as a complete universe of self. The purpose of the science is to extend the knowledge of what makes up the self—the beliefs, attitudes, and patterns of action —in short, the complex of individual behavior. The psychologist seeks to determine the factors that cause behavior, the organization of these factors that bring about certain patterns of behavior, and the intensity of various factors required to bring about particular patterns of behavior. He conducts his research through experimentation, careful observation of general behavior in particular situations, case studies of single individuals, and interviews. Often he uses statistical procedures to indicate the significance of his findings.

Because of his reliance upon psychology in coping with his problems of organizing learning and because of his particular view of the science, the elementary social-studies teacher may tend to regard psychology as too abstract for children, or perhaps not really relevant to social studies as content. Such opinions are erroneous. When a teacher guides his pupils in the study of biographies of great men and women, he is actually teaching aspects of psychology in a very direct way. The study of such great persons as Clara Barton or Jane Addams, George Washington or Abraham Lincoln, Thomas Edison or George Washington Carver are case histories, somewhat biased and in error to be sure, but case histories nevertheless. As children study these case histories, they learn about the importance of self-direction as a force in human motivation. They learn the meaning of adversity, resourcefulness, and courage. They may be inspired to develop the traits of resourcefulness and courage which serve so well in the lives of great persons.

In an indirect sense, the study of people everywhere and in every era leads children into studying human motivation as a factor which contributes to the ways that people approach problems of all kinds.

Psychology as a social science contains understandings that, if well taught, serve to help the individual develop attitudes and patterns of action that will promote his own well-being. He will see the need for self-control. Furthermore, he will gain insights into understanding other persons and peoples.

SOCIOLOGY

In some respects, sociology, like psychology, is not entirely new to most elementary teachers. They study aspects of it during their professional preparation, but this study is sufficient only to the task of managing and understanding children. Social-studies teachers need to know more about sociology as a basic area of study.

As an area of study, sociology is centered on man's group behavior and the extension of knowledge about this behavior that man may better control the direction and impact of his social actions. The sociologist seeks to define what is meant by *group* in its many manifestations in the life of man. He seeks to know why groups form and how they form, how they function and how they change, and why some are long-lived and others disintegrate. Often he deals with the pervasive problem of social disintegration.

For the elementary social-studies teacher, sociology is a social science which may be taught directly or indirectly to children. When he teaches sociology directly, the teacher is concerned with both skills and content. As primary children undertake group tasks in social studies, the teacher guides them in learning and using communication and interaction skills to form groups, organize them, and to make them function toward desired ends. In the later grades, he helps them to develop these skills to higher levels of sophistication. He guides them toward greater independence in deciding when to form groups to accomplish certain tasks. In the primary grades, the teacher often guides children through various studies of the community so they may acquire basic learning about social interdependence. In the later grades, he may organize units dealing with propaganda and social problems such as interracial relations, delinquency, and care of the aged. Indirect teaching of ideas from sociology is more frequently found in the later grades as the pupils are guided into considering the social problems existing in other times and places.

As both content and skills, sociology offers the elementary social-studies teacher a repository of understanding and patterns of behavior necessary for life in a democratic society. When these are well taught, children learn when to engage in group activity and when to refrain from it and how to select a group activity in which to become involved. They gain insight into social problems due to cultural change and technological advancement.

SOCIAL PSYCHOLOGY

As a social science, social psychology is often difficult to differentiate from sociology or psychology. It is concerned with both individual and group behavior. However, it has its own specific universe—the universe of self and other—with a particular emphasis on the study of the intricate relationships obtaining between self and other, the development of these relationships, their structure, and their stability at various levels of social interaction. The point of departure and the point of return is always the self. The social psychologist seeks to define more fully the impact of cultural and social expectations on the behavior of the individual. He tries to discover ways to help society resolve conflicts between the individual and his society and culture. In a very real sense, he is the champion of the individual, for if the conflicts are not resolved, it is most likely that the individual would be destroyed. He carries on his research through careful observation, experimentation, case studies, and the analysis of propaganda and opinions.

As far as the elementary social-studies teacher is concerned, social psychology as an area of study offers little in the way of content with which children may become involved over an extended period of time. However, from time to time, through the use of roleplaying, sociodrama, and other projective techniques, children may be brought into contact with ranges of acceptable personality traits within the culture being studied. They may be guided into considering the changes necessary in their own attitudes and patterns of action so they may interact with the people of such a culture with the least amount of conflict for themselves and the people with whom they are having contact. Occasionally, a class may have to consider how to cope with personality problems that arise during social studies. An attempt may be made to reduce the conflict without harm to individuals or to the task of the class as a group.

In the study of a culture, children may be guided into determining the personality characteristics of a culture by studying its art, music, and literature, either as folk or individual creative expression, and by looking at the conflicts encountered by children growing up.

Social psychology, then, as an area of study, contributes most richly to social studies in a supportive sense rather than as basic content to be studied.

Actually, the parallel between social studies and social psychology is closer in intent than that between social studies and any other social science. As stated before, the basic objective of social studies is the development of a citizen. Implicit within the function of a citizen is the development of the personality of a citizen who in his lifetime will be called upon to operate effectively at several levels of social interaction—as sibling and child, as spouse and parent, as worker and voter, as inhabitant of a neighborhood and world traveler. Social studies is an applied form of social psychology dealing with the growth of self as a result of a richer knowledge of other.

A PROGRAM OF SELF-STUDY

Structures and important ideas inherent in the social sciences, here expressed most briefly, are at best a shallow introduction. The prospective teacher or the elementary teacher who wishes to improve his teaching of social studies must do much more than read and study this digest. He should develop a personal program for extending his knowledge of the social sciences. Such a program entails making the best use of available educational resources. Any of the following will prove helpful:

1. Taking or auditing courses in a nearby junior college, college, or university. Often these institutions offer evening courses, many of which are introductory, in the various social sciences. These courses are also frequently offered during summer sessions.

2. Organizing an independent study and reading program. Due to the recent great increase in paperback-book publication, almost every drugstore or stationery store in America contains a supply of excellent books, many of which deal with the social sciences. Self-study aids, such as the *College Outline Series* published by Barnes and Noble, are available. In this series, almost every social science is represented in a simply written, easily understood book. Most large bookstores now have entire sections devoted to the display and sales of paperback books. Every college bookstore is well supplied.

Some elementary social-studies teachers prefer to read and study college textbooks on their own. They carefully read college-catalog course requirements to see whether a particular course is one that they would like to take. If the course appears applicable, they buy the textbook recommended by the instructor. Frequently a college or university instructor will be glad to recommend an introductory book that may be readily available.

Another excellent resource for social-studies background is children's books written about the social sciences. In recent years, more and more of these books are being written and sold.

3. Taking advantage of every opportunity provided by the district. Many large school districts have in-service or institute programs which include interesting lectures and presentations by social scientists. In most instance, these programs are a painless means of acquiring background.

In recent years, some school districts have hired social scientists to present the basic ideas from their discipline to groups of teachers. Often these social scientists offer suggestions on how to teach these ideas to children.

There is little reason for any teacher not to have the social-science background necessary for conducting a good program in social studies.

Because of the paperback-book "explosion" of the past decade or so, many excellent, well-written books dealing with the social sciences and social-science topics are readily available at a small expenditure. [Books available in paperback listed in this section will be indicated with an asterisk (*)]. A teacher can acquire the necessary background for guiding children in social studies by expending a small amount of money and a reasonable amount of energy. This section will be devoted to suggestions, and recommendation of a few books, for the teacher who wishes to prepare himself to a greater depth in the social sciences generally or to refresh his background in selected social sciences.

Social scientists have an almost undefinable spirit which lends a particular verve to their thinking and inquiry. This spirit is often reflected as an attitude balanced between logical objectivity and a rich interest in human activity, between an ax-to-grind, case-to-win mission and a sincere desire to inform. The teacher of social studies, regardless of grade level, needs something of this spirit as he guides children in inquiry into the world of man and his problems. Stuart Chase's book *The Proper Study of Mankind** (New York: Harper & Row, Inc., 1956) stimulates the development of this spirit as well as a curiosity about the social sciences generally, although anthropology is the science most extensively treated in the book.

Books somewhat less exciting but more objective in point of view can also stimulate the development of the spirit of the social scientist and curiosity about social-science ideas. The following are recommended as simply written, well-illustrated general introductions to the social sciences:

Watson, Jane Werner, *The Sciences of Mankind*. New York: Golden Press, 1960.

The World's Social Structure. Introduction by Ashley Montague. International Pictorial Treasury of Knowledge. Englewood Cliffs, N.J.: International Graphic Society, 1963.

The following books present an excellent introduction to the social sciences at a higher level of abstraction:

Bierstedt, Robert, Eugene J. Meehan, and Paul A. Samuelson, *Modern Social Science*. New York: McGraw-Hill Book Company, 1964.

Bonner, Thomas N., Duane W. Hill, and George L. Wilber, *The Contemporary World: The Social Sciences in Historical Perspective*. Englewood Cliffs, N.J.: Prentice-Hall, Inc., 1960.

Berelson, Bernard, ed., *The Behavioral Sciences Today**. New York: Harper & Row, Publishers, 1963.

Handy, Rollo, and Paul Kurtz, *A Current Appraisal of the Behavioral Sciences*. Behavioral Research Council Bulletin, Great Barrington, Mass.: Behavioral Research Council, 1964.

Michaelis, John U., and A. Montgomery Johnston, eds., *The Social Sciences: Foundations of the Social Studies**. Boston: Allyn and Bacon, Inc., 1965.

It is helpful for the social-studies teacher to have a grasp of research methods in the social sciences. The following are recommended:

Berelson, Bernard, and Gary Steiner, *Human Behavior: An Inventory of Scientific Findings*. New York: Harcourt, Brace & World, 1964.

Gee, Wilson, *Social Science Research Methods*. New York: Appleton-Century-Crofts, Inc., 1950.

Each of the social sciences has its own unique spirit, method, and concern, and the teacher of social studies must have some appreciation and understanding of these. Each unit he constructs tends to be a study in history, geography, anthropology, or the like, depending on the topic or issue to be explored. The following recommendations will be directed largely toward six basic disciplines most often included in lists of the social sciences.

A very forthright and readable introduction to the spirit, method, and concern of history is Henry Steele's Commager's *The Nature and Study of History* (Columbus, Ohio: Charles E. Merrill Books, Inc., 1965). For teachers who wish a more philosophical, abstract presentation, the following are suggested:

Collingwood, R. G., *The Idea of History**. New York: Oxford University Press, 1956.

Cohen, Morris R., *The Meaning of Human History**, 2d ed. LaSalle, Ill.: Open Court, 1961.

For those who wish a rapid review of the panorama of world history, the following will prove helpful:

Brosse, Jacques, Paul Chaland, and Jacques Ostier, *100,000 Years of Daily Life.* New York: Golden Press Inc., 1961.

McNeill, William H., *The Rise of the West**. New York: The New American Library, 1963.

An excellent source to be consulted for an economically acquired grasp of the thought and method of the geographer is Jan O. M. Broek's *Geography: Its Scope and Spirit** (Columbus, Ohio: Charles E. Merrill Books, Inc., 1965). The following are recommended as review books in the area of geography:

Doerr, Arthur H., and J. L. Guernsey, Eugene Van Cleef, ed., *Principles of Geography**. Great Neck, N.Y.: Barron's Educational Series, Inc., 1959.

Wheeler, Jesse H., Jr., J. Trenton Kostbade, and Richard S. Thoman, *Regional Geography of the World,* rev. ed. New York: Holt, Rinehart and Winston, 1961.

Cole, J. P., *Geography of World Affairs**. Baltimore: Penguin Books, 1959.

Economics as a discipline is so rich in abstraction that the uninitiated become lost without a few definitive concepts. The following books offer simply defined economics concepts:

James, Clifford L., *Principles of Economics**. New York: Barnes and Noble, Inc., 1956.

Murad, Anatol, *Economics Problems and Principles**. Paterson, N.J.: Littlefield, Adams, and Co., 1963.

For an introduction to economics in terms of system and method, *Economics** by Richard S. Martin and Reuben G. Miller (Columbus, Ohio: Charles E. Merrill Books, Inc., 1965) is recommended. The following offer interesting insights into economics in human activity:

Cochran, Thomas C., *Basic History of American Business**. Princeton, N.J.: D. Van Nostrand Company, Inc., 1959.

*Economic Forces in the U.S.A. in Facts and Figures**. The U.S. Department of Labor, Bureau of Labor Statistics, in cooperation with International Cooperation Administration, Washington, D.C.: U.S. Government Printing Office, 1960.

Oxenfeldt, Alfred R., *Economic Systems in Action**. New York: Holt, Rinehart and Winston, 1957.

For an appreciation of political science as a social science, a sense of man's struggle to develop and maintain with his fellows a political structure through which to act and express himself is required. Such a sense may be developed through reading *The Web of Government** by R. M. MacIver (New York: The Free Press, 1965). For an introduction to the functions and problems of a more immediate political structure, Scott Greer's *Governing the Metropolis** (New York: John Wiley and Sons, Inc., 1962) is recommended. *Political Science: An Informal Overview** by Francis J. Sorauf (Columbus, Ohio: Charles E. Merrill Books, Inc., 1965) offers precisely what its title indicates. It includes an extremely readable introduction to the method of the political scientist. The following books offer applications of political thought in which social-studies teachers often find themselves involved:

Andrews, William G., *European Political Institutions**. Princeton, N.J.: D. Van Nostrand Company, Inc., 1962.

Barnett, Vince M., Jr., ed., *The Representation of the United States Abroad**. New York: Frederick A. Praeger, Publishers, 1965.

Corwin, Edward S., *The Constitution and What It Means Today**. New York: Atheneum, 1963.

Doyle, David Cushman, *The United Nations**. New York: The New American Library, 1965.

A semantic grasp of anthropology rests upon an appreciation of its paradoxical characteristic of objective intimacy with man everywhere. Perhaps the easiest approach for a social-studies teacher to an appreciation of this characteristic lies in reading *Childhood in Contemporary Cultures**, a fascinating book edited by Margaret Mead and Martha Wolfenstein (Chicago: The University of Chicago Press, 1955). For an overview of anthropology as a social science, *The Study of Anthropology** by Pertti J. Pelto (Columbus, Ohio: Charles E. Merrill Books, Inc., 1965) is recommended. The following books present forthright introductions to anthropology:

Kluckhohn, Clyde, *Mirror for Man**. Greenwich, Conn.: Fawcett World Library, 1944.

Kroeber, A. L., *Anthropology: Culture Patterns and Processes**. New York: Harcourt, Brace & World, Inc., 1948.

Jacobs, Melville, and Bernhard J. Stern, *General Anthropology**. New York: Barnes and Noble, Inc., 1952.

An adequate introduction to sociology as science and method is *Sociology: The Study of Man in Society**, by Caroline B. Rose (Columbus, Ohio: Charles E. Merrill Books, Inc., 1965). For a more extensive and deeper preview, *An Introduction to Sociology**, by Joseph A. Roucek and Roland L. Warren (Paterson, N.J.: Littlefield, Adams and

Company, 1957) is recommended. The following books probe somewhat more deeply into important areas in sociology:

Goode, William J., *The Family**. Englewood Cliffs, N.J.: Prentice-Hall Inc., 1964.

Mayer, Kurt B., *Class and Society**. New York: Random House, Inc., 1955.

Stein, Maurice R., *The Eclipse of Community**. New York: Harper & Row, Publishers, 1964.

There is much concern today for knowledge about the "hot spots" in various areas of the world. The social-studies teacher desiring up-to-date, penetrating information about Africa, Southeast Asia, China, the Middle East, and Latin America will find the following interesting and helpful:

Dean, Vera Micheles, *The Nature of the Non-Western World**. New York: New American Library, 1957. (Although somewhat dated, this book provides rich insights into problem areas.)

Bascomb, William R., and Melville J. Herskovits, eds., *Continuity and Change in African Cultures**. Chicago: The University of Chicago Press, Phoenix Edition, 1962.

Gibbs, James L., *Peoples of Africa*. New York: Holt, Rinehart and Winston, Inc., 1965.

Goldschmidt, Walter, ed., *The United States and Africa*. New York: Frederick A. Praeger, Publisher, 1963.

Hapgood, David, *Africa: From Independence to Tomorrow*. New York: Atheneum, 1965.

Butwell, Richard, *Southeast Asia Today and Tomorrow**. New York: Frederick A. Praeger, Publisher, 1964.

Henderson, William, ed., *Southeast Asia: Problems of United States Policy*. Cambridge, Mass.: The M. I. T. Press, 1963.

Hickey, Gerald Cannon, *Village in Vietnam*. New Haven and London: Yale University Press, 1964.

Mills, Lennox A., *Southeast Asia*. Minneapolis: University of Minnesota Press, 1964.

Chai, Ch'u, and Winberg Chai, *The Changing Society of China**. New York: New American Library, 1962.

Myrdal, Jan, *Report from a Chinese Village*. New York: Pantheon Books, 1965.

Baer, Gabriel, *Population and Society in the Arab East*. New York: Frederick A. Praeger, Publisher, 1964.

Cooke, Hedley V., *Challenge and Response in the Middle East*. New York: Harper and Brothers, 1952.

Alexander, Robert J., *Today's Latin America**. Garden City, N.Y.: Anchor Books, 1963.

The above list is at best an exceedingly small sample of current sources for information about these areas.

At first it is advised that the social-studies teacher seeking background in the social sciences choose those areas in which he will be immediately involved. For example, the upper-grade teacher who knows that his yearly commitment is largely restricted to history and geography would do well to study these areas first and to follow up with preparation in political science and economics. The primary teacher will most likely profit from studying somewhat more deeply in sociology, economics, and political science. The other social sciences should be sampled eventually to prepare the teacher more amply, for all the social sciences are richly interrelated and knowledge in one makes each of the others encountered all the more interesting and understandable.

No recommended reading has been suggested for some disciplines. Included among these are social psychology, psychology, psychiatry, law, and linguistics. With the exception of psychology, some foundation is given in the disciplines already discussed. They await the social-studies teacher whose interest carries him beyond the disciplines more commonly held as tangent to the elementary curriculum. Psychology is such a common foundation in all teacher-education programs that it was not felt necessary to include books relating to it as a discipline.

Unfortunately, few if any books are available for primary-grade social-studies teachers who are expected to guide children in the study of workers and processes. These studies are usually centered in the community and ideally the community can be used as the basic resource for gathering information. If the district provides field trips and qualified resource persons, the children can be guided in seeking information in a most realistic way. However, the adequacy of the guidance may be questioned if the teacher himself is not somewhat informed. When the teacher is uninformed, a richly dynamic study of transportation or communication deteriorates into a study of vehicles which guides children toward anthropomorphisms as concepts. It is recommended that the teacher who is to teach children about communication, community services, transportation, or some industrial process visit terminals, stations, headquarters, or industrial plants to explore and learn for himself the processes involved. If photographing is permitted, he should take notes with a camera. Prior to making his study visit, the teacher may inform himself somewhat by studying the following sources if they are available:

For an introduction to workers in all fields including community services: *Occupational Outlook Handbook*. Bulletin No. 1375, U.S. Department of Labor, Washington, D.C.: U.S. Government Printing Office, 1963.

For an introduction to industrial processes: Cooke, Donald E., *Marvels of American Industry*. Maplewood, N.J.: C. S. Hammond and Company, 1962.

For an introduction to communication as a process: Ruesch, Jurgen, and Weldon Kees, *Nonverbal Communication*. Berkeley: University of California Press, 1956.

SUMMARY

The social sciences as a total area focus on man and his activity. The social sciences commonly accepted as significant to elementary social studies include cultural geography, history, economics, political science, anthropology, sociology, psychology, and social psychology.

Ideas within the social sciences reflect overlapping and divergency. The overlap is due to a shared concern for man, interborrowing of ideas, and similarities in methods of research among the various social sciences. The divergency of ideas is largely a result of the social scientists' questioning attitude about the ideas in their various disciplines. A sense of the overlapping and divergency within the social sciences is helpful in acquiring background.

A basic controversy in the social sciences relates to where the focus of scrutiny should be directed. Some social scientists feel that it should be placed on logically developed models, while others feel that it should center on man's behavior. The social-studies teacher has a choice of either side of the controversy.

History deals with the past and change. Geography encompasses the study of region and its influence on man's ways of living. Economics deals generally with the problems related to the production, distribution, and consumption of goods and services. Political science treats of the problems of power and authority. Anthropology centers upon the complex patterns of ways of living developed by man everywhere for the conduct of effective living. Psychology is the study of man's individual behavior. Sociology searches into the group life of man. Social psychology looks into the effect of group life on the individual.

General approaches to the acquisition of background include taking courses, developing an independent program of reading and study, and taking advantage of every opportunity provided by the district to help teachers acquire background.

Exercises for Further Understanding

1. Obtain a copy of a textbook used for a beginning course in one of

the following: anthropology, economics, sociology, or political science. Read the introductory chapter and make a list of the "big" ideas presented. Think carefully about these ideas and find at least one application of each within your own living experience.

2. Obtain a copy of a textbook used for a college course in history. Select a chapter and read it carefully to determine whether the chapter deals primarily with political science, economics, or anthropology ideas.

3. Obtain a copy of a textbook used for a college course in cultural or regional geography. Select a chapter to read. Read it carefully to determine the facts related to dependency and interdependency.

4. The following are terms used in the social sciences. Attempt to define each in your own words, then look up each in two different social science textbooks: (1) money, (2) property, (3) division of labor, (4) culture, (5) group, (6) population, (7) natural resources, (8) government, (9) family, and (10) communication.

5. Using general references such as encyclopedias, almanacs, and atlases, make yourself an "instant" expert on two widely different nations. Then consider the kinds of information that you would really like to have. Express your lack of information in questions. The depth and breadth of your questions will reveal your background generally in the social sciences. Too few questions will usually indicate a need for further study.

Selected References

Note: Chapter 3 contains an extended discussion of general reference books. These books serve as *Selected References* for this chapter.

4

Organizing Content
in Social Studies

As the teacher seeks to acquire background, he has two essential aims: (1) to become acquainted with the "big ideas" or generalizations within the social sciences, and (2) to arrive at a sense of the structure of facts and ideas that support the generalizations. At the same time he may be thinking about a classroom of pupils and the requirements specified in his course of study, for after he has acquired the necessary background, he will select a generalization to serve as a guide for unit construction. This chapter deals with the problems involved in selecting a generalization from a social science and translating it in terms of social studies.

GENERALIZATION AS A PROCESS AND PRODUCT

Some teachers have difficulty in working with generalizations, due in part to their continuing concern for two basic elements, the matter being taught and the psychological aspects of the teaching-learning act.

The difficulty with the term *generalization* is that it can easily be used to describe both basic elements. Generalization has several meanings which describe what takes place from a psychological point of view when a child learns. Generalization may refer to the *process* of generalizing, or drawing experiential facts together to accomplish a task. This sort of generalization occurs when a person attempts to learn a second foreign language after he has already mastered one. He brings the skills learned while studying the first foreign language to the study of the second one. As a result of generalization, the second foreign language is easier to learn than the first.

Generalization may also refer to the *product* of having generalized or drawn experiential facts together to accomplish a task. In a sense, every act performed by a human being is a generalization. The child who pushes a stepstool closer to the kitchen counter as an aid to getting a cookie from a jar is expressing a generalization which takes into account his desire for something and the utility of certain objects in satisfying his desire. The little boy who stands very straight when the flag passes is expressing a generalization about the meaning of the flag and his behavior toward it in a particular situation.

Frequently the expression of a generalization includes language. The child who grimaces, snorts with disgust, pushes his salad to one side, and howls, "I don't like tomatoes," has expressed an easily understood generalization about tomatoes and their value to him.

Often the greater burden of the expression of a generalization is assumed by language, particularly when the generalization is a product of penetrating analysis and synthesis of facts. Scientific principles are examples of such generalizations, as are significant generalizations in the social sciences. It is social-science generalizations which are of concern to the social-studies teacher, for he will select one as the focal point around which to plan a teaching unit. The generalization will stand as a concise statement of the subject matter to be treated in the unit.

In terms of unit construction, generalization refers primarily to a product. To the social-studies teacher, the product will exist in the minds and behavior of his pupils as a result of his efforts to arrange experiences for them in which they will come in contact with social-studies facts. Because the generalization is first in his mind, he expresses it first in any written statement of content. He then expresses the facts the children must know before they can be expected to arrive at the generalization.

However, the social-studies teacher does not forget that there are aspects of process implicit in his use of the word *generalization*. Implicit are the assumptions that facts must be acquired, analyzed, and synthesized before a generalization can be reached.

Confusion about the term often stems from the teacher's difficulty in understanding that the generalization as subject matter may occur first in any expression of subject matter, but represents an objective to be reached in the teaching-learning act. In a factual book about the subject matter, the generalizations (in many instances, topical sentences in paragraphs) occur first and each is followed by supporting ideas and facts. In the teaching-and-learning act, the facts and supporting ideas often come first, followed by generalizations. This order is more obvious when the pupils are guided in inductive learning. It is to a certain extent apparent in deductive pattern of learning, where the generalization is held in doubt until a sufficient number of facts have been gathered and weighed to attest to its truth. The generalization is not arrived at until proved.

In building a unit, the teacher's first task is to determine what the content of the unit should be. In expressing this content, he uses a subject-matter orientation, that is, the generalization first, then the supporting ideas and facts.

In this discussion of the process-product aspect of a generalization, another aspect of it has been introduced—the generalization as expressed in observed behavior. The generalization as physical action alone, as physical action accompanied by language action, and as language action primarily, then, is a behavioral statement.

GENERALIZATION AS A BEHAVIORAL STATEMENT

Behaviorally speaking, a generalization may be defined as a statement of a concept at a given level of sophistication. The key term in this definition is *concept*. An educational psychologist,[1] a student of linguistics,[2] or a curriculum theorist[3] may each have his own way of de-

[1]Lee J. Cronbach, *Educational Psychology* (New York: Harcourt, Brace & Company, 1954), p. 281.

[2]Bertil Malmberg, *Structural Linguistics and Communication* (New York: Academic Press Inc., 1963), pp. 8-10.

[3]Paul R. Hanna, "Generalizations and Universal Values: Their Implications for the Social Studies Program," in *Social Studies in the Elementary School,* Nelson B.

fining or describing what the concept is, and each will find his definition or description to be highly useful, although it may differ from that of the others. Such is the nature of operational descriptions or definitions. Operationally, then, a *concept* is here defined as a behavioral "package" related to an item of matter, a particular quality, a function, or an idea. A generalization, as a statement of concept, presents the package in terms of its size and variety of content. Thus the generalization of the concept that a four-year-old has about an automobile will be less complex than the generalization of the same concept held by the automobile manufacturer.

Let us suppose that we wanted to communicate to a friend a generalization of the concept of automobile held by a four-year-old. We could choose among several methods. First, we could take our friend to observe the four-year-old as he reacts to an automobile in a variety of situations. After a number of observations, say a couple of dozen or so, the generalization, perhaps not quite the same as we have but similar to it, would be communicated. Second, we could take our friend to observe the four-year-old reacting to an automobile; as the child reacted to it, we could point out verbally certain aspects of his behavior. After two or three observations, the generalization would be communicated. Third, we could tell our friend the generalization. In the last instance, behavior is translated into language, as social-science thinkers translate highly abstract views of human behavior.

As far as the social-studies teacher is concerned, a social-science generalization is a behavioral statement of a concept at a given level of sophistication translated into a verbal statement.

To examine briefly the *level of sophistication* aspect of a generalization, let us consider the concept *man* as it may exist in the minds of several individuals:

1. *Man is a big moving thing that makes nice noises and plays with me.*
2. *Man is a big two-legged thing that wears pants, a shirt, and sometimes a necktie, has a deep voice and short hair, and is very strong.*
3. *Man is many workers who drive trucks, wear special clothes, and do all kinds of things such as deliver milk, letters, laundry, and clothes; sell gasoline, groceries, clothes, and toys; fight fires; and watch traffic.*
4. *Man is a being who depends on others of his kind for the goods and services that he needs, and they in turn, depend on him.*

Henry, ed. The Fifty-Sixth Yearbook of the National Society for the Study of Education (Chicago: National Society for the Study of Education, 1957), p. 29.

5. *Man is a thinking being who continually strives to control his environment for his own survival and betterment.*

An analysis of the above list of generalizations shows that the generalizations from 1 through 5 reflect ever-increasing levels of sophistication. The first is the simplest of all, 2 is less complex than 3, 3 is less complex than 4, and 5 is the most sophisticated of all. Possible categorizations are given within the list of generalizations. From a curriculum point of view, generalizations 1 and 2 are preschool generalizations learned by children during their early years in the home. Generalizations 3 through 5 are those that would be studied in school—3 would serve well in the primary grades, 4 in the intermediate grades, and 5 in the upper grades.

In the above statements, presented to show differences in level of sophistication, the concept being generalized, *man*, remained the same. Because the generalizations were definitions, there was little doubt as to what concept was being generalized. Definitions leave little doubt; other generalizations may leave more. If generalizations are descriptive, one's attention tends to be attracted to the descriptive element, as shown below:

1. People are *interdependent in the production, distribution, and consumption of goods.*
2. Transportation *functions to bring persons, goods, and services together at moments of necessity.*
3. George Washington was *the Father of our Country.*
4. Man is *unique, yet everywhere he is the same.*
5. Men *form into groups to accomplish tasks necessary to both their individual and social welfare.*

The descriptive element, as attractive as it is, is not the concept being generalized. The structural order of the statement demands that the language structure in the *subject* position be regarded as the concept. Thus the concepts being generalized above are *people, transportation, George Washington, man,* and *men.* The descriptive element in each statement serves to identify the direction of generalization. The same usually holds true for generalizations expressing relationships:

1. The *past* influences the present in many ways.
2. *The abundance and accessibility of natural resources in a given region* often contributes toward the standard of living of the people in that region.
3. The greater the density of population, the greater *the need for governmental regulation of behavior.*

4. The more prolonged the interaction between two peoples, the more will *they* become similar.
5. If wages rise, *prices* rise.
6. *We* appreciate the work of farmers.

The italicized language structures in the generalizations above indicate the concept being generalized. In 2, aspects of concept have been narrowed to include *abundance, accessibility,* and *in a given region*—all as they relate to *natural resources.* In 6, *we* is the concept. This state of affairs is natural and logical because the generalization indicates an attitude, and the study of it indicates a possible change in the concept of self.

So far, we have treated the social-science generalization as a behavioral statement, which, for purposes of formal unit organization, must be translated into a verbal statement. Language as a tool for communication and thought makes possible such a verbal statement for future direction and guidance, but sometimes at an exorbitant price. Language can as easily hang as a thick veil over concept as it can cast a revealing light into it. On the surface, a verbal statement of a generalization expresses no more than it says, but a verbal statement symbolizing a behavioral statement signifies much more. It signifies, particularly for social studies, not only the facts and subideas that support it, but ideas about attitudes and patterns of action as well. Therefore, the social-studies teacher must provide for the learning of at least a sufficient number of subideas and facts to assure a logical arrival at the generalization. He must also make provisions for the children to make inquiry into attitudes and patterns of action related to the generalization.

WORKING WITH GENERALIZATIONS TO DEVELOP UNIT CONTENT

As he works with generalizations to develop content for a social-studies unit, the teacher is concerned with both the cognitive and the affective aspects of knowledge. Nothing prevents him from scrutinizing first the affective aspects, then the cognitive, or from trying to consider the two simultaneously. However, most teachers tend to think about the cognitive aspects first, and to consider the affective aspects later. For this reason, the procedures suggested here will follow this way of thinking.

The procedures involved include selecting a generalization, restating it in terms of the topic of the unit, developing or recasting it to indicate attitudes and patterns of action, and preparing an outline of content. These procedures are presented in greater detail in the remainder of this section.

SELECTING A MAJOR GENERALIZATION

Some teachers can develop generalizations to be used in social studies. Others will have to consult a source of generalizations of one kind or another. The majority of teachers will have to consult sources which present generalizations in more specific form. One such source is an authoritative list[4,5]. Another source is a list developed by curriculum workers in a district, such as this list developed in the San Diego State College Laboratory School:

GENERALIZATIONS FROM GEOGRAPHY

Thematic Generalization: To exist, man must utilize natural resources.

Kindergarten
Man's basic natural resource is himself.
(Primary restatement: We must learn to take care of ourselves.)

Grade One
Next to himself, man's nearest natural resource is other men.
(Primary restatement: We must learn how to get along, work, and play with
others.
We depend upon many people for the things we need
and use.)

Grade Two
1. People working together are interdependent in the process of making things needed by everyone.
2. People working together are interdependent in the process of performing services for everyone.
3. Division of labor makes people more interdependent and at the same time

[4]John A. Michaelis and A. Montgomery Johnston, eds., *The Social Sciences: Foundations of the Social Studies* (Boston: Allyn and Bacon, Inc., 1965), pp. 308-339.
[5]Bernard Berelson and Gary A. Steiner, *Human Behavior: An Inventory of Scientific Findings* (New York: Harcourt, Brace & World, Inc.), 1964.

provides them with more goods and services than they would have if each man provided these things for himself.

Grade Three

1. A community, such as the local community, is a complex of many interdependent groups of people producing goods and services for community use.
2. A community is interdependent with other communities, sometimes for needed goods, sometimes for needed services, and often for both.
3. Communities differ in size and in the goods and services they produce.

Grade Four

1. A state is a large community composed of many different kinds of communities interdependent with each other for goods and services.
   a. Many of these communities work at processing natural resources into raw materials to be sold directly or to be manufactured into useful goods.
      (1) These natural resources must be used carefully to assure enough raw material for needed goods.
      (2) New ways to use natural resources must be found.
   b. Many of these communities work at manufacturing raw materials into useful goods.
   c. Large communities may have workers changing natural resources into raw materials and workers manufacturing raw materials into useful goods.
   d. Many communities are interdependent with communities outside the state for raw materials and manufactured goods.
2. The state as a community is interdependent with other states for raw materials and manufactured goods.

Grade Five

1. Our nation is a large community composed of states interdependent with each other for goods and services.
   a. Some of the states are grouped together in regions characterized by the natural resources available in them.
   b. There is manufacturing in all the states, but some states are leaders in manufacturing.
   c. The cities in these states often have large populations which work in the factories and consume many of the things they manufacture.
   d. Natural resources converted to raw materials are shipped from many states to these cities; manufactured goods are shipped everywhere within the nation.
2. Our nation is an industrial leader because of its abundance of natural resources, including human resources.
3. Our nation produces much more of some raw materials and manufactured

goods than it can use; it cannot produce enough of others; therefore, it is interdependent with other nations of the world.

4. Our nation has established a particular pattern of economic interdependence with Canada.

Grade Six

1. Latin American nations differ in the abundance and kinds of natural resources which they have available.
2. All nations are part of a global system of economic interdependence.

GENERALIZATIONS FROM HISTORY

Thematic Generalization: The historical past influences the present.
Kindergarten
1. Some important things happened long ago.
2. Some important men lived long ago.

Grade One
1. Long ago people lived in a different way from the way we do today.
2. In some ways, we live like people did long ago.

Grade Two
1. Long ago people made and distributed things in ways different from the ways used today.
2. Some of the old ways are still being used.

Grade Three
1. Almost every modern community shows evidence of change in the ways that people live and produce things.
2. Changes in the ways of doing things may occur when people desire change and when a way of bringing about a change is available.
3. Changes in the ways of doing things may occur as a result of important events in other places.
4. The work and deeds of outstanding men contribute to the founding and growth of a community.
5. The direction of change is not always the same.

Grade Four
1. Our state has a unique cultural history, evidences of which are manifested in its people's speech, holiday celebrations, architecture, and ways of thinking because:
   a. Various groups of people with different ways of living settled in the area now a state.
   b. Various groups of people settled the area now a state for different reasons.

c. The various groups coming to the state have made a series of adjustments to each other and to the resources available.
2. Our state has a unique political history because:
   a. The basic source of public authority changed from era to era.
   b. The goal of statehood led the people to a series of actions which culminated in a series of significant events.
   c. Outstanding men assumed roles of leadership.
3. Our state has a unique economic history because:
   a. It attracted people with particular interests and abilities.
   b. Developments in transportation and communication helped the state to develop unity and stronger relations with the rest of the nation.
   c. Developments in land-use patterns increased production.

Grade Five

1. Our nation has a unique economic history because:
   a. It has a rich and varied abundance of natural resources, including human resources.
   b. It attracted people with particular interests and abilities and provided a cultural climate that fostered the development of ideas in the solution of technological problems in manufacturing, agriculture, transportation, and communication.
   c. Many persevering thinkers and experimenters made important contributions.
2. Our nation has a unique political history because:
   a. Early it accepted and implemented a deep commitment toward democracy as a way of life and a form of government.
   b. It assumed gradually a role of leadership in international political affairs.
3. The economic and political history of Canada is similar in many ways to that of the United States.
4. Canada and the United States share a common cultural heritage with modifications unique to each nation.

Grade Six

1. The Latin American nations have a unique political history because:
   a. Hispanic culture was established early as the dominant culture with particular political values and practices.
   b. Hispanic political ideas and practices were modified by the culture of indigenous Latin American societies and by the immigration of large numbers of Europeans from other cultures, and by the transmission of political ideas from other emerging democracies, particularly the American democracy.
2. Each Latin American nation has a unique political history because:

a. The rate of settlement varied from one nation to another.

b. The mother cultures of the settlers varied from one nation to another.

c. Communication with other nations varied from one nation to another.

GENERALIZATIONS FROM ANTHROPOLOGY

Thematic Generalization: Man is man, yet everywhere he is unique.

Kindergarten
People in other places are different in the ways they do things.

Grade One
Families and schools are different in other places.

Grade Two
1. People wear different clothes and eat different foods in other places.
2. People in some countries are very much alike in the clothing they wear and in the food they eat.
3. All people need food and clothing.

Grade Three
1. Indians, like the members of any culture, were born into particular ways of doing things, such as:
   a. Providing for food needs
   b. Providing for shelter needs
   c. Providing for clothing needs
   d. Ways of communicating
   e. Ways of transporting.
2. Indian cultures varied in ways of doing things.
3. A fairly common characteristic among Indian cultures was the direct use of natural resources in their immediate environment to obtain the things they needed for living.
4. The direct use of natural resources influenced the division of labor within the family and community, thereby affecting the ways of family and community life.
5. The different resources within the various parts of the United States account in part for the variety of Indian cultures.
6. Our culture is indebted to Indian culture for some of our popular foods, words in our language, clothing design, and types of recreation.

Grade Four
1. The early Spaniards had ways of doing things quite different from those found in California today:
   a. Clothing, shelter, and food
   b. Language, ways of communicating and transporting
   c. Ideas about wealth

d. Ideas about religion

e. Ideas about the value of people

2. The Spaniards changed some of their ways of doing things by borrowing from the Indians and by modifying their ways of making use of natural resources and human resources.

3. The Spaniards, because their culture was stronger in many ways, changed many of the Indian's ways of doing things, but not completely.

4. Spanish culture was in turn replaced by a stronger American culture, but not completely.

5. Our culture in California is indebted to the early Spaniards for ideas in architecture, ideas about land-use patterns, certain kinds of food, words in our language, and ways of celebrating state and local holidays.

Grade Five

1. The culture into which we are born is characterized by democratic ways of living and a highly developed technology.

2. Our culture has borrowed much from other cultures; in a sense, we are a "melting pot" of cultures, but from the "melting" has come uniqueness.

3. The culture most closely related to ours is English culture.

4. We share this characteristic with Canada.

Grade Six

1. A culture is socially learned and consists of the knowledge, beliefs, and values which human groups have invented to establish rules of group life and methods of adjusting to and exploiting the natural environment.

2. Hispanic culture influences the ways of living in most Latin American countries.

3. Various Indian cultures have strongly influenced the ways of living in some Latin American countries.

4. Cultures in Latin America are varied from country to country.

GENERALIZATIONS FROM POLITICAL SCIENCE

Thematic Generalization: Two essential functions of government are to serve and regulate in the public interest.

Kindergarten

Signs and signals are for our protection.

Grade One

Firemen and policemen are hired by our community to protect us and our property.

Grade Two

1. We respect the property of others and they respect ours.

2. We keep our property clean and free of litter out of respect to others and to ourselves.

Grade Three

1. Our community elects officers who are responsible for maintaining services for everyone in the community.
2. A community pays for these services through taxes.
3. Transportation between communities is kept orderly by laws.
4. A community maintains schools for the education of everyone.

Grade Four

1. A state has a government consisting of a governor, a law-making body, and a system of courts.
2. Most of the members of the state government are elected by the people.
3. The state government maintains services for the people of the state.

Grade Five

1. Our nation has a government which consists of a president, a congress, a supreme court, and many workers.
2. The president and the congress depend upon the voters of the entire nation to become accepted as part of the government.
3. The voters depend upon the president and the congress to govern well by doing, among other things, whatever is needed to:
   a. Provide for the national defense
   b. Promote the general welfare of the people through
      (1) regulating business
      (2) regulating labor
      (3) regulating transportation
      (4) regulating communication
4. The most important task of our government is to safeguard the freedom of the individual citizen.
5. Through our government, our nation exercises a role of leadership in solving world problems.
   a. This role of leadership has been assigned and accepted on the basis of political strength and economic wealth.
   b. This role of leadership brings many responsibilities.

Grade Six

1. Because Latin American countries share a cultural heritage different from that of the United States, there are certain basic differences between United States and Latin American governments in structure:
   a. Ways of conducting elections
   b. The powers of the president
   c. The powers of legislative bodies
   d. The powers of government as a whole
2. Because of different bases for economy, the Latin American governments differ in governmental structure.

3. Because of wide variations in political ideas, Latin American governments differ in governmental structure.

GENERALIZATIONS FROM ECONOMICS

Thematic Generalization: Productive resources are scarce and human wants are unlimited; however, economic welfare is a goal in most, if not all, societies.

Kindergarten
By using wisely, we have them when we need them.

Grade One
1. The bank and the people at the bank help us to save money.
2. If we save our money, we can buy things that we want.
3. People earn money by providing needed services or producing needed goods.

Grade Two
By having people produce different goods and services, we have more goods and services than if we tried to produce them all by ourselves.

Grade Three
1. Within a local community, the productive resources are used to produce goods and services needed in the community.
2. No modern community can produce all the goods and services it wants; it must depend upon other communities, and, in turn, provides other communities with goods and services.

Grade Four
1. Economic welfare in California reflects a high standard because of the availability of both natural and human resources.
2. California contributes to the welfare of the nation because of its industrial leadership in agriculture, manufacturing, and mining.

Grade Five
1. Economic welfare in the United States reflects a high standard because of the availability of both natural and human resources.
2. Human resources in America have led to a high standard of living because of the private enterprise system, rapid technological development which leads to the better use of available resources, new uses for materials once not considered as resources, and specialization of labor.
3. Maintaining a high standard of living brings problems.

Grade Six
1. Economic welfare varies from one Latin American country to another; therefore, the standard of living varies from one country to another.

2. In some countries, private enterprise is inhibited for a very large majority of the population because land and resource ownership resides in the hands of a few people or is controlled by foreign interests.
3. In some countries resources are limited.
4. In some countries there is little technological development other than that borrowed from the United States or European countries.
5. Specialization of labor is limited for a large number of the population.

GENERALIZATIONS FROM PSYCHOLOGY

Thematic Generalization: Human behavior is purposive and goal-directed.

Kindergarten
1. We do some things for our own health and safety.
2. At other times we have choices among the things we can do.

Grade One
1. In some ways we are all very much alike in how we do things.
2. In some ways we are quite different in how we do things.
3. We work to get things done.
4. Sometimes we work together to get things done.

Grade Two
1. All people need things to eat and wear.
2. They work to obtain these things.
3. Sometimes we work in one group; at other times we work in another group.

Grade Three
1. All people need food, shelter, clothing, and to be with other people.
2. People in the community work to earn the things they need.
3. People must work together to provide for their needs.
4. Good work is satisfying to a worker.
5. People do things in certain ways because that is the way they learned to do them.
6. People living in a community identify themselves as members of that community.

Grade Four
1. People living in a state or county identify themselves as members of that state or county.
2. People move from one part of the country to another for basically the same reasons; generally, people move to improve themselves and the way they live.
3. People who come to a new area group or enter groups as a means of answering their common needs.

Grade Five

1. The citizens of a nation develop understandings, attitudes, and patterns of behavior related to membership in the national society.
2. Traits of leadership are those which are instrumental in guiding a group in the solution of problems common to the group.
3. Personal, social, cultural, political, and economic problems give direction to individual behavior.
4. The ways of thinking and behaving characteristic of the American democracy are the products of interpersonal and intrapersonal interaction over a period of years.

Grade Six

1. The members of national groups possess certain common values and characteristics.
2. People in the different societies of the world have learned different ways of perceiving, thinking, feeling, and behaving.
3. Social groups at the national level tend to resist change, or tend to want to give direction to change.

GENERALIZATIONS FROM SOCIOLOGY

Thematic Generalization: Man is a social being.

Kindergarten

1. We are a group that lives, works, and plays in a classroom.
2. Each of us belongs in the group.
3. Often we must work together.

Grade One

1. We are members of different groups—the family, the classroom, the school, and the neighborhood.
2. We are members of a larger group.
3. We depend upon others to protect us.
4. We depend upon others to have the things and services that we need.
5. Others depend upon us for what they need.

Grade Two

1. Groups of people work together to provide the things they need.
2. Groups of people work together to produce things and services for other groups of people.
3. Communication is a way of exchanging ideas.
4. People communicate to solve problems.
5. People communicate in different ways.

Grade Three

1. The people who live in a city are an interdependent group.
2. They depend upon each other for goods and services.

3. They depend upon other groups outside the city and in other cities for the things and services they need.
4. The groups must work together for people to have all the goods and services they need.

Grade Four
1. The people in a state are basically a political group.
2. The people in a state interact to maintain a government.
3. There are community groups of various sizes within a state.
4. The size of community groups is determined in some ways by what is available in the environment to provide for the needs of people.
5. Groups make changes in their environment to be able to meet their needs better.

Grade Five
1. The people in a nation are a large interdependent group.
2. Groups of people within a nation are interdependent socially, culturally, politically, and economically.
3. National migration develops cultural diversity within a group and cultural diffusion among groups.
4. Changes in population are accompanied by social, cultural, and economic problems.
5. Modern inventions have extended the communities of man.

Grade Six
1. Social classes form as a result of the development of status factors which may include heredity, wealth, education, occupation, and others.
2. Persons and groups migrating to a new environment lose the modes of behavior already acquired and gradually take on those of the new society.

GENERALIZATIONS FROM THE STUDY OF BIOGRAPHY

Thematic Generalization: Great men work to preserve and enrich a cultural heritage.

Kindergarten
1. Some great men lived long ago.
2. Great men are brave.

Grade One
1. Some great men lived long ago.
2. Some great men had to work very hard to succed.

Grade Two
1. Some great men lived long ago.
2. Some great men were leaders of men.

Grade Three
1. Some great men lived long ago.
2. Great men are leaders in many kinds of work.
3. Great men are resourceful and do not give up easily.
4. Great men come from all walks of life.

Grade Four
1. Great men lived and worked during different times in history.
2. Some great men have shown their greatness by suffering hardships to achieve important goals for the good of others.
3. Some great men have shown their greatness by blazing trails through wilderness.

Grade Five
1. During times of stress, great men cooperate to accomplish important goals for a nation.
2. The accomplishments of great men sometimes bring them great personal rewards and always better the lives of a vast number of people.
3. Great men share the same characteristics: courage, resourcefulness, and perseverance; and as such they serve as models of behavior.
4. Every society owes a debt to its great men for their contributions.

Grade Six
1. Every nation has its great men.
2. Some men achieve greatness through their work in international affairs.

If the district or county includes generalizations in its social-studies guide or course of study, the guide or course of study should be regarded as the primary source. Other sources, if available, should be consulted as an aid in determining the final statement of the generalization. If no guide or course of study is provided, the teacher should feel free to consult any available source.

The teacher or curriculum worker must consider several factors as he goes about selecting a major generalization for a unit. These factors include the specifics listed in the guide or the course of study, the characteristics of the children to be taught, the materials available, and the teacher's own teaching style.

The teacher should have some voice in choosing the content which he is to teach, but he should also recognize that his choices are limited by his guide or course of study (if he is provided one), and rightly so. The guide or course of study represents an attempt by the district to articulate social-studies learnings through the grades. Such articulation assures continuity of learnings for children. If there is no attempt at articulation, children are often guided into areas recently covered in the previous grades or into areas meant for the following grade.

The pattern of articulation of learning through the grades is often expressed in terms of topic or unit titles of what should be studied in each grade. The teacher should analyze these specifics for clues as to the nature of the social-studies content to be taught. Sometimes the topics or unit titles indicate the social-science emphasis to be reflected in the social-studies program. For example, if the topic assigned is *thrift,* the unit to be developed should be built around economic ideas, or reflect an emphasis in economics. If the topic specified is *historical backgrounds of our government,* the unit should be built around ideas from history and political science. If the topic or unit titles are so brief that there are few clues as to the emphasis to be struck in the unit, the teacher may find it helpful to consult his administrator and other teachers in his school or district to determine what emphasis, if any, is given within the various topics.

Often an inexperienced teacher will select a major generalization on the basis of a preferred area of study, only to find that the district has provided no materials for children to use in studying a generalization within that area. For example, a teacher who has just successfully completed a course in political science may decide that his pupils in third grade need to take a careful look at the structure of government. With carefully prepared materials, pupils in third grade can profit from such a study, but the teacher finds that there are no materials available for a study of government in that grade. His choices are to (1) seek another generalization for which there are available materials, or (2) develop his own materials.

Before he attempts to select a generalization, the teacher should review carefully the materials available for the pupils. First he will survey the available materials to see whether basic and supplemental materials are provided. He will want to know whether there are basic textbooks and basic references such as maps and globes, encyclopedia, atlases, almanacs, and the like, and how many of these are provided. Of particular interest to him will be the abundance and variety of supplemental materials, such as fiction and nonfiction books, films, filmstrips, and picture series.

The teacher should also make a quality check of the materials. He will have to examine the basic textbooks to see whether there is a marked emphasis or a lack of emphasis within the book. For example, a teacher in grade eight may find that the basic textbook in United States history tends to emphasize only the political development of the United States, or he may find that the textbook reflects equal emphasis on political, economic, and cultural development. The teacher should examine the other materials as well to determine the nature of the emphasis in them. Whenever he surveys books, he should gauge the readability of the books and note how well they are organized. Whenever possible, he should preview films, filmstrips, and picture series to see precisely what information these materials convey.

If, as a result of his survey, the teacher finds that an area is well presented within the materials provided, he will tend to choose as a major generalization that statement which is well supported in the materials.

One factor gives the teacher considerable leeway in the choice of generalizations, regardless of the abundance or lack of materials and regardless of the limitations imposed by a guide or course of study. That factor is the teacher himself. If his knowledge of an area is solid and if he knows the basic ideas inherent in the area, he often may be able to provide pupils with an excellent contact for information. Through simple chalkboard illustrations, simply made illustrations such as charts, graphs, maps, and picture series, and through excellent use of community resources, he may guide his pupils toward acquiring important social-studies ideas far more effectively and economically than could be done with the most attractive textbooks, films, filmstrips, and the like. Such a teacher may choose almost any generalization as a basis for a unit, provided, of course, there is some justification for his choice within the course of study.

Occasionally, a teacher, particularly the new teacher or the teacher hired at a long distance from where he is going to teach, cannot check the recommendations in a course of study or guide and cannot survey the materials. In most instances, he can determine the topic area with which he is to teach. With this limited information, he can make a choice of a major generalization. He knows from his professional training and laboratory experience what can usually be expected in terms of materials. He goes ahead and constructs a unit, fully expecting that he may have to alter his construction as he works with his pupils.

RESTATING THE MAIN GENERALIZATION

Once the teacher has selected the major generalization for the unit, he examines it carefully to see whether it needs to be restated in more precise terms. Restatement will more than likely be necessary, and the extent required will depend on the source from which he selected the generalization. If he selected it from an authoritative list, he may have to restate it. The generalizations in such lists are stated in terms significant to a social science. A generalization chosen from such a list is usually not specific enough in terms of a topic area. For example, a teacher of grade four could select the following as the generalization about which to construct a unit:

The historical past influences the present.

The teacher restates the generalization to reflect the history of Oregon, in this way:

The ways of living of the early Oregonians can still be seen in our ways of living today.

If the teacher has selected the generalization from a list published by a district other than his own, he should restate the generalization in terms of the topic area specified by his own district. For example, a teacher of grade six who wishes to teach a unit about Africa selects the following generalization from a list developed by a district other than his own:

Because of wide variations in political ideas, Latin American governments differ in governmental structure.

The teacher restates the generalization to reflect the political structure of African countries, like this:

Because of wide variations in the development of political ideas, African governments differ in governmental structure.

The teacher in this instance is well aware of the differences between Latin America and Africa as complexes of countries. He has reflected his knowledge in the restatement of the generalization.

Often the generalization chosen by the teacher will be too broad and sweeping; therefore, he will want to restate it in terms more specific to a topic. In his restatement, he will also want to identify more specifically the subareas of concentration. For example, a teacher of grade three has selected the following generalization as the basic statement around which to construct a unit:

Culture consists of the knowledge, beliefs, and values which human groups have invented to establish rules of group life and methods of adjusting to the natural environment.

The teacher, whose topic area is *the Nez Perce Indians*, makes the following restatement:

Nez Perce culture consists of the ways the Nez Perce Indians developed for providing themselves with food, shelter, and clothing, for expressing themselves, for governing themselves, for educating themselves, for the use of leisure time, and for fulfilling religious needs.

In this restatement, the teacher has expressed the generalization in terms more understandable to children in grade three. He has also identified subareas of concentration—ways for providing food, shelter, and clothing, ways for expression, ways for self-government, and the like.

Restatement of the generalization serves two purposes: (1) to translate the generalization in the specific terms of the topic, and (2) to express the generalization in terms of the children who are going to study it. The first purpose, once fulfilled, answers the teacher's need for a more precise guide for organizing content in the unit. It has been discussed to this point. The other purpose, somewhat implicit in the examples given, will receive further consideration.

As the teacher attempts to restate the basic generalization that he has chosen as the base for the unit, he considers the characteristics of the children whom he is going to teach. Through the sources available to him, such as report cards from the previous year, former teachers of the children, cumulative records, and the administrator, he checks as carefully as he can the experiential and intellectual background of the children.

The experiential background of the children reflects the opportunities that the children have had for contact with a much wider area than just home-and-neighborhood space. Since home-and-neighborhood space is basic, the teacher will probe as deeply as he can the nature of the community in which the children reside. Children in farms, cities, and small towns have different needs in terms of contact with a wider life. Each has a quite different experiential base. More important, perhaps, than the kind of neighborhood, is the cultural level of the neighborhood. If the people who live in the neighborhood are prone to travel widely during summers, are relatively well educated, make wide use of transmission media such as newspapers, radio, television, magazines, and libraries for current information, and subscribe generally to a high standard of living and conduct, their children will quite likely be able to profit from the study of more abstract generalizations. If the cultural level of a neighborhood indicates deprivation, the children of such a neighborhood will more than likely have to be guided into the study of simpler generalizations.

The intellectual background of the children reflects the richness of contact, regardless of how wide the area of contact may be. Children who have a high ability in the areas of abstract thinking and skills, as measured by standardized tests, or children who are highly successful in school, will be able to study more abstract generalizations. When children have difficulty with abstract thinking and skills, or do not enjoy a high level of success in school, they will have to be guided into the study of less abstract generalizations.

The chronological age of the children to be taught also influences the teacher's restatement of the generalization. In some instances, a generalization which is a definition or an expression of an abstract statement is too abstract for younger children. The teacher may then recast it into a strongly descriptive statement which relates to some aspect of the selected generalization. For example:

The selected generalization: *Leaders in government are given the power to make decisions and are held responsible for the wise use of that power.* The recast generalization: *Our president has many important jobs.*

The recasting in this instance touches upon only one essential aspect of the generalization, that is, the responsibilities of a leader. This aspect will lead toward ideas about his power, a very important element in the generalization. Younger children may not learn much more about the generalization profitably.

The teacher's restatement of the basic generalization represents his best assessment of what his pupils need within the specific framework of his district. As far as the unit under construction is concerned, this restatement becomes the main generalization.

RECASTING THE MAJOR OR MAIN GENERALIZATION

Usually, the generalization chosen and restated as a major generalization pertains more to subject matter or informational area than it does to attitudes or patterns of behavior. It is probably of direct significance to a social science. Therefore, the social-studies teacher must recast it to develop generalizations pertaining to desirable attitudes and patterns of behavior. In this recasting, social studies emerges from the synthesis of social-science facts and principles and children's needs as citizens now and tomorrow. As far as social studies is concerned, any statement chosen as a first major generalization is an incomplete learning statement. The extent of its incompleteness becomes apparent when one applies an attitude of skepticism to the generalization. One may exercise this skepticism by merely asking, "What difference does that make?" or "So what?" after hearing or reading the generalizations under consideration. For example:

The historical past influences the present. So what?
Economic resources are limited; human wants are unlimited. What difference does that make?

The social-studies teacher helps children ask these questions and find answers for them. In so doing, he is teaching social studies. The first major generalization as restated merely sets the stage to make possible this kind of teaching. The teacher begins to provide for such teaching by recasting the first generalization to correspond to attitudes related to it.

An attitude, or a disposition to act or respond in a certain way to a complex of factors, is a product of experience and learning; it stems from knowledge. From a social-studies point of view, it is assumed that an attitude may be acquired through formal learning, particularly when the desired attitude is known by the teacher and serves as an objective for learning. Since the content objective of social studies comprises facts and principles about natural resources, people and peoples, their ways of doing things, and their problems, it follows that attitudes, part of the subjective content of social studies, will relate to these facts and principles. As he works to recast the first major generalization in terms of an attitude, or set of related attitudes, the teacher thinks of the language necessary for expressing attitudes.

An attitude, stated verbally, usually identifies a referent and a way of acting, but not the details of the fact itself. Frequently, the statement of attitude indicates the referent through the use of such terms as *we, people, man,* or *everyone.* It is clear to the reader of such a statement that it is *he* who is really the referent. For example, the attitude *We should appreciate our cultural heritage,* appeals to the reader in such a way that he personally recites to himself, "I should appreciate our cultural heritage." The identification of the way of acting is expressed through terms of feeling such as *be enthusiastic about, respect,* or *appreciate.* Occasionally, the identified way of acting may be made more demanding through the use of terms of demand such as *should, ought to, must,* or even the more urgent *have to.* The following statements of an attitude reflect the shades of meaning possible through the change of referents and the use of terms of demand:

> We appreciate our cultural heritage.
> Man appreciates his cultural heritage.
> Everyone should appreciate our cultural heritage.
> People ought to appreciate their cultural heritage.

Generally the referent *we* serves well; *must* and *should* are about as far as one needs to go in the use of terms of demand.

The final step in developing a statement of attitude is to relate it to the content of the main generalization and to add a *therefore* statement indicating the attitude, in this way:

> *Economic welfare in California reflects a high standard because of the availability of both natural and human resources.* (Main generalization)
> *Economic welfare in California reflects a high standard because of the availability of both natural and human resources; therefore, we appreciate the availability in both natural and human resources in California.* (Attitude added in the *therefore* statement)

Such a cumbersome statement is not necessary. The attitude statement can just as well stand by itself:

> *We appreciate the availability of both natural and human resources in California.*

Note that only the most significant part of the first major generalization is used in the statement of attitude, in this case, *the availability of both natural and human resources.*

The teacher who thinks clearly and can express himself well will develop a paraphrase statement of attitude:

> *We appreciate the richness of resources in California.*

When the main generalization has been stated and stands before such a statement, the meaning of the statement is clear.

Occasionally a list of generalizations will include attitude generalizations as well as objective-content generalizations, as does the one developed from an authoritative list for use in the Laboratory School at San Diego State College. The following pairs of generalizations, one dealing with objective content and the other with attitude, are taken from that list:

The voters depend upon the President and the Congress to govern well by doing, among other things, whatever is needed to:
  a. Provide for the national defense
  b. Promote the general welfare of the people through
    (1) regulating business
    (2) regulating labor
    (3) regulating transportation
    (4) regulating communication.
The most important task of our government is to safeguard the freedom of the individual citizen.

The early Spaniards had ways of doing things quite different from those found in California today.

Our culture in California is indebted to the early Spaniards for ideas in architecture, ideas about land-use patterns, certain kinds of food, words in our language, and ways of celebrating state and local holidays.

In many instances, the teacher may not be able to find in a list another generalization expressing attitude directly related to the objective-content generalization. He will have to develop a generalization or series of generalizations as a statement of attitude. The following are a few statements, each of which could be used as a first major generalization in a unit, and the statements, or generalizations, of attitude related to them:

The bank and the people at the bank help us to save money.
We appreciate what the bank and its workers do for us.

George Washington was a courageous, resourceful, and persevering man.
We owe much to George Washington.

Our community elects officers who are responsible for maintaining services for everyone in the community.

We respect these officers for the service that they provide the community.

Social groups at the national level tend to resist change, or tend to want to give direction to change.
We respect the efforts made by others to resist change or to give it particular direction.

Recasting the main generalization to reflect attitude basically involves identifying the referent and identifying a way of acting (a logical extension) as it is related to the main generalization.

Another recasting is necessary to indicate a pattern of action directly related to the main generalization. This recasting, too, is a logical extension. It completes the answer to "So what?" or "What difference does it make?"—the questions which may be reasonably asked after the statement of the objective-content generalization. It identifies what the individual does (either by himself or in a group), what he can or may do, as a result of knowing something and feeling in a particular way about it. As illustrated below, it is the final "therefore" statement.

Thomas Edison was a resourceful man who did not give up easily; therefore, we admire Edison for his resourcefulness and courage; therefore, we strive to develop habits of resourcefulness and courage.

Much of what has been discussed related to developing a statement of attitude applies as well to the statement of pattern of action. A personal referent, such as *we, people, man,* or *everyone,* is usually a part of the statement. Occasionally, the identified pattern of action is couched in terms of demand such as *should, ought to, must,* or even the more urgent *have to.* And again, the personal referent *we* serves well, and there is little need to go beyond *must* or *should* in terms of demand. A pattern of action, as is an attitude, is more directly related to the most significant part, or referent, of the first major generalization. The following are examples of objective-content generalizations logically extended to include both attitude and pattern of action:

Denver is a complex of many interdependent groups of people producing goods and services for community use.
We appreciate the many people who work together to provide us with the goods and services we need in Denver.

We can make life more pleasant for these people by using goods and services wisely.

The United States has a unique political history because early it accepted and implemented a deep commitment toward democracy as a way of life and a form of government and because it assumed gradually a role of leadership in international political affairs.

We appreciate the many advantages of living in a democracy and the role which the United States must play in international affairs.

As Americans, we must work to guarantee the advantages of democracy for posterity and for other peoples in the world.

New York has a government consisting of a governor, a law-making body, and a system of courts.
Our state government is an expression of ourselves.
We must participate in state government.

In some Latin American countries both natural and human resources are limited.
We admire the economic progress made in some Latin American countries despite the lack of resources.
We must work to find ways to help certain Latin American peoples to improve their ways of using resources.

The people in Japan wear different clothes and eat different foods.
We appreciate these differences.
We look forward to real experiences with the Japanese people.

Recasting the main generalization to reflect a pattern of action basically involves identifying the referent and identifying a pattern of action (a logical extension).

The teacher's purpose in recasting the main generalization into statements reflecting attitudes and patterns of action is to develop verbal reminders to serve as signposts to learning activities leading into the affective objectives of the unit. Identifying the referent and a way of feeling and acting (plus occasionally an expression of urgency such as *ought, should,* and the like) results in understandable signposts. However, some social-studies educators feel that signposts constructed in this way are too exhortative and moralistic. They prefer more objective signposts—those that suggest a greater number of choices for the learner.

Recasting the main generalization into attitudinal and action signposts of an objective type requires another way of thinking. The teacher examines the generalization to develop a strong statement of relationship between or among the factors within the generalization. Such a statement invites the inference of attitudes and patterns of action. This is true of statements such as the following:

1. The greater the exercise of the free vote and the greater the majority of votes cast for a candidate or slate of candidates, the more solid the basis for authority in government.
2. The greater the abundance of natural and human resources, the higher the level of economic welfare in a region.
3. If the cultural interaction between two societies is intensive and of long duration, the two societies will tend to have fewer conflicts.
4. Improvement of world transportation rests upon the following:
   a. World recognition of the need for improvement.
   b. Positive relations among the various nations.
   c. Technological advancements.

ORGANIZING INFORMATION

Once the teacher has developed the main generalization and statements of attitudes and patterns of action for the unit, he has the basic framework for the unit. He is now prepared to complete the framework in greater detail. As he works in selecting, restating, and recasting the main generalization, much of what he does is influenced by what he already knows about the topic area that he plans to teach. He has completed a careful survey of the topic area in books and whatever other sources are available to him. He has a fund of notes in outline form. The process of information gathering has left him with a point of view and a sensitivity that have given direction to his work with the generalization. His next task is to merge his background with the generalization to express more precisely what the content of the unit is to be.

The main generalization is the objective-content generalization. Children may be expected to arrive at it only after experiencing the social-science facts placed after it in the unit.

1. Analyze the generalization to determine what basic background is required before studying the basic facts directly related to the generalization. For example, if the topic area has to do with a manufacturing process, the children should have a general idea of what a factory is, as well as the product manufactured. If the topic area is Holland, the children should have some idea about its general location. This basic background should be expressed in a few statements, and if necessary,

supporting facts should be added. (Examples of this expression may be seen in the first section of each unit presented in the Appendix.)

2. Analyze the generalization to determine its areas of content. In the following generalizations, the verbal clues to the areas of content are printed in italics:

The Hopi Indians, like the members of any other culture, *learned from their parents and others in their society particular ways of doing things, such as: providing for food needs, providing for shelter needs, providing for clothing needs, communicating, and transporting.*

The Iowa State government *maintains services for the people of Iowa.*

The people of Peru have learned different *ways of perceiving, thinking, feeling, and behaving.*

The areas of content in the first generalization are rather clearly indicated, but in the second and third generalizations they are given only in general terms. The teacher must state these terms more specifically. Each area of content is expressed in a statement or series of statements, with such supportive statements and facts as are necessary. The result is an outline of objective content which fully extends the first major generalization. (Examples of this expression may be seen in the units presented in the Appendix.)

The first extension of the main generalization is into subjective-content generalizations that deal with attitude development. If children are to be able to form these generalizations, they will have to have experiences with facts that appeal to feelings of sympathy, empathy, appreciation, respect, and the like. For example, if children are to appreciate fully the policeman and his work, they may have to know what the qualifications of a policeman are, what his arduous training is like, and how he risks his life to protect persons and property. If they are to appreciate the level of technological advancement of a people, they will need to see that level of advancement as effective for the people who have developed it, and thus to be commended.

The teacher analyzes each attitudinal generalization to determine the kinds of ideas needed to guide the children toward developing a worthwhile attitude or set of attitudes as related to the first major generalization. He expresses these ideas in a series of statements and supporting facts. Often the supporting facts are similar to those learned during the study that leads to the first major generalization; therefore, they need not be repeated again in the unit. However, the development of attitude may demand that these facts be examined from another point of view. (For examples of statements listed after the second major generalization or as extensions of the main generalization, examine the third section of each unit in the Appendix.)

The second extension of the main generalization is into the subjective-content generalizations pointing the way for the development of a pattern of action. If children are expected to form these generalizations, they will need to be guided into experiencing ideas which give or suggest a pattern of action. For example, if children know what natural resources are, how they are used, and how important they are to human life, they must consider the kinds of things that can be done to conserve natural resources. If children come to know and learn to appreciate a people, they must consider how their actions affect the people and what needs to be done to improve interactive relationships.

The teacher analyzes the main generalization for clues as to ideas that lead toward a pattern of action, or several closely related patterns of action. Then he develops a series of statements to serve as guides toward patterns of action. These pinpoint the condition that demands something be done and suggest the pattern of action to be developed. Usually it is not necessary to list facts after each statement. (Examples of these statements are to be found in the units in the Appendix.)

MAKING PROVISIONS FOR VERIFICATION OF KNOWLEDGE

The main generalization and its extensions completely detailed in outline form appear to comprise a neat, self-contained parcel of knowledge. This parcel is an illusion, for no knowledge can be tied into a neat bundle and stored in a library or cerebral compartment to remain for all of time. Knowledge changes. Sometimes the change is no more than increase in volume; more often it is growth in precision. If the social-studies teacher is to deal realistically with knowledge, he must make provisions for its growth or extension. These provisions are reflected in the content of the outline of the matter to be learned and taught.

The extension is made from the objective-content generalization. This extension is really a verification of the generalization. The teacher guides the children toward a skepticism of what they have just learned. This skepticism follows these lines: Is what we have learned really true?

In all places? In all times? Has anything occurred recently to challenge its veracity?

The direction of the extension is generally the teacher's choice. He may choose to make it a historical extension. For example, his pupils' view of communication today may reflect that they take much for granted; therefore, he guides them into taking a quick look at communication in other times.

Frequently a teacher chooses to guide the extension of knowledge in the direction of geography. After his pupils have made a careful study of government, he guides them toward scrutinizing the government of other states or countries. This scrutiny serves to clarify their recent learnings as well as to unleash further interest in government.

Perhaps the best extension is that which leads into the current-events or current-affairs program. The study of the main generalization and its extensions have provided the necessary background to understanding what occurs within a particular topic area. For example, the children may have just completed a study of Latin American culture, economics, and governments. They continue to study Latin American problems by discussing current news. When the current extension is used, the objective and subjective content of the unit has no abrupt end to make way for the study of a new unit. The unit continues to grow and develop in the minds of children long after the last bulletin-board display has been removed and stored away.

Since the verification is basically of the main generalization, there is no need to develop further restatements of it. The teacher thinks of the areas (historical, geographical, or current) in which verification is to occur and expresses them in terms of teaching and learning activities. (Examples are provided in the units in the Appendix.)

The social-studies teacher who works to develop a content outline from generalizations, statements, and facts to use in the construction of a unit needs to keep the following in mind: (1) A generalization is a verbal statement indicating what pupils may be reasonably expected to arrive at as a result of acquiring and relating facts, and (2) the content outline is a brief statement of the content to be taught. The outline is uniquely his—it has meaning for him that it cannot have for others.

SUMMARY

The term *generalization* has both a process and a product meaning.

As far as elementary social studies is concerned, its process meaning relates to the act or series of acts performed in analyzing and synthesizing facts and ideas to arrive at a "big idea," and its product meaning relates to the "big idea" logically reached. As a teacher works at selecting subject matter for unit construction, he is primarily concerned with the generalization as a product. It is a concise statement of the subject matter to be taught.

A generalization is also a behavioral statement which may be expressed through physical action, physical action accompanied by language action, or primarily through language action alone. If the statement expresses highly abstract behavior, it is likely to be expressed through language action. As a working definition to be used by the social-studies teacher while constructing a unit, a generalization is defined as a behavioral statement of a concept at a given level of sophistication translated into a verbal statement. The clue to the concept being generalized resides in the language structure standing in the subject position of the statement. Implicit in the social-science generalization selected for unit construction are the facts and ideas that support it and the attitudes and patterns of action related to it.

The social-studies teacher may develop or select a generalization to be used in unit construction. Most teachers will make a selection from an authoritative list or curriculum guide. As the teacher makes his selection, he considers specifics listed in his guide, the characteristics of the children to be taught, the materials available, and his own teaching style.

Once the generalization has been selected, the teacher usually recasts it in terms of a specified topic area and attempts to express it in simpler terms. When working with a generalization to be used in a unit for younger children, he is likely to select a strongly descriptive aspect of it as his recasting. The recast generalization is labeled as the first major generalization or as the main generalization.

The teacher extends the main generalization into statements which identify attitudes and patterns of action. He may use value terms such as *we, should, must,* and the like in his expression. The results are generalizations stating attitudes and generalizations indicating patterns of action. Statements of relationships which invite the inference of attitudes and patterns of action may also be used.

The next step is to supply the facts and ideas that support the generalizations. The result is a content outline of subject matter to use in constructing a unit.

The final step is to select an area of verification for the main generalization or the main generalizations. The verification may be historical, geographical, or in current conditions.

Exercises for Further Understanding

1. The list of generalizations given below represents some selections made by a curriculum worker about to develop a course of study or a guide for his district. Good choices are generalizations of sufficient breadth and depth to be worthy of study; poor choices are those too narrow and shallow to be suitable for study. Read the following list carefully and decide which of the generalizations are good choices.

(a) Families everywhere are very much alike in some ways and very different in others.
(b) The head of the bank is called a banker.
(c) A community hires firemen, policemen, and trash collectors to help make the community a safe place in which to live.
(d) Many of the names of cities and towns in Wisconsin are French because French people settled there early in the state's history.
(e) In the making of shoes, many raw and processed materials from many places are brought together in a factory where the shoes are made.
(f) Communication takes place through person-to-person contact or through exposure to ideas as transmitted through various devices.
(g) Most of the people in our state government live and work at Topeka, the capital of our state.
(h) Theodore Roosevelt, our twenty-fourth president, stayed in office from 1901 until 1908.
(i) Theodore Roosevelt served in the legislature of New York, on the Civil Service Commission, as governor of New York, and as President of the United States.
(j) The Mexican way of life as it is known today is the result of a mixture of several ways of life in the past.

2. Given below is a list of generalizations which are supposed to be statements of attitudes. Some are, and some are not. Select from the list below those which indicate attitudes.

(a) Eskimo children eat many strange foods, have many strange customs, and speak their own strange language.
(b) The excellent use of the productive resources in Seattle helps to give us a happy, comfortable life.

(c) We should work hard also to make our community a safe place in which to live.

(d) We appreciate Abraham Lincoln for his hard work which helped all of us to be free.

(e) The freer the lanes of communication, the better the communication.

(f) Each new group was assimilated into the group that preceded it.

(g) Our lives would be much less pleasant if it were not for the honesty and hard work of our state government.

(h) We appreciate the quality control that goes into the manufacturing of automobiles, busses, and trucks.

(i) We appreciate all the things that Theodore Roosevelt did to get things done.

(j) To us, all families are important.

3. The list of generalizations given below are supposed to indicate patterns of action. Some do, and some do not. Select from the list those generalizations which indicate a pattern of action.

(a) We should use the bank.

(b) Like Theodore Roosevelt, we try to manage to get important things done.

(c) The communication process involves interaction at intrapersonal, interpersonal, intergroup, and international levels.

(d) We make good use of the services provided us by our state government.

(e) We are grateful for the abundance of natural and human resources that support our high level of economic welfare.

(f) Although our community hires helpers to make it safe, we must also do our part in making our community safe for ourselves and others.

(g) We must find ways of helping the shoe workers improve their working conditions.

(h) We should do all that we can to get ready to take our place in the world of workers.

(i) We follow the example set by the Pilgrims by celebrating Thanksgiving Day in a very special way.

(j) Because they are different in so many ways, Eskimo children are interesting to study.

4. The generalizations below are suitable for unit construction. Study each carefully, then compose a generalization based upon it and reflecting an attitude or set of attitudes related to it. After you have done this, compose another generalization based upon it but reflecting a pattern of action related to it.

(a) Thomas Jefferson was a great thinker and statesman.

(b) We depend on diary farmers and workers for milk products and they depend on us to buy and use their products.

(c) Modern transportation is a product of the desire to do things better and many inventions.

(d) The Watusi, like people everywhere, have the same basic problems in providing for existence.

(e) There is a variety of ways for establishing an effective public authority.

Selected References

Berelson, Bernard, and Gary Steiner, *Human Behavior: An Inventory of Scientific Findings*. New York: Harcourt, Brace & World, Inc., 1964.

Billings, Neal, *A Determination of Generalizations Basic to the Social Studies Curriculum*. Baltimore: Warwick and York, Inc., 1929.

Brownell, W. A., and G. Hendrickson, "How Children Learn Information, Concepts, and Generalizations,"*Learning and Instruction*, pp. 92-128. Forty-Ninth Yearbook of the National Society for the Study of Education, Chicago: The University of Chicago Press, 1950.

Davis, Gary, "A Note on Two Basic Forms of Concepts and Concept Learning." *Journal of Psychology*, 62:249-254 (March 1966).

Dimond, Stanley E., "The Role of Generalization in Teaching Social Studies." *Social Education*, 22:232-234 (May 1958).

Hanna, Paul R., "Generalizations and Universal Values: Their Implications for the Social Studies Program," *Social Studies in the Elementary School*, pp. 27-47. Fifty-Sixth Yearbook of the National Society for the Study of Education, Part II, Chicago: The University of Chicago Press, 1957.

_____, and John R. Lee, "Generalizations from the Social Sciences," *Social Studies in Elementary Schools*. Thirty-Second Yearbook of the National Council for the Social Studies, Washington, D.C.: National Education Association, 1962.

Joyce, Bruce R., *Strategies for Elementary Social Science Education*, Chap. 2, "The Analysis of the Social Sciences." Chicago: Science Research Associates, Inc., 1965.

Michaelis, John U., *Social Studies for Children in a Democracy*, Chap. 2, "Foundations of the Social Studies." Englewood Cliffs, N.J.: Prentice-Hall, Inc., 1963.

_____, and A. Montgomery Johnston, *The Social Sciences: Foundations of the Social Sciences*. Boston: Allyn and Bacon, Inc., 1965.

Scriven, Michael, "The Structure of the Social Studies," in G. W. Ford and Lawrence Pugno, eds., *The Structure of Knowledge and the Curriculum*. Chicago: Rand McNally & Company, 1964, pp. 87-105.

Wesley, Edgar B., and Mary A. Adams, *Teaching Social Studies in Elementary Schools*, Chap. 18, "Developing Concepts and Generalizations." Boston: D. C. Heath and Company, 1952.

Taba, Hilda, and James L. Hills, *Teacher Handbook for Contra Costa Social Studies, Grades 1-6*, Chap. 7, "Generic Teaching Strategies;" and Chap. 8, "Teaching Strategies for Cognitive Skills." Hayward, Calif: Rapid Printers and Lithographers, Inc., 1965.

5

Planning Social-Studies Units

In Chapter 4, the problem of planning what to teach was treated. Once he has solved this problem, the teacher copes with the problem of how to teach. This problem is more complex because it involves arriving at decisions about guiding children into and through effective learning activities. This chapter presents only an introduction to the ways of deciding how to teach. Subsequent chapters will offer greater detail.

Discussion will be centered on the social-studies unit as an expression of the teacher's thinking after he has arrived at firm decisions about learning activities dealing with selected aspects of an idea in depth, and about the order in which the activities are to occur. In short, a teaching unit in social studies is a comprehensive instructional plan specifying the what, the how, and the when of teaching a "big idea." Just as we would examine a poem to learn more about how to express ourselves in poetry or a table to obtain ideas about building one, we shall examine some units and their structure to get insights about planning for effective teaching and learning in social studies.

Some teachers make paper-and-pencil plans of units similar to those presented here; others utilize other forms of expression. Sometimes a unit plan is expressed as a series of checks after entries designating activities and materials in a district social-studies guide or resource unit.

A unit plan may be contained in several folders of materials which the teacher uses in teaching. Frequently the teacher's notes about what was done the last time he taught the unit are included with the materials. Some units can be expressed only in process, that is, as the teacher teaches them. However, for purposes of examination here, carefully developed "blueprint" forms will be presented.

All of the units to be examined will share certain common characteristics. All will be constructed to guide children toward understandings, attitudes, and patterns of behavior related to the same "big idea." All will reflect decisions about how to guide the children into a unit, how to guide them in acquiring facts and ideas, and how to guide them in tying ideas together. However, each will reflect a different strategy and somewhat different tactical measures to assure learning.

AN OVERVIEW OF STRATEGIES

Plainly put, an instructional strategy is a scheme to assure effective learning. The scheme reflects a commitment to a total act or a closely related series of acts which will bring about a desired end. When applied, it is followed through to the end and is subject to change only when it is recognized for certain to be inefficient. Although it is in itself a rigid design, the strategy allows for flexibility in the variety of tactical measures or procedures permitted for its accomplishment. One who selects and applies a strategy assumes that certain conditions exist and that any error in these assumptions will be corrected by changes in tactical measures. Let us review some of the strategies that have been applied in social-studies education.

Perhaps the oldest strategy is that which can be described in this way: Children will learn what they need to know about social studies by reading from cover to cover the basic social-studies textbook and answering all of the questions listed therein. When he uses this strategy, the teacher assumes that the textbook is prepared by competent authorities and that all the children can read it and answer the questions. If he is wrong in these assumptions, he can read the textbook to the children and help them formulate answers to the questions. For obvious reasons, this strategy is not highly regarded.

A later strategy, which takes more fully into account the characteristics of children, may be described in this fashion: Children will learn what they need to know about social studies by being encouraged to manifest their interests in topics and areas and being guided in extending and amplifying those interests. The teacher who selects this strategy assumes that children have interests in their physical and social environment that will emerge through teacher-pupil planning of "doing" activities related to areas and topics. Sometimes activities consist of individual projects; at other times, group projects. If interests are slow in emerging, the teacher changes his pattern of stimuli, provides for readiness activities, examines his pattern of action for too much self intrusion, or shifts to another area of study. This strategy based on children's interests is highly regarded by some social-studies educators.

Another strategy enjoying acceptance by some educators is that children will learn what they need to know about social studies by being guided in solving problems arising in their physical and social environment. By working with these problems, the children not only become aware of the problems which their society must treat, but learn as well the process and techniques necessary for treating problems. The teacher using this strategy assumes that children can and will use group process in solving problems. If they cannot, he reduces the complexity of the problem and guides them into learning activities which will promote growth in the skills of group process.

The strategies presented to this point reflect both the social-studies standard and two later innovations discussed in Chapter 1. It was also pointed out that social studies today is a mosaic of curriculum organization and practices. This mosaic has brought about a strategy more commonly accepted than any discussed so far. This *basal strategy* represents an attempt to pull the strengths of the various strategies together into the most telling strategy of all: Children learn what they need to know about social studies by having their interest stimulated in the topic or area, by expressing their interest in the form of questions about the topic or area to be studied, by seeking answers to their questions as independently as possible, and by drawing together and expressing their findings in a way that they select, both as individuals and as groups. Problem solving is utilized when the need for it arises.

Support by many school districts for this strategy is reflected in social studies-guides and the materials made available to teachers. It is regarded as the basal strategy to be implemented with newer ideas by inserting provisions for thinking. Two changes are involved: (1) The criterion of scope is changed from a broad topic or area, such as *transportation* or *Africa,* to a "big idea," and (2) instead of guiding children into a new unit after a flurry of expressive activities marking the close of the old unit, they are guided in applying their learning to problem situations.

This combination of newer and older ideas results in a *synthesized strategy*. It is described in this way: Children learn what they need to know in social studies by having their interest stimulated in an area of facts and ideas; by expressing their interests in the form of questions about this area to be studied; by seeking answers to their questions as independently as possible; by drawing together and expressing their findings in a way they select, both as individuals and as groups; by verifying their findings; and by applying their findings to problems introduced by the teacher. Among the units presented in this chapter, that prepared by Teacher X reflects the synthesized strategy.

A very recent strategy now being recommended by social-studies educators with a strong social-science orientation may be described in this way: Children will learn what they need to know about social studies by learning social-science concepts through following designs for inquiry similar to those used by the social scientists themselves. The unit developed by Teacher Y utilizes this *social-science strategy*.

In the opening chapter of this book, it was pointed out that "big ideas," or social-science generalizations, placed greater emphasis on thinking. As has been explained in the two paragraphs above and will soon be seen in the units themselves, the synthesized strategy and the social-science strategy both include provisions for encouraging children to think and inquire in order to learn. In the synthesized strategy of Teacher X, the children are encouraged to pull their learned facts and ideas together to arrive at a generalization and then to solve problems related to the "big idea" as a means of understanding it further in application. In the social-science strategy of Teacher Y, children are stimulated to think, as demonstrations and experiments are performed by the teacher, and later are encouraged to pull their findings together and to apply them. Much of the thinking is stimulated and directed by the teacher to guide children in acquiring facts.

Another strategy places a greater emphasis on reflective thinking. This *thinking-emphasis strategy* is identified as follows: Children learn what they need to know about social studies by stating what they think is true about a state of affairs, inquiring to prove or disprove their own statements, and verifying and extending their proven statement in a variety of ways. The unit prepared by Teacher Z utilizes this strategy.

No claim is made for the superiority of any one of the three strategies over the other two. The synthesized strategy offers much to teachers who are now working in districts which implement the basal strategy. The social-science strategy frees the teacher who has specialized in a study of the social sciences and who is proficient in developing demonstration and experimentation situations to help children learn social-science concepts as social scientists learn them. The thinking-emphasis strategy, like the synthesized strategy, is not too different from what many teachers are doing. At the same time it incorporates some of the practices supported by the social-science strategy.

THE BASIC STRUCTURE OF A UNIT

A unit has both a vertical and a horizonal structure. The horizontal structure usually contains three parts, the "what," "with what," and "how," that is, a listing of content, a list of materials, and a list of procedures, arranged in any horizontal sequence. The vertical structure is a rigid arrangement of parts dealing with the "when" of the unit and indicating basic procedures. This vertical structure also has three parts, each of which has a particular function and sometimes subfunctions, depending on the strategy and tactical measures adopted by the developer of the unit. These parts may be identified generally as the part devoted to stimulating children's interest in the idea or area of facts and ideas to be studied, the part which indicates the facts and ideas to be learned and the learning activities to be used, and the part in which learnings are tied together, verified, and examined for applications.

The units here will be presented in a broken fashion to facilitate comparison of the various parts. The chart following page 100 presents an over-all outline of each unit, to allow comparison of the variation in emphasis.

STIMULATING CHILDREN'S INTEREST

After the teacher has chosen the "big idea," implemented it with the necessary supporting ideas and facts, and arrived at statements reflecting attitudes and patterns of behavior related to the "big idea," he must reach a decision as to how to guide children into the unit.

Teacher X, who works in a large city school district that provides him with ample guides and materials adequate to supporting suggestions in the guides, has decided to use the synthesized strategy. One of his tactical measures is an arranged environment which the children explore. It presents sufficient variety to assure each child's finding something of interest to which he can react. Other tactical measures include having children explore the contents of their basic textbook and encouraging them to express their interest in terms of questions. Read Section I of Teachers X's unit to obtain a grasp of the decision he has made and how he has implemented it.

TEACHER X'S UNIT
Communication as a Process

SECTION I. INITIATION OF THE UNIT

Teaching purposes:
  a. To stimulate interest in the unit.
  b. To present an overview of communication.
  c. To elicit questions about communication to be answered during the study of the unit.

Elements to Be Included in the Overview

Communication as an interpersonal process.
Social factors which influence communication.
Physical factors which delay communication.
Communication as a means of social control.

Materials for Introducing the Unit

• A bulletin-board display showing the elements of communication in silhouettes and diagrams to represent persons, vehicles of communication, symbols, a problem, transmission, and interaction. Accompanying caption: COMMUNICATION.

• A bulletin-board display showing some of the social factors: two stick figures in a group and ten stick figures in a group, a boy blindfolded and a girl gagged, and a list of words with the same meaning but given in foreign languages. Accompanying caption: WHEN IS COMMUNICATION MORE SUCCESSFUL?

• A table display consisting of a large picture showing high mountains and a wide lake, a telephone, and a telegraph key. Accompanying caption: WORDS ACROSS LAKES AND MOUNTAINS.

• A counter display consisting of soap and food advertisements from magazines and newspapers. Accompanying caption: WHO IS COMMUNICATING WITH WHOM?

* Basic textbook: *Passwords to People*, Carol Denison.

Procedures for Introducing the Unit

Encourage the children to circulate freely around the room to examine the bulletin boards and displays. Take notes of their reactions.

Guide the children in examining the table of contents and other parts of *Passwords to People*.

Share with the children some of the questions expressed by individuals as they looked at the bulletin boards and displays. Encourage the children to discuss these and to contribute other questions that were raised in their minds as they looked at the bulletin boards and displays and explored their textbooks.

Guide the children in arranging their questions in study order.

Teacher X could have used other tactical measures. He could have arranged for a field trip to a museum containing a communication display; shown a series of pictures, a filmstrip, or a film in which communication was richly involved; read aloud a story in which faulty communication interfered with the solution of a problem, or a poem about communication; or encouraged a discussion about one or more objects related to communication, such as a telephone, a mirror, a drum, a signal flag, or the like.

Teacher Y has a rich background in the social sciences; therefore, he chooses the social-sciences strategy. His tactical measure is to stimulate each child to think of someone like himself and consider his potential role as a communicator. As a result, the child begins to consider what communication is and question his own ideas. Examine Section I of Teacher Y's unit to understand his decision and how he plans to put it into effect.

TEACHER Y'S UNIT
Communication as a Process

SECTION I. INTRODUCING THE UNIT

Teaching purposes:
   a. To guide the children in "warming up" toward a definitive study of communication.
   b. To stimulate curiosity about communication to the point that questions are asked.

General Feeling to Be Established

There is more to communication than just talking.

Materials for the "Warm-up"

• A picture of a ten-year-old boy standing erect with his hands at his sides. His face is expressionless.

Procedures for Accomplishing the "Warm-up"

Showing the picture, ask the children to consider whether the boy depicted can communicate. Have them establish what they would have to know about the boy to be able to answer whether he can communicate. Encourage the expression of as many pertinent ideas as possible.

Announcing that the boy can communicate, have the children consider whether he will. Encourage them to think of as many conditions as they can. Guide the children in a review of their responses to see whether they can develop a sentence which tells what communication is.

Guide the children in developing questions which they will need to answer before they can have an adequate understanding of communication.

Teacher Y could have used the same materials as those listed for Teacher X, but he would have used them differently. He would be prone to encourage children to make responses to which they would react in a more penetrating fashion later. An aura of questioning skepticism would prevail to heighten the urgency of inquiry.

Teacher Z feels that children should be as independent as thinkers as they can be. For this reason, he chooses the thinking-emphasis strategy. He uses three tactical measures. The first is to establish what level of knowledge the children already have about communication, the second to place the "big idea" in issue before the children, and the third to develop a design for inquiry. Read Section I of Teacher Z's unit for a better understanding of his decision about how to stimulate children's interest in the unit.

TEACHER Z'S UNIT

Communication as a Process

SECTION I. STIMULATING INTEREST IN THE UNIT

Teaching purposes:

 a. To establish a level of knowledge background about communication as a process.

 b. To place in issue the "big idea" about communication as a process.

 c. To develop a design for inquiry to lead toward acquiring the "big idea."

Ideas and Facts, Necessary Background Knowledge for the Study of the "Big Idea"

Communication is all around us.

 1. Much of our time spent in speaking and listening to others.

  a. Upon greeting.

    b. When doing things together.

    c. When studying in a classroom.

    d. When someone wants information.

  2. Some of our time spent at reading and writing.

    a. Writing and reading notes, invitations, and letters.

    b. Reading signals, signs, billboards, and notices.

    c. Reading directions of all kinds as we study.

    d. Reading books, magazines, and newspapers.

  3. Many mechanical devices in our homes and at school.

    a. Telephone.

    b. Tape recorder.

    c. Radio.

    d. Television.

    e. Loudspeaker system.

Materials for Establishing a Level of Background Knowledge

• A bulletin-board arrangement consisting of magazine pictures of the following: People conversing in various situations; people writing, reading, and responding to signals and billboards; various devices used for communication purposes.

Procedures for Establishing the Level of Background Knowledge

Encourage the children to discuss the pictures on the bulletin boards to make them aware of the various aspects of communication in their daily lives.

Guide the children in clarifying that all the pictures tell something about communication—the actions of persons in listening, speaking, and writing to others and reading what has been written by others.

Guide the children in sensing the difference between person-to-person communication and agency-to-group communication as used on billboards, radio, and television.

The "Big Idea" Being Studied in the Unit

Communication is a process of interaction in which people use symbols as a means of controlling their social environment in the solution of problems.

Instruction Model for Placing the "Big Idea" in Issue and Leading toward the Development of a Design for Inquiry.

• Magazine or newspaper pictures showing the following: A boy writing, a man sleeping, a woman doing a household chore, a girl walking, a soldier holding his rifle over his head, an announcer framed within a television screen, a sailor beside a signal lamp, a baby playing with blocks.

• A cartoon strip showing conversation.

Procedures for Placing the "Big Idea" in Issue and Developing Design for Inquiry

Showing the pictures and the cartoon strip, one at a time, have the children select those which show communication.

Expressing doubt over such selections as the writing boy and the sailor beside the signal lamp, encourage the children to express why these depict communication.

Guide the children in summarizing their ideas into a definition of communication.

Encourage the children to challenge the certainty of their definition.

Guide the children in developing questions to be answered to establish the validity of their statement about communications.

As you have probably noticed, Teachers X, Y, and Z use different labels for the first part of their unit. Teacher X uses *initiation* (a term long in use in social studies), Teacher Y uses *introducing,* and Teacher Z uses *stimulating interest in the unit.* All are functional. One is no better than any of the others. What is important is that children in some way be engaged in what is to be studied and that the start be consistent with the strategy chosen.

The term *teaching purposes* was also introduced. A listing of these purposes serves the teacher as a reminder of immediate goals that he has for himself as he goes about his teaching task.

GUIDING CHILDREN IN ACQUIRING FACTS AND IDEAS

After interest has been stimulated in the "big idea" or the area of facts and ideas (usually accomplished during one or two social-studies periods), anywhere from three or four daily to several weeks of social-studies periods are characterized by learning activities of one kind or another. The purpose of these activities is to acquire the facts and ideas necessary to adequate generalization.

Because of his commitment to the synthesized strategy, Teacher X holds as firmly as he can to tactical measures which place as much responsibility as possible for the acquisition of facts and ideas on the pupils themselves. After he has guided the pupils in clarifying the questions, he releases them to find the answers in available resources. He may have to review certain aspects of investigative skills before he releases the pupils totally or he may have to work with individual pupils whose skills are weak. Independence in the use of these skills is an essential goal which he holds for all his pupils.

However, his commitment to independence in these skills for his pupils is not so great that he rejects learning activities that require anything other than individual reading, map study, and the like. If he feels that the available resources are inadequate or that facts and ideas may be acquired more economically in a learning activity in which he has a directive role, he does not hesitate to assume that role. It is a tactical measure which he may or may not use.

Another tactical measure which Teacher X uses to assure effective learning is expressive activity. Through such activity his pupils are given opportunities for integrating the facts and ideas they have acquired.

For a better understanding of Teacher X's decisions on tactical measures to assure that his pupils acquire the necessary facts and ideas for generalization, examine Section II of his unit.

TEACHER X'S UNIT

SECTION II. ACQUIRING INFORMATION

Teaching purposes:

a. To gather facts and ideas about communication as a process.

b. To improve reading skills necessary to acquiring information.

Information to Be Learned

Language developed as a system of symbols as human beings sought ways of answering to their needs through communication.

1. Needs: foods, protection, and ways of expressing fear and pleasure.

2. Communication: a way of sharing ideas with others to solve problems, requiring:

a. Two or more persons (usually)

b. A vehicle of transmission; voice or vision

c. A medium of symbols common in meaning to the communicators

d. A problem

e. A transmission; a message sent from A to B

f. An interaction; a message sent by A and received by B.

3. Language: a system of symbols, developed first in oral form, then in written form, having common meaning among a group of people.

Materials for Guiding Children in Acquiring Information (A)

• A chart of the questions which the children had developed during the introduction to the chapter.

*Chapter I, *Passwords to People,* Carol Denison.

• A sound tape of interactions and transmissions.

• A diagram of communication between Sender A and Receiver B.

• A sound tape of conversations to be analyzed for problem content.

Procedures for Guiding Children in Acquiring Information (A)

Refer to the question or questions on the chart which refer to the definitive aspects of communication. Clarify these through discussion.

When children have a clear idea about the question or questions to be dealt with, guide them into reading Chapter I of *Passwords to People* to find the answers.

Guide the class in discussing the answers to the questions.

Using the communication diagram, guide the children toward an understanding of the factors and functions involved in communication.

Using the sound tape of interactions and transmissions, have the children analyze it to determine which are interactions and which are transmissions.

Using the sound tape of conversations, have the children analyze each conversation for the problem.

Guide the children in expressing independently an interaction and a transmission, first in words, then in diagram form.

Guide the children in developing a summary of their learning for later reference.

Information to Be Learned (B)

Obstacles of various sorts hinder communication:
1. Increased number of persons in the communicating group.
2. Restriction of the vehicle for transmission to voice or vision.
3. The use of symbols confusing to one or both of the communicators.
4. Weak human interrelationships.
5. Low acceptability of the problem.

Materials for Guiding Children in Acquiring Information (B)

• A chart of questions which the children had developed during the introduction to the unit.

*District Instructional Pamphlet No. 67, *Communication and You.*

Procedures for Guiding Children in Acquiring Information (B)

Refer to the question or questions on the chart which refer to the factors which make communication work. Clarify these through discussion.

Have the children read the pamphlet *Communication and You* and take notes to answer the question or questions involved.

Guide the class in discussing the answers to the questions.

Using the diagrams in the pamphlet, encourage the children to contribute examples of situations dealing with interrelationships and the acceptability of problems. Have them express their ideas in roleplaying.

Guide the children in developing a summary in outline form that reflects their learnings.

Information to Be Learned (C)

Obstacles of various sorts delay communication:
1. Physical barriers between communicators.
2. Space and time barriers.
Human innovation has reduced these barriers through
1. Early uses of light and sound.
2. Development of telegraph, telephone, radio, and rapid mail service.

Materials for Guiding Children in Acquiring Information (C)

- A chart of the questions which the children had developed during the introduction to the unit.

*District Instructional Pamphlet No. 68, *Messages to Everywhere.*

Communications, C. B. Colby.

The Wonderful World of Communication, Lancelot Hogben.

Passwords to People, Carol Denison.

Procedures for Guiding Children in Acquiring Information (C)

Refer to the question or questions on the chart which ask about how communication is delayed. Clarify these through discussion with the children.

Using the questions as guides, have the children read the pamphlet *Messages to Everywhere* and take notes about their findings.

Guide the children in a discussion of the answers to the questions.

Stimulate the children to develop a time line showing the ways that man has invented to overcome the obstacles to communication.

Have each child choose one of the various devices for improving communication to be examined further and present his findings in report form to the class.

Information to Be Learned (D)

Individuals are subject to the control of distant others through communication.
1. Control by the warning sign and the traffic signal.
2. Control through advertisement by print, radio, and television.
3. Control through the editorial and cartoon.
4. Control through a story or book.

Materials for Guiding Children in Acquiring Information (D)

- A chart of the questions which the children had developed during the introduction to the unit.
- *Chapter 5, *Passwords to People*, Carol Denison.
- Some photographs of warning signs.
- A chart showing a traffic signal light.
- Some photographs of billboards.
- A collection of newspaper and magazine advertisements.
- A collection of recent newspaper cartoons and editorials.
- A list of titles of stories read by the children in their reading textbooks.

Procedures for Guiding Children in Acquiring Information (D)

Refer to the question or questions on the chart which ask about communication as a means of controlling people. Clarify these through discussion with the children.

Have the children read Chapter 5, *Passwords to People*, to answer the questions.

Guide them in a discussion of the information found.

Extend the information found by discussing how warning signals and signal lights control the behavior of people, discussing how billboards influence people's actions and ideas, having the children analyze advertisements for the kinds of promises made, having the children analyze editorials and cartoons for restricted points of view, and having them recall the "message" that the stories they had read seemed to contain.

Encourage the children to develop posters which advertise a promise; have a total class evaluation of these.

Encourage the children to draw cartoons which reflect a single point of view; evaluate these in a total class discussion.

Guide the children in developing a summary of their learning.

As you probably noticed, Teacher X plans to guide his pupils into each idea (A, B, C, and D) and its supporting facts as a complete structure of learnings. For each of these structures he has provided a set of procedures which reflects an order of activities that remains the same for each idea, that is, clarify purposes, work at answering purposes, check to see how well purposes have been answered, express, and summarize. This order does not necessarily have to be so invariable. Teacher X could have chosen to guide the children in summarizing before expressing. His decision in this matter could have been governed by the belief that children's expressive products are freer and more individual when summarization is delayed, or that summarization is facilitated by having the children express their learnings first.

Teacher X's teaching purposes indicate a concern for the improvement of reading skills in social studies, yet no direct indications of what he plans to do about it appear in Section II of his unit. He plans to work at this goal as the need for it arises.

Teacher Y's provisions for the acquisition of facts and ideas are strongly influenced by his commitment to the social-science strategy. Although we shall find that the ideas and facts that his pupils are to acquire are about the same as those to be acquired in Teacher X's unit, we shall also find that he regards them somewhat differently. What were Ideas A, B, C, and D to Teacher X are Concepts 1, 2, 3, and 4 to him. In his way of thinking, he looks upon *communication* as the concept to be learned, and Concepts 1, 2, 3, and 4 represent a breakdown of the concept. Another way of expressing it is offered in this simple formula: communication = Concepts 1, 2, 3, 4. If children are to learn what communication is, they must learn and synthesize each of the concepts.

Teacher Y's view of the teaching-learning process also differs from Teacher X's. He has some concern for the exercise of independent skills in acquiring information from available resources but, whenever possible, he wants his pupils to learn social-science concepts in much the same way as social scientists learn them, that is, from direct observation of social phenomena. For this reason, he will guide his pupils into activities in which they will learn about communication as sociologists and social psychologists learn about it. Whenever possible, he will encourage children to express "hunches" as ideas and to check them experimentally. Reading and other independent skills involved in the study of available resources have a place. When contact with reality can be made in no other way, or when children wish to compare their finding with those of others, resources will be used. Social scientists make use of resources in this way.

Examine Section II of Teacher Y's unit closely to see how he has decided to guide children in acquiring facts and ideas.

TEACHER Y'S UNIT

SECTION II. ACQUIRING BEHAVIORAL IDEAS AND FACTS

Teaching purpose: To guide the children in establishing concepts about communication.

Concept 1 Expressed as Idea and Fact

Certain conditions have to be satisfied before communication can be said to take place:

1. Two or more persons (usually).
2. Availability of a vehicle of transmission; voice or vision.
3. Availability of a medium of symbols common in meaning to the communicators.
4. A problem.
5. A transmission; a message sent.
6. An interaction; a message sent and received.

Materials to Be Used to Help Children Acquire Concept 1

• A chart showing "go" and "stop" in several foreign languages.

Procedures for Guiding Children toward Concept 1

Have a child absent himself from the classroom for about thirty seconds and have the others determine a way to say "Good morning" to him.

Have the class determine as many ways as possible to transmit "Hi!" to each other.

Using several different foreign languages command the children to go and stop. Show the chart for further analysis.

Using the tape of conversations, have the children analyze them for the problem being treated in each.

Using the tape of conversations and transmissions, have the children analyze them for differences.

Clarify transmission and interaction with chalkboard diagrams.

Concept 2 Expressed as Idea and Fact

Obstacles of various sorts hinder communication:

1. Increased number of persons in the communication group.
2. Restricting of the vehicle for transmission to voice or vision.
3. The use of symbols confusing to one or both of the communicators.
4. Weak human interrelationships.
5. Low acceptability of the problem.

Materials to Be Used to Help Children Acquire Concept 2

• A sound tape of commands and requests given in a variety of ways from harsh to appealing.

• A sound tape of brief monologues in which persons are considering various kinds of acts.

Procedures for Guiding Children toward Concept 2

Using two children as demonstrators, have them decide together before the class who should lead the pledge to the flag tomorrow. Have this activity timed.

Using ten children as a demonstrating group, have them decide who should lead the pledge on the day after tomorrow. Have this activity timed.

Guide the class in comparing the time required by each demonstrating group, and discuss reasons for differences in the time required.

Ask a child to bring you a pencil. Then ask a child to bring you a "graphite eradicator" (eraser). Give him clues until he brings it. Have the children compare the time required for each act.

Using the sound tape of commands and requests, have the children analyze each to determine which of the persons they would like to communicate with further. Pinpoint "feelings" as encouraging or discouraging to communication.

Using the sound tape about various acts, have the children decide which they would like to communicate about further. Encourage them to substantiate their choices to underscore the acceptability of the problem.

Concept 3 Expressed as Idea and Fact

Obstacles of various sorts delay communication:
1. Physical barriers between the communicators.
2. Space and time barriers.

Human innovation has reduced these barriers through:
1. Early use of light and sound.
2. Development of telegraph, telephone, radio, and rapid mail service.

Materials to Be Used to Help Children Acquire Concept 3

• A screen, a mirror, and a flashlight.
• A relief map showing mountains and wide bodies of water.
• A sufficient number of the following books for classwide distribution:
*Passwords to People, Carol Denison.
*Communications, C. B. Colby.
*The Wonderful World of Communications, Lancelot Hogben.
• The materials and tools needed for constructing simple telegraph apparatus and telephones.

Procedures for Guiding Children toward Concept 3

Have one child step behind the screen. Encourage another to attempt to communicate a simple message to him by a visual means. Encourage the child to experiment with the flashlight and the mirror to develop a message.

Using the relief map, have the children isolate the barriers and relate them to the time and means of transmitting messages across each.

Guide the discussion toward the question of how man has reduced these barriers. Have the children substantiate their knowledge through consulting the available books.

Divide the children into groups with these specific tasks: building a telegraph transmitter and receiver, building several simple telephones, and devising codes.

Have the children test their codes on the telegraph apparatus.

Guide the children in conducting several experiments with the simple telephones such as "one-way" telephones, telephones with crossed wires, and the like. Simple tasks are to be performed and timed under various conditions.

Concept 4 Expressed as Idea and Fact

Individuals are subject to the control of distant others through communication:
1. Control by the warning sign and the traffic signal.
2. Control through advertisement by print, radio, and television.
3. Control through the editorial and cartoon.
4. Control through a story or book.

Materials to Be Used to Help Children Acquire Concept 4

- Some simple sketches or pictures of warning signs and a traffic signal light.
- A collection of magazine and newspaper advertisements about soaps and food.
- A collection of relatively simple political cartoons and newspaper editorials.

Procedures for Guiding Children toward Concept 4

Presenting the sketches of the warning signs and the traffic signal light, have the children consider how these communicate to them. Have them consider their response patterns to these and whether one may communicate "back" to them.

Have the children react to the advertisements. Encourage them to think of why they react in particular ways. Again have them consider the possibility of "answering back."

Guide the children in analyzing the cartoons and editorials for the intent of the cartoonists and the editors. Encourage them to react to these intents. Have them consider the "answering back" aspects.

Encourage the children to discuss some books that they have read recently and how these books have affected them. Have them discuss what they believed the intent of the authors to be. Again have them consider the "answering back" aspect.

As you may have noticed, Teacher Y has but one teaching purpose —to guide children in acquiring concepts. This purpose is in keeping with his chosen strategy.

Teacher Z's basic concern is for thinking. For this reason, he places Ideas A, B, C, and D (the same as those used by Teacher X and Teacher Y) in issue in a fashion similar to that in which the "big idea" was placed in issue in the first part of his unit. However, the instructional models tend to be more simple and usually there is no attempt to develop a design for inquiry for each idea. Although he plays a directive role (often similar to that of Teacher Y), he provides for investigative activity in which children work more or less independently to acquire facts and ideas. Like Teacher X, he recognizes the value of expressive activity as a means of encouraging children to integrate learnings.

Examine Section II of Teacher Z's unit to gain a clearer understanding of his decisions about helping children to learn facts and ideas.

TEACHER Z'S UNIT

SECTION II. ACQUIRING FACTS AND IDEAS
Teaching purposes:
  a. To guide the children in investigative activities for facts and ideas related to communication as a process.
  b. To improve children's inquiry skills.
  c. To improve children's investigative skills.

Idea and Facts Supporting the "Big Idea" (A)
Certain conditions have to be satisfied before communication can be said to have taken place.
1. Two or more persons (usually).
2. Availability of a vehicle of transmission; voice or vision.
3. Availability of a medium of symbols common in meaning to the communicators.
4. A problem.
5. A transmission; a message sent.
6. An interaction; a message sent and received.

Materials for Acquiring Idea and Facts (A)
• A chart showing the children's statement of what they believe communication to be.
• Two hand puppets.
*Basic textbook: *Passwords to People,* Carol Denison.

Procedures for Guiding Children toward the Facts and the Idea (A)

Review the children's statement with them and invite them to suggest changes in it.

Refer to their design for inquiry and the question relating to how communication works.

Using the puppets, present two situations as an instructional model. In Situation 1, a puppet alone says, "Hello, George." In Situation 2, one puppet speaks and the other replies. Have the children decide which is communication and why it is. Introduce the terms *transmission* and *interaction* and demonstrate several times. Have pairs of children use the puppets to demonstrate the terms.

Branching out from Situation 2, use the two puppets to demonstrate the other conditions of communication—the need for a vehicle of transmission, the need for common symbols, and the need for an exciting problem.

Encourage the children to devise situations with the puppets in which communication may or may not take place.

Have the children verify the ideas just learned by reading Chapter 1 of *Passwords to People*.

Idea and Facts Supportive of the "Big Idea" (B)

Obstacles of various sorts hinder communication.
1. Increased number of persons in the communicating group.
2. Restriction of the vehicle for transmission to voice or vision.
3. The use of symbols confusing to one or both of the communicators.
4. Weak human relationship.
5. Low acceptability of the problem.

Materials for Acquiring Idea and Facts (B)

- A chart showing a pair of persons face to face and a circle of ten persons facing inward.
- A chart showing the front view of a person's head and shoulders, a similar view with the person blindfolded, and another with the mouth covered.
- A magazine picture showing two persons in close proximity.
- A sound tape supposedly representing three attempts of the persons to communicate with varying results—one person asks for something that the other knows nothing about, one person tries to begin a conversation but the other informs him that he does not know him and refuses to speak further, and one person asks the other to brush his teeth for him and receives an abrupt refusal.

Procedures for Guiding Children toward the Facts and Ideas (B)

Refer to the question from the children's design for inquiry that relates to what makes communication good or poor, OR

Refer to the previous day's work and have the children consider what makes communication good or poor. List their statements on the chalkboard for future reference.

Present the chart showing persons in a pair and in a circle and have the children consider which would have the most difficulty in communicating. Encourage them to develop an experimental situation to test their ideas. Present the magazine picture and encourage the children to decide whether the persons are communicating or not. Have them give reasons for their answers.

Play the tape and have them analyze what they hear to discover how confusing symbols, weak human relationships, and low acceptability of the problem affect communication.

Focus the children's attention on their earlier statements. Guide them in relating their findings to these.

Encourage the children to find newspaper or magazine pictures of people in close proximity and to develop ideas about whether good or poor communication is taking place and how they can tell.

Idea and Facts Supportive of the "Big Idea" (C)

Obstacles of various sorts delay communication.
    1. Physical barriers between communicators.
    2. Time and space barriers.
Human innovation has reduced these barriers through
    1. Early uses of light and sound.
    2. Development of telegraph, telephone, radio, and rapid mail service.

Materials for Acquiring the Facts and Ideas (C)

- A diagram showing an office area equipped with desks and persons.
- An acetate overlay for the diagram showing the partitions between the desks.
- A cardboard screen large enough to conceal a seated child and containing a slot large enough to admit a 3″ x 5″ card.
- A physical map of a continent.
- A sketch of a scientist with an innovation.
- *Communications*, C. B. Colby.
- *The Wonderful World of Communication*, Lancelot Hogben.
- *Passwords to People*, Carol Denison.
- Standard references, that is, almanacs, encyclopedias, and the like.

Procedures for Guiding Children toward the Facts and Idea (C)

Refer to the question from the children's design for inquiry that relates to what makes communication good or poor, OR
Refer to the previous day's work.

Stimulate further thinking by presenting the diagram of the office area and having the children decide between which persons communication will be good or poor. Encourage the children to substantiate their ideas and to think of other factors that may possibly delay communication.

Place the overlay over the diagram to help the children discover that physical obstacles between communicators delay communication.

Show the screen to the children and group ten of them seated in a circle.

Encourage the class to develop and perform several experiments showing how a physical obstacle delays communication.

Using the map, guide the children in generalizing between their findings and the barriers on the map.

Guide the children toward an understanding of space as a barrier by presenting a few problems about persons wishing to communicate over areas in which there are few if any other obstacles.

Using the sketch of a scientist with an innovation, have the children consider how the scientist is going to make his innovation available for people a hundred years from now. List the children's ideas and challenge them for completeness.

Returning to the diagram and the overlay, identify it as an engineering office preparing some plans to be sent halfway around the world in six hours or less. Encourage the children to think how this is to be done. List their ideas and challenge them for completeness.

Guide the children into reading available resources for more ideas. Encourage them to relate their findings to the problem. Have them develop alternate plans for meeting the six-hour deadline.

Idea and Facts Supportive of the "Big Idea" (D)

Individuals are subject to the control of distant others through communication.

1. Control by the warning sign and traffic signal.
2. Control through advertisement by print, radio, and television.
3. Control through editorial and cartoon.
4. Control through a story or book.

Materials to Help Children to Acquire Facts and Idea (D)

- Two hand puppets.
- A sketch of a policeman and fireman.
- A sketch of a boy about to buy a baseball glove. He is looking at three different advertisements making different promises.
- A duplicated copy of a recent editorial and a cartoon taken from a local newspaper.

*Selected excerpts from Lois Lenski's *Cotton in My Sack* and Robert McCloskey's *Homer Price*.

*Chapter 5, *Passwords to People*, Carol Denison.

Procedures for Guiding Children toward the Facts and Idea (D)

Refer to the questions from the children's design for inquiry that relate to how communication works, OR
Refer to previous learnings.

Using the puppets, present an argument between the two. One stoutly maintains that he can make up his own mind without extra information, the other argues strongly that that is quite impossible and that he must always seek information before making decisions. Encourage the children to decide which is correct and to substantiate why. Help them to refine their points of view.

Presenting the sketch of the policeman and the fireman, have the children consider whether these men need to be present at a scene to make their influence felt.

Present the sketch of a boy about to buy a baseball glove and have the children analyze the advertisements for the most valid promise.

Encourage the children to develop advertisements on posters, making various promises.

Guide the children in analyzing the editorial and cartoon to discover how these make an appeal to opinion and action.

Encourage the children to develop simple editorials and cartoons to appeal to the opinions and actions of others. Conduct a class analysis of the products.

Have the children write individually about their opinions of migrant workers, then read an excerpt or two from *Cotton in My Sack*. Encourage the children to write what they think now about migrant workers. Conduct a class analysis of the results.

Have the children write individually what they think about comic books, then read them the story about the Super-Duper in *Homer Price*. Encourage them to write again what they think about comic books. Conduct a class analysis of the results.

Returning to the situation presented with the puppets, have the children consider which person was more correct.

Perhaps you noticed that Teacher Z included three teaching purposes in Section II of his unit. Of special note is his concern for thinking for which he makes as many provisions as he can in the study of each idea. Like Teacher X, he reflects a concern for the skills involved in seeking and gathering information, but he makes no specific mention of procedures to be used. We may assume that he will deal with improving investigative skills as needed, either on an individual or classwide basis. These tactical measures fit his thinking-emphasis strategy.

This second section of the unit will require several weeks of daily social-studies periods. Each teacher will consult his unit from day to day to develop daily lesson plans (treated more extensively in Chapter 6).

TYING IDEAS TOGETHER

As soon as the children have completed the acquisition of facts and ideas, they are guided in tying the ideas together at several levels. The third section of the unit contains the provisions made by the teacher to guide his pupils in the thinking necessary for these tasks.

In Section III of the unit, Teachers X, Y, and Z face similar problems and tend to solve them in similar ways. Each must guide his pupils in arriving at the "big idea," verifying it, and relating it to appropriate attitudes and patterns of action. Although to this point their procedures have reflected marked differences, their procedures in this section of the unit will reflect, with an exception or two, marked similarities. The teachers share a concern for the processes and products of thinking as aids to learning.

Teacher X uses an instructional model and summary charts (prepared at the close of the study of each idea in the second section of his unit) to bring his pupils to the point of generalization. After the generalization is reached, he guides the children into expressive and verifying activities, and then into problem-solving situations in which they discover attitudes and patterns related to the "big idea." Examine Section III of Teacher X's unit to see how he provides for the activities.

TEACHER X'S UNIT

SECTION III. CULMINATING THE UNIT.
  Teaching purposes:
    a. To summarize the subject matter learning about communication as a process.
    b. To integrate learning in expressive activities.
    c. To verify learnings.
    d. To apply learnings to problems in communication.

The "Big Idea"

Communication is a process of interaction in which people use symbols as a means of controlling their social environment in the solution of problems.

Instructional Model Used in Guiding Children to Arrive at the "Big Idea"

- Summary charts made at the close of studying each idea about communication.
- Magazine or newspaper pictures showing the following: a boy writing, a man sleeping, a woman doing a household chore, a girl walking, a soldier holding his rifle over his head, an announcer framed on a television screen, a sailor beside a signal lamp, a baby playing with blocks.
- A cartoon strip showing conversation.

Procedures to Be Used in Guiding Children in Arriving at the "Big Idea"

Guide the children in analyzing the pictures and the cartoon strip to determine situations in which communication is taking place. Encourage the children to substantiate their choices. Use the summary charts as aids in helping children to recall facts and ideas.

Guide the children in developing a definition of communication based on their choices among the pictures and the cartoon strip.

Choices of Expressive Tasks to Be Performed

1. Developing a mural about communication as a process.
2. Developing conversational sequences reflecting differences in problems and human interrelationships.
3. Developing a visual code for transmitting messages.
4. Developing an advertising program for an imaginary product.
5. Developing political posters and other visual materials for a boy or girl running for school office.

Materials to Stimulate Children to Become Involved in Expressive Tasks

- A mural completed by another class.
- A sound tape used previously for study.
- A short message in a simple visual code.
- Advertisements about a selected product.
- Political advertisements and other materials.

Procedures for Guiding Children in Expressive Activities

Present the various products and have the children decide which task they would like to work on.

Form the children into groups in accord with their choice of the expressive task to be performed.

At the close of group work, guide the children in evaluating the products for accuracy.

Verifying the "Big Idea"

Does the "big idea" hold true in a variety of situations?

Materials to Be Used in Guiding Children in Verifying the "Big Idea"

- The summaries developed at the close of each section of the unit as well as the summary statement of the "big idea."

- A cardboard screen large enough to conceal a seated child. The screen has a slot large enough to admit a 3" x 5" card.

- A series of sketches or pictures of persons in various kinds of situations and relationships: a police sergeant inspecting a squad of policemen; a pair of guards, each representing a different nation, at an international boundary line; a family seated around a dinner table; a fire inspector talking to the owner of a house; NATO representatives talking about problems; a striker picketing a place of business.

Procedures for Guiding Children in Verifying Their Learning

Guide the children in thinking about ways that they can test what they have expressed in their summaries. Help them to get started with experimenting by having pairs of children communicate in the solution of problems of varying difficulty while the rest of the class observes. Increase the number of pupils in communicating groups to see what occurs. Organize ten children in a communication circle as an experimental arrangement. Alter conditions by using the screen to separate communicators. Vary the nature of the problems. Encourage the class to report their observations and to analyze them to see whether their summary ideas hold true.

Guide the children in analyzing each of the pictures to establish that the conditions of communication are apparently in force in the situation presented. Encourage the children to identify the problems, human relationships, and symbols used. Have them consider whether anything pictured does not really fit into the scheme of communication that they have learned.

Help the children understand that the differences in problems, relationships, and symbols do not deny what they have learned about communication as a process.

Ideas about Attitudes and Patterns of Action Related to Communication as a Process (A)

We appreciate the importance of maintaining open lanes of communication.

We value those human interrelationships which serve to keep the lanes of communication open.

We hold as acceptable for solution through communication those problems which do not require us to violate our own integrity.

To improve communication between ourselves and others, we strive to strengthen interrelationships by doing the following:

1. Seeking and weighing information about others before arriving at an opinion about them and acting upon it.
2. Becoming involved with others in joint efforts to solve acceptable problems.
3. Trying to see others as they would have us see them and helping them.

Materials to Be Used in Guiding Children toward Understanding These Ideas (A)

• A series of problems:

Problem 1. A new pupil who appears to be very shy and fearful has been assigned to your classroom. Should you try to open a lane of communication with this person right away or should you wait? Why? Once you decide to open a lane of communication, how should you go about it?

Problem 2. A group of your very closest friends invite you to go with them to play in an old house in which no one has lived in years. Your father has warned you to stay away from the house because its floors are rotted. What will be the conversation between you and your friends? Explain why the conversation will work out in this way.

Problem 3. Your best friend and you have an argument because he will not share his eraser with you. In anger both you and your friend promise not to speak to each other. Later you are sorry. Will you try to open a lane of communication with him or will you wait until he tries? Why?

Problem 4. The mayor of your city wants the city council to spend tax money for a new hospital. One morning you see the following headline in the newspaper: COMMUNICATION BREAKDOWN BETWEEN MAYOR AND COUNCIL. What you you think must have happened? The city really needs a new hospital. What should the mayor do? What should the council do? What kinds of things can the mayor or the council do to open a lane of communication?

Problem 5. A boy is transferred from another classroom to yours. You have heard that he makes trouble and sometimes hurts people. The teacher assigns him a seat next to yours. What are you going to do?

Problem 6. On a television newscast you see several high-ranking officers leaving a conference room. The announcer says that this is the end of a very important meeting about keeping an airbase in another country. The officers of one country think it is necessary; the officers from the other country are afraid to have it so near one of the big cities. The officers are shaking their heads. No agreement has been reached. What can be done to improve the communication among these officers?

Problem 7. All through the school year your fifth grade has been the only one in the school. Suddenly it is decided that another fifth grade is to be transported from somewhere else in your school. What can your fifth grade do to make this new fifth grade become a part of your school? How can you make sure that there is an open lane of communication between your grade and the new grade?

Procedures to Be Used in Guiding Children toward Understanding These Ideas (A)

Guide the children in reacting to the problems listed above through role-playing, individual statements, group statements, or story writing. Focus the children's attention on the communication aspects.

Ideas about an Attitude and Pattern of Action Related to Communications as a Process (B)

We appreciate the mass media of communication as sources of information, but we realize that we must be careful in judging the information and using it to solve problems.

We discriminate carefully between well-based opinion and poorly based opinion as we use mass media as sources for information.

Material for Guiding Children toward Understanding These Ideas (B)

• A series of problems:

Problem 1. Present a series of advertisements about bicycles to the children. Have them study carefully the specifications and qualities of the bicycles as advertised and encourage them to determine which bicycle is the best buy. Encourage several volunteers to go to a bicycle shop to determine what a good bicycle is and what it should cost. They report their findings to the class; then analyze the advertisements again.

Problem 2. Present a series of letters to the editor about an issues. Have the children read them carefully to identify differences in point of view. Encourage them to decide with which point of view they agree. Alert them to watch the newspapers for the next few days for more objective news about the issue. Then guide them in reexamining the point of view that they had accepted earlier.

Problem 3. A famous sports hero has just published a book about how boys and girls should be trained to be good citizens. He thinks that all boys and girls should have at least three hours of homework every night and that they should be punished severely when they do not do their lessons in school. Many people buy his book. He appears on television programs. A newspaper publishes his articles every day. What do you think is going to happen to boys and girls? What do you think people should do?

Procedures for Guiding Children toward Understanding These Ideas (B)

Guide the children in reacting to the problem situations listed above through roleplaying, individual statements, group statements, or story writing.

Teacher X has made provisions for all his teaching purposes. He refers to the business of tying ideas together as culminating the unit. *Culminating* the unit or the *culmination* of the unit are terms that have been long in use in elementary social-studies methodology.

Teacher Y has a different view of what he is doing in the Section III of his unit, as can be seen in its title, *"Acquiring Behaviors."* His teaching purposes are expressed differently. Yet his procedures do not differ greatly from those of Teacher X. The main difference is that he omits expressive activity. However, like Teacher X, he uses an instructional model as a device for helping children to bring their ideas together to arrive at a generalization, or the "big idea" under study; has the children verify it; and then guides them in problem-solving situations to help them discover attitudes and patterns of action. For a better understanding of his point of view and his procedures, examine Section III of Teacher Y's unit.

TEACHER Y'S UNIT

SECTION III. ACQUIRING BEHAVIOR

Teaching purposes:
a. To synthesize learnings about communication as a process.
b. To verify learnings about communication as a process.
c. To examine learnings to determine possible behavior.

The "Big Idea"
Communication is a process of interaction in which people use symbols as a means of controlling their social environment in the solution of problems.

Instructional Model for Helping Children Synthesize Learning into the "Big Idea"
• Magazine or newspaper pictures showing the following: A boy writing, a man sleeping, a woman doing a household chore, a girl walking, a soldier holding a rifle over his head, an announcer framed in a television screen, a sailor beside a signal lamp, a baby playing with blocks, a cartoon strip showing conversation.

Procedures for Guiding Children in Synthesizing Learning
Showing the pictures and the cartoon strip one at a time, have the children select those which show communication. Encourage them to substantiate their choices. List their reasons. After the pictures and cartoon strip have been analyzed, guide the children in examining their reasons to develop a definition of communication.

Verifying

Is the "big idea" really true?

How true is it true in other times and places?

Materials Used in Guiding Children in Verifying the "Big Idea"

- A series of sketches depicting the following: Two Spartan boys, an American Plains Indian man and an Indian woman somewhat older than he is, an army general and a private, a businessman and his secretary.

Procedures for Guiding Children in Verifying the "Big Idea"

Ask the children how sure they are about their definition. Have them consider whether communication is always what they think it is everywhere and at all times.

Present each of the pictures and clarify that Spartan boys were taught to cheat, lie, and steal as soldiers; that in some Plains Indian tribes a man could not speak to his mother-in-law; and that in some instances communication is mostly one-way between superiors and subordinates. Have the children consider whether these situations in any way alter their definition or make it less true.

Ideas about the Communication Process Offering Orientation to Behavior (A)

The more open the lanes of communication, the better the chances of problem solution.

The stronger the human interrelationships among the communicators, the more open the lanes of communication.

The greater the acceptability of the problem among the communicators, the greater its chances of solution.

Materials for Guiding Children toward Sensing These Ideas (A)

- A series of roleplaying situations:

Situation 1. Family and school problems in which one communicator, or several, decides not to speak to the others, or to communicate only in writing, or to communicate only at selected times.

Situation 2. Family and school problems between individuals and groups of individuals—sibling and sibling, parents and children, boys and girls in different classrooms, older and younger children.

Situation 3. Neighborhood and community problems—obtaining a park, home beautification, the need for more schools.

National- and international-level applications similar to the above.

- A series of reaction stimulators:

Write about expectations of visiting a certain city section or a certain country, investigate available resources, review original ideas.

Consider doing a task jointly with another classroom, decide on task, do it; review the results in terms of human interrelationships.

Decide feeling about a certain group of people, seize an opportunity to do something for them, then reexamine feelings.

Procedures for Guiding Children toward Sensing These Ideas (A)

Guide the children in roleplaying the various situations. Those not immediately involved analyze the performance and may from time to time assume roles with different personal interpretations.

As the children play each series of situations, guide them toward ideas about *lanes of communication and human interrelationship.*

Guide the children into the various reaction stimulating situations. Encourage individual reaction and class discussion of reactions.

Ideas about the Communication Process Offering Orientation to Behavior (B)

The more contact with mass media, the more discriminating the individual must be in accepting information and governing his actions by it.

Materials for Guiding Children toward Sensing These Ideas (B)

• A series of current advertisements, editorials, and cartoons.
• A selection of television commercials to be analyzed and compared.
Who's Who and other available references.

Procedures for Guiding Children toward Sensing These Ideas (B)

Guide the children in analyzing the advertisements and commercials for obviously untrue promises and "hidden" promises.

Guide the children in analyzing the editorials and cartoons for point of view. Encourage them to look for cartoons and editorials and letters to the editor in conflict with each other.

Guide the children in examining points of view about an issue for the information that stands behind each. If possible, consider also the reputation of the author as support to a point of view.

Perhaps you are wondering about such statements of Teacher Y's as *the more this . . . the more that . . .* as verbal ways of describing attitudes and patterns of action. They contrast sharply with the *We this . . .* and the *We that . . .* statements listed in Teacher X's unit. The statements used by Teacher Y contain implicit attitudes and patterns of action and as such tend to point toward their formation with considerable force.

You may have noticed that Teacher Y is not as specific as Teacher X in terms of problem situations for developing attitudes and patterns of action. He prefers to leave these more open in order to utilize better problem situations that may occur in the classroom, or current happenings reported in newspapers and magazines.

Teacher Z's procedures are similar to those of both Teacher X and Teacher Y. The only real difference between the third section of his unit and either of theirs is that he reintroduces the instructional model used in the first part of his unit as a means of helping children to arrive at a generalization of the "big idea." The children reexamine their original hypotheses in the light of their findings acquired in the second part of the unit. In so doing, they arrive at the "big idea." For a more complete picture of Teacher Z's procedures, see Section III of his unit.

TEACHER Z'S UNIT

SECTION III. TYING IDEAS TOGETHER ABOUT COMMUNICATION AS A PROCESS

Teaching purposes:
   a. Generalize to arrive at the "big idea" about communication as a process.
   b. Reexpress the "big idea."
   c. Verify the "big idea."
   d. Tie the "big idea" to related attitudes and patterns of action.

The "Big Idea"

The "big idea" to be arrived at is the same as that placed in issue in Section I. The materials to be used to help children in generalizing include the instructional model (pictures of a boy writing, a man sleeping, a woman doing a household chore, and others) used in placing the "big idea" in issue, and the children's statement or statements about communication made then.

Materials for Guiding Children in Verifying the Big Idea and in Expressive Activity

• A series of pictures showing persons in various kinds of situations and relationships: An officer of high rank inspecting men of low rank, a small child and its mother, a Boy Scout and his Scoutmaster, representatives of nations at a United Nations meeting at a conference table, an American soldier and a foreign soldier, a policeman giving a ticket, a line of strikers or demonstrators carrying signs.

• A communication model illustrating a condition of communication in which various obstacles and interrelationships prevail, expressed in conversation and sketch sequences.

Procedures for Helping Children Arrive at and Verify the "Big Idea"

Post the pictures on a bulletin board and write the children's original statements on the chalkboard. Have the children again look at the pictures and examine their original statement or statements. Guide them in analyzing the statements for accuracy. Encourage them to make necessary changes.

Have each suggested change substantiated by the individual suggesting it. The statement or statements as changed reflect the "big idea."

Challenge the truth of the children's statement or statements and invite them to test them by thinking about the ways that they communicate with their parents and teacher. Discuss the kinds of problems that are treated and the differences in the problems discussed with parents and a teacher. Guide the children in analyzing each of the pictures to see whether any run counter to their statement or statements. Encourage the children to consider differences in problems, relationships, and symbols used.

Help the children to understand that although there are differences in problems, relationships, and symbols, the process of communication as they have expressed it remains essentially the same.

Showing the models, encourage the children to make several models themselves. They may write conversational sequences or develop sequences of sketches. Isolate certain conditions and have the children group to complete tasks.

Statements that Reflect Ideas about Attitudes and Patterns of Action Related to Communication as a Process (A)

We appreciate the importance of maintaining open lanes of communication.

We value human interrelationships which keep communication lanes open.

We hold as acceptable for solution through communication those problems which do not require us to violate our own integrity.

To improve communication between ourselves and others, we strive to strengthen interrelationships by doing the following:
  a. Seeking and weighing information about others before arriving at and acting upon an opinion about others.
  b. Becoming involved with others in joint efforts to solve problems.
  c. Trying to see others as they would have us see them, and helping them.

Materials for Guiding Children toward Sensing These Ideas (A)

• A series of common classroom and playground problems presented at the communication stage: A group of sixth graders insist on playing in the same play area as the fifth graders, a third-grade group insists that the fifth graders' play equipment is theirs, a group of seventh graders invites some fifth graders to join them in playing a trick on some sixth graders, a group of fifth graders are to build a puppet stage.

• A series of community situations presented at the communication stage: A fire inspector visits a home, a mayor works at a transportation problem with the city council, a bagboy at the grocery store causes a customer's groceries to spill out on the floor, a service-station attendant neglects to watch what he is doing and thereby puts more gasoline in the tank than the customer wants and can pay for.

Procedures for Guiding Children toward an Understanding of Attitudes and Patterns of Action Related to Communication (A)

Guide the children into roleplaying these various situations under conditions when the lanes of communication are open and when one communicator decides to close the lanes. The children not roleplaying at any given time evaluate what they see and from time to time assume roles as they see them.

Have the children consider the human interrelationships in some of the situations. Encourage them to perform roles under various conditions of human interrelationships.

Use some of the situations as reaction stimulators in which individual children catalog their ideas, roleplay, and then reexamine their ideas.

Statements that Reflect Ideas about Attitudes and Patterns of Action Related to Communication as a Process (B)

We appreciate the mass media of communication as sources of information, but we realize that we must be careful in judging the information and using it to solve problems.

We discriminate carefully between well-based opinion and poorly based opinion as we use mass media as sources of information.

Materials to Be Used to Guide Children toward Sensing These Ideas (B)

• A descriptive situation about a family that has just learned that a power-hungry individual has just seized control of all the mass media of communication in a nation.

• A series of advertisements about articles of use to children such as bicycles, transistor radios, and the like.

• A collection of cartoons which present conflicting views about a community problem.

Procedures for Guiding Children toward an Understanding of Attitudes and Patterns of Action Related to Communication (B)

Encourage the children to develop individual creative stories about the family that has just learned that the mass media are now in the control of a power-hungry man.

Have the children analyze the advertisements to arrive at decisions as to which leads toward the best buy. Have the children consult with local experts to determine which is best.

Invite the resource person to the classroom to discuss the merits of various products of the same type.

Guide the children in analyzing the cartoons to decide which ones appear to tell the larger truth.

Have the children check in available resources before arriving at a decisions about an issue depicted in cartoons.

Units are complete structures which assure a full knowledge of ideas including understandings, attitudes, and patterns of action. The completeness, however, is a convention which indicates that the "big idea" treated has been studied to a certain level of sophistication. It may be studied again the following year or several years later. In the meantime, emphasis on it has ceased. From time to time the learnings acquired may be manifested in the current-affairs program or in life situations. To this extent the study of the unit is not finished.

Three units for further study, each prepared with a different strategy, have been included in the Appendix.

SUMMARY

A unit in social studies is a comprehensive instructional plan specifying the content related to a generalization and the materials and procedures required for its teaching and learning. It may be expressed in a variety of ways.

A unit reflects the teaching strategy chosen by the teacher. A strategy is an instructional design which indicates a belief and a commitment to a way of working with children to assure effective learning. Some of the strategies among which social-studies teachers may choose are (1) the basal strategy, which places emphasis on large areas and topics and independent, factual learning; (2) the synthesized strategy, which is similar to the basal strategy except that it is organized around a "big idea" and includes provisions for thinking as an aid to learning; (3) the social-science strategy, which places emphasis on children's learning social-science concepts in much the same way as social scientists and includes provisions for thinking as an aid to learning; and (4) the thinking-emphasis strategy, which centers on inquiry as a way of learning social-studies ideas. No claim is made for the superiority of any of the last three strategies over the others.

A unit has a horizontal and vertical structure. Its horizontal structure consists of specifics in terms of content and the materials, and learning activities required for teaching the content listed. The vertical structure consists of three parts. The first part indicates content, materials, and activities involved in building interest in the unit; the second lists content, materials, and learning activities involved in acquiring facts and ideas; and the third presents content, materials, and learning activities involved in arriving at the "big idea," verifying it, and relating it to appropriate attitudes and patterns of action.

Exercises for Further Understanding

1. Obtain a guide or resource unit prepared by the curriculum office of the county or district in which you plan to teach. Analyze it carefully to determine how much unit construction is left to the teacher. Note the variety of suggested procedures, the variety of materials provided, the specific provisions made for individual differences and for inquiry.

2. Professional magazines such as *The Grade Teacher* and *The Instructor* often contain units. Examine several issues of both of these magazines and analyze the units offered in them to determine whether they are resource units or teaching units. Try to make a personal assessment as to the utility of these units, particularly the teaching units. Can you picture the class of pupils for which each teaching unit is developed?

3. Prepare a two- or three-day teaching unit leading toward a deeper understanding of a national holiday such as Thanksgiving Day, Washington's Birthday, Lincoln's Birthday, Memorial Day, or the like. After this unit has been carefully evaluated, keep it as a basis for evaluating your growth in unit construction.

Selected References

Benjamin, William F., "The Teacher and Learning in the Social Studies." *National Elementary Principal,* 42:35-39 (May 1963).

Drummond, Harold D., "Separate or Merged—Sound Experiences Are Vital." *National Elementary Principal,* 42:27-30 (April 1963).

Dunfee, Maxine and Helen Sagl, *Social Studies through Problem Solving,* Chaps. 1-12. New York: Holt, Rinehart and Winston, Inc., 1966.

Hamilton, Jean F., "Creating a Learning Situation." *Social Education*, 18:15-17 (January 1954).

Hanna, Lavone A., Gladys L. Potter, and Neva Hagaman, *Unit Teaching in the Elementary School*, Chap. 5, "The Unit of Work," and Chap. 6, "Developing a Unit of Work." New York: Rinehart and Company, Inc., 1955.

Hill, Wilhelmina, "Designs for Social Studies Units," *Social Studies in Elementary Schools*, pp. 262-270. Thirty-Second Yearbook of the National Council for the Social Studies, Washington, D.C.: National Education Association, 1962.

————, ed., *Selected Resource Units: Elementary Social Studies*. Curriculum Series, No. 11, National Council for the Social Studies, Washington, D.C.: National Education Association, 1961.

Jarolimek, John, *Social Studies in Elementary Education*, 2d ed., Chap. 3, "The Development of Social Studies Units." New York: The Macmillan Company, 1963.

Joyce, Bruce R., *Strategies for Elementary Social Science Education*, Chap. 10, "The Depth Study." Chicago: Science Research Associates, Inc., 1965.

Merritt, Edith P., *Working with Children in Social Studies*, Chap. 4, "The Unit of Work." Belmont, Calif: Wadsworth Publishing Company, Inc., 1961.

Michaelis, John U., *Social Studies for Children in a Democracy*, 3d ed., Chap. 7, "Planning Units of Instruction." Englewood Cliffs, N.J.: Prentice-Hall, Inc., 1963.

Muessig, Raymond H., "Bridging the Gap between Textbook Teaching and Unit Teaching." *Social Studies*, 54:43-46 (February 1963).

Park, Joe, "Three Views of the Problem of Instruction." *Social Studies*, 52:54-58 (February 1961).

Preston, Ralph C., *Teaching Social Studies in the Elementary School*, Part Two, "Social Studies Units." New York: Rinehart and Company, Inc., 1958.

Smith, James A., "Teaching through Process Units," *Social Studies for the Middle Grades*, pp. 40-52. Curriculum Series, No. 5, National Council for the Social Studies, Washington, D.C.: National Education Association, 1960.

6

Lesson Planning in
Social Studies

As shown in Chapter 5, a teaching unit in social studies is an over-all plan for an extended period of time. It serves the teacher as a general guide indicating what is to be taught, when and how it is to be taught, and the materials to be used. Although it reflects considerable detail, it usually lacks the specificity required for a daily teaching plan. The purpose of this chapter is to present procedures for daily planning.

Because of the abstract nature of social studies, much of its content is difficult to teach either with or without a daily plan. In and of itself, a daily plan does not assure effective teaching; it does assure that the teacher will give some deliberate thought to what he is going to do and what he is going to guide children in doing to reach daily objectives. The plan eases the difficulty of teaching to the extent that the teacher feels less apprehensive about himself and his teaching ability. Assurance takes him a step or two toward effective teaching. The rest must be left to the quality of his planning and to his alertness as a teacher to make the necessary, usually minor, on-the-spot changes in plans. Change may involve no more than selecting an alternative procedure considered during the planning stage but rejected in favor of another which appeared to be better. Thus it is that quality of planning may be greater than that reflected on a neatly developed paper-and-pencil plan clearly indicating the decisions made before the moment of teaching.

Quality of planning is the key factor, but it has a dual aspect. A daily lesson plan may be said to be adequate on the basis that its application did bring about effective learning, or it may be said to be adequate in terms of how well it reflects an understanding of a particular classroom of children and an ability to translate knowledge into teaching-learning increments in proper sequence. Upon this latter aspect of quality, this chapter will focus in a general way.

Frequently the idea of making daily lesson plans is criticized as being so much nonsensical busywork. This criticism is not directed toward the idea of daily planning, but toward the ways that such plans are expressed. In particular disfavor are long, carefully structured statements. The most frequent argument against them is that experienced teachers seldom use them. This argument does not imply that these teachers have not planned; a few ideas noted on a slip of paper or kept in mind suffice for them. But for novice social-studies teachers, the extended, carefully structured statement of plans serves two purposes: (1) it is a basis for preperformance criticism from a supervisor, and (2) it is a means of mastering the thinking methods of a social-studies teacher. In this chapter such statements will be presented as models to introduce the patterns of thought characteristic of a social-studies teacher as he plans lessons.

As is to be expected, the teacher's commitment toward a strategy of teaching will be reflected in his plans, although not so apparently as it is in his unit. Frequently teachers using different strategies will use similar tactical measures from day to day. Except for certain small differences, the models presented here will be applicable within all the strategies introduced.

THE STRUCTURE OF LESSON PLANS

Similarly to the unit, the lesson plan is structured to reflect the basic teaching-learning theme: establish goals, work to reach goals, and evaluate to see whether goals have been reached. Like the unit, it will contain listings of facts and ideas, materials to be used, and procedures to be followed. It will differ from the unit in that it will deal with much less content and specify more narrowly the materials to be used and the procedures to be followed.

The usual pattern of thinking in developing a lesson plan is generally as follows: Review the facts and ideas to be learned or treated as objectives, review the resources or materials to identify more specifically the elements to be used, and develop a sequence of teaching-learning activities to arrive at the selected objectives.

DEVELOPING DAILY OBJECTIVES

The first step in planning a day's lesson is to develop a statement of the objective or objectives to be met in the course of a social-studies period. If the unit has not been completely developed and expressed beforehand, the teacher will need to develop a structure reflecting the objective to be taught. Let us suppose that a teacher of grade four in California decides that his pupils need to learn about the location of their home state and how this location generally influences the lives of the people living there. He develops a structure such as this:

UNIT: CALIFORNIA AS A STATE COMMUNITY

Objective. An understanding of the following:

California has a unique location
1. Among the southwestern states.
2. Among the Pacific Coast states.
3. Among the western states.
4. In the United States.
5. On the continent of North America.
6. In the Pacific community
7. In the world.

California's location influences the way its people live.
1. Nearness to the sea provides for recreation, commerce, and industry related to the sea.
2. Southerly location contributes to a very comfortable climate enjoyed by many people and inviting to certain industries.

This structure is expressed as an objective when the label *An understanding of the following* is attached. The objective so expressed in total form can serve now as a guide in the selection of materials and in the development of learning activities.

The matter of developing a statement of objective or objectives would have been much simplified if a unit had been completely developed and expressed previously. The teacher would merely have studied the content outline in the unit, selected a comprehensive element from it (similar to the outline included in the objective above), and developed a simple statement of objective such as the folowing:

An understanding of the location of California and the ways the location influences the lives of Californians.

The structure of the objective will vary with the aspect of behavior to be taught. In the above example, an understanding about facts and ideas has been treated. If the behavior has to do with an attitude or a pattern of action, the structure of the objective will reflect this difference.

Another factor which influences the structure of the objective is the teaching strategy which the teacher plans to use. Models such as the above would be suitable for certain moments during the course of a synthesized-strategy unit or during a thinking-emphasis unit. A teacher using the social-science strategy would be likely to structure the statement of objective or objectives in this way:

Understanding of the following:
    Location is the placement that an entity has in relation to other identified entities.
    Location influences the function of an entity.

These models have treated only of the structure of the objective characteristic of the second section of the unit, in which emphasis is placed on acquiring supportive facts and ideas. Lesson plans dealing with the first part of the unit, in which interest is stimulated, will have objectives structured to meet the requirements of the teaching strategy used. However, since the purpose of this part of the unit tends to be open-ended and largely processive, a more specific plan than that given in the unit itself is little needed. If a unit has not been fully expressed previously, the teacher will need to develop a plan which closely duplicates what Teachers X, Y, or Z have included in the first section of their units.

Some teachers feel that they do a better job of teaching social studies if they show some concern in their plans for the skills used in social studies. In the structure of objectives they include a reference to skill objectives. Often these are listed in this way: practice in reading reference skills, practice in notetaking skills, practice in reading maps, and so on. If the teacher plans to give minor emphasis to a skill, that is, to lead the pupils in a discussion about the skill, or to have the pupils practice the skills briefly under his immediate supervision, or to review the efficacy of the skill, then the skill should be listed. The skill or group of skills need not be listed unless some instructional emphasis is to be given to the skills listed. A list of skill objectives, especially if it is quite long, tends to look like so much pedagogical whitewash with which the teacher deludes himself or others who may be evaluating his plan.

SELECTING MATERIALS

The second step in planning the lesson is to determine exactly which materials are going to be used. As the teacher examines the materials listed in his unit, he assesses them carefully. When he first drew up this list, he had in mind a "typical" class. How typical is his class? Does he need materials of less abstraction? Of greater abstraction? At this point, he is as much concerned with the differences in background and the range of intellectual ability in his class as with the accuracy and pertinence of materials. He is already thinking ahead in his plans, for he is considering the use of materials. He arrives at his decisions about materials in accord with the needs of his class and within the limitations of immediate availability. He lists the materials to be used in a very exact way giving exact page numbers, picture titles, map titles, and the like. He may also review the materials to see whether they contain passages, illustrations, diagrams, and the like which would be helpful in creating interest and evaluating learning. If he finds such aids, he lists them and their page locations or titles.

DEVELOPING TEACHING PROCEDURES

The third step in lesson planning is to develop a series of teaching-learning activities that will lead toward the objective(s). Depending on the detail and precision with which these are expressed, and depending somewhat on the strategy that gives direction to the planning, as many as ten or twelve may be listed, but in most instances at least three are essential. The three basic instructional procedures are: establishing goals, working to reach them, and checking to see how well they have been reached. If more than three teaching-learning activities are listed, they are generally categorized under one or the other of the three basic procedures.

The first of these teaching-learning activities indicates the roles of the teacher and the pupils in the matter of developing interest. Whatever the teacher does and whatever the pupils do are listed in sequence under a functional heading such as *defining purposes, establishing purposes, motivation,* or the like. The two factors which contribute strongly to the selection and development of these activities are the nature of the teaching moment and teaching strategy being used.

If the demand of the teaching moment is the stimulation of interest at the beginning of the unit, the proponent of each strategy will make lists of activities as follows:

Synthesized strategy

> Activity 1: Introduce an arranged environment or a slice of reality as represented in a film, filmstrip, object, or the like.
>
> Activity 2: Encourage the children to examine whatever has been presented.

Social-science strategy

> Activity: Conduct a general discussion about the central concept being studied as a "warm-up".

Thinking-emphasis strategy

> Activity 1: Through discussion develop a level of knowledge about a basic idea within the generalization.
>
> Activity 2: Place the "big idea," or generalization in issue to prompt inquiry.

If the demand of the teaching moment is the stimulation of interest in a supporting idea to be studied, the strategists will make a listing as following:

Synthesized strategy

> Activity: Guide the children in discussing and clarifying the question to be investigated.

Social-science strategy

> Activity: Present a demonstration which the children observe to secure an idea.

Thinking-emphasis strategy

> Activity 1: Place the idea in issue.
>
> Activity 2: Guide the children in developing a design for inquiry.

If the demand of the teaching moment is to maintain children's interest in the seeking of ideas and facts, the strategists develop the same activity:

Activity: Guide the children in a review of the facts and ideas studied to this point.

If the demand of the moment is to stimuate children's interest in arriving at the "big idea," the various strategists develop activities as follows:

Synthesized strategy
Activity 1: Guide the children in developing a summary of the learnings acquired in the unit.
Activity 2: Presenting an instructional model, guide the children in examining it for conflicts of ideas.

Social-science strategy
Activity: Presenting an instructional model, guide the children in examining it for conflict of ideas.

Thinking-emphasis strategy
Activity: Presenting the children's original hypothesis(es), guide them in examining the hypothesis(es) in the light of their findings.

If the demand of the moment is to stimulate interest in verifying a "big idea" and discovering attitudes and patterns of action related to it, the various strategists plan similar activities:

Verifying a "big idea"
Activity: Place the idea in doubt.

Discovering attitudes and patterns of action
Activity: Guide the children into a projective activity.

The second basic teaching-learning activity (or group of activities) deals with the more active involvement of children in the learning process, and it is again the demand of the teaching moment and the selected strategy that guide the teacher in developing activities. These activities are listed under such functional labels as *contact experience, purpose fulfilling, involvement, work, investigative activities,* or the like.

If the demand of the teaching moment is to involve children immediately following the stimulation of interest in the unit, the strategists develops activities as follows:

Synthesized strategy
  Activity: Guide the children in discussing what has been introduced to them.
Social-science strategy
  Activity: None. (The general discussion listed previously assumes the continued involvement of children.)
Thinking-emphasis strategy
  Activity 1: Encourage the children to make hypotheses and substantiate them.
  Activity 2: Guide the children in selecting the hypothesis or hypotheses which appears to be the most reasonable.

If the demand of the teaching moment is to involve children in seeking more facts related to a supporting idea, the strategists develop activities as given below:

Synthesized strategy
  Activity: Guide the children in consulting resources for facts.
Social-science strategy
  Activity 1: Present a demonstration for the children to observe and discuss, OR Guide the children in developing a demonstration to discover needed facts.
  Activity 2: Same as either of the above as needed.
Thinking-emphasis strategy
  Activity 1: Guide the children in consulting resources for facts, OR Present a demonstration for the children to observe and discuss, OR Guide the children in developing a demonstration to discover needed facts.
  Activity 2: Any of the above as needed.

If the demand of the teaching moment is to involve children in arriving at the "big idea," the strategists develop the following activities:

Synthesized strategy
  Activity: Guide the children in resolving the conflict of ideas through recalling previous learnings that are directly pertinent.
Social-science strategy
  Activity: Guide the children in resolving the conflict of ideas through recalling previous learnings that are directly pertinent.

Thinking-emphasis strategy
> Activity: Guide the children in making the changes necessary in their original hypothesis(ses).

If the demand of the teaching moment is to involve children in verifying a "big idea," the strategists develop learning activities as follows:

Synthesized strategy
> Activity: Guide the children in examining various resources to see whether the "big idea" holds true in other places, AND/OR
> Guide the children in examining various resources to see whether the "big idea" holds true in other times, AND/OR
> Guide the children in examining various resources to see whether the "big idea" holds true in current life.

Social-science and thinking-emphasis strategy
> Activity: Any activity listed above plus any of the following wherever possible—Guide the children in developing experimental situations to verify the idea, AND/OR Guide the children in checking their statement of the "big idea" with statements made by various authorities.

If the demand of the teaching moment is to involve children in the discovery of attitudes and patterns of action, all the strategists plan a replication of projective activities.

The third basic teaching-learning activity (or group of activities) deals with the integration and synthesis of learning. Here, too, the demand of teaching moment and the selected strategy influence the choices made by the teacher as he plans lessons. He lists these activities as entries under such functional headings as *checking purposes, evaluation, evaluative activity, synthesis,* or the like.

If the demand of the teaching moment is to determine purposes after the children's interest in the unit has been stimulated and they have had opportunities to delve into the possibilities of study inherent within the unit, the strategists develop activities as follows:

Synthesized strategy
> Activity 1: Guide the children in developing questions to serve as a guide.
> Activity 2: Guide the children in arranging their questions in investigative order.

Social-science strategy
> Activity: None. (The general discussion listed previously terminates with an established general curiosity.)

Thinking-emphasis strategy
　　Activity: Guide the children in developing a design for inquiry to guide further investigation.

If the demand of the teaching moment is to have children synthesize facts into an idea, the strategists develop activities reflecting the following:

Synthesized strategy
　　Activity 1: Have the children contribute their findings from available resources.
　　Activity 2: Guide the children in integrating the facts into the statement of an idea.
　　Activity 3: Guide the children in expressing the idea in a selected medium.

Social-science strategy
　　Activity 1: Present a demonstration or guide the children in an experiment which brings previous learning together.
　　Activity 2: Guide the children in a careful analysis and synthesis to discover the idea.

Thinking-emphasis strategy
　　Activity 1: Have the children present their findings resulting from investigative activities.
　　Activity 2: Guide the children in relating their findings to their hypothesis(es) about the supporting idea.
　　Activity 3: Guide the children in developing a statement of the discovered idea.
　　Activity 4: (Not always) Guide the children in considering an expressive activity to reexpress the idea in their own terms.

If the demand of the teaching moment is to bring children to the point of making a statement of the "big idea" as a generalization, the strategists plan activities as follows:

Synthesized strategy
　　Activity 1: Guide the children in inferring a statement that synthesizes their learning.
　　Activity 2: Guide the children in an activity (or several activities) in which they express the "big idea" in a chosen medium.

Social-science strategy
　　Activity: Guide the children in inferring a statement that synthesizes their learning.

Thinking-emphasis strategy

Activity 1: Guide the children in developing a precise statement of the generalization.

Activity 2: Guide the children in an activity (or several activities) in which they express the "big idea" in a chosen medium.

If the demand of the teaching moment is to terminate study at the close of the period at a point before all the facts necessary for an idea have been studied, the strategists develop a similar activity: Guide the children in a review of the learning acquired during the period.

If the demand of the teaching moment is to have children synthesize findings to verify the "big idea," the strategists incorporate similar activities in their plans as follows: (1) Guide the children in contributing their findings; (2) have them determine whether a parallel exists between their findings and the "big idea"; (3) guide them in establishing whether lack of parallel is real or apparent; and (4) if necessary, have them restate the "big idea" to reflect new findings.

If the demand of the teaching moment is to have children synthesize their findings to discover attitudes or patterns of action, the strategists plan activities in much the same way: (1) Have the children examine their findings to select those which are the most appropriate; (2) guide the children in testing their choices in real or projective activities.

As shown in the above, each turn of the teacher's daily planning is called by the demand of the teaching moment and by the strategy to which he is committed. Teaching strategies were introduced in the previous chapter and clarified more fully in this chapter as forces which influence the teacher's selection of teaching-learning activities as tactical measures. The new idea introduced has been that of the teaching moment. Each is characterized by a particular purpose and activity. The general moment is determined by an aspect of the basic theme of instruction and learning for example, motivation, involvement, or evaluation. A diagram of the scheme of these moments is presented below.

The general moment in the lesson plan is often broken down in a series of specific moments. Here, strategy and the teacher's individual style of teaching and thinking exert an influence on the plan. No prediction can be made as to the number of these specific moments. However, it is likely that the greater the number of instances in which the teacher is directly involved, the greater the number of specific moments in the plan. This theory will be shown more clearly in fully developed lesson plans in the following section.

Scheme of Teaching Moments

	Teacher's Involvement	Children's Involvement
Stimulating interest in the unit	1. Introduce the unit	1. Determine general directions to follow
Acquiring facts and ideas	2. Introduce the area of facts	2. Determine specific directions to follow
	3. Introduce a direction to follow	3. Review findings
	4. Check progress in a given direction	4. Summarize findings to this point
	Repeat as necessary	Repeat as necessary
	5. Introduce total findings of ideas for analysis and synthesis	5. Arrive at the supporting idea
	Repeat above steps with each supporting idea	Repeat above steps with each supporting idea
Tying ideas together	6. Introduce total findings of ideas for analysis and synthesis AND/OR	6. Arrive at the "big idea" AND/OR
	Guide children in examining possibilities of expressive activities	Evaluate results for accuracy
	7. Introduce verifying activity	7. Arrive at verification
	Repeat as necessary	Repeat as necessary
	8. Introduce attitude-discovery activity	8. Discover attitudes
	Repeat as necessary	Repeat as necessary
	9. Introduce pattern-of-action discovery activity	9. Discover pattern of action
	Repeat as necessary	Repeat as necessary
	10. Introduce activity for testing attitudes and pattern of action	10. Evaluate attitudes and pattern of action
	Repeat as necessary	Repeat as necessary

MODELS OF LESSON PLANS

In social studies, children study reality. They make immediate contact with reality, but more often than not contact is mediated. A lesson plan reflects the teacher's role as a mediator. His role may call for him to mediate continually all through the lesson or it may call for him to release children to work largely on their own for a period of time.

Let us follow the work of a teacher as he makes a plan in which he is serving as a mediator throughout the lesson. First he glances at his complete unit. He selects the following entries:

Content:

The idea to be acquired: California has a unique location.
  Supporting facts:
    1. Among the southwestern states.
    2. Among the Pacific Coast states.
    3. Among the western states.
    4. In the United States.
    5. On the continent of North America.
    6. In the Pacific community.
    7. In the world.

Another idea to be acquired: California's location influences the way its people live.
  Supporting facts:
    1. Nearness to the sea provides for recreation, commerce, and industry related to the sea.
    2. Southerly location contributes to a very comfortable climate enjoyed by many people and inviting to certain industries.

Materials: An outline map of California with only the outline showing, physical-political maps of California, the United States, and the world; a world globe; a piece of string about three feet long.

Procedures:
  1. Using the outline map, stimulate the children's interest in finding out about California's location.
  2. Guide the children in analyzing maps and globe to locate California more precisely.
  3. Have the children discuss the location of California as a factor influencing the lives of its people.
  4. Using the outline map of California again, have the children assist in making it more precise in terms of location.

He develops this plan:

PLAN 1

Objectives:
1. An understanding of the location of California and the ways the location influences the lives of Californians.
2. Practice in map-reading skills.

Materials:
- A physical-political map of California.
- A physical-political map of the United States.
- A physical-political map of the world.
- A world globe.
- A piece of string about three feet long.

Procedures:

Defining purposes: "Boys and girls, pretend for the next few minutes that you are writing a letter to someone who has no idea where California is. You are trying to tell this person where it is. Take a sheet of paper and write the paragraph that tells about the location of California." Allow five minutes for the writing, then have volunteers read their paragraphs quickly. Use the paragraphs as a basis for further exploration of the location of California.

Learning activities:
1. Using the physical-political map of the United States, have the children locate California with respect to the states immediately surrounding it. Heighten sense of direction and location by having children respond to such questions as: If you travel to the north from here, what will be the first state you would come to? If you traveled southeast from here? To the east?
2. Using the physical-political map of the United States, guide the pupils in discovering the characteristic that California shares with Washington and Oregon.
3. Using the physical-political map of the United States, guide the children toward an understanding of the location of California with respect to the states west of the Mississippi River. Clarifying what is meant by "West" and "western" states, have the children respond to such questions as: Which is farther away from California, North Dakota or Texas? How much farther? In what direction?
4. ... the physical-political map of the United States, establish California's location with respect to the entire United States. Have the ... respond to such questions as: If you started from San Francisco ... traveled due east, what states would you cross before you

came to the Atlantic Ocean? Which is farther away from Sacramento: Albany, New York, or Talahassee, Florida? In what direction does each of these lie from Sacramento? Suppose someone who had never been to the United States were to ask you where California is in the United States; what would you tell him? Suppose that person planned to enter the United States at Galveston, Texas. What would you tell him?

5. Using the physical-political map of the world, guide the children toward an understanding of the location of California in North America. Ask such questions: If you wanted to visit a foreign country, and you didn't want to travel very far, where would you go? What foreign country would you come to if you traveled to the north? Suppose that you wanted to fly to Labrador, Canada. In what direction would you go? How far would you travel? To British Columbia? To Baja California, Mexico? To Yucatan, Mexico? (Be sure to point out that these are states or provinces in foreign countries.)

6. Using the physical-political map of the world, have the children locate California with respect to the Pacific community, including Hawaii, China, the Philippine Islands, Australia, Japan, Formosa, the Fiji Islands, and so on. Ask such questions as: If you were in the Philippine Islands, and you wanted to return home to California, in what direction would you go? How far would you have to travel? Suppose that you were in Australia and you wanted to "island-hop" home to California; what route would you take?

7. Using the physical-political map of the world and the globe, establish California's location in the world by having the children respond to such questions as, Which is closest to California: London, England, or Hong Kong, China? Buenos Aires, Argentina, or the North Pole?

8. Guide the children toward seeing that location has an influence on the ways Californians live, by asking: Do you see any advantages to living in California because it is placed where it is? If necessary, guide with such questions as: Why is such a long coastline a good thing for a state to have? How does this make a difference in the ways that people live in California? Does being down in the southern part of the country have anything to do with the people living in California?

Checking purposes:

1. Have the children reexamine the paragraphs written at the beginning of the lesson in the light of the learnings in the lesson.

2. Further clarify what is meant by *location* by having the children give as many different locational descriptions of California as they can and by having them review the differences that location makes in the lives of people.

In his daily lesson plan, the teacher extends considerably the procedural entries taken from his unit. Four teaching moments were listed in the unit. They were extended into eleven moments. This extension was due largely to the teacher's interpretation of his role as constant mediator.

In the next plan, the teacher interprets his role in two ways. Examine it carefully to find these ways.

PLAN 2

Objectives:
1. An understanding about Argentina's trade relations.
2. Practice in reading for information and notetaking.

Materials:
   Living in Latin America, pp. 321-327
   Neighbors in Latin America, pp. 222-227 (203, 222, 227 for slow group).

Procedures:
   Defining purposes:
   1. "Yesterday we learned about the regions of Argentina and we decided that Argentina was basically an agricultural country. What do you suppose this means for the people of Argentina?" The most likely response: The people of Argentina have enough to eat and wear.
   2. Have the pupils consider whether this agricultural abundance assures the Argentinian people of all their needs and wants to the extent that Argentina is basically independent economically. Guide the pupils into making a statement which expresses their opinion on this point. If several statements are given, have the children select the one that appears to be the most reasonable.
   3. Have the pupils consider what trade relations with the U.S. must be, in the event that Argentina may have to depend on other nations (this may have something to do with the hypothesis, or hypotheses arrived at in 2). Guide the pupils into developing a statement most reasonable to them to be checked.
   4. Focus the pupils' attention on the statements to be checked to determine precisely what kinds of information will be needed. Clarify investigative purposes by developing questions to be answered, such as:
      a. What are Argentina's products?
      b. What products are produced and used mostly in Argentina?
      c. What products does Argentina need?
      d. From what countries does it obtain these products?
      e. What does it obtain from the United States?
   5. Review notetaking: writing the reference point, or question, on the

notepaper; writing the answer to the question in a few words; and writing bibliographical information.

Investigative activities:

1. Make reading assignments:
    a. Pupil 1's group, *Living in Latin America,* pp. 321-327.
    b. Pupil 2's group, *Neighbors in Latin America,* pp. 222-237.
    c. Pupil 3's group, *Neighbors in Latin America;* start by looking at the diagram on page 203.
2. Provide for pupils with high interest in social studies by giving page references in the *World Almanac* and the *Information Please Almanac.* Suggest that they also check in the other textbook to see how well the two agree.
3. Provide for pupils with low reading ability by guiding them in an analysis of pages 203, 222, and 227 in *Neighbors in Latin America.*
    a. Guide the pupils in a review of what had been studied the day before by having them examine carefully the map on page 203. Help them interpret the legend of the map to see that Argentina is basically an agricultural country because of its extensive farming and grazing lands. Guide the pupils in a discussion of the kinds of agricultural products that Argentina might possibly produce.
    b. Have the pupils check their responses about Argentina's agricultural products by having them study the product map on page 222.
    c. Ask this question, "Do you think that the people of Argentina use all these cattle and other products themselves, or do you think they have enough to sell to other countries?"
    d. Guide the pupils in checking their responses to the questions in c above by studying the picture graph on page 227. Help them to understand what tallow and *quebracho* are. Have them analyze the graph carefully to see which of the products are exported to the United States. Ask: "Why do you suppose that Argentina does not export much meat, corn, and wheat to the United States?" Guide them into considering what some of the important agricultural products of the United States are.
    e. Review findings by going quickly over the maps and graph studied.

Evaluative activity:

1. Check notetaking.
2. Guide the pupils in checking their original statements by discussing the results of their information gathering.
3. Guide toward Generalization 1 by asking whether any modern country can get along economically by itself.
4. Guide toward Generalization 2 by asking whether patterns of interdependence are the same among all nations.

5. Guide the pupils into considering whether all the sources are in accord on the information presented.
6. Suggest that these ideas will be checked again in the study of other Latin American countries.

In the above plan, the teacher served as a constant mediator for part of the class all through the period, while another part of the class worked on its own. This mediation was necessary because a group of children was unable to work independently. The teacher had to make the necessary adjustments for this in his plan.

Let us see how well this lesson plan would work in use. The class consists of thirty-one sixth-grade children, a somewhat greater number of which is boys. Attendance has been taken and the children have just sat down after saying the pledge to the flag.

Mr. Wilson, a sixth-grade teacher, sweeps the class briefly but thoroughly with his eyes, and, when every face is turned toward him, he says, "Yesterday we learned about the regions of Argentina and we decided that Argentina is basically an agricultural country. What do you suppose this means for the people of Argentina? Jimmy?"

"Most of them are farmers?"

"Yes, we can say that. Anything else? Helen?"

"I would think that they raise a lot of cattle and sheep, maybe a lot of horses."

"That is a reasonable idea, Helen. Let's turn our thinking in another direction. Take a look at the bulletin board that shows the difference between the standard of living of people in South America and that of people in the United States. If Argentina is an agricultural country, what can we say about the standard of living of its people?"

All faces are turned toward a large bulletin board on the left wall of the classroom. Two-thirds of the board is covered with two charts, one showing a home, characteristic foods, and an average income for an American family, and the other illustrating similar aspects for a South American family. The remaining third of the board contains a chart written in manuscript as follows:

We think that the people in South America have a lower standard of living than ours because:
1. They do not have many natural resources; and
2. They do not know how to use their natural resources well.

Questions to be answered:
1. What natural resources do the various countries have?
2. How are the natural resources used in the various countries?
3. How well are they used in the various countries?

Instantly several hands are raised. The teacher recognizes this multiple response by saying "Several of you have ideas. Let's hear Dick's first."

"Well, if Argentina is mostly an agricultural country, the people should have enough to eat and wear."

Mr. Wilson goes to the chalkboard and, as he begins to write Dick's response, encourages the children to take over the discussion by asking, "Dick, would you call on one of the others who had an idea as I write yours up here?"

Dick quickly scans the upraised hands and solves his problem of choice by saying, "Helen, you speak first, and then you may call on one of the others."

"I was going to say that the people of Argentina *probably* have enough to eat and wear. Mary?"

"They probably have simple homes and low income, too. Pete?"

"With all that agricultural land, I'd think that the people would have plenty to eat and wear. And they could have pretty nice homes and a good income. Dick?"

"I don't know how you can say that. Those charts of Mr. Wilson's show that South American people do not live as well as we do."

"Some countries could be different," replies Pete.

Mr. Wilson breaks in at this point.

"You've given three ideas so far, and here they are. Are there any other ideas that can be added now?"

Attention is riveted on "should have," "probably have," and "have plenty" within the statements written on the chalkboard. One hand is raised and Mr. Wilson recognizes it. "Emily? Do you have another idea?"

"Well, we could say perhaps that the people of Argentina do not have enough to eat and wear, but it does not seem right. Not with all that farming land."

"Do you think I should list it up here with the others? (Pause) Does anyone think that it should be included with these others? (Pause.) It looks as though we have all the ideas we need to consider. Which one can we agree upon as being the right one? What do you think, Bob?"

"I think that Mary's idea is the best one."

"Why?"

"It just sounds better, I guess."

"Perhaps you mean that it appears to be the best statement that we can make now. What do the rest of you think? Pete?"

"I still don't see how we can say the people probably have enough to eat and wear. I think that they should have plenty and that their country is maybe one that is different from all the others. Mary?"

"But we really don't know. I don't know how you can say that."

"Well, look at the farmers in our own country. They make a lot of money raising wheat, cotton, corn, cattle, and pigs."

Mr. Wilson intervenes by suggesting, "Let's use both Mary's and Pete's ideas for further thinking. Let us suppose that the abundance of farming land provides enough or plenty of food and clothing for the people of Argentina. Can we now say that Argentina is completely self-supporting, that it can support all the food and clothing needs of its people?"

Pete raises his hand and, after a nod from Mr. Wilson, asserts strongly, "It sure can!" He glances quickly at some of his classmates to note with satisfaction several affirmative nods.

"I see that several people are in agreement with Pete. Does everyone agree with him?" asks the teacher, turning to write Pete's statement on the chalkboard.

"Mr. Wilson!" Jimmy calls for recognition.

"Yes—."

"I can't go along with Pete. The people may have plenty of leather and wool because of Argentina's cattle and sheep, but they may need cotton. They'd have to get that from some other country."

The teacher turns from the chalkboard, nods in a matter-of-fact way, and says, "That could be. Mary?"

"I've seen a program about sugar on television, and it, I mean the man on the program, said that there are only a few places where sugar cane grows well in the world. Maybe the people in Argentina have to get their sugar from another country. Eric?"

"I know that tea and chocolate grow in certain places, and I can't remember ever hearing about tea and chocolate as things coming from Argentina. If the people use these things, they would have to be obtained from some other country. Pete?"

"Well, people everywhere don't use the same things. Maybe the people in Argentina do not wear cotton clothing. Maybe they don't use coffee, tea, and chocolate. They could have other things to use instead. Tim?"

"That's right. Some people eat toasted grasshoppers, like in Africa."

"And snails in France!"

"What about cannibals! They eat people!"

A momentary survey of food oddities brings a raft of chuckles and hideous grimaces.

"All right! All right, now!" asserts Mr. Wilson firmly but with a trace of humor. "People do eat different things, to be sure. And some are very strange. And Pete does have a good reason for thinking the way that he does. Our bit of fun underlined that. At the same time, Jimmy's way of thinking is backed by good reasons. Let's review these ways of thinking quickly."

Mr. Wilson points to these statements written on the chalkboard:

Argentina can provide for all the food and clothing needs of its people.
Argentina cannot provide for all the food and clothing needs of its people.

And goes on to say, "I'm sure right now that the whole class would not agree on either of these as being the most true. Using either of these ideas, consider whether Argentina has any need for products from the United States. Stan?"

"Well, if you think the first idea is right, you could think that the people in Argentina need little or nothing from the United States. Some of our products to be sold in other countries are wheat and cotton. If you think the second way, Argentina would need products from the United States."

"What do you think, Bill?"

"I go along with the idea that Argentina can provide just about all the things that the people need. I don't think that it needs to buy food and clothing from the United States."

"Ellen, what do you think?"

"I think that Argentina can raise many of the things it needs. Perhaps it raises so much that it can sell to other countries."

"You bet it can!" states Pete firmly. This time the number of affirmative nods shows an increase over the last time.

"Mary, what would you like to say?"

"I'm beginning to agree with Pete. I think that there is a good chance that Argentina has extra things that it can sell in other countries. I think that I would change what I had said earlier to: the people of Argentina have enough to eat and wear, and they have so many agricultural products that they can sell them to other countries."

Mary's capitulation solidifies the climate of opinion in the classroom.

Mr. Wilson seizes the moment to say, "Do most of you think that we can accept Mary's idea as being the most reasonable that we have had so far?" Common assent permits the teacher to erase what has been written on the chalkboard and to write: *Because Argentina is mostly an agricultural country, its people have what they need to eat and wear and it has extra agricultural products to sell to other countries.* As he dusts his hands, he asks, "Do you think that the United States and Argentina trade agricultural products?"

This question quickly brings a rejection. The idea that Argentina would most likely have better trade relations with countries that have a need for its products is quickly established. Mr. Wilson now plants the seed of doubt by saying, "I think that the discussion we have had so far has brought us as far as we can go without further information. Only with more information will we know that our statement is true or needs to be changed in some way. Let's get ready to look for more information. What questions do we have to ask ourselves to find the information that we need? Jim?"

"I can think of one: What does Argentina produce?"

(As each question is suggested, the teacher records it on the chalkboard.) "Any others? Betty?"

"Which of its products are used mostly by the people in Argentina?"

"A good question. Jane?"

"What does it produce to trade with other countries?"

"Very good. Is there another question? Pete?"

"What does it trade with the United States and what does the United States trade with it?"

"Any others? (Pause.) I think that another question we could use would be this: What kind of trade takes place between Argentina and other countries in the world?"

After this last question is recorded, Mr. Wilson has the children prepare for investigating. Books, pencils, and packets of notes are removed from inside desks and placed on the working surface. Several boys go to a bookshelf to obtain almanacs which are distributed at two clusters of desks. The children at the remaining cluster of desks have individual copies of one of the textbooks being used, while at the other two clusters of desks the children have four different sources of information, two textbooks and two almanacs. When the noise subsides, Mr. Wilson guides the children toward investigative activity by pointing to the questions on the chalkboard and asking, "As you use an index to find where to read, what entry word are you going to use?"

Argentina is established as the primary entry word and *products, trade, agriculture* are developed as secondary entry words to be found listed after *Argentina*.

Then the children's attention is directed toward notetaking skills. One of the children brings one of his previously made notes to the front of the classroom to illustrate a properly taken note. He points out the question at the top of the notepaper, its answer written as briefly as possible, and the bibliographical notation including the name of the source and the page on which the information was found. After being thanked for his assistance, he returns to his seat. Investigative activities begin at two clusters of desks after the teacher says, "As soon as you finish investigating your questions in one textbook, check to see whether the other book contains the same information. Some of you may wish to check your information further in one or both of the almanacs."

Mr. Wilson sits down with the pupils at the cluster of desks where the only source for information is a textbook. Casting a sweeping glance over the children at work at the other clusters of desks, he begins to guide this group of children in their investigation: "Let's take another look at the map that we studied yesterday, the one on page 203. Do you remember what area on the map represents Argentina? Allen? Hold up your book and show us."

"It's this part right in here," Allen announces as he traces with his finger the heavy black line that separates Argentina from the rest of the land area of South America.

"Thank you, Allen. Yesterday we talked about how big Argentina is. Do you remember what we found out? Tim?"

"We said that it is about as long as it is from San Diego to New York. It would take us about a week to drive from one end of Argentina to the other."

"That's right, Tim. Suppose that we were going to drive from one side to the other there at the widest part. About how long would it take us? Debby?"

"About two days."

"That is a good estimate. Argentina is a large country. Now let us suppose that we were going to drive across that widest part from east to west. What kind of land would we start in—what would the land be used for? Frank?"

"That would be grassland. It would be good for cattle, sheep, and horses."

"How do you know that it would be that kind of land?"

"Because down here in the corner of the map it says that that kind of shading means grassland—good grassland."

"Good for you, Frank. Can the rest of you find what Frank is talking about?"

The children study the legend of the map for a moment and compare what the legend offers with what is indicated on the map.

"Let's continue our trip to the west. Would we continue to travel in grassland all the way across? What do you think, Debby?"

"No, we would come to farm land with pasture or forest."

"And what would be the next kind of land that we would come to? Allen?"

"More grazing land, but it would be like some of our western range land —mountains and prairies, like that."

"Good. Now, can you find the largest city in Argentina? What is it, Frank?"

"Buenos Aires, where that big black dot is."

"Right. Has everyone found it? Now let us suppose that we go up that river there to Rosario. Have you found it? What different kind of land would we see?"

As the children discover a new shading on the map, they learn there is an area of rich cropland in Argentina. The teacher guides them in a brief summary of the land-use patterns of Argentina, and then asks, "What do you think would be the most important products to come from this country? Frank?"

"Cattle and sheep and meat and wool."

"Can any of you think of some others? Debby?"

"With that cropland there they could raise wheat and corn."

"Any others? Frank?"

"Grains—different kinds of grains besides wheat and corn. Maybe leather, too, because of all the cattle hides."

"Anything else? If not, let's turn to the map on page 222. It will help you to see whether you are right about some of the products."

The children quickly find the new map and are apparently quite pleased with their guesses. The picture map shows clearly the basic farm products of Argentina—cattle, sheep, goats, wheat, and corn. They soon discover that the productive center of Argentina lies within cropland and rich grassland area. The teacher guides them further in their inquiry by asking, "What kinds of products do the people in Argentina use for trade? What products do they have so much of that they have some left over to sell?"

The children readily agree that meat, wool, wheat, and corn are most likely to be the most important products to be used for trade. To check their guesses, they are directed to turn to a picture graph showing the products that Argentina raises for export. They are encouraged further to find that their ideas are quite accurate. Deeper study of the graph ensues when Mr. Wilson asks this question, "Which of these products are traded with the United States? This graph gives us this information. Can you find it? Frank?"

"Well, at the top of the graph it tells that each of the pictures in blue tells how much of that product is sold to the United States. The pictures in all black show what is sold to other countries."

"All right. How many products can you find that are sold to the United States? Debby?"

"Wool is. I can't figure out what some of those others are."

"Try the word clue, Debby."

"Hides."

"Good. Any others? Allen?"

"Linseed oil? What's that?"

"It is an oil made from the seed of the flax plant. It is used in the making of paint used in painting homes. Are there any other products which Argentina sells to the United States? Tim?"

"Dairy products, and something else. I can't make out what it is."

"That's tallow. That is the fat removed from cattle. It can be used for making soap. That one just below dairy products and tallow is *quebracho*. Look at it and say it several times after I say it—*quebracho* (pause), *quebracho* (pause), *quebracho* (pause). It is a tree the wood of which contains tannin. This tannin is used for making animal hides into leather. What do you suppose that that little blue boot stands for? Tim?"

"Leather?"

"Right. And that line of pictures at the bottom of the graph stands for a variety of special goods that Argentina sells to the United States. It includes handicrafts and small amounts of other kinds of items. Now what about the products that Argentina sells to other countries and not to the United States?"

Working in much the same way as illustrated above, the teacher guides the children first toward seeing that Argentina does not sell meat, corn, wheat, or other grains to the United States. The children readily understand that these are products which the United States also produces in large quantities and sells to other countries. As far as these products are concerned, the United States and Argentina are competitors.

Mr. Wilson has noticed that for the last few minutes there has been a flurry of activity at the clusters of desks where the children have been working by themselves. Textbooks have been exchanged. Several children are trying to find their way in an almanac. He begins to bring his direct supervision of Frank, Tim, Allen, and Debby to a close by reviewing with them the questions that were to be answered during the day's investigation. The children see that they can contribute during the discussion and are set to work at trying to complete one note by themselves. The teacher circulates around the room briefly examining the children at work and some of the notes that they have completed. He discusses the work completed or the work in progress with several children. Finally he comes to the front of the classroom and raising his voice to its usual pitch for guiding the entire classroom, he brings the investigating period to a close: "I see that most of you have finished. Let's close our books and discuss what we have found. Be sure to have your notes handy."

The children place their books to one side. Some quickly peruse their notes while others stack them neatly before them or spread them on the desk for easy reference.

Mr. Wilson establishes an immediate, direct contact with the children by stating, "I just had a brief chance to take a quick look at some of your notes. Those that I saw were quite good—the question legibly written at the top of the notepaper, your written answer in no more words than necessary, and the bibliographical data at the bottom of the card—quite good. Quickly look at your notes to see how complete they are. How about the number of the page at the bottom of the note? No, don't try to write in the number of the page now. Try to remember next time."

The teacher gestures toward the hypothesis on the chalkboard: *Because Argentina is mostly an agricultural country, its people have what they need to eat and wear and it has surpluses to sell to other countries.* He reads the hypothesis, and asks, "Can we accept this statement as being true? Pete?"

"It is. It said in both of the books that the people eat meat three times a day."

"In one way that could mean that the people have plenty to eat. In another way it could mean that the people have not enough to eat. Mary?"

"There are many other products grown in Argentina besides meat. Vegetables and fruits and dairy products are also grown on rich farms."

"Frank, is there something that you would like to add?"

"They grow a lot of corn and wheat, too."

"Any other grains? Dick?"

"Barley, oats, and rye."

"Anything else? Eric?"

"Sugar cane, rice, and cotton."

"Yes, Helen."

"There was nothing in my book about those things."

This assertion brings an affirmative nod from several children.

"Did anyone else find the same facts?" asks Mr. Wilson. "Eric?"

"I found them, all right. They are on page 327 in *Living in Latin America*. I have it on my note here."

"So do I." "Me, too." Expressions of agreement echo around the room.

"Did anyone find the same information in *Neighbors in Latin America?*" asks the teacher. "Jim?"

"Yes, I found it on page 233. I also looked in the *Information Please Almanac* and found that sugar cane and cotton are considered to be important crops. It was given on page 624."

"Thank you, Jim. Any other agricultural products? Debby?"

"That stuff that they make oil from."

"You mean flax. The seeds are used to make what? Allen?"

"Linseed oil"

"Yes, Dick?"

"Well, they grow the leaves for a special tea. It's called yerba mate. They grow it on farms in Argentina, but it grows wild in other parts of South America."

"That is true, Dick. Now what about our statement here. How accurate is it? George?"

"The first part of it appears to be true, but we have not said much about clothing. I suppose that they have enough wool, cotton, and leather to take care of that. I would say that the first part of the statement is all right."

"What do you think about that, Tim?"

"I think so, too."

"Does anyone feel that we need any more facts to support the first part of the statement? (Pause.) All right, then, let's consider the second part of the statement. Does Argentina produce enough agricultural products to trade them with other countries? Tim?"

"I know that they trade meat, corn, and wheat."

"Yes. Anything else? Tim?"

"Wool and hides."

"Good. Any other products that are traded? Debby?"

"Linseed oil."

"Others? Eric?"

"Well, there are some other grains, like barley and oats. Then there are some products that are not strictly farming products, like leather goods and q-something-or-other."

"Do you mean this?" asks Mr. Wilson as he writes *quebracho* on the chalkboard.

"Yes, that's it."

"It's pronounced kay-BRAH-cho. Say it, everyone. (Pause.) Did you find out what it is good for? Allen?"

"It is used in making hides into leather, and it is made from wood."

"Other information about *quebracho?* Frank?"

"It is a real hard wood. It's name means *ax-breaker* or something like that."

"It seems to me that we have found a lot of things that Argentina grows or produces from agricultural products to be traded with other countries. How about our whole statement now? Do our facts make it true? (Pause.) Let's spend a few minutes thinking about Argentina and the United States and how they feel toward each other as far as trade is concerned and the trading they do. You thought that they would not trade agricultural products. How true is that? Mary?"

"That is true, too. The United States is a big producer of wheat. Argentina grows wheat, too. They have to work against each other to sell their wheat sometimes."

"Yes, Frank."

"They couldn't trade wheat for wheat. That would be sort of dumb."

"Well, is there anything that the United States could trade with Argentina so that it could obtain something that it needed? Pete?"

"It would not be an agricultural product most likely. The United States could trade machinery for some of that *quebracho* and maybe leather goods."

"Did you find some facts that support what you are saying? Allen?"

"On that page that we looked at, where those pictures are, it showed what Argentina sells to other countries. The little blue pictures showed what is sold to the United States. It's in the red book."

"Perhaps all of us need to look on that page. Did any of the rest of you find it? What page is it? George?"

"Page 227. I have the things here that it sells to the United States. Wool, hides, linseed oil, dairy products, *quebracho,* leather goods, and other exports."

"Thank you, George. Do you think that it would be a good idea for all of us to examine that page for a minute or two? Let's turn to that page."

Class-wide examination of the picture graph on page 227 of *Neighbors in Latin America* reveals what many pupils have already recorded, but no one had carefully analyzed the graph for how much of Argentina's total output in goods is traded with the United States. With Mr. Wilson's guidance, the class discovers that less than one tenth of Argentina's total output of export goods is sold to the United States. Several children report their findings in the *Information Please Almanac*. This supports what the children have discovered in careful study of the graph and yields further information, some of which has already been found in the textbooks, for example, Argentina's best customers are the United Kingdom, the Netherlands, and Italy; its leading suppliers are United States, West Germany, and the United Kingdom; and its greatest need is for machinery, motors, vehicles and parts, and iron and steel goods. At this point the teacher directs the children's attention toward their previously made hypotheses: "Are we agreed that it is true that Argentina produces enough agricultural products for the needs of its people? (General assent.) And that it produces surpluses to sell to other countries? (General assent.) And that trade relations between the two countries are not good? Pete?"

"I don't think that would be quite true. I can't think of why right now."

"Eric has an idea. What is it?"

"It seems that would be true in one way and not in another."

"Perhaps we need to think like Argentinians and then like Americans. If you were an Argentinian, what would you think about trade relations with the United States? George?"

"I wouldn't like them. The United States sells more to Argentina than it buys."

"What do the rest of you think about that? Any other ideas? Pete?"

"Well, if Argentina got more money for its products than the United States did for its products, it might not be so bad. The trade relations could be quite good."

"I wonder if that is the case. George?"

"It is not. I found in the almanac, that one, that Argentina must spend much more money for the things that it buys from the United States. On page 607 it shows that the United States receives more than three times as much money for its exports."

"Any other facts? Now let's look at this relationship as Americans. How is it for us? Mary?"

"Very good. Argentina is a good customer."

"What kind of statement can we make, then? Eric?"

"Trade relations between the Argentina and the United States are good for the United States but poor for Argentina."

"Let me write that on the chalkboard. The rest of you look at it and decide whether it should be changed." The statement proves acceptable. One child manifests an insight through a question:

"What would we say if both countries traded about the same amount?" asks George.

The children feel that that would be an example of good trade relations.

Mr. Wilson alerts the children to tomorrow's work: "Tomorrow we shall begin to consider the same ideas for Brazil." The class prepares for work in another curriculum area.

As can be seen in the description of the lesson, the plan for it serves as a guide, not as a complete prediction of what the lesson would be. Compare the description of the lesson with the lesson plan and note that the teacher had made a somewhat poor choice as to the initial question that he asked to guide the children in defining purposes. However, his poor choice became apparent as soon as the children began to respond it to and, using instructional resources immediately available, he made a very quick adjustment. Closer examination of what the teacher planned to say and what he said will reveal some differences also. Despite these differences, the lesson followed the direction established in the plan and the objectives were reached. This result is about the best that can be expected.

The primary teacher is almost always serving as constant mediator in social studies. Usually there are only a few instances when he can release children to work on their own. Read the following plan to find the instance in which he has them work independently:

PLAN 3

Objectives:
1. An understanding of the relationship between the size and design of trucks and their uses in transportation.
2. An understanding of how the uses of trucks require the work of men and other machines.

Materials:
Study print series, *Trucks*.

Procedures:
Motivation:
1. Relate from previous day's experience as expressed in drawings reflecting that day's learnings to the content for today's lesson: "Yesterday you drew pictures of trucks you have seen loaded with things. You also drew the things on the trucks. Let's see what you drew." Pupils tell about their pictures showing trucks loaded with oranges, cattle, furniture, construction materials, and the like.
2. Establish study purposes: "I've noticed that you have many different kinds of trucks. Are there really different kinds of trucks? How are they

different?" Some are bigger, some pull trailers, and so on. Guide toward more exact ways of describing differences—the different jobs, distances traveled. "Do you have any ideas why they are so different?" Suggest that they will find out for sure as they study the pictures. "And I see that almost everyone has a driver in his truck. Are there other people who work with trucks? Perhaps we'll find out about that too as we study the pictures."

Involvement (using the picture series):

1. Discuss study standards: "As we study our pictures, what must we remember as we sit up here so close together? And when we want to say something? And when we say something?"

2. Guide children into seeing the differences in trucks: as each print is presented, ask if they know what the truck is. Identify it for them if they do not know—the pickup truck (Prints 1 and 2), the tractor (Print 3), the van trailer (Print 5), the refrigerator trailer (Prints 6 and 7—clarify *perishable*), the tanker or tank truck (Print 8), the slide-top trailer (Print 9), and the flat-bed trailer (Print 10).

3. Guide children toward understanding the different uses of trucks: Relate size to function—"Which truck carries a smaller load?" (Prints 1 and 4). "Which carries a bigger load?" "Which carries loads longer distances?" Relate structure of trucks to function: "How are these trucks built to carry special loads?" (Prints 7, 8, 9, 10).

4. Guide children toward an understanding of how men work with trucks: "We wondered about the men who work with trucks. We already know that a truck needs a driver. Is that the only worker that a truck needs?" (Print 4) "If a truck has just one driver, what else does he have to do?" (Print 1) "Does he have to do all the carrying and lifting himself?" Clarify *fork-life*.

5. Guide the children toward an understanding of trucks and workers with trucks by having them discuss this question: "What do you suppose would happen to us if all the drivers, trucks, and loaders stopped working?"

Evaluation: Recall the two questions about why there are different trucks and that workers are needed on trucks. Encourage the children to use the study prints as they deal with these questions. Briefly review the importance of workers and trucks. Guide the pupils in an evaluation of their work as a group.

Expressive activity: "We know so much more about trucks and the men who work with them. We should be able to draw much better pictures about them. What kinds of trucks can we draw? What can we show the men doing? Some of you may want to write a word or two that tells what your truck is or its parts. What words can we use?" List words in manuscript. Help children to remember words that they do not recall immediately.

At the close of the lesson, the teacher guided the children into independent expressive activity. The number of teaching moments, as well as their specific nature, indicates the constant mediating role of the primary teacher. The mediation continued until the point for expressive activity was reached.

Often in grades four through nine several days will be devoted to finding facts for reaching an understanding of an idea. This time span changes the mediating role of the teacher. The number and nature of the teaching moments change, as can be seen in the following plan:

PLAN 4

Objectives:
1. (Continued) An understanding of the technological and economic burgeoning of European countries that contributed to the development of America.
2. Practice in reference skills for finding information.
3. Practice in notetaking.
4. Practice in analyzing facts and arriving at a conclusive statement.

Materials:
- As specified in previous plans.
- Notes taken by pupils during the past few days.

Procedures:
Defining purposes: Having the pupils consult their notes, review the facts and conclusions drawn from the study of the Portuguese explorations— that Portuguese explorers had contributed much toward the development of sailing and navigating skills, but it would not be likely to be one of the nations competing for holdings in what is now the United States. Guide the pupils into considering briefly whether they have sufficient facts to make a conclusive statement about Spain. Since the pupils have gathered only the basic facts about Columbus, they will have to seek more facts. Clarify that the significance of his discovery and explorations, as well as the other Spanish explorers, will have to be researched. Write these items on the chalkboard as guides.

Investigative activities: Most of the pupils continue to read and take notes. The more able pupils are encouraged to check their findings in the various sources available. The teacher works with the less able pupils.
1. Using the discovery and exploration map of the New World, have the

pupils find the routes followed by Columbus on his various voyages. Help them in notetaking.

2. Review Columbus' basic purposes. Have the pupils consider whether he had fulfilled his purpose. Guide them in the reading of pages 23-24 of *The Story of America* to find out. Have them formulate notes of their findings.

3. Have the pupils consider what more needed to be done before it was really known that a New World had been considered. Have them check the map for clues. Identify Magellan and Balboa as men who explored for Spain. Guide them into a discussion of the exploits of these men and their contributions in establishing that there was a New World. Guide them in checking their ideas on page 24 and 26 in *The Story of America*. Help them to develop notes.

Checking purposes: Draw attention to the guides written on the chalkboard earlier in the period. Have the members of the class contribute their findings. After the exploits of Columbus, Magellan, and Balboa have been documented as fully as possible, have the pupils attempt to arrive at a statement about the possibility of Spain's having great influence on the New World. Suggest that, although the evidence is strong for Spain, perhaps the class should wait until they had learned more about the explorations sponsored by other countries.

Except for the moments when he was briefly involved with the children in determining directions for the day's work and guiding them in considering possible new directions, the teacher mediated little for the bulk of the class. He continued his role with children whose investigative skills needed support.

When the social-studies period is devoted to expressive activity, the teacher's role as mediator is reduced as he assumes a role as organizer and administrator, as reflected in the following plan:

PLAN 5

Objectives:
1. To make a series of wall panels comparing medieval western European culture with eastern European culture of the same period in the following areas:

   a. Social forces (religion, education, security)

   b. Use of natural resources.

   c. Technological development.

   d. Economic organization.

   e. Contact with other cultures.

2. Practice in organizing a group for a particular task.

3. Practice in following group assigned roles.
4. Practice in illustrative and graphic arts.

Materials:
- Two roughly made sketches depicting a comparison of the level of technological development of the American Indians with that of modern America. These sketches, made on large sheets of tagboard, serve as an example of how the comparison charts can be made.
- Pupils' notes on this area of study.
- Sketching paper.
- Ten to twenty large sheets of white tagboard.
- Five sets of poster paints.
- Ten bottles of India ink.
- Twenty lettering pens, fine point.

Procedures:

Showing the comparison sketches, help the pupils to identify what the sketches represent.

Have the pupils consider how they could use similar sketches to illustrate the differences between western European culture and Middle Eastern culture. Guide them into a discussion of the possible content for sketches in each of the various areas—social forces, use of natural resources, technological development, economic organization, and contact with other cultures. Make brief notes of the discussion on the chalkboard.

Begin organization of groups by listing the content areas across the chalkboard and asking for indications of interest by a show of hands. Make group assignments by recording one name, under each content area first, then the second person for each group, and so on until every pupil in the class has an assignment in a group.

With the pupils' help, rearrange the furniture into five study areas. Have the pupils go to their group areas. Give them their first group assignment—the selection of a chairman and a recorder.

Clarify the group task with the pupils by having them suggest the kinds of things a group will have to do to make comparison charts—review their notes to find items to illustrate, to select the best items for illustration, preliminary sketching, and division of production tasks.

The groups begin to work. The teacher goes from group to group and enters into the group work only when the group has difficulty working. At five minutes to the end of the hour, the pupils stop working.

The group chairmen or recorders report the work of each group quickly. The chairmen give a brief idea of the work to be done the next day.

With the pupils' help, rearrange the furniture for the next period.

SUMMARY

Although a daily lesson plan in social studies in and of itself does not assure effective teaching, it contributes toward effectiveness. It becomes an instrument of high promise when the quality of planning is adequate and the teacher using it is prepared to make immediate changes as needed.

A daily lesson plan is developed usually from entries listed in a teaching unit. Its structure reflects a studied concern for implementing children's arriving at a selected understanding, attitude or set of attitudes, or pattern of behavior. It includes a statement of objective(s), a precise listing of materials, and a listing of procedures which indicates the teaching moments of the lesson. The choice of these procedures and their expression is a function of the teaching strategy to which the teacher is committed and his teaching style.

A daily lesson plan presents the role of the teacher as mediator between children and the reality that they are studying.

Exercises for Further Understanding

1. Three sets of lesson plans are offered below. Each set is comprised of two plans, each of which has similar objectives. These represent plans made by two different teachers whose classes are about the same as far as ability is concerned. Read both plans carefully, then select the one which you think is the better of the two. List briefly your reasons for the selection of one plan over the other.

LESSON PLAN FOR TUESDAY, APRIL 14 (GRADE 2)
UNIT: SHOEMAKING, A NECESSARY INDUSTRY

Set A, Plan (1)

Objectives:
1. Content objectives: Leather is made from animal hides.
   a. Cleaning the hides.
      1. Hides with hair still on them soaked in a special liquid to remove hair and loosen tissue.
      2. Scraping off the tissue by machine.
      3. Final cleaning in an acid bath.
   b. Tanning the hides.

1. Vegetable tanning.
    (a) Soaking the hides in a tanning liquid.
        (1) Eight vats containing tanning solution.
            (2) Hides soaked in each vat, then stacked and left to dry somewhat before going into the next vat.
            (3) Last vat contains a bleaching agent.
        (b) Processing the soaked hides into leather.
            (4) Hides hung up to dry.
            (5) Rubbed with oil on the grain side a few days later.
            (6) After a few days, hides smoothed between heavy steel rollers.
            (7) "Curried," or treated with oil.
            (8) Hides stretched to dry.
            (9) When dry, ready to use as leather.
        (c) The process requires from three to six months.
2. Skill objectives: to improve listening, discussion, and thinking skills.

Materials:

• A small piece of animal hide obtained from a slaughter house.

• A piece of shoe upper from a discarded shoe.

• A flow chart showing the conversion of hides into leather.

Procedures:

Help the children to recall their findings from yesterday, that is, most of the parts of a shoe are made from leather.

Using a piece of hide and a piece of leather, encourage the children to hypothesize about the steps in the process of changing hide into leather.

Introduce the flow chart as a means of finding out.

Encourage the children to respond to each panel in the chart.

1. First panel—cleaning the hides: soaking, scraping, and bath. Clarify *acid*.
2. Second panel—the tanning process. Clarify *vat, tannin*.
3. Third panel—the final curing; drying, treating with oil, smoothing, treating with oil again, stretching for final drying. Clarify *curry*.

Have the children examine their original hypotheses. Encourage them to use the chart to support their ideas.

Guide the children in the writing of a group summary about leather making.

Set A, Plan (2)

Objectives: Same as for Plan (1)

Materials:

• The shoe we dismantled yesterday.

*Book: *Marvels of American Industry*, by Donald E. Cooke, pages 117-118.

• A list of guide questions on a chart, to include: What is leather made from? How is it made?

Procedures:

Creating interest:

1. Using the dismantled shoe, review for the children their findings from yesterday, that is, most of the parts of a shoe are made from leather.
2. Encourage the children to guess what they are going to learn about today.
3. Introduce the book, *Marvels of American Industry*, to the children. Show them some of the pictures and pages. Impress upon them that it is a very fine book meant for grownups and that if they listen well as it is read, they will learn how leather is made.
4. Present the chart of questions. Have several children read them aloud. Inform the children that they are to listen for the answers as you read.

Acquiring the facts:

1. Review listening standards.
2. Read the chosen selection a paragraph at a time. At the close of each paragraph, encourage the children to relate the information that the paragraph offered. Clarify such items as *vats* and *tannin*.

Evaluation:

Encourage the children to respond to the questions.

Have the children draw a picture of the parts of a shoe made from leather.

LESSON PLAN FOR THURSDAY, MAY 4 (GRADE 5)

UNIT: NIGERIA, AN EMERGING NATION

SET B, PLAN (1)

Objectives:

1. Content objectives: Nigerian homes are unique and varied.
    a. In some of the cities.
       a. Modern homes similar to ours.
       b. Also crudely built homes of mud and plaster with metal roofs.
    b. In northern Nigeria.
       a. Herdsmen's homes made of grass and branches.
          (1) Easily moved and built.
          (2) Permanent homes not needed because the families follow their herds from place to place.
       b. Farmers' homes.
          (1) Round mud huts with thatched roofs.
          (2) A family lives in a cluster of huts surrounded by a wall.
          (3) Some huts made completely of mud and without windows.

c. In eastern Nigeria.
    a. Homes constructed of concrete, wood, bamboo, and mud.
    b. Built in clusters.
    c. Roofed often with mats woven of palm branches.
d. In western Nigeria.
    a. Homes constructed of wood, bricks, mud, and concrete.
    b. Often roofed with corrugated iron.
e. Furnishings.
    a. Many village homes sparsely furnished.
    b. Some city homes furnished like ours.
f. Nigerian homes are changing.
    a. Concrete blocks replacing mud as a building material.
    b. More furnishings.

2. Skill objectives: improving reference and notetaking skills.

Materials:

Africa with Focus on Nigeria, pages 55-60.

How People Live in Nigeria, pages 67-69.

Procedures:

Building interest:

1. Encourage the children to discuss their learnings acquired during the past few days.
2. Have the children discuss news articles about Nigeria.
3. Announce today's topic for study—Nigerian homes.

Work period:

1. Make reading assignments: high group, pages 55-60 in *Africa with Focus on Nigeria;* low group, pages 67-69 in *How People Live in Africa.*
2. If members of the high group finish early, have them also read the low group assignment.

Evaluation:

1. Have the children discuss what they have read.
2. Play a vocabulary game with terms already studied: *Hausa, Fulani, Kunari, Yoruba, Edo, Ibo, Ibibio, Niger, Benue, Gulf of Guinea, Lagos, Ibadan, Kaduna, Kano, Enugu, Port Harcourt, ground nuts, millet, gari, agbada, fila, turban.*
3. Remind the children to look for more news articles about Nigeria.

SET B, PLAN (2)

Objectives: Same as for Plan (1).

Materials: Same as for Plan (1).

Procedures:

Establishing purposes:
1. Initial statement: "Yesterday we learned about the foods that the Nigerians eat and how they obtain them. Our next area to learn about has to do with Nigerian homes. What questions must we ask ourselves to learn about Nigerian homes?"
2. Stimulate the development of questions by having the children consider whether the homes, like the foods, will present a picture of variety from region to region.
3. Have the children prepare note papers.

Gathering facts:
1. Set the larger group of children to work in *Africa with Focus on Nigeria*. They are to use their reference skills to decide where to read in the book.
2. Guide the slow group in studying the pictures on pages 68 and 69 of *How People Live in Africa*. Then guide them in reading the two paragraphs at the top of page 68. Have them make simple notes from their reading.
3. Work with individuals in the larger group to check adequacy of skills.

Checking purposes:
1. Have the children review and discuss their notes.
2. Pinpoint the variety of homes in Nigeria by having the children analyze the kinds of homes in their community and compare the results with their findings about Nigerian homes.

LESSON PLAN FOR MONDAY, FEBRUARY 7 (GRADE 8)
UNIT: AMERICA BECOMES AN INDUSTRIAL POWER
SET C, PLAN (1)

Objectives:
1. Content objectives:
   a. The Industrial Revolution begins in Europe.
      (1) In England, the transition from hand labor to machine labor.
         (a) Textile industry first.
         (b) First step in development—division of labor in the making of cloth.
         (c) Second step in development—machines to replace hands.
            [1] Spinning—Richard Arkwright, 1769, a machine to replace twenty persons at spinning wheels.
            [2] Weaving—Edmund Cartwright, a weaving machine.
         (d) Third step in development—discovery of a new source of power: James Watt, 1769, the first workable steam engine which was rapidly improved in the following years.

(e) The new source of power improved production and distribution of goods (steamships and locomotives).

b. The Industrial Revolution changes the economic structure of a country.

(1) Factory system replaces the home system of manufacturing.

(2) Urban areas near factories replace farms as home sites for many people; cities grow in number and size.

(3) More goods available at lower prices for home consumption.

(4) More goods available for competing in international trade.

2. Skills objectives: Improvement in reading and thinking skills.

Materials:

• Worksheets completed by the class yesterday.

*Basic textbook: *Story of the American People,* pages 329-332.

• Worksheet for today as follows:

1. Match the following:

a. Early British clothmaking	—Spinning machine
b. Later British clothmaking	—A great change
c. Richard Arkwright	—Steam engine
d. Edmund Cartwright	—Factory system
e. Industrial Revolution	—Weaving machine
f. James Watt	—Home system

2. Make a list of the changes brought about in the lives of people by the Industrial Revolution.

a.

b.

c.

d.

Procedures:

Distribute yesterday's worksheets.

Review by discussing the worksheets.

Define *Industrial Revolution.*

Distribute the worksheets for today and make the reading assignment.

Circulate around the room to assure independent work.

When the pupils have finished their worksheets, guide them in evaluating their work.

Collect the worksheets.

Using the sketch on page 330 in the textbook as a point of departure, tell the pupils how the early craftsmen worked.

Using the sketch on page 332, have the pupils contribute what they know about early transportation and transportation today. Have one pupil record the responses of the others on the chalkboard.

Analyze and discuss the recorded responses.

SET C, PLAN (2)

Objectives: Same as for Plan (1).

Materials:

- A chart showing the export-import pattern of the United States today.
- *Basic textbook: *Story of the American Nation,* pages 329-332.
- A taped reading of the above listed pages and the equipment necessary for listening.
- *Basic History of American Business,* pages 23-26.

Procedures:

Developing purposes:

1. Encourage pupils to participate in discussing yesterday's learnings.
2. Guide the discussion toward the nature of American trade with other nations. Using the chart, prompt a comparison of American trade today with what it was during the post-Revolutionary period. Have the pupils offer ideas as to what accounted for this change. Record their ideas on the chalkboard. Establish that the accuracy of these ideas is to be investigated.

Work period:

1. Discuss notetaking briefly.
2. Make the class reading assignment: pages 329-332 in *Story of the American Nation.*
3. Suggest that those who are interested in understanding more about labor, production, management, and distribution of goods during this period read pages 23-26, *Basic History of American Business.*
4. Work with pupils who find the textbook difficult to read.
   a. Conduct a brief study of the sketches on pages 330 and 332 in the textbook to clarify the nature of the change explained in the textbook.
   b. Clarify the term *Industrial Revolution.*
   c. Have the pupils listen to the tape while following the printing on the pages.
5. Generally supervise the reading and notetaking.

Checking purposes:

1. Direct pupils' attention to the ideas recorded previously on the chalkboard. Encourage them to determine which are accurate and to support their choices with facts.
2. Determine whether anyone has read the pages in *Basic History of*

American Business. Have these people report informally about how early American business was conducted.

3. Focus the discussion on changes to occur in the lives of people as a result of the Industrial Revolution.

2. If possible, observe an entire social-studies lesson taught in a nearby elementary school. Take notes and then try to reconstruct the plan that the teacher used.

3. Choose a topic of interest to you and one ordinarily treated in social studies. Isolate an aspect of the topic that you would like to teach and prepare a lesson plan that you could follow to teach the objectives which you have outlined.

Selected References

Beck, Robert H., Walter W. Cook, and Nolan C. Kearney, *Curriculum in the Modern Elementary School,* 2d ed., Chap. 4, "Motivating Educational Behavior;" and Chap. 9, "Principles of Learning." Englewood Cliffs, N.J.: Prentice-Hall, Inc., 1960.

Bell, Thomas, "Why Not a Social Studies Lab?" *Social Studies,* 54:181-183 (October 1963).

Bigge, Morris L., and Maurice P. Hunt, *Psychological Foundations of Education,* Chap. 15, "How Is Learning Related to Teaching?" New York: Harper & Row, Publishers, 1962.

Dunfee, Maxine and Helen Sagl, *Social Studies through Problem Solving,* Chap. 3, "Planning Cooperatively to Solve Problems;" and Chap. 4, "Experiencing to Achieve Goals." New York: Holt, Rinehart and Winston, Inc., 1966.

Jarolimek, John, "Curriculum Content and the Child in the Elementary School." *Social Education,* 26:58-62ff (February 1962).

Jenkins, Marion, "Teacher Planning for a Specific Class," *Social Studies in Elementary Schools,* pp. 284-292. Thirty-Second Yearbook of the National Council for the Social Studies, Washington, D.C.: National Education Association, 1962.

Kranyik, Robert, "The Elementary Classroom as a Human Relations Lab." *Social Studies,* 57:16-22 (January 1966).

Lewis, Gertrude M., "For Whom Are We Planning: Children of Grades 4, 5, and 6," *Social Studies for the Middle Grades,* pp. 6-20. Curriculum Series, No. 5, New Edition, National Council for the Social Studies, Washington, D.C.: National Education Association, 1960.

Melby, Ernest O., "Improvement of Teaching in the Social Studies," *Social Studies in the Elementary School,* pp. 285-305. Fifty-Sixth Yearbook, Part II, of the National Society for the Study of Education, Chicago: The University of Chicago Press, 1957.

Michaelis, John U., ed., *Social Studies in Elementary Schools,* Chap. 2, "Social and Psychological Foundations." Thirty-Second Yearbook of the National Council for the Social Studies, Washington, D.C.: National Education Association, 1962.

Ojemann, Ralph H., "Social Studies in Light of Knowledge about Children," *Social Studies in the Elementary School*, pp. 76-119. Fifty-Sixth Yearbook, Part II, of the National Society for the Study of Education, Chicago: The University of Chicago Press, 1957.

Reynolds, Robert W., *et al.*, *Guiding Children through the Social Studies*, Chap. 2, "Perspectives for the Social Studies." Washington, D.C.: National Educational Association, 1964.

Sears, Pauline S., and Ernest R. Hilgard, "The Teacher's Role in the Motivation of the Learner," *Theories of Learning and Instruction*, pp. 182-209. Sixty-Third Yearbook, Part I, of the National Society for the Study of Education, Chicago: The University of Chicago Press, 1964.

Taba, Hilda, and James L. Hills, *Teacher Handbook for Contra Costa Social Studies, Grades 1-6*, Chap. 4, "Selection and Organization of Content." Hayward, Calif.: Rapid Printers and Lithographers, Inc., 1965.

7

Guiding Children
into Inquiry

When the social-studies teacher has completed a content outline, organized within what he considers to be implicit in the main generalization of his unit, he directs his thinking toward the procedures to be used in bringing his pupils into contact with the small area of reality circumscribed by his unit. Since he believes that this contact should be through inquiry, his first problem is to develop ways to guide children into inquiry. This chapter presents ways of solving this problem.

The social-studies teacher will have to arrive first at his own view of inquiry as a way of learning, and then at a decision as to how to implement inquiry in his unit.

SOME VIEWS OF INQUIRY

About as many views of inquiry exist as there are people who advance them. Definitions will vary. Let us begin, then, by viewing inquiry in its simplest and most common forms.

INQUIRY AS A LIFE ACTIVITY

A simple act all of us have performed on different occasions is that of deciding between two or more things we want, or several courses of action in one situation or another.

Suppose that you have no automobile and are faced with the problem of getting to and from work, which is five miles away. Your choices are to ride on a public bus, obtain a ride with a fellow worker, or buy your own automobile. After investigating each of the choices, your findings are: the public-bus schedule will require you to rise an hour earlier and to wait forty-five minutes after work before being picked up to be brought home, at a cost of three dollars per week; no one of your fellow workers is willing to take you for a fixed fee, but several would like you to join a pool in which you would drive every fourth week; and a down payment on a reliable automobile will take all your savings. You weigh the evidence. Bus service is intolerable; you do not meet your fellow workers' standards for cooperation; your savings will be depleted if you buy an automobile. Your decision: use the intolerable bus. This choice is apparently the only one open to you if you wish to maintain your present level of financial solvency. For the moment the inquiry is closed. Later, after you save some money, inquiry will begin again if you decide to buy an automobile and have to consider which one to buy.

As we examine this example, we discover certain basic conditions necessary to inquiry: a desire to be satisfied, two or more choices, an investigation of the choices, and a decision that one is more suitable. This inquiry is problem oriented.

Let us examine another kind of inquiry. Again we find ourselves scrutinizing a simple act—the act of acquiring information about something of interest. Suppose that you find yourself quite taken with antique American house furnishings. You may begin visiting antique shops. Before long you are reading authoritative books and examining special collections in museums and historical centers. Public auctions of household goods become exciting events as far as you are concerned. In time you become a knowledgeable expert as a result of following a line of inquiry. This inquiry is ~~problem oriented~~. *interest centered.*

In the regular course of life, one kind of inquiry may give rise to the other. For example, an individual with a transportation problem may discover an interest in old automobiles as a result of having to cope with his problem. The self-made expert in antiques may find himself faced with the problem of deciding whether to maintain his interest at a book-ish level or to cater to his interest by buying antiques.

Neither kind of inquiry is superior over the other in daily life. We use them as the situation demands.

And as individuals going about the daily business of living, we accept inquiry as a natural activity. We do not regard it as mysterious or particularly awesome. It merely exists.

INQUIRY IN ELEMENTARY SOCIAL STUDIES

Inquiry has an important role to play in social studies. Inquiry skills tend to be placed high when skills to be learned in social studies are considered. [1,2] Concern for the place of inquiry in the elementary social-studies curriculum[3] and the ways in which it may be implemented[4,5] are often reflected in the literature. Although research in the uses of inquiry in social studies is somewhat limited, particularly at the elementary level, evidence supports inquiry as an effective way of learning.[6] At this time, however, it must be admitted that the support of inquiry in elementary social studies is primarily philosophical. Because of the absence of objective data attesting to the superiority of problem-oriented inquiry over interest-centered inquiry, or vice versa, a controversy has arisen.

One side of the controversy holds that interest-oriented inquiry is most suitable for children. The teacher guides the children in establishing an interest, and then in a series of dynamic demonstrations, experiments, and activities. He guides them in extending their concept of a selected aspect of social life.

[1]Millard H. Black et al., "Skills and Processes in Social Studies," Social Studies in Elemetary Schools. Thirty-second Yearbook of the National Council for the Social Studies, John U. Michaelis, ed. (Washington, D.C.: National Council for the Social Studies), pp. 150-218.

[2]Helen McCracken Carpenter, "There Are Specific Skills to Be Taught," The Instuctor, 72:89-92 (March 1963).

[3]Ruth Ellsworth, "Critical Thinking—Its Encouragement," The National Elementary Principal, 42:24-29 (May 1963).

[4]Shirley H. Engle, "Decision Making: The Heart of Social Studies Instruction," Social Education, 24:301-304ff (November 1960).

[5]Byron G. Massialas, "Revising the Social Studies: An Inquiry-centered Approach," Social Education, 27:185-189 (April 1963).

[6]Findlay C. Penix, "Teaching Social Studies in Elementary Schools," in New Challenges in the Social Studies, Byron G. Massialas and Frederick R. Smith, eds. (Belmont, Calif.: Wadsworth Publishing Company, Inc., 1965), pp. 63-88.

The other side of the controversy maintains that the problem-oriented inquiry more closely meets the dual requirement for an effective way of learning and skill in critical or reflective thinking. The teacher, using a selected paradigm of reflective thinking, guides children in examining a problem, hypothesizing, selecting a hypothesis, investigating or testing it, relating findings to the original hypothesis, arriving at a generalization, and verifying it. Paradigms vary and there is no agreement as to which is best for classroom use.

The backers of the interest-oriented inquiry advance strongly the argument that children should learn about man and his physical and social environment in the ways that social scientists do.

The advocates of the problem-oriented inquiry counter this argument with the assertion that the basic objective of social studies is the development of the citizen, not of the social scientist.

A sound point of view may be presented without any pretense at ending the controversy. Upon occasion we guide children into either form of inquiry, depending upon prevailing instructional conditions and how we interpret them. Some of us will find that interest-oriented inquiry will be effective at any time we are guiding children in expanding concepts. Those of us who work with young children will tend to guide our pupils in interest-oriented inquiry. When we are guiding children in relating ideas, in developing values, and in undertaking group projects, we will guide them into problem-oriented inquiry.

OPEN AND CLOSED INQUIRY

Inquiry may also be regarded as open or closed. Examining it in this way serves as an aid to acquiring a deeper understanding of both forms of inquiry.

Inquiry which follows a course determined by one discovery growing out of another may be classified as open. Such inquiry begins with an initial discovery and continues until the inquirer tires, is satiated, or discovers another area of inquiry which has greater promise. Ideally, interest-oriented inquiry will take this course.

Closed inquiry follows a series of reflective-thinking acts concerning a problem. The focal point of inquiry is the problem. Inquiry begins with an examination of the problem to ascertain the forces in conflict. A series of "best guesses," or hypotheses, about its solution follows. The "best guess" which appears to offer the most promise is investigated or tried out in some way, and the findings related to the original problem. If the solution is not satisfactory, the inquirer may reexamine his ways of investigating or testing, change them, and try again, or he may select another hypothesis to work with. Inquiry is closed when a satisfactory solution is found. The satisfactory solution marks the end of problem-oriented inquiry as viewed ideally.

In comparison, open inquiry has no end; closed inquiry begins with a particular end in view. Open inquiry has a psychological basis; closed inquiry has a logical basis. The differences between the two suggest differences in use. The two methods are used differently in elementary social studies.

In the synthesized strategy, the unit begins with an open inquiry, becomes a series of closed inquiries, draws toward an end with a greater closed inquiry, and finishes with open inquiry.

In the social-science strategy, the unit begins with an open inquiry, continues with a series of open inquiries, draws toward an end with a closed inquiry, and finishes with open inquiry.

In the thinking-emphasis strategy, the unit begins with a closed inquiry which continues until closure is made, and then ends with open inquiry.

Under ideal circumstances, if a child comes to the social-studies teacher with a problem related to social studies, he is guided into closed inquiry. If he evinces an interest in a social-studies concept, he is encouraged to follow open inquiry.

Although there appears to be a greater reliance on one form of inquiry as opposed to the other in the various strategies, as presented in this book, no strategy rejects either form completely. When working with an individual child, the nature of his concern determines the inquiry to be used.

Much of the foregoing suggests that inquiry has been foreign to social studies in the past. What passes for universally poor teaching in social studies, that is, study by reading the textbook and answering the questions at the end of each chapter, is a form of closed inquiry. However, it is poor closed inquiry because it is completely teacher-dominated. Perhaps the greatest issue in the use of inquiry is the role of the teacher.

THE ROLE OF THE TEACHER IN INQUIRY

When we examine the uses of inquiry in the business of daily life, we can see that nothing stands between the individual and his interest or problem. He can select an interest and follow a path of inquiry in almost any direction and for as long as he wants. He may ignore some problems and accept others. He does not, and obviously cannot, have quite the same freedom when the area of interest and problems is restricted to social studies and when the number of peers in the classroom requires that both interests and problems be to a large extent common to all. Within these conditions, it is the role of the teacher to guide the children into and through inquiry.

The teacher guides inquiry in the following ways:

1. He contrives situations and settings in which interests and problems may be found.

2. He encourages children to deal with these interests and problems in thinking ways. Their thoughts and ideas are elicited and are treated in such a way that a child is the first to withdraw his contribution as being in some way not germane to the interest or problem at hand.

3. He provides resources for investigating or testing hypotheses that bring all children into investigative or testing activity.

4. He fosters the development of the spirit of free inquiry in the classroom. He meets the emergence of each individual interest and problem as an opportunity for inquiry.

The danger implicit in the use of inquiry, open as well as closed, in the classroom is that it may become teacher-dominated. The teacher who attests to a strong belief in open inquiry but persists in contriving all the experiments or demonstrations and playing the role of the know-it-all during discussions removes the power from inquiry. So does the teacher who in the name of closed inquiry forces a specific closure which resides in his mind but not in the minds of his pupils.

BEGINNING THE UNIT WITH OPEN INQUIRY

So far our concern has been for the general aspects of inquiry. Now we direct our attention to procedures to be used to implement specific aspects of inquiry.

Inquiry has been involved in elementary social studies for some time. A negative example teacher-dominated closed inquiry was cited. Positive examples of the uses of inquiry, characteristic of older practices and those current in elementary social studies today, can serve as spring-boards to newer practices. Let us consider open inquiry first.

Teachers today often guide children into open inquiry, as often perhaps in science as in social studies. The classical example of an open-inquiry activity is "sharing" (or "show-and-tell," "news," or the like). This activity, which often opens school work at the beginning of the day and is most frequently found in the kindergarten and primary grades, may reflect open inquiry. It begins with an individually chosen item of interest, discovered by the sharer and about which he has made some inquiry. Inquiry may continue as other children contribute similar experiences or related knowledge. The line of inquiry may become so compelling that further investigation is made immediately or extended over a series of "sharing" periods for several days in succession.

As children progress through the primary grades, certain limitations are usually imposed by the teacher in positive ways. The children are encouraged to "share" about the world around them rather than themselves, their pets, and their families. In some schools, "sharing" soon comes to mean reporting on items in the news. Both the items of interest to be "shared" and the sources from which they may be drawn are limited. However, as long as a fairly wide margin is allowed in the matter of the selection of items of interest and further inquiry is encouraged as the situation demands, open inquiry occurs.

In the intermediate and upper elementary grades, "sharing" activity is replaced by reporting about items in the news. The period devoted to this may be known as the "news" or current-events period. When the conditions outlined in the previous paragraph prevail, open inquiry occurs.

Often during a science or social-studies period, a definitive term regarding matter, function, behavior, relationship, or the like inspires interest immediately. As children are encouraged to state their views and interpretations and to investigate further, open inquiry takes place.

The above instances of open inquiry are primarily incidental. They are for the most part short-term examples of inquiry incidental to the accomplishment of other goals. They occur more as a result of a teacher's automatic response to an immediate learning need as expressed by his pupils than to a careful reflection on what the learning needs are and what his response should be. If time is limited, he is just as likely to discourage inquiry by giving an answer or redirecting the would-be inquirers to another activity.

Let us examine the uses of open inquiry as a tactical measure which the teacher consciously applies. The teacher using the synthesized strategy sets the stage for inquiry through a contrived situation which narrows the area of interests and at the same time provides for the discovery of interests. The most elaborate contrivance is the arranged environment in which children become saturated immediately with a welter of interests related to a topic area and a generalization. Let us suppose that a teacher had prepared an arranged environment for the study of a unit on the culture of early Hawaii. On the evening before the day on which the unit is to begin, he arranges the environment to reflect the topic and the generalization as follows:

A small bulletin board to the left of the chalkboard at the side of the classroom shows an early Hawaiian in a communicative mood. Beside him is a large chart containing a list of common Hawaiian words and phrases with translations in English.

Below the bulletin board there is a tape recorder and several sets of earphones. The tape contains words and phrases in Hawaiian along with translations. Hung over the chalkboard are several pieces of tapa cloth.

To the right of the chalkboard is another bulletin board containing pictures of traditional Hawaiian homes. On a table below the bulletin board is a model of an outrigger canoe.

The large bulletin board to the front of the classroom contains three picture displays showing early Hawaiians preparing and enjoying a luau.

A large display table at the back of the classroom contains Hawaiian artifacts such as grass skirts, a canoe paddle, a war club, musical instruments, and household utensils. Textbooks and tradebooks open at pictures illustrating the use of some of the artifacts complete the display.

This arranged environment reflects at attempt to bring early Hawaiian culture within the confines of the classroom.

The next morning the children come into the room. There is an air of excited anticipation as they go to their seats. Some linger hesitantly at a bulletin board or display. The teacher is enthusiastic as he performs the necessary administrative tasks with dispatch. The moment arrives. After a word or two about care to be taken with some of the artifacts on display because they are on loan from the museum, the teacher releases the children to explore the environment.

Giggles and chattering in a low key prevail at first. A boy picks up a grass skirt and gives an experimental wiggle or two, much to the amusement of a bystander. A pair of boys peer intently at the model of the outrigger canoe and discuss it quietly. A girl taps another on the shoulder and invites her to listen to the other set of earphones at the tape recorder. They grin with wonder at the sounds of another language and self-consciously try to mouth the syllables that they hear. Clusters of children form at the various displays and then break and change as a new one arrests their attention.

The teacher wanders from display to display noting the children's reactions on a small pad. He is cataloging interests as they emerge. Such remarks as the following are noted:

"This club is made of wood. I wonder why they didn't use steel?"

"It must have taken a long time to build that canoe."

"What a funny language! It doesn't sound at all like English or Spanish."

"Feel that cloth. It feels just like paper."

"The men didn't dance!"

"I heard that the Hawaiians found out first about surfing, but I don't see any surf boards around here."

At the close of a twenty- or thirty-minute period, the children return to their seats. Open inquiry begins as the teacher invites the children to comment on what they found to be the most appealing. Gradually, common interests begin to emerge as the teacher interweaves into the discussion the remarks that he heard during the exploration of the environment. Directions which the inquiry is to take are established.

As soon as directions are established, open inquiry narrows. Questions to be answered are developed and organized. Open inquiry will likely terminate in a series of closed inquiries. Yet the essential fact remains—open inquiry marked the beginning of the unit.

The teacher using the synthesized strategy may use less elaborate contrived situations to prompt open inquiry. For example, open inquiry could be instituted in any of the following ways:

Showing a film depicting aspects of early Hawaiian life and encouraging the children to project from the aspects shown to others not depicted. (A similar activity can be used with a filmstrip, a series of pictures, or a single picture.)

Reading an authentically based story about early Hawaiian life and encouraging the children to note happenings and strange conditions which have strong appeal to them.

Beginning a general discussion about life in early Hawaii and inviting the children to contribute their knowledge gleaned from picture magazines, movies, television, and the like to establish points of interest.

Having the children examine an early Hawaiian artifact or two and guiding them in establishing points of interest through general discussion.

Having the children listen to several Hawaiian folk tales or legends and building upon their curiosity about people with such beliefs to establish interests. (A similar activity can be used with excerpts of music, language, and examples of art.)

Establishing a date when the early Hawaiians had control of their territory and encouraging the children to wonder about aspects of life in those days. Points of interest are established in accord with the amount of curiosity shown.

Inviting the children to explore quickly the contents of a social-studies textbook about early Hawaii and encouraging them to indicate the points of interest that they find.

At the close of these activities directions are established, and again it is likely that open inquiry will be replaced by a series of closed inquiries.

Let us consider the applications of open inquiry made by the teacher who uses the social-science strategy. His is a strong commitment to open inquiry. He may use contrived situations similar to those used in the synthesized strategy, including the arranged environment, but with this essential difference—the situation will be contrived in such a way that a discovery or series of related discoveries will occur. For example, after an initial discussion in which it is established that Hawaii is an area of islands located generally in the mid-Pacific and that it was once inhabited by a group of people somewhat different from those living there today, the teacher shows some pieces of tapa cloth to the children, announces that they are products made and used by the early Hawaiians, and urges that a careful examination be made of the products. After review is made of the discoveries about texture, weight, size, and design, the teacher guides toward another finding by wondering about the uses of the product. After suggestions are made to the effect that the product could be used as wrapping paper, wallpaper, a wall decoration, or cloth, the teacher directs the children's attention to a series of pictures showing the uses of tapa cloth. This brief investigation brings to light that the product is indeed cloth. At this point the teacher asks the children whether they have any ideas about how this cloth was made. This question leads into a general discussion about how cloth is made within the children's own culture. The results of this discussion are that it is most likely to be made by hand from a vegetable fiber. The discussion prompts the showing of a filmstrip depicting the making of tapa cloth. Attention is arrested by the designs printed on the cloth. The period of study ends. The matter of design and the limitations of design will likely lead into examining various kinds of taboo during the next study period.

As can be seen, the "open" aspect of inquiry in the social-sciences strategy is a function of the teacher's guidance and preparation in providing for one discovery to grow out of another. He is prepared to go in any of several directions. The area into which he feels that inquiry should lead has to do with beliefs which the early Hawaiians had about the world around them. If the children had manifested knowing about tapa cloth, its uses, and its manufacture, their scrutiny would have been invited toward design immediately. If they had shown themselves to have been very little informed about Hawaii, the teacher may have initiated the study by having the children examine the cloth to determine whether they would care to wear it and encouraging them to think about the nature of the people who wore it and the conditions within which they lived.

As this type of open inquiry continues, children are carried on by the impetus of what they learn, now discovering, now synthesizing what they have learned for new discoveries, barely conscious that they are learning. Variety is constant in learning activities—examining artifacts and representations of all kinds; listening to and interviewing resource persons; probing into their own feelings, beliefs, and practices and comparing them to the feelings, beliefs, and practices of others; reading the accounts of others about processes, products, and the lives of other peoples; experimenting; observing demonstrations; developing demonstrations and experiments, now with the teacher, now in groups, now as individuals. Almost every social-studies period is a kaleidescope of different learning activities, yet each activity adds to a line of inquiry, half of which exists in the mind of the teacher and the other half of which takes form in accord with the interests and responses of children. The area and dimensions of knowledge are large enough to accommodate both, at least as far as the social-science strategist is concerned.

The thinking-emphasis strategist makes little use of open inquiry at the beginning of his unit. He recognizes the need for children to have certain background; to determine whether this background exists, he may use an open-inquiry technique such as encouraging children to relate their experiences about some aspect of the generalization to be studied. For example, children about to study about the farm as a productive unit could be invited to contribute their experiences of living on farms, visiting farms, seeing farms along the highway, seeing farm life depicted on television, reading about farms, and so on to establish a common concept of farm necessary to further study about the farm as a productive unit. This discussion would occur not long before the teacher began to guide the children toward closure about a common concept about farm.

Open inquiry, then, has its uses in launching units within all the strategies being treated, but it receives its fullest use in the social-science strategy. It has an important role to play in the synthesized strategy, but occurs only at a low level in the thinking-emphasis strategy.

BEGINNING THE UNIT WITH CLOSED INQUIRY

Closed inquiry used in positive ways is not particularly new in elementary classrooms. It is frequently used as an approach to establish classroom control. For example, when the children are about to be guided into work which places an undue burden on their self-control, the teacher guides them in inquiring into modes of effective behavior. The children probe into their own experience and values to develop a pattern of behavior which they feel will work. Then it is tested. Modifications are made, if necessary, and the established pattern of behavior is maintained (some individuals will need help). A problem may arise over the use of a space or equipment in the classroom or on the schoolyard. At this moment the teacher guides the children in examining the problem to determine forces in conflict, developing hypotheses about solutions, selecting a hypothesis, and testing it in classroom or schoolyard practice.

Another use of closed inquiry characteristic of older and current practices occurs when children are guided into project construction. The children work together in groups in a series of inquiries—clarifying the task, developing a plan, and determining the materials to be used.

Often these kinds of inquiry occur within the conduct of the social-studies program. As can be seen, these examples of closed inquiry occur when problems arise relating to children's values concerning their own behavior and to the production of an article of one kind or another. Let us see now how this inquiry is used with intellectual problems related to learning more about people, their ways of living, and their problems—in short, as a method of instruction.

The teacher using the synthesized strategy follows a practice long common in many social-studies programs. As was discussed in the previous section, the initial open inquiry, which serves to cause interests to emerge, terminates in a series of closed inquiries guided by questions developed as expressions of interest. As soon as these questions have been organized, they tend to be regarded as a contract entered into by the pupils when they expressed their interests and were encouraged to arrange them in order. Unfortunately, as a contract this may prove to be a harsh contract. To prevent this, the teacher strives to renew interest, as each new question or cluster of questions is approached, by encouraging the children to reexamine each question for meaning and possible meanings. As a comprehensive section of content is covered, he guides the children in integrating their learnings through expressive activity. From time to time he guides them in examining the progress they have made and encourages them to think about the content to be probed into as they continue their study.

Much of the children's time is spent at information-gathering activity in textbooks, reference books, at maps, globes, and the like. Although the children may be using similar sources, they are encouraged to do so independently. Almost every social-studies period closes with a pooling of findings to determine the most accurate answer to the question or questions involved, thus closing inquiry.

Children being guided through social studies by the teacher using the synthesized strategy are very conscious of learning. They also have an opportunity to practice and refine skills learned during other periods in the school day as well as skills unique to social studies.

During the course of his unit, the teacher using the social-science strategy makes little use, if any, of closed inquiry, although he may use it as a means of closing the unit. This use will be discussed in the next chapter.

The thinking-emphasis strategist has the strongest commitment of all to closed inquiry. As was mentioned in the previous section, his first tactical measure, to establish the level of background about a concept or idea basic to understanding other learnings in the unit, begins similarly to open inquiry but soon turns into closed inquiry. This progression, of course, follows his intent. He may use any of the following procedures:

He may encourage children to tell their experiences about the basic understandings. From time to time, he may also contribute some of his experiences to serve as a guide.

He may ask a thought-provoking question which prompts discussion and serves as a guide into the background to be checked. He guides the discussion through questions.

He may present materials related to the background and guide the children into the background to be checked.

He may encourage the children to reflect their level of knowledge through roleplaying or sociodrama.

For example, in a history unit about the economic aspects of the early settlement of America, the teacher uses a bulletin board or a set of display panels showing in contrast the various levels of economic welfare acceptable within the United States. As the teacher guides his pupils in any analysis of the bulletin board or display panels, they arrive at a definitive view of what is meant by levels of economic welfare and its range of acceptable levels in the United States. An idea of the meaning of these terms is necessary to further learning in a unit dealing with human motivation and the part it played in the beginning of America.

Or, the teacher could establish a level of knowledge of these ideas through a discussion begun in this way, "Let us suppose for a moment that we have the task of telling some foreign students about our American standard of living. We would want to describe the kinds of things that we believe are necessary for decent living—the kinds of homes we have, the kind of food we eat, the kind of clothing we wear, and so on. Exactly what would we tell them?" Through occasional guide questions, the teacher could direct the pupils' scrutiny toward the various acceptable levels within the American standard of living.

Or, the teacher could initiate the discussion by asking this question: "What is generally meant by this often-repeated statement, 'Americans enjoy the highest standard of living in the world'?"

Or, the teacher could stimulate the pupils to probe into their ideas about standard of living as related to level of economic welfare by encouraging them to respond in dramatic form to situations. Such a situation could be a family discussion at dinner. One group of pupils could interpret the family that enjoys a high level of economic welfare; another group, the family that enjoys an average level; and a third group, the family that lives at a low, but acceptable, level.

No one way is best for beginning the discussion to establish a level of knowledge. Most teachers find that presenting materials seems to offer pupils something tangible as a point for discussion. Such a presentation tends to encourage discussion and wider participation among the members of the class. Roleplaying or sociodrama, if carefully controlled and seriously accepted by the pupils, offer the same advantages. Many teachers, particularly those with an intense interest in social studies and children, can establish a level of knowledge through asking thought-provoking questions. Others, particularly teachers of primary children, find it easier to have the children share their experiences and pool their knowledge.

Whatever the means of beginning the discussion, it is continued until the teacher is reasonably sure that the pupils have the basic background for understanding the unit. Occasionally the teacher may be able to elicit only weak responses from his pupils. The teacher may have chosen a level of knowledge too low to challenge his pupils, or his device for stimulating discussion may be too weak. He may have chosen a common-level knowledge beyond his pupils' comprehension, or a device that is too intricate. When the responses are weak, the teacher should close the discussion, guide the pupils into another activity, and think through once more what the level of knowledge should be and what the device should be for stimulating discussion.

Once the level of knowledge has been established, the pupils are prepared for the presentation of the problem itself. This moment is crucial, for at this time the spark of interest in an abstract intellectual problem is generated. The problem, as defined, is presented in veiled form—veiled in the sense that the problem forces are shown, but not the solution.

Several assumptions underlie the presentation of the problem in such a way. It is assumed that an intellectual problem has a psychological dimension; the individual who examines it becomes aware of and accepts the disparity between his ignorance and the knowledge needed to solve the problem. He wishes to reduce the disparity. It is also assumed that the most difficult aspect of work with an intellectual problem is the definition of it in terms of the known and the unknown. For this reason, the teacher defines the problem and presents it in a form that identifies the known and points toward the unknown. These assumptions support the general assumption that the presentation of the problem defined in veiled form heightens conflict within the learner, thus creating and building interest in the problem presented.

To present a problem in veiled form, the teacher devises an instructional model. In its simplest form, an instructional model is a statement of a generalization with something omitted, usually a key idea which, when found, makes possible a complete statement. The instructional model is an incomplete statement expressed with symbolic representations, such as situational descriptions, objects, graphs, maps, charts, films, filmstrips, or the like. It is a statement which cannot be completed at the moment without a hypothesis. It is hypothesis-demanding, provocative, and interest-stimulating. Some teachers may find it easier to regard the instructional model as a question which leads toward a hypothesis, but a question asked in a subtle way, as reflected in the following examples

1. *The unit:* Shoes—A Factory Product.
   Generalization: Many people must work together to make our shoes.
   Instructional model: A pair of discarded shoes, one whole and the other dismantled.
   Use of the instructional model: The teacher encourages the children to examine the shoes. They discuss the different materials and parts to be found in a shoe. The teacher guides them into hypothesizing by asking: "How many pairs of hands do you think were needed to make these shoes?"

2. *The unit:* The Policeman, Protector of Life and Property.
   Generalization: Policemen are hired by our community to protect us and our property.
   Instructional model: A toy village display and some toy automobiles.
   Use of the instructional model: The children study the village and identify its various parts, including the residential area, the business area, churches, schools, and so on. Using imaginary names, the teacher leads the children into making hypotheses by developing situations, such as: "One day Mrs. Brown was driving down this street and Mrs. Smith was coming up this street. Neither one could decide who was to stop. They ran into each other. This happened with other people several times during the day. Finally the people of the village decided to do something about it. What do you think they did?" The children hypothesize about a police department, how it is organized, the duties of the policeman, and how the community controls the policeman and his work. (See Figure 3.)

3. *The unit:* California, A Leading Producer of Goods.
   Generalization: Economic welfare in California reflects a high standard because of the availability of both natural and human resources.
   Instructional model: A large bar graph or a chart showing the per capita yearly income of various states, including California.
   Use of the instructional model: The teacher guides the children in an analysis of the graph or chart to assure their understanding of what it

depicts, then encourages them to hypothesize by asking: "How can we account for the high income of Californians?"

4. *The Unit:* America, the Great "Melting Pot."

Generalization: The ways of thinking and behaving characteristic of the American democracy are the products of interpersonal and intrapersonal interaction over a period of years.

Instructional model: Groups of pictures to include the following:

1. Customs of greeting: An Italian embracing a relative; two Japanese bowing; two Americans shaking hands.
2. Sports: A scene from an European soccer game; a scene from an English rugby game; a scene from an American football game.
3. Eating: A Filipino child sucking a piece of sugar cane; a Mexican child nibbling at a taco; an American child munching a hotdog.
4. Dress: An Indian wearing a turban; an Arabian wearing a headcloth; an American wearing a hat.

Use of the instructional model: The teacher arranges the pictures on the

FIGURE 3. FIRST-GRADE CHILDREN, USING AN INSTRUCTIONAL MODEL, DISCUSS WHAT A COMMUNITY MUST DO ABOUT TRAFFIC PROBLEMS.

chalk tray or on a bulletin board and guides the children in identifying the Americans in each group. Hypothesizing begins when the teacher asks: "Why do we have these particular customs in greeting, sports, eating, and dress?"

5. *The unit:* Communication, A Way of Helping to Get Things Done.
   Generalization: People communicate to solve problems.
   Instructional model: A telephone.
   Use of the instructional model: The teacher has the children demonstrate the ways in which they use the telephone and the ways they have heard and seen others using it. He guides them into hypothesizing by asking, "What is a person really trying to do when he uses the telephone?"

6. *The unit:* Theodore Roosevelt, a Great President.
   Generalization: Our society owes a debt to Theodore Roosevelt for his contributions to government and to conservation.
   Instructional model: A series of pictures of Theodore Roosevelt showing him as a speechmaker, a rancher, a big game hunter, a soldier, and a president.
   Use of the instructional model: The teacher displays the pictures on the chalk tray or on a bulletin board. The pupils examine the pictures and identify the various roles depicted. The teacher invites hypotheses by asking, "In what ways do you suppose this man made his greatest contributions to our country?"

7. *The unit:* The Historical Background of the American Economic System.
   Generalization: Our nation has a unique economic history because it attracted people with particular interests and abilities and provided a cultural climate that fostered the development of ideas in the solution of technological problems in manufacturing, agriculture, transportation, and communication.
   Instructional model: A physical-political map of the United States, one of Canada, and one of Australia; a chart for each country showing its area, population, and gross national product expressed in dollars.
   Use of instructional model: The teacher presents the maps and charts for class analysis during which the pupils' attention is centered on population size and size of gross national product. The teacher encourages hypotheses by saying, "These countries share similar characteristics in size and background traditions. What do you suppose accounts for the greater population and greater gross national product of the United States?"

8. *The unit:* Indians of the United States.
   Generalization: Indian cultures varied in ways of doing things.
   Instructional model: The teacher gives a verbal description of a situation.

Use of instructional model: The teacher says, "One day I heard two boys having an argument. One boy said, 'The Indians were about the same everywhere.' And the other boy said, 'The Indians were quite different from place to place.' The boys argued and argued, but they could not agree. Which of these boys do you agree with? Why?"

During the application of the instructional model, the teacher records or remembers the hypotheses made. These hypotheses are the basic material from which the children organize a design for inquiry. As the design for inquiry is being organized, the teacher works to help them develop the best design that they can devise. If the hypotheses have been recorded (this procedure is usual in grade three and above), the teacher directs the pupils' attention toward their stated hypotheses as written to determine whether any are repetitive. If the hypotheses have not been recorded (this procedure is usual in the primary grades), the teacher reviews them and guides the pupils toward seeking for repetitions in this way: "As I remember, John said . . . , and Mary said . . . , and Phil said . . . , and Jimmie said . . . . Are each of the things that they said different, or have some of the people said the same thing?" If this procedure is used, the teacher should be prepared for corrections by the children whom he is quoting. If deletions are to be made, they are made on the basis of class decision.

When the children have arrived at a list of statements that stand as separate, discrete hypotheses, the teacher guides them toward determining which hypothesis is the most reasonable. Expressions such as the following are used: "Which of these statements do you think is the best explanation of . . . ?" or "Which of these explanations do you think is best?" or "John said . . . and Mary said . . . and Bill said . . . . Who do you think is right?" When pupils make choices, they are encouraged to tell why they made this choice or that. The teacher reacts to each choice and substantiation of choice with complete equanimity, reflecting neither approval nor disapproval of what has been said. After the children have reacted to all the hypotheses listed, the teacher tries to help them to establish a unanimity as to which hypothesis or hypotheses is the most reasonable. Usually, a group of pupils has little difficulty in seeing which hypotheses listed are the more reasonable and which can be discarded. However, the group often has difficulty in deciding which of two or three hypotheses is to stand as the most reasonable of all that have been offered. Although it may be somewhat simpler to guide children in investigating the tenability of a single hypothesis, the simplicity gained is of little value if it has been assured through abrogating children's right to think. Abrogation occurs when the teacher forces children to select but one hypothesis from several given. It is better to have several hypotheses and thus to preserve the climate for thinking. Actually, the several hypotheses lend an aura of suspended judgment as a result of effort in thinking and reflect a desire to wait until more facts have been found. These conditions indicate a healthy, realistic view of the thinking process.

The selected hypothesis is the basic design for inquiry. Sometimes only this basic design is used. If it is, the teacher suggests that from time to time the class will be examining its hypothesis to determine how accurate it is in the light of their findings. Frequently when the teacher uses a bulletin-board display as an instructional model, he will leave the display posted all through the study of the unit as a constant reminder of the hypothesis which the class had developed at the beginning of study.

Sometime the thinking-emphasis strategist feels that it is necessary to extend the basic design. This extension is accomplished through encouraging the children to develop questions for which they must find the answers in order to acquire the facts and ideas necessary for checking the tenability of the hypothesis. Usually, these questions reflect the supporting ideas for the incomplete generalization presented in the instructional model. However, questions developed at this time may have to be forced from the children. If this is the case, time and effort expended at eliciting questions may well destroy the interest just created.

An instructional model should also be used in introducing an idea that stands at the head of a parcel of content. It is at this point that designing an extended structure for inquiry becomes particularly vital. The children are going to be dealing with specifics; therefore, they should devise the questions instrumental to checking the hypothesis that has been selected. The teacher may invite the development of such questions by asking, "What questions will we have to ask ourselves to find whether this statement is true?" or "What information do we need to find now?"

Because of the intricacy involved in the procedures used in initiating closed inquiry, the following examples at two grade levels are presented. Note in each of the examples how the teacher establishes the level of knowledge, introduces the problem, and guides the children in developing a design for inquiry.

Miss Mills, the first-grade teacher, helps her twenty-six first-grade boys and girls arrange themselves on and around the rug at the front of the class-room. A little more than half the children are seated in chairs around the edge of the rug, while the remaining children are seated at the rug. Miss Mills, who is working on her last probation year, is seated in a chair at the front of the rug. She is holding on her lap a set of large pictures face down. A nearby easel stands empty. When the children are ready, she announces quietly. "We are going to study some pictures about something that you already know. The pictures will show parts of the thing, and after we finish talking about each one, I shall ask what the thing is that we are talking about. Here is the first picture. I'll put it on the easel here so that you can see it easily. Who can tell me what it is? So many hands! What is it, Dell?"

"It's a church."

"How do you know?"

"It has windows like a church and there are a lot of people around it."

"Yes, it must be Sunday. Or it could be another day, maybe a special day. Do you know now what thing we are really talking about? It has a church, or even many churches. Can you guess? Pam?"

"A street?"

"That is a good guess but that is not it. Boyd?"

"It's people!"

"No, not people exactly. Perhaps we had better look at another picture. All of you know what this is. Say it."

"It's a house!" "It's a home!"

"Sure, it is. Each one of us lives in one. This thing that we are studying about has many homes in it. Can you tell me what it is? Dell?"

"The place all around our school."

"Sorry, Dell. You are really thinking, but we are talking about something that is bigger than just the place around the school. Perhaps this will help you. What is this? Tony?"

"It is a big building."

"That is what it is. Do you have any idea what it is used for? Have any of you ever seen a building like this? Bobby?"

"I've seen buildings like that. They are on the side of the road when you go downtown."

"Yes, Bobby, when we go downtown from here, we do see many build-ings like this along both sides of the street. Yes, Marvin?"

"My daddy works in a building like that. Once he showed me a building like that. We were going downtown and the building was on (pointing) that side of the road."

"A big yellow building?"

"Yes, with big, funny writing on the outside."

"What kind of work does your father do in that building?"

"I don't know. He just works there."

"That building is a factory. It is where things are made from plastic. Many things are made in factories. Almost everything in this room is made in a factory—the tables, chairs, chalkboards, paper, pencils, the clothing you are wearing, just about everything. Marvin?"

"Were all these things made in the same factory?"

"No, some factories make furniture. Others make paper. Still others make other things. Well, can you think of something that has churches, houses, and factories? Arthur?"

"All I can think of is a street."

"No, that is not it. Let's look at another picture."

Miss Mills shows a picture of each of the following: a park, a school, a store, a service station, a library, and a city hall. Each of these is discussed briefly. Only the city hall needs a more detailed explanation. After the last picture is discussed, Miss Mills displays them on the chalk tray at the front of the room and encourages the children to think what all these pictures show parts of.

"Think carefully," she reminds them, "I'm sure you know what has all these things."

Hands begin to rise.

"Don't say it," she admonishes them, "I'm going to come around to each of you and have you whisper it to me. Why don't we stand? That will give you a chance to stretch a little while each of you tells me what we are really talking about."

Miss Mills makes her way around the group quickly. Most of the children can tell her quickly; some need a few questions to help them know; two or three need to be told quickly. These grin somewhat self-consciously at not being able to think of it immediately.

"Almost everyone knew. It is a city. Let's sit down again and think some more about it."

When all the children are settled again, Miss Mills guides the children in discussing how all the things pictured are used by people or why they are important to people.

"Just why do we have to have all of these things in a city?" she asks. "Philip?"

"Well, we have to have schools. Boys and girls have to go to school to learn things."

"And what about the grown-up people? Where do they go? Billy?"

"The fathers go to work. They work in the factories?"

"That is true. Do all the fathers work in factories? Charles?"

"Some of them work in stores. My father works in a store."

"Any other places where fathers work? Lynn?"

"My father is a school teacher. He works in a school. And I see men working in service stations."

"And how about the mothers. Where do they go? Donna?"

"Some of them work, too. My mother works in an office."

"Quite a few mothers work. Some of them work in factories, schools, and stores. What other kind of work do they do? Gerry?"

"My mother works at home. She takes care of the baby and cleans the house."

"Many mothers work at home. We have talked about the work of people and where they work, and we have mentioned almost everything in our pictures. Can you see any that we haven't talked about? Bobby?"

"There's the library. We haven't talked about that."

"And how do people use it?"

"They go there to get books to read."

"Anything else? When your mother takes you to the library, do you see other people in the library? Marvin?"

"I go there every Saturday and I see many people there. Some are bringing books back and some are taking books out. And I see some at tables looking at books."

"Very good, Marvin. You really have your eyes wide open. We see many people at the library because people want to learn more about things or they like to read for fun. It is often a place that people like to go to when they are not working. Any other places that we haven't talked about? Boyd?"

"There is the park. People go there to have picnics and to have fun."

"Right. And how about that other building there, the city hall. What is that used for? Pam?"

"That's where the men who run the city work."

"Do you know how those men get their jobs? Dell?"

"Do they go to school for a long time and then they get their jobs?"

"Not exactly. You know how we decide who is going to be team captain? How do we decide? Lynn?"

"We vote."

"Well, these men who work in city hall get their jobs by votes. Your mother and father do the voting. Most of the mothers and fathers in the city vote for the men who are going to run the city in which we live. The city hall and all the other things are important for a city. Sometimes we call a city by another name. Can you think of it? Tony?"

"A town?"

"A town has fewer people than a city. It is a smaller place, but sometimes we use another word. We can also use it when we are talking about a town. What do you think it is? Bobby?"

"A state?"

"That is much larger than a city, but sometimes we can use the same word for it, for town, and for city. You have heard the word, I'm sure. Your parents have said it many times when you were around. Can't think of it? The word is *community*. Can you say it? Good. A community is a place where people live, where they work, where they buy and sell things they need, where they have fun, and where they decide together who is to look after things for everyone who lives in a place."

"Let's pretend that we are living in a new community. It is the community that we saw in the pictures. One day Marvin's mother is bringing him to school. Pam's mother is also bringing her to school. These two mothers are traveling down two different streets. (Miss Mills goes to the chalkboard and draws two lines representing two intersecting streets.) Dell's mother is coming down this street and Pam's mother is driving on this street. They meet at this corner, but they do not see each other in time. There is an accident! No one is hurt, but the cars are damaged. What are the mothers to do now? Bobby?"

"They are going to try to fix their car."

"They could try to do that. What else could they do? Charles?"

"They can call a policeman."

"But this community is so new that it does not have any policemen. How do you suppose that it is going to get policemen? Gerry?"

"Maybe they can get some from another place."

"Maybe they could. Are there any other ways that you can think of? Billy?"

"Some of the fathers could take turns being policemen."

"That's an idea. Yes, Donna."

"My father could not be a policeman. He does not have a policeman suit and he does not have a gun."

"My father could!" pipes Boyd. "He has a whole lot of guns!"

"Perhaps he could. Do you have any other ideas of how this community can get the policemen that it needs? Bobby?"

"The people in the community could vote for them."

"That is a way. Any other ideas? Arthur?"

"Maybe the people in the community could find out who would like to be policemen. Then they'd let them be policemen."

"That is another way. Can any of you think of another way? No other ideas? Listen as I tell you the ideas that we have so far: the community could get them from another community, have the fathers in the community take turns being policemen; the people could vote for policemen, or they could find out who would like to be policemen and let those men be policemen. Which of these ideas do you think is the best?"

In the discussion that follows there is a strong feeling that perhaps the community should find the men who would like to be policemen and then have them work as policemen. Miss Mills encourages the children to decide on what they should find out about first to see whether this idea is true. The children agree generally that they should investigate how the community learns what men would like to be policemen.

As can be seen in the foregoing, the idea of *community* has to be developed first. Once it has been established, the fictional accident is presented as a means of provoking interest and stimulating thinking. Hypotheses are made and considered and the design for inquiry, in this case the aspect of the problem to be treated first, is developed. As is to be noted in the above, younger children will make rational hypotheses but will not always be able to arrive at a precise one. Several may be quite near accuracy. Usually a complete design for inquiry is much more than younger children can accomplish. However, they can decide on a reasonable initial point. The following is representative of what occurs when older children are guided through establishing a level of knowledge, meeting the problem, and developing a design for inquiry.

". . . and one of the city engineers in Rio de Janeiro said that a new drainage system would have to be planned for the city. Any questions?" asked the slender sixth grade boy at the front of the classroom. "Harry?"

"Jim, I'll bet their storm wasn't much worse than the one we had a few weeks back. I guess our city engineers must be thinking the same as that one down in Rio."

A ripple of laughter from the boys and girls at their seats indicates that the deluge of a few weeks ago has become an amusing event in ancient history.

Mrs. Adams, the teacher, rises from the vacant seat where she has been sitting with the boys and girls as they conducted a brief discussion about current events taking place in Latin America. "Perhaps so, Harry," she says with a wise, indulgent smile, "but this event in the news and our own recent sad experience does point up one thing. Do you know what it is?"

"I don't think I see the point."

"Well, Harry, the remark that you made in fun really indicated something to the rest of us. It showed a point of view we have here about the storm. You said it as a reaction to a similar point of view expressed by a citizen of Rio de Janeiro. And the two of you are thousands of miles apart."

"Well, I guess we have the same problems, and we do and think the same things."

"Did that occur to any of the rest of you? Dorothy?"

"I was thinking that way as I listened to the reports about the storm."

"Others among you were probably thinking the same way. For a moment it seems that our city of Los Angeles and Rio de Janeiro are very close."

With the self-assurance of twenty years of coping successfully with the instructional problems of fifth- and sixth-grade children, Mrs. Adams walks briskly to the front of the classroom, picks up a large outline map, and invites the children's attention to it by saying, "This is a map of a country much closer to Rio and Brazil than it is to Los Angeles and the United States. Is it familiar to any of you?"

The children peer at the map to seek clues. The map, prepared on tagboard with felt pen, shows an area of three regions from north to south—desert, grassland, and tropical rain forest. A river system and scattered mountains are represented. The southern boundary shows a coastline on the Gulf of Guinea. Latitude and longitude are indicated along the margins on the map. A scale is also indicated.

"What country do you think this is. Doug?"

"That Gulf of Guinea at the bottom of the map shows that the country is not any of the continents that we have studied so far. It is not on North America or South America."

"Right, Doug. What are the possibilities, then? Diane?"

"Africa, Asia, Australia, and Antarctica, but I think that we can forget about Antarctica. It would not have those different parts."

"Good thinking, Diane. It must be on Africa, Asia, or Australia. Which of these is most likely to be the continent on which this country is found? Fred?"

"That Gulf of Guinea there. Maybe it could be near New Guinea. That's not too far from Australia."

"That is a possibility. Examine the clues on the map more closely. Harry?"

"I'd throw out Australia. It is in the south latitudes. This country is in the north latitudes, about four degrees north of the equator. Hey, it must be just above the equator, like Venezuela in South America!"

"You're beginning to locate the country. If it is above the equator, just where is it? Polly?"

"It must be Africa!"

"How can you be sure? Jerry?"

"Well, the map also shows that the lower lefthand corner of the country is at about four degrees east longitude. That means that it is not far from the prime meridian which runs down through Greenwich, England. Most of Europe lies to the east of it. Farther down, south of Europe lies Africa. I think that the country is in Africa."

"Let's check it, then. Donald, will you please pull down the world map and see what you can find at about four degrees north latitude and four degrees east longitude? Emily, will you try to find the same location on the globe?"

In a moment both Donald and Emily have located a point and are wait-
ing to report their findings.

"Tell us what you have found, Donald."

"It's a place called—ah, Neye-GEER-ee-ah, I think."

"Perhaps you can write it on the board. (Pause.) Did you find the same
place, Emily?"

"Yes, Mrs. Adams, but isn't it pronounced Neye-JEER-ee-ah?"

"That's right, but we can't always be sure about foreign names. The two
of you can go back to your seats now. George, will you pull down that map
of Africa and find Nigeria on it for us?"

In a few moments Nigeria is located on the map of Africa. Walking over
to the wall map, Mrs. Adams guides the children in an examination of Nigeria
on both the outline map and the wall map. The mountains and the river system
are discussed. Relative size of the country is treated. Mrs. Adams informs the
class that the country covers roughly the same area as Texas, Arkansas, and
Louisiana. Consulting a large wall map of the United States, the children
arrive at a clearer understanding of the size of the country and its regions.
They note the similarity between the Gulf of Mexico and the Gulf of Guinea
and the difference between the Niger River and the Mississippi River with
respect to relative location in the areas being compared.

At this point Mrs. Adams guides the children in a distance study as a
means of clarifying the location of Nigeria with respect to their own location.

"Let us suppose that we were going to go to Nigeria from here. Let's consider air routes first. What do you think would be the shortest route? Brad?"

"The polar route would most likely be the closest, probably from here
to London, and then from London to some city in Nigeria."

"Why don't you find out about that? You will find a yardstick and a
piece of string over there by the globe. You will find the city of Lagos,
L-A-G-O-S—perhaps you'd better write on the board there for reference—in
southern Nigeria. Use that as your Nigerian destination. While Brad is finding
that information, we can use the wall map to consider other routes. If we did
not use a polar route, what other routes might we consider? Margaret?"

"We could fly to New York first."

"Will you go to the world map and measure the first leg of our trip?"

By having the children work at the various maps and the globe, Mrs.
Adams encourages them to discover the following: in terms of travel distance,
Lagos, Nigeria, is about 9,000 miles from Los Angeles; in flight hours, the
distance is about fifteen hours by jet as compared to about four hours to
New York; in sailing days, the distance is about eighteen days on the usual
passenger liner. The children explore routes westward from Los Angeles as
well as from large Asiatic cities. The result is a well-established idea of

Nigeria's location. Facts about size and regional divisions have contributed to the development of a basic geographical idea of what Nigeria is.

Mrs. Adams guides the children toward considering a problem area by saying, "Nigeria became an independent nation in 1960. In this sense it is a new nation, and all new nations have special problems to attempt to solve. Here is an example of one problem that Nigeria has. Listen to this news article as I read it to you. (The article gives an account of an attempt of rebellious army troops to assume control of the government. The prime minister and the finance minister have been kidnapped and their whereabouts are unknown. It is rumored that the heads of government in two of the regions have been assassinated. It is said that the reason for the revolt is dissatisfaction with the government. Hope for a return to peaceful conditions seems to rest on the control of the capital, Lagos, by loyal army elements.) What is this problem? Eleanor?"

"It is the problem of not having a strong government. Maybe some of the African countries are like some of the Latin American governments."

"From this one news article that seems to be true, Eleanor. Did our country ever have this problem? Doug?"

"Sure. After the War for Independence, Washington, Jefferson, and the others had to work hard to set up a strong government in the United States."

"Yes, and as we learn more about these new nations in the world today, it is more than likely that we'll find that most of them have difficulty in establishing a strong government. Here is some evidence of another problem."

Mrs. Adams presents two picture graphs. Each graph contains a hundred figures, each representing one hundredth of the working population. The graph depicting the working population of the United States shows ten figures holding hoes. These are the farmers. The ninety other figures represent the other occupations combined. The graph depicting the working population of Nigeria shows eighty figures holding hoes. The remaining twenty represent the percentage of working men in other occupations. She encourages the children to examine these graphs closely by having them analyze the graphs to determine the statement which each makes. When these statements are clearly understood, Mrs. Adams uses the difference between the statements to encourage the children to hypothesize.

"Why do you suppose that so many of the working men in Nigeria work at farming? Len?"

"Is it because the people don't know how to do anything else?"

"Do you want to make that as your hypothesis?"

"O.K. There are so many men working in Nigeria as farmers because the people don't know how to do other things."

"What makes you think that?"

"There are a lot of natives in Africa. They may not know much besides hunting and simple farming."

"Can any of the rest of you think of some other reasons that appear to support his hypothesis? Phyllis?"

"Well, it could be that the people are just learning how to farm after years and years of hunting for food."

"Phyllis, that is really another hypothesis. Can you tell us what makes you think this?"

"I'm not exactly sure, but I think it was something I saw on television. It told about how people go through stages. A long time ago men just gathered food, and then they learned how to become good hunters. Later they learned how to raise plants. All the time they were making better and better tools. It could be that the people in Nigeria are at the farming stage."

"Yes, Gary."

"I saw that program, too."

"Perhaps quite a few of you saw it. (Several nods in the affirmative.) That seems quite reasonable. Do any of the rest of you have a hypothesis to make. Doug?"

"I think that so many men are needed to farm in Nigeria because the people do not know how to get the most out of their soil."

"Why do you think that?"

"Look at our own country. When it started out it was mostly farmers. Then ways of farming improved—better plows, tractors, threshing machines, reapers. Now some of our farmers have huge farms where they raise large crops with the help of just a few men."

"What do you think about that, Terry?"

"I agree, I mean—I know that is true."

"Any other hypotheses? Harry?"

"We know that poor natural resources make people work harder to get the things they need. The people in Nigeria could have very poor natural resources, so it would take the work of most of the men to get the things needed by the people."

"Do you know of another place where that is true?"

"Not really. But I was thinking about the rain forest in Brazil. The few people in the jungle have to work so hard to gather the rubber, medicine plants, and lumber. They don't really need those things, but they can be sold to get the money to buy what they need."

"It is not exactly the same, but your thinking is pretty sound. Doris?"

"You just read us that article about the trouble they're having with their government down there. Maybe they're so busy fighting they don't have enough time to really work their farms. That's why it take so many of them."

"That is possible. Any other ideas from the rest of you? All right, then, let's choose a hypothesis from among those given. Which do you think seems to explain best why so many Nigerians work at farming? Dorothy?"

"I think that I go along with Doug's hypothesis. Even though only four persons out of a hundred in our country are farmers, there are still many farmers who cannot use their land well."

"What do the rest of you think?"

In the ensuing discussion, the children consider the other hypotheses given. They find it impossible to agree on one hypothesis. Opinions appear to cluster around the following: (1) So many of the men must work at farming in Nigeria because natural resources are so poor; and (2) most of the men in Nigeria work at farming because the people do not know how to get the most out of the soil.

Mrs. Adams guides the children in developing some questions that must be answered in order to determine which of the two hypotheses is the more accurate. The following questions are quickly suggested:

1. What are the natural resources of Nigeria?
2. How do the people of Nigeria use these resources to get what they need for living?
3. Can the Nigerian people enter world trade? If they can, what can they offer?
4. How do the Nigerian people look at the problem?

As can be seen in the above, older children can hypothesize more accurately and can develop a more complete design for inquiry. They also bring facts learned from several sources to bear upon any problem. However, the same procedures were followed, that is, a level of knowledge was established, a problem was presented in an interest-provoking way, and a design for inquiry was developed.

Closed inquiry used as a starter for the unit brings into being directions for inquiry as well as a series of short-term inquiries related to it. Children are aware that they are making inquiry and that what they are doing is purposeful. The information gathered is to support as well as to establish a point of truth which has previously been left in doubt. The teacher guides children into closed inquiry so that they determine the inquiry and its direction from his instructional model, a contrivance which brings into view the problem forces in conflict. Once the inquiry begins, the teacher continues to guide children toward points of truth by presenting the investigative activities and materials that he feels are necessary and within the ability of the children. Children are to use independent fact-gathering skills when feasible. The teacher may devise charts, experiments, demonstrations, and the like, which he presents to children as a means of gathering facts. He helps them to analyze these devices to acquire facts.

By this time, it should be apparent that the teacher who utilizes inquiry approaches, either open or closed, is a master of the skills of contriving for learning.

SUMMARY

Inquiry is a human activity which is a part of daily living. Sometimes it is interest-oriented inquiry in which an individual motivated by curiosity seeks after more information about something that has taken his fancy. At other times it may be problem-oriented inquiry in which an individual seeks to establish a choice through hypothesizing, selecting a hypothesis, and testing.

Inquiry may be regarded as open or closed. Open inquiry tends to be interest-oriented. It follows a course developed by an initial discovery which gives rise to another, which in turn leads to another, until the inquirer tires, is satisfied, or finds a new line of inquiry to follow.

Closed inquiry is much the same as problem-oriented inquiry. It begins with a problem and follows one model or another of reflective thinking.

Both open inquiry and closed inquiry have uses in learning. One factor which determines the efficacy of their use in learning is how the teacher interprets his role. He should regard himself as guide.

Neither open inquiry nor closed inquiry is to be regarded as new in elementary teaching practices. Both have been used for some time to accomplish certain learning tasks.

No teaching strategy among those treated totally disregards either form of inquiry. One form may lead to the other, depending on the teacher's interpretation of the learning situation.

The use of open inquiry in beginning a unit follows these patterns: in the synthesized strategy, the teacher uses an arranged environment, or some other contrivance, as a means of helping children to discover interests. However, open inquiry becomes a series of closed inquiries when the children express their interests in the form of questions. The teacher using the social-science strategy uses a contrived situation which serves as a means of helping children to make a discovery. He follows with a series of contrived learning situations, some of which are determined by children's responses, which keeps the line of inquiry open and carries along. The teacher using the thinking-emphasis strategy begins his unit with a form of open inquiry, but soon guides it toward closed inquiry about a basic idea necessary to further learning in the unit.

The use of closed inquiry in beginning a unit follows these patterns: in the synthesized strategy, the teacher guides children into a series of closed inquiries once common interests have been identified. The children are encouraged to use independent skills in seeking and gathering information. The teacher has to make special provisions for maintaining interest at a high level. As the social-science strategist guides his pupils in the beginning of the unit, and beyond, he makes little or no use of closed inquiry. The teacher using the thinking-emphasis strategy begins with a closed inquiry which establishes a basic concept, and then, using an instructional model, guides the children into closed inquiry related to the generalization. The children are encouraged to hypothesize and select the hypothesis which appears to be the most reasonable. They may be guided into developing a design for inquiry in the form of questions that will need to be answered to determine the tenability of the hypothesis. Interest in carrying on inquiry is promoted by placing each subidea in issue and developing an inquiry related to it and by examining the greater line of inquiry from time to time.

The uses of inquiry demand ingenuity in contriving learning situations.

Exercises for Further Understanding

1. Given below is a list of topic areas as well as the grade levels in which they are usually taught:

> The Family—Kindergarten
> Clothing Manufacturing—Grade 2
> Agricultural Production in Our State—Grade 4
> Life in Latin America—Grade 6
> The Founding of Our Country—Grade 8

Choose one of the above and do the following:

(a) Make a brief outline of notes describing an arranged environment that you would use to guide children in finding interests within your topic area.

(b) Find a story or poem that would be suitable for use in helping children to find interests within your chosen topic area.

(c) Find a picture or an object or artifact which you could use in helping to discover an interest in your topic area. Develop a series of learning activities that would lead the children toward making at least two more related discoveries.

(d) Select an idea from your topic area which you feel would have to be known by the children at a common level if they are to continue studying effectively within the topic area. Decide how you are going to establish this level of knowledge. Express your decision in terms of materials (if any) and a list of procedures.

2. Given below are some generalizations which could serve as guides in developing units. Devise an instructional model for each.

(a) *(Your town or city)* works as a community to provide some of the products and many of the services for its people.

(b) As people came to desire more and newer products, the ways of using land *(in your state)* changed.

(c) Modern inventions have extended the communities of man.

(d) The most important task of our government is to protect the freedom of the individual citizen.

(e) It is the job of the family to provide for the needs of its members.

3. If possible, arrange to visit a classroom on the day that the teacher is going to introduce a unit. Take particular note of the practice that he follows. Which strategy does he use? If he has to make a transition from open inquiry to closed inquiry, does the children's level of interest remain the same?

Selected References

Black, Millard H., *et al.,* "Critical Thinking and Problem Solving," *Social Studies in Elementary Schools,* pp. 150-175. Thirty-Second Yearbook of the National Council for the Social Studies, Washington, D.C.: National Education Association, 1962.

Burton, William H., Roland B. Kimball, and Richard L. Wing, *Education for Effective Thinking.* New York: Appleton-Century-Crofts, Inc., 1960.

Cox, C. Benjamin, Emily S. Girault, and Lawrence E. Metcalf, "Review of Research in Social Studies: 1965." *Social Education,* 30:348-359 (May 1966).

Dunfee, Maxine, and Helen Sagl, *Social Studies through Problem Solving,* Chap. 3, "Planning Cooperatively to Solve Problems." New York: Holt, Rinehart and Winston, Inc., 1966.

Ellsworth, Ruth, "Critical Thinking—Its Encouragement." *National Elementary Principal,* 42:24-49 (May 1963).

Getzels, J. W., "Creative Thinking, Problem Solving, and Instruction," *Theories of Learning and Instruction*, pp. 240-267. Sixty-Third Yearbook, Part I, of the National Society for the Study of Education, Chicago: The University of Chicago Press, 1964.

Goldmark, Bernice, "Critical Thinking: Deliberate Method." *Social Education*, 30:329-343 (May 1966).

Joyce, Bruce R., *Strategies for Elementary Social Science Education*, Chap. 3, "Introducing Organizing Concepts to Children;" and Chap. 4, "The Social Sciences and Approaches to Content." Chicago: Science Research Associates, Inc., 1965.

_____, "The Modes of Inquiry Problem." *Social Education*, 30:181-183 (March 1966).

Kaplan, Abraham, *The Conduct of Inquiry*. San Francisco: Chandler Publishing Company, 1964.

Mallan, John, and John Vaughn, "Social Inquiry; Knowledge in Transition." *National Elementary Principal*, 45:30-35 (June 1966).

Massialas, Byron G., "Revising the Social Studies: An Inquiry Approach." *Social Education*, 27:185-189 (April 1963).

Michaelis, John U., *Social Studies for Children in a Democracy*, 3d ed., Chap. 4, "Developing Thinking Processes." Englewood Cliffs, N.J.: Prentice-Hall, Inc., 1963.

Miel, Alice, and Peggy Brogan, *More Than Social Studies,* Chap. 10, "Helping Children Increase Competence in Democratic Problem Solving." Englewood Cliffs, N.J.: Prentice-Hall, Inc., 1957.

Reynolds, Robert W. *et al., Guiding Children through the Social Studies*, Chap. 3, "Guiding Children through the Social Studies in the Primary Grades;" and Chap. 4, "Guiding Children through the Social Studies in the Intermediate Grades." Washington, D.C.: National Education Association, 1964.

Russell, David, *Children's Thinking*. Boston: Ginn and Company, 1956.

Wann, Kenneth D., Miriam S. Dorn, and Elizabeth Liddle, *Fostering Intellectual Development in Young Children*. New York: Teachers College, Columbia University, 1962.

8

Guiding Children in Closing Inquiry

In the last chapter open inquiry and closed inquiry were introduced. Their uses in starting a social-studies unit within the various strategies were treated. This chapter will treat further uses of both types of inquiry in bringing the unit to a close. Mid-unit inquiry, as well as procedures for guiding children in tying facts and ideas together at several different levels and in continuing open inquiry about the "big idea," will be discussed.

MID-UNIT INQUIRY

For the moment let us consider the graduate student at work on a thesis or dissertation. With the help of an advisor he develops a research proposal. His feeling of accomplishment is high when his proposal, which includes a carefully defined problem and a design for research, finally meets with the approval of his advisory committee. His elation is short-lived, however, for the wearying and time-consuming data soon occupy him. A similar state of affairs may prevail for children engaged in a series of closed inquiries once common interests have been established (as they are in the synthesized strategy) or a "big idea" has been placed in issue (as occurs in the thinking-emphasis strategy), but with an important difference. The graduate student, sustained by his usually intrinsic motivation, manages to gather the necessary data and to organize them without loss of interest in his problem. Children guided into a series of closed inquiries in a school situation frequently do not have such a strong force sustaining their interest. Therefore, the big problem for the teacher who uses the synthesized strategy or the thinking-emphasis strategy is the maintenance of children's interest at a high level. Some procedures both teachers may follow; others are unique to their strategy.

Both strategies rely to a certain extent on children's independent ability to gather facts. Children's inability to gather facts, for whatever reason, could destroy the interest developed during the introduction of the unit. Any or all of the following procedures may be used to cope with this problem:

1. Carefully examine resource materials to assure that the facts to be sought are presented in them.
2. Check the level of sophistication of presentation in resource materials to assure that children of various abilities are guided to the resource or resources most suitable for them.
3. Made special materials and provisions for children who lack certain formal skills.
4. Develop a variety of learning activities demanding different fact-gathering skills.
5. Carefully check the children's skills instrumental to fact gathering—reading, map and globe skills, reference skills, and the like—before beginning units which place a heavy burden on these skills. When it is found that skills are deficient, remedy them before work in the unit begins.

More specific suggestions for procedures to be followed in the above areas are presented in greater detail in Chapters 9, 10, 12, and 14.

At various times during the study of a unit, the teacher using either the synthesized or the thinking-emphasis strategy may guide his pupils in expressive activity. Interest in following the line of inquiry may be lost if certain procedures, such as the following, are not applied:

1. Vary expressive activities to include many media.

2. Carefully check the children's expressive skills before encouraging their use for expressing learning.

More detailed suggestions for procedures to be applied in the above areas are presented in Chapters 11, 12, and 14.

The more involved children are in working with the points of inquiry, the greater the possibility that they will maintain an interest in it. If they are denied this involvement because the teacher is unable to relinquish discussion to the class or because the teacher and the same four or five pupils always become the active discussants, most children soon forget that inquiry is taking place. For specific suggestions about this problem, see the section about discussion skills in Chapter 12.

The procedures for maintaining interest unique to each of the strategies, although treated to some extent in the previous chapter, will be discussed in greater detail here.

In the synthesized strategy, children working in the middle of the unit are guided in finding the answers to questions which they have developed themselves. The repetition of the same activity day after day (reading to find the answers to questions) will be likely to deaden the interest awakened earlier. All too often the daily social-studies period becomes routinized in accord with the following guide-questions:

"What did we find out yesterday?"
"Which question are we going to answer today? Will someone read it aloud? Does everyone know what it means?"
"Which books are we going to use?"
(Children read.)
"What did we find out today?"

This method is little more than a teaching "crutch" which supports the basic requirements of the teaching-learning moment—determining a purpose, involvement, and checking to see how well the purpose has been fulfilled. It does little to maintain interest. The following procedures serve to refresh interest within the requirements of teaching-learning:

1. Encourage open discussion of the question or questions to be treated during the period. Some of the following devices may prove helpful:
   a. Have the child who originally contributed the question chair the discussion about the meaning of the question.

b. Reintroduce the picture or artifact that prompted the question originally and have the children reexamine the question.

c. Introduce a picture or artifact that activates interest in the question.

d. Have the children examine the question to determine subquestions that will need to be answered before a total answer can be found.

e. Invite the children to develop possible answers to the question and then to select the best possible answer to investigate.

f. Present the question with several possible answers from which the children choose one to investigate.

2. Delay closing inquiry on any question until the children arrive at the answer as a guided group.

3. Provide opportunities for children to cope with the problem of organizing and integrating facts and ideas in a variety of expressive activities.

Understandably, overuse of any of the above can result in deadly, obvious routinization. The keynote is variety, not for sake of it, but in natural order when a procedure and device appear to be the most appropriate.

The thinking-emphasis strategy in its carefully contrived closed inquiries within a larger closed inquiry is less prone to routinization than the synthesized strategy, but it is to a certain extent subject to it. If every "big idea" and every subidea supporting it are always placed in issue in much the same way, the initial interest in inquiry as well as in the topic being treated deteriorates. To maintain high interest, the teacher utilizes the following procedures:

1. Constructs instructional models of various kinds rather than placing reliance on one or two types favored because of ease of construction or as a personal choice.

2. Alternates between offering wide choices and narrow choices when composing questions to be used for inviting hypotheses. Examples:

a. "Were the early difficulties between the settlers and the Indians due to the naturally warlike spirit of the Indians or to the failure of both groups of people to understand each other?" (Narrow; two choices—either this or that.)

b. "Were the Indians fair in their dealings with the early settlers?" (Narrow; three choices—either *yes* or *no,* or sometimes *yes* and sometimes *no.*)

c. "There are several opinions about why there were difficulties between the early settlers and the Indians. These include:

The two groups of people had widely different ways of living.

The Indians were naturally warlike and distrustful of other peoples.

The early settlers regarded land as private property, not as common property.

The settlers required more land than the Indians for their enterprises.

The Indians wanted the settlers' tools and weapons for their own use." (Narrow; five choices.)

d. "Why do you think that there were difficulties between the Indians and the early settlers?" (Wide; almost unlimited choices.)

e. "What do you suppose will happen when these European settlers begin to interact with Indians?" (Wide; almost unlimited choices.)

3. Varies the medium in which children express hypotheses by encouraging them to draw pictures, cartoons, diagrams, maps, charts, and the like, or having them dramatize or write brief creative stories, to state what they believe to be true.

4. Occasionally guides children into an open-inquiry sequence in the middle of a unit.

   The thinking-emphasis strategy, much the same as the synthesized strategy, may lose much of its appeal as far as children are concerned if allowed to degenerate into a series of routinized steps. Variety and ingenuity are required to maintain interest at a high level.

   The social-science strategy is the least prone to routinization of any of the strategies. Inquiry occurs within a variety of learning activities, and because it is open, there is no system of acts to be performed in a regular sequence. The sequence of logic, whatever it may be, shifts and darts in accord with the teacher's interpretation of what the children are learning and discovering and how he must respond to keep the inquiry open and moving. His concern is constant for children's interest in both learning itself and in what is being learned. This concern may be a weakness as well as a strength. The social-science strategist may need to ask himself these questions from time to time:

1. Were the discoveries during class today arrived at by the children? Or did I force the discoveries?

2. Were the discoveries commonly understood by most of the members of the class? Or was I preoccupied with the few who seem to share a kindred spirit with me in a love for ideas and working with them?

3. Were there moments when the children worked on their own in experimenting and demonstrating? Or was I always the experimenter and demonstrator, regardless of the number of opportunities that occurred in which children could have worked on their own?

These questions merely reflect that if inquiry is to be carefully teacher-fostered, as it is in the social-science strategy, the teacher needs to be wary of getting in his own way. If he does, children's interest dies and no inquiry really occurs.

A basic procedure for helping children to maintain interest in inquiry and the unit, regardless of strategy, is to introduce activities in which they come to appreciate applications of learnings already acquired. The following devices may be used:

1. Present a story, poem, picture, picture series, filmstrip, film, or news clipping that reflects facts and ideas already studied. Have the children examine critically whatever is presented.
2. Point out to the children applications in other subject areas such as reading, science, or the like.
3. Encourage the children to seek applications within the community and in newspapers and magazines to present to and discuss with the rest of the class.
4. Invite the children to project themselves in roleplaying or creative expression in situations demanding applications of facts and ideas.

In summary, mid-unit inquiry, either open or closed, requires that the teacher constantly apply ingenuity in developing teaching-learning activities. Failure to do so results in children's loss of interest. When organizing a social-studies unit, the teacher makes provisions for a wide variety of teaching-learning activities.

INQUIRY PATTERNS IN BRINGING THE UNIT TO A CLOSE

As has been suggested in the previous chapter, social-studies units always close with a continuing open inquiry into the area in which concentrated study has just occurred. The formal aspect of this inquiry will be reflected primarily in the current-events program, for it is through this program that children continue to test and refine acquired ideas. The major differences among the various strategies lie in the procedures to be followed just prior to establishing conditions for a continuing open inquiry.

When the synthesized strategy is used, as shown in Teacher X's unit in Chapter 5 and as discussed in Chapter 7, the teacher culminates the unit by placing the "big idea" in issue with the children. After guiding them in reviewing, summarizing, and expressing the facts and ideas already acquired, he presents an instructional model (see Chapter 7) which brings the children to the point of hypothesizing. The children are encouraged to contribute any hypothesis which they deem reasonable. As each hypothesis is contributed, it is substantiated in terms of the learnings already acquired. The likelihood exists that only one hypothesis will be contributed, but through discussion it will be altered in accord with known facts and ideas. If more than one hypothesis is advanced, and one is vastly different from the other, the idea placed in issue before the children reaches a level of controversy. When this occurs, the children review their learning by reexamining their earlier findings, reconsulting resources, and investigating any new resources available. Inquiry draws to a narrow close when a hypothesis is accepted as tenable. The generalization or "big idea" has been reached. For study purposes, inquiry is reopened, and remains open thereafter, when the children are guided in verifying the "big idea" historically, geographically, or in current happenings. Further open inquiry is followed as the children explore for attitudes and patterns of action related to the "big idea."

The teacher using the social-science strategy has several choices open to him as he considers tactical measures to apply in closing the unit:

1. When he finds himself having to employ many interest-supporting activities, he may decide to allow the inquiry to cease and the unit to come to an end. The end is marked by the beginning of inquiry into a new idea and topical area. He assumes that learning has been acquired through intrinsic motivation, that each individual has integrated it to the extent that he is able, and that development of attitudes and patterns of action has occurred automatically as the "big idea" has been studied.
2. He may use any or all of the procedures used in the synthesized strategy. (The unit presented in Chapter 5 as prepared by Teacher Y reflects such a pattern.)
3. He may guide the children into an extended verification of the "big idea" studied. They may explore more widely in their local community, establish a communication lane with children in other countries, and seek more extensively for verifications in different eras and areas.

Whatever method the social-science strategist chooses, the choice is purely his to make. The justification for his choice, as for his choice of strategy, resides within his philosophy of teaching-learning and such rationale as he can abstract from it.

When using the thinking-emphasis strategy, the teacher culminates the study of the unit by having the children reexamine the original hypothesis or hypotheses made at the beginning of the unit when the "big idea" was placed in issue. Reexamination is characterized by a review, summarization, and expression of the facts and ideas studied, and another look at the instructional model used at the beginning of the unit. The close of the unit proceeds from this point in much the same way as it does in the synthesized strategy.

In short, units taught within the synthesized strategy or thinking strategy are brought to a close in much the same method. Both strategies use closed inquiry, then guide toward open inquiry. The same procedure may be used within the social-science strategy, although several other choices are available.

GUIDING CHILDREN IN TYING FACTS
AND IDEAS TOGETHER

In the discussion above, several basic acts necessary to closing inquiry were mentioned. These acts included summarizing, expressing, arriving at a generalization, relating attitudes and patterns of action to it, and verifying it. Each represents a tying together of ideas.

These acts may be organized in a chronological order of occurrence as procedures in bringing inquiry to a close. A certain rigidity prevails in this order in that summarization must precede arriving at the generalization, and the generalization must be arrived at before it can be verified, or before attitudes and patterns of action can be related to it. Some flexibility is possible. Expressing may occur almost any time within the sequence. Verifying the generalization may precede or follow the development of ideas about attitudes and patterns of action, and the development of ideas about attitudes may precede or follow that dealing with patterns of action.

The acts may also be regarded as existing at different levels of difficulty in terms of intellectual effort. At the easier level are expressing (if adequate control of the expressive medium is assumed) and summarizing. The latter requires a selection of the essential facts and ideas to develop an abridgement, abstract, or digest of ideas. Next in order of difficulty are those acts requiring the tying together of the generalization to ideas about attitudes and patterns of action and those acts performed in verifying the generalization. Most difficult of all is arriving at the generalization.

In guiding children in performing these acts, the teacher brings the children to the threshold of performance. Through the presentation of materials and verbal clues, he suggests the act to be performed. As the children respond, he serves as a guide, suggesting that certain clues be included, that they may have to be restructured, that interpretation may need to follow a certain line, and the like. This role is a function of the teacher's alertness, his ingenuity, and his respect for and understanding of children; therefore, not much information of a sequential, procedural nature can be offered as a guide to teaching. However, definite procedures may be utilized in bringing children to the point of summarizing, arriving at a generalization, and so forth. The remainder of the chapter will be devoted largely to these procedures.

PREPARING CHILDREN TO SUMMARIZE

Chapter 11 presents procedures for introducing children to the summary as a specific communicative form and for guiding them in learning the skills involved. For purposes of discussion, it is assumed that children are acquainted with this idea of summary and these skills. Our concern is for the procedures and practices necessary to bring children to the threshold of summarizing.

Children's success in the act of summarization rests on the fulfillment of two conditions. The first condition is that the facts be well acquired; the second is that a device be available to facilitate the recall of facts. Frequently both conditions are fulfilled through the use of the pupils' expressive products which, if carefully made, are a measure of contact with facts and ideas and how well they have been acquired. Devices other than expressive products are also frequently used.

A device favored by teachers using the synthesized strategy is directed toward the implementation of the fact of summarization itself. This device is a review of the daily log. A daily log is usually a record of what has occurred during the social-studies period for a particular day. It may include any or all of the following: (1) a list of the purposes for investigation; (2) the results of investigation; and (3) a list of the activities performed, particularly those having to do with group or committee work. This log is usually made at the close of the period, or it may be kept throughout the period. Frequently the log for the previous day is the point of departure for the day's work. The teacher maintains a file of the logs, and when the time for summarization arrives, he displays them about the room or presents them in chronological order. Perhaps the greatest advantage gained from log keeping is that it provides for a series of daily records for future reference, and thus it facilitates summarization.

Since summarization is such an important level of work in tying ideas together, some teachers feel that it is essential always to guide their pupils in maintaining logs. This practice is questionable, especially when writing the log marks the close of the social-studies period every day. The procedure becomes so reliably predictable that most of the pupils of the class come to regard it as a boring task and one easy to avoid. Log keeping as a daily activity is also of questionable value when it dominates the program. So much time must always be devoted to it that other worthwhile activities have to be omitted. Actually, when log keeping dominates the social-studies program, the basic emphasis of the program is learning how to keep records, and learning in social studies becomes secondary.

If it is really desirable to keep a log, perhaps the best practice to follow is to guide children into regarding the log as a device to help them remember the important facts and ideas studied. Log keeping does not occur every day, but when the facts merit it.

Another device favored by some teachers is the review of individually written summaries. Such summaries are really little more than individually kept logs, sometimes written at the close of the period or after a structure of facts has been studied. Such summaries present many of the same advantages and disadvantages as the log. A particular advantage is that responsibility for summarization is shifted from the group to the individual. If individually written summaries are to be reviewed as a device for developing a general class summary, it is the teacher's responsibility to check to see that everyone has accurate summaries for all the facts studied.

Like log keeping, summary writing should not be used as a teaching "crutch" to maintain continuity of the social-studies program.

The review of expressive products has been found to be a successful device for helping primary and slower children to summarize. The children perform expressive activities before the moment of summarization. This order makes little difference as far as learning is concerned. The children analyze all the expressive products, or a representative number of them, to help them recall the important facts and ideas learned.

Teachers of older or brighter children may use a similar device.

Pupils are referred to the notes they have taken and the reports they have written to develop the class summary. The review of products as a means of bringing facts and ideas to mind for the development of a summary is a useful device at any grade level.

If the teacher has been using a thinking-emphasis strategy throughout his teaching of a unit, he has available a device which can prove most useful in helping children to recall facts and ideas for a summary. This device is a review of the hypothesis elicited from the pupils at the beginning of the unit itself or at the beginning of study of an area of content. The point of summarization is clear, for it centers on the hypothesis. The summarization becomes a subtle act, something less than a formal step in instruction, because it becomes instrumental in the check and perhaps in the restatement of a hypothesis. Some review of expressive products may be necessary. Usually the act of generalization is immediate.

When guiding pupils in the act of summarization, some teachers find it helpful to have individual pupils express statements as they recall them. The statements are listed on the chalkboard or on a large chart. When all the statements have been elicited, the teacher has the pupils, as a class group, analyze the list for accuracy of order and statement.

Once the children have completed the act of summarization, they have a manageable abridgement, abstract, or digest of facts and ideas. Almost at a glance they can perceive the whole complex of what they have studied. It becomes possible to examine and interpret facts and ideas further and, most important of all, arrive at the generalization.

PREPARING CHILDREN FOR ARRIVING
AT THE GENERALIZATION

The completion of the task of summarization stands as one aspect of preparedness for arriving at the generalization. However, something more will need to be done to bring the children to the moment of synthesizing to discover the generalization. Some guideposts for thinking have to be provided.

The teacher using the synthesized strategy and the social-science strategist use an instructional model as a device for providing guideposts for thinking. The model, since it is in effect an incomplete statement of the generalization, serves as a means of helping children to identify critical elements to be tied together in some way. For example a first-grade teacher who has guided his children through a careful study of policemen, firemen, and trash collectors may present a large picture as a model to guide toward this generalization: *Our community hires policemen, firemen, and trash collectors to help make our lives safe.* The picture shows a group of city employees including policemen, firemen, and trash collectors receiving their checks at the pay window in the city hall. Uniforms and mode of dress make the various persons easily identifiable. After a brief discussion of what these people do and why they receive their pay in the city hall (facts and ideas come tumbling forth because of a recent summarization), the teacher guides the children toward the generalization by asking, "What are these policemen, firemen, and trash collectors being paid for?" From this moment onward the model serves as a focal point around which discussion and thinking take place. Responses may range from general ideas such as "For what they do," "For their work," to "Policeman are paid for doing thus and so . . . ." The teacher guides the children by giving another clue: "Suppose that we did not pay our taxes and our city government could not hire these workers. What do you think would happen to us then?" Eventually the generalization is arrived at, not as a random or desperate guess, but as a result of working with facts and ideas. As responses indicate that the direction toward the generalization has been set, each response is carefully deliberated and substantiated.

For the thinking-emphasis strategist, summarization and arriving at the generalization may occur in close conjunction. As was pointed out in the previous section, he may present the children's original hypothesis as the device to focus attention on what is to be summarized and the act of summarization itself. He may reintroduce the instructional model as an aid in helping children to recall their hypothesis. The moment at which summarization is completed is also the moment of arriving at the generalization. The nature of the act of summarization into which the thinking-emphasis strategist guides his pupils is quite different from that into which children are guided within the synthesized strategy and the social-science strategy.

The difference may be clarified through examining the general clue-questions with which the teachers guide the children in summarizing. Teachers in the synthesized and social-science strategies would tend to use the following:

What are the essential facts and ideas?

What are the facts and what are the ideas?
Which facts go with each idea?
What should the order of the facts be after each idea?
What should be the order of the ideas?

The thinking-emphasis strategist asks the following:

Is our hypothesis true or untrue? OR
Which of our hypotheses is accurate?
What makes you think so?

The children respond in accord with the desire to substantiate a point of view. Facts and ideas are contributed as substantiations. And when the hypothesis is substantiated, and changed if necessary, the generalization has been reached.

In effect, the thinking-emphasis strategist is actually guiding children in summarizing and generalizing at the same time.

PREPARING CHILDREN FOR EXPRESSIVE ACTIVITY

Expressive activity always requires some knowledge of the medium to be used. Some activities, such as the more directly projective activities (spontaneous dramatics, for example), require little formal knowledge; others, such as report writing, require considerable knowledge. The point for the social-studies teacher to remember is that children should not be guided into expressive activities requiring skill in a medium before they have acquired the necessary skills. Chapter 11 presents procedures and practices used in assuring that children have these skills.

The elementary-education program should make provisions for teaching expression in the various media, and the teacher should utilize this program fully to assure his pupils of a variety of ways for expressing themselves. Then he needs to do no more than to guide the children in generalizing their skills to various purposes, such as expressing ideas in social studies. This procedure is one he can follow to help his pupils in their task of tying ideas together through expressive activity.

Another way he can help his pupils is by checking carefully their ability in the medium preferable for use in tying ideas together. Checking should be done during the period preceding the one in which ideas will be tied together. If he checks their ability, and finds that it is lacking, he should take the time to teach the necessary skills.

It is also essential that the teacher establish with the children the latitude of creativity to prevail during expressive activity. The latitude depends on how the teacher presents the expressive task to the children. The greater the number of limitations, the more restricted the latitude for creativity. The latitude is narrow, with both medium and content limited, if the teacher states: *We shall use this medium to express this idea or complex of ideas.* The latitude is broadened through providing choices of either medium or content if he states: *Choose any idea, combination of ideas, or complex of ideas and express your choice in this medium,* or *Choose the medium you prefer to express this idea or complex of ideas.* He provides a wide latitude for creativity if his behavior is reflected in this statement: *Choose any idea, combination of ideas, or total complex of ideas and use any medium to express it.*

No hard-and-fast rule determines how great the latitude should be. The teacher makes a decision in keeping with the needs and abilities of his pupils as he interprets them. If he is going to restrict content, expressive activity is preceded by a class discussion of relevant content. Often a completed summary gives direction to this discussion. If no summary has been developed, a discussion somewhat similar to but less rigid than formal summarization occurs. If he is going to restrict the medium to be used, the presence of the expressive materials announces the restriction. A review of the skills necessary for the adequate use of the medium may have to be conducted. If choices in medium are to be made, he guides the children in considering the possibilities inherent in each and encourages them to make a choice. Whatever the latitude, limitations of space will usually require that adequate provisions be made for the organization, distribution, collection, and storing of materials and tools. Review or organization of patterns of acceptable behavior may also be necessary for members of the class as they work to express themselves.

Expressive activity is felt to be a function of individuality, but practice in social-studies teaching in recent years supports much group expression. Such expression is justifiable, in that it helps children to learn how to plan and perform tasks together and it increases the number of expressive activities in which children may become involved. However, the teacher should exercise certain precautions before guiding his pupils into group expressive activities. He should assure himself that the social climate in the classroom will permit group activity in which the members of the group are not at all times under the direct supervision of the teacher. He should also make certain that his daily program will permit the use of large blocks of time. His classroom should be amenable to organization for the best use of space and for the establishment of work centers. He may need to plan for both individual and group activities at the same time. While some of the members of the class work at a group task, the others will be occupied at worthwhile independent tasks. He divides his time and effort between the two groups. Frequently individual interests emerge as the class moves from one aspect of study to another. Such interests may appear in the children who favor social studies or in those who have an interest related to the social-studies topic at hand. The teacher should make provisions for those individual pupils who show an interest in the entire topic or in some aspect of it. Such provisions usually include making materials easily available, scheduling times for individual conferences to check the accuracy of the work under way, and assuring recognition for individual work. Such recognition comes when the individual shares his work with others.

Preparing children for expressive activity involves the following: making certain that children have the necessary skills, establishing the latitude of creativity that will prevail, and following basic administrative and instructional procedures to assure that all children have sufficient physical and social freedom within which to work.

PREPARING CHILDREN TO INQUIRE INTO ATTITUDES

As the teacher guides his pupils into developing attitudes related to the generalization, he is guiding them into another area of inquiry in social studies. The task always involves the problem of bringing social-studies ideas into parallel with personal ideas about attitudes. The direction of inquiry always proceeds from recently acquired social-science ideas as a working base into the complex of feelings that the children already have as a result of life experience.

This transitional point in the pattern of inquiry begins in much the same way as closed inquiry, in that children are invited to hypothesize and to select a hypothesis as being the most tenable. From this point onward inquiry is open. Only a partial closure is made for the moment and future modification of closure, either narrowing or widening, is left to the individual learner, to be determined by his future accretions of knowledge and experience. From a humane and philosophical point of view, this state of affairs is usually desirable. Complete closure of inquiry represents indoctrination, which in most instances is undesirable.

As the teacher works with children in developing a hypothesis about attitudes, he is helping them to develop what amounts to the best possible guesses that can be made with the ideas and facts at hand. More ideas and facts later will bring change. The hypotheses, verbal or behavioral, are statements of value regulative of behavior within the individual who has it integrated within himself. The complex of ideas about attitudes listed in his unit is the guide which the teacher uses to determine the direction toward which he guides his pupils.

After the pupils have ended the direct study of the social-studies generalization, they are ready to begin their inquiry into attitudes. A good moment for the teacher to guide inquiry into attitudes is immediately after the evaluation of the major activity or series of activities that occurs at the close of the study of the generalization. Another good moment occurs immediately after a review of the instructional model that was used to build interest at the beginning of the unit. Either the evaluation of the major activity or the review of the instructional model anchors the objective content in the mind of the pupils.

The teacher may use any one of a number of teaching devices to stimulate inquiry, some no more sophisticated than a direct question such as "How should we feel about these people?" or "What do you feel about conserving the wildlife in our forests?" However, subtlety is usually more effective. Some teachers have enjoyed success with some of the following procedures.

A. The teacher pinpoints the need for dependence or interdependence inherent within the generalization, and then suggests that the need cannot be provided for. Examples:

1. A teacher in grade two has guided his pupils through a study of shoe-making to arrive at the generalization: *People working together are interdependent in the process of making shoes needed by everyone.* The children have expressed themselves by making a large bulletin-board flow chart which depicts the making of shoes from raw materials to the finished product. As the pupils study their product, the teacher asks, "And what do you suppose would happen if the men who run these machines (shoemaking) refused to do their work?" The teacher guides the discussion to the point at which the pupils understand that they themselves depend on the workers. They go on to discuss how they would feel about being such workers.

2. A teacher in grade four has guided his pupils through a study of the history of their state to arrive at the generalization: *Our state has a unique cultural history because various groups of people with different ways settled here for a variety of reasons and finally became a single people.* The children have expressed themselves by making a comparison chart of the various peoples who came to the state. The chart shows, among other things, the contributions made by each group. The teacher invites the pupils' attention to these contributions on the chart and asks: "Let us suppose that this group of people had not come to our state. Do you suppose that it would have made any difference in our lives today?" The teacher guides the discussion to the point at which the pupils realize that life today would be quite different if it had not been for the coming of a certain group of people to the area. They go on to discuss how they should feel toward these people.

B. The teacher guides the children into roleplaying as a means of surveying attitudes. After an initial "warmup" period in which the children play roles common to their everyday experience, the teacher presents a situation to a few children, encourages them to assume and play roles while the remainder of the class observes. All the pupils are guided into analyzing the attitudes displayed during the roleplaying. If differences arise, other children play the roles until there is fairly common agreement among the members of the class on the adequacy and appropriateness of a particular set of attitudes. Examples:

1. A teacher in grade six has guided his pupils through a study of Mexico to arrive at the generalization: *Hispanic culture influences the ways of living in Mexico.* The children have expressed themselves by painting a large mural consisting of four panels. Each panel expresses a theme about a different institution, including social kinship, biological kinship, religion, and education. After the pupils have carefully examined and discussed their product, the teacher presents this situation: "A Mexican boy of about your age has come to visit you on the first of May, and he plans to stay for about two weeks. Shortly after his arrival, you and he are sitting in the living room. Your father enters the room. The Mexican boy reacts in the same way that he would at home if his own father were to enter the room. Who would like to act out what the Mexican boy does? What the American boy does? What the father does?" The pupils play the roles, and arrive at an appreciation of Mexican familial practices. Other situations will include the Mexican boy's behavior on the morning of Cinco de Mayo (one of the important national holidays in Mexico), on Sunday morning, and when he visits an American elementary school.

2. A teacher in grade one has guided his pupils in the study of policemen to arrive at the generalization: *Policemen are hired by our community to protect us and our property.* The pupils have expressed themselves by constructing a small community on a large area of floor space. This small community has stores, a police station, "beats" for policemen, patrol cars, vacant lots, schools, and the like. After a teacher-pupil discussion about the many things the policemen do, the teacher presents this situation: "You and some of your friends are playing on this vacant lot. It is not a very safe place to play, because a building has just been torn down there, and there are many boards with nails sticking out of them. There are bits of sharp glass and wire lying about. But you and your friends begin to play there anyway. A policeman drives up in his patrol car. He gets out and comes over to where you are playing. What do you think is going to happen? What is the policeman going to say? What are you going to say? Who would like to be the policeman? The playing children?" The pupils play the roles, and arrive at greater respect for the policeman and his job. Other situations will include a lost child, a store robbery, and a traffic violation.

C. The teacher presents a situation in which some individuals have shown questionable attitudes. The situation may be made up for the occasion, well depicted in a film, shown in a picture, or drawn from a program from a television series. The children are guided into analyzing the situation for accuracy of attitude and are encouraged to justify their point of view. Through discussion of the situation, the pupils are guided into developing ways of feeling that agree with the facts and ideas that they have learned. Examples:

1. A teacher in grade three has guided his pupils in the study of Indians to arrive at the generalization: *Indians need food, shelter, clothing, and to be with other people.* The children have expressed themselves by developing a series of plays reflecting one day in the life of an Indian boy and girl in each of the major groups of Indians that once lived in the United States —the Woodland Indians, the Southeast Indians, the Plains Indians, the Northwest Indians, the Southwest Indians. After the pupils have performed their plays, the teacher guides them into a discussion of a recent television program in which a major force within the story was a strong dislike for Indians. The children discuss the feeling displayed in the program and suggest the attitudes that persons should have toward Indians, particularly since they are people who have the same needs as other people.

2. A teacher in grade five has guided his pupils in the study of the European emigration to America during the nineteenth century to arrive at the generalization: *National migration develops cultural diversity within a group and cultural diffusion among groups.* The children have expressed themselves by making a large wall map showing from where large numbers of immigrants came. A legend indicates some of the ideas these peoples brought with them. After the pupils have reviewed their map, the teacher reads them the story "A New Pioneer," by Dorothy Canfield. They analyze what Magda, the heroine of the story, brought with her to her new school and neighborhood, and what she learned as a result of her experience. The children conclude that newcomers from abroad should be welcomed for the richness that they bring.

   D. The teacher may present an open-minded situation in which the children supply the attitudes. The attitudes are listed as given. Then the children analyze the list to determine which attitudes are the most suitable within the ideas and facts they have. Examples:

1. A teacher in grade two has guided his pupils, in the study of communication, to arrive at the generalization: *When groups of people specialize in producing services in a community, the people of the community benefit from more and better services.* The children have expressed themselves by making a series of narrative charts showing the events involved in the sending of a letter, a telegram, and a telephone message. After the children have reviewed their charts, the teacher suggests that the children try to develop ways in which a single individual would attempt to assume the total responsibility for sending a message to another person. The pupils come to see that so much time would be lost and that so much effort would need to be expended. They arrive at the idea that living in a modern community is to be welcomed.

2. A teacher in grade eight has guided his pupils in the study of American history to arrive at the generalization: *Our nation has developed a private-enterprise economic system which contributes greatly to our high level of economic welfare.* The pupils have expressed themselves in a series of individual reports. The teacher presents a large bulletin board display showing the traditions of the private enterprise system and its basic factors. Among the factors are the citizens of tomorrow indicated by a largely printed "YOU" on the bulletin board. The pupils are guided toward considering their attitudes about the various factors in the private-enterprise system. They express the various attitudes that they hold about these

factors and attempt to arrive at a consensus about various attitudes expressed.

As the teacher works with pupils in developing attitudes, he must remember that the statement of attitudes and the agreement upon them needs to be flexible. As a teacher he cannot be insistent or adamant about one set of attitudes or another. He may close the study of attitudes by indicating directly that the attitudes derived during the period of inquiry are subject to some change. He may also suggest, particularly if local provincialism prevents the pupils from accepting certain positive attitudes, that all should exercise suspended judgment until further study and more experience points to a clearer delineation of attitudes.

Basically the development of attitudes requires that the teacher be certain that the pupils have the objective content ideas firmly in mind as a base from which to think and work. Then, using such subtlety and ingenuity as his teaching style permits, he guides his pupils toward developing favorable attitudes related to the objective-content ideas just acquired.

PREPARING CHILDREN FOR INQUIRING ABOUT
PATTERNS OF ACTION

Much of what has been presented about inquiring about attitudes in the previous section also pertains here. The same humane and philosophical assumptions prevail; similar kinds of ends are desired. Inquiry into patterns of action marks another transitional point from closed to open inquiry. However, there are some differences.

One difference is that the children have more ideas to work with. They have not only the social-studies generalization but ideas about attitudes as well. However, this difference does not much influence the ways of working in inquiry.

Another difference sometimes lies in the immediate testing of a selected hypothesis. For example, if the children have studied a significant generalization about conservation, it is quite possible for them to develop a pattern of action dealing with the conserving of goods or materials. They may organize a campaign to conserve school supplies in the classroom or food in the school cafeteria. After a relatively short time, the pupils can learn how effective their pattern of action is. Changes may be made in the pattern or a new pattern may be evolved. This procedure may continue until the children arrive at an effective pattern suitable to all. Much the same procedure may be used after the study of banking, the organization of government, or the organization of a procedure for the settlement of problems.

Whenever possible, the teacher should guide pupils in developing a pattern of action which actually can be tested. Testing cannot always be done; it depends on the nature of the generalization studied.

The ideas about patterns of action listed in the unit serve the teacher as a guide in planning teaching-learning activities.

After the pupils have made their inquiry into attitudes, they are directed into inquiry about a pattern of action. Some teachers find it easier to direct their pupils' effort into inquiry about attitudes and a pattern of action at the same time. When situations or roleplaying are used as a means of probing into attitudes, it is often difficult to prevent analysis from dealing with a pattern of behavior as well. Actions as well as feelings are displayed, and separation of the two may be difficult. Dealing with attitudes and a pattern of action at the same time may be more suitable for some objective-content ideas, or may be more amenable to a teacher's style of teaching. If either condition prevails, the teacher should feel free to deal with the development of both at the same time. It is recommended here that, for the sake of clarity and the logical extension of ideas, the teacher deal with each set of subjective ideas as separate, though related. A separate inquiry is made into each.

The teacher may use any of the suggestions offered for the development of attitudes. He may invite inquiry by asking a simple, direct question such as: "What should we do about this?" or "What are the kinds of things that we can do to show our understanding of this?" Subtler procedures are recommended, such as roleplaying or reacting to situations.

If the pattern of action is one that can be applied immediately, an excellent way of developing such a pattern is to offer the task to groups of children organized for that purpose. For example, if the object content has treated of government, the children may be offered the task of organizing a government for their classroom. After a period of small-group work, the children are brought together to discuss the ideas developed in the various groups.

In most instances when the pattern of action developed may not be applied directly or immediately, the pupils should be guided toward a projective expressive activity, such as producing a play, writing creative stories, making cartoons, making sketch stories of action, or developing stories to be told with the illustrative aid of flannel-board figures. The teacher guides them into the problem by suggesting a situation of conflict such as may arise between a traveler and a native, between a native and an immigrant, between persons who hold different opinions about prevailing conditions, or between persons caught in the whiplash of a significant current event. Often pictures from such magazines as *Life* and *Look,* news accounts, and television documentary programs listed in advance can be used with good effect in lending realism and currency to the situations involved. The teacher's approach always reflects this line of reasoning: In the light of what we know, what we feel, and what we have decided is the way to act, what should we do in this instance?

This projective activity requires the same preparation as an expressive activity. The problems must be carefully discussed. Some attention must be given to the medium through which the projective activity is to occur. When the projective activity is through written language, the teacher will need to help younger or slower children with their difficulties in spelling and composition.

The following are some examples of the guidance given pupils to stimulate them toward projective activity:

a. The children in first grade have just completed their study of the supermarket. They know the work involved in running a supermarket, they appreciate the service that it provides the community, and they have developed a pattern of action to follow when they are in the supermarket. The teacher shows an amusing picture of a pudgy boy sitting in the midst of what was apparently once a display of canned goods. The children are guided into analyzing the picture in terms of the kind of boy he is and the appropriateness of his behavior. They are encouraged to invent a name for the boy and to tell his story as they imagine it. The teacher may serve as the secretary for the group in writing a story or may have the individual pupils prepare narrative sketches of the story as each one sees it.

b. The children in the fourth grade have just completed their study of Japan. They have learned about the culture of Japan, including family structure, social kinship practices, education, religion, and recreation. They appreciate the similarities and differences between Japanese culture and American culture. They have developed a pattern of action related to Japanese people as human beings. The teacher relates a story about an American boy who visits a Japanese family for the first time. The boy's behavior is appropriate at times; at other times it is questionable. After the pupils have analyzed the story, the teacher guides them in creative dramatic activity in which a similar situation is developed.

c. The children in the sixth grade have just completed their study of

Mexico. They have learned about economic conditions in Mexico and the status of Mexico as a world producer of goods; they have sympathy for the large number of poverty-stricken people in Mexico and respect the nation for what it contributes to the world market; they have developed a pattern of action which Americans could follow to improve economic conditions in Mexico. The teacher presents some pictures showing members of the Peace Corps at work in a Latin American country, and then suggests that each of the children consider himself to be the child of a technical assistant who has been sent to Mexico to help the farmers improve their agricultural practices. Each is to imagine that he meets the child of a Mexican farmer who resents the presence of the technical assistant. Individual stories are written about this problem and its solution.

d. The children in the seventh grade have just completed their study of the culture of America as influenced by the large number of immigrants who came to the United States during the nineteenth and early twentieth centuries. The children are well-acquainted with the pattern of motivation that brought so many people to America. They appreciate the diversity that these people brought to American culture. They have developed a pattern of action to follow when interacting with immigrants. The teacher has the pupils watch a documentary television program describing the establishing of quotas of persons to be admitted from the various European countries. After a class discussion of the program, the pupils are guided into preparing editorials which could appear in American or European newspapers.

e. The children in the eighth grade have just completed their study of the cultural geography of Europe. They know the natural resources of Europe and the different organizations of economy that exist in Europe, as well as some of the factors which contribute to the various organizations of economy. They appreciate the efforts made by some European countries to improve their level of economic welfare and sense what this means for the American economy. They have developed a pattern of action which they feel will benefit both Europeans and Americans if it were ever applied. Using a recent magazine article about the European Common Market as a base for discussion, the teacher guides the children in considering what would happen if the Common Market fell completely apart or became more firmly united. The children compose cartoons to reflect the feelings and actions of all involved. The results are discussed.

The teaching of patterns of action may occur at the same time as the teaching of attitudes with the use of similar procedures, or each may be taught separately using procedures that are nearly the same. The point of analysis makes the difference; the class analyzes for either attitudes or patterns of action, or for both. When the question is one of a pattern of action which can actually be applied and tested, group work is recommended as a means of developing the pattern to be used. If the pattern of action is one which cannot actually be applied, the pupils should be guided toward making application through projection into a creative activity. The teacher does not regard a pattern of action as something to be mastered; rather, it is something that will grow and change. Therefore, he does not insist that a particular pattern is the only correct one.

PREPARING CHILDREN FOR VERIFYING GENERALIZATIONS AND RELATED LEARNINGS

The verification of the generalization and other learnings marks the third point of transition from closed to open inquiry. Social scientists tend to regard all the generalizations which stand as the products of their study and thinking as tentative statements subject to further proof and modification. The social-studies teacher can do no less than guide children toward sensing that these generalizations, as well as related attitudes and patterns of action, are also subject to reexamination and change. In three areas he may bring the children to the threshold of verification of ideas—history, geography, and the here and now.

One way to verify ideas is to subject them to the test of history. The teacher guides his pupils in applying this simple criterion in question form: Has this idea just learned been true for all times? Applying the historical criterion is the test, applicable with many ideas at all levels of sophistication. For example, children in kindergarten who have just learned much about the family as an economic organization may be guided into examining family life in other times through the use of pictures or simple stories. Children in the eighth grade who have just completed a study of the development of democracy as a means of establishing a public authority in the United States may be guided toward looking at the development of Greek democracy in an attempt to strike a parallel. The application of the test of history guides children toward a true sense of history—a sense of the people, their lives, and their efforts in the past—and not just a gloss of sophistication which guarantees the "correct" response to such stimuli as 1066, 1215, 1492, or 1776.

Another way to verify ideas is to subject them to the test of geography. The teacher guides his pupils in applying this simple geographical criterion in question form: Does the idea just learned hold true in all places? This method of verification is also applicable to many ideas held within the various levels of ability among children. For example, children in first grade who have just learned the pattern of interdependency that exists between the community and the policemen that it hires may be guided toward examining the policeman in a Mexican community and a Congolese community to see whether the same pattern of interdependency exists. Again, pictures and simple stories can provide the contact areas within which investigation is made. Children in the fourth grade who have just completed formal study of the state in which they live may be guided into taking quick glimpses at other states to see whether a similar agricultural organization exists in other places. Seventh-grade children who have just studied the economic development of the United States could be encouraged to examine the economic development of Latin American countries. Applying the test of geography leads children to a more accurate idea of what geography is as a concept. More than maps and globes and topography and natural resources and romantic names, geography is people as seen here and there, a concept of space in use.

Perhaps the most important verification of ideas is accomplished through the test for current application. Its simple criterion is this: How reliable is this idea? What changes need to be made in it? With a few exceptions, this test is applicable to all social-studies ideas. The vehicles for content are the newspaper, the news magazine, the television and the radio, and the skills involved include reading, listening, and viewing. The application of this test lies at the heart of the news or current-affairs program which will be discussed in a later chapter.

AN EXAMPLE OF TYING IDEAS TOGETHER AT THE CLOSE OF A UNIT

The following illustrates the various levels of tying ideas together in a third-grade class toward the end of the school year:

A large bulletin board running along one side of the classroom contains children's pictures rendered in wax crayon and carefully written paragraphs on separate sheets of paper. A caption, written on a long strip of tagboard in large manuscript handwriting, reads: "Trees, from Plants to Useful Things." The pictures illustrate steps in logging, converting logs into useful products, and the uses of various products. Another bulletin board at the back of the classroom is a collage of pictures clipped from magazines and labels and small items manufactured from wood such as a pencil, swatches of rayon cloth, a plastic dish. A cryptic caption in the middle of the melange reads: "From Wood." This latter bulletin board has been fashioned largely by the children during their study, while the former is a teacher-made arrangement of children's products made during the study of the unit.

Mrs. Johnson, now in her third year of teaching third grade, guides her pupils in the day's work by saying, "As I promised yesterday, I have looked through your folders and have chosen from each one a picture or a paragraph that you made while we were studying about forests and logging. If you look carefully at the large bulletin board, you will find something of yours, either a picture or a paragraph. As you can see, all these pictures and paragraphs put together really tell the story of what we have been studying. Let's start with the first picture there in the left-hand corner. Whose is it? Carla?"

"It's mine. It's a forest with tall trees."

"And a very beautiful forest it is with all those yellows and greens. There is a paragraph partly covering it. Do any of you recognize that as yours? Pat? Will you go over to the bulletin board and read us your paragraph?"

"This is what I wrote: 'A forest is where many tall trees grow. Some of them are more than a hundred feet tall. There are many small trees, too. In the forest near us the biggest trees are Douglas firs, hemlocks, and cedars.'"

"Thank you, Pat. Now the picture just below Carla's. Who made it? Lee? Tell us something about it."

"Well, it's a Douglas fire. I have made it very tall because it is one of the tallest trees in our forest. You can see that the trunk is very long and the branches are high up."

"You've done such a good job that everyone can tell that it is a Douglas fir. And there is a paragraph that goes with it. Who wrote that? Frank? Will you please go over and read your paragraph to us?"

"The Douglas fir is a very big tree. Sometimes it is three hundred feet tall. That is higher than any building we have around here. It has cones. The cones have seeds in them. The trees grow from these seeds."

Working in this way, the children review the facts and ideas that they have been studying and expressing for the past five weeks. The names of workers, such as logger, "catskinner," high climber, forester, and ranger, are used meaningfully with such terms as undercut, backcut, slash, yarding, spar tree, sawtimber, arch, crosscut saw, chain saw, wedge, sledge, and second growth. The discussion in interlarded with references to "cats," climbing irons, slashers, loaders, jackladders, trimmers, circular saws, and planers. The industrial chain stretching from the forest through the sawmill and lumberyard and hardware store to buildings, furniture, and the like, is established as the children begin to examine the bulletin board at the back of the classroom.

"All through our study," reminds Mrs. Johnson, "we have been filling our back bulletin board with examples of useful things or products that come from the forest. Who would like to go back to that board and find three things made from forest trees? Henry?"

"Here is a picture of a floor in a house, and the boards that are put up on the inside of a wall—they sort of hold the rest of the wall, and here is some cloth. I can't remember the name of it."

"Several of your friends who know have their hands up. Would you like to call on one of them?"

"Keith."

"That's rayon."

"Of course, Keith would remember. He found out how wood is made into rayon and told us about it. Thank you, Keith, and thank you, Henry. Who would like to go to the board to find three more uses of wood? Sarah?"

"Here is paper. This is a plastic dish made from wood. And this piece of cellophane, too."

In this way the children examine the board fully. When the children complete this activity, they are prepared to do the thinking required to arrive at the generalization the facts and ideas of which they have been studying. Mrs. Johnson guides them toward arriving at the generalization by encouraging them to summarize their learnings. She directs their attention again to the large bulletin board along the side of the classroom and suggests the task by saying:

"Let's look again at the big bulletin board containing your pictures and paragraphs. The first part, which includes Carla's picture and Pat's paragraph and all the pictures and paragraphs underneath them express an idea that can be said in one sentence. What do you think it it? Steve?"

"Well, they're all about the forest and the kinds of trees that grow in it. I guess the idea is: The forest has many big trees."

"Thank you, Steve, let me write that idea on the chalkboard (pause). Do all of you agree with Steve? What do you think is the idea which the pictures and paragraphs are all about? Jeff?"

"I think that it says that the forest is a place where many big trees grow."

"I'll write that. (pause) What do the rest of you think? Do you think that that part of the bulletin board expresses one of these ideas or another. Keith?"

"Jeff's idea is a good one. It tells what a forest is. Steve's idea tells something about the forest."

"Steve, what do you think about that?"

"Jeff's idea sounds better, I think."

"Any other suggestions or ideas? Janet?"

"Jeff really says Steve's idea and a little bit more."

"That is true. Shall we use Jeff's idea? (pause) You seem to think that we should. I'll erase Steve's sentence. Look at the next set of pictures—Don's picture and Mary's paragraph, and all the pictures and paragraphs underneath them. What idea do they express? Sally?"

"The loggers cut the trees down?"

"That is a question, Sally. Is that what all the pictures and paragraphs say or are you making a guess?"

"The pictures show men cutting trees and that's what the paragraphs are about. Yes. The loggers cut down the trees. That's the idea."

"All right, Sally, I'll write it here beneath Jeff's sentence. (pause) Does anyone else think that the pictures and paragraphs express another idea? (pause) There seems to be no disagreement. Now take a look at the next set of pictures and paragraphs—Keith's picture and Tom's paragraph and all the pictures and paragraphs under them. What is the idea all these tell us? Sarah?"

In this way the summarization of ideas occurs. The bulletin board at the back of the classroom is included in the summarization of ideas which looks like this in its final form as recorded on the chalkboard:

The forest is a place where many big trees grow.
Loggers cut down the trees.
Workers load the logs on trucks or trains or put them together in rafts to be floated to the sawmill.
Workers in the sawmill change the logs into lumber or small pieces of wood.
Workers use lumber for building and making things.
Workers change wood chips into paper, cloth, or plastic.
We use many things made from wood.

The point of generalization has been reached. To aid the children in arriving at it, Mrs. Johnson introduces the instructional model used when the unit was begun and the hypotheses resulting from its presentation. The instruction model consists of four tools used by loggers—a crosscut saw, an ax, a sledge, and a wedge. The hypotheses, written on a tagboard chart, are:

We could not live very well without the men who use these tools.
If we lived in a forest, we could live very well without the men who use these tools.

After quickly helping the children to recall what had transpired on the opening day of the unit, Mrs. Johnson directs the children's attention to their original hypotheses by saying, "These are the ideas that we had as we began our unit. You remember that we decided that one of these ideas must be true, but we could not agree on which one. Do you suppose that we can decide now which of these ideas is true? Paul?

"I think that first idea is the right one."

"Why do you think that?"

"Well, the men who use those tools have to cut down the trees before the other workers do their jobs. And if they don't do their jobs, we don't get the things we need."

"Henry has something to say. What is it, Henry?"

"I still think that we could get the wood things that we need if we lived in a forest. We'd have to learn to use the tools ourselves. Then we could get the things we need."

"Keith, you have your hand up and so has Sally. First, you, then, Sally."

"Maybe that is true, but I don't think that we could make things like paper and plastic and cloth. They take chemicals and very special machines."

"Sally."

"If we really knew how to use those tools, maybe we could live very well in a forest, but it would take a lot of work. I don't think we'd have the time needed for other things like gathering or growing food."

"Do any of the rest of you have any ideas about this? Bert?"

"If we lived like people did in the old days, we would know how to use those tools, but today we don't. Today we use lots more things and we are used to them. We couldn't have them even if we lived in a forest and knew how to use the tools."

"What do you think about that, Carla?"

"I think Bert is right."

"I see that many of you are nodding your heads in agreement. Is there anyone who does not? (pause) It seems, then, our first idea on the chart is right. Let's think in another way for just a moment about the workers in the forest, in the sawmills, and in the factories. How do you think they would get along without us? Frank?"

"We buy the things that they make and the money we pay is used to pay them. Then they can buy the things they need."

The generalization was reached when one hypothesis was known to be accurate. Its meaning was extended by inviting the children to look at the facts and ideas from another point of view.

On the following day Mrs. Johnson sets the stage for expressive activity. A mural about sea life has been tacked over the large bulletin board at the side of the classroom, and a flow chart of sketches showing cotton from the seed to cloth covers much of the front chalkboard. A tape-recorder at the front of the room is ready for operation. Mrs. Johnson encourages the children to think about expressive activity by introducing expressive products in this way: "Last year the third grade class that my friend taught made some things after they had learned many things about sea life. I thought that perhaps you would like to do something similar to what they did. There is their mural over there. What do you think about it? Sally?"

"I like that. I think that it would be fun to make one."

"Bert?"

"We did one of those in second grade. It was kind of fun."

"Keith?"

"I think that I'd rather make a big chart like that on the front. It tells all about something."

"There is something else here. Perhaps it will give you an idea or two. Last year one of our fifth grades in this school did this. Listen."

Mrs. Johnson turns on the tape recorder. The voice of a narrator explains that many people came to the new world for several reasons and that the first play would tell one important reason. The audience is to listen to a conversation in a Pilgrim home in 1609. The rustle and bustle of several children trying to find a place near the microphone are heard. A moment of silence, then an exchange between young voices telling why they had left England and why they are so grateful to be in a place where they could worship as they pleased. After the first play, Mrs. Johnson turns off the recorder to say, "What do you think about something like that?" The decision is reached quickly. The class will develop a series of little plays and tape them.

After several days of work at developing dramatizations in groups and a final recording, Mrs. Johnson guides her pupils toward developing attitudes about the forest and workers in the forest. She begins the day's study by having them relate how they feel when they know they are going to the forest and when they arrive at the forest. This activity establishes the natural beauty of forests and its relaxing yet exhilarating effect on most persons. Then she suggests that forests can make people feel another way. After encouraging the children to listen to determine the feeling expressed, she reads the poem "What Do We Plant?" by Henry Abbey, an expression of gratitude for all that a tree can provide to fulfill human needs. To reinforce this attitude, she reads the poem "Trees," by Harry Behn, which expressed a somewhat similar theme. Then, she encourages the children to discuss what the world would be like without forests and trees. A positive note is again struck when she presents the children with the simple task of writing a sentence which expresses how they feel about trees. A class evaluation of the content of the sentences as they are read orally closes the period.

On the following day, Mrs. Johnson guides the children in their inquiry for attitudes toward the workers in the forest. After a review of what the workers in the forest do, she guides the children in developing pantomimed sequences of actions of the loggers at their work. The conditions are changed from hot days to cold days. The children sense the endurance and strength that is required for such work and quickly develop respect and admiration for such workers. A review of the summary prepared on tagboard underscores the necessity for such workers to provide things needed for everyday living. At the close of the period Mrs. Johnson encourages the children to look through the newspaper in the evening to find items about the forest and forest workers.

The next day she encourages the children to report on the items that they have brought, only to discover that at the moment there are no items available. She uses this situation to have children consider when forests and forest workers are most likely to be in the news. This brings the topic of forest fires to the fore. She reads several news clippings about forest fires that had taken place during the previous autumn. As she guides the children toward thinking about fire-prevention in the forest, they respond with information gleaned from posters and television, particularly as it relates to the recommendations of Smokey, the fire-prevention bear. At this point the children are encouraged to roleplay a family planning to have a campfire in the forest. In one instance, the family is in a forest in which a permit is required; in another instance, there is no permit required. The highlights of each roleplaying are the selections of the place to build the fire and extinguishing the fire after it is used. The period closes with the making of simple posters bearing information on correct behavior in the forest to prevent forest fires.

Mrs. Johnson again encourages the children to look in the newspaper for items about the forest and workers in the forest. She prepares a bulletin board with the caption "Forests in the News," to serve as a reminder. In the days that follow, news clippings are brought to school, discussed, and posted on the bulletin board. From time to time Mrs. Johnson reports on magazine articles about the forest. In this way the unit dealing with forest and logging remains alive for a long period during the school year.

In the foregoing description, the tying together of ideas is a series of acts—summarizing and synthesizing ideas, expressing ideas, relating ideas to attitudes and patterns of behavior, and verifying ideas. All of these acts are necessary for complete learning in social studies. Devoting several days, perhaps as much as several weeks, to these acts is thus easily justifiable.

SUMMARY

Guiding children in mid-unit inquiry usually presents the social-studies teacher with the problem of helping children to maintain interest in inquiry as well as in the topic being studied.

The teacher using the synthesized strategy or the thinking-emphasis strategy supports children in maintaining interest by assuring that they have the skills they need to perform investigative and expressive tasks and that they participate as directly and fully as possible.

The teacher using the synthesized strategy needs to vary his approaches to daily learning activities to assure a high level of interest.

The thinking-emphasis strategist makes careful use of ingenuity in constructing instructional models and presenting them to help children maintain interest.

The social-science strategist may need to examine his practices from time to time to assure that his self-intrusions do not destroy interest.

Regardless of strategy, teachers can help children to maintain interest by guiding them into activities which help them to appreciate what they have learned.

Bringing the unit to a close involves introducing a closed inquiry (within the synthesized strategy and perhaps within the social-science strategy). The social-science strategist may reject closed inquiry for terminating a unit.

Closing a unit, particularly within the synthesized and thinking-emphasis strategy, includes activities in which children tie ideas together. These activities include summarizing, expressing, arriving at a generalization, relating it to attitudes and a pattern of action, and verifying it. In guiding children in performing these acts the teacher brings them to the threshold of performance by preparing them. He sets the stage to make the acts possible.

Summarization requires that provisions be made for children to recall learnings and that children have the necessary skills.

Expressive activity requires that the children have skills in the use of various media, that they know the latitude of creativity, and that they have sufficient physical and social freedom to work.

If children are to arrive at a generalization, provisions for stimulating and directing thought must be made.

Developing attitudes and patterns of action and verifying generalizations and related learnings are the transition points from closed inquiry to open inquiry. The teacher guides the children toward partial closure of inquiry and then leaves it open for future change as a result of further knowledge and experience on the part of each learner. This occurs through life.

Guiding children in the development of attitudes and patterns of action is largely a matter of having children explore these through projective devices. Depending on the content of the generalization, children may be guided into testing a selected pattern of action. It is recommended that this be done whenever warranted.

Verification of the generalization and learnings related to it occurs in three areas of exploration—historical, geographical, and current.

Exercises for Further Understanding

1. To prove the value of tying ideas together, try this experiment on yourself. Select a nation that interests you. Then read carefully about this nation in an almanac. After several days sit down and try to jot down the facts and ideas that you remember from reading. Select another nation of interest to you. Read about it in an almanac, then make a crude map of it. Label the map profusely, then put it aside for a few days. Then, without referring to your map, write down as many facts as you can remember. Compare the results with your earlier attempt to recall facts and ideas.

2. Arrange to visit an elementary classroom on a "review" day or when the teacher begins to bring a unit to a close. This may involve a conference with the teacher to explore the possibilities of your being informed when either of these events is to occur. Observe carefully for the following:

    (a) What provisions has the teacher made for pupils' recall of facts and ideas?

    (b) How does the teacher guide the pupils through the act of summarization? Are facts drawn together into ideas? Are ideas synthesized into ideas of greater significance?

    (c) At what level of tying facts and ideas together does the day's work end?

3. Arrange to visit an elementary classroom while the usual work of gathering information is in progress. Be particularly attentive toward the close of the lesson to see how the teacher guides the pupils in wrapping up the day's work.

4. The following is a generalization reflecting an attitude or set of attitudes.

We appreciate the many services provided us by our city government.

Using the suggestions given in this chapter, develop four different approaches for guiding children in their inquiry for the attitudes inherent in the generalization.

5. The following is a generalization reflecting a pattern of action.

We do those things which will assure us an efficient, honest city government.

Using the suggestions given in this chapter develop several different approaches for guiding children in their inquiry for the patterns of action implicit in the generalization.

6. Select a generalization from among those presented in Chapter 4. Think through the kinds of facts and ideas that the children have studied as well as the attitudes and pattern of action that may have resulted from inquiry. Then develop a brief list of projective activities into which you guide children who had completely studied the generalization.

7. This chapter concludes the basic aspects of unit construction. At this time you should review the units presented in Chapter 5, select a generalization within a topic area suitable and prescribed for a grade which you intend to teach, and begin the construction of a unit.

Selected References

Aschner, M. J. McCue, "Asking Questions to Trigger Thinking," in Byron G. Massialas and Andreas M. Kazamias, eds., *Crucial Issues in the Teaching of Social Studies,* Englewood Cliffs, N. J.: Prentice-Hall, Inc., 1964.

Ausubel, David P., *The Psychology of Meaningful Verbal Learning,* Chap. 7, "Learning by Discovery." New York: Grune and Stratton, Inc., 1963.

Blair, Glenn Byers, R. Stewart Jones, and Ray H. Simpson, *Educational Psychology,* 2d ed., Chap. 8, "Interests and Attitudes." New York: The MacMillan Company, 1962.

Burton, William H., Roland B. Kimball, and Richard L. Wing, *Education for Effective Thinking,* Chap. 18, "Teaching for Thinking: Social Studies." New York: Appleton-Century-Crofts, Inc., 1960.

Chesler, Mark, and Robert Fox, *Role-Playing Methods in the Classroom.* Chicago: Science Research Associates, Inc., 1966.

Crow, Lester D., and Alice Crow, *Educational Psychology,* Chap. 13, "Attitudes, Interests, and Motivation." New York: American Book Company, 1963.

Dewey, John, *Democracy and Education,* Chap. 11, "Experience and Thinking;" and Chap. 12, "Thinking in Education." New York: The Macmillan Company, 1916.

Dressel, Paul L., and Lewis B. Mayhew, *Critical Thinking in Social Science.* Dubuque, Iowa: William C. Brown Company, 1954.

Dunfee, Maxine, and Helen Sagl, *Social Studies through Problem Solving,* Chap. 11, "Culminating an Area of Learning." New York: Holt, Rinehart and Winston, Inc., 1966.

Hullfish, H. Gordon, and Philip G. Smith, *Reflective Thinking: The Method of Education.* New York: Dodd, Mead & Company, 1961.

Jones, Samuel H., "Generalizing in the Social Science Classroom." *Social Education,* 21:358-362 (December 1957).

Kranyik, Robert D., "The Elementary Classroom as a Human Relations Laboratory." *Social Studies,* 57:16-21 (January 1966).

Muessig, Raymond H., "Attitudes Formation—Its Nature, Complexity, and Its Importance to Education in a Space Age," in John Jarolimek and Huber M. Walsh, eds., *Readings for Social Studies in Elementary Education.* New York: The Macmillan Company, 1965.

National Society for the Study of Education, *The Integration of Educational Experiences,* Nelson B. Henry, ed. Fifty-seventh Yearbook of the N.S.S.E., Chicago: The University of Chicago Press, 1958.

Otto, Henry J., *Social Education in Elementary Schools,* Chap. 11, "Learning Procedures in Social Contexts;" and Chap. 12, "Learning in the Social Studies." New York: Rinehart & Company, Inc., 1956.

Russell, David H., *Children's Thinking,* Chap. 8, "Concept Formation;" Chap. 9, "Problem Solving;" and Chap. 10, "Critical Thinking." Boston: Ginn and Company, 1956.

9

Improving Immediate- and
Intermediate-Contact
Investigative Skills

In Chapters 7 and 8, our concern was with inquiry and its uses in teaching social studies. Chapters 9 and 10 discuss the practices and procedures necessary to improve children's ability in selected investigative skills supportive of inquiry.

Children are guided into making contact with physical and social aspects of reality. Open and closed inquiry devices offer the immediate purposes for making this contact. The richness of the contact depends upon the clarity of the purposes, the extent to which the children accept them, and the nature of the contact itself. Throughout this chapter we shall be preoccupied with the latter.

Contact may be categorized roughly in terms of the distance between the learner or investigator and the area of study. Immediate contact occurs when he is situated next to or within processes and products in actuality. Intermediate contact involves an intermediary person who mediates between the investigator and the area being explored. The intermediary person, usually known as a resource person, is one who is an expert in the area under scrutiny. Distant contact occurs when the investigator explores an area by examining symbolic representations of it. The distance factors include actual distance in time and space, the level of complexity of symbolic representation, and the ability of the investigator to abstract meaning from symbolic representations.

The difficulties in guiding children in making effective distant contact require a separate chapter (Chapter 10) for adequate discussion on how to improve children's skills. This chapter will be devoted to ways of helping children improve in making immediate and intermediate contact with physical and social reality for investigative purposes. For the moment let us examine briefly some of the investigative skills generally applied by students of problems.

An oceanographer, a scientist and student of the problems having to do with ocean life and its uses, must apply certain investigative skills for acquiring information. He may study the entire ocean as a universe which he explores with a specially equipped ship. In order to peer beneath the surface he may need diving gear of one kind or another, or he may use cameras, viewing devices, or sensitive instruments. Whatever his equipment, he will be knowledgeable in its use, make penetrating observations, and record his observations as accurately as he can. Perhaps the oceanographer will study a part of the ocean as a universe abstracted from the whole ocean. With meticulous care he will prepare tanks containing the specimens he wishes to examine closely in a live state. Gauges, thermometers, and the like aid him in maintaining the desired conditions and serve to provide him with precise data. His knowledge, his eyes, and his instruments assure him a sustained contact as he makes painstaking observations and records. The oceanographer may wish to make a preliminary investigation before he begins a projected investigation, or perhaps no equipment is available for him to use in making a direct exploration of the ocean; therefore, he makes a careful study of the reports of others. As a reader he must be able to interpret charts, diagrams, graphs, and maps of various kinds as well as printed passages devoted to description and explanation. An oceanographer may use any of these ways of investigating. His choice is limited by the nature of his problem and the availability of resources.

A sociologist, a social scientist and student of the problems dealing with the structure and functions of human groups, must also apply certain investigative skills for acquiring information. He may make a study of society in immediacy by visiting a city, town, or neighborhood. He observes the people as they go about their affairs, listens to them as they interact for various purposes, interviews individuals, makes notes of what he experiences, and finally examines his notes carefully to determine what he has found. Or the sociologist may wish to study a society within selected areas of opinions and actions. Perhaps he will interview selected subjects, or he will test them for aspects of personality. He may decide to send questionnaires to selected individuals who are representative of a particular population. He examines the results of his interviewing, testing, or polling to determine his findings. The sociologist may want to know about a society or a segment of a society which he cannot visit, or one whose members he cannot interview, test, or poll. In these instances, he must peruse the reports of others. He must be able to interpret figures of various sorts and to deal with printed passages which present procedures, findings, and conclusions. Like the oceanographer, his choice of mode of investigation and the skills to be used are limited by the nature of his problem and the availability of resources.

To a large extent both the teacher and the pupils in social studies are restricted in much the same way in their choice of mode of investigation and the skills to be used. The teacher in his role as the most knowledgeable person in the classroom must guide the pupils toward the most reasonable choice, but, from time to time, the pupils must be permitted freer rein in selecting and implementing a mode of investigation. This freedom should be given after the pupils have had much experience with the various modes of investigation. The freer rein is necessary to provide for the growth that will bring the pupils to the level of sophistication at which they can make independent investigations.

The task of helping children improve in investigative skills may be primarily a matter of developing and following a good social-studies program, or it may be a matter of developing and following two programs, one in social studies and another in a skill or complex of skills instrumental to investigation. Improving close-contact skills such as "doing" activities, viewing processes in action, or examining artifacts is primarily a function of the social-studies program. Improving intermediate-contact skills and distant-contact skills is generally a function of both programs.

IMPROVING IMMEDIATE-CONTACT
INVESTIGATIVE SKILLS

Immediate contact is that which places the learner within or immediately adjacent to the universe which he is to investigate. He becomes deeply involved when duplicating a process such as scrape weaving or bread baking. When viewing a process such as road building and clothing making in action, his involvement may not be so deep, but it is broadened as he perhaps momentarily assumes the various roles of the persons at work within the process. When he is encouraged to roleplay and when he is asked to examine products of the present and artifacts of the past, his involvement is complex, for he is trying to determine the roles of others which he is to interpret. Often the facts with which he must work are limited. The skills which he must use include action-analysis, critical observation, and analysis of objects. (See Figure 4.)

These skills consist of complexes of acts so variable from individual to individual and so psychologically intricate that they cannot be broken down easily into separate acts which occur in any predictable sequence. Usually they are not amenable to direct, sequential teaching. Improvement of these skills then procedes along lines other than drills on isolated acts and on combining the acts into usable skills to accomplish this purpose or that; rather, the improvement results from the use of skills in purposeful situations. They improve to the extent that they are used fruitfully, and fruitful use will always depend on how well the purposes for their use have been defined and on how well they are seen to work. Careful purpose-setting and purpose-checking are explicit in the effective use of such skills as action analysis, critical observation, and analysis of objects. However, each has its own particular requirements in the way that purposes are established and checked and in the way the skill is exercised.

Action analysis as an investigative skill almost always requires that the learner have some basic information before the skill can be applied. For example, children who are going to make soap as an investigative activity must have some ideas about the process before becoming involved with it.

The facts and ideas to be acquired through action-analysis tend generally to be those most accurately expressed in deeply internalized understandings and attitudes. Expression of such learnings in terms of words and other symbols fails to reflect precisely their nature and intensity. For example, children who work at the process of tanning a hide in pioneer fashion acquire insights into the time, effort, and unique sensations that accompany such a process. They experience a dimension of pioneer life that could not be acquired in any other way.

Frequently a teacher may guide his pupils into an action-analysis to clarify in their minds the events in a process. For example, at the close of a study of how a bill becomes a law, the teacher guides his pupils toward trying this process themselves with a school rule but using the same limitations stated within the Constitution. The process becomes

FIGURE 4.

FIRST GRADERS DEAL WITH DISTRIBUTION PROBLEMS THROUGH ROLEPLAYING.

more clear in two aspects: first, the events and sequence of events are more firmly established; second, as the pupils assume various roles, they come to appreciate the feelings and actions of persons ordinarily at work within the process of law making. The latter constitutes the added dimension.

Action-analysis may often be used to prompt further investigation. This use of the skill is most frequent in the primary grades in association with block work or with a continuing project. For example, children who are studying the city use their new learning each day in building a community of blocks. As they evaluate what they have done each day, they are guided into considering what new things they need to learn about; they establish a new aspect. During the evaluation period, they discover new aspects to be included in the days that follow.

When roleplaying is used to determine a level of knowledge, it is also action-analysis. For example, a group of fifth-grade children could be guided into playing the roles of miners during the Gold Rush. In their roleplaying, they reflect what life must have been like in those days while the rest of the class watches their performance and finally evaluates the accuracy of their presentation. They make further investigations to verify their findings.

Whatever learning is to occur as a result of action-analysis depends on the point for analysis established before the action or "doing" takes place, or upon its completion. In most instances, learning is most effective when the point for analysis is established at the close of action. To follow the latter procedure is to encourage contribution of more facts and ideas to the action being performed. If, for example, children were to explore the roles of a father in a family, and the roleplaying was preceded by detailed discussion, the children would be likely to reflect only the content of the discussion. A freer contribution of facts and ideas tends to ensue when the discussion is brief and general and the point for analysis is delayed until after extensive roleplaying has taken place.

Critical observation as an investigative skill requires that the learner be placed at a point from which he can observe a process as it works. The use of this skill usually requires a field trip. In most school districts the administrative procedures for taking children on field trips are well established. A list of places approved for field trips will be maintained in the school or district offices. The teacher chooses from this list, files an application for the trip, and waits for approval. When approval is granted, the teacher knows that on a specified date a bus will be available to transport the children. All he needs to do is to send a pupil-release form home with his pupils to be signed by their parents and have his pupils prepared for the field trip on the specified day.

In some schools or districts only limited help is given the teacher. A list of places approved for field trips will be provided. After the teacher makes his choice, he must make the arrangements for transportation himself. Perhaps he will contact parents who would be willing to use family automobiles to help in transporting pupils. If a public conveyance is to be used, he may have to ask parents to provide money for fares.

Sometimes a teacher may wish to take his children to a new place. In this case, it is his responsibility to clear his intention with the principal and to make a preliminary visit to the destination for the field trip to obtain permission from persons in charge and to see what safety precautions need to be taken.

The procedures for arranging and taking field trips other than those on a list vary so much from one education system to another that it is always advisable for a teacher to check soon after he takes a position in the district to see exactly what provisions are made. Procedures to be followed when the teacher takes his class on a walking trip to a point near the school may be provided. Often such trips are very valuable and can be easily arranged.

The teacher himself is completely responsible for certain administrative procedures. It is his responsibility to see that his pupils understand what standards of behavior are to prevail during the trip. If the time set aside for the trip includes the noon hour, he must make certain that each child knows that he is to bring an appropriate lunch.

From an instructional point of view the effectiveness of the field trip as an aid to investigation will be determined by how well the teacher prepares the pupils to make critical observation. If information gathering is the basic purpose for taking the trip, the teacher guides the pupils in the development of general questions to be answered. Such questions reflect a "let's-find-out-about" attitude. Children visiting a supermarket may want to know the answers to these questions: Who are the workers in the supermarket? What does each worker do? If the children visit a men's clothing factory, they may want to investigate these questions: What are the steps in making a garment? What machines are used?

If the purpose for taking the field trip is to find a structure of information, the teacher guides the pupils in a review of the process as studied and encourages them to develop additional questions to clarify the process. Children studying the fire station may seek the answers to questions such as these:

1. How do firemen clean and dry hoses?
2. What happens if they receive an alarm when they are cleaning hoses?
3. How long does it take for a fire truck to be ready to go after an alarm has been received?

Whenever possible, children should be encouraged to feel free to ask questions arising during the visit.

Since memory is not always a reliable faculty, the teacher will need to make provisions for recording or having recorded what transpires during the observation period. In the primary grades the teacher takes notes. In the later grades the children take notes. Sometimes certain individual pupils assume the responsibility for taking notes that answer specific questions, or every pupil is responsible for taking his own notes. Note cards should be prepared before the trip. Extra cards may be provided for each pupil to take notes on facts of particular interest to him.

For the most effective learning, the teacher should guide the pupils in processing their information as soon after the observation period as possible. Ideally, the processing of information should occur near the point of observation. Such a practice help pupils to recall more accurately what has been observed and often assures a recheck of vague facts at the scene of observation. Usually a review of findings occurs as soon as the pupils return to school and become settled in their classroom.

Analysis of objects, or product analysis, as an investigative skill usually requires that the learner take a field trip to a depository of products or artifacts such as a museum, a trade fair at which the products of a country or a group of countries are displayed, a county or state fair, or any specifically arranged display of artifacts. The administrative procedures for such a field trip are similar to those already discussed. If the teacher can visit the display before the class makes the trip, he can make the venture much richer. Occasionally displays of artifacts are made available to classrooms by nearby museums. Since these displays are allowed to remain in a classroom for an extended period of time, they may be studied in detail, thereby enriching the study at hand.

The effectiveness of product analysis as a means of acquiring information depends on how well the teacher clarifies the purposes for examining the product or display of products. If the pupils are studying artifacts to gain basic insights into the ways of people past or present, the teacher guides the pupils toward investigating these ways. If pupils are studying a primitive African culture, they should be encouraged to ask questions such as these:

1. What kinds of tools do these people have?
2. How are these tools used? By whom?
3. How are the tools made?

If the pupils are studying American pioneer life, questions such as these help them to analyze more carefully:

1. How are the things used by pioneers different from what we use today?
2. What things were found in a pioneer home but are not to be found in ours today?
3. How were these things used to produce food and clothing?

If the pupils are to acquire a view of the economic structure of a nation through an examination of its products, questions related to structure should guide the analysis:

1. What products are produced in Japan for export?
2. Which products appear to be the most important?
3. What raw materials appear to be most available to Japanese industries?
4. What skills appear to be the most in demand by Japanese industry?

In some instances the pupils have already had an extended contact with the facts and ideas inherent in a particular historical or cultural unit and a deeper appreciation of ways of life is desired. For example, after studying a unit on American colonial life, the pupils may examine the artistic productions characteristic of the period, including such items as china, glassware, and metal objects of silver and pewter. In this case the teacher will need a knowledge of what makes these objects unique and how they reflect the spirit and values of the period. If the teacher lacks background and no expert is available to guide the pupils in their scrutiny of the objects, little is to be gained from examining them.

Occasionally, the study of a display of objects or artifacts may be used as a means of verifying what has just been studied from books and other materials available in schools. The display is studied to determine whether new ideas should be added to those already acquired. For example, pupils who have just completed the study of agriculture in their county may visit the county fair to see how well their facts parallel what is displayed. New information will be acquired and added and certain ideas will be changed.

When the pupils study an object or a display of objects there is usually little need for taking notes. If classroom study is involved, the extended presence of the objects helps pupils to retain their discoveries about the objects. If the pupils have taken a field trip, they may purchase informative materials for nominal cost at the display or may obtain free materials. Often guides or specialists are on duty at displays to answer questions and to explain materials.

Each of the investigative skills for immediate contact requires for its effective use a careful delineation of purposes and an assessment of information as soon as possible after the contact experience. Action-analysis as an investigative skill usually requires that the point of analysis follow the action that has just taken place. It should be noted that each of the investigative skills is limited in terms of the purposes for which it can be used. It should also be noted that immediate-contact investigations demand rigorous use of community resources.

IMPROVING INTERMEDIATE-CONTACT SKILLS

A resource person is defined as one who serves as an intermediary between the learner and the area of contact. Usually he lives in the community or is easily available and by his experience is better qualified than the teacher to talk about a topic or issue.

The intermediate-contact skills needed by pupils for acquiring facts and ideas are listening and listening combined with interrogation or interviewing. Improving the effectiveness of these skills involves developing purposes and ways of working with purposes, providing a rich area of contact, and developing listening and interviewing skills.

Developing purposes and ways of working with purposes for listening to and interviewing a resource person is determined by the role which he is to assume. Frequently the resource person assumes the role of a guest lecturer. Usually such a person will bring with him a collection of artifacts, pictures, photographic slides, or a motion-picture film with which to illustrate his presentation or to serve as the basis for it. In preparation for the guest lecturer's appearance, the teacher guides the pupils in reviewing what they already know to seek out vague areas. These vague areas are expressed in the form of questions which may be used in several ways. They may be submitted to the guest lecturer beforehand to help him select the facts and ideas that will be of greater interest to the pupils, used as references to special points to be listened for and reviewed after the resource person leaves, or used as the basis for an interview of the resource person after he has made his presentation. Most resource persons like to have questions asked about the topic or issue treated in their presentation, but some do not. It is advisable to learn the resource person's preference in this matter before he makes his visit.

The other role played by the resource person is that of consultant, a role in which he fully expects to be interviewed about a topic or issue. The teacher guides the pupils in preparing for the interview. They develop the questions to be asked, and the teacher informs the resource person about the questions. The class assigns the role of interviewer to one pupil or to several, in which case each interviewer is assigned a question to ask and pursue. In recent years more and more resource persons have been acting as consultants as the result of a new telephone development. An amplifier has been added to the telephone to make it possible for an audience to hear any conversation that occurs. In some schools a tape recorder is attached to the amplifier and the entire interview is taped for later study. This new telephone, called the Spokesman, makes it possible for busy people who ordinarily could not make a classroom visit to serve as resource persons.

Improving intermediate-contact investigative skills through providing a richer area of contact is accomplished in part through carefully selecting resource persons from the community and preparing them for each presentation. In part, it is accomplished through the teacher's deeper understanding of his role as a resource person. Selecting resource persons usually presents few problems for the teacher because most schools and districts maintain an approved list of suitable persons who have been successful in presenting facts and ideas to children. If these lists have been carefully maintained by an annual review of persons no longer available and new persons to be added to the list, they are most useful. If a teacher wishes to have an unlisted resource person, he should first clear the person with the administration, consult the person to assess his manner, language, and preparation, and then to try him in a classroom appearance or telephone interview. If the person serves well as resource person, the teacher should see to it that his name is added to the list.

Preparing the resource person for his contact with children should include some explanation of the children's background and what the class wishes to know.

Developing listening and interviewing skills for use with a resource person may be considered an area of emphasis in both the language-arts and the social-studies programs. Sometimes few provisions are made for these skills in the language-arts program, or the program may deal only with the general aspects of these skills. The social-studies teacher may have to introduce and teach these skills. More than likely, he will have to extend the skills in terms of specific uses in social studies.

The listening skills used when a resource person is presenting facts and ideas include establishing a purpose, remaining "tuned in" during the presentation, selecting pertinent data, and retaining the data for use. The first of these skills is essentially a function of the social-studies program. The second, third, and fourth may be treated in a direct manner.

Remaining "tuned in" is a skill which usually has its beginnings in the kindergarten where the children learn the overt behavior of a good listener. A few simple standards, consistently discussed, and ample rewards of praise when standards are followed, help in the teaching of the skills. Such standards may be stated as simply as this:

> When a person is telling us important things
> we are polite to him,
> we look at him,
> we keep our hands and feet still,
> we speak to no one,
> and we listen carefully.

In kindergarten and the first grade, these standards may be represented pictorially on a chart, or the teacher may guide the pupils in a flannel-board sequence in which hands, feet, eyes, ears, and mouth have particular functions to perform during the act of listening.

In the later grades, once the purposes for listening have been established, the act of listening is taught as a matter of courtesy to both the speaker and the other listeners. Usually pupils have little difficulty remaining "tuned in" with a resource person because his appearance is a welcome novelty.

Selecting pertinent data while listening to a resource person is a skill amenable to improvement through concentrated practice. In the primary grades, the teacher may prepare short oral recitations, the first of no greater duration than fifteen or twenty seconds, during which the children listen for a fact or two. The children are alerted to the fact or facts to be listened for, listen to the entire recitation, and then relate the fact or facts. After the children have learned to listen for a fact or two, the recitations are lengthened and based on sets of related facts such as the steps in a process, a role that someone plays, the use of a tool, what something is like, the reasons for some event or happening, the deeds of persons, and the like. In the later grades similar practices may be followed with more sophisticated recitations longer in duration. Older children should be guided to listen for an opinion and its related facts and to judge whether the opinion is well based or poorly based. Usually the skill of selecting pertinent data will need to be recalled before the resource person arrives or is contacted by telephone.

Retaining data from a resource person's presentation for future use is basically notetaking, a skill not amenable to formal practice in most of the elementary grades. Children's handwriting skills are not sufficiently developed for notetaking from an oral presentation until at least grade seven, and it is often advisable to delay teaching the skill until a later grade. However, all through the grades, teachers can do much to prepare children for learning the skill. In kindergarten and grade one the teacher can guide the children into a discussion about the presentation and arrange for an expressive activity immediately at the close of the resource person's talk. In grades two and three the teacher may guide the pupils in a class recall of the facts and ideas and the development of a record of what was learned. In grades four through six the teacher may have the children write individual summaries about the presentation or he may assign to certain children individual responsibilities for taking notes on specific questions. Simple note cards upon which the question to be answered is written and a space left for the note or notes required to answer it are prepared before the presentation. Later the children pool the results of their notetaking and share them with the rest of the class. In grades seven through nine the teacher introduces notetaking as a coverage skill. From his carefully prepared recitations the pupils learn how to select main ideas and supportive ideas and how to record them.

The effectiveness of listening skills will be improved through direct practice. The guarantee of the effectivenes of these skills is assured only when purposes are clearly defined and commonly accepted by the listeners.

The interviewing skills used to acquire information from a resource person include establishing a purpose, establishing rapport with the interviewee, pursuing a point, and retaining data for future use. As with listening skills, the purposes for interviewing skills are a function and product of the social-studies program. Skill at pursuing a point is also largely a function of the social-studies program in which the direction and extent of pursuit are determined. Establishing rapport and retaining data for future use are somewhat amenable to formal instruction.

Once the purposes for an interview have been determined through teacher-pupil interaction, the pupils are ready to structure the interview within the dimensions of purpose. If the dimensions of purpose are small, the dimensions of the interview will be small. Usually a small-dimension purpose is characterized by requiring only facts not readily obtainable from the available resources for its fulfillment. For example, some children in grade two could develop the following framework of questions about clothing making:

1. How many shirts can be made in a day?
2. How long does it take to make a shirt?
3. Where do the shirts go after they leave the factory?
4. How much does it cost to make a shirt?
5. How many different sizes of shirts are there?

The dimension of purpose is small because the children are prepared to ask questions requiring only a few facts.

A purpose of large dimension demands opinion supported by facts. Children in sixth grade studying about Latin America could develop the following:

1. Is the low level of technological development in many Latin American countries one cause for difficulties in government in many of the countries? What makes you think so?
2. Would you say that low technological development is the major cause? Why? (Why not?)

When the dimension of purpose is large, there is a need for pursuing a point—the point being an opinion to establish or clarify on the basis of as many facts as possible. When the dimension of purpose is small, the point is no more than factual answers to a few questions.

When it has been decided that a resource person is needed for obtaining information and the purposes have been generally defined, the teacher guides the pupils in structuring the interview. The questions to be asked and the order in which they will be asked are developed. Then the role of interviewer is assigned. Pupils selected by the class or the teacher may have the responsibility for asking a particular question, or the class may desire to maintain a more fluid interview by assuming that anyone may ask a question and that everyone will assume the responsibility for seeing to it that all the questions are answered.

If the purpose of the interview is of small dimension, the pupils should be alerted to the need for getting understandable answers to the questions developed. If the resource person does not mind, the pupils should be encouraged to ask questions about the terms that he uses. If the pupils are not to ask questions other than those developed precisely for the interview, the teacher will need to listen carefully for technical terms. At the close of the interview he may make a request such as this, "I'm not sure that all of us understand what you mean by————. Would you please tell us what it means?"

If the purpose of the interview is of large dimension, the questions should be arranged to encourage a train of thought leading to a conclusion, as exemplified in the following:

1. What are the characteristics of government in Brazil?
2. Is the government usually classified as a democracy?
3. Can everyone, rich or poor, man or woman, vote in Brazil?
4. What percentage of the eligible voters usually vote during a national election?
5. Do voting privileges and the way they are used have a direct effect on the government and its efficiency?
6. What, in your opinion, is the cause for recent instability in the Brazilian government?

If the children have already made hypotheses, the contact between the resource person and the pupils can be made much richer by having the class present its statements or hypotheses for the resource person's reaction. For example, a member of a class studying global geography could present a hypothesis in this way: "We think that the lines of economic interdependence between newly emerged nations in Africa and the industrial nations are about the same. Each country ships out its surplus and each receives what it needs. The people in both regions should be able to live without want. What do you think about that?" Such a statement begins an open-ended discussion between the members of the class and the resource person. If the resource person enjoys this kind of contact, the ensuing give-and-take results in deeper, more exciting learning. If this procedure is used, the teacher may need to have the pupils consider carefully the practices of courtesy which should prevail during such a discussion. Also it is likely that the teacher may have to serve as moderator from time to time during the interview.

Establishing rapport between the interviewer(s) and the interviewee may be regarded as building an "interviewing climate." This climate, basically, is nothing more than an exercise of courtesy. The teacher guides the pupils in making provisions for the introduction of the resource person to the class (which may include an outline of his background), in giving thought to ways of addressing the resource person, and in expressing thanks to the resource person for making himself available. During this aspect of preplanning with the pupils, the teacher is guided by the spirit, not the letter of courtesy. Cordial, sincere expressions stated simply are all that is required. Formality and exaggerated eloquence too often lend artificiality to the interview. Sometimes a brief run-through of courteous practices before the arrival of the resource person is helpful. In the primary grades, creating a pictorial chart or a simply written chart of interviewing standards with the pupils often helps them to contribute to the "interviewing climate." Much the same as any other skill, the skill of establishing rapport grows with carefully evaluated practice. The preplanning merely assures the success of that learning.

Much of the foregoing applies to establishing rapport with the resource person when he is being interviewed by telephone.

Making provisions for retaining information from an interview is similar to the procedures used to assure the retention of information from listening to a resource person's presentation. The difference between the two situations is that the interview is usually structured into specific questions to be asked. In the kindergarten or first grade, the teacher helps the pupils retain information by leading them into a discussion of the questions asked the interviewer and the answers he gave, as well as of other information that was obtained. Immediate expression of the information after the discussion is also helpful. In grade two or three, the teacher has the pupils recall the interview and reconstruct it. The reconstruction is recorded and carefully examined for accuracy. In grades four through six, the pupil who asks the question may be required to record the information received on note cards, or each interviewer may have another pupil working with him as a recorder. The interviewers share their notes with the other class members, who also check the notes for accuracy. The information obtained is then related to the topic or issue being studied. In grade seven or eight, responsibility for retaining the results of an interview is more individual. Although only a few individuals may be involved with conducting the interview, all the pupils participate by attempting to take notes on the interview. Direct practice is often helpful. The pupils may interview each other, or may interview school personnel on various topics.

In recent years the use of the tape recorder as a means of retaining the results of an interview has become more prevalent. Permission to tape the interview should be obtained from the resource person when the interview is being arranged. After the interview the tape is played back and analyzed. The new information is related to the topic or issue being studied. In general, the effectiveness of interviewing skills is largely determined by the planning that occurs before the resource person arrives or is contacted by telephone.

The foregoing discussion has treated the use of the resource person who is invited to the classroom or who has been contacted by telephone. However, since the basic responsibility and objective of social-studies teaching is the development of the citizen who functions individually and independently, the highest level of sophistication in the use of resource persons for information occurs when the learner seeks him out and interviews him. Whenever possible, pupils should be encouraged to interview workers within the community whom they meet on their way to and from school. In the later grades, children may be guided toward inquiring about resource persons, making arrangements for interviews, and conducting interviews. The problem of the personal security of children is to be considered. Persons working in public places present little or no risk. If private persons are to be interviewed, it is advisable that arrangements be made for the teacher or a parent to accompany the interviewer.

SUMMARY

The use of immediate-contact and intermediate-contact skills for investigation requires the utilization of human resources and community resources. Children guided into action-analysis, be it the duplication of a process in the classroom or roleplaying, bring to bear all their experiences related to the topic or issue at hand and then examine those experiences critically. Children investigating at the scene of a process within the community observe firsthand the dynamics of the process and project themselves into it. When they visit a depository of products or artifacts, they study a community expression about an industry, an economy, or a historical era. When they communicate with a resource person, they gain most richly from the experience of another person who is a part of their community.

The use of immediate-contact and intermediate-contact skills demands that the children have purposes for making contact and that they have the skills necessary for profiting from contact. The purposes emerge from the social-studies program itself. Action-analysis requires little if any formal skill on the part of the pupil, but establishing and maintaining contact with a resource person may require several kinds of listening and various interviewing skills. Teaching these skills may be incidental or may involve a carefully organized instructional program.

The particular value of the application of immediate- and intermediate-contact skills whenever possible lies within the dimensions of learning. Because the child's contact is closer to himself as he applies these skills, his learnings are more real to him. Through the exercise of these skills he acquires understandings not accessible to him in any other way. All children, not just the very young and the very slow, need opportunities for immediate and intermediate contact with social-studies reality.

Exercises for Further Understanding

1. Given below is a list of processes which children can and have duplicated in the classroom. Select one, research it to learn exactly what the process is, and then make a list of the provisions required for this to be an effective learning experience for children.

(a) Baking bread.
(b) Making soap.
(c) Making candles.
(d) Branding.
(e) Building a log cabin.

(f) Weaving.

(g) Making pottery.

2. Choose a social-studies topic in which you are most knowledgeable. Assume that you are going to serve as a resource person for this topic in a given classroom. Make the preparations that you believe would do honor to you as well as be most beneficial to the children. Show these preparations to a classmate for his reactions.

3. Choose an area of community study in social studies which is all but completely foreign to you. This may have to do with the policeman, the fireman, the work of the city council, a service, or an industrial process. Develop a framework of questions about it and arrange for an interview with an expert in the field. Make the interview and decide for yourself the value of preparation.

4. If you are student teaching and a resource person is available for the topic under study, make all the arrangements necessary for his visit. Prepare the children for his visit and guide them in participating. Judge for yourself how well this has worked for you and for your class. What will you do next time to make such a visit more beneficial to the children?

5. If you are student teaching and the social-studies curriculum specifies a community study of one kind or another, arrange to take your pupils on a walking trip to a nearby place where learning can be enhanced through observation and interviewing. Plan the trip carefully. After the trip, decide what you will do next time to make it a more effective learning experience.

Selected References

Colman, Gould P., "Taped Interviews and Community Studies." *Social Education*, 29:537-538 (October 1965).

Dale, Edgar, *Audio-Visual Methods in Teaching*. New York: The Dryden Press, 1946.

Dunfee, Maxine, and Helen Sagl, *Social Studies through Problem Solving*, Chap. 6, "Drawing on the Community to Solve Problems." New York: Holt, Rinehart and Winston, Inc., 1966.

Hauser, Frances M., "World Map Study in the Community." *Social Education*, 19:65-72 (February 1955).

Kemp, Jerrold E., *Planning and Producing Audiovisual Materials*. San Francisco: Chandler Publishing Company, 1963.

Kinder, James, *Audio-visual Materials and Techniques*. New York: American Book Company, 1959.

Menser, David, "Ideas and Objects, the Artifact Kit." *Social Education,* 30:343-345 (May 1966).

Merritt, Edith, *Working with Children in Social Studies,* Chap. 6, "Learning through Doing, Looking, and Listening." Belmont, Calif.: Wadsworth Publishing Company, 1961.

Michaelis, John U., *Social Studies for Children in a Democracy,* 3d ed., Chap. 15, "Audio-Visual Materials;" and Chap. 16, "Community Resources." Englewood Cliffs, N.J.: Prentice-Hall, Inc., 1963.

Muessing, Raymond H. "Using Projective Pictures." *Social Education,* 22:250-252 (May 1958).

National Council for the Social Studies, *Social Studies in Elementary Schools,* Thirty-Second Yearbook, John U. Michaelis, ed., Chap. 6, "Skills and Processes in the Social Studies;" and Chap. 7, "Instructional Resources." Washington, D.C.: National Education Association, 1962.

Preston, Ralph C., *Teaching Social Studies in the Elementary Schools,* rev. ed., Chap. 13, "Using Audio-Visual Aids." New York: Rinehart & Company, Inc., 1958.

Tiegs, Ernest W., and Fay Adams, *Teaching the Social Studies,* Chap. 15, "Audio-Visual Materials and Procedures." Boston: Ginn and Company, 1959.

10

Improving Distant-Contact
Investigative Skills

Most of the contact which children have with social-studies reality is distant contact. Although distant contact is likely to be to the most abstract of contacts and the most difficult for pupils to cope with, it is most often the only contact that can be provided. Studies of distant processes and products, peoples in other places, and peoples in other times can be instrumented only through films, filmstrips, series of pictures, maps, globes, charts, cartoons, and verbal representations. Occasionally a resource person may be available, or a process may be viewed on a field trip or duplicated in the classroom. But for the most part, learners must be dependent on the teacher for guidance into the best representations available, and for instruction on how to cope with problems in symbol interpretation. The improvement of distant-contact skills is determined by the teacher's success in presenting problems to the learners, and the extent to which they understand and accept the purposes that grow out of the problem presentations; in providing accurate representations for the learners to analyze; in providing representations suitable for learners at their stage of experiential and intellectual development; and in teaching the skills instrumental to investigation.

Providing accurate representations for learners to analyze is a constant problem for social-studies teachers, although a problem that many teachers do not perceive. These teachers assume that all the representations provided by the district must be accurate, or the district would not have provided them. Unfortunately, too often the representations provided are inaccurate. A film on the dairy farm made ten years ago does not accurately reflect the dairy farm today; books about Latin America published seven or eight years ago may present a political or economic picture that does not reflect Latin America today. The assumption that all the materials provided by the district are accurate is often not warranted.

Some teachers, who do perceive that the representations provided are inaccurate, then either guide their pupils into many purposeless "doing" activities or become fountains of wisdom from which lectures flow.

The teachers who fully perceive the problem of providing the most accurate representations possible work with it in several ways. One way is to develop careful outlines of content based on authoritative sources and to use them as guides. Such outlines are revised from time to time to make them current with more recent events and conditions. Another way of dealing with the problem is to use the provided materials in valid ways. Outdated materials are often excellent sources of historical evidence of change. Often some aspects of a representation are inaccurate but other aspects are quite accurate. The teacher uses only those segments which are accurate. Some teachers make certain that both accurate and inaccurate materials are available for analysis, and the learners are guided into assessing the accuracy. Still another way of working with the problem is to prepare simple representations, such as flannelboard sequences, narrative charts, tables, graphs, and maps, for pupils to analyze with guidance.

Providing representations suitable for learners at their stage of experiential and intellectual development presents a two-aspect problem. The first aspect involves the suitability of representations for an entire classroom of pupils at a particular grade level. No matter what type of representation is being considered, it should present facts and ideas at a level within the understanding of all or most of the members of the class. This criterion is general. The application of other criteria is specific to types of representations. As the teacher considers a sound film, a filmstrip with a transcription accompaniment, or a transcription, he will want to make certain that the monolog or dialog is within the comprehension of his pupils. As he selects filmstrips or series of pictures, he will examine critically the breakdown of events or the arrangement of aspects to be studied. The greater the distance between the events being depicted or the aspects presented to view, the more advanced the level at which ideas are being presented. As the teacher takes stock of the various reading materials he has available, he will examine them for the following: how logically they are organized, how well basic terms are defined within the text, how long the sentences are, how complex the vocabulary is, and how well the text is illustrated with pictures, charts, tables, diagrams, and maps. He will determine how much the author respects children (a writing style in which the author continually asks himself questions and answers them, or in which he uses infantile language in an attempt to reach "their level," or in which a pair of perfect children ask a know-it-all Mr. Smith about facts and ideas does not reflect much respect for children as thinking human beings). He will need to check single pictures, wall maps, dioramas, wall charts, and wall diagrams for the clarity in which ideas are expressed.

The second aspect of the problem of suitability of representations as sources for information involves suitability for independent work at the various levels of ability within the class. An ideal fondly held by many teachers is that they would be provided with representations that offer the same facts and ideas at different levels of sophistication. Textbooks and reference books would be provided for children at each level of ability—low, average, and high—and the same would hold true for filmstrips, picture series, maps, charts, and the like. However, much less than the ideal exists.

Most teachers cope with the problem of varying ability levels by attempting to find materials suitable for each level within the classroom. For example, a teacher in grade six may find that his slower pupils can learn much about Latin American culture through the study of pictures, his average pupils can profit from reading a section in the textbook, and his faster pupils will learn much from an analysis of a set of cartoons. The pupils are studying about the same idea but are seeking within different representations to find out about it. Sometimes the same type of representation is available for all pupils. For example, some pupils may be reading a periodical article while another group is reading the textbook. A third group may be reading a brief printed passage about the topic written by the teacher, who has reduced the vocabulary load and sentence complexity. Another way of coping with this problem is to guide the pupils into suitable materials and have them contribute findings whenever they appear to be pertinent. Brighter children work with more complex ideas in more abstract representations; slower children work with simpler ideas in less abstract representations.

Defining problems with children, providing accurate representations, and selecting representations suitable for children as members of a class, as members of various ability groups, and as individuals may be all that is necessary for effective investigation, but often something more is necessary. This additional requirement is ability with a particular skill or complex of skills. The skill or complex of skills needed is usually determined by the type of representation being used. Films or transcriptions require little more than well-defined purposes and fundamental viewing and listening skills. Certain kinds of charts, such as organization charts (showing the structure of the lines of responsibility in government, military command, production, or the like), evolution charts (showing the development of an artifact over a period of years), pedigree charts (showing a "family tree"), narrative charts (showing the steps in a process or the events contributing to a crisis or important change), or comparison charts (tabular or pictorial representations arranged to bring differences into sharp relief) require some specific purposes and fundamental reading skills. The same may be said for filmstrips and series of pictures. However, representations such as single pictures, diagrams, globes, maps, graphs, and printed verbal representations require skills that need to be carefully taught. These skills include picture-analysis skills, diagram-analysis, graph-analysis skills, map- and globe-study skills, and certain reading skills.

PICTURE-ANALYSIS SKILLS

A picture may well be worth thousands of words for expressing an idea; as a source of information, it may give rise to the expression of many more words in support of a multitude of ideas or clusters of ideas. A picture is no more than a representation of an event in time, space, and function. The problem that a learner faces when he attempts to use a picture as a source of information is to determine precisely which event it reflects. The purposes he has accepted serve as a guide.

Picture analysis consists of three skills: skill in identifying the items (including persons) and functions depicted; skill in interrelating items and functions (items with items, items with functions, and functions with functions) to arrive at the event depicted; and skill in relating the event within a chain of past events and future events or a complex of current events. These skills are generally applied in the order just given. See Figure 5. In the following teaching-learning sequence, the teacher guides children in picture analysis. Note that he guides children in such a way that he encourages them to bring to bear on the task whatever background and analytical powers they possess. He provides information from time to time, but only that which is necessary to the direction of analysis.

Teacher: Yesterday while we were talking about clothing some of you were able to give the steps that your mothers follow when making a dress. Can you remember the steps?

Pupil A: My mother buys a pattern, pins it on the cloth, cuts the cloth, and sews it together.

Teacher: Anybody's mother use different steps?

FIGURE 5. FOURTH GRADERS REACT TO A CARTOON
ABOUT A SERVICE PROVIDED BY THE STATE.

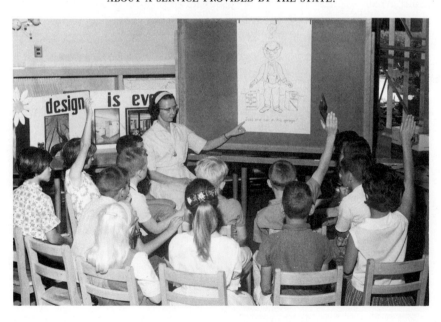

Pupil B: Sometimes my mother borrows a pattern from one of her friends.

Teacher: That's another way to obtain a pattern. Does she use other steps? Does she do anything different?

Pupil C: Yesterday I think that we mentioned that mother fits the dress to herself before she begins sewing.

Setting the Purpose

Teacher: I think we included that as a step yesterday, and we decided that in a dress factory dresses were made by teams of people working together—one person getting a pattern, another pinning it on the cloth, another cutting it out, another fitting it on a person, and another sewing it together. Today we are going to look at a picture which may help us to know better how clothing is made. Where do you suppose that this picture was taken?

Pupil D: It looks like the inside of a clothing factory.

Pupil A: I think that's what it is.

Pupil E: Me, too.

Identifying Items

Teacher: What makes you think so?

Pupil B: On those big tables there are many pieces of cloth, and the people are doing something with the cloth. It must be a clothing factory.

Identifying a Function

Teacher: That lady worker at the right of the picture—what does she appear to be doing?

Pupil F: Pinning the pattern on the cloth.

Pupil G: No, she isn't. She is tracing a pattern on the cloth. She has what looks like some chalk in her hand and I can see white lines on the dark cloth.

Relating Items and Function

Teacher: Any other ideas about what the lady worker is doing? All of us seem to agree that the lady is tracing the pattern on the cloth. What do you suppose happens next?

Pupil H: It has to be cut.

Teacher: Can you see anyone in the picture busy at cutting cloth?

Pupil I: I see a man there. He looks as though he is cutting something with a saw—some kind of power saw.

Pupil A: And he is cutting through a thick bundle of cloth. Those pieces of cloth that we see on those tables there are piles of cloth cut in the same shape.

Teacher: Does everyone see that?

Pupil G: He could be sewing the cloth.

Pupil A: No, he isn't. That thing there holds the motor and it has a blade on it. He's cutting the cloth.

Teacher: Do you suppose that he could use scissors?

Pupil C: Well, he could, but I don't think that he could cut through so much cloth at one time with a pair of scissors.

Teacher: Do you see other people in the picture doing other things?

Pupil H: There are some other people back there. It's hard to see exactly what they are doing, but they seem to be doing the same things as these people up here.

Teacher: What do you think would be a good name for this part of the factory?

Pupil J: I think I'd call it the cutting room.

Pupil K: I think it should be called the pattern tracing and cutting room.

Identifying the Event

Teacher: Any other ideas? Well, most factories are divided into departments. Each department has its own work space and workers. It does one job. I think that we could call this part of the factory the cutting department. Can you think of other departments that might be in this clothing factory?

A similar teaching-learning sequence may occur at a more sophisticated level as shown in the following picture analysis. In this instance a cartoon is being analyzed.

Purpose Setting

Teacher: We've been discussing freedom of speech and what it means for our individual behavior. In this cartoon we see another interpretation of freedom of speech. Let's see what this cartoonist really means. What is he saying in the left-hand part of the cartoon?

Pupil A: Those closed doors there stand for government secrecy. The label above the door shows that.

Teacher: Government secrecy is used a lot nowadays. What does it mean?

Pupil B: Well, it means that men in government are working with things that others should not know anything about.

Teacher: Can you give an example?

Pupil B: Military secrets. Like the development of a new bomb.

Teacher: Yes. Can any of the rest of you think of examples?

Pupil C: The people in city government might want to meet in secret to decide on where to build a new city hall. They would want to keep it a secret so that people would not buy the land in a certain place to sell it to the government at a high price.

Items

Teacher: A good example. Who do you think that fellow is who is trying to pry open the doors with the huge pen?

Pupil D: Somebody who want to know what's going on behind the doors. A newspaper man maybe.

Pupil E: It must be a newspaper man, because the pen that is used as a bar to pry open the door says on it, "Freedom of the Press."

Teacher: Could there be anyone else who would also be very much concerned about the freedom of the press?

Pupil F: We, as people—as citizens—we should be concerned. That man who is working so hard could stand for any one of us.

Teacher: That is a possibility. What do the rest of you think?

Pupil G: Who is that funny-looking little man there at the right supposed to be?

Pupil B: He just seems to sort of balance out the picture. But he seems to be interested in what is going on.

Pupil D: Could that silly little man be *us*?

Pupil I: I think so. Everytime that I look at a cartoon on the editorial page of the newspaper I see cartoons like this one. Often there is just such a figure in cartoons. He is a simple-looking man. Sometimes he has a label but I can't remember what is it.

Teacher: John Q. Public?

Pupil D: That's right. He does stand for us, each of us as a spectator.

Teacher: Let's return to government secrecy for a moment. Do you think it is right or wrong?

Pupil A: There has to be government secrecy sometimes. If we did not keep our latest developments in rocketry and missiles secret, others could use the information to make better missiles and rockets than ours.

Teacher: And what is wrong with others having better rockets and missiles?

Pupil A: They might be able to destroy us.

Functions

Teacher: Or we could say that government secrecy is sometimes necessary to maintain the safety of the people. But if it is safety of the people that is the important thing, why can't the people themselves know about the secrets? After all, it is *their* safety that is at stake.

Pupil E: The people might talk about the secrets to the wrong people who could be spies.

Pupil H: Or they might not understand the secrets very well and become frightened by them.

Teacher: Then should all government business be kept secret?

Pupil I: No! The people have a right to know what the government is doing. The people elected the men who work in government, and those men have a responsibility to the people to keep them informed of what they are doing.

Relationships

Teacher: We seem to be saying that government secrecy is both right and wrong. Would you agree that most of the time the business of government should be open, but when secrets will best serve the people's interest and safety, there should be government secrecy? All of you seem to agree. What about the freedom of the press? What should it have to do with government secrecy?

Pupil C: It is the business of the newspaper to report all important events, including events in government.

Teacher: And if there is government secrecy, the freedom of the press is curbed. Is that right or wrong?

Pupil E: If the freedom of the press is curbed, a newspaper cannot do its job. It cannot report to us what is going on. That is wrong. But if government secrets are for our own good, they should not be open to anyone—not even the press. That is right.

Moment

Teacher: Well, then, what do you think that this cartoonist is trying to tell us?

The cartoon as a picture presents considerable difficulty to the learner as he attempts to deal with it as a source of information. In this medium of expression characterized by economy, exaggerated picture metaphors carry the burden of meaning. Most often, a critical comment composed of a single kernel of truth is selected from many and presented as the significant kernel because all others are for the moment concealed or purposefully omitted. For children, the symbolism of both facts and ideas is often difficult to understand. Carefully guided discussion is required to assure their understanding of items, functions, relationships, and the significance of the idea presented.

In the examples offered above, the teacher is an important agent in guiding the pupils in analyzing pictures for investigative purposes. Many teachers willingly accept this role, particularly when teaching primary children or slower children who cannot read. Unfortunately many teachers in the later grades relegate picture analysis to use with nonreaders. This limited use is an error because picture analysis is a valid, respectable means of investigating. Often the most accurate resource available is a picture. All pupils, regardless of reading ability or intellectual capacity need to know how to analyze pictures for information. Furthermore, picture-analysis skills should be taught to the extent that picture analysis can be used at an independent level.

Ordinarily the picture-analysis skills are taught as needed and practice is given within the expressed need. After the purposes at hand have been fulfilled, there is no more practice until another need for information from pictures arises. No separate area of the curriculum is known as picture analysis, and rarely is any consideration given to it during reading or language-arts instruction. However, much can be done to sharpen children's picture-analysis skills.

One way to help children develop picture-analysis skills is to organize and index a file of pictures based on the social-studies units studied. Such a file could be used in kindergarten by putting small pictures on the index tabs, but it is usually used in grades one and two. When a child or group of children wants information about some aspects of study, the file is consulted. The correct index section is selected and the pictures are quickly examined until one that offers the desired information is found.

Another way to help children learn independent picture-analysis skills also involves a file of pictures. The teacher makes a selection of pictures that offer information about social-studies topics. Each picture is mounted on cardboard or tagboard or pasted in a file folder. On the back of the card or on the opposite side of the folder or above or below the picture, the teacher attaches an exercise which he has composed. The exercises for the various pictures may be controlled for difficulty within each of the skills. The following is a simple breakdown of suggested exercises for the skills.

Identifying items or functions:

Easy:
1. Counting the items listed.
2. Counting groups of items listed.
3. Identifying items and functions listed. (Items and functions on the picture have holes punched at the places where they are depicted and the child runs a string attached to a word symbol through the hole; the picture and exercise are covered with a sheet of very thin plastic and the child marks responses with a crayon; the items and functions on the picture are letter-keyed with brush pen or India ink and the child matches the letters with the symbols numbered on his answer paper.)

Difficult:
4. Choosing the items and functions depicted from those on a list.
5. Listing items and functions.

6. Listing the items and functions that appear to be the most important as related to a question.

Relating items with functions:

Easy:

1. Relating workers with tools or machines.
2. Relating people with tasks.
3. Relating one group of workers with another.

Difficult:

4. Deriving climate from land use, or vice versa.
5. Relating topography with land use.
6. Relating level of technology with land use.
7. Relating esthetics with the feeling and values of a people.
8. Relating ways of living with a people or an era.

Relating to other moments:

Difficult:

1. Relating the event depicted with the events just completed.
2. Relating the events depicted with the events about to take place.
3. Relating the event depicted within a chain of events.

When the children can read, the exercises may be made self-correcting with separate answer cards or an answer booklet. The children should be taught how to maintain records of the results of their work with exercises, and from time to time the teacher should counsel with each child to see how well he is doing.

Another way to guide children in the development of independent picture-analysis skills is through the use of specially devised materials now available. These materials, published by Science Research Associates, Chicago, Illinois, are devised for use with pupils individually, in small groups, or in an entire class. The materials are self-correcting, require a minimum of direct teacher supervision, and guide toward the development of independent picture-analysis skills.

Usually the development of picture-analysis skills occurs during social studies or when the pupils have free time after completing other work.

DIAGRAM-ANALYSIS SKILLS

A diagram as a representation reflects only what is essential about a structure. Diagrams are used to represent floor plans of buildings of all kinds and cross-sectional views of ships, airplanes, machines, mechanical devices, manufactured articles, and the like. Attractive diagrams are to be found in magazine and newspapers, but these are of limited utility for instructional purposes. The structure in these diagrams is often limited and sometimes distorted for commercial or propaganda purposes. The diagrams found in textbooks, reference books, and the more scholarly publications serve to clarify knowledge through concise expression, and such expressions are usually carefully keyed or labeled to aid comprehension.

The use of accurate diagrams for information requires the application of two skills: relating the symbolized structure of the diagram to a real structure and interpreting the labels or key.

Basic to the use of diagrams for investigative purposes is a sense of the nature of symbols, particularly when the symbol is so much reduced in size that it reflects few details. Whenever primary children are guided into the use of a diagram they will need to be reminded of what a symbol is, that it is very much reduced in size in comparison with the actual size of the thing symbolized, and that the reduction in size has also reduced the number of details that can be observed. Most primary children have little difficulty with learning that a symbol stands in the place of something real.

Relating the symbolized structure of the diagram to a real structure is an automatically exercised skill when the structure symbolized is part of children's everyday environment. For example, a diagram of a shoe, an automobile, a service station, or a supermarket presents little difficulty to children. They can readily relate the diagram to the thing symbolized in terms of size and loss of detail.

However, when the diagram symbolizes a structure unfamiliar to children, the teacher must guide them carefully in establishing referents. For example, if a group of children in Nevada were studying the diagram of a cross section of an ocean freighter, they could be encouraged to use the size of the classroom, the school building, the play yard, a city block, or perhaps several of these, to determine the length, width, and depth of the ocean freighter. They may be guided into study of other details of the ship—hold-to-hold and deck-to-deck transportation within the ship, the speed of the ship, and so forth—through the use of pictures.

Interpreting the diagram labels or key is a skill requiring practice if the children are to be able to use diagrams independently. Children should be guided into examining the labels on a labeled diagram one by one, using their word-analysis skills to determine the pronunciation of words and using the terms to relate the items and functions depicted. When a key is provided, an additional step is required. Numbers or letters in the diagram must be related to the numbers or letters on the key. It is generally better for the children to work from the diagram to the key.

Because diagrams are not often available for investigative purposes, teacher usually do not make special provisions for formal practice in their use. Whenever a diagram is found, the teacher guides the children in its use. If a teacher wanted to make additional provisions to help children learn diagram-analysis skills, he could use procedures similar to those listed for picture-analysis skills. In materials published by Science Research Associates, diagram-analysis skills are given considerable emphasis.

GRAPH-ANALYSIS SKILLS

A graph represents a concise statement of quantitive information which, if expressed in verbal symbols, would be a long, involved statement. It may be a comparison which reflects differences, such as the differences in population among the largest cities in the world, the differences in the amounts of the average worker's dollar expended for his basic needs and wants, and the like. Or it may be the statement of a trend established over a given period of time, such as the growth of the gross national product for the past twenty-five years, the decrease of the relative number of agricultural workers over the past fifty years, or the general stability of the average annual rainfall in a region for the past twenty years. Concise statement in a graph is accomplished through the use of common units of number expressed on a labeled grid or through the use of selected symbols.

Graph-analysis skills include graph orientation, determining the basic unit, interpolating within unit expressions, and synthesis.

Children at work investigating in social studies find simple picture graphs and bar graphs in their textbooks and reference books. Sometimes they have occasion to use line graphs and circle graphs, particularly when they have the ability to investigate in materials devised for adult use. Although each of these types of graphs is different, they are similar in the general skills required for their accurate interpretation. Teaching children these skills is largely a matter of helping them to develop a graph "conscience" which prompts the learner to bring himself to the task of graph interpretation with those questions:

1. What is this graph telling about? (Orientation)
2. What are the units or symbols of expression? (Unit or symbol analysis)
3. How are the units or symbols broken to show more exact expression? (Interpolation)
4. What idea does the graph express? (Synthesis)

The development of graph "conscience" may be approached either incidentally or directly. The difference between the approaches is primarily an administrative difference. Basic procedures do not differ greatly. In the following discussion the procedures for the incidental approach will be treated. Organizing for direct instruction will be dealt with later.

The incidental approach involves teaching graph-analysis skills when they are needed. Each time the class, group, or individual meets with a graph during investigation, the teacher gives instruction.

The first step is guiding the learners into graph orientation by having them make a quick analysis of the title of the graph, the general aspects of the graph, and the legend, if any, for what the graph is about. A conversational sequence reflecting this step would be as follows:

"Let's see what we can find that tells what this graph is about. What is the title? Now look at the graph. Is there anything there that gives you any clue to what the graph is about? And the legend down below. Does it tell you anything more about the graph?"

The second step in teaching graph-analysis involves guided study of the units symbols or both used in the graph. The direction of study will be determined by the type of graph being examined.

If the graph is a picture graph, such as one showing the exports of a country, in which each export is represented by a small picture (an ear of corn for corn, a locomotive for heavy machinery, a hammer for tools, and the like), the pupils identify each symbol. Then, examining the legend, they determine what quantity each symbol represents. It may be a percentage or a representative quantity.

If the graph is a bar graph, such as one showing the gold production of the leading gold-producing states during a given year, the pupils are guided into a study of the bars. They find the longest bar and the shortest bar and identify the state for which each bar symbolizes a quantity of gold. If the bars are not presented in order of length, the pupils rank them in order of length. Finally the pupils examine the grid to determine the quantity represented by each square which the bar crosses. The numbers on the abscissa, or bottom, of the graph are carefully analyzed and related to units of measurement. In a bar graph such as the one described above, each square will represent so many metric tons.

If the graph is a line graph, such as a graph showing automobile production for the past twenty-five years, the pupils are guided first into the study of the abscissa of the graph to determine the value in years represented by each square in the horizontal rows of the graph. Next the ordinate, or left-hand margin of the graph, is analyzed carefully to determine the unit value of each vertical square from bottom to top. In the line graph cited above, each square is likely to represent one hundred thousand automobiles. Sample readings are made at various points where the vertical and horizontal lines meet.

If the graph is a circle graph, such as a graph showing the expenditure of the tax dollar, the point that the graph represents a whole divided into parts must be clarified for the pupils. The pupils are then guided in determining the largest part and the smallest part and in ranking the parts in order of size. The pupils attempt to arrive at approximations of the size of each part in terms of common fractions.

The third step in the teaching of graph-analysis skills is guiding the pupils in interpolating within the units or symbols or both, used in the graph. Again the direction of study will be determined by the type of graph under consideration. In a picture graph, the pupils will analyze each symbol fragment to determine its value and will then add the value to that of the line of whole symbols. In a bar graph, the pupils will discuss the value of each square, including unlabeled squares, and the common divisions of each (halves, quarters, fifths, and tenths). The precise reading for each bar will then be determined. In a line graph, a procedure similar to that used with the bar graph will be used for the vertical lines of squares upon which values are usually measured. Discussion should clarify that the horizontal squares represent the points in time at which measurements are taken or observations made. Precise reading follows an up-and-across orientation. In a circle graph, the pupils are encouraged to read each part to the nearest tenth or hundredth. A large circle on a chart divided into a hundred parts will help familiarize the pupils with hundredths.

The final step in teaching graph-analysis skills is guidance in determining the general idea the graph expresses. The pupils are guided into a reexamination of the graph to develop a statement or a few statements reflecting the idea expressed in the graph. Depending on the type of graph, statements may be similar to the following:

The chief exports of _____ are _____, _____, and _____.

The leading gold-producing state is _____. Other important gold-producing states are _____, _____, and _____.

For the past twenty-five years. automobile production has increased. Peak years were _____, _____, and _____. Particularly poor years were _____, _____, and _____.

Most of our tax dollar is spent for _____. Other important expenditures of our tax dollar include _____ and _____.

If a teacher follows the steps listed above each time his pupils study a graph, and if graph study occurs frequently, the pupils will learn graph-analysis skills. However, since graph study does not occur frequently, the incidental program is not likely to be very effective. If children are to learn to read graphs independently, a more concentrated program which places a direct emphasis on graph-analysis skills is required.

Some teachers find an analysis-application approach effective. The type of graph which the teacher wishes to teach is selected and duplicated in such a way (individual copies, chart, or projection with the use of an opaque or overhead projector) that all pupils can study it. Using the steps listed for the incidental approach, the teacher guides the pupils in analyzing the graph. After the analysis, the pupils are given data for a graph which they make individually under careful supervision. Through exercising the skills necessary in graph making the pupils gain insights into analyzing graphs for information.

Some teachers have devised materials for pupils who can read to use in independent learning activity. The teacher collects graphs from current sources such as magazines, newspaper, and promotional literature and mounts them on 9" x 12" sheets of tagboard or chipboard. An exercise for each graph is developed and mounted on the back of the tagboard or chipboard. The exercises should be varied for the sake of interest. The exercise on one graph could duplicate the steps on graph analysis through the use of multiple-choice items in which the pupil selects the best title for the graph, the meaning for basic unit or symbol, the interpolation of a unit or symbol segment, and the ideas which the graph expresses. On another card may be a list of true-false statements about a graph, a series of items to be matched, or a series of blanks to be filled. It is advisable to introduce the types of graphs to be studied in a classroom presentation in which the teacher guides the pupils in a discussion of graphs and the forms they may take. The exercises may be made self-correcting through the use of answer cards or an answer booklet, or the teacher may correct the exercises himself. In the latter instance, the scores on exercises should be discussed individually with pupils.

Recently a set of materials devised for helping children to learn graph-analysis skills has been published by Science Research Associates. These materials are designed for class, group, or individual use.

Although graph-analysis skills are generally not taught formally before grade four, the teacher in the primary grades can introduce the graph as a means of expressing ideas. For example, a picture graph showing the occupations of the fathers of the children in the classroom can easily be made and understood. A point-to-point relation (one symbol = one father) should be maintained. Children studying the weather may keep a bar graph showing the temperature in the classroom each day over a long period. Even the circle graph can be used. For example, the children attending a school which serves the needs of a population which is both urban and rural can develop a circle graph showing the population distribution of urban and rural children within the classroom. Each child could color a circle segment representing the area in which he lives and paste it on the circle.

MAP AND GLOBE SKILLS

Maps and globes are at best representative reduced-scale symbols of space which serve to bring space under control for scrutiny. The fundamental concepts necessary for an intelligent understanding of maps and globes are the concept of space, the concept of reduction of space, and the concept of representative symbol.

"Space" may refer either to volume or to surface area. Both are involved in map and globe reading, but surface area, which is a conventional series of connected points within space, is basic in the learning involved. It is given emphasis in concept teaching for the understanding of maps and globes.

Children are aware of spatial facts and use them. They know what is near or far. They know how to make their way through the neighborhood. Their basic point of reference is the self or the home. In the home certain spatial rights have been accorded the child—his place at the table, his bed, storage space for his belongings, play space, and the like. These rights are closely tied in with the child's concept of self. When he leaves the home, it becomes a point of reference, the beginning point. Other points of reference are learned, related to each other and to the beginning point, and used as a means of maintaining direction. For example, a child going to school reacts to his points of reference in this way, "I go out the walk and turn toward Jimmie's house. It's down there. I pass Jimmie's house and keep on going down to the corner where there is a mailbox. I am at the mailbox. Here I cross the street and go toward the big fence around the playground. There is the school building. I pass it. Here is the playground gate. I go through it and I am at school."

As has been shown, a child, even a very young child, has a concept of space very rich in facts exhibited in demonstrable understandings, attitudes, and action patterns. This richness goes beyond surface-area facts. The child is aware of the space above the surface. The contrail of a jetliner high above him, the eggbeater chatter of a helicopter, the persistent hum of a small airplane, the negative worrying of a kite at the end of an invisible string, the kaleidoscopic effect of sunlight on a flight of pigeons, the swift darting of swallows, a column of smoke, and the parade of clouds above the horizon are facts of space—the space of "up." Indeed, the total dimension of space is deeply imbedded within the child's consciousness, but it is subjective. Guiding his learning in the use of maps and globes is a matter of making him objectively aware of surface space and its symbolic representation. One approach to teaching children map and globe skills involves analysis and discovery which leads toward basic generalizations which can be extended for further understanding. Basically, six generalizations support map and globe skills. They are as follows:

1. *Directions are constant points of reference in space.* This generalization can be taught in grade one or two through the use of procedures similar to the following:

Guide children into beginning to think about directions by having them discuss the routes by which they come to school or go to the store. Several children should be given an opportunity to tell the routes they take to get to the same place. (Usually children describe the routes they follow in much the same way as that described in an earlier paragraph.) Help the children to see that the various things that they mention are really "markers" that help them to know that they are following the right route to a place.

Introduce the compass by having the children consider how a person would find his way from one place to another without such markers as roads, streets, churches, stop signs, service stations, and the like. Permit children to handle the compass to discover that its needle always points in the same direction. This direction is North.

Clarify the idea of North by taking the children outside and helping them to find North with the use of the compass. Help them to choose a "marker" for North in the distance—a church steeple, a tall tree, a dip in the hills, a peak, or the like.

Introduce the directions South, East, and West with reference to North. Establish "markers" on the horizon for these. Guide the children in practicing finding the directions and saying them. Have individual pupils take turns at facing or pointing in the various directions while the rest of the class determines the direction indicated.

Extend the applications of directions by returning the class to the classroom and having them decide where signs labeled with the various directions should be placed. Use these signs to play games in which individual pupils give directions to others to have them go from one point in the room to another. Example: "Stand up. Turn East. Walk one step. Turn South. Walk seven steps. Take three more steps South. Turn East. Walk six steps. Take six more steps." Another pupil could try to give directions to have the person return to his starting place. The game should be played in several places outside the classroom.

Encourage the children to describe the routes they use to come to school or to go to the store using the directions as learned. Then have them try to give the reverse route.

Discuss the meaning of the directions "Up" and "Down."

Use directional terms whenever practical during instruction.

2. *A map is a picture of space usually reduced in size.* This generalization can be taught in grade one or two through the use of procedures similar to the following:

Prepare an area to be mapped by arranging common articles such as a book, a pencil, a ruler, and a paper clip on a drawing board or any other similar board.

Prepare a series of charts to include:
  A simple sketch showing a three-quarter view of the drawing board and the articles arranged on it.
  A chart showing a "map" of the drawing board showing the arranged articles in some detail.

A chart showing the same "map" but reduced in size. Some of the detail cannot be shown because the size of the symbols has been reduced.

Three more charts, each representing the "map" in more reduced form until the last chart shows only the book and the ruler. Items such as the pencil and paper clip (if these have been used) have disappeared because of the reduction of the size of symbols.

Introduce the lesson by having the children discuss what they think a map is. Accept all ideas, but inform the children that as they work together they will discover which of their ideas are correct.

Present the drawing board with the objects arranged on it. Have the children identify the objects.

Present the chart showing the simple sketch of the drawing board and guide the children toward seeing that the difference between the sketch and drawing board is that the drawing board and objects are real things to be picked up, handled, and used, but the things on the sketch are symbols. These symbols stand for the things really on the drawing board as well as the drawing board itself.

Present the chart showing the "map" of the drawing board and guide the children toward seeing the difference between the sketch and the "map." The map shows an arrangement of articles as though one were looking down at them. The sketch does not. The detail on the map is not the same.

Present the remainder of the charts in order of the size of the maps on them, from largest to smallest. Guide the children in seeing what happens to the symbols on the maps as the maps become progressively smaller. Occasionally direct their attention toward the drawing board to remind them that no matter how small the map becomes, the area represented in the map remains the same size.

Recall some of the ideas which the children had given at first about what a map is. Guide them in analyzing their ideas and arriving at the generalization.

If the children have studied directions, have them decide where the directions on one of the larger "maps" should be, depending on the way in which the drawing board and its objects are situated within the room. Present a simple map compass and have the children decide how it should be placed on the map.

Guide the children in using the drawing board or a large sheet of tagboard and symbols for tables, desks, cupboards, or the like made from construction paper to make a map of the room. Distribute the symbols and have the children place them one by one on the board or tagboard sheet.

Encourage the children to draw maps of the top of their tables or desks, the school, or some area that they can see from the school. If a sandtable is available, have the children construct a relief map of a common area in the community. They make the symbols from easily available materials.

3. *A globe is a symbol of the earth very much reduced in size.* This generalization is also one that can be taught in grade one or two. Procedures similar to the following would be used:

Gather the following materials: a primary globe and an orange. Make a "play" orange from clay or a mixture of salt, flour, and water. Paint it orange and be sure to include a little dot to symbolize the stem.

Begin the lesson by having the children explore the similarities between the real orange and the "play" orange. After identifying the objects, the children should be guided in considering the uses for each. The real orange can be eaten, but the "play" orange cannot be. It can be used *instead* of a real orange when playing store. Establish that the "play" orange is a symbol for a real orange.

Guide the children into considering how much bigger the real orange is than the "play" orange. A rough approximation is all that is necessary.

Present the globe and have the children consider whether it is a symbol. Establish that it is a symbol of the earth upon which we live. Clarify that it is many times smaller than the earth.

Introduce the children to symbolization on the globe of the things found on the surface of the earth by having them examine again the real orange and the "play" orange. Have them consider why they identified the "play" orange as an orange, to bring them to an understanding of color as a symbol—orange for the outside of the orange and green for its stem. Then direct the children's attention to the colors on the globe. Establish that the blue areas symbolize water and the brown areas symbolize land.

Clarify the limits of symbolization by having the children again compare the real orange with the "play" orange to see whether the "play" orange is exactly like the real orange except for size. The children find that the roughness of the orange rind, due to little indentations on its surface, is not duplicated on the "play" orange. It cannot be seen because the symbol is so small that such detail cannot be reproduced. The globe is much the same way. Houses, people, roads, and the like cannot be symbolized on the globe because it is so small.

Have the children explore the globe to see what it tells about the earth.

Guide the children in establishing directions on the globe.

Help the children to find their location on the globe.

4. *A map is the whole globe or a section of the globe flattened out.* This generalization can be successfully taught in grade one or two through the use of procedures similar to the following (See Figure 6.):

Gather the following materials: A primary globe, a world map, a large sheet of newsprint (24″ × 36″) or any other kind of paper, a sheet of paper (9″ × 12″), and a rubber ball at least six inches in diameter. The rubber ball should be cut in half. Using a brush pen, draw a square, a triangle, and a couple of dots (Figure 6A).

FIGURE 6A.

Then, with scissors make cuts from the outer edge of each hemisphere (Figure 6B).

FIGURE 6B.

When the scored hemisphere is spread apart, it shows distortion (Figure 6c).

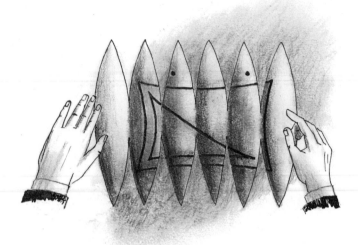

FIGURE 6c.

Using the globe and the world map, guide the children toward seeing that the same things are symbolized on the map and globe. Then have them compare the size and location of continents as shown on the map and globe. Clarify that the continents are not proportionately the same size and shape on the map and globe. Encourage the children to hypothesize the differences.

Have the children check their hypotheses by trying to fit first the large piece of paper and then the small one around the globe. This will help the children understand the difficulty of depicting exactly a round surface on a flat one.

Further clarify the distortion on maps by having the children experiment with the rubber hemispheres fashioned from the rubber ball. The size and shape of the square and the triangle are changed. The two points on the hemisphere are farther apart and are changed somewhat in location. Flattening the hemisphere on the blackboard or on a piece of paper and linking the figures with drawn lines will help the children understand better the distortion of figures on a map.

Encourage the children to examine the hemispheres to determine where the figures tend to remain the same size regardless of whether the hemisphere is flattened or round. Have the children identify which kind of hemisphere was used in making the world map.

Leave the hemispheres on a table where children can manipulate them during free time.

5. *The representation of a particular area varies in size from one locational aid to another.* This generalization is related to the second generalization treated above, but is sufficiently different to warrant separate attention. It can be taught in grades three or four through the use of the following procedures:

Gather the following materials: A map of the state, a map of the nation, a map of the continent, and a map of the world; a globe; maps of smaller geographical areas such as the city, county, or township, if available. A map of a local area such as a valley, fire-control area, the school, or the like may be used if available.

Arrange the maps at the front of the room in an order depicting the smallest area first and the largest area last.

Guide the children in making an analysis of the map showing the smallest area to discover all the details that it presents. If this map is of a nearby area with which most of the children are familiar, have them relate their knowledge to that shown on the map. Whatever is depicted in this first map analyzed serves as a basis for comparison and discovery in the remainder of the maps.

Have the children analyze the map by finding the area depicted in the first and comparing the amount of detail shown with that shown on the first map. Use the same procedure with the remainder of the maps.

Clarify that the representation of an area varies in size, but the area depicted really does not change size; that the larger the representation of an area, the greater the amount of detail likely to be shown. This clarification usually occurs as the children analyze one map after another.

Give the children various places to locate on the maps and globe. Encourage them to give the reasons for a place being shown on one map and not another or why a place is shown on one map and not on another or on the globe. Encourage them to make approximations of the location of a place by locating a point indicated on the map near the place being sought. For example, children living in Livermore, California, cannot find their city on a globe, but they can approximate its location by finding San Francisco.

Identify the scale on the maps and globes. Help the children to relate the scale to the size of representation on the various maps. Establish that the scale indicates accurately the size of the representation being studied.

Introduce the use of a piece of string or paper tape with the scale to determine the distances between cities, the breadth and length of countries and continents, the width of oceans, and the like. Places should be found on all the maps available and the globe, and comparisons should be made of findings for the same exercise. For example, the distance between Los Angeles and New York should be on a national map, on a map of the continent, on a world map, and on the globe. The findings should be compared.

6. *The world is marked off in a grid of imaginary lines.* This generalization may be taught in grade three or four through the use of
procedures similar to the following:

Make a large map of the classroom on the blackboard or on a large sheet
of paper pinned to a bulletin board. Use care in depicting the furniture in
the classroom. The children should be able to identify easily the area depicted.

Encourage the children to locate various points in the room such as
their desk or table, the teacher's desk, display tables, and the like through
verbal descriptions in which the map is used.

Place grid lines on the map. These should be the same distance apart
vertically and horizontally. If the map is drawn on the chalkboard, the grid
lines may be drawn directly on the map with the help of a liner or yardstick
as a guide. A few dots drawn along the edge of the map will make the drawing
of the grid easier. If the map is pinned to a bulletin board, strands of yarn
or string may be used as grid lines. Pins stuck along the edge of the map at
the appropriate distance apart will help in making the grid quickly.

Encourage the pupils to use the grid to locate points. This will lead them
to seeing the need for labels on the lines of the grid. Letters for the horizontal
lines and numbers for the vertical lines may be used. If the map is drawn on
the chalkboard, the labels for the lines may be written around the margins of
the map. If the map is pinned to a bulletin board, paper tabs may be pinned
in the appropriate places. Have the pupils practice locating points within the
room using the grid label.

Clarify that the grid lines are imaginary lines. Have the pupils find the
grid lines on a map and on the globe. Identify the vertical lines as longitudes
and the horizontal lines as latitudes. Make certain that the children understand that these are also imaginary lines but that they serve the same purpose
as the grid lines on the map of the classroom.

If a large map is available, attach grid labels to the grid lines and have
the children practice using them in locating points.

If a large globe, such as a 24" globe or larger, is available, attach labels
to the grid lines and have the children practice at locating points.

These six generalizations are basic to learning how to use maps
and globes for investigative purposes. More sophisticated work with
maps and globes is an extension of these generalizations. For example,
the generalization about grid lines supports the accurate use of latitude
and longitude in expressing exact locations. In grade four or five the
children can learn to read the lines as given. In grades six, seven, or
eight they learn to interpolate between the lines given. However, learn-

ing these skills is tangent upon an understanding of the nature and function of the grid.

In the grades later than those recommended as appropriate for the learning of generalizations the teacher should check carefully to see whether the children have an understanding of the generalizations just discussed. If they do not, the teacher should use procedures similar to those recommended above.

Another approach to teaching map and globe skills involves the use of textbooks and workbooks specifically designed to aid children in learning about maps and globes. These materials are generally suitable for pupils in grades three and four. Using them, the teacher guides the pupils into a unit or series of units on map and globe skills.

Recently a set of materials developed specifically to help children learn map and globe skills has been published by Science Research Associates. These materials are deviced to introduce basic ideas about maps and globes and to guide children to the limits of their potential in the skills. The materials may be used by an individual, group, or class.

READING SKILLS

The program of instruction in the reading skills necessary for investigation is comprised of three complexes of skills: reference skills, retention skills, and exploratory-discovery skills. Each of those complexes of skills must be carefully taught if children are to be expected to exercise inquiry through reading effectively.

The reading-reference skills, sometimes called the location skills, are the skills needed for coping with the problem of determining the kind of book or source to be used and the problem of finding the place within the book or source in which the precise information may be found.

The following procedures are helpful in teaching children how to select the best reading source:

Make individual assignments to specific pages in various references to implement the study at hand. For example, a class may be studying a geographical unit and the basic source for information is the textbook. While most of the class is working in the textbook, individual pupils consult individual pages in the World Almanac, the Information Please Almanac, an atlas, and a section in an encyclopedia. Also one pupil may be reading a trade book on the area being studied. These individuals share their information with the rest of the class.

Guide the entire class into consulting several sources as they seek information related to the problem, topic, or issue at hand. The class discusses the accuracy, depth, and breadth of information found in each source.

After the pupils have had a considerable amount of practice with the above, encourage them to generalize about the potential of various sources for different kinds of information. The generalizations could be similar to the following: Atlases are good for locational information and brief descriptions. Almanacs provide precise, current information about economics, politics, and history. Encyclopedias usually offer broad, general coverage of a topic. Magazine articles provide current information about issues and events. Trade books offer detailed information about a topic.

Constantly encourage pupils to analyze the expression of purpose that they are working with for clues as to the kind of source that may prove to be the most fruitful. The expression of purpose, a question to be answered or a topic or issue to be explored, often reflects a breadth of demand in purpose which determines the usefulness of this source or that. For example, if the pupils are seeking to determine whether political factors, cultural factors, or economic factors are dominant as causes for living conditions in certain Latin American countries, the breadth of demand of purpose indicates that an encyclopedia, an almanac, or an atlas will not be much help. Magazine articles and books written about South America, particularly conditions in South America, will be the best sources.

The second problem involving the location of information within a source is treated somewhat more fully in the literature dealing with the teaching of reading skills. In most classrooms some emphasis as prescribed by the district as placed on learning the skills associated with locating information in printed sources. Besides the procedures recommended in textbooks written for teacher preparation and in district and county guides, the following will also be found to be helpful:

Introduce the structures of reference to the pupils by having them examine the table of contents and index as guides to the information found in a book. If a basic textbook is provided for all pupils, use this textbook for the introduction. Guide the pupils in a comparison of the two structures of reference to clarify the organization of each. The table of contents presents a guide to information through a list of chapter and section headings given in the order in which they occur in the book. Page numbers of the various headings are given. The index presents a list of the terms used in the book. The terms are arranged in alphabetical order and after each term there is a list of numbers and other symbols.

Establish the point-to-point relationship that exists between the content of purpose and the indication of content given in a structure of reference. Several instructional steps are required:

a. Guide the children in an analysis of the expression of purpose, either the social-studies question to be answered or the topic to be investigated, to find the term to be used as an entry idea or word in a structure of reference. Simple expressions of purpose such as the following should be worked with first:

How is *coal* mined?
When is *cotton* harvested?
What are the materials needed for *shoe making?*
The *Policeman's* Day.
How a *Law* Is Made.

b. Direct the children's attention toward finding the word or ideas as they are given in a table of contents. Encourage them to skim the table of contents quickly until they find a heading or several headings that have possibilities. If several headings are given, have the children examine the expression of purpose more carefully to select the one that most closely approximates the content in the expression of purpose. For example:

How is coal mined? Entry word or idea: coal.

Table of Contents

Finding Coal 13
Mining Coal 16
Coal Products 20
Iron Deposits 25

Mining Coal most closely approximates *How is coal mined?* Then the children find the page on which they should begin reading to find information about the question or topic.

c. Have the children find the word in the index where it is expressed as an entry word. When the word is found, guide the children in examining the locational data after the entry word to determine where the best source for information would be found. For example:

How is cotton harvested? Entry word or idea: cotton.

Index
alfalfa, 24, 36, 42

automobiles, 42, 47, 48-53, 61
barley, 23, 26, 27, 42
bronze, 123
butter, 3, 5, 8, 10-12
coal, 94-98, 103
cotton, 23, 43-45, 68

Question: Where would you begin to read to find how cotton is harvested? Answer: Page 43, because it is the first of several pages all of which are about cotton. It is most likely that the information desired will be found within a cluster of pages devoted to a topic. If there are no clusters of pages listed, the reader has no choice but to begin reading on the first of the single pages listed.

d. During succeeding lessons extend pupils' sophistication in finding the word or idea that serves as an entry word to include the following levels:

1. Choosing a term from several possible to use. Example:

How much *coal* is mined in *Pennsylvania?*
What kind of *religion* did the *Indians* follow?

Usually these terms are arranged in a hierarchy within an index. Most likely any place name or name of a person is listed first and specific kinds of facts are specified after it.

Pennsylvania   Washington, George
  Area   Early life in Virginia
  Agriculture   French and Indian War
  Coal   War for Independence
  Industry   Constitutional Convention
  Iron   Presidency

2. Using cross-references.

3. Developing reference terms or inferring them from the expressions of purpose. Example:

How did the Indians send messages? *Communication.*
What do the Mexican people do for amusement? *Recreation.*
What kinds of schools do they have in Japan? *Education.*
What are their chief crops? *Agriculture.*
How important are the uranium deposits in Canada? *Minerals.*

4. Making full use of the symbols used to clarify the kind of information to be found on a particular page. Examples:

$$m. = \text{map.}$$
$$t. = \text{table.}$$
$$p. = \text{picture.}$$

e. Guide children into the value of skimming as a skill used for finding information quickly. Practice of the skill occurs as the final act in the use of reference skills for investigating. Encourage the children to read section headings and side headings quickly to determine whether the section or passage following the heading is most likely to contain the desired information. Once the promising heading is found, skimming stops. Scanning begins.

Retention skills are used to make the information found more easily available at a future date. The skills are note taking and outlining.

In recent years the need for teaching note taking as a skill of children in the later elementary grades has received somewhat greater attention, particularly in grades seven and eight. Occasionally some attention is given to the skill in grades four, five, and six.

A good way to introduce the learning of the skill is to clarify the purposes which it serves. Most children have suffered the experience of knowing an answer to a question or having a contribution to make during a discussion only to forget it when the opportunity for sharing it is finally granted. Citing such an instance and having the children think of ways to avoid such a situation usually leads to the suggestion of a note to serve as a reminder. At this point the teacher may suggest the usefulness of notes for another task commonly arising during social studies—the task of gathering information for an individual project or report.

After the purposes for which note taking has been introduced to the children, the teacher presents the structure of a note. The simplest structure of a note consists of an expression of purpose and the fulfillment of the purpose. The simplest note is a question as an expression of purpose and its answer written in a few words. The teacher may teach this structure in several ways:

Using a large sheet of tagboard and a brush pen the teacher makes a large facsimile of a note on a note card. At the top of the note is a neatly written social-studies question, and just below the question its answer is given. The teacher guides the children in analyzing the chart to determine what a note is and of what it consists. Then, under the teacher's supervision, the children make up note cards or note sheets for a list of social-studies questions, find the answers to the questions, and evaluate their new skill.

Working at the chalkboard, the teacher draws a large note card and demonstrates how it is prepared for note taking and its appearance after the note has been taken.

Once the idea that notes serve as handy reminders has been introduced to the children, they are encouraged to take notes on social-studies questions. Cards (5″ x 8″) are distributed to the children and they take notes. After the discussion period, the children's attention is directed toward their note cards and how they may be used. As the children talk, the idea that there must be an expression of purpose and fulfillment of purpose is usually suggested by several class members.

Teaching note taking is generally more successful if the teacher exercises care in the selection or preparation of questions for the pupils to treat during their first experience. The following is a list of the types of questions arranged in the order in which they should be presented to children:

Questions requiring a single fact as an answer:

How long was George Washington the President of the United States?
What was Thomas Edison's most important invention?
What is Brazil's most important product?
How many policemen do we have in our city?

Questions requiring several facts as an answer:

How are animal skins made into leather?
What were the causes for the War for Independence?
Why do people move so much from one part of the country to another?

After the children have become successful at taking notes as answers to questions, the teacher guides them into taking notes on topics or aspects of topics. The topic or aspect of topic is copied at the top of the card and the fact or facts pertaining to it are listed after it in the order in which they are found while reading.

Usually an issue is raised about how the fulfillment of purpose is to be expressed on a note card. Some teachers and curriculum workers feel that the children should write every note as a complete sentence. The reason usually given for this practice is that children need practice in writing complete sentences as an aid to developing accurate written expression. Other teachers and curriculum workers feel strongly that a child should write only the words that he needs as a note. If the expression of purpose is a question, then the question and the few words required for its answer constitute a complete statement. When the expression of purpose is a topic or aspect of topic, a constant demand for complete statements encourages pupils to become plagiarists as they copy complete sentences from sources or forces them to write infantile sentences. Actually, if the object of note taking is to obtain facts and record them as quickly as possible, there is no real basis for demanding notes as complete sentences.

A complete note is one which includes a bibliographical reference to the source from which information is taken. At the beginning of instruction in note taking it is somewhat easier for the pupils to concentrate on making sure that the note includes an expression of purpose and a fulfillment of purpose. When the ideas are fairly well established, the children are introduced to the necessity for including bibliographical data. The children should be guided toward seeing that including these data may help to solve future problems. If a dispute should arise over the accuracy of facts and ideas, it can often be resolved by having several persons check in the source from which facts and ideas were taken. If the bibliographical data are readily available, much time can be saved. Sometimes the facts and ideas need to be reviewed; if the reviewer knows precisely where he found these facts and ideas in the first place, he does not need to search through his memory or to trace his steps back along a blind path.

At first only the minimum essential of bibliography are taught, that is, the title of the book and the page or pages upon which specific information was found. When the entire class is working with the same group of books, perhaps only the initials of the title of the books are necessary. As soon as the habit of always including bibliographical data is·established, the teacher should guide the pupils into more precise indications of bibliography, such as the name of the author, the name of the publisher, and the date and place of publication. Instruction is usually more effective when each of these aspects is introduced separately.

The biggest problem involved in teaching children how to take notes has to do with paraphrasing information. If a child is reading a book written for the use of children, it will most likely be a simply written book, and the language used will be most difficult for a child to paraphrase. It cannot be paraphrased "down" because the text is so simple. Most children do not have the vocabulary and language skills necessary for paraphrasing "up." If the language of the book reflects a sophisticated level of expression, the child may somehow be able to relate his expression of purpose to what is found in the book, but it is likely that his vocabulary and language skills are not adequate to the task of an honest paraphrase. Too frequently the child resorts to copying not just sentences but entire paragraphs of text. As stated earlier, the insistence that everything written by a child be expressed in complete sentences may force him into copying as a means of survival. It is recommended that the children always be encouraged to write their notes in their own words and to copy the words, phrases, or sentence fragments necessary as "reminders." If a child finds that for the moment he is not sure about his selection of notes from a sentence, a group of sentences, or a paragraph, he may copy the passage but he should indicate on his note card that it is a quotation.

Outlining, the other retention skill, is really a form of note taking. It differs from the note taking just discussed in the purposes for which it is used and the demands which these purposes make. The purposes for outlining generally have something to do with a digest or structure of ideas. A person may outline a passage to procure a digest of ideas from a resource of limited availability, such as a reference book maintained in a reference library and not circulated outside the library. Sometimes a person outlines to obtain a structure of ideas as a means of furthering his understanding about a topic or issue or as a readily available framework for review. Or he may outline to obtain a structure of ideas for a report or a project. The teacher introduces his pupils to outlining through presenting these purposes as the reasons for learning to outline.

As the teacher guides his pupils into learning the skill of outlining, he should make certain that the pupils have an initial experience with outlining material that can easily be outlined. The style in which a passage is written determines the ease of outlining. If the writer uses an informational-journalistic style, he will tend to cluster the facts supporting an idea into a single paragraph. The idea itself must be inferred from the facts given. This means that the pupil doing the outlining will have to infer the main ideas. He will find very few topical sentences which present main ideas. If the writer uses a critical-instructive style, the written text which he produces will differentiate between main ideas and supporting ideas and facts, using topical sentences and summary sentences. Such material is much easier to outline. Many social-studies textbooks are written in informational-journalistic style;

therefore, they will contain few passages which can be easily outlined. When the teacher presents outlining as a skill to his class, he should present simpler material written in critical-instructive style. At a later time he can guide his class in coping with the problems inherent in outlining material written in informational-journalistic style.

In its simplest aspect an outline is a linear, hierarchical arrangement of facts and ideas expressed in the most economic way and it is this rather definitive notion of an outline that children will need in order to be able to outline a printed passage. A simple topical outline may be introduced to children in grade two or three, or a complex outline with sections, main ideas, supporting ideas, and supporting facts may be introduced to children in grade seven or eight. Whatever the complexity, one of the best ways to introduce the outline to children as a structure is to guide them in an analysis of a printed passage and its outline. As they see the relationship between the contents of passage and outline, they learn what an outline is.

Instruction in outlining is most effective when each level of complexity is introduced separately. The topical outline, or the outline of main ideas, is treated first. Children learn how to make this outline in the later part of grade two or in grade three. The simple understandings which they work toward are these: (1) every paragraph in a passage tells about an idea, (2) this idea is the main idea, and (3) in an outline the main idea is expressed briefly and labeled with a roman numeral. When a child has mastered these understandings, he is introduced to the next level of complexity, supporting ideas in an outline. In a total elementary curriculum, learning about supporting ideas in an outline occurs in grade four or five. The children are guided toward these understandings: (1) usually there are other ideas in the paragraph besides the main idea; (2) these ideas tell more about the main idea; (3) they are the supporting ideas; and (4) presented in the order in which they occur in the paragraph, they are expressed briefly and each is labeled with a capital letter. The more extended outline which includes supporting facts is generally taught in grade six: (1) facts are related together to express ideas; (2) frequently there are several sets of facts in a supporting idea; (3) these facts make the idea more clear; and (4) presented in the order in which they occur in a main idea, they are expressed briefly and each is labeled with an Arabic numeral. More extended levels are possible in an outline. The number of levels is a function of the complexity of presentation and organization of ideas in the written passage. In grades seven and eight, children may need to outline complex passages. Little more than an extension of the numeral-letter sequence of ideas and the necessary indentions are required as the tools of outlining. The following are among the label systems sometimes used:

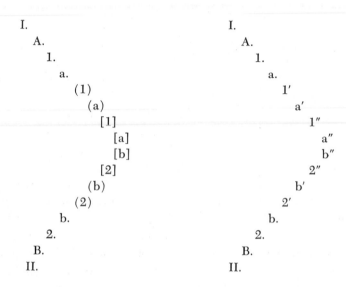

Curriculum specifications for teaching outlining skills differ. Sometimes specifications are few. If a teacher finds that his pupils in the later grades cannot outline or have poor outlining skills, he should begin at the very simplest level, the topical outline or the outline of main ideas, and build from that level to more sophisticated levels.

Recently a kit of instructional materials which includes material dealing with the note-taking and outlining skills just discussed has been published by Science Research Associates. These materials are organized to guide children toward understanding notes and outlines and to provide practice in the skills. The materials are designed for children of various ability levels and for classroom use with an entire class, with a group, or with individuals.

The third complex of reading skills with which the social-studies teacher must be concerned consists of the exploratory and discovery skills. These skills are most closely related to the fundamental reading skills taught during either the reading period or language-arts period. They represent the independent exercise of reading fundamentals for the purposes of social studies. Although the purposes are for social studies, they must also be purposes which the individual reader heartily accepts as worthwhile, for it is the setting of individual purposes by the pupil himself that makes exploratory and discovery reading a fruitful experience.

Of the two kinds of individual purposes, the first is to find out all about a topic or issue. This purpose will involve learning the basic vocabulary associated with the topic or issue, discovering the structure of ideas within which the topic or issue is usually discussed, and recognizing the applications of basic ideas. The second kind of individual purposes are those having to do with the acquisition of more useful ideas. The reader seeks to find a more valid principle. This principle may parallel an opinion he holds; therefore, he reads for a change of opinion or for a strengthening of conviction.

The setting of these individual purposes comes in part through the social-studies program and in part through a personal acceptance of these purposes. The purposes are the social-studies teacher's basic responsibility, but his responsibility does not end with them. He must teach his pupils the skills which will assure the effectiveness of exploratory-discovery skills. One way is to teach a complex of acts that remain always the same. Almost always these include a preview or survey of the material to be read to become familiar with the general content, skimming to identify purposes as suggested by topic sentences or side headings and italicized words, reading to answer the established purposes, and synthesizing the results into a retainable digest of pertinent facts and ideas. The teacher may reduce this process to a formula such as ESSS (explore, skim, scan, study) or PQRR (preview, question, read, review). Unfortunately, the factors in the formula frequently conceal the complexity of the acts to be performed. Each act has to be carefully taught and related to the others in the sequence. The following is a program that a fifth-grade teacher could follow:

First day: Using a social-studies textbook, guide the children in leafing through selected, previously unread sections or chapters to determine what they are about. Have the children discuss their findings.

Second day: Using a social-studies textbook carefully organized with side headings and italicized terms, guide the children in skimming the contents to find points of reference. As each point is found, help the children through discussion to develop a questioning attitude about it and to formulate a question or statement of purpose. Follow this with careful reading to answer the question or purpose.

Third day: Guide the children in a review of the acts performed so far. Help them to see the relationship between the acts, present an independent task in which these acts are performed, and have the children work independently. At the close of the period the children compare individual results.

Fourth day: Introduce the use of note cards as a means of recording findings and guide the children into another independent task. Guide them in examining their cards and developing an outline or summary of facts and ideas. Immediately administer an objective test on the material treated to help the children see the value of a systematic approach to reading material when they are responsible for establishing purposes.

Thereafter, the teacher occasionally guides the children into situations in which the skill is demanded.

Guiding children in the use of formulae does not occur before grade four or five.

Another way of helping children establish purposes for exploratory-discovery reading is an individualized approach. The teacher works with the child to help him to formulate questions about his point of interest. Using these, the child reads and discusses his findings with the teacher or class.

Another way to help pupils develop individual purposes is to encourage them to jot down an opinion, belief, or conviction about the topic or issue under study. In short, they are encouraged to make a self-survey. Then they read to test their own accuracy of opinion, belief, or conviction. This procedure is most frequently used in grades seven and eight.

As a social-studies teacher examines his responsibility as both a teacher of social studies and a teacher of reading, he often wonders where one responsibility ends and the other begins. The teacher in the self-contained classroom has much less difficulty with his problem, except in those instances in which the curriculum is rigidly prescribed. The teacher at work in the departmentalized situation has much greater difficulty. If the teachers in the language-arts department are incooperative and subject-matter lines in the curriculum are drawn according to absolute criteria, the difficulty is increased. However, if children are to be expected to investigate primarily through reading, the social-studies teacher has no choice other than to accept his responsibility as a reading teacher and to do the best that he can within rigid guidelines.

One way to work within rigid guidelines is to prepare and teach a reading-skills unit at the beginning of the school year or semester and to alternate skills units with content units. The unit is concentrated and carefully prepared. Usually it comprises two measuring devices and practice materials developed from the basic social-studies textbook. The practice materials are developed in a series at various levels of sophistication, at least three exercises per level. At the beginning of the unit, the teacher introduces the ideas that support the effective use of the skill involved, uses one of the measuring devices to see how much his pupils know, and then assigns individuals to the levels of materials which meet their needs. After most of the pupils have finished the final level of materials, the teacher uses the measuring device to determine how much the pupils have achieved. The results are discussed with the pupils, who are guided into generalizing about their learning and are encouraged to use the generalizations as guiding principles when they need to apply the skill. Such a unit may require from two to four class periods.

Some teachers find it easier to work within rigid guidelines by teaching a combination skills-content unit. A basic-content unit required for understanding later more complex units is selected. Such a unit may be one of the following: *Physical Geography, Factors of Production, Organization of Government, Culture,* or the like. The introductory materials, the tests, and the practice materials are developed from the content of the unit. The preparation of materials and the procedures followed are similar to those in the skills unit. When the teacher guides his pupils in evaluation, they evaluate content learning as well as skills learning.

Many teachers, particularly those working in grades seven and eight in departmentalized situations, prefer to teach the skills in accord with individual pupil needs. These teachers have on hand the practice materials necessary for instruction. During investigative periods, the teacher carefully observes his pupils at work. Whenever he sees a pupil having difficulty, he consults with him immediately to learn the nature of the difficulty. On the basis of his findings, he assigns practice materials to the pupil, some of which are to be accomplished during class time and after school, the rest to be completed as homework. During available class time and after school the teacher counsels with the pupil to assure his learning the needed skill.

None of these procedures is superior to the others. The teaching style of the teacher and his ways of perceiving pupils' difficulties may make one procedure more workable than the others. What is important is that the pupils' investigative skills in reading be improved to the limits of his capacity so that he may learn how to inform himself about topics and issues in human affairs, and ideas significant to social studies.

Much of the foregoing is applicable only to children who have reached a high level of sophistication in the fundamentals of reading. However, much can be done in the primary grades to prepare children for the more concentrated program in reading skills used in social studies in the later grades. Each complex of skills has its beginning somewhere in the primary grades.

The foundation for reading-reference skills can be laid in the kindergarten. The basic idea to be taught is that books are valuable sources in which to seek information. The teacher teaches this idea by reading excerpts from various books as a means of acquiring information.

The foundation for reading-reference skills is extended in the primary grades. Alphabet skills, so necessary to finding one's way through an index, are taught. Toward the end of first grade, children can be taught how to use a very simple table of contents and index as a means of pinpointing the location of information. By late second grade, many children are ready to learn how to analyze simple topic titles and questions for entry words. By late third grade, some children are prepared to learn how to skim side headings as a means of locating information on a page or two.

Certain aspects of retention skills may be begun as early as second grades. Those children whose writing skills may still be quite primitive can "draw" their notes in simple sketches or pictures. They can take notes when a large part of the handwriting chore is removed. The questions which they are to investigate may be duplicated at the head of newsprint note sheets. They find the answer and record it in a few words. Some children will be ready for the simplest aspects of outlining when the material to be outlined is carefully written and well organized. They can make an outline of main ideas properly labeled with roman numerals.

The exploratory-discovery skills may be practiced as children read accounts in their weekly newspaper. The purposes remain ever the same: What was the newspaper story about? What did it say? What was important about it? These general purposes, learned first as the teacher questions the pupils orally about their reading and later when following a chart on which these purposes are simply expressed, help children to learn about the logical organization of ideas and how to express purposes.

With such a profusion of skills to be taught, teachers often ask how and when they can be taught within a curriculum already overloaded. Several procedures may be suggested. Such skills as map and globe skills, graph-analysis skills may be regarded as those of particular use in social studies; therefore, time can and must be found during the conduct of the social-studies program to teach these skills. If the teacher organizes his units carefully, time will be available. The reading skills which can be generalized to serve in science and the study of health can be taught better during the reading or language-arts period. Such a practice could serve well to improve the program in all the content areas of the curriculum, particularly in the later grades.

SUMMARY

Children's contact with social-studies reality is most likely to be through representations of it. If the contact is to be effective, children will need to be taught the skills necessary to interpreting and dealing in other ways with symbols, regardless of the medium in which they are presented. Teacher who are deeply concerned about children's problems in working with symbols provide representations carefully selected on the basis of accuracy of content and the adequacy of children's skills, and guide the children through carefully developed instructional programs to assure a fundamental mastery.

Most of the skills programs are amenable to either incidental or systematic approaches to teaching. The teacher chooses whether a skills program is to be incidental or systematic. His choice will be influenced by the content of his unit and the needs of his particular class.

The skills programs include the following: skills in picture analysis, diagram analysis, graph analysis, in map and globe study, and in reading. The reading skills to be treated are reference, retention, and exploratory-discovery skills. Most of the skills can be broken down into sub-skills which can be directly taught and interrelated.

Picture-analysis skills consist of identifying the items and functions depicted, in interrelating them, and in arriving at a statement of meaning. The teacher may help children to learn these skills through carefully guided picture study as required in the unit or through specially developed materials which focus precisely on each subskill. Picture-analysis skills are as essential to the average and above-average pupils as they are to below-average pupils.

Skill in diagram analysis rests on the ability to interpret labels or the key and the ability to relate the diagram to the real structure in terms of size and function. Not many opportunities for the exercise of diagram-analysis skills exist in elementary social studies. For this reason, the instructional program is usually incidental.

Although graph-analysis skills differ somewhat in accord with the type of graph (bar, line, picture, or other), children will need to be guided carefully in the skills of graph orientation, unit or symbol analysis, interpolation, and synthesis. Incidental and systematic approaches to instruction in these skills differ only in the extent to which children have extended practice in the various subskills. Sometimes children are brought to a better understanding of how to interpret graphs by being guided into graph making.

The learning of map- and globe-study skills usually requires a systematic program of instruction. Most of the learning is inherent within six generalizations relating to directions, a map as a representation, a globe as a representation, the relationship between a map and the globe, scale, and grid.

The instructional approach to teaching the various reading skills necessary to social studies is usually systematic. Reading-reference skills include skills in locating an appropriate source and skill in finding the place within it at which to begin reading carefully. Skill in the latter resides for the most part in the ability to analyze the statement of purpose to determine the entry word or idea to use when consulting a table of contents or an index. The reading-retention skills, note taking and outlining, require carefully delineated purposes. Note taking involves developing complete statements on note cards or paper in which purpose, information, and source are indicated. Paraphrasing presents the greatest difficulty to children in this skill. Outlining, the business of developing a digest of ideas from a source, frequently presents difficulties to children because of the style in which the material to be outlined is written. Informational-journalistic material is more difficult to outline than that written in critical-instructional style. The exploratory-discovery reading skills are exercised when children's individual purposes are involved. This purpose emerges from the social-studies program. Sometimes children can be taught simple formula systems of approach to this form of reading.

The social-studies teacher is also a teacher of reading. Depending upon his teaching situation, he may see the need for teaching units of instruction which are pointed largely toward helping children improve in selected reading skills.

The foundation for the various reading skills necessary to social studies is laid in the primary grades.

Exercises for Further Understanding

1. Select a picture or a cartoon that would be useful to an elementary class as a source of information. Think through as carefully as you can how you would introduce it to the children and how you would guide them in analyzing it.

2. Select a picture depicting social-studies content and develop a self-correcting exercise that would be helpful to a child in learning how to read pictures.

3. Develop the materials and a plan necessary for introducing children to reading a diagram. One of your aids should be a diagram of something familiar to the class, such as a classroom, a home, or an automobile. A key should be provided. Your other aid should be a diagram of something relatively unknown to the children.

4. Develop a simple bar graph showing social-studies content. Use it in developing a simple, independent, self-correcting exercise which would be helpful to a child learning how to read graphs.

5. Several basic procedures for teaching how to read maps and globes have been presented in this chapter. Study one set of these related to the teaching of a basic map or globe idea. Study it carefully. Then plan a lesson which would logically extend the procedures presented.

6. Using a social-studies textbook written for children, develop a simple, independent, self-correcting exercise which would help a child to learn the skills involved in using a table of contents or an index.

7. Carefully scan a social-studies textbook written for children to find several passages suitable for outlining. As a "proof" of suitability, outline the passages yourself. If possible, persuade a classmate to outline the same passage. Compare the results to see how closely the two of you agree.

8. Develop the materials and a plan necessary to introduce children to note taking.

Selected References

Barton, Thomas Frank, "Functional Play." *Social Education,* 19:210-212 (May 1955).

Burrows, Alvina Treut, "Reading, Research, and Reporting in the Social Studies," *Social Studies in the Elementary School,* Fifty-Sixth Yearbook of the National Society for the Study of Education, Part II, Chicago: The University of Chicago Press, 1957.

Chace, Harriet, "Map Skills in the First Grade." *Social Education,* 19:361-362 (December 1955).

————, "Map Skills at the Third Grade Level." *Social Education,* 20:13-14 (January 1956).

Hanna, Lavone A., Gladys L. Potter, and Neva Hagaman, *Unit Teaching in the Elementary School,* rev. ed., Chap. 9, "Developing Skills of Inquiry and Research." New York: Holt, Rinehart and Winston, 1963.

Harris, Ruby M., *Handbook of Map and Globe Usage.* New York: Rand McNally & Company, 1959.

Jarolimek, John, *Social Studies in Elementary Education,* 2d ed., Chap. 6, "Reading Social Studies Materials." New York: The Macmillan Company, 1963.

McAulay, J. D., "Some Uses of Social Studies Textbooks." *Social Education,* 21:23-24ff (January, 1957).

McCracken, Mary E., "Learning about Mexico through Maps." *Social Education,* 22:361-362 (November 1958).

Michaelis, John U., *Social Studies for Children in a Democracy,* 3d ed., Chap. 10, "Reading Materials, Reading Skills." Englewood Cliffs, N.J.: Prentice-Hall, Inc., 1963.

Sabaroff, Rose, "Map-Making in the Primary Grades." *Social Education,* 24:19-20 (January 1960).

Sawyer, Richard P., "A Reading Teacher in the Social Studies Class." *Social Education,* 20:364-366 (December 1956).

Spache, George D., *Toward Better Reading*, Chap. 4, "What Is the Nature of Comprehension?" Chap. 5, "How Shall We Teach Critical Reading?" and Chap. 18, "Study Skills." Champaign, Ill.: Garrard Publishing Company, 1964.

Tinker, Miles A., and Constance M. McCullough, *Teaching Elementary Reading*, 2d ed., Chap. 12, "Reading in the Content Fields." New York: Appleton-Century-Crofts, Inc., 1962.

11

Improving Expressive Skills

The two preceding chapters have dealt primarily with the procedures and practices to be followed in helping children be more independent in the acquisition of social-studies facts and ideas. This chapter presents ways of guiding children to become more independent as users and integrators of facts and ideas through expressive activity. The acquiring function does not cease, for as children integrate acquired knowledge through expression, they discover new ideas about social studies and themselves. The integration of facts and ideas and the discovery of new ideas are accepted by some social-studies educators as the purposes for expressive activity.[1,2,3,4]

Teachers using the synthesized strategy and that of thinking emphasis tend to regard these purposes as essential. In so doing, they are

[1]Maxine Dunfee and Helen Sagl, *Social Studies through Problem Solving* (New York: Holt, Rinehart and Winston, Inc., 1966), pp. 202-228.

[2]Edith Merritt, *Working with Children in Social Studies* (San Francisco: Wadsworth Publishing Company, Inc., 1961), pp. 217-242.

[3]John U. Michaelis, *Social Studies in a Democracy* (Englewood Cliffs, N.J.: Prentice-Hall, Inc., 1963), pp. 525-572.

[4]Ernest W. Tiegs and Fay Adams, *Teaching the Social Studies* (Boston: Ginn and Company, 1959), pp. 394-398.

following practices based upon interpretations of John Dewey's philosophical findings[5] as well as the findings of others.[6,7] As do many other
curriculum specialists, they see expressive activity as supportive of mental health, personality development, development of worthwhile leisure-
time activity and creativity. With respect to the last-named area, these
strategists follow the assertions that creativity does not develop and
grow in a vacuum, but requires careful stimulation, and they live with
the criticism that their concern for product appears to be greater than
it is for process.[8] True, children's creative products are often used as a
source of data on how much has been learned and the extent to which
it is understood. This use need not inhibit the growth of creativity.[9,10,11]

Although the teacher using the social-science strategy is not barred
by his commitment from following beliefs similar to the above, he may
choose another viewpoint. He may reject much of the above and justify
his rejection by indicating the paucity of empirical data supporting the
theory that expressive activity works in the ways it is believed to work
with normal elementary-school children. He does not reject expressive
activity as a part of the social-studies program. He views it in this way:
If in their inquiry children need to use an expressive mode of the social
scientists, they are guided into using it. If they need additional instruction in its use, they are given it.

The teachers using the other strategies will also have instructional
programs in the use of a variety of media for expression. Depending on
the organization of curriculum in the district, these programs may be
included as aspects of the social-studies program or of the art and
language-arts programs. Occasionally the unfortunate circumstance

[5]John Dewey, Democracy and Education (New York: The Macmillan Company, 1916), pp. 241, 274, 352.

[6]Henri Bergson, *The Creative Mind,* translated by Mabelle L. Andison (New
York: The Wisdom Library, 1946), pp. 81-84.

[7]Benedetto Croce, *Aesthetic,* translated by Douglas Ainslie (New York: The
Noonday Press, 1953), p. 11.

[8]Pauline Johnson, "Art for the Young Child," *Art Education,* Sixty-Fourth
Yearbook of the National Society for the Study of Education, Part II (Chicago:
The University of Chicago Press, 1965), p. 79.

[9]Charles D. Gaitskell, *Children and Their Art* (New York: Harcourt, Brace &
Company, Inc., 1958), pp. 36-55, 342-345, 355-356.

[10]Blanche Jefferson, *Teaching Art to Children* (Boston: Allyn and Bacon, Inc.,
1959), pp. 250-256.

[11] Viktor Lowenfeld and W. Lambert Brittain, *Creative and Mental Growth*
(New York, The Macmillan Company, 1964), pp. 49-51.

occurs in which no specific provisions are made in any instructional program for the expressive skills necessary to social studies. In this instance, the teacher develops programs as he sees the need for them. The suggestions offered in the following sections are workable within any of the strategies.

As the teacher considers his task of teaching the necessary skills he will find it helpful to regard them as being primarily verbal or nonverbal skills. The instructional procedures for teaching various verbal skills tend to be similar; those for teaching various nonverbal skills also tend to be somewhat similar. Although American elementary schools tend to give some emphasis to all the expressive skills, by far the greatest emphasis is given to the various kinds of verbal expression; therefore, the remainder of this chapter will reflect much more detail in the discussion of verbal skills. The discussion dealing with nonverbal skills will tend to be more general.

IMPROVING NONVERBAL-EXPRESSION SKILLS

Nonverbal expressive products—murals, desk pictures, clay figures, and the like—share a common characteristic: Each tends to be a statement of a single idea. If the teacher accepts nonverbal expression as statement making, and not just as release from the tensions or pressures that characterize the busy school day, or as simply drawing, painting, constructing, or the like, he strives to help children make statements. If he lends the cast of communication to his thinking and procedure, he holds certain basic conditions central to statement making, that is, that there be something to say and that there be the ways and means of saying it. He assures himself that these conditions prevail as his pupils approach the task of expressing their social-studies learning through the use of nonverbal media.

To assure that his pupils have something to say, the teacher carefully builds interest in the ideas being studied and guides the pupils through fruitful investigations. These procedures comprise the continuing aspect of assuring that children have something to say. In an immediate aspect, the teacher helps his pupils recall the facts and ideas to be expressed, especially when expression follows a number of investigative periods over several days. Children usually cannot recall facts and ideas by themselves. Frequently the expressive period occurs after a summary has been made on the previous day. The summary is reviewed and discussed briefly. Little if anything is recorded during this discussion to leave the choice of ideas for expression open.

If the children are to express before a summarization has occurred, as often happens daily in a primary grade, the teacher guides the pupils in a review of the facts and ideas studied and then encourages them to think about the main idea studied and to express it. Sometimes the children are encouraged to express what was just studied.

If the expression is to be primarily an individual task, the teacher must make certain provisions for the "ways" of expression. This administrative task includes making certain that each child has a place to work at a table, at an easel, or on the floor. Children may have to be grouped according to space and facilities available. (See Figure 7.) Ways for distributing materials will have to be organized. Perhaps materials will

FIGURE 7. FOURTH GRADERS USE SAND, PAPER, CLAY, AND
STICKS TO EXPRESS LEARNING.

be placed at or near the work space before expression begins, or distributed cafeteria style as the children file by a materials center, or distributed by monitors. Provisions will need to be made for the gathering of materials, cleanup at the end of the expression period, and the disposition of finished products. Many teachers feel that the success of expression depends largely on how well the administrative details for expression have been organized and how well the children understand these provisions.

Early in the school year it may be necessary for the teacher to guide his pupils in determining the standards of behavior to prevail during the expression period. The teacher guides the pupils in developing standards about how much conversation is to be permitted, how much movement is to be made about the classroom, how to obtain help when it is needed, and what a child is to do when he finishes early. Some teachers find that by extending the expressive period for the first few times during the school year they have the necessary time for habituating children to these standards. Later only a reminder is necessary to assure positive, productive behavior during the expression period.

If the expression is to be primarily a group task, the teacher guides the pupils in the use of group process to determine what the organization of the classroom is to be during the expression period. When the groups are involved in a task, their work usually requires an extended time, perhaps a half day or a whole day or all the social-studies periods over a week or more. Time is required for groups to plan as well as to do what they plan. Each group must meet to decide what it is going to say in its expression, how it is to be said, the materials needed, where the work will take place, and to determine individual assignments within the group. The standards for the behavior of individuals within groups should have already been established before the children divide into groups.

The third major concern of the teacher as he provides for expressive activity is the "means," or the thinking and psychomotor skills necessary for accurate and satisfying expression. The "means" are provided in part by the elementary program in art. (See Figure 8.) This program provides opportunities for children to make discoveries about the use of materials and techniques. These discoveries should be made before children are guided into expression in social studies. Because expression in social studies is primarily an application of skills learned in the other areas of the elementary curriculum, providing for the "means" of expression will consist mostly of product analysis. For example, if children are to paint a mural, their point of departure will be an analysis to determine precisely what the mural is as a means of expression. As they analyze the mural, they begin to see it as a statement made through the use of media and techniques they have learned previously, as a precise application of media and techniques. Often children who have had few opportunities to learn art techniques will have inklings of what they are to do just through analysis of an art product.

FIGURE 8. THIRD GRADERS USE THEIR OWN WAY AND THAT OF
ANOTHER CULTURE TO EXPRESS IDEAS.

Many art teachers, specialists in teaching many forms of nonverbal expression, introduce each new medium or technique with a product analysis. This product is often fashioned by the teacher. The social-studies teacher may not have the skills required for making products for children to analyze, but he need not be deterred from guiding his pupils in product analysis. He may have the children analyze children's products made by his previous classes. Often children are willing to leave their products with the teacher. The product used for analysis should reflect the use of a medium in making a statement but it should not deal with the same content that the children in the current class are going to express. For example, children who are going to express themselves through making figurines of the native Hawaiians should examine figurines of Mexican people or people of some other culture. These figurines provide opportunity for an analysis of the use of a medium but offer little encouragement for copying. Another source of art expressions is the many commercial reproductions of art products. Reproductions must be used with care because they often suggest standards of perfection which children cannot hope to reach.

As the teacher guides the children in making an analysis of the art product, he directs them toward two points of analysis: the statement that the expresser has attempted to make in his product and the means used in making his statement. The teacher encourages the children to react verbally to the attempt of the expresser (the artist, the sculptor, the author, the person who made the graph, map, chart, or the like.) These verbal reactions are pooled and synthesized to determine the statement made. The second point, dealing with the means used by the expresser, will be limited by the teacher's knowledge of nonverbal expression. This analysis may involve little more than directing the children's attention toward aspects of composition, the center of interest, and simple figure-ground relationships, or it may be more sophisticated, including such aspects as the integration of elements, rhythm, proportion, the dynamics of line, form, color, texture, space, and unity. These aspects are not treated as principles, rules, or even precautions, but as means of making a clear statement. The discussion should be simple, not belabored too long, and directed toward a few aspects, not all of them. The need for discussion of particular aspects should be determined by pupil need within the class.

Many teachers find that product analysis as the introduction to expressive activity makes children more eager to commit themselves to the act of expression. They readily recall the facts necessary for expression and willingly accept whatever organization is needed for the distribution of materials, arrangement of work space, and control of individual behavior. Furthermore, product analysis yields a basis for evaluation in terms of tangibles.

The teacher's final concern as he works with children expressing themselves is to make provision for continued growth in their ability to express ideas. He reflects his concern by guiding his pupils in evaluating their work to see whether they have met the objectives to which they had been committed. First they examine their expressive products to determine whether they have "said" what they meant to "say" and whether their statements agree with the facts and ideas acquired through investigation. Then they take a careful look at how well they have applied their expressive skills and what they need to know more about.

Many teachers find that group evaluation is helpful to pupils. The group examines the products of those individuals who have no qualms about showing their work. The group discusses the accuracy of statement first, and then the application of skills. The group feels free to ask the expresser how he solved certain expressive problems and he is encouraged to ask the group for suggestions on how he could have solved certain problems.

Some teachers feel that greater depth is assured when each pupil evaluates his own work with the help of the teacher. During this procedure the pupil comes to know his strengths and the areas in which he needs to learn more. The evaluation often results in the organization of a self-improvement program which the pupil accepts wholeheartedly.

Some teachers attempt to help pupils improve in expressive skills by exhibiting only the best products. More often than not this procedure encourages those who do well to do better and those who do less than well to do as little as possible. The display of products can incite all children to learn more, but only when every child has an equal chance to see his product displayed.

Much of what has been discussed to this point has been directed toward the teacher who maintains an instructional program in a self-contained classroom. The social-studies teacher who works in a departmentalized situation may have to make different provisions for nonverbal expressive activities in which painting, modeling, or constructing are involved. Many teachers in such a situation guide their pupils into individual projects. The success of such an approach depends on the variety of projects considered acceptable by the teacher. If he is flexible he is more likely to meet the needs of his pupils. Usually pupils provide their own materials and work at home. The teacher will have to provide for individual conferencing with pupils, perhaps during his free periods or after school, to encourage the production and completion of projects. Pupils who complete projects should be given an opportunity to show and discuss their products with the class.

Occasionally the teacher in the departmentalized school may guide his pupils into group projects. Sometimes the projects are undertaken and completed in the classroom on specified days after school. Sometimes the art teacher is willing to cooperate by providing materials, time, and work space during the art period for the pupils from a particular class to work on a project. An art teacher may also assume the responsibility of helping a group of pupils learn more about the use of the media necessary for a project.

Social-studies teachers in departmentalized schools tend to assign projects which are primarily language activities. This practice penalizes many pupils, particularly those who do not write well. The pupil may have acquired the facts and ideas that have been studied, but he cannot express them well because the medium favorable to him is rarely included in expressive activity. A pupil who is unable to write an acceptable report or term paper may well be able to produce a series of watercolor paintings illustrating events leading to a significant change, or illustrate a process vital to government on a large chart, or construct a diorama reflecting early Roman life.

IMPROVING VERBAL-EXPRESSION SKILLS

Although expressive products such as maps, globes, diagrams, and graphs are usually regarded as nonverbal expressions, the use of verbal symbols on them is so necessary in many instances that they could be classified as a special type of verbal expression. Often the nonverbal symbols on such products are virtually meaningless without labels, legends, and keys of various kinds. In the following discussion, maps, globes, diagrams, and charts will be regarded as brief, economic statements in which the economy is accomplished through the use of nonverbal symbols, sometimes conventional and sometimes invented, to bridge between the various arrangements of verbal symbols.

In some respects, improving children's expressive skills in map, globe, diagram, and graph making is similar to improving their skills in nonverbal expression. The teacher must make provisions for the pupils to have something to say and for the "ways" and "means" of expression. Facts must be recalled, materials and work space must be allotted, an expressive product must be analyzed, and the result of the expressive attempt must be evaluated. However, unlike the program to improve nonverbal skills, the program of improvement of these special expressive skills has little or no support from the other areas in the elementary curriculum. Map and globe making is an expressive skill taught almost entirely within social studies, and much the same is true with diagram making. Graph making may be treated in the arithmetic program, depending on content organization, or the science program, depending on the strength of the program in which maintaining complete and careful records during the observation of phenomena is emphasized. In many schools, teaching graph making as an expressive skill will be the responsibility of the social-studies teacher. The programs in improving skills in map, globe, diagram, and graph making will generally be taught during the social-studies period, with a primary program and a program for the later grades.

MAP AND GLOBE MAKING

Map and globe making in social studies may be justified in two ways. First, learning how to make a map or a globe supports learning how to interpret maps and globes. Frequently a teacher guides children into making maps immediately after they have learned what a map is. Children learn how the symbols on a map are used to convey information and then are encouraged to use similar symbols to express ideas on a map. Second, a map or globe is a good way to arrange certain kinds of information for presentation; in many instances, a map is the best way. Data about topography, climate, political relationships, economic relationships, and cultural relationships can often be more clearly expressed on a map or globe than in any other way.

Generally a map serves better than a globe as a vehicle for expression. A globe tends to be a static structure unamenable to many different kinds of arrangements. Furthermore, a globe represents such a reduction of space that it is of limited utility. As a construction it presents many difficulties in terms of class time and room space. A map is not so static. It is amenable to many different kinds of rearrangements to show many different kinds of relationships. A map may be used to represent any space, including a space within the child's perception; it is a common form of expression and is relatively easy for individuals and groups to construct.

Little is done in the primary grades with globe making. Occasionally children in grade two or three are guided into fashioning individual globes from paper mache. Sometimes a ball of crumpled paper or an inflated balloon is covered with paper mache. The resulting form is painted and labeled to represent the classroom globe. Often the basic reason for making a globe is just to make a globe like the classroom globe. Globe making is somewhat helpful to children as they try to learn the placement of continents and oceans.

Once these globes have been made, they may be used for expressing other learning such as the different kinds of clothing worn, the different kinds of food eaten, the different kinds of homes built, and the different kinds of animals used around the world. The pupils make small paper figures and paste them at the approximate locations. Such an activity teaches the child that space and distance may be defined or described by the ways that people live and do things. Care must be taken that erroneous learning does not occur. For example, a child who has pasted representations of a grass hut in Africa and another in South America, of a conventional house in North America and Europe, and of a pagodalike structure in China and Japan, may come to the erroneous understanding that all the people in Asia live in pagodalike structures, and so on. The teacher should help pupils to understand that their symbols represent the ways of some, not all, people in an area.

A teaching sequence for guiding primary children into globe making is presented as follows:

1. Make a globe in the way that children are to make it. Paste on it representations showing the distribution of something other than what the children are studying. For example, if the children are studying clothing, prepare the globe to show the distribution of ways of providing shelter around the world. They can see the use of the globe for showing distribution and then deal with the problem of using it to show differences in clothing around the world.

2. Show the globe to the children and guide them toward seeing what is expressed on it. Then guide them toward thinking how they can express what they are studying on a globe.

3. Using the materials needed for making a globe, show the children how

it is made. This procedure should be reduced to simple steps to be followed.

4. Distribute the materials and give help to the pupils who need it.

Globe making in the primary grades is a time-consuming venture. Before guiding children into it, the teacher should give consideration to several factors, including the time available, the maturity of the children or their ability to do the task with a minimum of supervision, and the worthwhileness of the task.

Map making in the primary grades is a basic part of learning how to interpret maps as each new learning about a map is applied. After children have learned what a map is and the function of symbols on maps, they are ready to begin to make maps. The following sequence is recommended for guiding children into map making:

1. Take the children on a field trip to a geographical area rich in contrasts—hills and valleys, meadows and streams, and so on. An area close to the school and somewhat familiar to the children is preferable. Guide the children in observing the details of the area. Only the large, more easily observable details should be treated.

2. Immediately upon returning from the field trip, have the children express what they observed by constructing a simple relief map. A sand table is preferred for this activity. An outside sand pit may be used. By distributing the sand to make land forms and fashioning symbols for details such as streams, roads, groves of trees, or the like, the children construct a map which reflects what they observed. If no sand table or sand pit is available, a relief map can be made from a discarded sheet and crumpled newspaper. The newspaper is crumpled to represent rises in the land and the sheet is laid over them and pressed down to represent depressions.

3. Guide the children into making a "flat" map of the same area on a large paper surface laid out on the floor.

4. If the children have already learned about directions, guide them into putting directional indicators on the map.

5. Have the children make maps of areas familiar to them such as the classroom, a bedroom, the home, and the school.

The above sequence will assure most children of a "feel" for maps.

Using maps for the expression of ideas learned in social studies is an easily learned step after a sequence of learning activities similar to the one above. Several effective procedures may be used to help children make the bridge from what they know about maps to using maps for expression. If the children have been using maps of an area—a city, harbor, airport, or county—in investigating, the suggestion that similar maps be used for the expression of ideas is generally well received by them. Frequently teachers in the primary use a functional map which they make themselves as an investigative source for children. This outline map consists of the shape of an area cut from large sheets of heavy, durable paper or from a large sheet of oilcloth and symbols fashioned from wood, plastic, or paper. The teacher needs only encourage expression with a map and invite the children to use it to express the facts and ideas that they have learned. It is assumed that the facts and ideas will be other than those which were expressed on the map previously.

Or the teacher may show a map already made expressing ideas similar to those being studied. This map may be commercial, one that the teacher has made, or one made by another class. Frequently a visit to another classroom to see one of its products heightens children's desire to make a similar product.

Or the teacher may make the outline map and encourage the children to use it for their own expression.

Preparing the outline portion of any map may present difficulty to children in the primary grades. It is advisable for the teacher to do this work himself and leave to the children the responsibility of making symbols and placing them on the map. Some care needs to be taken in guiding children toward making symbols of proportionate size. For example, in the map of a harbor the symbol for a lighthouse and the one for the breakwater should bear an approximate size relationship as do the objects in reality.

In most instances, map making in the primary grades is a group venture. It usually occurs at the end of the unit when ideas are being tied together.

Characteristically, the areas studied in the later grades are the larger areas such as states, provinces, countries, regions, and continents. If the primary program has been strong, the "feel" for maps serves to make expression with maps a logical choice for individuals or for groups. If the primary program has been weak, the teacher may find it necessary to teach what a map is and the function of map symbols. Although older children are usually able to work at higher levels of abstraction, the teacher may want to organize a program in which many of the learning activities are similar to those in the good primary program. If a sand table or a sand pit is available, older children will profit from making a relief map of a familiar geographical area. Mapping familiar areas is an experience essential to both map interpretation and expression through maps.

Maps can be used in a wide variety of ways to express many different statements, some of which are listed:

With color as a basic symbol, maps may be used to express:
1. Land-use patterns.
2. Topography.
3. Political divisions.
4. Political relationships.
5. Economic relationships.
6. Cultural relationships.
7. Religious relationships.
8. Population density.
9. Climate, or aspects of climate.
10. Distribution of resources.

Through the use of conventional or invented symbols, maps may be used to express:
1. Any of the ideas listed for color, but with substitutions of cross-hatching or visual textures.
2. Production, total of selected items.
3. Distribution of fauna and flora.
4. Clothing, shelter, and basic foods in various areas, total or selected.
5. Population.
6. Military power.
7. Routes of all kinds.
8. Centers of commerce.
9. Communities of various sizes.
10. Points of historical interest.

Three-dimensional maps most adequately express topography and land-use patterns.

Rearranged maps (maps in which location and size of nations and continents are distorted to express significant relationships) are particularly good for showing:
1. Political relationships.
2. Economic relationships.
3. Cultural relationships.
4. Religious relationships.

Most classrooms in the later grades have wall maps, most frequently

political-physical maps or political and physical maps, the latter sometimes labeled as topographical or elevation maps. Most textbooks and
reference books contain maps, including different kinds of production,
population, and historical maps. Teachers may feel that they are giving
their pupils practice in expressing ideas through maps by having them
copy a map from one source or another. Copying is not expression. However, the many maps that children have available to them may often
be used well in product analysis to help them acquire ideas as to ways
of making maps for expression.

Three-dimensional maps and rearranged maps are rarely found in
elementary classrooms. Three-dimensional maps are quite expensive,
and rearranged maps are not popular. Because rearranged maps are
purposely distorted to express ideas more clearly, they present views of
the earth's surface that are shocking to those who hold that maps are
primarily for navigational purposes. Physical geographers may tend to
be somewhat chary of rearranged maps. Those concerned with social-
studies teaching continually warn of the distortion inherent in maps. The
result is that most teachers shy away from any distorted artifact. Publishers also steer clear of that which is not traditional. Teachers and
those who would be teachers rarely have experience with rearranged
maps. However, a map of the earth's surface in terms of gross national
product of each nation presents most clearly and dramatically certain
economic differences among nations.

The fact that three-dimensional maps and rearranged maps are not
often to be found in elementary classrooms makes them an excellent
choice as maps for expressing social-studies ideas. The three-dimensional
map has long been a favorite, but it is often poorly used. Children have
little idea of how distorted the maps are, especially when each child
produces his own small relief map of his state or country or of a distant
continent. Worse still, these small relief maps lead children into thinking
that states and continents are islands.

Perhaps the best use of a three-dimensional map for expression is
as a means of group expression. A much larger area can be expressed
with less distortion. Practice in the use of scale for more precision can
be provided. Once the map has been completed it is highly useful for
continued study and reference. However, since its construction requires
a lot of time, the teacher will have to organize his daily program
carefully.

As has been pointed out, the rearranged map is obviously distorted in terms of physical distance and location, but it often clarifies other kinds of distance. A map showing the free world in the center surrounded by "buffer" nations between it and the Communist world clarifies ideas about political distance. A map with the industrial nations in the center ringed by nations that produce, primarily, raw materials reflects economic distance. A map with Spain in the center surrounded by the nations of the world in which Hispanic culture influence is strong gives a picture of cultural distance. Considerable care must be exercised in guiding children in the making of such maps. They must be thoroughly aware of why the map is to show a rearrangement. Although it should be obvious to them, it may be necessary for the teacher to point out that such a map cannot be used for navigation across the surface of the world.

Although product analysis of each of the various types of maps may be necessary to provide pupils in the later grades with insights into the task of expression through map making, after the first few experiences with map expression the pupils' imagination will likely be sufficient to make clear statements with maps. If product analysis is necessary, a procedure similar to that recommended for map and globe expressive skills in the primary grades should be used.

Because children in the later grades are more likely to be studying ideas amenable to worldwide application, globe making as a way of expressing is somewhat more feasible than it is in the primary grades. To assure a globe of sufficient size for real usefulness, the teacher should guide his pupils toward making a globe as a group project. Small, individually made globes are of little use in the later grades. The globe can be much larger than the classroom globe and may be made to show a three-dimensional arrangement of the earth's surface. Usually chicken wire fashioned into a hollow ball and covered with paper mache is used in the construction of such a globe. Sometimes the globe may be constructed in hemispheres which are permitted to rest on the floor. The globe or hemispheres may be used over again for the expression of ideas by removing and adding symbols. For example, a fifth-grade class could show the routes of explorers, then the routes of pioneers, and finally modern sea and air routes. Strands of yarn used as symbols could be removed and replaced with each new area of study, or they could all be left on the globe. To construct a large globe or large hemispheres is quite an undertaking for any class. To construct such an artifact just for the purpose of constructing it seems hardly justifiable. If it is to be used again and again for expressing ideas, it is a most worthwhile project.

DIAGRAM MAKING

Essentially there is not much difference between a diagram and a map, except in terms of the area represented. A map may represent a very large or a very small area, relatively speaking. It is generally used to represent natural areas. Almost always it presents a surface view. A diagram usually shows a smaller area and is often used to picture precisely some manmade object. It may present a cross-sectional view.

The teacher's problems in guiding children into diagram making are basically the same as those encountered in guiding children into map making. Just as children need to know what a map really is before trying to express ideas with maps, so will they need a definitive idea of what a diagram is before trying to use it as a means of making a statement. Usually social-studies textbooks contain few diagrams. Some encyclopedias make good use of them and occasionally simple diagrams are to be found in magazine and newspapers, particularly in advertisements. A diagram duplicated and enlarged on a large sheet of paper, or a diagram duplicated for class distribution, or even the small diagrams included in dictionaries will serve as the focal point for analysis. As the teacher guides children in their examination of the diagram, he will need to clarify that a diagram is a simply drawn "map'" of a building or some other structure. A good diagram is usually well labeled or keyed. The children will need to understand why labeling or keying is so important —that it is essential to the viewer for a complete idea of what is being diagrammed. The teacher should remember that if children are to grasp how expressive diagrams can be they must learn how to develop them. Copying diagrams is not an expressive activity.

Making diagrams may be difficult because the children may not have the necessary practical, firsthand experience at measuring and making preliminary sketches. Much of this difficulty can be reduced by helping children to estimate, perhaps by using their height or the height, width, and length of their classroom as a basic unit of measurement. Sometimes more exact measurements can be obtained from an easily accessible source. For example, children making a diagram of an airliner may be able to obtain size information from an airport. During field trips, such as those to the bakery, the fire station, the grain elevator, or the like, the children's attention should be drawn to the dimensions of the structure visited.

A good initial experience with diagram making is to make a diagram of the classroom, labeling and keying it. A "flat" diagram (very similar to a map) may be made. This exercise should be followed by the making of a simple cross-sectional diagram of the classroom. Simple diagrams can also be drawn of desks and other furniture. Each of these should be provided with labels and a simple key.

Simple diagram making may take place in all the grades. However, a three-quarter view of a cross-sectional diagram is usually too difficult for children in the elementary grades.

GRAPHS

Perhaps one of the most widely used forms of expression for social-studies information is the graph. The graph is used for showing comparison of some aspect within an entity or among entities, and for showing trends. Often one needs to do little more than to glance at a graph to grasp an idea which would require many words for exposition.

The primary program in graph making is almost the total program in graph skills. Rarely do primary children have any need for graph interpretation skills because their sources for information usually do not contain graphs. However, they study facts and ideas that are easily expressed in graph form. (See Figure 9.)

The first graphs made in the primary grades are one-to-one relation-

FIGURE 9. SIXTH GRADERS USE SOCIAL SCIENCE SKILLS TO EXPRESS
RELATIONSHIPS.

ship graphs which are particularly useful in community studies. In the first one-to-one relationship graphs, the picture symbol represents one easily identifiable entity. For example, if children were to use a graph to show the distribution of occupations of their fathers, and sixteen fathers worked in factories, six worked in construction, eleven worked in services, and one was unemployed, four different kinds of figures would be developed to mount on the graph. Sixteen simple man figures shown entering a door would represent the factory workers, six figures of men carrying boards would represent the construction workers, eleven figures of men standing behind counters would represent those employed in services, and one sitting figure would represent the unemployed. This kind of one-to-one relationship graph is often referred to as a picture graph.

The next level of sophistication in graph making involves the use of abstract symbols in a one-to-one relationship. For example, the graph just discussed might be expressed in this way: after a small sketch of a factory, sixteen small black discs; after a small sketch of a store or shop, eleven discs; and after a small sketch of a home, one disc.

Picture graphs and graphs in which abstract symbols are used in a one-to-one relationship are simple bar graphs which prepare children for the more elaborate bar graphs. As children begin to work with these, the one-to-one relationship is maintained as a structure for expression. Ideas such as the following may be expressed:

1. Almost any kind of comparison, such as the different numbers of people in the classrooms using various kinds of transportation to reach school; the different numbers of people using community services, such as the laundry pickup service, the laundromat, and home washers; the communication devices; the homes represented in the classroom population, and so on.

2. Trends, such as the rush hours for traffic outside the school on school days, the number of items of a type used or wasted in a day, the number of persons in the classroom banking money over a period of weeks, daily temperature, and so on.

About the only limitation to bar-graph making in the primary grades is the extent of knowledge that children have about number. It is not likely that there will be much bar-graph making in the early first grade, but by late first grade most children have enough number ability to make graphs.

The teacher must make certain that the children understand the pattern of the bar graph, that each square in the grid represents one of something. The children will have to understand the cumulative aspect of a graph and its bottom-to-top or left-to-right orientation.

The simple one-to-one relationship may be maintained for the making of simple area or circle graphs. The making of such graphs will almost always require the teacher's direct assistance. Children will have to know that they are making a representation of a whole divided into parts. As they begin their experience with the circle or area graph, children should work with a whole familiar to them, such as the whole represented by all the members of a classroom. Using a large circle and circle segments, the teacher can guide them in making a variety of statements about the whole which represents their classroom. For example, they can make statements of comparison about the number of boys and the number of girls in the classroom, the number of boys and girls who walk to school and the number that come by bus, the number of boys and girls who bring their lunches and the number eating at the school cafeteria, or the like. At the beginning comparisons should be between two aspects. More complex comparisons should be delayed until the children have a better background in the knowledge of fractional parts.

In the primary grades the program in graph making is generally restricted to expressing one-to-one relationships. However, children of high ability in the second half of grade two and in grade three may be introduced to making graphs in which the symbol structure reflects a one-to-two, one-to-five, and one-to-ten relationship. At first a picture symbol should be used to express the statement. Later the abstract symbol may be used.

In teaching graph making, guided product analysis is generally an effective procedure. The following sequence of teaching-learning steps may be used:

1. Select an example or several examples of the kind of graph to be introduced. Sometimes the teacher will have to make them; at other times examples may be found in magazines and newspapers. The example or examples selected should be duplicated for class distribution, or reproduced on a large chart, or shown through an opaque projector, or prepared in such a way that projection is possible through whatever device is available, such as an overhead projector or the like.

2. Present the graph and guide the children in analyzing it to discover what it says and how it says it.

3. Challenge pupils to see how the way of expressing just discovered can be used to express a statement of ideas and facts recently studied.

4. Working at the chalkboard or using flannel-board materials and acting as recorder of the children's ideas, guide the class in making a graph. Encourage them to develop the steps to be followed and to direct you as the graph is being made.

5. If the pupils reflect a good grasp for graph making throughout Step 4 above, present a problem in expression taken from facts and ideas already studied for individual pupil solution through graph making. Distribute materials and supervise individual work.

If the pupils have difficulty throughout Step 4, do not have individual practice immediately. Either repeat Step 4 as soon as possible or, whenever the occasion presents itself, guide the pupils through a graph-making experience in which the teacher acts as recorder. Repeat this procedure until pupils reflect a grasp for graph making. Thereafter guide the pupils into graph making whenever the situation merits it.

6. Present each new type of graph in the same way.

If graph making as an expressive activity has been a part of the primary social-studies program, the children make an easy transition into graph making in the later grades. The more difficult types of graphs, including the line graph and the more complex bar and circle or area graphs, remain to be studied. The basic factor of complexity is working with relationships greater than the one-to-one relationship, which involves learning to interpolate to express more precisely.

If the children have learned how to express change over a period of time on a bar graph (a bar graph used in this way is often called a histogram), they understand the basic idea necessary for making a line graph. The difference between the two graphs is that one uses shaded bars beneath a given point to represent quantity more clearly and the other joins a series of plotted points with a line. If the lower portion of a line graph is shaded, it is quite similar to the bar graph. Children can usually perceive this similarity easily when they are given an opportunity to compare a line graph and a bar graph expressing the same statement.

The teacher can assure children's success with interpolation in expression by carefully controlling the kinds of information with which the children work and by providing working materials that make interpolation a simpler task. At the beginning stages of working with more complex bar and line graphs, children should work with elements of quantity easily divisible and easily understood. For example, degrees of temperature, inches of rain, sheets of paper saved each day, amounts contributed in a classroom drive of one kind or another, or the like, can be easily worked with and divided in twos, fives, and tens. More extended amounts such as millions in population, thousands of metric tons, tens of thousands of cattle, or the like can be introduced later. In most instances the first graphs should be drawn on a very large grid. The teacher can have the pupils make their own graph paper with a ruler or prepare it for them in duplicated form. Commercial graph paper can be used later.

Interpolation in expression on the area or circle graph requires that the children be relatively sophisticated in identifying the fractional parts of a circle. Frequently the teacher will find it necessary to lay off a large circle in halves, fourths, twelfths, and twenty-fourths to guide the children in its study and use. Because circle or area graphs very frequently use units expressed in percentages, some teachers prefer to introduce the circle laid off in tenths and twentieths. As they try expressing the parts of a whole in an area or circle graph, the children must be guided first in establishing the total or whole and then in establishing fractionally or percentage-wise the magnitude of the part as compared with the whole and the remainder of the parts. Much work with a carefully laid off circle is sometimes necessary.

If the graph-making program has been neglected in the primary grades, the teacher in the later grades may have to introduce graph making as a separate program or as a part of the graph-reading program in the social-studies curriculum. One effective way is to develop a program which will require several successive periods of social studies for two or three days. Such a program could consist of the following sequence of teaching-learning activities:

1. Prepare these materials:
   a. A bar graph showing a comparison, a bar graph showing a change over a period of time, a line graph, and a circle or area graph. Prepare for class distribution or for projection.
   b. For each graph prepare a paragraph which offers the same information as the graph. Prepare for class distribution or for projection.
   c. Develop at least three paragraphs offering information amenable to graphic expression for each type of graph. These will serve as problems to be solved by pupils, and should be prepared for class distribution.
   d. Obtain or prepare graph paper suitable for the solution of problems developed for practice as outlined in c.
2. Present the graphs and their accompanying paragraphs and establish

through discussion the utility of graphs—that through their use one can express clear, easily readable statements.

3. Using one of the paragraphs offering information amenable to expression through a bar graph showing comparison, guide the class through the making of the graph. For this step-by-step procedure, the teacher works at the chalkboard and pupils work at their desks.

4. Using the remaining two paragraphs, have the pupils work individually at making graphs. This work should be carefully supervised.

5. Repeat Steps 4 and 5 with the bar graph showing a change over a period of time; the line graph; and the circle or area graph.

6. Have the pupils file their work in folders or their notebooks for future reference. Whenever the occasion presents itself, guide the pupils into graph making. Encourage them to use their previous work as a reference aid.

The above is really a "crash" program perhaps most suitable to grades six, seven, and eight. Some teachers prefer to prepare the materials listed above and to teach graph making when the need for each type of graph arises. This method assures the decided advantage that the children will be working with facts and ideas recently required within the unit. However, the "crash" program also has an outstanding advantage in that it makes children more aware of how graphs can be used for expression.

As children learn more about graphs they should be encouraged to use them as means of presenting information in a direct, clear way. Graphs make excellent illustrative material in either the written or oral report. Frequently a graph may serve as the basic element in a report.

CHARTS

Generally the chart as a means of expression presents the fewest difficulties to children in expressing facts and ideas. However, children must cope with two basic problems. The first is a problem in the mechanics of language because words and letters are used so frequently in charts. The words must be accurately spelled and must be written in legible handwriting or hand lettering. The second problem is a thinking problem dealing with the development of symbols and their arrangement to reflect facts and ideas.

The problem of symbol development and arrangement is often easily solved by carefully examining the nature of the content to be expressed. Charts may be categorized in terms of basic arrangements of symbols for making statements. The following is a list of basic types of charts in terms of arrangements and the kinds of ideas which they may express:

1. The narrative chart, an extended left-to-right arrangement of facts and ideas for expressing:
   a. The events in a process such as shoe making, oil cracking, or the like.
   b. The events in the development of a significant issue to its point of resolution or to present status (sometimes a time limit). Examples: the events leading to the separation of the American colonies from England, the events leading to the establishment of the idea that an individual should be free and that he should have a voice in his own government, the events leading to increased regulation of business by government.
   c. Technological improvement over a period of years such as improvement in transportation, communication, manufacturing.
2. The tabulation chart, a left-to-right, top-to-bottom arrangement of facts and ideas for expressing:
   a. Numerical data for making comparisons.
   b. Lists of products, mountains, rivers, or the like in selected areas.
3. The cause-and-effect chart, usually a limited left-to-right arrangement of facts and ideas for expressing:
   a. Relationship between standard of living and such factors as economic system, availability of natural resources, level of technological advancement.
   b. Relationships between a culture and neighboring cultures.
   c. Relationship between rights and responsibilities.
   d. Relationship between a complex of conditions and change or conflict.
   e. Relationship between the elected and the electors.
   f. Relationships between community workers and the community which supports them.
4. The chain chart, a circular or semicircular arrangement of facts and ideas for expressing:
   a. Transitions, such as the transition from raw materials to useful products.
   b. Cycles, such as the water cycle and crop rotation.
5. The evolution chart, a left-to-right arrangement of facts and ideas for expressing:
   a. Changes in specific items from beginning to date, perhaps with projections into the future. Examples: origin of the automobile and its subsequent development, early basic homes and changes in basic homes to date.
   b. Changes in standards in food consumption, length of work week, purchasing power of a dollar, or the like.

If the facts and ideas are well understood by the pupils, the arrangement often suggests itself. Charts are of so many different forms that it is difficult to isolate a basic idea or two specific enough to lend direction to all chart making. Perhaps the best procedure for the teacher to follow is to present the idea of chart making as a task and to encourage pupils to discuss and develop arrangements. If the basic textbook contains many different types of charts as illustrative material, or if the teacher has a few examples of charts taken from newspapers, magazines, or other sources, these may be examined by the pupils to stimulate their thinking.

The legibility of lettering and handwriting and the accuracy of spelling on charts generally depends on the teacher's success in helping children to develop a "conscience" in these matters during the regular spelling and handwriting programs and as this learning is applied in other school work. If the teacher holds children to reasonable standards of accuracy and legibility in the application of language mechanics in all that they do, the "conscience" will develop. No absolute standard of perfection exists for every child in the classroom to meet. The teacher must give attention to individual differences in skill and coordination for detailed work.

Often the development of "conscience" is hastened by the teacher's careful analysis of the skills to be applied to certain areas in which he can help children. He can help children to write and letter better by diversifying his handwriting program to include both cursive and manuscript writing, particularly in the later grades. Block lettering and lettering in all capitals can be a part of the handwriting program in all the grades. Sometimes showing children how to make templates and use them is helpful. The least that a teacher can do is to post some facsimiles of block letters and capital letters about the room when children make charts.

The teacher can also provide additional aids in spelling. Many teachers guide their class in maintaining a list of words to be used during social studies. As soon as a new term is encountered and discussed in the social-studies program, it is listed on a large chart or in individual notebooks for future reference. Some teachers guide children toward independence in spelling difficult terms by directing attention to the many different sources for the correct spelling of words available at a pupil's desk. Indices in textbooks and reference books can serve as lists of correctly spelled social-studies words.

The primary program in chart making is usually more successful when it is first a group venture. In the very earliest attempts, the teacher reduces the complexity of the task by having the children determine only the arrangement on the chart of entities to express an idea. Often this exercise occurs after the children have drawn pictures or sketches about a process that they have been studying. As a class the children examine and select from all the pictures or sketches made those that will be needed to depict the entire process. They decide the order in which these should be placed on the chart. Usually the teacher uses a bulletin board as the chart and the various representations are pinned on it. Large sheets of wrapping or butcher paper may also be used, either taped over the chalkboard or laid on the floor, with the representations pasted on the paper. The teacher supplies the labels as they are developed by the class.

Sometimes the teacher may place the labels on a bulletin board and encourage the children to produce pictures, sketches, and the like, or select pictures from magazines to fill in the chart.

After the children have had considerable experience making charts in the above ways, they may be guided toward independent group production of a chart. Using group process, the children determine the content to be placed on the chart, assign roles to various members of the group to prepare representations and labels, do the necessary work, and complete the chart. Occasionally a gifted primary child, or one who is highly interested in social studies, may be encouraged to make a chart as an individual project.

The program in chart making in the later grades should involve both group and individual tasks. Ideally chart making is best suited for group task work. However, it should also receive emphasis as an individual task, for it provides a child with practice in organizing ideas and presents him with another way to tranmit information effectively and economically. A chart will often serve as a basis for a report or as an illustration within a report. Children who have difficulty retaining facts and ideas can be helped to overcome the difficulty through opportunities for expression with charts.

SUMMARIES AND REPORTS

Summaries and reports are the forms of verbal expression most frequently used in social studies. Their preparation is most demanding in terms of thinking and language skills; therefore, the social-studies teacher needs to give considerable attention to teaching these skills, whether during his language-arts program or during his social-studies program. It is quite likely that a certain amount of time in both programs wil be devoted to teaching the skills necessary to adequate preparation of summaries and reports. The teacher in a departmentalized situation may often find himself totally responsible for teaching the skills, because the departmentalized language-arts program may be devoted primarily to aspects of general composition. Whatever the situation in curriculum or school organization, the skills must be taught.

As a child progresses from kindergarten through grade eight or nine, he at first deals with facts and ideas orally, then moves on to a combination of oral and written treatment, until he reaches a stage where he is expected to deal effectively with the problems of expressing himself in either oral or written form. In kindergarten, the sharing, show-and-tell, or news program, in which the child deals with what is often social-studies content, is purely oral. Or he may be encouraged to summarize or report about social-studies content at the close of the period by being asked a question similar to the following: "And what did we find out today about the father's job in a family?"

In the first and second grades the practices mentioned above continue to be followed. A new aspect, writing, is introduced. At first the teacher serves as a recorder of what the children express and the result is an "experience chart." Occasionally time may be set aside for individual children to dictate "stories," which may be summaries or reports of what they have learned in social studies. Sometimes late in first grade and during second grade the children are encouraged to write individual "stories" which are often summaries or reports.

In the later grades, usually beginning with grade three, the terms *summary* and *report* begin to be used more extensively. The teacher may do much of the recording, particularly in the early part of grade three, and with slower children until grade seven. Usually emphasis on individual responsibility in expression is established in grade three and emphasis is increased in each grade thereafter.

Although much time and effort is expended in summarizing and reporting, children in the later grades frequently manifest behavior which reflects that the skills have not been well taught. When asked to write a summary, a child in grade five may respond by writing something related to the topic. Facts may be omitted, erroneous facts may be included, or facts may be out of order. It is a summary only in the sense that it is his response to the task of writing it. It may not indeed be a summary. Or, when asked to write a report, he may do one of several things. He may copy an article out of an encyclopedia or some other source; he may exhaust his memory and his effort in writing down everything that he can recall about the topic; or he may write stilted paragraphs about some aspect of the topic. None of these is really a report. A child in seventh grade may be required to write an extended report on a topic usually identified as a "term paper" or a "notebook." His response may be to copy several encyclopedia articles, or to limply paraphrase the articles at best, to insert the copied articles in a folder, to prepare some small drawings to be inserted between the pages and at least one to be pasted on the cover of the notebook, and to submit the product to his teacher. Only by a wild stretch of the imagination can such a product be called a report.

The instructional program in the language and thinking skills necessary to the adequate preparation of summaries and reports needs to be carefully organized. This organization can be done in several ways. Much of what follows consists of suggestions which may be used for organizing such a program.

The primary program should be characterized by a directness which permits the young learner to know what he is doing. At the very beginning in the kindergarten and first grade he should become used to hearing the terms *summary* and *report*. The teacher can introduce the idea of a summary after a period of study in a way similar to this: "Let us see if we can remember the important ideas we learned this morning. We are making a summary of the important things we learned about this morning." The term *report* can be used just as easily and just as meaningfully as "share" or "show and tell." For example, a teacher can use an expression similar to this: "Who has something to report?" to begin the reporting period. The teacher may encourage children to *report* about the things they have or the things they have seen and heard. When children are encouraged to ask their parents or other people for information, they can be asked to report what they learned. When the social-studies period is the first of the day, it is often the practice to open the period with reporting. It is just as reasonable to have the reporting period toward the close of the period and to call it *social-studies reporting*.

The child should begin early to acquire ideas about organization of thoughts and ideas. The teacher guides through verbal clues. As the children work with the summary, the teacher guides in a way similar to this: "Now that we have heard all the ideas that we learned this morning, let's see if they are in the right order." The teacher repeats the ideas as given by the pupils. "Which idea should we have first?" "Which comes next?" "What do you think is the most important idea of all?" "Shall we say it first or last in our summary?" As the child begins to work with reports the teacher gives him clues to the organization of thoughts and ideas in this way: "Tell us what your report is about." "Tell us what you know about it." "What is the thing you liked best about it?"

As the child begins to learn reading and writing skills, the teacher begins to teach written language skills and to extend his understanding of structure. The teacher serves as recorder. As he guides the children as a class in the writing of a summary, he elicits from them statements of ideas which he copies on the chalkboard or on a large chart. Then, using another section of the chalkboard or another sheet of chart paper, he encourages the children to offer suggestions on how the ideas should be rearranged. In accord with their suggestions he copies the rearranged summary. Much copying can be avoided by writing the children's statements on strips of paper or tagboard. After all the necessary ideas have been expressed in sentences, the teacher guides the children in determining the order in which the strips should be placed. The children have also an early introduction to the written report. The teacher offers clues in much the same way that he does when guiding children through oral reports. "First a sentence that tells us what the report is about . . . And now sentences that tell the facts . . . Now we need a sentence that tells the most important thing to remember." After children have had many experiences such as these for both the summary and the report, the teacher may work with the children to develop guide charts. The charts may be similar to the following:

How to make a summary
1. Say the important ideas.
2. Say the most important idea.

How to make a report
1. Tell what the report is about.
2. Tell the important facts.
3. Tell the most important fact of all.

These charts are posted as the children work with the summary and the report.

The primary program in learning how to summarize and report as suggested above provides a strong foundation for continued learning in the later grades.

If children have had the benefit of a strong program in summary and report writing during the primary grades, their program in the later grades becomes one in which they are guided gradually into sustained, more detailed expression. They learn how to maintain the point of the report, how to write more carefully organized paragraphs, and how to prepare reports several paragraphs in length. They develop skill in developing summary statements. Much of this learning occurs as the result of guiding children in editing their summaries and reports.

If the primary program has not been strong, teachers in the later grades will need to apply procedures which guide children toward a definitive view of what is a summary and what is a report. This definitive view helps the child to direct his efforts toward a known product in much the same way as a poet's knowledge about a sonnet's structure helps him to produce a sonnet. The teacher may choose from three general procedures—one which is primarily inductive, another which is primarily deductive, and another which is applicative.

An inductive procedure is one that guides children in making analyses which lead toward discoveries. The following is a sequence of teaching-learning activities developed to help children learn inductively what a summary is. Their learning guides their practice in writing summaries.

1. *Preparing a summary for pupils to analyze.* From a textbook or other source select a short (two or three paragraphs) passage which the pupils can read easily. Then write a summary of the passage. Prepare it for class distribution or for projection.
2. *Guide the pupils through an analysis of the passage and its summary.* Refer the pupils to the passage in the textbook and present the summary to them. Through discussion, help them to determine the relationship between the passage and its summary. Establish that a summary has the following characteristics:
   a. A summary contains the main ideas from a selection of paragraphs.
   b. The main ideas in a summary are in the same order as they occur in the selection.
   c. A summary statement tells what the whole selection is about.
   d. A summary statement may come either at the beginning or end of the summary.

3. *Provide for pupils' supervised practice.* Refer the pupils to another passage of paragraphs. Serving as a recorder, encourage them to develop a summary together. As suggestions are made, write them on a chart or on the chalkboard. Working together, the class determines what the summary should be. They use their learning from the analysis as guides. Continue with more supervised practice if pupils have a poor grasp initially of what a summary is as reflected in class work.

4. *Provide for individual practice.* Refer pupils to another passage in the textbook. Have each individual write a summary. At the close of the activity, guide the pupils in comparing their work. OR Whenever the occasion arises, have the pupils write a summary. Review the learnings from analysis before the pupils begin to write. Guide the pupils in a class evaluation of their summaries. Also evaluate each summary individually with its writer.

Another step can be introduced in the above sequence. During the preparation step the teacher selects four or five passages and prepares a summary for each. These summaries should vary in quality. One or two should be accurate. The others should be incorrect in some aspect, perhaps the omission of a main idea or two, the omission of a summary statement, or ideas out of order. At the close of step two above, the teacher has the pupils analyze these summaries and the passages to determine which summary (or summaries) is accurate and which ones are poor. The pupils are guided into substantiating why a summary is good or poor.

A similar sequence of teaching-learning activities may be organized for helping children to learn the definitive aspects of a report. The sequence is as follows:

1. *Prepare reports for pupils to analyze.* Select a topic from the current study of social studies and write an acceptable report about it. Such a report should reflect the following structure: It should have a beginning, middle, and end (a paragraph for each part should suffice). The beginning should introduce the topic, the middle should develop the topic, and the end should conclude it. Prepare several more reports to serve as foils. The latter are incorrect in some way, perhaps reflecting an omission of one or two parts.

2. *Guide the pupils through an analysis of the report.* Present the reports to the pupils and have them determine as a class which of the reports is a good report. Having them examine the good report and its foils, establish the following:
   a. A good report has three parts, a beginning, a middle, and an end.

b. The beginning of the report tells what the report is about.

c. The middle of the report presents the facts.

d. The end gives the conclusion or the most important idea remembered.

3. *Provide for pupils' supervised practice.* Have the pupils choose a report topic from current study, a topic already studied. Working as a recorder, encourage the pupils to compose sentences of the report. Write them as they are given. When the report is finished, guide the pupils in editing it. Encourage the use of the learning resulting from the analysis in Step 1. Repeat this step until pupils reflect a grasp of the structure of the report. This practice should not be concentrated, but rather practice as the situation in social-studies demands. If there is opportunity for report writing about a topic, guide the pupils in writing a class report.

4. *Provide for individual practice.* Choose a topic the facts about which are well known by the pupils. Have each pupil write a report about it. Supervise carefully to help pupils having difficulty. Conduct a class evaluation of the reports written. Also make provisions for evaluation of the report on an individual basis during a brief conference with each pupil. Whenever there is an opportunity for expression through report writing, guide the pupils into it.

A deductive procedure is one in which definitions, rules, or principles are placed before the learner, discussed with him, and then turned over to him for application. The following is a sequence of teaching-learning activities useful in teaching children deductively how to write a summary:

1. *Prepare to transmit the definitions, rules, or principles about the summary to pupils.* Prepare a chart defining the summary. A series of short statements similar to those listed under Step 2 on page 340 is better than a single long statement. Select a two- or three-paragraph passage from the social-studies textbook and write a summary of it which reflects a careful application of the definitions of a summary presented on the chart. The summary should be written on a large chart prepared for projection, or duplicated for class distribution.

2. *Guide the pupils in the study of definitions, rules, or principles. Present the chart defining a summary.* Use the selected passage and the prepared summary to illustrate the application of the definitions on the chart.

3. *Provide for pupils' supervised practice.* Using a textbook passage of two or three paragraphs in length, lead the pupils in writing a summary cooperatively. The pupils compose the sentences and the teacher writes them on the chalkboard or on a large chart. The product is carefully evaluated by the class to determine whether the definitions of a summary writing is

necessary. When most of the pupils have grasp of what is involved in summary writing, they may be guided into individual summary writing.

4. *Provide for individual practice.* If in the first trial, Step 3 above is successful, present a passage selected from the textbook and have the pupils write individual summaries. When these are completed, have the class evaluate some of the summaries to see how well they have been written. Later confer individually with each pupil on the summary that he has written. Whenever summaries are written during social studies, confer with each pupil who has difficulty with summary writing until he can write summaries independently.

Deductive procedure for introducing children to report writing is much the same as the above, except that children are learning about the report. The sequence of steps remains quite the same:

1. *Prepare to transmit the definitions, rules, or principles about the report to pupils.* Prepare a chart defining the report. A series of short statements similar to those listed under Step 2 in the sequence about report writing on page 340 would be appropriate. Write a report about a topic the facts of which are well known to the pupils, reflecting a rigorous application of the definitions listed on the chart. This report should be written on a chart prepared for projection, or prepared for class distribution.

2. *Guide the pupils in the study of the definitions, rules, or principles.* Present the chart defining the report. Use the report to illustrate how the definitions are applied.

3. *Provide for pupils' supervised practice.* Have the pupils select a topic which they have studied recently or one about which they know the facts. Guide them into writing a report about the topic as a cooperative effort. As the pupils compose the sentences, write them on the chalkboard. After the report has been written, guide the pupils in examining it carefully to see whether it meets all the criteria listed on the charts. Make changes as recommended. If the pupils have difficulty during cooperative writing, repeat this step whenever report writing is necessary. When most of the pupils have a grasp of what is involved in report writing, they may be guided into writing reports individually.

4. *Provide for individual practice.* If Step 3 above is successful with the first trial, have the pupils try their hand at individual report writing with a topic with which all are knowledgeable. When these are completed, have the class evaluate some of the individual reports to see how well the criteria for the report have been met. Later, confer briefly with each individual on the report that he has written. Whenever reports are written during social

studies, confer with each pupil who has difficulty until he can write reports independently.

An applicative procedure is one in which the child learns the skill by applying it step-by-step under the direct guidance of the teacher. A teaching-learning sequence for summary writing follows the steps listed below:

1. The teacher briefly defines a summary by saying something like this: "A summary tells the important ideas." He then leads into the task of summary writing: "We have studied many ideas today. What are the important ones that we have studied today?"
2. The teacher elicits and records the ideas in complete statements as the pupils give them. After the statements have been written on the chalkboard, he has the pupils carefully analyze them to see whether all the important ideas have been given and whether the ideas given are really important.
3. The teacher invites the pupils to examine the order of the ideas listed. If there is a need for rearrangement of ideas, they are listed in order on the chalkboard.
4. The teacher briefly defines a summary statement, perhaps in this way: "All the ideas that we have listed really say one thing when put together. This is a summary statement. Can you make a summary statement?" The teacher writes suggested statements on the chalkboard and guides the pupils in selecting the one most appropriate.
5. On successive days, the teacher guides the pupils in reviewing their learnings and writing a cooperative summary at the close of the social-studies period. When the pupils as a class appear to be able to perform the task of summary writing, the teacher has them attempt as individuals to write a summary of the important ideas covered during the study. Some of these summaries are subjected to class evaluation. The teacher confers with each pupil individually about his summary. Whenever summaries are written, the teacher guides individuals who have difficulty in summary writing in an evaluation of their product.

(The above sequence is designed for learning to summarize facts learned during social studies. The task is similar in teaching learning to summarize important ideas that are read. Only the material is different. The children work with selected printed passages.)

The use of the applicative procedure in guiding children into report writing follows generally the same steps outlined for summary writing, except that it is the report that is involved. Because the report is a more extended type of discourse, the teacher may wish to work with it part by part over a period of days. A suggested sequence is as follows:

1. The teacher defines briefly the structure of a report. Then he has the pupils focus their attention on the beginning of a report about which they know the facts.

2. The teacher elicits facts or ideas which should be included in the beginning of the report. He copies them on the chalkboard as they are given. Then he has the pupils examine the facts for relevancy, completeness, and order.

3. The teacher invites the pupils to express the facts or ideas in sentences. When this task is completed, they read their product and discuss it.

4. Steps 1, 2, and 3 are repeated, first for the middle of the report and then for the end of the report. (Some teachers prefer to work with the report and its facts as a whole. They follow this procedure: elicit and record all the facts for the report, categorize the facts in accord with where they should appear in the report, order the facts in each category, write the report.)

5. Whenever there is an opportunity later for writing a report, the teacher guides the pupils in a cooperative writing effort. He continues to do this until they have a grasp of the skills necessary for organized report writing. If the pupils grasp the skills readily with the first guidance through applicative procedure, they may be guided into writing individual reports about a common social-studies topic. A few of these are evaluated by the class. Then he makes provisions for brief individual conferences with his pupils about their reports. On the basis of the results of these conferences, he continues to confer with individuals who have difficulty after each report writing. He continues this practice until all his pupils can write organized reports independently.

No brief can be made for the superiority of any one of these procedures over the others. What is effective for some teachers may not be for others. What works with some children may not work with others. However, some recommendations can be made about the use of each of these procedures. The applicative procedure, which is so similar to what many primary teachers use, is usually effective with children in grades three and four and with children of low ability in the later grades. The inductive approach, in which emphasis is on analysis and discovery, is generally quite effective with children in grades four, five, and six. The deductive approach requires much less time at the beginning stages and is usually most effective with children in grades seven and eight. The effectiveness of any one of the procedures is determined largely by the teacher's patience and willingness to guide children as long as they need assistance in learning.

Earlier, it was pointed out that in the primary grades experience with the oral summary and the oral report precedes experience with the written summary and report. In the later grades the opposite is true— written experience precedes oral experience. There are several reasons for this shift of emphasis. Although children in the later grades can deal with more abstract topics and are capable of maintaining oral discourse about a topic over a longer period of time, they frequently have difficulty maintaining the point of the topic and remembering the ideas which they wish to present. If they have experience first with the written report, they learn to think in deliberate fashion about what they want to say and how they wish to say it. Their written product serves as a record of performance which can be analyzed critically to assure further improvement. Spoken discourse is transient and difficult to analyze. As the use of tape recorders becomes more widespread, it is likely that it will make little difference which summary and report, oral or written, will be treated first in the classroom.

After the summary and the report have been presented and practiced in written form, the teacher guides the children in refining their organization skills. As he guides them in this refinement, he helps them to lay a foundation for oral skills. The basic skill involved is that of making an outline. The general structure of an outline of a summary will present the skeleton of a summary and the outline of a report will present the skeleton of a report. From their written experience the children will know the definitive aspects of the summary and the report. They are guided in the use of this knowledge in making an outline—an outline for a summary will consist of a list of ideas, the first of which is the main idea and the remainder being supportive ideas given in numbered order. An outline for a report will reflect hierarchies of ideas briefly expressed and listed in this order: first, the topic of the report introduced in a main idea, and then its supporting ideas indented and given in numbered order; second, the major aspect of the topic presented briefly in a main idea and followed by a list of supporting ideas indented and in numbered order; and third, the conclusion of the report expressed briefly in a main idea and followed by supporting ideas indented in numbered order. As a child works to develop an outline for a summary, a structure similar to the following serves as a general guide:

Main idea

1. Supporting idea.
2. Supporting idea.
3. Supporting idea.

And as he develops an outline for a report, the following is his general guide.

Topic

I. Introduction to the topic.
   A. Supporting idea.
   B. Supporting idea.
   C. Supporting idea.
II. Major aspect of the topic.
   A. Supporting idea
   B. Supporting idea.
   C. Supporting idea.
III. Conclusion of the topic.
   A. Supporting idea.
   B. Supporting idea.

As he makes an outline, listing briefly the entries in it, the child fills in the general outline from the specifics acquired from his study. Once this outline is made, it may serve as a basis for either a written or an oral report. Each entry serves as a clue to a statement to be written or spoken. If the report is an oral report, the pupil is encouraged to use his outline as a set of notes. He studies the notes carefully, develops statements to express them, and practices with an audience which may be a friend of his or the members of a report team. They give him suggestions and generally criticize his effort. Later he makes his presentation before the class, and it is indeed an oral report. It is not a written report read orally to the class. It is likely that if he were to present it several times, its substance would not change but the wording about the substance would differ with each presentation.

If a tape recorder is available, the teacher can use it to good advantage to help the oral reporter improve in reporting skills. The reporter can hear what he said and can evaluate it to assure his improvement in the same task in the future.

When teaching oral reporting directly to a class, any of the procedures (inductive, deductive, or applicative) may be used. However, it is more feasible to bridge from the written summary to the oral summary and from the written report to the oral report.

CREATIVE LANGUAGE

A striking parallel exists between one interpretation of the basic purposes of social studies and the traits common among creative persons. Creative persons have a deep awareness of the problems of human existence. One purpose of social studies is to make children aware of the problems of human existence. A creative person has a compelling desire to react to such problems. Another purpose of social studies is to build within children a desire to react to such problems. A creative person has an essential mastery over an art medium. A purpose of social studies is to provide children with a growing ability in the use of thinking and action skills necessary for the solution of problems in the American democratic society. The parallel appears to end when the purposes of creativity and social studies are compared in terms of what is to be controlled. The creative person exerts a projective, personal control over what may have been or could be. Social studies helps children learn to control what is.

Although there is this difference in what is to be controlled, the creative product, particularly that presented in the medium of language, frequently reflects an influence exercised by the reality that is. Significant events represented in cultural, social, political, and economic events are regarded by the writer as the subject matter of human experience. In his creative product he illuminates these events, places them in perspective, and suggests patterns of action.

Valid decisions implemented by effective patterns of action are of first value as far as our society is concerned; therefore, the skills, attitudes, and understandings which assure valid decisions and effective patterns of action receive the basic emphasis in social studies. Within this emphasis there is a place for guiding children into creative language activity. For several reasons, this place is accorded to creative language. First, through projection of self (the creative writer's act) ideas may be brought into the open and tested. Second, the creative language product exerts an influence on decisions and actions to be applied. For example, the war novel which emphasizes heroism may make war a subject of fascination; the war novel which emphasizes human suffering makes war horrible. Such novels affect our thinking and acts. Such creative products vie for our attention in books, on radio, and on television. Through experience in trying to develop creative products, children learn a way of bringing ideas into the open and subjecting them to tests for truth. They learn to sense the need for authenticity and the power of a kernel of truth.

A child should be guided in the study of the various creative-language products before he is faced with the task of developing one. Almost all creative-language products share these characteristics: Each deals with a problem, in which the conditions which give rise to and support the problem are presented; each reflects a particular expressive structure, that of a story, a play, or a poem; and each represents a careful exercise of word choice and arrangement to express clearly. Children need to know something about these characteristics.

The teacher will find many products available for guided analysis. The reading textbook is usually filled with excellent stories. Although many television plays fail to meet highest standards of craftsmanship, some do meet these standards. Educational transcriptions are often quite excellent. The social-studies teacher who wishes to guide his pupils in integrating their ideas through creative language expression does not have to go far to find products for children to analyze to acquire ideas on how they could develop similar products.

The primary program in creative language as a form of expression in social studies is for the most part an oral program in which there is much dramatic activity. Most primary children lack the skills needed for sustained individual speaking or writing. The teacher works first at developing readiness for dramatic activity as expression. During the reading or language-arts period the children dramatize stories they have heard and, later, the stories they have read. Sometimes they dramatize through the use of flannel-board figures or with puppets. Perhaps they may be encouraged to pantomime a story as it is read for a second time.

Dramatization of social-studies ideas and facts is an easily accomplished venture after a strong readiness program. Young children eagerly participate in teacher-pupil discussion of the problem and the characters necessary for dealing with the problem. Puppets and flannel-board figures, articles of dress, and artifacts help children deal with the problem of dramatization. These materials may be made by the teacher, but they have more meaning if the children make them. Usually it is better to guide children scene by scene or act by act in producing and performing their play. Eventually they reach the point where they can present a sustained performance. Voice and pronunciation problems are treated gently but consistently all through dramatization practice. The first plays in a primary grade are usually produced through teacher-pupil planning followed by group performance and evaluation. Later the children may work in groups to define problems and plan their dramatization.

Evaluation is an important step in assuring the growth of children both in the use of social-studies ideas and facts and in dramatizing. If the children have been following teacher-pupil planning and group performance in their work, the children should be guided toward offering suggestions for improving the performance. Suggestions may be made diplomatically for the improvement of individual performance. When the play or some part of it has been prepared from beginning to end by a group, the class members must first be guided in evaluating the accuracy of the definition and solution of the problem and the dramatic presentation of the facts supporting the solution. Then they deal with the quality of the play and the quality of performance.

Occasionally poetry is included in the primary program. The program in readiness is characterized by having the children listen carefully to poetry of the type which they can be reasonably expected to write. Free verse such as that written by Carl Sandburg or Hilda Conkling and repetitive poetry such as that written by Vachel Lindsey are suitable. As they listen to these products, children must be guided in trying to determine what the poetry is trying to say.

Often poetry writing by the whole class or by a group produces remarkable results. The teacher guides the children in giving their impressions about a process or worker in social studies. Individual impressions are elicited. Particularly euphonious lines may be chosen for repetition. Finally all the impressions are capstoned with a line that sums up all the impressions. This kind of poetry writing provides an opportunity for individual expression with very little structuring by the teacher. Later, when the children have acquired writing and spelling skills, they may be encouraged to try individual poetry writing.

A rich program in the use of social-studies facts and ideas in dramatization and poetry writing in the primary grades is a foundation for the use of creative language in social studies in the later grades. The program does not provide many definitive ideas about creative form, but the ideas learned are accurate. The richest contribution made by such a program is the formation of positive attitudes about creative language as a means of expressing facts and ideas learned in social studies.

The program in creative language in social studies in the later grades is much more sophisticated, including both oral and written expression. Generally emphasis is considerable on the use of creative language in grades four, five, and six. Emphasis often continues in grades seven and eight, but it is a diminishing emphasis which gives way to a heavier emphasis in "factual" writing—the more formal report or the "term paper." Occasionally in social studies, programs for the gifted include provisions for guiding children into integrating facts and ideas learned through creative language.

Usually the program reflects a heavier emphasis in written expression. Occasionally some emphasis may be given to dramatics, but the venture often becomes time-consuming, involving formal play writing, scenery building, and the like. Sometimes a teacher will guide his pupils in developing a choric verse expression or into individual poetry writing.

Although the program in literature, either in the language-arts, reading, or English program, is a necessary foundation to the use of creative language for expression in the later grades, it is often not sufficient to assure children the background they need for expressing ideas acquired in social studies. A more penetrating analysis may be required. The creative story will need to be seen as the expression of human problems through characters caught up in the web of issues or events and pinpointed in time and space through "local color." Much the same is true of the play. Analysis of choric verse should touch upon the broad theme of feeling as transmitted through the spirit of words, their music, their rhythm, and their repetition. Poetry needs to be revealed as an analysis of a moment and the poet's interpretation of that moment.

Generally these analyses occur during the reading, language-arts, or English period, and sometimes analyses are followed by guided experience in expressing in the form analyzed. The understandings and skills are generalized into use in social studies as ways of tying ideas together. This generalization can be accomplished easily in the self-contained classroom and in the core program in which social studies and English are combined. In the departmentalized situation the social-studies teacher may be able to enlist the aid of the language-arts or English teacher.

Social studies is often a rich source of ideas for children in grades four, five, and six as they make efforts in creative dramatics. Often the social-studies content in these grades is rich in historical and cultural content which lends itself easily to dramatic expression. Social studies is also a rich source for ideas to be developed in choric verse in all grades, particularly grades seven and eight. In these grades children are more likely to have a deepened historical sense and a more refined sense of dramatic feeling. Children in these grades often reveal a rich esthetic feeling toward the geography of their own country and that of the world.

As children project themselves through the use of creative language into events or issues that may have been or could be, they reflect within their limited language the deepest understandings of what they have learned often far deeper and far more factual than those reflected on any test.

SUMMARY

The purpose for expressive activity is to provide opportunities for children to integrate learnings or to discover new ideas. Teachers using either the synthesized or the thinking-emphasis strategy freely accept this purpose. The social-science strategist may also. However, he may reject this idea and give emphasis only to those expressive activities used by social scientists.

The instructional programs in the various skills may be a part of social studies or included in the art and language-arts programs. When they are not formally provided for, the social-studies teacher develops programs as needed.

The expressive skills necessary to social studies include nonverbal skills (drawing, painting, clay modeling, constructing, and the like) and verbal skills (map and globe making, summary writing, preparing reports, and the like).

When working with children to improve their nonverbal skills, the teacher regards expression as a form of communication and guides children in learning to use various media to make statements. Product-analysis is used as the basic device for guiding children into insights about process. When expressive products are evaluated, two areas are scrutinized: the representation of social-studies ideas and the use of the medium.

The social-studies instructional program in the expressive verbal skills dealing with maps, globes, graphs, diagrams, and charts is usually considered an aspect of social studies. Again product-analysis serves as an effective instructional device.

The more purely verbal skills may be taught through the use of deductive, inductive, or applicative procedures. The deductive and inductive approaches are built around product analysis. The applicative approach involves clueing children in on what is required and guiding them in making responses.

Exercises for Further Understanding

1. Select an art medium in which you feel yourself to be passably proficient. Using the medium, make an expressive object which you could use for a product analysis with children. As you make the object, make a job analysis of what you do. Be sure to include time as a factor in your analysis. Then think through carefully the provisions that you will have to make to guide children in producing a similar object.

2. Select a topic area in elementary social studies which contains ideas that can be expressed on a map. List the ideas that can be expressed and describe briefly both teacher-made and child-made materials that could be used for expressing these ideas.

3. Prepare an example of a bar graph showing a change over a period of time, a line graph, and a circle graph to be used as instructional aids in introducing graph making to a sixth-grade class.

4. Prepare an instructional chart which will help children in the primary grades or intermediate grades to form the idea that a report contains at least three parts and that each part has a particular function to perform.

5. Prepare three reports which children could analyze to discover what a suitable report is. All the reports should be about the same topic and only one should be really suitable.

6. Go to the children's section of your local library and find several children's books in which stories are told about people living in historical times or people living in foreign countries. The stories should be realistic, that is, they should deal with problems real to the era or area. Plan ways of introducing these stories to children and guiding them in discovering ways in which real facts and real events are used in the telling of the stories.

Selected References

Anderson, Paul S., *Language Skills in Elementary Education,* Chap. 8, "Written Composition." New York: The MacMillan Company, 1964.

Applegate, Mauree, *Freeing Children to Write.* Evanston, Ill.: Harper & Row, Publishers, 1963.

_____, *Helping Children Write.* Evanston, Ill.: Row, Peterson and Company, 1954.

Dunfee, Maxine, and Sagl, Helen, *Social Studies through Problem Solving,* Chap. 7, "Constructing and Processing to Solve Problems;" and Chap. 9, "Enriching an Area of Learning through Creative Activities." New York: Holt, Rinehart and Winston, Inc., 1966.

Gaitskell, Charles D., *Children and Their Art.* New York: Harcourt, Brace & Company, Inc., 1958.

Green, Harry A., and Walter T. Petty, *Developing Language Skills in the Elementary School,* Chap. 11, "Developing Specific Oral Language Skills;" and Chap. 12, "Developing the Written Language Skills." Boston: Allyn and Bacon, Inc., 1959.

Hanna, Lavone A., Gladys L. Potter, and Neva Hagaman, *Unit Teaching in the Elementary School,* rev. ed., Chap. 10, "Using Basic Skills in Reporting and Sharing Information;" Chap. 11, "Dramatic Play and Dramatizations;" Chap. 12, "Construction Activities in a Unit of Work;" Chap. 13, "Providing Aesthetic Experiences." New York: Holt, Rinehart and Winston, 1963.

Jefferson, Blanche, *Teaching Art to Children.* Boston: Allyn and Bacon, Inc., 1959.

Johnson, Pauline, "Art for the Young Child." *Art Education,* Sixty-Fourth Yearbook of the National Society for the Study of Education, Part II, Chicago: The University of Chicago Press, 1965.

Lowenfeld, Viktor, and W. Lambert Brittain, *Creative and Mental Growth,* 4th ed. New York: The Macmillan Company, 1964.

McPhie, Walter E., "Student Reports in the Social Studies." *Social Education,* 30:96 (February 1966).

Marksberry, Mary Lee, *Foundation of Creativity.* New York: Harper and Row, Publishers, 1963.

Merritt, Edith, *Working with Children in Social Studies,* Chap. 9, "Organizing and Expressing Ideas through Art." Belmont, Calif.: Wadsworth Publishing Company, Inc., 1961.

Michael, John A., "Art Experience during Early Adolescence," *Art Education,* Sixty-Fourth Yearbook of the National Society for the Study of Education, Part II, Chicago: The University of Chicago Press, 1965.

Michaelis, John U., *Social Studies for Children in a Democracy,* 3d ed., Chap. 17, "Enrichment Experiences." Englewood Cliffs, N.J.: Prentice-Hall, Inc., 1963.

National Council for the Social Studies, *Skill Development in Social Studies,* Helen McCracken Carpenter, ed., Thirty-Third Yearbook of the N.C.S.S., Washington, D.C.: National Education Association, 1963.

Preston, Ralph C., *Teaching Social Studies in the Elementary Schools,* rev. ed., Chap. 12, "Planning Creative Experiences." New York: Rinehart & Company, Inc. 1958.

12

Improving Group Work
in Social Studies

So far our concern has been for social studies in the usual classroom milieu in which the teacher and the children have been equally committed to the tasks of inquiry. Now we shall concern ourselves with those moments in which the responsibility for inquiry rests more with groups of children than with the teacher and the class as a total group. This chapter presents a rationale for group work in social studies and procedures for guiding children into it.

The work aspect in group work is viewed here in keeping with John Dewey's idea of work—purposeful activity directed toward a result so deeply desired that both effort and intelligence meet strong demands.[1] It follows, then, that whenever children are to be guided into group work, the task and its result must be clear, the task must be commonly accepted by the members of the group, and the children must be able in both the knowledge and skills necessary to the task.

[1]John Dewey, *Democracy and Education* (New York: The Macmillan Company, 1916), p. 239.

The group aspect of work follows what one sociologist chooses to call an "associational group," that is, persons who freely acknowledge their membership in the group, who interact with each other, and who recognize and participate within an organization or group.[2] Membership, interaction, and organization are the factors which support the completion of a task.

Within the ideas expressed in Chapters 7 and 8, group work is problem-oriented. Problem solution by the group tends to follow the line of closed inquiry. In most instances, the primary sources for information are the experiences, beliefs, and attitudes of the members of the group.

THE PLACE OF GROUP WORK
IN SOCIAL STUDIES

The inclusion of group work in social studies is supported basically by historical precedent and the logic of curriculum development.

In Chapters 1 and 2 it was explained that the general purpose and objective of social studies focus on one intent—the development of citizenship. It logically follows, then, that in the development of curriculum adequate provisions be made for the teaching-learning of citizenship behavior within assumptions about the rationality of the citizen, how it operates, and how its growth is fostered. One set of widely accepted assumptions supports that thinking, both individual and group, be implemented in the elementary social-studies curriculum.

In Chapter 1 it was pointed out that social-studies teaching is directed toward guiding children to react to conditions of people near and far. Reaction is behavioral, influenced by objective facts and ideas and by feelings and patterns of action related to these. Not only the reaction of the individual defined as a single universe is considered, but that of the social individual as a member of a group formed to bring about a change in conditions in some way intolerable to the entire group.

Our news media constantly reflect examples of group action, both destructive and constructive. Constructive action, obviously preferred, requires the skills of deliberate, reflective thinking and inner control of the group. The responsibility of elementary social-studies instruction is

[2]Robert Bierstedt, Eugene J. Meehan, and Paul A. Samuelson, *Modern Social Science* (New York: McGraw-Hill Book Company, 1964), p. 134.

to guide children toward the mastery of these skills, not as the only or the main agent, but as a strong support.

Historically, group work has had a place in social studies. As was pointed out in Chapter 1, group work has been accepted and made a part of the mosaic of social-studies instruction as a result of thinking occurring during the 1930's. Actually the foundation for group activity as an essential part of social-studies instruction was laid in the child-centered innovation that appeared in the first quarter of the twentieth century. A concern for the socially controlled aspects of individual interest and the ways of developing such interest had given a place to group activity within the earlier innovation.[3] In the later society-centered innovation, new emphasis was to be given to group activity. The social-studies program, constructed around social problems to be solved through group work, was to be the core of the curriculum. This idea, though not widely accepted, served to keep teachers and curriculum specialists aware of the need for group work in elementary social studies.

In short, group work has a place in the elementary social-studies program. However, its role is difficult to determine. The difficulty appears to stem from two conditions: (1) the pervasive use of groups to administer to instructional needs, and (2) a general misunderstanding of what group work is and what it involves.

USES OF GROUP WORK IN SOCIAL STUDIES

During the course of social-studies instruction, several different types of grouping may be seen in operation from time to time. Occasionally administrative grouping is used to make the best use of available space, which may include grouping children near the materials which they are to use or grouping them to reduce noise. For example, one group may be at the front of the classroom, another at the back, and another just outside the classroom but within the view of the teacher through the windows.

Occasionally children will be grouped according to ability. In social studies, children are often grouped by investigative ability. Several groups of children may work with materials of different levels of difficulty while another group studies sets of pictures. Children may also

[3]Dewey, *op. cit.*, pp. 37-39.

be grouped in accord with expressive ability—one group of children may be writing individual reports and another group may be painting individual pictures. The teacher uses such groupings to supervise more adequately the use of skills.

Sometimes children are grouped according to their interest in a topic. Children who have the same interest work in the same area and share materials and resources. Such groupings aid children in maintaining and extending interests that emerge during social studies.

Administrative, ability, and interest groups are essentially teacher-selected task groups; they help the teacher to conduct his social-studies program. Through the use of such groupings, the teacher can go a long way toward providing optimal conditions for learning in a classroom, providing for individual differences, and coping with "problem" children.

Another general form of task group is the teacher-pupil group, which occurs almost every day during the social-studies period. Most often the group consists of the whole class and the teacher working together to define or redefine purposes at the beginning of the period and to check the fulfillment of purposes at the close of the period. Occasionally the teacher-pupil task group may be organized to solve a problem of values or a problem concerning the rights of individuals to certain materials or space. From time to time, the group may consist of the teacher and a group drawn from the membership of the class. The characteristic which distinguishes this form of grouping from the teacher-selected task group is that both the teacher and the children are equally committed to the task.

The types of grouping discussed to this point may be found within the other instructional periods of the day. However, one general form of grouping is more likely to be found during the social-studies period than during any other instructional period. It is the pupil task group.

The pupil task group may be differentiated from the other forms of grouping in several ways. One basic difference exists in the roles played by the teacher and pupils. In the teacher-selected task group the role of the teacher is that of director; the pupils have roles as followers. In the teacher-pupil task group the teacher follows the role of the most mature member of the group. Leadership of the group passes from the teacher to various pupils, frequently going from one pupil to another and, from time to time, back to the teacher. The role of follower is shared by all the members of the group, including the teacher when he is not the leader. Whether he be leader or follower, the teacher never relinquishes his role as the most mature member of the group and thus guides the children in the solution of their problem. In the pupil task group the teacher assumes the role of a distant supervisor and occasionally that of an advisor whose services may be called upon. The pupils develop the role structure by determining who is to be leader and who are to be followers, the functions of the leader and those of the followers in terms of the task at hand. The task is defined and implemented by the pupils themselves. The completed task is regarded as the result of a group venture.

Another way to differentiate the forms of grouping is on the basis of the task to be implemented through grouping. If the task is to maintain conditions for teaching and learning, it is the teacher's to perform. If the task is to maintain direction in study and to assure a social climate for study, it is a task shared by both the teacher and the pupils. If the task is to complete group expressions of learnings or to decide issues rising from social studies, it is basically a task for pupils.

Pupil task groups, the most valuable for learning group work skills, present the greatest challenge to the social-studies teacher. If he is to be at all successful with it, he will need to develop within his classroom a social climate which permits and supports such grouping and its action.

The most decisive factor in the development of a social climate in a classroom is the way in which the teacher interprets through his actions his general role in the classroom. If he interprets his role as that of the head of a rigid hierarchy, as though he were a colonel in command of a regiment, he follows certain actions. He maintains a system of one-way communication—he orders and the children obey. He develops the rules and regulations by which children are to govern their behavior, makes all the rewards, inflicts all the punishments, and arrives at all the decisions. If he looks upon his role as that of the servant of children's whims, he follows other actions. He guides the children into positive ways of satisfying their desires; acknowledges no hierarchy to the extent that he is one with the children most of the time; avoids making decisions, rules, or regulations; and seeks to maintain the direction of learning through rewarding lavishly, coaxing, cajoling, and sympathizing. Such interpretations of the teacher's general role in the classroom make the pupil task group impossible.

However, if the teacher interprets his role as that of the responsible person who works to maintain a flexible structure for the purposes of teaching and learning, the pupil task group is possible. His actions are varied and suited to the learning situation. In some instances, he must guide and the children must follow; the children know and accept this state of affairs. On other occasions, the children develop guidelines for action with his very necessary help, and the children recognize these occasions. At times, the children develop the guidelines, calling upon him for help only when they deem it necessary; they recognize the conditions which make this activity appropriate.

The second most decisive factor in the development of a social climate suitable for such grouping is the nature of the classroom group of children. If, by the time the children arrive at his classroom, they have worked successfully in such groups in other classrooms, they bring with them expectations about social climate as well as about pupil task-group work. All that the teacher needs to do is to guide them in establishing their expectations in terms of their new classroom, their new teacher, and the new group in which they find themselves. If the children arrive at his classroom with a poor background of experience or with no experience at all with such task work, the teacher works carefully to establish a social climate. This climate can be established with little difficulty when the children come from neighborhoods and homes relatively free of conflicts due to social, cultural, or economic conditions. The teacher may have cnsiderable difficulty in establishing a positive social climate when the children bring hostilities from their homes and neighborhoods, that is, hostilities induced by social, cultural, economic, or psychological deprivations.

As the teacher works to establish a social climate adequate to pupil task-group work, he takes care in establishing positive teacher-pupil relations and positive pupil-pupil relations. Some of his practices support the development of both kinds of relations:

1. Regarding each child as a worthwhile individual. Each day, or as often as possible, he makes an individual contact with each child. This positive contact is characterized by friendly commendation or reassurance.

2. Giving patient guidance to children with problems. Frequently this involves sharing the burden of the child's problem. The teacher is aware of the child's problem and lets him know about his awareness. Working together, they determine realistic goals for improvement of behavior, work at reaching the goals, and evaluate progress. Frequently the teacher must be satisfied with relatively short gains over long periods of time.

3. Being circumspect when discussing individual problems. When-

ever a child needs his attention directed toward his own questionable behavior, the teacher chooses a time and place in which the child's attention, and not that of the whole class, can be focused directly on his behavior.

4. Sharing administrative responsibilities with children. He has children help in the distribution and collection of materials, the collection of money, in delivering reports to the office, in keeping the classroom in good order, and in carrying on routine matters in general. Often he will help the children develop a class government to implement routine functions.

The following practices support the development of positive pupil-pupil relations:

1. Guiding children through problems arising from playground or cafeteria activity and the shared use of space and materials. Whenever possible he avoids the roles of "judge" and "executioner." Whenever a difficulty arises, he encourages the presentation of all sides of a grievance, the selection of a solution, and a solution trial.

2. Providing every child with a chance at "choice" responsibilities. Whenever the room monitor or assistant structure is being developed he selects or guides children in selecting candidates with fairness. The structure will be changed often to make certain that all have an equal chance.

3. Seating children with consideration for their preferences. He helps children to find their preference for a "permanent" seat near people whom they like. Whenever they must regroup for some purpose, he respects their preferences. Sometimes he finds it necessary to clarify that when individuals sit next to or near people whom they like, all share the responsibility for maintaining the proper conditions for study and work.

Another aspect of establishing a positive social climate in the classroom is helping children become accustomed to working together more or less on their own. Tasks such as distributing materials, preparing the physical classroom for expressive activity, taking down bulletin-board displays, and putting the classroom in order after an expressive activity may be accomplished by small groups of children working together. The teacher presents the task and selects the members of the group. As the group begins its work, a leader usually emerges to guide activity, not as "boss," but as coordinator. The group structure is freely accepted and the task is accomplished. At the same time children have practice in working in a group.

Certain "open-ended" tasks related to learning activities may be accomplished by small groups of children. Both the "warm-up" to roleplaying and roleplaying itself are instances in which quickly selected groups of children participate and learn almost unconsciously how to work with others. For example, a sixth-grade teacher guiding his pupils in the study of Mexico may at a particular point of study ask for volunteers to dramatize the first meeting of Montezuma with Cortez. A few minutes are afforded for a group of four or five pupils to go to a corner to plan the dramatization. The group reviews the facts, assigns roles, and presents the dramatization. Many opportunities for working together in situations similar to these enrich the social climate and help children attain readiness for pupil task work. The use of "buzz" groups in dealing with a variety of problems also affords children practice in working as groups. For example, when developing behavioral standards related to a particularly activity, the teacher carefully outlines the task, divides the class in groups of three or four, and encourages the groups to explore ideas for a restricted time. Again a group structure is quickly established and work takes place.

Establishing the social climate necessary for pupil task-group work may require various amounts of time. In some classrooms the greater part of a school year will be required; in others, only a few weeks will be necessary. Regardless of the time required, it is essential that it be developed before the teacher attempts to guide his pupils into pupil task-group work. It is just as essential that children have experience with pupil task-group work every year, for the skills inherent within it are the foundation for citizen task-group work in the years to come.

GROUP STRUCTURE AND FUNCTION

The establishment of a positive social climate alone is not sufficient to such group work. Other conditions related to group structure and function are also necessary. Provisions must also be made for physical arrangement of the members of groups to facilitate discussion, helping children to know and understand the structure and function of a group, and helping children improve in discussion skills. Research in communication supports, among other things, that the fewer the obstacles between communicants, the more effective the communication for task completion. Many classrooms are organized permanently to reduce communication. Seats or desks are arranged in rows so that those who would communicate will see only the chalkboard and the backs of heads. However, in social studies, task-oriented communication for the solution of problems is frequently needed; therefore, carefully aligned rows of seats or desks facing in one direction need to be rearranged during the social-studies period to bring individuals into face-to-face positions. If the desks or seats are permanently attached to the floor the teacher cannot do much. If the seats or desks are movable, almost any closed or semiclosed arrangement is possible. The ideal arrangement of desks or seats is a hollow circle, square, or rectangle. A semicircle, an open square, or an open rectangle often works well. When desks or seats are fastened in rows on runners, they can often be pushed into a double-U or double-L arrangement. This same kind of arrangement can often be used to good advantage when space is restricted in the classroom in which seats and chairs are movable. If the entire social-studies period is going to involve the entire class as a discussion group, the rearrangement can be made quickly at the beginning of the period. Many teachers can guide children into appropriate behavior during individual work without having to place obstacles among them to discourage communication. Often these teachers maintain an arrangement amenable to communication as a permanent arrangement.

Frequently it is easier for the primary teacher to arrange the physical setting to encourage communication. The furniture in primary classrooms is usually of the movable type. Often there is so much space available that chairs can easily be arranged in a circle in a separate area or the children may be seated in circle on a rug.

Research in communication supports, among other things, that persons facing each other tend to communicate more than persons sitting adjacent to each other; therefore, the social-studies teacher should from time to time change the arrangement of pupils. The same individuals should not always be sitting across from each other and the same pupils should not always be seated directly across from the teacher during discussions. Furthermore, the teacher will need to use a form of discussion that tends to move communication into the group and around it. Too often the class discussion becomes a series of exchanges between the teacher and four or five pupils.

To a certain extent, the care that the teacher exercises in the arrangement of furniture and persons to encourage communication influences the care which the pupils take in arranging for adequate communication as they move into pupil task-group work, but this concern is not enough. As the children separate into small groups, the teacher will need to help them arrange themselves in ways that promote rich discussion. When the room is furnished with tables and chairs or individual, movable desks, arrangement is neither difficult nor time-consuming. If these are chairs, these can easily be moved into small circles with perhaps one table provided for the person who serves as recorder. Frequently classrooms equipped with stationary furniture have vacant spaces at the front and rear of the room where pupils can meet in small groups. Sometimes folding chairs that can be brought to the room for these purposes are available from the auditorium. School policy may frown on the idea of having pupils sit on the tops of stationary desks, but where this is permitted small groupings may be easily formed. However, a continued lack of comfort may lead to further difficulty in group work. Some schools are equipped with patios or corridors outside the classrooms which can be used for group work.

If children are to be expected to work in pupil task groups, they must have some definitive ideas about the structure and function of a group. They must understand leadership and followership.

When working in pupil task groups, most children manifest a deep concern for who is to be the leader. They recognize the need for leadership and hold the position of leader in high regard. Many want to be the leader of the group, for to be leader is to be "boss," particularly in the case of younger children. Some teachers take a hand in structuring the group by assigning leaders on a rotation basis. Teacher involvement may be necessary at the beginning of pupil task-group work, and may be further justified as a practice to aid in discovering who has leadership ability.

Many children welcome the role of follower, but there are always some who do not accept it gracefully. A child who covets the role of leader will often openly reject the leader of the group by declining any assigned role, attempting to divide the group in such a way that he controls a faction of it, or striving to become the functional leader of the group and making the appointed or elected leader accept a figurehead role. Young children sometimes have difficulty relating themselves to a leader who is no bigger physically than they. When such conditions prevail, the teacher guides the children in investigating the role of a follower and applying their findings.

Two basic approaches are useful in helping children learn about the roles of leaders and followers. One is a precautionary approach in which the children are guided in reviewing their ideas and experiences to determine what they think leaders and followers should do in groups.

The teacher leads them into thinking about and discussing these issues and often a tangible result in the form of a set of behavorial standards is produced. For example, the class may establish the following standards of leadership behavior:

> *When I am leader*
> I give everyone a chance to speak,
> I listen to others,
> I help others decide what to do,
> I ask others in a nice way to do things, and
> I keep our work going.

The class may define followership behavior in this way:

> *When I am in a group*
> I wait my turn to speak,
> I speak quietly,
> I give ideas,
> I listen to others, and
> I work with the leader and
> others to get the job done.

These standards of behavior are written on a large chart and posted. For younger children who cannot read, a similar chart depicting the standards in simple sketches can be used. Often teachers have the children practice these standards with a simple, teacher-assigned task such as getting all the boys and girls to the playground in good order or supervising a cleanup after expressive activity. The behavior of the leaders and followers is carefully evaluated in a teacher-class discussion.

The other approach to help children learn about the roles involved in group work places emphasis on discovery. After the groups have been formed and the tasks accepted, the teacher releases the children to work. Usually conflicts arise and group work ceases. The teacher re-forms the groups into a class again, and guides the children in reviewing what was taking place within the groups. The children are encouraged to explore ideas for improving work within the groups. If one group has been successful, it reviews what it has done. Solutions to group problems are considered, which may relate to changes in the behavior of leaders or followers. Changes are tested and retested in group work until the groups begin to function efficiently.

Neither of the two procedures is of much value if the findings are not continually tested and evaluated. The simplest of classroom administrative tasks can often serve as a proving ground for followership behavior in a working group. Whenever children are involved in pupil task-group work, they will need to be guided in examining their behavior to detect areas in need of improvement. Often a child who has a reasonable grasp of his role as leader can evaluate the work of the members of his group objectively without identifying too harshly those who have difficulty. For example, such a leader may give a general appraisal of how the followers worked and follow his appraisal with mentioning those members who did an especially good job.

Helping children to learn how to do group work also requires that the teacher give individual children the support that they need. Occasionally the child emerging as the leader of a group has difficulty in assigning roles to others or in moving his group in the direction it must follow to complete a task. Followers from time to time find it difficult to accept leadership or responsibility for performing a job. The teacher works with these children to help them develop a deeper understanding of group work and how they are to function within it.

Much of what has been discussed so far has been focused upon the structure of groups and functions within groups. Children need also to know why a group functions. Often they find themselves involved in pupil task groups with only the vaguest idea of why the group was ever formed. The group's function, or what it is supposed to do and why it is supposed to do it, is not clear. As children are guided into group work, they should be convinced that the task to be completed cannot be performed very well by an individual and, for that reason, a group is required. They should also feel that the task to be performed is one that has a real place in learning social studies. Pupil task-group work is not to be regarded just as a procedure introduced to break the tedium of usual class work or as a way of studying or finding out about things as a common, everyday occurrence.

The social-studies teacher can help children to acquire insights into what tasks groups can do and why they do them by guiding his pupils into group work only when it is warranted and indicating the utility of such work. Children can easily recognize that an expressive project such as developing a mural or producing a play will require the efforts of a group or several groups and that such a project is a good way of expressing what they know about a topic. When guided into exploring the various sides of an issue, they can see that a commitment to one side or another divides the class into groups and provides each group with a task that helps the members to clarify their ideas for a presentation. The same is true when children find themselves involved with the task of determining the best pattern of action to follow when certain conditions exist. All the members of a group are committed to improving conditions since the need for improvement is obvious. And most children understand the need for saving time. During the investigative phase of study it is often better to have groups investigate for applications of ideas already learned. (See Figure 10.) For example, a group of seventh-grade children have just learned that economic motivation played a large part in the colonization of what is now the United States. Each individual in the class has investigated in as many sources as are available and each has this idea clearly in mind. They begin to ponder whether this motivative force has contributed toward the colonization of other areas in the world. They divide into groups to check on the colonization of ancient Spain by the Greeks, of ancient Gaul by the Romans, of South America and Africa by modern Europeans, and of Australia by the British. Each group presents its findings and, as a result,

FIGURE 10. FIFTH GRADERS WORK AT A GROUP TASK.

the original generalization is somewhat modified. Time has been justifiably saved. However, it is difficult to justify pupil task-group work near the end of the semester when the pupils are divided just to be sure that material is covered.

Knowing the structure and proper function of a group frees children to become effectively involved in discussion, the communication skill that lies at the heart of pupil task-group work and assures the accomplishment of tasks. Through communicative discussion, terms are given a common meaning. Through group work, the use of these terms assures everyone a knowledge of what is being done and how much of the task has been completed. At the same time, the meaning of the terms is extended and deepened. Through discussion, suggestions are made, opinions are given and substantiated, choices are made, roles are assigned, directions are asked for and given, and work is checked and evaluated.

However, many children are relatively unacquainted with discussion as a communication skill. They know something about arguments, to be sure. They hear and use arguments, but rarely do they hear or participate in a discussion. And, unfortunately, few teachers discuss or allow children to discuss.

Several kinds of communicative action occur frequently between teachers and pupils during social studies. One is "jug filling" in which the teacher "pours" a stream of facts and ideas and the children are supposed to "fill" like so many jugs beneath a spout. They are so busy being "filled" that there is no opportunity for them to utter a meaningful sound.

Another form of communication often occurring between teachers and pupils is "tooth extracting." The teacher extracts from the children by asking questions at the close of the investigative period. Each fact or idea experienced during the investigative period is the "tooth" to come out. A brief example of such a discussion goes something like this:

Teacher: Now let's close our books and see what we remember. When was George Washington born? John?
John: 1732?
Teacher: Right. And when did he die? Philip?
Philip: 1826?
Teacher: No. Thomas Jefferson and John Adams died that year. When did Washington die? Mary?
Mary: 1799.

Teacher: Very good. You read carefully, Mary. And what occupation did he learn as a young man? Bill?

Bill: He learned to be a soldier.

Teacher: Not right. Ellen?

Ellen: Governor?

Teacher: No. Anybody know? John?

John: He was a surveyor.

Teacher: Right. And—

This communication action continues until the teacher asks all his questions or the period is closed by the bell or another curriculum area is introduced.

Another form of communication in which teachers and pupils become involved is "thread spinning." The teacher serves as a guide of thought and works with his pupils to develop logically a strand of facts and ideas. It works something like this:

Teacher: Today we were concerned with learning why we celebrate Washington's Birthday. What did you find out? Jane?

Jane: Because he was our first president.

Teacher: That is true. That fact gives us one clue to why we celebrate his birthday. Can anyone else think of another? Fred?

Fred: He was also the commanding general of our armies during our War of Independence. He was very famous as a general.

Teacher: Another important clue, Fred. Is there another that we can bring to mind? Bob?

Bob: Well, he took that message from the governor of Virginia to the French governor.

Teacher: Do you think that would have any bearing on why we celebrate his birthday today?

Bob: (Shakes his head in the negative.)

Teacher: Perhaps carrying the message showed how resourceful and courageous he was going to be later on in life when he was faced with a difficult problem. Can you think of another fact which gives us a clue to why we celebrate his birthday? Ellen?

Ellen: He worked hard at the Constitutional Convention. One book that I read said that he kept the men at the convention working together until the Constitution was made.

Teacher: Another important fact. Any others? (Pause.) Well, I think that we have enough facts to work with. We know that Washington was a capable general who led his army to victory during the War for Independence, that he was a statesman at the Constitutional Convention, and that he was the first president. How are these facts related to our practice of celebrating his birthday? We have other men in our history who were soldiers, statesmen, and president during their lifetime, but we don't celebrate their birthday. Jack, have you an idea?

Jack: Is it because he was *first* in all these things?

Teacher: Well, in part, yes. Boys and girls, we have a very special way of describing George Washington, a special name we sometimes give him. Have you ever heard it? (Pause.) Can't think of it? Perhaps this will help you. Admiral Rickover is often called the Father of the Nuclear Submarine. Sometimes we use an expression like this when we talk about George Washington. Yes, Jack?

Jack: The Father of Our Country?

Teacher: Yes. Now if we do some careful thinking, we'll be able to see how the facts we know tie in with our calling George Washington Father of Our Country. Let's concentrate now on why George Washington has been given credit for being the *father* of our country. Let us think of what a good father does for his child.

This discussion would continue until the children would understand more or less that we celebrate Washington's Birthday because he was the Father of Our Country.

Examination of this form of discussion reveals the following: The teacher is in complete control throughout the discussion. He heads the discussion by indicating correct facts and ideas and by giving clues. Keeping the discussion to the point, he leads from one fact to another and from one synthesis of facts to another. He knows exactly where the discussion is to lead.

The types of communication action described to this point are generally termed as *discussions* and, commonly accepted as such, they comprise the idea of the discussion act as it exists in the minds of teachers. Actually these forms of discussions are little more than teaching devices. "Jug filling" has extremely limited utility in transmitting information from the teacher to the children. "Tooth extracting" is of somewhat questionable utility in seeing how well children retain acquired information. "Thread spinning" is usually of high utility in helping children to recall recently acquired facts and helping them to see the relationships among facts and how facts may be tied together. However, these types of discussions cannot serve in any way as models for a child leader or a child follower to use when involved with pupil task-group work. The type of discussion required for work in pupil task groups, as practiced by a teacher working with children, is exemplified in the following:

Teacher: As we began our study of George Washington, some of you pointed out that we celebrate his birthday each year, but we do not celebrate the birthday of any other president with the exception of Abraham Lincoln. Some of you decided that we should not celebrate Washington's Birthday, because he lived so long ago that no one really knows him. Besides, you said, it would be only fair to celebrate the birthdays of all the presidents. Others of you said that we should celebrate his birthday because he was the first president. We decided that we would find as many facts as we could to see whether we should celebrate his birthday. What did you find out? Henry?

Henry: I found out that when Washington was president, he had a lot of respect for his job. He tried to be as perfect a president as he could be. This was an example that he set for all the presidents who followed him. I think that this is really important.

Teacher: Do you have something to ask Henry? All right, go ahead.

Pete: Henry, I read the same thing that you did, but I don't think that his example was really that important.

Henry: Well, then, Pete, suppose that he had been careless. Suppose that he had not cared how he looked or about what he said. Or suppose that he had taken advantage of his job as president to make money? The other presidents who came after him would want to do the same thing. We would not have a very good government today.

Jane: I'm with Henry and I have another fact about how great Washington was as an American leader. Some men came to him and asked him to be king. They were sure that the people would elect him to be king. George Washington would have nothing to do with the idea. What would have happened if he had accepted the idea? Maybe today we would have a king to run our country, a king that we did not elect.

Bob: I wouldn't like that.

Jim: Me, neither.

Teacher: Any more ideas? Helen.

Helen: When he was a general during the War for Independence, he did not have a large army. Sometimes his men were hard to handle. Often he did not have money to pay them, even to feed and clothe them. But still he led them. And finally the war was won. If he had not stayed with his difficult job, the war might not have been won. Perhaps our country would still belong to England.

Teacher: George, and then you, Rachel.

George: Why not celebrate his birthday? We need all the holidays we can get.

Teacher: We are trying to get true facts about Washington to see whether we should celebrate his birthday. Rachel?

Rachel: The author of my book said that we really should celebrate his birthday because he was the Father of Our Country.

Eric: What did he mean by that?

Rachel: I'm not sure.

Teacher: Does anyone know what that means? Alec?

Alec: I read the same book, and the author tells what he means, but I can't remember it exactly. It's somewhere near page 98 in the red book. That's the one, *America's Presidents.*

Teacher: Perhaps Alec has given us a good lead. Should we check to see what the author says in his book?

And the discussion would continue until the class had reached one decision or another, presumably toward the appropriateness of celebrating Washington's Birthday. Throughout the discussion the teacher relinquishes control other than to move the group along in its work. The pupils, or the members of the group, become highly involved and carry the discussion. Through his way of conducting the discussion the teacher provides an example of how a leader guides a discussion. His example serves as a means for children to learn what a discussion really is and provides insights into the various roles involved.

An analysis of the sample discussion above reveals the role of a discussion leader. He presents the task clearly, listens to the discussion, encourages the clarification of statements, and helps the members of the group to pull facts together into ideas. Another way of regarding the role of leader is to look upon him as the agent of thinking. He sets the stage for thinking, maintains an atmosphere for thinking and expressing, interferes only when thinking is drifting away from the point, and guides toward conclusions. The teacher can give children practice in this role by abdicating his role of leader once the task is presented and appointing a chairman to assume the role. Ultimately the teacher may encourage an appointed chairman to present the task, provided that it is one having its genesis in the previous day's work, and to guide the discussion.

Much of the teaching of this type of discussion results from the teacher's seizing every opportunity to use it with children during social studies. If the teacher uses a problem-oriented, inquiry approach to social-studies teaching, there are many opportunities. When he is building interest in the unit or in ideas within the unit, discussion may logically ensue. The presentation of the instructional model prompts pupils to make statements, and the teacher regards every statement as valuable as any other. He gives no indication as to the "rightness" or "wrongness" of a statement. This attitude frees every child to make whatever statement seems reasonable to him. The discussion passes around the classroom as the teacher invites children to substantiate their statements and encourages all children to react to what has been said. Whenever ideas are being tied together in summaries, the task is clear—to arrive at a summary statement of what has been studied. The teacher can easily encourage a pupil to guide the discussion leading toward the formulation of a summary. With this kind of practice, children begin to learn the process of discussion necessary for effective pupil task-group work.

At first the children may appear to be somewhat puzzled by this pattern of discussion. Children seem lost who have learned to "trial-and-error" their way through discussion by making guesses in which answers are given as questions. The teacher can prepare children for discussion by refraining from immediately labeling as right or wrong every answer given by a child. He can bring the attention of the class members to any statement and invite them to consider whether it is right or wrong. Some teachers use the simple technique of having children call on each other during a discussion. When a child makes a statement, the others are invited to comment about it. When another child signifies that he has something to say, the child who made the statement calls upon him to make a comment.

More direct procedures may be necessary, particularly in the later grades. The teacher may guide his pupils in making an analysis of two or more discussions such as the samples provided in this chapter. These discussions may be tape-recorded or read as plays before the class. The pupils listen and decide which is the "real" discussion and determine what makes it so effective. They may be guided into generalizing about its effectiveness and use their generalizations as guides whenever discussions arise. The applications of generalizations will always require evaluation if growth is to occur.

Another way to help children develop their skill to discuss as exemplified here is to begin with a group failure. The members of the group are encouraged to examine the discussion that occurred and, as a result, develop some procedures to try. The procedures are tried and modified in accord with experience until the children arrive at the point that they know the roles inherent in discussion and are able to follow them.

Sometimes the teacher finds that attempts to use discussion are hindered by failure to develop early a simple means for an individual within a group to communicate to the leader that he has something to say. Any commonly understood signal will do—an unobtrusive hand signal, eye contact and gesture, a nod of the head. Often the leader of the group is given the task of indicating the speaking order of the members of a group.

If the children do not have skill in pupil task-group discussion, it is not likely that what they have managed to learn about group structure and function will prove of much benefit to them.

ORGANIZING FOR PUPIL TASK-GROUP WORK

The other sections of this chapter have dealt with aspects of organizing for group work. The necessity of establishing a positive social climate within the classroom, the need for children to be knowledgeable about the structure and function of a group, and practice in democratic discussion are readiness aspects of organizing for group work. Specific conditions to be checked and specific plans to be made for pupil task-group work will be treated in this section.

When the social-studies teacher begins to develop an organization for pupil task-group work, he will do well to ask himself these questions:

Are my pupils ready for pupil task-group work?
What is the group task to be?
How is the task to be introduced to the group?
Who are to be the members of the various groups?
Who is to be the leader of each group?
How can I be assured that my pupils will grow in their ability to use group work skills?

Assessing readiness for pupil task-group work involves judging the adequacy of the social climate in the classroom and the ability of the children to perform in groups under more or less direct supervision. When checking for the adequacy of the social climate in the classroom, the teacher should observe carefully the group situations in which children are committed to working and playing together daily or frequently. One of the best indicators of the adequacy of social climates is positive relations on the playground. If the children can play amicably in various school or classroom groupings during the play periods of a school day, the social climate in their classroom is quite probably adequate for pupil task-group work. Another good indicator of a positive social climate in the classroom is the prevalence of friendly behavior in neighborhood groups as they come to school or leave it. Probably the best indicator of an adequate social climate is the display of positive interpersonal feelings and attitudes of children as they perform simple group tasks such as straightening the room or cleaning up after an expressive period. Often such groups reflect an amazing ability to divide responsibilities without conflict. Of course, occasional friction is to be expected, but when the usual pattern of behavior reflects children's ability to do things together, it is likely that they are ready for pupil task-group work.

The teacher should also check the general level of behavior within the classroom. If the classroom is usually a relatively quiet, relaxed, businesslike place and if the children can make the regularly scheduled changes without confusion, the teacher should feel free to introduce pupil task-group work.

Before guiding children into pupil task-group work, some teachers observe children's attitudes toward each other in the classroom. Of particular importance are the attitudes which children display toward those who have difficulties in the classroom. If the children have an understanding of the limitations of some of their less fortunate fellows, they show it by accepting both them and their limitations, and group work can take place. If this condition is not widespread throughout the classroom, the teacher has little choice other than to contrive that children with problems work only with the individuals who can understand them. Children's attitudes toward the teacher also have a part to play in pupil task-group work. If they feel that he trusts them and respects them to the point that they are secure without his personal guidance all the time, they will be able to engage in pupil task-group work.

Another area which the teacher should check in assessing his pupils' readiness for pupil task-group work is their ability with group skills. He makes careful note of the ways in which the children respond to events inherent in a formal group situation when he himself directs the class as a group. As he works in organizing the structure and function of the class group, the children respond to accepting responsibility, to being given a role, and to having the opportunity to assign a role. During discussions, he will observe to see how well the various children respond to the freedom to make suggestions, express opinions, and make criticisms, and how they react to criticism. Of particular interest to him will be how readily the various children commit themselves to the solution of a problem.

Occasionally a teacher may find that a group of his pupils are ready for pupil task-group work, but the rest are not. In this case, he works with the group to get them started with group work and has the others do individual work. As more children become prepared, he guides them into group work when group work is warranted. Sometimes one of these capable groups can be used as a demonstration group for the rest of the children to give them insights into what group work is about.

As the teacher sets about determining the group task, he is concerned with two aspects of suitability, the suitability of the task for group work, and the suitability of the task for a specific group of children. Earlier in this chapter the task was mentioned as an important consideration in deciding whether group work or individual work is to be done. Due regard must be given to the development of individual integrity. At times, the American citizen must seek information about problems and issues as an individual. At other times, particularly when applying information to determine a decision for the common good of the group, he becomes involved with group work. Children need to learn how to differentiate between the two situations; therefore, the teacher must exercise care in considering the task toward which to guide children. A reasonable criterion to use in the selection of the task for group work is this: If the task is ordinarily performed by a group in our society, it is a task suitable for children using pupil task-group work.

Later in the chapter, reference was made to the kinds of tasks that are suitable to pupil task-group work. These tasks included group expression, deciding an issue, and determining a necessary action. However, certain conditions must be met before these tasks can be considered suitable. The first of these conditions is that the pupils reflect a common concern for the necessity of the task; the second is that the children have the skills necessary for the task.

When guiding younger children into group work, the teacher often breaks the task down into subtasks, and each of these is accomplished in order during several social-studies periods. For example, the children in a first grade are to produce some large wall pictures expressing their learning about community workers. The groups are organized around the topic of the work performed by each of the following: the fireman, policeman, postman, trash collector, and street repairman. A group is concerned with each of these. The first subtask, deciding what the content of the wall picture is to be, is accomplished on the first day. On the second day, the children decide what materials will be needed and who will do the various jobs. On the third and fourth days, each group works on its wall picture. The product is presented to the rest of the class on the fifth day—the end of the task.

Group work for younger children is generally restricted to expressive tasks.

In the later grades, children are guided into group work with intellectual tasks as well as with expressive tasks. Any idea which fractions the class along lines of differing opinions is a suitable matter for group work. Opinions may differ when a generalization is to be verified, when an issue arises during study, when a definite play of action is to be developed and tested, or when a classroom value is to be examined and placed on trial. A single social-studies period, or several, may be required for these tasks.

Generally, as the teacher deals with the problem of selecting a task to present to a group, he should apply a list of criteria, such as the questions below, to any task being considered:

Is this a task usually performed by group action?
Is this a task for which my pupils have the required skills?
Is this a task toward which pupils will make a strong commitment?

If the answers to these questions are in the affirmative, the task is suitable for presentation to the group.

Introducing the task to the group usually presents little difficulty. Under ideal conditions the task grows out of the regular class work in social studies. When an issue arises and the children can see several sides to it, they are inclined to want to do something about it—to prepare for a debate, a panel discussion, or a round-table discussion. When an idea has been learned and the teacher suggests strongly that it may not be true in all times and in all places, the children want to verify it. The atmosphere in the classroom is often expressed clearly in such suggestions as: Why don't some of us check on this idea and some of the others check on that idea? Children brought face-to-face with conservation needs show by their behavior that they want to do something about it. Learning about how our Constitution was developed almost always generates interest in developing a constitution for the classroom. The dramatic content of great events and the lives of men often prompt children to suggest play production as a means of group expression. In a sense the task often seems to introduce itself.

Sometimes a more direct introduction to the task is necessary. The teacher may cite the need for the resolution of an issue by offering a challenge which may be no more than the simple question: And what do you think about that? Perhaps he will devise an instructional model which presents the conflict clearly. To stimulate children to want to verify an idea, he may present materials to the children which suggest that the idea is not as valid as it seems. For example, children who have learned through a study of their own society that man must utilize his natural resources in order to live may be brought to the level of skepticism by being shown some pictures of a primitive society. If the task is to determine what a pattern of action is to be, the teacher begins by asking for suggestions of what can be done and then leads directly toward the task by asking: What can each one of us do? or What can we do? When the task is to be some form of group expression, the teacher can stimulate children to want to undertake the task by having them view the finished product of another class. In every instance a measure of subtlety must be used. If the direct introduction is nothing more than a command, the pupils' commitment to the task is likely to be low.

Determining the membership of the various groups sometimes causes the teacher some problems. Essentially, two views exist. One holds that to assure learning is the teacher's responsibility; therefore, it is his responsibility to organize groups in such a way that learning will be most effective. Occasionally this view must prevail, particularly when the children are just beginning to do pupil task-group work. The majority of the children will be ready but quite a few others may not be. Often children, particularly very young children, are not sophisticated in making choices. They do not consider that the task must receive the most consideration, and not the personalities of their colleagues. Some children may be deeply hurt by the way that other children make choices.

The second view about determining the membership of groups holds that children need practice in the uses and skills of democracy. This view should prevail as often as possible. It can prevail when children understand the place of authority in a democracy, when they understand the need for exercising tolerance and helpfulness, and when they recognize that the task is central. Children may not reach this level of sophistication until the later elementary years. Some classrooms of children in grades four, five, and six may reach this level toward the end of the school year. Sophistication depends largely on the number of opportunities they have had to use pupil task-group work successfully during the year.

A teacher can help himself to make more accurate choices in the formation of groups through the use of sociometric devices. These devices are usually brief questionnaries requesting children to make choices with regard to whom they would like to work on a given task. The questionnaire below is an example of a sociometric device:

NAME

In the blanks below, list the names of the boys and girls with whom you would like to work at painting a mural. List your first choice after 1, your second choice after 2, your third choice after 3, and so forth.

1. _____
2. _____
3. _____
4. _____
5. _____

It should be noted that the device is task-oriented. The children should be formed into groups largely in accord with their choices. Children who are least chosen should be assigned to groups but carefully supervised as they work with others.

The simple device of asking children their choices individually can be used in the primary grades.

The use of a sociometric device presents the teacher with a generally accurate view of the social structure of the classroom as it is related to a task. If the teacher uses such devices, he must be prepared to use his findings to organize groups. If he does not, further use of the devices offers results of questionable reliability. Since the use of sociometric devices can be quite time-consuming, some teachers prefer to use other procedures.

Another procedure often used in the selection of groups is to have the children indicate which group they would like to work in as an expression of interest. Hand-raising and chalkboard tabulating is a poor way to have children indicate choices. The teacher may question the children individually or may have them list their choices on cards or slips of paper. The teacher consults the data and forms the groups. The children's choices are to be honored, for once they have been asked to make a choice, a promise has been made. If the teacher cannot follow through on the promise, the child who cannot have his choice may have difficulty in accepting the task of the group. The disadvantage to this procedure for determining group membership is that there is usually no way to control the size of groups. Sometimes having the children list several choices helps. The choices of children usually should be accepted as valid. Groups that are too large can be split and both groups can work at the same task, each in its own way. A group of one seems ambiguous, but if that is the way that choices of interests turn out, it is better to accept it. Frequently the "group of one" will decide that he would like to join another group.

A very questionable procedure is that of selecting leaders and having them openly choose the members of their groups. Children who have difficulty in adjusting to the social structure of the classroom are left standing and the leaders do all that they can to avoid choosing them. If the leaders are to choose their group members they should work at the back of the classroom with a class roster. No child knows then who was chosen first and who was chosen last.

The size of pupil task groups should range generally from five through seven. Sometimes the task will determine the number of persons necessary for its completion. Some tasks may be performed in groups of two, three, or four. Often working first in these smaller groups provides a background for working in larger groups. Groups larger than eight or nine either will impede group work or will make for difficulty within the group. Too many members cannot become directly involved, and the members who cannot work gainfully with the others find other things to do.

The issue arising when teachers select group members also arises when leadership is being determined for the groups. The same views and conditions exist. Sometimes the teacher selects the leader, at other times the group selects him. The use of sociometric devices is particularly good as an aid in selecting leaders. The individuals who are most frequently chosen as persons to work with are leader material. Younger children are likely to choose most frequently those children who are most popular and more athletically endowed; therefore, their leaders will always need to be guided carefully. Older children will usually choose most often those individuals who will most suitably act as leaders in a particular task.

If the teacher finds that he has more than the usual number of individuals who can serve as leaders in his classroom, rotating the responsibility of leadership and appointing coleaders sometimes helps. Sometimes the teacher does no more than to make sure that the group membership includes leadership material. As the group begins its work the real leader emerges.

The more sophisticated children become in their understanding of the structure and function of a pupil task-group, the more qualified they become for selecting a leader from within the group. (See Figure 11.) When the teacher has groups assume the responsibility for selecting their own leaders, small popularity contests often ensue. This situation can be avoided somewhat if the teacher selects a leader whose job it is to lead until the structure of the group has been determined. The temporary leader presents the act of selecting a leader in these terms: Who among us knows the most about the task we are to do? Who can help us to get the job done? The teacher makes this temporary leader's responsibility clear by instructing him openly before the group about

FIGURE 11. THIRD GRADERS WORK TO DETERMINE GROUP STRUCTURE.

what he is supposed to do. Another procedure which the teacher may follow is to encourage groups to delay establishing the structure of the group until they have talked about the task for a while. During the free discussion the leader emerges.

Growth in group skills tends to be gradual. By no means are the skills mastered by the end of the elementary school years. Each new task presents a new group structure and function. Each year brings changes in class groups and changes in teachers. To assure growth the teacher must apply procedures that encourage growth. These procedures involve little more than the application of the simple but vital practices that support effective learning. As in the practice of any difficult task, practice in group work must be carefully supervised. The teacher moves from group to group. He helps groups and individuals having difficulty. Sometimes it is necessary for him to establish a signal for stopping group work so that everyone can examine his behavior—perhaps the sounding of a few notes on the piano, the ringing of a bell, switching the lights on and off.

Constant evaluation also assures growth. During the initial stages of pupil task-group work, the teacher will have to direct the children's attention toward group work standards at the beginning and end of the period. Areas needing improvement will need to be isolated and worked at. As groups begin to work smoothly, evaluation of group behavior may become the task of the group leader. At times he will need to make no mention of group behavior. He will report only on the work accomplished. The arrival of this moment signifies that the children have come a long way in learning how to work at pupil task-group work.

SUMMARY

Group work in social studies refers to the learning activity in which groups of children accept tasks, organize to accomplish them, and complete them.

The place of group work in social studies is established by historical precedent and exercise of the logic of curriculum development. Although the place is firmly established, it is not specific.

Groups used in social-studies instruction may be differentiated on the basis of for whom the task is being performed. Group work is involved when the pupils accept the task, develop a group structure to implement its completion, and work together to complete it.

If children are to be guided into group work, the teacher must recognize his role as guide, a positive social climate must be established, and the children must understand the structure and functions of a group.

Group work requires that the physical environment be arranged to facilitate interaction.

Formal instruction in the structure and functions of groups may be conducted in two ways: (1) the children may be guided in drawing up standards of behavior for leaders and followers and testing them, or (2) they may be guided in discovering the necessary behaviors through trying to work in groups and examining the results. Children's evaluation of their work is essential to their growth in group skills.

The teacher must also provide for support of individuals in group work. He also exercises care in selecting tasks toward which groups are to be guided and serves as a model for the communication skill necessary to group work.

Before guiding his class into group work, the teacher carefully studies the children to determine whether social interrelationships exist at a level which will support group work. He also examines the results of his instructional program in group work skills. Group work is launched as the teacher guides children in accepting tasks and helps them to form into groups.

Exercises for Further Understanding

1. The richest resource that a teacher can bring to guiding children into and through group work is experience with adult groups, either careful observation of adults at work in various kinds of groups or participation in a council, an executive board of one kind or another, or a committee which has a project to complete. To gain objective insights into groups do as many of the following as you can:

    (a) Observe a crew at work doing some kind of repair or constructing. How well do the crew members respond to authority? How well do they cooperate? How much of the conversation is directed toward the task and how much toward maintaining group equilibrium? Can you make some "educated" guesses about the source of authority and the complexity of the task in relation to the efficiency of the group?

    (b) Attend a meeting of the executive board of an organization to which you belong or a public meeting of the board of education, a municipal commission, or a city council. In what person does the authority reside? In your opinion, is he a strong or weak leader? What makes you think so? Can you identify any member of the group who seems to compete with the functional leader for leadership of the group? Does there appear to be a place for humor in the conduct of the meeting? Are all the members of the group interested in the task at hand? What are the characteristics of the members of the group that makes work possible?

(c) Recall an instance in which you were a group member. If you were the leader, what were your biggest problems? If you were a worker, how well do you think the task was accomplished? How could it have been accomplished more quickly and efficiently? What would you have done if you had been leader?

2. Make arrangements to visit an elementary classroom in which group work is taking place. Observe one group for the following:

(a) Is what is being done indeed called group work, or something else?

(b) How deep and how widespread is the commitment of the members of the group to the task?

(c) How well do the children understand the roles of various members of the group?

(d) What provisions are made for the group to know how much progress they have made?

Selected References

Bany, Mary A., and Lois V. Johnson, *Classrom Group Behavior*. New York: The Macmillan Company, 1964.

Bierstedt, Robert, Eugene J. Meehan, and Paul A. Samuelson, *Modern Social Science*, Chap. 4, "Social Organization." New York: McGraw-Hill Book Company, 1964.

Bradford, Leland P., and Dorothy Mial, "The Individual and the Group." *National Elementary School Principal*, 41:30-34 (January 1962).

Brookover, Wilbur B., and David Gottlieb, *A Sociology of Education*, Chap. 10, "The School as a Social System;" Chap. 14, "School Climates and the Socialization Process;" and Chap. 15, "Teacher-Pupil Interaction, Teacher Models, and Learning." New York: American Book Company, 1964.

Fox, Robert, Margaret Barron Luszki, and Richard Schmuck, *Diagnosing Classroom Learning Environments*. Chicago: Science Research Associates, Inc., 1966.

Hare, A. Paul, Edgar F. Borgatta, and Robert F. Bales, *Small Groups*. New York: Alfred A. Knopf, Inc., 1955.

Harnack, R. Victor, and Thorrel B. Fest, *Group Discussion*. New York: Appleton-Century-Crofts, Inc., 1964.

Jarolimek, John, *Social Studies in Elementary Education*, 2d ed., Chap. 7, "Developing Skills Needed in Group Situations." New York: The Macmillan Company, 1963.

Margolin, Edythe, "The Kindergarten: Social System and Laboratory." *Educational Leadership*, 23:157-160 (November 1965).

Merritt, Edith, *Working with Children in Social Studies*, Chap. 5, "Group Guidance in Social Studies." San Francisco: Wadsworth Publishing Company, Inc., 1961.

Michaelis, John U., *Social Studies for Children in a Democracy*, 3d ed., Chap. 8, "Group Work Skills." Englewood Cliffs, N.J.: Prentice-Hall, Inc., 1963.

Miel, Alice, and Peggy Brogan, *More Than Social Studies*, Chap. 8, "Helping Children Feel Good about Themselves;" Chap. 10, "Helping Children Increase Competence in Democratic Problem Solving;" and Chap. 12, "Creating the Democratic School Setting." Englewood Cliffs, N.J.: Prentice-Hall, Inc., 1957.

National Society for the Study of Education, *The Dynamics of Instructional Groups*, Nelson B. Henry, ed., Fifty-ninth Yearbook of the N.S.S.E., Part II. Chicago: The University of Chicago Press, 1960.

Porter, Robert M., "Relationship of Participation to Satisfaction in Small-Group Discussions." *Journal of Educational Research*, 59:128-132 (November 1965).

13

Providing for Individual
Differences in Social Studies

From time to time throughout this book the matter of individual differences has been briefly discussed. The moment has arrived for us to examine these differences more closely to see what they imply for elementary social-studies instruction. Our particular concern will be with children whose pattern of learning behavior is different, for one reason or another, from the wide ranges of behavior regarded as typical for most children.

During recent years, both professional educators and the public have been showing a growing concern for the education of these children. Not too long ago, provisions for the education of children who were severely mentally retarded or emotionally disturbed were made only in the large metropolitan districts. Today, smaller communities are attempting to provide more fully for these children. A few years ago, few educational programs were designed for the children who are gifted intellectually; today, there are many such programs. A decade or so ago, the elementary classroom teacher was expected to conduct all the remedial programs necessary for his pupils;

today, special programs such as remedial reading staffed by specially prepared teachers are to be found in many schools. Concern is now growing for the children who have learning difficulties because of cultural disadvantages. The general picture today reflects many attempts being made to identify these children and to devise procedures to help them.

Providing for the needs of exceptional children in social studies is approached in several ways, depending largely on the policies developed by the school district. One such policy is to have pupils grouped homogenously in terms of intellectual endowment and achievement. When this policy is followed, children at the low extreme of intellectual endowment are grouped into separate classes small in size, provided with specially trained teachers, and generally administered as a separate branch within the district. The slow, the average, and the gifted children are grouped in separate classrooms. The provisions for social-studies instruction for children of low intellectual endowment varies from district to district. In some districts, no attempt is made to provide social-studies instruction because it is felt that these children do not have the skills required for the conduct of a social-studies program. This practice is questionable. Very slow children, the same as others, live in a world in which social, cultural, political, and economic ideas are continually impinging upon them; therefore, they need to understand these ideas to the fullest extent of their limited capacities.

Some districts, particularly the larger ones, develop special programs in social studies for very slow children. Sometimes the program reflects a careful differentiation of children on the basis of their capacity to learn how to read. It is assumed that slow children cannot learn reading skills to the point that they can use them efficiently for gathering facts in the materials usually available. Therefore, within a daily period and a program organized under the social-studies label, they are guided into craft activities in which they make articles useful to themselves or their families. Despite the label, this work is not social studies; it is crafts. Children in the later grades are guided into the study of units studied by normal primary children. This practice assures adequate materials requiring little reading, but it fails to take into account that slow children have needs similar to those of normal children of the same age. Too often the units reflect a dabbling in ideas, yet these children need to exercise their thinking to its fullest potential. The same is often true for children in the junior high years, where the units are similar in name to what normal children of their age study, but the emphasis is upon exercising reading skills and retaining a few facts considered necessary to citizenship. A more acceptable social-studies program for very slow children would include topic areas in content similar to those studied by other children, the use of simple, carefully devised resources, and much inquiry into attitudes and patterns of action.

When the policy of homogenous grouping is followed, the rest of the children, including the educationally handicapped, the average, and the gifted, are guided through a social-studies program which is about the same for every pupil in that similar topic areas and contents are used. Frequently the classrooms containing gifted children are provided with extra resource materials and audiovisual aids, but those containing educationally handicapped and average children use only the basic materials. The teacher's responsibility in these classrooms is to develop a specific program suitable to the needs of the children. The teacher of educationally handicapped children usually suffers the most severe hardships, because these children usually are deficient in abstract skills for one reason or another or for a number of reasons. Often these children develop problems intensified by frustration with school work. Because they can use so few materials efficiently, the teacher must use his ingenuity to devise the necessary materials. Usually he is so busy containing the problems in his classroom that he has neither the time nor the energy for such an undertaking. These conditions have given rise to several questionable practices, such as assigning poor teachers or inexperienced teachers to classrooms of slow children, or establishing a rotation system in which every teacher in the school takes his turn with the educationally handicapped children. Reasonably, a district which supports the policy of homogeneous grouping would provide not only the necessary materials for the instruction of all groups but the teacher incentives as well, to encourage the effective instruction of slow children. Reduced class size, adequate counseling and guidance services, and provisions for teacher self-identification through in-service programs and associations would go a long way toward remedying the situation.

Another policy popular in some school districts holds that exceptional children need to be provided for in a special way; therefore, special programs in social studies are developed for them. However, these programs are provided only for the gifted and sometimes for the culturally disadvantaged. The programs function in this way: A carefully selected teacher is sent to the school at a specified time or times during the week. The children to be served by the program are released from their classes to work with the special teacher. The social-studies curriculum is relatively unstructured, although the culturally disadvantaged children are usually guided toward a special study of the community. Gifted children are guided in developing a curriculum in accord with their interests. It is assumed that the children's usual social-studies needs will be answered in the regular social-studies program, but that the special programs will provide a strong support to the regular program by providing needed background to the culturally disadvantaged and challenge to the gifted. An outstanding disadvantage of the special programs in social studies is that they make it difficult for the regular classroom teacher and the special-program teacher to maintain a regular program. When the regular classroom teacher and the special-program teacher meet frequently to exchange information on what each is doing, this disadvantage is considerably nullified.

Homogeneous grouping and special programs often represent the best that a school district can do for these children in social studies in terms of available finances and personnel. Often the procedures are applicable only in the larger school districts. However, no matter how they are administered, they cannot completely solve the problems of providing for the social-studies needs of atypical children. Much remains for the classroom teacher to do regardless of the complex of intellectual abilities that may exist in his classroom. He may follow certain instructional procedures, sometimes in separate application, but more often in combined application. These procedures include extending readiness, exerting control over the investigative activities to be used, exerting control over the complexity of ideas being studied, enriching the social-studies curriculum, and individualizing the program.

EXTENDING READINESS

When a social-studies teacher is working with children of retarded mental development or with culturally disadvantaged children, he will more than likely have to spend more time at teaching the basic idea upon which fruitful study is built. When the children know the basic idea upon which a social-studies unit is constructed, they are ready to study the main idea of the unit. For example, children about to study how the community is dependent on the work of farmers will need to know basically what farmers are. In a typical class, a twenty- or thirty-minute discussion about farmers in general establishes a common level of knowledge about what farmers are. However, mentally retarded children or culturally disadvantaged children in the city may need much more than a twenty- or thirty-minute discussion period to establish the level of knowledge about farmers needed before the main idea about dependency can be pursued. An extended readiness period is required.

As the teacher works with his pupils to build readiness for the study of the main idea, he will be teaching definitive ideas for the most part. If he is working with mentally retarded younger children about to study the supermarket as an important service, he will have to help the children clarify in their own mind what a supermarket is. It may be necessary to take the children on a field trip to a supermarket to establish what it really is. The trip itself will not likely be sufficient; several social-studies periods will have to be devoted to discussion and further study with pictures, as well as some expressive activities dealing with the supermarket. A similar procedure is necessary when younger mentally retarded children are about to study community workers. The children will need to walk through the community to see who the community workers are. Later, several social-studies periods will have to be devoted to discussion with pictures and flannel-board figures and expressing definitive ideas about community workers. When younger mentally retarded children are to be guided in the study of a process, they will need to be guided in a careful analysis of the product that results from the process. They will have to explore what it is made of and its various uses before they begin to study the process itself.

Older mentally retarded children studying a geographical area will need to have the area delineated more carefully in terms of the area in which they live and in terms of their own experience. The various experiences of children living and traveling in other places will have to be completely explored and discussed. Seasonal and climatic differences will need to be analyzed carefully in terms of temperature, activities, and clothing habits. When these disadvantaged children are guided into the study of a historical era, they will need to be guided into a careful look at themselves and the world around them in terms of habits, modes of dress and food preferences, transportation, communication, and occupations. They will have to consider themselves in terms of their own daily needs, the drives that impel them to act in certain ways, and how these needs and drives are satisfied. When these children are guided in the study of units which are basically about social, cultural, economic, or political ideas, they will need to analyze their own needs for getting along with others, for basic ways of doing things, for goods and services, and for government.

Culturally disadvantaged children will require a cultural extension of the basic idea to provide readiness for the main idea in the unit. The direction and nature of the extension of the idea will be determined by the nature of the limitations or barriers to life experience with which culturally disadvantaged children live and grow. The culturally disadvantaged child who has lived in a large metropolitan area all his life tends to know only the beliefs, values, and practices necessary for survival within his neighborhood; these may be in conflict with those of the society-at-large. To aid him in developing an understanding of these differences, he must be guided in examining the conflict to discover what is of value, particularly of common value, in both his subculture and the culture within which it is located. He is likely to suffer from a lack of basic information, as well as the ways of acquiring it, about aspects of technology, time, and space removed from his neighborhood. Therefore, when he is being guided in extending a basic idea, his efforts are directed in exploring it fully and seeing its application in both his neighborhood and the greater world.

Because of their lack of skill in acquiring information from the usual sources, such as books, maps, and the like, culturally disadvantaged children living in a metropolitan area are guided into an extended readiness through field trips and the extensive use of visual aids such as films, filmstrips, series of pictures, charts of various kinds, and flannel-board sequences. Many of the field trips may be walking trips; others may be provided through the use of district-financed public conveyance or through school transportation facilities. The visual aids required may be difficult to obtain; therefore, every source for pictorial material will need to be exhausted. Teacher-made charts and flannel-board sequences will often have to be produced. Using field trips and pictorial aids, the teacher guides the children in analyses to clarify the differences between their world and the one that surrounds it and to acquire the basic information necessary for understanding further facts and ideas about relationships.

Listed below are a few general suggestions for the teacher to follow as he guides these children into usual social-studies areas:

If a study is being made of agricultural technology, the teacher uses films to build the idea of farm generally. Using pictorial materials, the teacher guides the children in an exploration of daily farm life to include the general work, patterns of daily living, habits, and dress of farm people.

If a study is being made of the workers in the immediate community, the teacher guides the children in developing a new perspective which reaches beyond the street and the immediate neighborhood. Field trips are taken to the city center of government, the main business center, residential areas, libraries, museums, and so on. Special efforts are made to help the children see certain community workers in a new light. For example, the policeman is presented as a protector, not as a threat. These ideas are extended further in discussion of pictorial aids and in roleplaying.

If a study is being made of communication, the teacher guides the children toward seeing the utility of the various vehicles for communicative transmission which goes beyond entertainment. The newspaper, the magazine, the radio, and the television are scrutinized carefully. Newspapers, magazines of various kinds, a radio, and a television are brought into the classroom to be studied.

If a study is being made of transportation, the children will need to see it as a process which ties the city together, not as a stream of noise to which one becomes accustomed or as the wherewithal for an exciting game. A walking trip to a busy corner where careful observations are made of the various kinds of transportation and their purposes helps to provide needed insights. Field trips to dispatch centers and travel and transportation terminals also help. Using a city street map and other pictorial devices, the teacher encourages the children to see that the busy streets that surround their homes are streams of necessary activity.

If a study is primarily geographical, the teacher takes the children on walking trips and other field trips to establish the geography of the area in which they live. This study should include the nature of the space in which they live, not only the essential aspects of surface space and its uses but also the air space above the surface. Then, using films and other pictorial aids, the teacher guides the children in examining the geography of the area to be studying in greater detail later to establish differences and similarities. Changes in use of space demanded by seasonal changes are also analyzed.

If a study is primary historical, the teacher guides children toward an understanding of change brought about with the passage of time. Since a city is itself a product of constant change, walking trips in the neighborhood and field trips to other parts of the city serve as an excellent means of study.

Architecture and historical landmarks represent easily studied products of change. Classroom discussions centered around pictorial aids and artifacts from the past and stories about people who live in the past brings an understanding of change. The teacher always makes certain that many comparisons are made between life now and life in the past.

If a study is about some aspect of culture, economics, or political science, the teacher guides the children in examining the needs and drives within their lives related to the aspect to be studied. For example, if the study is about the Constitution, the teacher has the children analyze the basis for government in their homes, in the school, and in the classroom. This study should guide them toward a basic understanding of the need for authority. It may also be necessary to review the structure of government in neighborhood groups to determine its basis.

Culturally disadvantaged children living in rural areas may have lived and grown under two different sets of conditions. Some of these children have existed in small, relatively backward rural communities all their lives; others have traveled extensively over some areas of the country as children of migratory agricultural workers. The latter will have a wider background for geographical studies, although the conditions under which they travel are not often conducive to rich experience. To such children, travel is often just a means of getting from one place to another, in a not-too-reliable vehicle, to find work. Travel is part of a means of survival, not a quest for information about other people and places or a seeking of natural wonders for enjoyment. However, travel does provide background for the child of the migratory worker. His most serious lack is his limited conception of community, because his community is his family and little more. The family is the only stable unit he knows; thus it must serve as the basic frame of reference from which his social-studies teacher helps him to extend basic ideas. His mobility must be taken into account when plans are being made for his social-studies instruction. The elementary teacher who knows that he will have to provide for the needs of the children of migratory workers will do well to plan short concise units with adequate provisions for exploring basic ideas fully. The direction of extension will have to lead from the family through the community in which the child finds himself at the time. Extensive use of the local community for field trips will be necessary. Other basic information will be acquired through teacher-guided analyses of pictorial material.

Culturally disadvantaged children living in isolated rural areas lack basic information because of immobility and few avenues through which to examine people and places beyond their immediate neighborhood. However, they can easily be guided toward a basic understanding of the community as a social unit in which all the social processes occur. As the social-studies teacher works with these children in extending basic ideas, he guides the children in making a direct analysis of the aspect or process as it occurs in their neighborhood and, by providing basic information about its application in the wider community, helps them to relate what they know to what occurs in the more extended area surrounding them. As many field trips as possible should be taken to the nearest metropolitan center. Extensive use of pictorial aids will be necessary.

Generally, extending readiness is a matter of guiding children in examining the basic idea as a unit through the use of community and audio-visual resources. The more abstract ideas may be extended through guiding children in scrutinizing the forces operant in the greater sphere of human activity.

In terms of the strategies much of the foregoing is applicable in all the strategies. Within the synthesized strategy, readiness is extended before the children are guided into working independently in the sources available to them. Within the thinking-emphasis strategy, the extension occurs before the "big" idea is placed in issue. The social-science strategy, if the necessary precautions are observed, is admirably suited to extending readiness because it emphasizes learning through direct observation. As a matter of fact, it reaches beyond extending readiness to the development of concepts. Similar procedures are used to guide children all the way through the learning of ideas.

CONTROL OF INVESTIGATION

Perhaps the most universally followed practice in providing for children who have learning difficulties in social studies is the control of investigation. Control is achieved through providing investigative resources which the various types of children in a classroom can use effectively. In every classroom, regardless of the criteria used to select the children for the various classrooms, individuals or groups of children will be above or below grade expectancy. In rooms in which an attempt has been made to group children homogeneously, several levels of ability will be found, although the range of levels may not be the same as in classrooms in which children are grouped heterogeneously. Every teacher, then, finds himself faced with the task of controlling investigation through providing a variety of investigative resources.

Patterns of control of investigative resources range from the use of materials extremely limited in scope and narrowly focused on a few ideas to materials that could be used by sophisticated adults. The pattern of control may have to encompass many levels of ability from one extreme to the other, or it may encompass only a few levels. The patterns will be determined by the classroom population and the range of abilities that exist within it.

In a classroom of young, extremely slow children, independent investigation is almost always completely out of the question. The teacher must always be present with the learners as they try to find out about topics or issues. The teacher must make use of as many dynamic representations as are available. Films and dioramas with movable figures are most helpful. In the latter, the movable figures serve as points of reference which children may use for projective activities, for expressing learnings, and for formulating questions. The teacher also guides the children in the careful use of many visual materials, such as pictures, simple charts, filmstrips, and series of pictures, as investigative resources. After the children have had an introduction to maps, they may be guided in the use of simple maps. Whenever possible, the teacher encourages the children to use whatever reading ability they possess. Often simple sentence strips can be used by the class or a group as a means of finding some important facts. Occasionally simple teacher-made expositions are used in a guided reading situation. Whenever the opportunity presents itself, the teacher reads simple texts and the children listen to acquire needed facts. Of course, the number of ideas that can be treated within a given period of time is often few. Investigation proceeds at a slow rate.

There will be differences in ability in a classroom of young, extremely slow children. Some children will be able to acquire facts only through carefully guided use of pictorial materials while others will be able to use more abstract resources. Some teachers prefer to cope with this situation by presenting every resource to the entire class. Those who can learn from the resource serve unconsciously as mediators as they verbalize their findings and the slower children listen. Other teachers prefer to divide the class into ability groupings and to present resources to each group in accord with its ability. While the teacher works with one group, the other members of the group perform an individual task in expression. Working with the children in groups is somewhat preferable to working with them as an entire class. The smaller the number of children working with a resource, the greater the opportunities for individual involvement and the longer can children stay with the task.

Older, extremely slow children may reach the level of independent investigation with simple materials. When they reach this level, the teacher makes certain that they understand the purpose for investigation and releases them to read, to study pictures, or to view a filmstrip. As they work at this activity, he guides the less able children in the use of other resources.

The usual practice in many school districts is to provide separate facilities for children suffering from severe intellectual handicaps, to provide specialized programs within each school for gifted children, and to assign the rest of the children by chronological age to regular classrooms. Control of investigation in these regular classrooms is a necessary procedure, for, regardless of the criteria used for assigning children to classrooms, every classroom will contain a group of educationally handicapped children, that is, children below expectancy in the skills required for responding to abstract representations, particularly verbal abstractions. If a policy of homogeneous grouping is followed, the classrooms containing children of demonstrated high ability will have at least a small group of children suffering an educational handicap; classrooms of children of average ability will have a group of children, perhaps as many as a third of the children, who are handicapped. A classroom of low achievers may consist of children who are handicapped at several different levels of disability. In these classrooms, the teacher assumes responsibility for two objectives, the children's acquisition of facts and ideas, and improving children's skills in investigation. The basic goal that he holds for educationally handicapped children is independence in investigation.

To help the educationally handicapped child achieve independence in investigation, the teacher guides him first in the use of skills which require little or no use of printed verbal symbols. The child's basic resources for facts and ideas are pictures, simple diagrams, and filmstrips. The teacher needs to take care in selecting resources, particularly picture series and filmstrips. The continuity must be clear and of sufficient detail that the printed accompaniment is not essential to understanding. Other resources will include texts which the teacher will read. The teacher begins by teaching the skills and carefully supervising individual practice. In many cases, supervised individual practice will have to continue for a considerable period before independence emerges.

Since the educationally handicapped child's usual disability is in reading and writing skills, the teacher may use a tape recorder to good advantage as a means of providing him with an investigative resource. The teacher may record informational passages from various references and through a "listening post" device transmit it to the child. Since the child's listening comprehension is likely to be normal, he can obtain authoritative information independently from the tape. He may not be able to make notes, but he can listen to the tape several times.

To encourage the use and improvement of reading skills for investigation, the teacher simplifies the reading task for the educationally handicapped child. Whenever possible, simple books about the topic are provided. These books, illustrated or not, should not be condescending or patronizing in tone. They should present direct, clear, well-organized prose. If the teacher can, he should rewrite passages to present only the important facts and ideas about the topic or issue under study. His prose should be simple and well organized and should reflect treatment of basic ideas only. The following is an example of the original text:

During the twentieth century, our ideas about conservation and where the responsibility for it lies have changed considerably. By the close of the nineteenth century, conservation as a movement was viewed as pertaining mostly to forests, rangelands, private farmland and, to some extent mines. As far as responsibility was concerned, it was placed firmly on the shoulders of the owners and managers of these land resources. It was generally accepted that it was they who were to assure the continued abundance of resources for future generations. Later came the idea that the responsibility for conservation should rest on the shoulders of all the citizens.

The rewrite follows:

Today, more than ever before, we know that we must use our natural resources wisely. These natural resources are forests, grasslands for cows and sheep, the soil on farmland, and such things as iron, coal, and oil. When we use them well, everyone has the food, clothing, and home that he needs.

Some years ago people did not think as we do now. They did not think that everyone had to use natural resources wisely. They thought that just the men who owned the forests, farms, and mines should worry about the use of natural resources. If they took care of the natural resources, there would always be plenty.

Then people began to change. They saw that everyone had to care about natural resources. Today we have the things we need because everyone began to care. If we also care, our children and all those who live after us will have what they need.

In the above rewrite, care was taken to see that a definitive idea about natural resources was given. The change of thinking, which is the main idea treated in the original paragraph, is developed simply and directly. If the reading ability of the children was very low, a rewrite such as the following would be prepared:

We need many things. We need food, clothing, and a house. We need cars and tools. All these are made from natural resources.

Soil is an important natural resource. The plants we eat grow in soil. The plants that animals eat grow in soil, and we eat the animals. Cotton grows in soil. We use cotton to make clothing. From the soil come many things we need.

A forest is an important natural resource. Its trees are made into boards. We use the boards for building houses. Wood from trees is used to make tables and chairs. Paper is also made from wood. From the forest we get many things we need.

A grassland is another natural resource. A grassland is a big piece of land on which grass grows. The grass grows wild. Cows and sheep eat the grass. If we had no grasslands, there could not be so many cows and sheep. Then we would have less milk and meat for food. We would not have wool and skins for making clothing.

Some natural resources are deep in the earth. Oil and iron are among the natural resources deep in the earth. We need oil. From it gasoline is made. We need gasoline for our cars. Iron is used to make cars and tools. Without oil and iron we could not have cars.

A long time ago, people did not care how they used natural resources. Sometimes they used only what they needed. Sometimes they wasted them. Then people began to care. They saw that their children might not have the things they needed. They wanted the men who had the natural resources on their land to be careful. These men must see to it that the natural resources are used well.

Today we know that all of us must care how our natural resources are used. We must not waste the things made from them. We must use only what we need. We must see that natural resources are cared for. If we do these things, we can have what we need. Our children will have what they need.

A rewrite such as the above is quite extended. Control of vocabulary as well as need for definitive ideas to be acquired through reading necessitate the extended treatment.

Another way in which the teacher may simplify the task of reading is to select passages from textbooks and reference books for the handicapped children to read under carefully guided supervision. The teacher should be present during the reading and should clue the children with guide-questions. Frequently a careful study of the difficult words before reading is begun proves helpful. However, if reading is really to be the skill to be used for obtaining information, the study should be restricted to aspects of word recognition.

Occasionally some teachers try to help handicapped children with their reading task by having children who cannot read well read with good readers as partners. This procedure can be very effective. If he is made dependent upon a peer who reads to him, the handicapped child may acquire the necessary facts and ideas, but his reading will not be improved. An undesirable relationship between the "partners" is also likely to develop.

Perhaps the most significant factor in helping educationally handicapped children in the classroom through the control of investigation is the way in which the teacher works with these children in the presence of the remainder of the pupils in the classroom. He establishes independence for these children as soon as he can. Although he works frequently with them, he also works with the other children from time to time. If he does not, both the children always being helped and the children always left much to themselves during investigative periods may develop negative attitudes in a devastating pattern. The handicapped children may resent the teacher's continual presence as a symbol of their inadequacy; the abler children may grow to resent both the teacher and the handicapped children who deny his working with them. Sometimes children become patronizing and arrogant toward those less able than themselves. The teacher can prevent the development of such attitudes by working with handicapped children as respected human beings and by considering all the children in his classrooms as pupils deserving of his time and attention.

Control of investigation is also a procedure used to provide for the needs of gifted or very able children. The direction of control is toward the most challenging of investigative resources. These resources include textbooks written at a high level of sophistication; special books devoted to the topic or issue under study—these may include books written at an adult level as well as books written for children; reference books of all kinds; films and filmstrips for independent study; critical comments about human affairs such as are found in editorials, cartoons, and essays; and community resources such as resource persons, historical libraries, local governmental agencies, industrial centers, and the like. Another direction of control leads toward independence in the selection and use of resources.

To encourage the use of many resources by the more able and gifted children in the classroom, some teachers establish investigative centers. One center may be located near a set of shelves on which the reference books are kept, another may be located at a large table containing books on the topic or issue being studied, and still another may be located near a stack of current magazines containing pertinent articles. (See Figure 12.) A collection of maps at the front of the room constitutes another center. When special audio-visual devices are provided, a center may be organized around these, such as a film-viewing center, a filmstrip-viewing center, and a listening center where a phonograph or a tape recorder is available for use. As individuals the children go to these centers to seek information.

This procedure is effective in a variety of classroom situations in which the more able children and gifted children are found. It will work just as well in classrooms containing faster children with typical children. In situations demanding that the needs of typical children be fulfilled also, the teacher provides materials at the various centers for these children. If slower children are also in the classroom, the teacher will work with them while the remainder of the children work at the centers.

To help the more able and the gifted child see the value of community resources, the teacher introduces the uses of these sources early in the school year. As a class, the children soon see the value of the field trip and the resource person contacted in person or by telephone. Once this value has been established, it is a relatively easy matter to guide the children toward seeking out their best community resources and making arrangements for their own visits.

In classroom situations in which few provisions are made for a wide variety of resources, the teacher guides the more able and the gifted child toward checking information in several sources. On the desks of the more able and the gifted children are several books other than the basic textbook. These may include a supplementary textbook, an almanac, an individual atlas, and perhaps a volume of an encyclopedia. The more able and gifted children check information in the several sources, report their findings, and indicate which source they believe to be the best. If the classroom contains children of typical

FIGURE 12. A SIXTH-GRADE PUPIL WORKS AT AN INDIVIDUAL PROJECT DEALING WITH A DEMOGRAPHIC PROBLEM.

ability, it is advisable that they each be provided with at least one extra resource within their ability. They are expected to work in much the same ways as the more able and gifted children. Such a practice, if handled correctly, prevents the establishing of a classroom "brain-trust."

Although it is widely followed procedure used to provide for the needs of atypical children in social studies, exerting control over investigation presents many problems to the teacher because of the paucity of suitable materials. Sometimes the scarcity of materials is more apparent than real, for often district or county education centers contain more than is realized. Occasionally free materials such as brochures, pamphlets, special maps, and the like are to be had for the asking. When specially prepared materials are needed, a group of teachers can work together to produce special materials which they share. Many inexpensive materials such as paperback atlases, paperback books, documentary publications, almanacs, and articles in newspapers serve as excellent sources of information. Often a teacher's alertness to the possibilities around him and willingness to work with others can provide him with precisely the materials that he wants and needs.

The practices outlined above are generally applicable in the synthesized and thinking-emphasis strategies and of limited applicability in the social-science strategy.

CONTROL OF COMPLEXITY OF IDEAS

Some confusion exists among curriculum workers in social studies as to what is meant by exercising control over the complexity of ideas. The traditional view, influenced by the "expanding horizons" concept to a certain extent, assumes that most children's horizons grow in the same direction, and that for some children the horizons expand more slowly than they do for most children. This view to a degree, is correct, but it has led to some questionable practices in social studies, to wit, making no provisions for social studies in the educational program of the young, very slow child and providing for the needs of older, very slow children with social-studies units generally used in the primary grades with typical children. As for the "expanding horizons" of gifted children, it is assumed that the rate of expansion is not too different from that of typical children. The difference is primarily in the ability to perform abstract skills. Therefore, the more able and the gifted children study the same units as typical children, but they are provided challenge through having to investigate in more difficult resources. Sometimes they are just required to do more work for the same facts and ideas. Such practices fail to take into account that even a very slow child accrues some learning and understanding purely as a function of having lived over a period of years and for that reason is "older" than his mental age would indicate, and that, on the other hand, a very bright child has the power of mind to reach far into abstract learning. The very slow young child can profit from a social-studies program organized around a few simple ideas; his older counterpart can cope with ideas of greater complexity than those usually studied in the typical primary grade, and the more able or gifted child can probe more deeply into complex ideas.

A somewhat more enlightened view of the control of complexity of ideas holds that most of the ideas in the social sciences can be fairly well contained within a few simple statements:

1. Geography. To exist, man must utilize natural resources.
2. History. The life of man has been and is influenced by change.
3. Anthropology. Man is man, yet everywhere he is unique.
4. Political science. Man seeks to establish and maintain a public authority through which to govern and be governed.
5. Economics. Productive resources are scarce and human wants are unlimited.
6. Psychology. Man's behavior is purposive and goal oriented.
7. Sociology. Man is a social being.
8. Social psychology. Man as a social being is both an individual and a member of groups.

These ideas exist as thematic ideas of wide application. Each can be broken down into smaller ideas which can be arranged in order of complexity from low to high. The following list of ideas represents a vertical continuum which can be logically subsumed under the thematic idea of history as follows:

1. As we grow, we change in the way we look, in the ways we work and play, and in our dependence on others.
2. Things change as they grow, as they are added to in some way, as they become old, or as they are worn away in some way.
3. As the years go by, people change their ways of living, homes, clothing, and ways of earning a living.
4. Today, we have better ways of overcoming the obstacles of space and time because of the many inventions of men in the past.

5. Man's continuing search for better ways of government has resulted in the development of a form of economic system which we enjoy today.

6. Man's continuous struggle to develop more effective ways of producing and distributing needed goods and services has resulted in the development of a form of economic system which we enjoy today.

7. Cultural development of natural and human resources, the impact of cultural interaction, political development, and economic development work as forces in the development of a civilization.

8. History reflects man as a being who grows slowly but surely in his ability to solve the problems of existence and survival.

The eight ideas listed above serve only as an example and are not to be considered as an eight-year curriculum in history. Nor are they to be regarded as an end-all in the organization of ideas in history. A more accomplished historian could extend the list further; a less accomplished historian would develop a shorter list. The important aspect of the list is that it does reflect an increasing complexity of ideas from top to bottom, but this complexity is not the only one involved. Each of these ideas can be reduced to a greater simplicity or extended to reflect greater sophistication. The list is extended to express greater simplicity and greater sophistication as follows:

Basic

1. As we grow, we change in the way we look, in the ways we work and play, and in our dependence on others.

Simple

As we grow, we change.

As we grow, we change in different ways.

Sophisticated

As we grow, we make predictable changes.

Each of us is what he is because of the life he has lived.

Basic

2. Things change as they grow, as they are added in to in some way, or as they become old or worn away in some way.

Simple

All the things around us are changing—some things faster than others.

The things around us change in different ways.

Sophisticated

Like those who came before us, we can make changes in the things around us by removing, replacing, or improving.

Everything around us is a product of change.

Basic

3. As the years go by, people change their ways of living, homes, clothing, and ways of earning a living.

Simple

The people who lived long ago did things differently from us.

People long ago lived in houses different from ours, dressed differently from us, prepared meals in ways different from ours, and worked at jobs different from ours.

Sophisticated

Persons living during a particular period of time work to bring about changes to make life better for themselves and others.

The direction and rate of change in the ways of living in the past influence our ways of living today and in the future.

Basic

4. Today we have better ways of overcoming the obstacles of space and time because of the many inventions of men in the past.

Simple

Long ago few men could travel far to talk to men who lived far away from them, but now many men can.

For a very long time men have worked to make things to help people travel and transport things faster and to talk to each other over long distances.

Sophisticated

Today, as in various periods in the past, "necessity is the mother of invention."

The success of any invention or discovery depends on the man, the people of his time, and the level of technological advancement of his time.

Basic

5. Man's continuing search for better ways of government has resulted in a form of government which we follow today.

Simple

Today we need a government to protect us; men long ago needed a government to protect them.

Today our government works to help us to defend ourselves and to see that everyone has what he needs; in the past governments sometimes worked in this way and sometimes they did not.

Sophisticated

The basic trend in man's development of government through the years has assured greater freedom for more people, thus we are freer today than people were in the past.

Our historical experience with government indicates the following: the government which governs least governs best.

Basic

6. Man's continuous struggle to develop more effective ways of producing and distributing needed goods and services has resulted in the development of a form of economic system which we enjoy today.

Simple

Today everyone must work if all are to have what they need; this was also true long ago.

Today work is divided to produce what everyone needs; in the past, work was divided, but in different ways.

Sophisticated

The basic trend in man's development of economic system has been directed toward the organization of a system that will produce in ever-growing amounts the goods and services needed by an increasing number of people to assure an ever-improving level of economic welfare.

Our historical experience has proved that only an individual enterprise system can keep pace with the constant demands of a growing population for an ever-increasing gross national product and a better standard of living.

Basic

7. Cultural development of natural and human resources, the impact of cultural interaction, political development, and economic development work as forces in the development of a civilization.

Simple

The ways we live, work, and govern make us a people; the ways that others have lived, worked and governed make them peoples different from us.

The ways that people lived, worked, and governed long ago have been passed on to other people and finally to us; these ways make us a people.

Sophisticated

Throughout the development of civilization, cultural, economic or political forces may be dominant at any one time, or all may contribute equal force at one time, and all operate at any one time in the growth of a civilization.

This moment in its every aspect is a product of all the significant historical moments that preceded it and is itself a moment leading toward other moments in the future.

Basic

8. History shows man as a being who grows slowly but surely in his ability to solve problems of existence and survival.

Simple

We could not be the people we are and have the things that we have if the people before us had not worked so hard.

As time goes on, people become better and better at discovering ways to find the answers to questions about work, government, and getting along with each other.

Sophisticated

In every civilization, past or present, the progress of man can be measured in terms of his solutions of problems of control of his physical and human environment to assure his survival and prosperity.

Within the limits of his time and age, man has strived always to control his destiny.

A construct of generalizations, derived from a thematic generalization and reflecting extensions toward greater simplicity and greater sophistication, serves as a spectrum of content objectives from which the social-studies teacher may select ideas to develop units for children of various ages and abilities. Teachers having classrooms of children who are similar in age and ability may select one generalization to serve as a guide in unit construction. (See Figure 13 in the illustration section.) The following is an example of the selections that teachers planning to teach historical units could make from the construct of generalizations:

1. For very slow six- or seven-year-olds, the simplest generalization given for basic generalization 1 or 2.

2. For very fast six- or seven-year-olds, the most sophisticated generalization given for basic generalization 1 or 2.

3. For very slow eight- and nine-year-olds, the simplest generalization given for basic generalization 3 or 4.

4. For very fast eight- or nine-year-olds, the most sophisticated generalization given for basic generalization 3 or 4.

5. For very slow children ten years of age and older, the simplest generalization given for basic generalization 5, 6, 7, or 8.

6. For very fast children ten years of age and older, the most sophisticated generalization given for basic generalization 5, 6, 7, or 8.

Teachers having classrooms in which there are no extremes in learning ability but in which there are children who are educationally handicapped in verbal skills, children who are fast learners but not gifted, and children who are generally classified as average in ability would select several generalizations from the spectrum in these ways:

1. For six- or seven-year-olds, basic generalization 1 or 2 plus the simpler

generalization for handicapped children and the more sophisticated generalization for faster learning children.

2. For eight- or nine-year-olds, basic generalization 3 or 4 plus the simpler generalization for handicapped children and the more sophisticated generalization for faster learning children.

3. For children ten years of age or older, basic generalization 5, 6, 7, or 8 plus the simpler generalization for handicapped children and the more sophisticated generalization for faster learning children.

Occasionally teachers may select two, four, or five generalizations, depending on the distribution of learning abilities in their classrooms. However, the teacher who makes a multiple selection of generalizations usually uses the basic generalization as an organizational guide. In his provisions for building interest in the unit, guiding children through investigations, and helping them to ideas together, he takes care of the needs of the various children in the classroom.

FIGURE 13. Third graders investigate the historical growth of their community at a level of complexity within their ability.

Constructs of generalizations similar to the one above can be made for all the areas in the social sciences. The one below is an example of a construct prepared in the area of economics.

THEMATIC GENERALIZATION: Productive resources are limited and human wants are unlimited.

Basic

1. We depend on many people for food, clothing, and the other things we need for living.

Simple

Our mother and father give us the things we need.

In our community people work to make and do things for us.

Sophisticated

Everything we need and use makes us dependent on many people in many places.

The greater our need for goods and services, the greater our dependence on other people.

Basic

2. We depend on many people for both the goods and the services necessary to our way of life, and many people depend on us to buy their goods and services.

Simple

Our parents buy the many things that we need and pay the bills.

The people who have stores and service stations help us to have what we need; they use the money from their work to buy what they need.

Sophisticated

People everywhere and we are interdependent in producing the goods and services that everyone needs and uses.

The greater our need for goods and services, the more tightly are we interdependent with people everywhere in all walks of life.

Basic

3. Through the division of labor we have more goods and services than if each of us tried by himself to provide just what he needed.

Simple

Father, and sometimes mother, works away from home at a job making something or giving service for many people to use.

Many workers are required to make what we need, and each must do his job if we are to have what we need.

Sophisticated

Division of labor not only makes possible the more efficient production of goods and services, but also makes many more jobs available.

The greater the need for goods and services, the more specialized labor becomes.

Basic

4. Every working person may be one or several of the following in the chain of producing what we need: an owner, a manager, a worker, or a "middle man," and is always a consumer.

Simple

Father, and sometimes mother, has a job that makes him part of a team that makes something or gives a service needed by everyone.

Sophisticated

Each of us has a unique relationship with each factor of production in terms of our work and the goods and services we consume.

Consumption serves as a guide for the use of the factors of production.

The more educated a person is, the greater his role as a producer and consumer.

Basic

5. If an industry is to be effective, it must be located near power resources, raw materials, markets, labor, and other industries of its kind.

Simple

In our community, there are certain jobs for our parents because only certain things can be produced in our community.

Each community is a producer of certain goods and services because of its location and population.

Sophisticated

A successful industry may be located in an area, provided that the richness of some factors compensates for the relative scarcity of others in the cost of producing and distributing goods.

The greater the abundance of natural resources, markets, and labor, the greater the possibility for an industry to thrive and grow.

Basic

6. If an industry is to be effective, it must have the form of business organization that will make it profitably productive.

Simple

Some people in our community run their own businesses; others run businesses owned by other people.

In our community some people own and run their own businesses, some people manage businesses for others, and some people buy parts of businesses.

Sophisticated

Because of increasing specialization in industry, large business organizations are assuming more control of and greater responsibility for the production of goods.

Big business contributes more than small business to the economic welfare of the society.

Basic

7. The price of whatever we buy is determined by its cost of production, to include cost of marketing and transportation, by competitive production, and by how much we need or want the item and the money we have available.

Prices change when the value of money changes.

Simple

When we buy somethings, we pay for the work of many people and we buy only what we have the money to pay for.

The price we pay for something includes its cost, how much of it is available, and how many people want it.

Sophisticated

If price levels are held constant, the economic welfare of society is improved.

In this construct, as well as in the construct developed for history, it is to be noted that at the more abstract, more sophisticated end of the spectrum generalizations occur which are not necessarily a reflection of truth. There is by no means agreement on the historical idea that man is improving if big business contributes more than small business to the welfare of a society. Skepticism is implicit. It is a facet of sophistication. It is assumed that any such generalization will be restated at the close of the study of the facts and ideas related to it and that the restatement will reflect something else, either another conviction or a suspension of judgment.

A teacher working by himself can develop similar constructs provided that he has the knowledge background. Generally, better constructs can be made by groups of teachers working together. The best constructs are developed by teachers working under the guidance of social scientists who have some insights in how children learn and who can see and grasp the simpler ideas upon which their disciplines are founded.

Once these constructs are made and teachers appreciate their value, definite social-studies programs can be developed for classrooms containing children of various abilities. Developing such constructs is applicable in all the strategies.

The three procedures just discussed—extension of readiness, control of investigation, and control of complexity of ideas—offer the greatest effectiveness in application when used in combined form. Used together, they provide for individual differences as well as group differences. If one procedure is used to the exclusion of the other, it often becomes little more than a well-intentioned use. For example, the teacher who carefully extends readiness for the children who need it and then fails to take into account the need for control of investigation and complexity of ideas has wasted his time and that of his pupils. However, at any one time one procedure may be predominantly in use, but when being used effectively, it will be related to the other two in some way.

ENRICHMENT

Many schools and school districts provide for the learning needs of fast-learning and gifted children through enrichment making available to these children the best learning resources available. The following list of provisions made for a special class of twenty gifted children, ages ten through fifteen, is an example of such enrichment.

1. A high priority for textbooks, reference books, films, filmstrips, and other resource materials at the country education center.
2. Three filmstrip projectors.
3. Two motion-picture projectors.
4. A Spokesman telephone.
5. A list of resource persons who are authorities in their field.
6. A bus available for field trips for which arrangements can be made twenty-four hours in advance.

As can be seen here, enrichment is basically an enrichment of contact with reality.

The provisions listed above represent an all-out effort to provide for the learning needs of fast-learning and gifted children. More often the provisions for enrichment in social studies will include the following:

1. An encyclopedia.
2. Several atlases.

3. Four or five copies of one or two almanacs.

4. A *Who's Who*.

5. A good assortment of maps.

6. Provisions for more field trips during the semester or year than are provided regular classes.

7. A filmstrip projector.

8. High priority on a motion-picture projector.

In classrooms which provided little more than basic textbooks and a few supplemental books, plus two or three maps, provisions such as the above are indeed enriching.

Enrichment as a procedure may be viewed as an aspect of control of investigation which was discussed previously. However, when enrichment is the basic procedure used as a means of providing for the needs of exceptional children, it touches only on the needs of fast learners and gifted children. It is often characterized by a relatively unstructured curriculum and an individualized program in the skills necessary to the adequate use of resources. The children are guided into selecting the social-studies topic or issue which they wish to investigate, are assigned a project, and work under the supervision of the teacher. He teaches the skills as necessary for each individual.

As a procedure for meeting the needs of exceptional children, particularly fast learners and gifted children, enrichment presents some very convincing advantages. Because of the practices that often accompany it, a respect is shown for the integrity of individual children. They are encouraged to make independent choices in line with their interests and to go as far as they wish in developing their choice. When used in a classroom which contains average learners as well as fast learners and gifted children, enrichment usually improves the learning for all the children.

An issue is raised as to whether enrichment for fast-learning and gifted children is really justifiable. Would not all the children in a school or district profit from enrichment? Yes, they would, but there are difficulties other than the usual financial ones. Enrichment for typical children and for slower children is often not feasible because an abundance of materials is not available for purchase. Research in learning and curriculum has yet to yield findings that indicate clearly the kinds of materials to be devised. However, there is a basic justifiability for enrichment as a procedure to be used with fast-learning and gifted children: Typical children and slower children generally require much more in terms of the need for the teacher's direct supervision; therefore, enrichment for other children is a legitimate compensation for having them work more by themselves.

It should be noted that enrichment is not very effective without careful guidance by the teacher. The teacher must be thoroughly knowledgeable in the ways that children learn, in the limitations which various materials impose, and in the social sciences. He must be capable in guiding children toward arriving at complex ideas. If he does not have these qualities, the provisions for enrichment may be more a curse than a blessing. Sometimes indiscriminate use of all the resources is forced just because they are available. Too often the availability of many resources is used as an excuse for setting difficult goals for children. Enrichment is applicable in all the strategies.

INDIVIDUALIZATION

Individualization of study in social studies is product- or project-oriented. In many instances the pupils are encouraged to choose a project to their liking and amenable to the topic or issue at hand; in other instances projects are assigned by the teacher. Once the project is assigned or decided upon, the pupil works independently, first seeking out facts and ideas and then pulling his findings together and presenting them to his teacher and his peers. As the children work on projects, the structure of the class is very loose and the teacher serves as a consultant to his pupils. Through teacher-pupil conferences he maintains control of the class and guides children toward the completion of their projects. In a very real sense, all social-studies instruction is geared to the production of projects.

Individualization as a means of providing for the needs of fast-learning and gifted children in social studies has grown in popularity. The practice is well supported by research which has clearly established the ability of most bright children to work independently. As a practice, it has been found to be most effective for older elementary children in grades seven, eight, and nine, the grades at which most bright children have achieved a basic mastery of investigative and expressive skills. However, it is also suitable with bright children in grades four, five, and six, but only when care is taken to teach the necessary skills. Individualization at these grade levels demands a strong and meticulously conducted program in the skills of investigation and expression. The projects themselves become important points for evaluation for growth in skills.

When individualization is practiced, the teacher must assume the responsibility for guiding children into projects suitable for them and accepted by them. This task is not easy. Some children who have been generally classified as gifted resist both projects and social studies because of a lack of interest in either the work or the area of knowledge. Frequently it will appear that a child has selected a project which when completed meets only the minimum requirements of acceptance and reflects very little, if any, originality. Some teachers attempt to work around this difficulty by making a basic assignment required of all children. This assignment most often takes the form of a report or a "term paper" of extended length. Then the teacher feels free to accept any child's proposed project, no matter how bizarre it may appear. Teachers who are content to allow the individualized program to build slowly and gradually spend an extended period of time helping children explore their interests in social-studies topics and issues and in the kinds of work they like to do. This exploration will involve working in short, two- or three-day units with a wide latitude allowed in the selection of expressive activities. The outcome is a gradual assumption of responsibility on the part of most children in the selection of a topic or issue and the project to be worked on. Some teachers maintain an alternating program, first the study of a unit as a class and then individual selection of topics or issues and projects. When all the projects are completed or nearly completed, the class is again directed toward the study of a unit. Any of the procedures cited can be effective, but their effectiveness is largely dependent on the teacher and the relationships he maintains with the members of his class.

Perhaps the greatest abuse of individualization as a means of helping fast-learning and gifted children is a tendency for many teachers to rely on the formal report or "term paper" as a basic project. Being called upon to complete report after report often jades pupil's interest in social studies and reports. Frequently the only motivation that supports the practice is the pupil's fear of a poor grade or mark or being dropped from the fast-learning or gifted program. Fortunately for some children, both they and their parents see through the artificiality of report after report to the point that they insist on a change. The child works again with a typical group of children.

Like the teacher who makes effective use of enrichment, the

teacher using individualization must also know the ways that children learn and be widely knowledgeable in the social sciences. He must also be ingenious in developing projects. One of the most effective directions for this ingenuity to follow is toward the well-established interests that many of the more able and the gifted children have. If a child is known to have a strong interest in mathematics, for example, the teacher will do well to guide him toward a project in which the use of mathematics is necessary. The following are suggestions that a teacher guiding children in the study of a unit which is primarily geographical in emphasis could use:

For children having an interest in mathematics
 Construct a relief map of the local area or any other selected area to scale;
 Develop a series of graphs;
 Develop a game dealing with travel across a given area during a specific period of the year (the child deals with the probability of the occurrence of hazards);
 Construct rearranged maps in which quantities are being expressed.

For children having an interest in science
 Develop a series of demonstrations to illustrate the movement of the earth's surface to include some treatment on how such movement influences the productive resources of man;
 Draw a series of diagrams illustrating the composition of the earth's crust and a brief discussion of how this composition affects man's use of the soil;
 Make a chart of the simple chemical reactions that occur in the soil and an explanation of how these reactions are significant to man;
 Preparing an ecological map of the local area or of a given area.

For children having an interest in language
 Write a short story having a locale in an area just studied and about a problem characteristic of the people in the area;
 Present a report of a critical study of some geographical aspect of a region and its significance in the lives of the people in the area;
 Write a play having for its theme man's continual struggle against geographical forces within a given area;
 Develop an annotated bibliography of periodical articles and books about a geographical problem.

For children having an interest in art
 Draw a dual series of cartoons reflecting opposing points of view about conserving natural resources.

Develop a poster of wide appeal about a selected geographic area (the poster should present the outstanding aspects of the area within an honest perspective);

Paint or draw a picture representing a selected geographical area and depicting accurately this theme: to exist, man must utilize his natural resources;

Develop comparative sketches about two very different regions in which geographical aspects are made clear and the human-use patterns of these aspects are reflected.

The following are suggestions which a teacher guiding children in studies the emphasis of which is centered in political science could use:

For children having an interest in mathematics

Develop a questionnaire about a student issue within the classroom, distribute it, and make a statistical analysis of the results;

Represent in a bar graph the results of the last presidential election;

Represent in an area or circle graph the percentages of state income from its various tax and fee sources;

Develop a graph projecting national income tax returns based on population growth and growth in the gross national product for the next year or for several years in the future.

For children having an interest in science

Using one hundred as a representative sampling, make an analysis of the characteristics of voters in a selected area in terms of sex, occupation, and political affiliation;

Poll the classroom on a selected student issue, then select a side of the issue to the extent that it would be unanimously accepted;

Make an objective analysis of two constitutions on the basis of their provisions for a check-and-balance control of governmental power;

Make an analysis of the workings of the British parliamentary form of government for weaknesses and strengths.

For children having an interest in language

Write a one-act play which takes place in the campaign headquarters of a candidate for the state legislature;

Write a poem reflecting the feelings of three voters, each of whom is from a different walk of life, as they enter the polls;

Prepare an opening statement for a debate on a critical student issue in school;

Interview a successful lawyer to obtain his opinions about the limitations of the law and report findings in a feature article.

For children having an interest in art

Draw a cartoon which expresses one side of a current political issue;

Develop a series of sketches showing how a city government legislates;

Develop a series of wall pictures to express this theme: Man seeks to establish and maintain a public authority;

Sculpt a figure reflecting man as a political being.

These examples of individual projects are obviously more suitable for fast-learning and gifted children in grades seven, eight, and nine. It is possible that some, particularly those listed for children having an interest in language and art, will be suitable for children of high ability in grades four, five, and six. As can be seen, emphasis on variety of expressive activities is the criterion used to guide the teacher's ingenuity. This basic clue defines what can be done in the early grades for young children of high ability. These children too can be guided toward suitable projects in which they work independently to complete expressive products such as graphs, pictures, stories, and the like.

Underlying the lists of projects given above is the assumption that there are individual differences among fast-learning and gifted children in terms of interests and abilities. Often some of these children will manifest a high interest in one social science and relatively little in another. Some have little interest in any topic or issue in social studies, no matter what the social-science emphasis may be, but through the use of interests and abilities in other areas of the curriculum as a means of building understanding, attitudes, and skills, these children come to learn what they need to know. Integration of areas in the curriculum in conditions such as these is most justifiable.

Individualization as a procedure used to meet the learning needs of fast-learning and gifted children requires that the teacher be gifted as a teacher, well-read in the social sciences, and highly skillful in guiding individuals in a variety of projects. He must have at least an essential grasp of a wide variety of skills. With these qualifications, he can be effective in individualizing a social-studies program. As a practice, individualization of instruction has a place in each of the teaching strategies.

SUMMARY

Generally, the procedures for working with children who have learning difficulties in social studies include the following: extending readiness, control of investigation, control of complexity of ideas, enrichment, and individualization. Extending readiness is a procedure often required to meet the needs of slower children and culturally disadvantaged children. Control of investigation and control of complexity of ideas are procedures which should be followed in every classroom, regardless of the extant range of abilities, be it narrow or wide. Enrichment and individualization are procedures often reserved for use with fast-learning and gifted children. These two procedures may or may not be followed; the others often must be followed if effective learning is to occur.

Exercises for Further Understanding

1. Make arrangements to observe an elementary class during social studies. Observe for the following:

(a) How the teacher makes provisions for atypical children.

(b) How effective the provisions appear to be.

If possible, interview the teacher to ascertain the range and variety of abilities in the class.

2. Make arrangements to observe an elementary class of mentally retarded children as they work in social studies. Observe for the following:

(a) The level of abstraction at which the children work.

(b) The kinds of investigative activities into which the children are guided.

(c) The level of independence at which the children work.

(d) Provisions made for tying ideas together.

3. Make arrangements to observe an elementary class of gifted children during social studies. Observe for the following:

(a) The level of abstraction at which the children work.

(b) The procedures used to meet the needs of the children.

4. Select one of the units presented in the Appendix and examine it carefully for changes that you would have to make in it to use it with gifted children. With mentally retarded children. With culturally disadvantaged children in a metropolitan area.

5. Choose a paragraph from your favorite book dealing with social-studies content. Rewrite the paragraph to make it more suitable for children.

6. Select a generalization from those presented in Chapter 4. Study it carefully. Then express it more simply. After doing this, express it to reflect greater sophistication.

7. Suppose that the unit into which you were guiding a group of gifted children was primarily a study of the history of transportation and that you were going to use individualization as a means of meeting the learning needs of the children. What kinds of projects would you guide the children toward?

Selected References

Beck, Robert H., Walter W. Cook, and Nolan C. Kearney, *Curriculum in the Modern Elementary School*, 2d ed., Chap. 8, "Social Class and the Curriculum." Englewood Cliffs, N.J.: Prentice-Hall, Inc., 1960.

Brookover, Wilbur B., and David Gottlieb, *A Sociology of Education*, Chap. 7, "Social Class and Education." New York: American Book Company, 1964.

Chace, Harriet, "Slow Learners in the Elementary School." *Social Education*, 21:122-124 (March 1957).

Chase, W. Linwood, "Individual Differences in Classroom Learning," *Social Studies in the Elementary School*, Fifty-Sixth Yearbook of the National Society for the Study of Education, Part II, Chicago: The University of Chicago Press, 1957.

Duffey, Robert V., "Challenging Above-Average Pupils." *Social Education*, 22:21-24 (January 1958).

Durrell, Donald D., and Leonard J. Savignano, "Classroom Enrichment through Pupil Specialties." *Journal of Education*, 138:1-31 (February 1956).

Epperson, David C., "Making Social Critics of Disadvantaged Children." *Social Studies*, 57:51-54 (February 1966).

Freehill, Maurice F., *Gifted Children*, Chap. 13, "Social Studies and Science." New York: The Macmillan Company, 1961.

Furman, Dorothy W., "Teacher-Pupil Planning with the Slow Learner." *Social Education*, 18:249-250 (October 1954).

Garton, Melinda Dean, *Teaching the Educable Mentally Retarded*, 2d ed., Chap. 5, "Units of Work;" and Chap. 10, "Audio-Visual and Other Sensory Training." Springfield, Ill.: Charles C. Thomas, Publisher, 1964.

Havighurst, Robert J., and Bernice L. Neugarten, *Society and Education*. Boston: Allyn and Bacon, Inc., 1957.

Hildreth, Gertrude, *Introduction to the Gifted*, Chap. 9, "Teaching the Gifted in the Elementary School." New York: McGraw-Hill Book Company, 1966.

Jarolimek, John, *Social Studies in Elementary Education*, 2d ed., Chap. 5, "Individualizing Instruction in Social Studies." New York: The Macmillan Company, 1963.

Johnson, G. Orville, *Education for the Slow Learners*. Englewood Cliffs, N.J.: Prentice-Hall, Inc., 1963, pp. 244-251.

Joyce, Bruce R., *Strategies for Elementary Social Science Education*, Chap. 12, "Depth Studies: Teaching Materials and Individual Differences;" and Chap. 15, "Social Studies for Disadvantaged Children." Chicago: Science Research Associates, Inc., 1965.

Ojemann, Ralph H., "Social Studies in Light of Knowledge about Children," *Social Studies in the Elementary School*, Fifty-Sixth Yearbook of the National Society for the Study of Education, Part II, Chicago: The University of Chicago Press, 1957.

Park, Frances Hauser, "Teaching Social Studies to Poor Readers." *Social Education*, 20:327-329 (November 1956).

Passow, A. Harry, ed., *Education in Depressed Areas*. New York: Teachers College, Columbia University, Bureau of Publications, 1963.

Ragan, William B., and John D. McAulay, *Social Studies for Today's Children*, Chap. 8, "Providing for Individual Differences." New York: Appleton-Century-Crofts, 1964.

Sand, Ole, and Bruce Joyce, "Planning for Children of Varying Ability," *Social Studies in Elementary Schools*, Thirty-Second Yearbook of the National Council for the Social Studies, Washington, D.C.: National Education Association, 1962.

Schmuck, Richard, Mark Chesler, and Ronald Lippitt, *Problem Solving to Improve Classroom Learning*, Chap. 5, "Cultural Influences on Classroom Problem Solving." Chicago: Science Research Associates, Inc., 1966.

Sowards, G. Wesley, and Mary-Margaret Scobey, *The Changing Curriculum and the Elementary Teacher*, Chap. 5, "Society, Culture, and Values: Guides for Curriculum." San Francisco: Wadsworth Publishing Company, 1961.

Strauchler, Jean, "Challenging the Rapid Learner." *Social Education*, 20:161-162 (April 1956).

Taba, Hilda, *Curriculum Development*, Chap. 10, "Social and Cultural Learning." New York: Harcourt, Brace & World, Inc., 1962.

Webster, Staten W., ed., *The Disadvantaged Learner*. San Francisco: Chandler Publishing Company, 1966.

14

Guiding Children in
Their Work with Issues

Each of the strategies discussed in the preceding chapters has been issue oriented. Social-science generalizations, attitudes, and patterns of action are the issues which children are guided into considering in a deliberate, reflective way. Other issues besides those treated in the formally organized social-studies curriculum are pressing and sometimes controversial. Some are so controversial that they are omitted from the formal program and many occur so unpredictably that little planning can be done before they find their way into the classroom. This chapter deals with the problem of coping with these issues.

WHAT IS AN ISSUE?

The term *issue* itself tends to have unpleasant connotations because it suggests a disturbing situation. Annoyance and discomfort are anticipated to the extent that they cloud not only the issue but also the sense of what an issue is. For this reason, as preparation for our work with issues which cause difficulties, we shall examine *issue* in a simple, definitive way.

An issue may be defined concisely as *a point on which a decision must be made to settle a matter*. All of us, including children, deal every day with issues, particularly those dealing with the matter of the daily existence and well-being of self involved with satisfying demands. Children at work in social studies will serve well as an example. Some matters and issues with which some of them may deal are:

The Matter	*The Issue*
1. To learn to read maps.	1. How best to profit from the teacher's instruction and the materials available.
2. To avoid embarrassment for not completing an assignment.	2. How to find a good excuse.
3. To pass a test.	3. How to prepare for a test.
4. To build a miniature stockade from toothpicks.	4. a. How to develop a plan and to make toothpicks stick together. b. How to divide the work so that everyone has an equal responsibility.
5. To receive an A in social studies.	5. To know what the teacher considers to be outstanding work.

As can be seen, the issues listed above are related to simple matters having to do with a pupil's everyday existence and well-being in school. Basically the matter is self, which may be expressed in dozens of different ways. The issue, no matter how expressed, also remains always the same; it is how best to maintain self. Concern for the world beyond the classroom is excluded. The only concern is for self issues, and for very narrow ones at that.

Some social-studies programs are basically oriented toward other-issues, to self-issues of much wider and deeper dimensions, and to issues of the future related to both self and other. Such programs guide children toward the areas rich in issues. The matter involved is always an objective idea drawn from a social science, and the issue related to it treats of an action, as illustrated below:

The Matter	*The Issue*
1. Natural resources and how they may be used.	1. How to use natural resources wisely and well.

2. Money and its uses.

3. Occupations and qualifications for each.

4. Private enterprise and its advantages and disadvantages.

5. The world market and its influence on our economy.

6. Democracy, its strengths and weaknesses.

7. A political party and how it functions.

8. A vote and how it works.

9. Loyalty to a nation and the ways in which citizens manifest it.

10. The ways of political expression.

11. Our government and its ties with other governments.

12. Individual rights and their limitations.

13. Groups and the functions of groups in a society.

14. Groups and their work.

15. Groups and their structure.

16. The roles in groups.

17. Culture and the differences among cultures.

18. Culture and change.

---

2. How to spend money wisely.

3. How to select and plan for the most suitable occupation.

4. How to participate in private enterprise to one's own good.

5. How the world market can be utilized best in the support of our level of economic welfare.

6. How to participate in democratic government.

7. How to participate effectively in a political party.

8. How to vote intelligently.

9. How to manifest loyalty to one's nation in the most effective way.

10. How to express oneself politically in the most effective way.

11. How best to participate in government to control its interactions with other governments.

12. How best to use and to protect individual rights.

13. How to regard and react to group differences in our society to assure the well-being of everyone.

14. How to participate effectively in a group.

15. How to select and work in groups to assure the performance of tasks.

16. How best to lead groups and to work with leaders of groups.

17. How best to accept one's own culture and other cultures.

18. How best to regard change and to control it.

Issues such as these serve as a point of focus toward the end of the study of a social-studies unit (in the synthesized strategy and sometimes in the social-science strategy), or they may serve as a point of departure and directional indicator for a social-studies unit (in the thinking-emphasis strategy). When the latter approach is used, the teacher presents an issue and the pupils are guided toward acquiring all the information necessary for making a decision. When the former approach is used, the teacher guides the pupils in acquiring facts and ideas related to a generalization and then engages them in treating an issue in which the generalization has to be applied to arrive at a decision.

Most of the issues listed above may be pursued to the point of controversy, a condition inherent in every issue that exists beyond the level of basic well-being. The point of controversy is reached when delay in arriving at a decision occurs because two or more opposing opinions of considerable strength exist as possible bases for making the decision. The problem is choosing the opinion which is to serve as the basis for action. Sometimes these opinions are well founded in fact, but in many instances they are ready-made in the sense that they are not the product of the gathering, weighing, and synthesis of facts that pertain to the issue. These ready-made opinions are a condition and product of culture, the result of cultural experience and cultural interaction over a long period of years. They exist as inherited values the rational bases for which have been long forgotten, but they have served as bases for action in the past. In their statement they are relatively unsophisticated but they are often in conflict, as can be seen in the following examples:

Opinion	*Opposing Opinion*
1. Labor, long down-trodden and disregarded, is dignified and worthy of taking a hand in its own destiny.	1. Labor is selfish and demanding; therefore, it needs to be controlled vigorously.
2. Destitute people are products of ignorance; therefore, they should be helped through education and financial aid.	2. All men are equal in the sight of God, but some men because of birthright, ability to assume responsibility, and wealth have more rights and privileges than other men not similarly endowed.
3. Conservation is primarily a matter of using natural resources wisely and preserving those difficult to replenish.	3. Conservation is primarily a matter of the use of human resources directed toward better and new uses of natural resources to

4. The government must impose regulations on the conduct of business to safeguard the general welfare of the people.

5. Every nation stands by itself; therefore, the primary concern of its people is for its survival.

6. Peoples of low technological development should be left to themselves to determine how they are to fulfill their cultural, economic, and political needs.

7. Increased automation improves the economic welfare of a people.

8. Capital punishment is a deterrent on crime; therefore, it should be maintained as a practice.

increase the level of economic welfare.

4. Government meddling in business destroys business and thereby harms the general public.

5. All nations today are inextricably interdependent; therefore, all peoples must share common concerns if all nations are to survive.

6. Peoples of low technological development must be encouraged to become modern nations lest they become the pawns of the opposing political power.

7. Increased automation brings about an improved economic welfare for some people and lowered level of economic welfare for many others.

8. Capital punishment is an inhumane practice out of place in a modern civilization; criminals should be treated as ill persons.

Any of these opinions could be used as a basis for making a decision about a related issue. Sometimes the distance between the decision-makers and the issue is a significant factor in determining the extent of controversiality and the opinion to be selected as a basis for action. For example, United States citizens may be in fundamental agreement on what the political and economic relations between India and Pakistan should be in terms of interdependence. Chances are that Americans will agree that these nations should recognize their interdependence and comport themselves in accord with it. However, chances are that Americans will disagree on what the relations between India and the United States should be. The nearness of the issues makes a difference.

Frequently the urgency of the issue lends force to the need for arriving at a decision. The stronger this force, the more likely is the choice to be made from available ready-made opinions. The force tends to conceal the need for thinking and deliberation necessary for the development of a more appropriate opinion to serve as a basis for arriving at a decision for action. Sides are taken on the basis of emotional commitment and conviction. At this point, the issue is controversial and remains so until a solution is forced or until thinking and deliberation can be applied. As long as the issue is controversial, it pervades the community and colors thought and action, often to the extent that the issue becomes a part of school life.

However, the community, at whatever level of organization—village, geographical area, neighborhood, city, county, state, or nation—usually objects to any act that brings the issue into school. Parents are often afraid that school treatment of the issue will make it difficult for the children to maintain loyalty to the parents' view of the issue. Because of school treatment of the issue, the children may entertain another choice of opinion which the parents feel reflects a lack of maturity and experience. Or the parents may feel that the teacher will not guide the children properly, thus they will become confused and disturbed by the issue. Telling some parents that the issue will be treated in the appropriate curriculum area, social studies, sometimes increases fears because the word *social* has its own dangerous connotation. Other parents take the matter-of-fact stand that children cannot do anything about issues; therefore, children should have nothing to do with issues. Besides, large issues have a way of resolving themselves in time.

Actually, the objection to controversial issues is neither to the issues nor to the controversies surrounding them, but rather to the ways these issues are likely to be treated in school. The depth and breadth of current issues measured in terms of parents' emotional commitments and convictions merely adds weight to the objection.

Frequently, dealing with controversial issues in school becomes itself a controversial issue which a school district may treat in one of several ways. Some school districts organize curricula bereft of issues and indoctrinate teachers to avoid issues. Other districts will develop curricula that deal only with the facts related to issues and then provide teachers with carefully spelled-out procedures to follow. The teachers are held to these procedures and are encouraged to feel that other procedures may not receive the sanction of the district. Some districts organize curricula that deal with all aspects of issues—understandings, attitudes, and patterns of action—and develop guidelines for teachers to use in dealing with issues, including controversial issues. Through in-service training, the teachers are helped to know how to use the guidelines. Parents are kept informed of these procedures. The last method appears to be logically the best, because it guides children toward seeing the world as it really is, makes provisions for maintaining the parents' confidence in the schools, and tends to reduce the unreasoning emotionalism that so often accompanies controversial issues.

Dealing with issues, even controversial issues, at a level beyond immediate well-being or existence should cause no difficulties in most instances as long as certain conditions are met. One condition holds that the school district express itself in policies which make provisions for the study of issues. A very necessary condition is that the teachers be well-informed and knowledgeable in what issues are, how to introduce them, and how to guide children in the study of them. The final condition is that children have the thinking and information-process skills, as well as available resources, necessary to investigate issues.

WAYS OF GUIDING CHILDREN
AS THEY WORK WITH ISSUES

During moments of stress within the immediate community, state, or national community, the issues involved are likely to find their way into the classroom. Newspaper, television, and radio transmit a barrage of information which tends to focus and hold attention. Sometimes the only information pouring through the communication lanes is that pertaining to the stress. When such a condition prevails, children begin to react by showing curiosity and sometimes fear. They develop a concern which they bring with them into the classroom. Although a teacher may force a submersion of the concern through a determined insistence on following the prepared curriculum, his better course, particularly for the sake of the children, is to deal directly with the concern. The procedures which he may follow do not differ greatly from those which he uses when guiding children in the acquisition of facts and ideas in social studies. Basically his teaching acts are comprised of the following: (1) clarifying with the children the issue that lies at the heart of the concern; (2) guiding them in identifying the different choices possible for deciding the issues; (3) encouraging them to explore the facts and ideas which support the issues; (4) guiding them in an analysis of the facts and ideas to determine bases for opinions; and (5) guiding them toward suspended judgment.

In most instances, particularly when the issue has entered the classroom during a high pitch of emotional involvement, children will be unable to clarify the point about which a decision is to be made; therefore, it is almost always the teacher's responsibility to clarify it. Clarification requires objectivity and background as well as the ability to think critically and quickly. As he begins to clarify the issue, in a very matter-of-fact way the teacher reflects this attitude: "This is what the excitement is all about." Simply and succinctly he presents the matter to be settled and the point on which a decision must be made. If, after he has made his brief presentation, he detects the presence of much feeling about the issue, he encourages the children to express their feelings and to relate them to aspects of the issue as clarified. Or the teacher may deal with children's feelings first. He encourages them to express what they think and feel before attempting to make any clarification, then he clarifies the issue and helps the children to understand their feelings through relating them to the points offered in clarification. If feeling runs so high that the teacher senses the futility of attempting to clarify the issue, he should encourage the children to talk out their feelings and guide them toward a wait-and-see attitude. Classroom consideration is ended for the time being, but the teacher may guide the children toward examining a clarification of the issue at a later time when the level of feeling has dropped.

If the children are ready to continue working with the issue, that is, they understand and accept the clarification of the issue, the teacher guides them into identifying the choices for deciding the issue. He may use any one of several points of entry into this procedure. Perhaps he will ask a question such as this, "What different things can people do to settle this problem?" Or he may encourage the children to think about different choices of action by having them identify the different groups of people who would have varying ideas about how the problem should be solved. Often a projective procedure is very effective. The teacher mentions individuals who are representative of various groups and factions and asks the children to assume their roles in a way similar to this: "Let's imagine that each of us is a man who is working in a factory. How do you think he feels about this strike? . . . Now let us suppose that he belongs to a union. How does he think and feel? . . . Let us think a little bit about the man who does not belong to a union. How does he think and feel? . . ." The discussion would continue and would include such persons as the factory owner, the manager of a grocery store, and the farmer who lives just outside the community. Or the teacher may guide the children in identifying choices for deciding the issues by encouraging individual children to state what they think and then to express another point of view if they can possibly see one.

Once the various choices for deciding the issue have been identified, the teacher directs the children's inquiry into the rational base for each choice of action. The nature and depth of the inquiry will depend on the nature of the issue itself and the level of sophistication of the children. Younger or less sophisticated children working with simpler issues may be able to do little more than to make an inquiry into the feelings of the persons involved in the issue. Frequently the terms used in stating the issue and other information will have to be provided by the teacher. When less complex issues are being treated by older or more sophisticated children, a teacher-guided discussion is sufficient to unearth the necessary facts for defining terms and attitudes. Complex issues are less likely to impinge upon younger or less sophisticated children, and when they must be treated by these children, treatment will not get much beyond a review of possible attitudes. When older and more sophisticated children work with a complex issue, the teacher guides them toward making a more independent inquiry. Such an inquiry may follow several pursuits to discover facts for building rationales for the several choices of action.

There are several basic patterns of inquiry for facts. To this point, inquiry into attitudes and definition of terms have been established as essential. With able children, pursuit of the latter is made in available sources. If no sources are available, the teacher conducts a discussion in which he elicits from children what they know and gives required information until the children arrive at a workable definition of terms. After this groundwork has been completed, the children as individuals investigate in available resources to determine authoritative points of view. The sources may include books and pamphlets related to the issue, editorials, cartoons, news magazine articles, and the like. The facts may then be synthesized into the various points of view. However, inquiry may be guided toward seeking historical precedent for the various rationales. In some instances, inquiry may be directed toward finding geographical applications of various points of view and their adequacy. The inquiry for facts to establish rationales for the various choices of action may require several days.

After the rationale for each choice of action has been established, the children are prepared to make an analysis of the facts to determine the choice which appears to be the feasible one as far as they are concerned. Individual reactions, statements of opinion, and substantiation of opinion are encouraged. The point of view during this work is: How does this choice of action affect us? Then the children consider the various choices in the light of what would be best for all the persons concerned and considering that the decision must be left in the hands of others held responsible for making the decision. This consideration may lead into the need for compromise or developing a new choice for action or it may result in a desire to suspend judgment. It is likely that the latter will be more feasible.

Guiding children in suspending judgment usually presents some difficulties. Probably the worst event that could occur would be an insistence on voting. Perhaps the best antidote to this state of affairs is a clear, forceful explanation to the children that the issue is not theirs to decide and that they will have to wait and see what happens. Each is to be encouraged to make his own choice as of the moment, but to think more about it and to be on the alert for more pertinent information. The teacher should feel free to express his own favored choice for action and to substantiate it, but he points out that he too is limited in what he can do about making the final decision. He can somewhat assuage fears by suggesting that the other choices for action have strengths to be considered.

The use of the procedures just discussed assumes that there is a common concern among the children about the issue, that the teacher is well-informed about the issue, and that he has the ability required for guiding children through an issue for which he may be the basic source for information. To protect himself, the teacher should report the emergence of an issue in his classroom and what he has done about it to his principal on the day that the issue emerges. The principal, who usually has a good grasp of community feeling, may advise the teacher to terminate work on the issue. The teacher has no choice but to close the study by no longer encouraging inquiry and by guiding toward suspended judgment.

Occasionally, older, more sophisticated children will bring up an issue most unexpectedly, not because they are particularly curious or frightened, because they want to see how the teacher will react to it. The teacher may respond by turning the issue adroitly back to the questioner or by having the entire class respond to it. When the children have given their points of view, he presents his own in a most matter-of-fact way.

Some teachers, particularly those teaching in the later grades, feel so strongly about the necessity for children to be prepared to handle issues that they start with issues as a basic approach to social-studies teaching. They build interest in the study at hand by making a provocative statement related to the topic or topic area to be studied. This statement, stimulating because it is exaggerated, harsh, satirical, or humorous, deeply involves many children. The children prompted to express their opinions freely and ultimately to clarify the issue, to determine the possible choices for action, to investigate them thoroughly, and to debate to determine the best choice. Such an approach is admirably suited to preparing children to deal with issues, but there must be a total commitment by all the members of the class to working with the issue. Children who are not committed to the issue may quote the provocative statements out of context. For example, a child at the dinner table with his parents could disturb several digestion systems by remarking casually, "My teacher at school thinks that Congress is filled with a bunch of old boobies." True, the teacher may have referred to Congressmen as being "old boobies," but his statement may have been a paraphrase of what one segment of the population thinks about Congress. Other statements as provocative may have been used to express other points of view. The child simply did not hear them. Beginning with provocative statements related to issues can be most effective, but it is necessary that the children understand the purpose of the teacher's devices for stimulating interest.

Although few schools and school districts have developed careful, positive policies regarding controversial issues in the classroom, teachers must deal in some way with these issues when they enter the classroom. Children need some preparation for dealing with these issues. Preferably the curriculum should be organized in such a way as to make the necessary provisions. When provisions are specifically denied, the best that the teacher can do is to guide children to work as rational, intelligent human beings with the issues near them. Few indeed are the classrooms and schools in which no difficulties arise from the use of materials and space in the classroom, the playground, the cafeteria, and the neighborhood. Practice in working with these issues is also a preparation for dealing with an issue of greater magnitude. If an issue of greater significance is brought into the classroom, the procedures used in treating the smaller issues can be applied.

The one provision that many school districts make to bring children into contact with issues is the current-events program usually organized as a part of the social-studies curriculum. However, more often than not, the stated purpose of the program is not to bring children into contact with issues, but rather to habituate children to read the newspaper to become informed. Sometimes the program is called the "news" program. Regardless of the stated purpose of the program, it remains as a possible channel through which children become aware of issues and concerned with decisions about issues.

THE CURRENT-EVENTS PROGRAM

Probably the one factor that has contributed most to the development of current-events programs in schools is the publication of inexpensive weekly newspapers and periodicals for children. Composed and edited by experts with the help of outstanding professional educators, these publications present news to children as well as items which are in themselves interesting to children. Cartoons, jokes, riddles, curiosities of various kinds, and science articles help children to learn the various uses of a newspaper or periodical. In the preparation of these materials, very careful attention is given to the control of reading difficulty. Vocabulary load and sentence length are regulated. Often special exercises are provided to help children improve in word-analysis and comprehension skills. An excellent guide for the teacher is often provided. Although the publication of these weekly newspapers and magazines has encouraged classroom current-events programs, it has also served as a deterrent to the consideration of vehicles other than newspapers for the study of current events.

The modern citizen who wishes to remain abreast of current events does not just read his newspaper each morning and evening. He may place an even greater reliance on the radio for hourly reports on current events. Whenever possible, he will watch news programs on television and is often rewarded by pictorial coverage. Most people today have several sources of information at their disposal for keeping themselves informed about current events. Children learn about these sources early; therefore, they need to learn how to use these sources as well. A more acceptable objective for the current-events program today would be to help children to develop an interest in the use of all the news-transmission vehicles and to improve in the skills which assure the effective use of these vehicles. Implicit here is the use of the various vehicles for information about issues.

In recent years the television newscast has begun to serve children as a source for information in the study of current events. Some primary teachers are successful in having children accept responsibility for watching a newscast and reporting their findings to the class. Success of such a venture usually rests on the children's having something specific to watch the newscast for. Occasionally children can be guided toward listening to the newscasts on radio. During the current-events program, the children report their findings and discuss them. Their reports are often surprisingly accurate. Often the smaller children can be accustomed to using television for information by watching and reporting the weather forecast.

For years, many schools and school districts have made a strong attempt to provide every classroom with a radio. Some schools, because of the use of television as a means of helping children to learn in various curriculum areas, have televisions in many classrooms. These could very easily serve as sources for information on current events. Both television and radio newscasts occur during the school day and could provide for immediate analyses of events both as a follow-up for trends in the news under study and as a means of establishing new trends in the news to be followed. Obviously, commercials can cause problems, but teachers can find ways of reducing their tendency to arrest attention.

However, despite the development and wide use of the various news-transmission vehicles in both homes and schools, most current-events programs are organized around the newspaper as the basic source for information. The practice brings several problems, the most difficult of which is guiding children to select suitable topics to report. Many teachers attempt to cope with the problem by specifying in very certain terms which topics are suitable. Most often these topics treat of political, economic, and technological events. Horrible accidents, gory crimes, and amusing incidents are tacitly forbidden. The unfortunate result is that children lose interest in current events, not because they like only the bizarre and the unusual, but because they do not understand the kinds of events that the teacher specifies as being suitable. Some teachers who take a more realistic view of what is suitable as a current event encourage children to report on events in sports, in the world of art and music, and in the lives of ordinary people. A few teachers regard reports on crime, corruption, and ghastly accidents in much the same way as legislators, editors, the clergy, and others who have an interest in public morality. To persons such as these, the occurrence of immoral or careless acts intensifies the need for society to reexamine the principles by which it governs its actions. A teacher of this persuasion may guide his pupils in examining horrendous events and pondering their significance in terms of needed attitudes and patterns of action.

A very successful procedure used by some teachers is to guide children in the development of criteria to be used in selecting news events. An excellent example of a single criterion developed by a group of children is this: Will the event be important enough to be included in history books twenty-five years from now? Primary teachers can encourage children to bring suitable events to report by presenting news events themselves for discussion and then having the children bring items of a similar nature.

Many teachers make it a point to have children submit their news clippings and reports to them for approval before the current-events period. If an item is unsuitable within the established guidelines, the teacher explains the unsuitability and encourages the child to seek another item for the current-events period at a later date.

Another problem brought about by the use of the newspaper as the basic source of information for the current-events program is persuading children to participate. This problem, often related to the restriction of the kinds of events to be reported, is also brought about by children's failure to understand what they are supposed to do as well as the reason for doing it. Some teachers help children to know what the current-events program is about and what is expected of them by maintaining files of newspaper clippings about the topic areas being studied in social studies. When current information is needed, the teacher presents the clippings for the children to consult and emphasizes that they contain the most current information about what is being studied. He encourages the children to extend the file by seeking newspaper articles about the same topic. Many teachers encourage children to participate by reserving the use of a bulletin board, preferably a large one, for current events. This board is carefully designed with an attractive inviting caption under which the children post their clippings after reporting on them. Sometimes an inexpensive world map is posted on the board and the clippings are pinned around it. Strips of yarn are pinned from each clipping to the place on the map where the event occurred. Often the board is divided into areas such as *local, state, national,* and *international,* or *government, industry, human interest, sports,* and *art.* As a further means of persuasion, some teachers make daily assignments on a "round-robin" basis, that is, everyone has his turn. If a child fails to bring an item on his assigned day, the teacher works with him in much the same way as he does for failure to complete work in any other area of the curriculum. This practice is acceptable only when the teacher makes adequate provisions for the child to obtain a news clipping. This may involve little more than remembering to bring his morning newspaper to school to serve as a class source. Often he may need to work individually with some children to help them assume an assigned responsibility. In some classrooms, the teachers help the children to make a survey of what is in the news for a period of several weeks during which news trends are established. On the basis of interest in a news trend, the children are grouped in committees which assume responsibility for watching and reporting the course of the trend to the rest of the class. One group serves as a committee to look for new trends. As old trends are exhausted, the children are regrouped and guided into the study of new trends. All the devices just mentioned can be successful if applied consistently and humanely.

Reliance on the newspaper as the basic source for information underscores the need for reading skills often far above many children's level of reading ability. With the exception of the few news articles prepared specifically for children, the readability level of most news items is too difficult for children, particularly for children in the lower grades. The vocabulary load is far too heavy and the sentences are too long and involved. The size and style of print presents difficulties to many children. Unfortunately, the teacher cannot do much to help children in any direct way to overcome their reading difficulties. The topics are so varied that vocabulary needs cannot be predicted with any exactitude, and rate of reading and comprehension is almost a function of growth in reading. However, the teacher in the lower grades can reduce the reading task by guiding children into seeking pictures accompanied by captions and short explanatory texts. The child is encouraged to bring his clipping whether he can read it or not. The teacher helps him with his reading task or reads the clipping for him. Some teachers encourage parents to help their children by reading their selected news clipping to them before they bring it to school. The practice is sometimes effective, but its effectiveness rests on how great the child's interest is in current events and the way in which his parents help him.

A problem not often mentioned in discussion about elementary current-events programs is the problem of lack of background, which contributes heavily to children's reticence to becoming involved in the current-events program. Many teachers deal effectively with this problem by conducting a carefully guided discussion in which the children are encouraged to contribute all they know and the teacher provides the necessary facts. When current-events topics are treated in such a way, children acquire background and, as a result, they begin to bring in more news articles dealing with the topics already treated.

As a teacher organizes the current-events program for his classroom he attempts to cope with these problems. Several approaches to developing the current-events program are possible, and each of the approaches reflects a concern for all these problems. However, each program is somewhat different in the emphasis which it places on coping with the various problems. The various approaches are the weekly newspaper or periodical program, the daily news program, the current-events unit, and the study of current events as an extension of a regular social-studies unit.

The weekly newspaper or periodical program is very popular in many schools because through school subscriptions to such publications as *My Weekly Reader* and *Scholastic* each teacher is provided a guide and each pupil is provided with current material prepared at his level of reading ability. It is obvious that the emphasis in this approach is centered on the problem of coping with reading difficulties. Often the current-events program becomes a part of the reading program, for one of the daily reading periods during the week will be devoted to reading and discussing the newspaper or periodical. This one reading period when all the children in the class can be stimulated to read about the same topic or idea makes for a pleasant change of pace for both the teacher and the children. Almost everyone can read to find out about it, because the publications are prepared at graded levels of reading and usually the same topic is treated in each graded issue. Most of the children can read about the topic independently, thus freeing the teacher to work with the children who have serious reading disabilities. Often the writing style used in preparing items for the children to read is excellent. Ideas are organized well and difficult words are carefully defined. Frequently, because these publications reflect so much concern for children's reading and comprehension difficulties, the reading period devoted to reading about current events is the most pleasant of the week.

The strength of this program in current events is often its weakness, for it easily becomes another period in reading instruction. Often the current events themselves become secondary or are not treated at all except as points about which one may read. The children may be given no opportunity to scrutinize the events in terms of how the various happenings influence their lives and the lives of others. As far as the teacher is concerned, the reading materials provided in the weekly newspaper or periodical provide him with an opportunity to help children know the difference between reading "stories" and reading facts.

Another serious weakness of this program is that the publications present an awry view of current events. Coverage of technological or cultural events is less affected by this weakness than is coverage of important events in political and economic life. By the time children have a chance to read about them, they are already history. Since the news publications are prepared for national distribution, only the current events about the nation and the world are reported. However, children need to know about events occurring at the local and state level.

The weaknesses of the weekly newspaper or periodical program make it a questionable program to serve as the sole means of meeting children's needs to be informed about current events, but its strength makes it a welcome supplement to any of the other current-events programs.

Another popular current-events program is the daily news program. Its basic emphasis rests upon children's participation in selecting news items and reporting them. Often it is an outgrowth of the "sharing" or "show-and-tell" period in the primary grades. Young children's perceptions about their world are encouraged to grow through seeking items of interest in the newspaper and reporting about them at school.

Pictures from the newspaper often serve as the basis for reports. With older children, beginning at grade three or four, the sharing period is replaced by the "news" period which usually consists of the first ten or fifteen minutes of the social-studies period. The children bring newspaper clippings to report about and to serve as a basis for class discussion.

This program, if guided well, is excellent. It provides for wide coverage of current events in all the areas of human activity and its reliance on the daily newspaper as the basic source of information provides a resource available to most children. In most instances, it could be improved by including radio, television, and the news magazine as sources for information. However, the program is difficult to organize, and in the hands of a weak teacher or a teacher who has no taste for current events it may degenerate into a program supported by extremes in gimmickry and coercion. In this case, the purposes for conducting the program are defeated.

Some teachers approach the task of developing a current-events program in much the same way as they develop a program in social studies; they construct brief units in currents events to teach from time to time. Sometimes these units are constructed around topics that are always in issue such as water-supply problems, population problems, transportation problems, and the like. In the construction of the unit, the teacher first guides the children in acquiring the facts and ideas necessary to understanding the topic and then encourages them to check in current sources to determine the status of the problems. The children arrive at a statement of the status of the problem and thereafter check in the newspaper and other sources for information to see whether the status changes. Often current-events units are largely impromptu, constructed around topics current in the news such as political difficulties in the Arabian countries, South America, or Europe. The teacher guides the children in examining the conflict and its historical background. Once the children have a background essential to understanding the topic, they check current sources to detect the outcome. The units are presented throughout the year, sometimes regularly at monthly intervals or at propitious times such as short school weeks caused by holidays or at the close of a regular social-studies unit. The emphasis in this approach is on the acquisition of background. Using current-events units throughout the year offers several outstanding advantages. There need be no concern about the suitability of the topic because the teacher chooses it. Control of the program rests in the teacher's hands as he acquires background and makes provisions for children to acquire it. The children have something definite to look for as they seek through the various sources available to them, ferret out trends, and observe change. Such a program supports a realistic view about the uses of sources of information, that is, a person seeks information in order to be informed about something, not just to be informed.

The major weakness of this program is that it locks children's attention to a single aspect of what is current. Since current events are not very predictable, the teacher may choose a topic which is suddenly thrust out of the news limelight by the beginning of a chain of significant events. A teacher who is current with what is occurring in the world usually finds no difficulty in guiding his pupils in following the shift in current-events topics.

If a teacher can accept that a social-studies unit is never really completed, even after the ideas have been tied together at several levels of abstraction, he has the basis for a current-events program which handily solves the problem of children's lack of background. His approach to developing a current-affairs program is to guide children toward extending currently the ideas learned in each social-studies unit. The children have the necessary background in facts and ideas and in vocabulary required for reading and discussion. Through current extensions, the children are encouraged to test through verification the ideas learned and to modify them in the light of current applications. It is possible that the statement of an idea may be modified in some way, but by far the greatest impact made on the learning of social-studies ideas by current extensions is the greater strength of conviction about the ideas and the clarity of direction for the development of attitudes and patterns of action related to the ideas. If the social-studies unit is extended through a study of current events, it remains alive. If a teacher wishes to develop his current-events program through extending social-studies units, he will have to construct his units around "big ideas" or generalizations, for these provide the definite guides in the current-events program. Children have something definite to look for.

A current-events program based on the extension of regular social-studies units has a gradual development through the school year. At the beginning of the school year, there is no program. It does not start until a unit is completed or nearly completed. Thereafter, as each unit is completed, the ideas studied in it are added to the program. It is likely that toward the close of the school year the children will be following the applications of several different ideas, perhaps as many as six or seven, in their current-events program. Some teachers prefer to encourage their pupils to make a daily check; others guide their pupils in gathering their information through the week and then reporting their findings during the last social-studies period of the week.

In many respects, developing a current-events program as a current extension of the regular social-studies units is similar to the program organized around current-events units. Its outstanding strength is that it provides adequately for background; its outstanding weakness is that it tends to neglect what is really current and pressing. This weakness can be remedied somewhat by developing a daily news program to accompany the program based on the extension of social-studies units.

Children must become informed about issues and must acquire the skills necessary for being informed. Since the current-events program is the one commonly accepted means of providing a contact for children with issues, a current-events program is a must. Whatever the program is to be depends basically on the teacher's interest in current events and his ability to guide children in their study. No approach is really best. The teacher selects the approach that he believes will provide the best program in terms of his teaching style.

All current-events programs can be richly improved through making provisions to guide children beyond the acquisition of objective facts and ideas. Children may easily learn why multitudes in India starve, why crops fail in China, or why world political figures seek the banner position in world affairs, but these are of little significance if children are not guided past the blasé "so what?" attitude. Children need to know how these events affect their society and themselves. If the current-events program does not go beyond objective content, it leads only into the abstract, which does not mean much to most children.

AN OVER-ALL LOOK

Our society's regard for children in school tends to be demanding in some respects and protective in others. On the one hand, it rigorously demands that all children have a fundamental mastery of skills within a common notion of what these skills are, and if the demands are not met, the child is considered to be immoral. On the other hand, children are to be protected from issues. Our society tends to hold that the school is a pure temple within which only the most pristine of traditional ideals are to prevail. The conflicts of the real world must not enter, which means that issues must not find their way into the school. If they do, the teacher is likely to be considered an immoral person.

Strangely enough, our society's regard for children at home and in the neighborhood is somewhat different. The child is subjected to a world of reality as far as family relationships are concerned. To be sure, conflicts vary in degrees of intensity, and he must become accustomed to these in order to survive. Often in his home and neighborhood the child is subjected to the worst of world reality. He sees it expressed in violence written large across the television screen, the comic book, and the covers of paperback books and magazines in the local supermarket and drugstore. From these he learns about the violent ways to solve personal problems, social problems, political problems, and economic problems. Quite frequently his favorite toys are the replicas of violence.

From a pragmatic point of view, our society's beliefs and practices about working with children in the school, the home, and the neighborhood are effective. Most children learn easily to differentiate between a genuine reality and a contrived one; therefore, the violence that they see on television and through other vehicles of transmission is not theirs to follow as they live their lives. Most children become self-supporting citizens and find ways to deal directly with many issues which impinge directly upon them. Therefore, there appears to be a real basis for society's objections to having children deal with issues in school. Due cognizance must be given to society's fears for having children deal with issues, because dealing with an issue requires that all strong opinions be considered. Children could accept a pattern of action odious to their parents. Perhaps they would have never had contact with it if the issue had not been explored.

However, there is evidence that the beliefs and practices about working with children in the school, the home, and the neighborhood are not working as well as they once did. Increases in juvenile crimes, incidents of group violence, unemployment, elections of political candidates who play upon the ignorance of voters, and the like, not only reflect the gradual breakdown of the old beliefs and practices but reflect as well that our people do not know how to recognize issues or how to cope with them. They are confused. Some want to return to our frontier traditions which supported the control of people through harsh ostracism, corporal punishment, quick, no-nonsense police action and justice, and a rigid practice of censorship. Others are maintaining that people must learn how to be aware of issues and how to deal with them at something beyond a survival level. Dealing with issues, then, has a place in school. Children are to be regarded as citizens-to-be and are to be respected as such, and not as depositories of evil that will out if given the slightest opportunity.

The school is one agency within the institution of education through which our society may assure that children learn about issues and ways of dealing with them. This learning begins in the elementary school, through the organization and application of a social-studies curriculum developed to guide children in working with issues. The issues may be the guidelines for organizing study, or they may be a way of study through inquiry and expressed as problems. The current-events program provides that children examine the issues as they present themselves in the current world. Teachers must be encouraged to guide children in examining issues, the sources for encouragement being clear policies to protect them, provisions for suitable materials for them to use, and in-service training programs which help them to become more adequate in working with issues.

Although the school can do much in helping children learn how to work with issues, it is not the only educational agency which has this responsibility. The family, the church, the neighborhood organization, and those who control the vehicles of mass transmission share the responsibility. If the school has a unique responsibility here, it is to help the others to explore and find the most effective ways of guiding children in working with issues.

Exercises for Further Understanding

1. For several days examine the sections of your newspaper which deal with local issues. A careful scanning of the local section of a large metropolitan newspaper often reveals the status of continuing issues

about the maintenance and control of needed utilities, transportation, education, recreation, housing, and the like. The critical nature of these issues is reflected on the editorial page and the letters-to-the-editor section. Analyze these sources to isolate the issues faced by your community to determine the following:

(a) How likely are the issues to enter the classroom?
(b) Which is the most critical?
(c) What are the various sides of the most critical issue?
(d) Would you guide children in examining this issue if they did not bring it into the classroom themselves? If yes, how would you go about this?

2. Isolate a local issue and become well informed about it by examining in a newspaper file at the newspaper office or at your local library.

3. Suppose that you are guiding some first-grade children in a study of the family. One first grader reveals in an open discussion that he has two families, a mother and a new father with whom he lives during the week and a father and a new mother with whom he lives on weekends. Another first grader asserts that the two-family child is not telling the truth. What would you do?

Suppose that the same issue occurs in an eighth-grade class in this way: during an open discussion about family relationships a girl suddenly rasps out, "What's wrong with divorce?" What would you do in this instance?

4. For several days make it a point to listen to newscasts and to study your newspaper to become aware of national and international issues. Select one which appears to be most critical to you, then become informed about it through consulting available sources. Seek at least one source, such as a book or periodical article dealing directly with the issue, which presents it in depth.

5. Arrange to visit an elementary classroom during the period devoted to the study of current affairs. Observe the teacher and children for the following:

(a) What approach does the teacher use to guide the children in the study of current affairs?
(b) How deep are the children encouraged to go in their study?
(c) How interested are they?
(d) Do they deal with any issues?

6. Suppose that you are being interviewed for a teaching position in a particular district. You have no idea of the district's policy or program dealing with current events or affairs. One of your interviewers asks, "How would you go about organizing a current-events program?" How would you answer?

Selected References

Ballinger, Stanley E., "The Social Studies and Controversy." *School Review*, 71:97-111 (Spring 1964).

Endres, Raymond J., "Criticism of Current Events." *Social Studies*, 57:8-16 (January 1966).

Fawcett, Claude W., "Teaching about Controversial Issues." *California Teachers Association Journal*, 60:25-26 (March 1964).

Fraser, Dorothy McClure, "Current Affairs, Special Events, and Civic Participation," *Social Studies in Elementary Schools*, Thirty-Second Yearbook of the National Council for the Social Studies, Washington, D.C.: National Education Association, 1962.

Lunstrum, John P., "School Policy and Controversial Issues," in Byron G. Massialas and Frederick R. Smith, eds., *Crucial Issues in the Teaching of Social Studies*. Englewood Cliffs, N.J.: Prentice-Hall, Inc., 1964.

————, "The Treatment of Controversial Issues in Social Studies Instruction," in Byron G. Massialas and Frederick R. Smith, eds., *New Challenges in the Social Studies*. Belmont, Calif.: Wadsworth Publishing Company, Inc., 1965.

Jarolimek, John, *Social Studies in Elementary Education*, 2d ed., Chap. 14, "Teaching of Current Affairs." New York: The Macmillan Company, 1963.

McAulay, J. D., "Current Affairs and the Social Studies." *Social Education*, 23:21-22 (January 1959).

Michaelis, John U., *Social Studies for Children in a Democracy*, 3d ed., Chap. 6, "Current Events and Special Events." Englewood Cliffs, N.J.; Prentice-Hall, Inc., 1963.

Ozmon, Howard A., Jr., "Challenging versus Supportive Teaching." *Clearing House*, 36:28-30 (September 1961).

Park, Joe, "Teaching Pupils to Inquire into Controversial Issues." *Social Studies*, 48:15-18 (January 1957).

Preston, Ralph C., "Children's Reactions to Harsh Social Realities." *Social Education*, 23:116-120 (March 1959).

Scholfield, Frank A., "Ideology and the Teaching of Social Studies," *Social Studies*, 48:57-59 (February 1957).

Simon, Sidney, and Harmin Merrill, "To Study Controversial Issues Is Not Enough." *Social Studies*, 55:163-166 (October 1964).

Wass, Philmore B., "Improving Current Events Instruction." *Social Education*, 25:79-81 (February 1961).

15

Evaluation in Social Studies

Motivation is central to learning. This basic principle of learning begins to be etched in the minds of teachers early in their training. Another basic principle, *evaluation is essential to learning,* is sometimes etched there, but not quite so deeply, yet this principle is fully as important as the first.

One reason for the importance of this principle is that evaluation is supportive of motivation, particularly when the motivation is toward a task similar to one previously performed by the learner. The success a learner has with a previously performed task contributes richly to the development of motivation toward another task similar to it. Learning procedes along a chain of links, each link a carefully forged alloy of motivation, involvement, and evaluation.

Another reason for the importance of the principle is that through evaluation both the teacher and the pupils come to know whether objectives have been reached, whether teaching and learning have really occurred. Defined most simply, evaluation is nothing more than examining the results of teaching and learning to determine how effective these processes have been.

This act of examining the results of teaching and learning has several different dimensions. The first dimension is circumscribed by each individual pupil, because children in the classroom are always evaluating themselves. They are concerned about how well they are doing. When work products are returned to children, their eyes rapidly scan each product to find the symbol of approval which the teacher has put on it—*Excellent! Very good! What improvement! A, B, C, D,* or *F; 1, 2, 3, 4,* or *5,* or whatever system the teacher uses. After they find the symbol, children cast their eyes about to catch a glimpse of the symbol that the teacher has put on the products of their peers. Perhaps the best indicator of a pupil's progress is the image of himself he sees reflected in his teacher's actions toward him. Warm, friendly sincere actions convince him that he is learning as well as can be expected of him; cold, hostile, bitterly patient actions convince him that he is not learning much and for that reason is being rejected. This dimension of evaluation, the most important of all, is too often neglected or ruled out as being of little significance.

Another dimension of evaluation involves both the teacher and the pupils in the classroom as they attend to their concerns in social studies. Very frequently, as a point of departure for the day's work or learning, the social-studies period begins with a review of the learning or work to date. Almost always, progress made during the day is examined at the close of the period. If the teacher has been guiding his pupils in inquiry, the inquiry has given force and direction to learning. Each evaluation of what is known and what remains to be learned makes clearer the direction to be followed, lends greater force to the inquiry at hand, and eventually indicates when the inquiry is completed. Into whatever area inquiry is directed—be it acquisition of facts and ideas or development of attitudes and behaviors that logically evolve from these, be it decisions necessary for carrying through an expressive project or development of school and classroom citizenship—the teacher and the pupils working together as a miniature society in the classroom make rich use of evaluation, both before and after the introduction of facts, to reach objectives.

A somewhat similar state of affairs prevails when children are working at group tasks. Leadership is different; instead of the teacher, a child or several children serve as leader.

The teacher working with an individual pupil constitutes another dimension of evaluation. From time to time every child is given an opportunity in social studies to express, in one medium or another, his learning. His product is the integration of the ideas he has learned and an exercise within his limitations of a skill or complex of skills. The integrity of the pupil's product must be respected, but the teacher must also be concerned with growth in terms of regard for accuracy and improvement in the skill exercised. The evaluation of a product is a joint venture of pupil and teacher. The result for the child should be a heightened respect for himself, a desire to improve, and some ideas about what he can do to improve. At times, individual children need help in learning how to live with themselves and others. Since behavior may also be interpreted as an expressed product based upon previous learning, the teacher works individually with these children, evaluating them in somewhat the same way.

The remaining dimension of evaluation is the teacher on a seat of judgment from which he surveys the perplexing but exciting, wearying but rewarding, process of teaching-learning in which he is, has been, and will be involved. His concern is for both his pupils and himself. He judges to arrive at important decisions for both his pupils and himself.

As the teacher works in this dimension of evaluation, the first area into which he probes is his effectiveness in the acts of teaching social studies. He asks himself questions such as these: How provocative and stimulating of thought were the instructional models which I developed for germinating the seed of inquiry in the minds of my pupils? How receptive was I to the many statements of hypotheses made by my pupils? How successful was I in guiding children toward a healthy skepticism of their most reasonable hypotheses? How well did I guide them in developing a design for inquiry? How effective were the provisions which I made for every child to have a rich contact with facts and ideas within the limitations of his investigative skills? How well did I guide children in synthesizing their acquired facts and ideas into definitions and principles of greater application? How efficient was my guidance of children as they made verifications of "big ideas?" How successful was I in encouraging children to suspend their judgment on issues and to continue verifying "big ideas?" How adequate were the provisions which I made for children to have opportunities to express the facts and ideas that they had acquired? As the teacher answers these questions, he finds evidence to support his decisions about what he will do as a teacher the next time he finds himself in similar teaching situations. He also finds evidence of weaknesses which he must remedy through independent study, consulting with experts, in-service training, and further college or university work.

The social-studies teacher also scrutinizes his growth as a person.

He examines his relations with children and his effectiveness in helping children to maintain positive relations among themselves and with other groups in the school and community. His findings often prompt him to exercise a greater perceptiveness in his work with children and to embark upon a program of study of children in a formal way.

Probably the most difficult aspect of this dimension of evaluation is arriving at accurate assessments of children's progress in social studies. Part of the difficulty lies in the lack of formal measuring instruments which when applied will gauge growth in each of the areas of social-studies objectives. To measure growth in social-studies learning requires a careful examination of the child in the light of his behavior as an inquirer and investigator; as one who retains, integrates, and applies facts and ideas; as an expresser of facts and ideas; as a member of a group; and as a person whose attitudes and actions are influenced by what he has studied. In some instances, objective measurements may be obtained; in many instances, subjective measurements will have to be made. The difficulty is heightened as the teacher struggles with the matter of validity and reliability of tests and observations, and with the decision as to whether he should rely more heavily on objective or subjective measurements.

Another aspect of the difficulty is arriving at a decision as to whether a child's progress in social-studies learning should be measured in terms of individual limitations and growth or in terms of expectancies for groups of similar age and experience. If the teacher decides in favor of the latter, the child may be destroyed as a learner; if he decides in favor of the former, the child and his parents may be misled as to the child's further success in school. Sometimes school or district policy provides at least partial relief, but regardless of the extent of relief, the ultimate decision remains with the teacher. He makes the decision and lives with it, and constantly strives to make it more accurately and with less agony. To encourage this striving, the bulk of this chapter will be devoted to presenting ways of gathering data about children's learning in social studies.

EVALUATING THE CHILD AS INQUIRER

In a social-studies program in which the basic approach to learning is inquiry, the child's growth as an inquirer receives first emphasis in evaluation. To make this evaluation the teacher must have firmly in mind the possible behaviors of a child as an inquirer. A careful examination of the inquiry process provides some valuable clues:

Inquiry into facts and ideas
1. Identifying the conflict in facts and ideas.
2. Hypothesizing as to why the conflict exists or as to whether it really exists.
3. Substantiating hypotheses.
4. Selecting hypotheses to be checked.
5. Formulating questions to be answered in checking the hypotheses.
6. Relating findings to the hypotheses.
7. If necessary, restating the hypotheses.
8. Verifying the hypotheses as stated.

Inquiry into attitudes and patterns of behavior
1. Identifying the aspects of a generalization which have or may have a direct bearing on one's attitudes and actions.
2. Isolating and expressing attitudes and actions that would be suitable.
3. Selecting the attitudes and actions that would be most suitable.
4. Whenever possible, developing a program in which attitudes and actions are tested.
5. Reviewing the results of the program.

Once the teacher has these behaviors firmly in mind, he is prepared to gather data on individual children through the use of one or several of the devices discussed below.

MENTAL NOTES

Making mental notes does not appear to be a very reliable device for gathering data, but it may serve quite well for the teacher who is thoroughly aware of inquiry as children use it. From time to time he gives a few moments of thought to each child in his class, recalling what the child was like at the beginning of the school year, recalling instances in which the child manifested knowledge of inquiry and how it is used, and making assessments as to how the child is growing as an inquirer. If he were to be questioned about his pupils' ability to use inquiry, quite likely he would be able to identify those who are sophisticated in the use of inquiry, those who appear to be able to do some things well within the inquiry process, and those who need further help. He manages to regard children both as children and as inquirers.

The teacher who is not thoroughly acquainted with inquiry or who has not yet developed a good working knowledge of children will find his judgments being influenced by the last few experiences with inquiry and by the behavior of children during moments when something other than inquiry is taking place. Such a teacher should use other devices for gathering data on children as inquirers.

OBSERVATION SHEETS

An observation sheet consists of a list of behaviors similar to those listed above as related to inquiry. As the teacher observes the child, or as soon as possible after the observation, he judges the child's behavior in accord with the items listed. Frequently this judgment is a matter of recording the date and the name of the child observed, and placing a check mark beside the behavior manifested. If the child shows examples of the same behavior more than once during the observation period, additional checks are added.

It is impossible to observe simultaneously all the children in a classroom in such detail. The teacher is advised to select four or five children at a time to observe during a period in which inquiry is being established and when its results are being examined. If the teacher follows this procedure, by the end of a semester or year he will have a good fund of data with which to assess pupils' growth in inquiry.

An observation sheet may be used to record findings in terms of behaviors for longer periods. At the close of several weeks or a month of social-studies instruction, the teacher may complete an observation sheet for each child in the class. In this case, a three-or-five-point scale is entered on the observation sheet as in the following examples:

Five-Point Scale	*Three-Point Scale*
Substantiates hypotheses	Substantiates hypotheses
_____Always	_____Frequently
_____Frequently	_____Sometimes
_____Sometimes	_____Rarely
_____Rarely	
_____Never	

The teacher rates the child's behavior from what he can remember during the observation period by placing a check mark under the adverb which seems to indicate most accurately the relative frequency of the behavior being examined.

ANECDOTAL RECORDS

An anecdotal record is a brief, objective account of a child's behavior, written as soon as possible after his behavior has been observed. As a teacher records what he saw and heard, he deals only with what he thinks is significant and avoids the use of value terms. The following is a well-written example of an anecdotal record:

Billy H., Nov. 12, 1966

Billy hypothesized that Fulton should be considered the inventor of the steamboat because he had seen pictures of old steamboats which looked like Fulton's. He felt that Fitch's steamboat probably didn't work very well because of the way it was built and that Fulton's invention served as a model for those built later. He rejected his own hypothesis when another member of the class suggested that maybe Fulton's success was due to people's wanting a better form of transportation. As the class developed the design for inquiry, Billy contributed these two questions: What kinds of transportation did they have in those days? Why should they want better kinds?

This record reveals exactly what happened. Compare it with the following:

Billy H., Nov. 12, 1966

Billy was very excited when saw the pictures of the two steamboats. Immediately he made an excellent and reasonable hypothesis. Later he rejected it for what he thought was a better one (which indeed it was). He participated in the following discussion in a very lively way. He is a very valuable member of our class when we begin inquiry.

This anecdotal record tells the reader next to nothing, and it is likely that exactly what Billy did will not be recalled the next time the teacher reads it.

Some teachers use anecdotal records to gather data on the behavior of children about whom they have a question in their minds, because other devices for gathering data do not appear to yield complete and appropriate information. However, the anecdotal record can be used as easily and effectively as the observation sheet for making a survey of the individuals of an entire class. Well-written anecdotal records can serve almost as well as videotaped records of behavior.

INFORMAL TESTS

Informal tests are those which teachers develop themselves to measure the learning which children have acquired under their direction. Simple tests for the measurement of children's ability in inquiry can be easily constructed. Such tests follow the order of inquiry as it occurs in the classroom. They begin with an instructional model similar to those which the teacher uses to stimulate children's interest in an area of facts and ideas. A few clue-questions which carry the inquiry process up to the point of investigation complete the test. The following is an example:

Many years ago some people lived on an island. Their ways of living were simple. They built their homes from poles which were covered with grass. Their food was the wild animals that they could catch and roots and fruits that they could gather easily. They made their clothing from bark and animal skins. They played simple games to amuse themselves. They made music with whistles and drums. They believed that there were many gods.

One day a strange new people came to the island. Their ships were larger and faster than what the people on the island had ever seen. The new people had ways of living that were different from those followed on the island. They knew how to grow their own food and how to preserve it. Their clothing was made of many different kinds of cloth. They used many materials making their homes. When they made music, they used many instruments made of wood, metal, and other things. In their religion, they believed that it was important to treat others fairly, especially parents.

Years and years went by. The new people became many. The island people did not change in number. The new people made their ways of living richer and richer. The island people still used their old ways. They changed very little.

1. What do you think is the hard thing to explain in this story?
2. Think of as many ways as you can of explaining this. Write them here.
3. Choose the way of explaining what you think is best. Write it here.
4. What questions will you have to answer to know that your way of explaining is best? Write them here.

As can be seen, the four clue-questions encourage the child to define the problem simply (the hard thing to explain), to hypothesize, to select a hypothesis, and to develop a simple design for inquiry to check the chosen hypothesis.

Some teachers will prefer a simpler test in which the child is presented with a forced choice, as shown in the following example:

A large, rich country wants to help a small, poor country. The people in the large, rich country are not sure how this should be done. Many of the people think that a gift of money should be sent to the little country. Just as many people believe that a gift of food, clothing, and other useful things should be sent to the little country.

1. With which of these people do you agree?
2. Why do you agree with these people? Write as many reasons as you can think of.
3. Choose your best reason. Write it here.
4. What questions will you have to answer before you know that your reason is right? Write them here.

In the above tests only hypothetical situations were used in the instructional models. It is necessary to remember that the situations used in an informal test for inquiry ability should not be closely similar to areas which the children have studied within the past year or two.

Tests such as the above should not be administered until the children have a fundamental mastery over the language-arts skills, probably not before the children are near the end of third grade or in the fourth grade. Such tests may be administered individually to children who lack the necessary reading or writing skills.

Occasionally the teacher may test for inquiry ability and stimulate interest in the unit at the same time. Instead of presenting the instructional model to the entire class and encouraging discussion by class members, the teacher presents a test with content based upon the facts and ideas to be studied. After every individual has completed the test, the teacher collects the test papers and prompts the class to begin inquiry from the instructional model. Later he examines the test results to determine individual growth in his pupils' ability to make inquiry.

A teacher can construct more sophisticated tests than those which have been offered as examples. Instead of prompting children to develop hypotheses, the teacher may offer a list of reasons from which a child is to choose those which appear to be the most reasonable to him. Such a test can go only about this far at one time, for if one reason in the next item is shown to be the most reasonable, nothing will keep a child from going back in the test and changing his responses in the earlier item. Another test may prompt the child to choose but one reason from many given. Then he is asked to develop the questions which need to be answered to check the accuracy of the reason.

When the teacher examines the results of tests for inquiry ability, he is not particularly concerned when the child develops hypotheses radically different from those that the teacher had in mind when he constructed the test. His chief concerns are how the child sees the problem, the general reasonableness of all the hypotheses offered, the number of reasonable hypotheses offered, and the completeness of the set of questions developed by the pupil as his design for inquiry.

The informal tests in inquiry suggested so far measure applications of aspects of the inquiry process to the point of investigation. Inquiry lends both force and direction to the investigation, but during investigation activities its dynamic aspects are at rest and do not function until the investigative activities draw to a close and the results are examined. Informal tests related to aspects of inquiry after investigative activities can also be developed without much difficulty. The following simple test measures the skill in the generalizing aspect of inquiry:

If all the ideas in the sentences below were put together, they would express a single idea. Each sentence tells something about this single idea. Read all the sentences carefully, then write the idea that all the sentences tell about.

1. A large number of people living in a small country must be very polite to one another.
2. A large number of people living in a small country must have careful laws to protect persons and their property.
3. A small number of people living in a large country may not see each other for long periods of time.
4. A small number of people living in a large country have fine ways of entertaining guests.
5. A large number of people living in a small country must care for their children for a while after they are grown up.
6. A small number of people living in a large country want their children to be men and women by themselves as soon as they can.

The above test requires the child to develop a statement, an act which demands expressive ability as well as the ability to think. Quite possibly a child may accurately sense the idea which all the other ideas support, but he may not be able to express that idea. If the teacher feels that many of the pupils of his class have this difficulty, he may extend the test by offering a list of statements from which one is to be chosen as the single idea which the other ideas support, such as the following:

A. Life in a small country with many people and life in a large country with few people are very different.
B. The number of people in a country and the size of the country have something to do with the way people treat each other.
C. It is more comfortable to live in a small country with a large number of people than it is to live in a large country with a small number of people.
D. Living in a small country and living in a large country may bring problems to the people no matter how many there are.

Often a hypothesis will be found untenable because it is too broad or too sweeping as a statement of truth. Examination of ideas which have been definitely established reveals the untenability and the need for restatement of the hypothesis. A replica of these conditions may be represented in a test such as the following:

Read this sentence carefully: The way that a people lives in a country depends on the topography of the country (mountains, valleys, rivers, and the like), its natural resources, and its climate.

Some of the sentences below explain the sentence above. Read each of the following sentences carefully. If a sentence explains the sentence above, write YES after it. If it does not, write NO after it.

1. A country that has many rich valleys also has many farmers.
2. Countries having short growing seasons usually cannot produce all the food needed by their people.
3. People learn from other peoples how better to do things, such as manufacturing, fishing, and the like.
4. Countries having many mountains often produce many minerals and metals because of many mines in the mountains.
5. Countries with long seacoasts often have large fishing and ship-building industries.
6. The people in some countries know how to make the best use of their natural resources; people in other countries do not.

Now let us suppose that all the sentences that you have just worked with are true. This means that the sentence at the beginning of this work is not true. How does it need to be changed so that each of the sentences above explains something about it? Write the changed sentence below.

This instance is another in which the teacher may wish to present the children with a list of statements from which the correct one is to be chosen.

The last act of inquiry in objective facts and ideas is verification of a discovered truth. In this verification of discovered truth ideas are placed in perspective and relationship with other ideas of equal significance. The simple test offered below is a replica of the act of verification in inquiry:

The following sentence gives an idea which many people believe. Read it carefully: The ways that people used in the past have something to do with the ways we use today.

Below are some sentences giving ideas which prove the idea in the sentence above. Read each sentence carefully. If the sentence proves the idea above, write YES after it. If it does not, write NO after it.

1. Long ago most people in our country rode on horses or in carriages; today most people travel in automobiles.
2. Long ago the people in our country traveled on the left side of the road; today automobiles and buses go on the left side of the street.
3. Long ago specially trained workers made beautiful candles; today beautiful candles are made in the same way by specially trained workers.
4. Long ago petroleum was used for making medicine; today people can eat all kinds of vegetables during the entire year.

All of the devices mentioned so far may be used for gathering data on how children perform when involved with the inquiry process as it relates to working within objective content. To gather data on how children perform when involved with the inquiry process as it relates to making inquiry into attitudes and patterns of action is quite another matter. It must be admitted that making mental notes, observations, and anecdotal records can be useful and that it is even possible to make informal tests which replicate the inquiry process or aspects of it. However, the facts and ideas that the children work with and the discoveries that they make are so deeply personal, so close to their being, that objective devices have limited utility in gathering usable data. Other devices are much better.

The first of these devices is creative projection through which children reflect their understanding of prevailing conditions and their empathy for persons existing within these conditions. The stories, plays, and poems that individual children write toward the close of the study of a unit often indicate clearly the attitudes and patterns of actions called for within certain sets of circumstances the objective content of which has already been studied. When children are called up to read their stories, act their plays, and recite their poems, they manifest feelings and desires for action which reach beyond the limitations of verbal expression.

A second device useful for gathering data on how well children work in the process of inquiry for attitudes and patterns of action is dramatization involving roleplaying and dramatic play. At first glance these appear to be another dimension of creative projection, which indeed they are, but they are different in that they are group projections. A child or group of children who play roles serve as an instrument through which the rest of the class find possible attitudes and patterns of action. The class watches the roleplaying and comments critically about it. In dramatic play, children work together to project their feelings and ideas about actions without any audience, but at some time or another they review for the rest of the class what they have done. The class as a group comments on the reasonableness of their attitudes and patterns of action.

Still another device is to deal directly in an open discussion with the problems of "How do we feel about this?" and "What should we do about this?" The children examine the objective facts and ideas, suggest attitudes and patterns of actions which are suitable, and finally decide that certain ones of those suggested are the most suitable. However, dealing directly with the problems of how one should feel and act as a result of having some objective information is a device not recommended for constant use. So often it deteriorates into an overbearing smugness or a nauseous self-flagellation.

A final device, not always applicable, is an actual project, a product of how children feel about an existing condition or set of conditions and what they do as a reaction to the condition or conditions. Children studying production, conservation, or government may develop a project in which they are highly involved with producing something to be sold, conserving useful goods, or establishing a form of classroom government which will benefit them.

When these last two devices are used, it is possible for the teacher to arrive at assessments of individual progress through making mental notes, observations, or anecdotal records.

Much can be said for all the devices listed here being useful for gathering data on children as inquirers, but none is so accurate that it alone is sufficient for giving a complete measurement of a child's ability as inquirer. Mental notes, observation sheets, and anecdotal records place a heavy burden on the memory and pupil-bias of the teacher. Paper-and-pencil tests are difficult for some children to use and they do not reflect the entirety of inquiry. Some children need to hear the ideas of others before they can begin participating in inquiry. Some children welcome the chance to project themselves individually into a creation, while others do not. Some children may always have to react to the projections of others in group situations. The best evaluation of the child as inquirer results when the teacher carefully selects the devices for gathering data in the light of the aspect of inquiry to be studied and the limitations of the device chosen, and pools his data. From his data, then, he may draw a profile of the child as inquirer.

EVALUATING THE CHILD AS A MEMBER OF A WORKING GROUP

As a social-studies teacher attempts to evaluate a child's growth in ability to work in a group, he gathers data on how the child reacts to authority and to other people. A child's reaction to authority may reflect that he seeks and uses it to guide the group in accomplishing its task; that he respects authority and looks toward it or consults it for guidance; that he has deep insights into the limitations of authority as he agrees with or challenges it. His reaction to others may reflect his assessments of others; he competes, cooperates, supports, or resists when he finds himself engaged with them. All of these reactions may be regarded as desirable as long as they move the group toward the accomplishment of its task.

The factors which influence a child's ability to work in task-oriented groups are so complex and varied in intensity from one moment to another that it is difficult to establish precise increments of growth. The social climate, the nature of the task, the abilities called upon to accomplish it, the diversity of children's personalities, and the status of children in the classroom and in a particular group rule against precision.

The teacher has two basic ways to gather data. He may determine the child's position within the total social structure of the classroom or group, or he may study the child for the occurrence of desirable behaviors.

Three devices which the teacher uses for gathering data on the frequency of various behavior have already been introduced. They include making mental notes, using observation sheets, and making anecdotal records. To use these devices, the teacher must have clearly in mind the behavior to note. The following lists define behaviors related to group work which the teacher may use as a basis for making mental notes, developing observation sheets, or writing anecdotal records:

The behavior of a child who seeks authority and uses it well
1. Vies with others for the position of authority.
2. Accepts the position when it is offered to him.
3. Exercises the responsibilities inherent in the position to help the group to accomplish its task.
   a. Asks for suggestions and opinions.
   b. Regulates the presentation of suggestions and opinions.
   c. Encourages the discussion of suggestions and opinions.
   d. Maintains the discussion on the point under consideration.
   e. Guides the processing of suggestions and opinions to determine which will prove most useful in the accomplishment of the task.
   f. Guides the implementation of suggestions and opinions into action.
   g. Assigns roles with careful attention to the abilities and desires of the various members of the group.
   h. Works with various members of the group as needed.
   i. Whenever necessary, convenes the group to consider emerging ideas and problems.
   j. Guides the group in examining its progress in the completion of its task.

The behaviors of a child who has respect for authority
1. Accepts the chosen leader.
2. Works to accomplish the group task.
   a. Offers suggestions and opinions.
   b. Listens to suggestions and opinions.
   c. Weighs suggestions and opinions.
   d. Contributes in the selection of suggestions and opinions to be used in accomplishing the task.
   e. Volunteers for roles of which he believes himself to be capable.
   f. Accepts roles as assigned.
   g. Works at assigned roles.

h. Asks for help from the leader during work.

i. Weighs each point toward completion and the final completion of the task itself.

The behaviors of a child who senses the limitations of authority

1. Works for the selection of the leader whom he feels best suited for the position.
2. Challenges the leader when he makes unilateral decisions.
3. Supports the leader during moments of confusion or indecision.
4. Presents syntheses of ideas after they have been presented.
5. Rejects roles for which he feels himself poorly suited.

The behaviors of a child who has respect for others in the group

1. Competes openly with others for the more desirable roles.
2. Cooperates with others.
3. Encourages others.
4. Helps others.
5. Seeks help from others.
6. Objects to untoward interference from others.

It would be unrealistic to expect any one child to manifest all of these behaviors during any one period of group work, or, for that matter, during an extended series of group work periods. Some children will vie successfully with others for the position of leader and will manifest most of the behaviors of an authority who exercises his responsibilities well; others may achieve the position of leader and fail in exercising the leader's responsibilities. Some children will fail to become leaders and will immediately assume the behaviors of those who respect authority; others who fail will immediately assume the role of the "gadfly" who senses the limitations of authority. Some may never aspire toward leadership. Some will be able to work with almost anyone within the group; others will be able to work with only one or two. What really matters is the frequency with which a child manifests behaviors directed toward the completion of a task. Change in the direction of increased frequency is an indication of growth.

In other data-gathering devices, the social-studies teacher may use the above matrices of behaviors as bases from which to work. These include group discussion, self-rating sheets, and teacher-pupil conferences.

GROUP DISCUSSION

To provide for improvement in the ability to work in a task-oriented group, it is always essential that the teacher direct the group's attention to its behavior in light of its perceptions of what persons are supposed to do when they work in groups. A set of standards or descriptions of acceptable behaviors established early in the course of group work serves as the criteria by which children judge whether they have been working successfully as a group and as members of a group. Often these standards describe generally what a group does in terms of general behaviors as it undertakes a task, what a leader does, and what a follower does. The standards may be quite simple, but as a result of further experience, these standards are extended and refined in accord with children's growing perceptions of what is involved in group work. In the extension and refinement of these standards lies evidence of the growth of the class or group as a whole. Discussion which determines how well the group and individuals within it met the standards, and which may ultimately bring forth the need for extension and refinement of standards, the data on how individual children are improving are revealed.

As the children freely discuss their behavior as a group, as the leader of their group reports his assessment of the group and the various members within it, and as the children assess frankly the behaviors of the leader, the teacher is given access to very valid information. The basis for validity is that the discussion is limited within the children's own perceptions. As the children examine their own group behavior critically, they are providing in a very real sense observations of individuals made by persons other than the teacher. The teacher can compare the data that he has gathered by himself with that gathered by the children and arrive at a more reliable assessment of what individual children actually do in groups and of how much they improve.

SELF-RATING SHEETS

Each child working in task-oriented groups needs to share with his teacher a concern for his improvement in his ability to work effectively in groups. One way in which to develop this concern is to have the child complete a self-rating sheet.

The development of the self-rating sheet should be a task in which all the members of the class are involved. After the standards for group work have been established, the teacher guides the children in organizing a self-rating sheet based on the standards. At the close of the group work, either before or after the group discussion, the teacher distributes the self-rating sheets for the children to complete. Occasionally, the self-rating sheets may be used instead of the group discussion, in which case the teacher should report a summary of the data to the class at the beginning of the next social-studies period.

An argument against the use of self-rating sheets is that children find it difficult to be honest with themselves and, as a result, rate themselves too high. This is not the case with most children. Their self-ratings often agree with the observations of the teacher and of their classmates. They are more likely to err by rating themselves too low.

The data which the child reveals about his behavior on a self-rating sheet represents another observation which the teacher may compare with his own and with the observations made by other members of the class or group to arrive at a more accurate assessment of a child's ability in group work. A series of these sheets representing ratings taken over a period of time will reveal a pattern of growth.

TEACHER-PUPIL CONFERENCE

By itself, the teacher-pupil conference can be a very effective device for gathering data on a child's ability to do group work. The particular advantage of this device for gathering data over the other devices discussed is that it can bring forth data not easily acquirable in any other way. The teacher can discover the child's attitudes toward group work and the basis for his attitudes, as well as his perceptions of what group work is, by asking such questions as: What do you think about working at something with a group? Do you like it? Why? Do you like (would you like) to be the leader of the group? What do you think a good leader should do?

When the teacher-pupil conference includes the examination of self-rating sheets and a review of events in recent group work sessions, it emerges as the most effective device for gathering data. The teacher and the child, reviewing the data which each have gathered, can arrive at agreement on which of the data are most accurate. The teacher has then the wherewithal to make a just assessment of the child's ability and to show the child where he needs to improve.

So far, the discussion has been focused primarily on devices for gathering data on how children work in groups. The use of each of the devices has been based on some definitive notions of what a child does as he works in a group. Emphasis has been placed on the process of group work. Another kind of data is needed, having to do with the child as a product or his status as a result of his having worked in groups within the classroom. The teacher gathers this data through the use of a sociometric device.

SOCIOMETRIC DEVICE

Simply defined, a sociometric device is a brief questionnaire to which children respond by stating their preference for working partners in a specific enterprise. Some examples are shown below:

With what person in this classroom would you like most to work on a mural? Write the names of your first, second, third, and fourth choices in the spaces below:

1. _____
2. _____
3. _____
4. _____

With what person in this classroom would you like most to plan a debate? Write the names of your first, second, and third choices in the spaces below:

1. _____
2. _____
3. _____

After decisions have been reached about the tasks to be performed by groups, the teacher develops the questionnaires and distributes them to his pupils to be completed. The pupils return the completed questionnaires to the teacher who organizes groups in accord with the findings. If the teacher follows these procedures each time the class is to engage in group tasks, and if he keeps the questionnaires for future study and comparison, he will have a series of data relating to the position that each child has in the social structure of his classroom. Upon reviewing the data, he will be able to determine whether a child is being more often preferred than he once was, whether he is receiving greater preference than he once was, or whether he is maintaining a relatively stable position within the pattern of preferences. The child's position, stable or changing, represents the synthesis of his capability, in the eyes of his classmates, for working in a group.

The sociometric device is a valid means of determining a child's position in the social structure of the classroom engaged in group work in social studies only when certain precautions are observed. The first precaution is to develop the device around a task that is actually going to be performed. Data relating to preferences for persons with whom to go to the movies, to go on a picnic, or to stay overnight are relatively useless. The second precaution is to apply the data when organizing groups. If the data are not used, the children soon become aware the questionnaires are of little significance as far as they are concerned and that any response at all will be adequate. The third precaution is to provide the child with as much privacy as possible while he completes the questionnaire. Each child should have his own questionnaire and should be encouraged to complete it by himself. The fourth precaution is to respect the integrity of each child by placing him with persons with whom he wants to work and by regarding all his responses on his questionnaire as confidential.

Again a variety of devices has been presented for gathering data on some specialized aspects of a child's behavior, and again, no definite prescription is given as to which of the devices is best or the frequency with which they should be used. The teacher's values as a social-studies teacher and his teaching style will determine which devices he will use and how often he will use them. However, the teacher is advised to have a systematic way of developing records of his observations as his pupils work at group tasks, involve the child in some way in scrutinizing his own behavior in groups, and be concerned with the child's position in the social structure as the class works in social studies.

EVALUATING THE CHILD AS AN INFORMED PERSON

When the social-studies teacher evaluates the child as an informed person, he examines the child's abilities at acquiring, retaining, expressing, and applying information. These abilities are closely interwoven into the inquiry process. As the child continues inquiry, the facts he has retained serve as a basis for seeking and acquiring new facts, the facts he has acquired are expressed in a way which communicates to others as well as to himself, and the facts are constantly applied in the tasks of integrating, expressing, and verifying ideas. A reciprocal relationship exists between inquiry skills and information-processing skills. Inquiry skills lend purpose and direction to information-processing skills, and information-processing skills serve to carry inquiry along toward completion. However, the reciprocity is somewhat limited. Inquiry cannot occur without information-processing skills, but information-processing can occur as a separate exercise. For example, the research librarian, once he has been given the questions to be answered, can unearth the desired information. The inquirer provides him with the questions. Given enough time, the inquirer can do his own library research but the research librarian cannot provide the questions. The immediate ends of elementary social studies include the development of the child as research librarian and acute observer of life and the development of the child as inquirer.

Traditionally, elementary social-studies programs have tended to support as an immediate and almost exclusive end the development of the child as a research librarian who, once he has discovered the facts, serves as a depository of facts. Somewhat less is expected of the professional research librarian, but children preparing for effective roles in the American democratic society must retain the facts for future use. Occasionally knowledge of facts is given so much emphasis that the function of research librarian is forgotten. Because practices in evaluation have been developed to measure factual retention and library research skills, the social-studies teacher has techniques of measurement and standardized tests at his disposal. The purpose of this section is to deal briefly with these as well as other means of gathering data on how well a child acquires, retains, expresses, and applies social-studies facts and ideas.

STANDARDIZED TESTS

A commercially prepared test for which norms of achievement have been established through extensive field trials with large numbers of children is generally known as a standardized test. The purchased test is accompanied by a manual which informs the teacher how to administer and score it and how to convert the score or scores to expression in terms of norms. Norms are usually expressed in centile ranking or grade-placement. The teacher administers the test to an entire class, scores it (in many larger districts the tests are scored by machine), and, consulting a conversion table, converts the score into norm expression. This expression reflects how a child's achievement compares with that of a large number of children used in the field trial of a test. For example, if a child is given a standardized test in social studies during his sixth month in the fourth grade and the number of correct responses shows him to have a grade-placement of 4-6 (or 4.6), he has achieved about as well as the children in the field test. He compares favorably.

Standardized tests are usually administered on a district-wide basis once or twice a year. More frequent administration is not advisable because the children become "wise" to them, thus distorting their validity as instruments of measurement. Furthermore, the tests are not really capable of measuring fine increments of growth. Standardized tests are of greatest use to the district in appraising its curriculum, provided that the curriculum is reflected in the test. They are of some utility in comparing the program in one school or classroom to that in another. For the classroom teacher attempting to evaluate individual children, standardized tests provide only a general indication of a child's achievement.

The use of standardized tests to gather data on a child's growth in social studies presents a bleak picture at best. Although elementary social studies curricula throughout the United States tend to have similarities in subject-matter content from grade five through grade nine, content still varies widely. It is all but impossible to develop a test which adequately reflects the subject-matter content and the emphasis with which it is taught in social-studies programs across the nation. If a district is addicted to the use of standardized tests in elementary social-studies subject-matter content, about the best that it can do is to find a test which closely parallels its curriculum.

The picture improves somewhat in the matter of standardized tests that measure growth in the skills of acquiring information. Such skills as map reading, reading of tables, charts, and graphs, evaluation of source suitability and use of the table of contents and index are presented well in some tests. The following are examples of such standardized tests:

Iowa Tests of Basic Skills. Houghton-Mifflin Company, 2 Park Street, Boston, Mass. Suitable for grades three through nine. Presents subtests in map reading, choices of references, index usage, dictionary usage, and alphabetization for grades three through five; presents subtests in map reading, choices of references, index usage, dictionary usage, and reading of graphs, charts, and tables.

SRA Achievement Series, Work-Study Skills. Science Research Associates, 259 East Erie Street, Chicago, Ill. Suitable for grades four through nine. Presents subtests in use of the table of contents, use of the index, choices of references, and reading graphs and tables for grade four through six; presents subtests in use of the table of contents, use of the index, reading charts, graphs, and tables, and map reading for grades seven through nine.

Metropolitan Achievement Battery. Harcourt, Brace & World, Inc., 757 Third Avenue, New York, N. Y. Suitable for grades five through nine. Presents subtests in map reading and the reading of tables, charts, and graphs.

Stanford Achievement Tests. Harcourt, Brace & World, Inc., 757 Third Avenue, New York, N. Y. Suitable for grades five through nine. Present subtests dealing with reading charts and tables, map reading, dictionary usage, choice of references, and the use of the index.

The *Metropolitan Achievement Battery* and the *Stanford Achievement Tests* also include factual subtests in history, geography, and civics.

A relatively new standardized test in social studies presents considerable promise. The *Sequential Tests of Educational Progress,* published by the Educational Testing Service, Princeton, New Jersey, include a test in elementary social studies which reflects the more recent thinking in social-studies curriculum and methodology. Rather than measuring factual retention or ability in library research skills, the test places emphasis on the thinking skills necessary for learning in social studies. The subject-matter content in the test assumes that the children have richly sampled history, geography, economics, government, and sociology; therefore the test tasks reach beyond factual retention into the manipulation of facts. If the social-studies curriculum of a district is organized around social-studies generalizations at increasing levels of sophistication through the grades, and if inquiry as a means of learning receives strong emphasis, it is likely that this test, or one similar to it, should be considered for use. Two levels of the test are available, one for grades four through six and one for grades seven through nine.

In summary, standardized tests in elementary social studies have limited utility. Much of this lack of utility is due to the inappropriateness of the tests in terms of subject-matter content. Some tests appear to measure library research skills adequately. Some improvement is evident in the development of standardized tests in elementary social studies. The best use for standardized tests is to determine the efficacy of the district or school program in social studies. The tests are of limited use as a source of data about an individual child's achievement.

TEACHER-MADE TESTS

When the social-studies teacher desires objective precise data on how well children gather, retain, and interrelate facts and ideas, he examines the results from tests which he has made and administered to the class. The preciseness of the data is due largely to the close relationship between the tests and what is actually taught. Sometimes the preciseness is distorted by the construction of poor tests, but given adequate time and a good reference on test construction, most teachers can make adequate tests.

Besides closely paralleling the actual social-studies program, teacher-made tests offer another rich advantage. Such tests can be so richly varied that the act of taking a test can be almost as interesting to a child as solving or putting together a puzzle. Another advantage is that tests can be made to measure growth in many different facets of learning. For example, a teacher may wish to see how well each of his pupils can synthesize ideas into facts. If he really knows what this task involves, he can construct a simple test in which children are given facts to synthesize. He may make the test at two levels of sophistication, one in which children view some facts to synthesize and then choose a statement of synthesis from several given, and another in which the children develop the statement of synthesis from a group of given facts. The greatest advantage which these tests offer is that they can be made a part of the teaching-learning program. The children may be guided in examining and discussing the results of the tests.

If a teacher can devise a way which will communicate to his pupils the questions which he wishes to ask and a way in which they can clearly record their responses, he can develop a test on fact gathering, retaining, and interrelating for almost any group of children. Young children, slower children, and children who have difficulty with verbal expression can mark pictures or draw simple lines or punch out precut discs under the *Yes* or *No* column on a cardboard strip after being given oral instructions.

Teacher-made tests fall into two categories—objective tests and subjective (or essay) tests. The line that separates the two kinds of tests is a very thin one. An objective test is one in which the teacher develops a series of statements to which the pupil responds in a very brief way. He may be asked to identify a statement as true or false or to give a yes or no answer to a question. He may be given a multiple-choice problem where he is asked to complete a statement by selecting the correct answer from several given, or to select a sentence fragment which completes the stem of a sentence. He may answer a "fill-in" question by writing a word in a blank. He may be asked to select the word from memory or he may be given a list of words from which to choose. He may be asked to match one list of items with another, or to arrange a list of statements in the proper sequence in accord with a stated criterion. In the objective tests mentioned, the pupil is relieved from the task of structuring a long verbal response. Occasionally he may have to recall a word or two. Memory and thought are left free to function without responsibility for spelling, handwriting, and arranging ideas.

A subjective test is one in which the pupil is presented with a topic or an issue to discuss or a broad question to answer. Not only must he recall the necessary facts and ideas, but he must structure these facts and ideas in communicative form as well. The "subjective" aspect of the test is that he must put so much of himself into his response.

In the hybrid test, somewhere between objective and subjective, the pupil is called upon to make a brief response and then to substantiate fully his response. The true-false test in which the pupil is required to tell why each false statement is false is an example. The "short-answer" test also falls in this in-between category.

Much can be said for all three kinds of tests, and the controversy about which is superior has given rise to an interesting but useless argument. Each teacher settles the controversy for himself and organizes a pattern of tests in keeping with his teaching style. The teacher of inquiry, regardless of whether he favors objective tests or subjective tests, will place greater emphasis on the application and interpretation of facts and ideas rather than the retention of them. Some examples follow:

Objective items

For kindergarten pupils studying the family
1. Oral directions: Draw a line across the persons who must decide the important things in this family. (Pictures: father, mother, and three children.)
2. Oral directions: Draw a line across the room where a family spends much time together. (Pictures: a kitchen, a bedroom, and a living room.)
3. Oral directions: Draw a line across the place that one person in the family more often goes than the others. (Pictures: store, church, and movie theater.)

For first-grade pupils studying workers in the community
1. Oral directions: Draw a circle around the person who is paid from tax

money. (Pictures: physician, fireman, salesman in a store, and a minister.)

2. Oral directions: Draw a circle around the person who has to go to school a long time before he can begin to work. (Pictures: fireman, gardener, dentist, service-station attendant.)

3. Oral directions: Draw a line across each of the workers who could be working for himself. (Pictures: a trash collector, a service-station man, a shoe repairman, a policeman.)

For second-grade pupils studying communication

1. Oral directions: Draw a line under the person who is trying to communicate with someone. (Pictures: a man standing with his back to a telephone, a man beckoning with one hand, and a man hammering a nail.)

2. Oral directions: Draw a line under the thing you would use to communicate with someone if you wanted an answer back right away. (Pictures: a letter, a note in a bottle, and a telephone.)

3. Oral directions: Draw a line under each of the things that communicate news to us every day. (Pictures: a letter, a newspaper, a telephone, a radio, a book, a magazine, and a television set.)

For third-grade pupils studying the community

1. Draw a line under the sentences that tell what will happen when the new freeway is built outside our city.
   a. We can go downtown easier.
   b. There will be fewer cars on our streets.
   c. Our gas stations will make more money.
   d. Our stores downtown will have more business.

2. Suppose the people in our city had no city government. What would happen? Draw a line under the things that would happen.
   a. No food for us to eat.
   b. No water for washing.
   c. No gas for cooking and heating.
   d. No clothing to buy or sell.
   e. No protection from fire.
   f. No safety in our streets.

3. Our city is a fishing city. Draw a line under the sentence that tells why it is a fishing city.
   a. The people in our city like to eat fish.
   b. Our city is near an ocean which has many fish.
   c. Fishing is all that our workers know how to do.

For fourth-grade pupils studying about Japan

1. Suppose a Japanese boy came to stay with you for a month. Check the

things below that you would most likely have to do to make him feel just the same as he would at home.

_____a. Make a bed for him on the floor.

_____b. Be more polite to your parents.

_____c. Feed him a lot of turkey and beef.

_____d. Take him to church every Sunday.

_____e. Make kites with him.

_____f. Play football with him.

_____g. Put your television away.

_____h. Have him take off his shoes before entering the house.

_____i. Take him to baseball games.

_____j. Shorten the legs on the dining room table.

2. There are many people in the small country of Japan, but the Japanese people have made their country very comfortable for themselves. Check the sentences below that tell how they did this.

_____a. They learned how to make good use of space.

_____b. They passed laws to keep other people out.

_____c. They worked out rules of politeness for everyone.

_____d. They encouraged most of their people to farm.

_____e. They used their natural resources carefully.

_____f. They became interested in beautiful things.

_____g. They fought wars to get more land.

3. A Japanese person coming to our country would find it hard to understand some of the things we do. Check the things below that he would not understand very well.

_____a. How we use our land.

_____b. How we use radios and television sets.

_____c. How children are treated.

_____d. How we build our homes.

_____e. How we entertain our friends.

_____f. How we do our shopping.

_____g. How we run our schools.

_____h. How we vote.

For fifth-grade pupils studying about the United States

1. Below are six reasons for which people today move from one country to another, or move from one part of the country to another:

a. To make a better living.

b. To have a change.

c. To find a healthier place in which to live.

d. To enjoy better government.

e. To worship God as they wish.

f. To get rich quickly.

The first reason is the most important today. The second is second in importance, the third is third in importance, and so on, until the sixth reason. It is least important today. How would you change the order of these reasons for the people who first came to this country? How would you change the order for the people living in this country in 1800? How would changes be made for the people living in this country in 1849?

2. Pioneers going to Alaska today have to know these things:

    _____a. How to use the machines available to clear the land.

    _____b. How to get medicines, doctors, clothing, and many food supplies from towns and cities to their homes.

    _____c. How to live in a very different climate.

    _____d. How to use wildlife and other natural things in order to live.

    _____e. How to use the land.

    The pioneers going to Boonesborough had to know some of the same things. Place a check before each of the things above that Daniel Boone and his friends had to know.

3. Columbus tried to find a new route to the Indies. We know the success that he had. What could we say would happen next?

    a. Many Spanish settlers would come to America.

    b. Other explorers would ask Columbus about his route.

    c. More explorers would sail to seek a new route.

    d. Spain would soon have all the spices it needed.

For sixth-grade pupils studying about Latin America

1. We know that Latin America is generally rich in natural resources, yet many of its people live poorly. Check the sentence in each group below that best explains this:

    a. *Labor.*

        _____1. The workers are not very ambitious.

        _____2. The workers do not have the necessary skills.

        _____3. The worker are poorly organized.

        _____4. The workers can't do much because of the heat.

    b. *Capital.*

        _____1. There is no money available for investing in capital goods.

        _____2. Machinery and other capital goods are not available.

        _____3. Most of the money is tied up in private bank accounts.

        _____4. The climate makes machinery hard to keep running.

    c. *Management.*

        _____1. Latin American businessmen dislike new ideas.

        _____2. Latin American businessmen are happy just to make a living.

        _____3. Businessmen are considered unimportant in Latin America.

        _____4. Businessmen are a small group in the population of Latin America.

2. Almost anyone could make the statements below. Because of Hispanic culture, it is likely that Latin Americans would make some of these statements more often. Put a check before each statement that a Latin American would be most likely to say.

_____a. I believe that a man should try very hard to be successful.

_____b. I believe that a man's honor is his finest possession.

_____c. I believe that a man should be true to God and himself.

_____d. I believe that a man should respect his government.

_____e. I believe that things should be thought over carefully before one acts.

_____f. I believe that my country should help me to live better.

For seventh-grade pupils studying about ancient Greece

1. The ancient Athenians had developed a democracy. We call our government a democracy, but we do some things in government that the Athenians did not do. Read the following list carefully and check the ideas that would seem strange to an ancient Athenian.

_____a. We elect important government officers.

_____b. We elect a congress to make our laws.

_____c. We permit citizens to vote.

_____d. Most of our people over twenty-one years of age are citizens.

_____e. We have judges and lawyers in our courts.

_____f. Most of our trials are jury trials.

_____g. Our trials often last for days.

2. The ancient Athenians contributed richly to our civilization. If you were walking down the main street of our city, you would find evidence of these contributions. Check the places and instances below where you would see this evidence.

_____a. A bus stop.

_____b. A bank front.

_____c. A dropped coin.

_____d. A newspaper headline about government.

_____e. A street with high curbs and deep gutters.

_____f. A music store show window.

_____g. A litter can on a corner.

_____h. A soldier in uniform.

_____i. A bookstand.

_____j. A telephone booth.

_____k. A lady shopper.

_____l. A theater notice: *The Men, A Tragedy of War!*

For eighth-grade pupils studying about government

1. Suppose that the following changes, and only these changes, were made in our government:

a. Only citizens forty years of age would be considered eligible for election to the United States Senate.

b. A term for a Senator would be ten years.

c. Elections of Senators would occur every five years.

How would these changes effect the operation of government as compared to its present operation? Place a check before each of the following that indicates how the operation of government would be effected:

_____1. Assure more sound decisions by the Senate.

_____2. Give the Senate more power than the House of Representatives.

_____3. Make the Senate the strongest.

_____4. Cause conflicts to arise between the President and the Senate.

_____5. Reduce the closeness of contact between the Senate and the people.

_____6. Make the Senate an honorary body rather than a working body.

2. As a member of the American democracy, you decide that baseball should be the only legal national sport. Check the ways below that would most likely work to make baseball the only legal national sport:

_____a. Write to your congressman.

_____b. Make speeches that convince others of your point of view.

_____c. Start a campaign to get people to attend no games except baseball games.

_____d. Join a group that believes the same as you do.

_____e. Convince as many people as you can that other games are harmful.

_____f. Tell everyone that you meet that baseball is the only really American game.

_____g. Become a member of a group attached to many other groups and make yourself heard.

_____h. Play baseball everyday in a place where many people can see you.

For ninth-grade pupils studying about world geography.

1. Study the chart below carefully.

	Nation A	Nation B
Area	20,000 sq. mi.	40,000 sq. mi.
Population	1,000,000	1,000,000
Per capita income	$700	$700
Annual potato production	2,000,000 bu.	2,000,000 bu.
Price of potatoes per pound	2¢	4¢

Place a check before each of the conditions below that best explains the difference in the price of potatoes in the two nations.

_____a. Nation B is a nation of rice eaters; Nation A is a nation of potato eaters.

_____b. Nation B uses a large part of its arable land for potato growing; Nation A uses a small part of its arable land for potato growing.

_____c. Nation B exports many of its potatoes; Nation A exports few of its potatoes.

_____d. Nation B is an agricultural nation; Nation A is an industrial nation.

_____e. Nation B has poor transportation facilities; Nation A has excellent transportation facilities.

_____f. Nation B is enjoying peaceful relations with its neighbors; Nation A is not.

2. Nation X is a sparsely inhabited, small equatorial country which is mostly mountains and desert. Its mineral resources are rich. Its religion discourages activity with other peoples. Its government is operated by a popularly elected parliament. Check the conditions below which are most likely to prevail in Nation X:

_____a. A high per capita income.

_____b. Low technological development.

_____c. An unhappy, rebellious people.

_____d. Simple patterns of life for survival.

_____e. Growing interest in the development of resources.

_____f. Concern for positive international relations.

Most of the items presented above are of a combination multiple-choice, true-false type. It would not require much effort to convert them to the more conventional multiple-choice or true-false items. However, as they stand, they present widened areas of facts and ideas within which the pupil is to think to determine answers. It would also be easily possible to convert most of the items above to subjective items by slightly rewording them and omitting responses from which the pupil is to select. To illustrate how younger children may be presented with subjective test items and the greater expressive latitude of subjective items, the following examples are offered.

For kindergarten pupils studying about the family

1. Oral directions: Paint the work of a father of the family.
2. Oral directions: Paint a family working together.

For first-grade children studying community workers

1. Oral directions: Draw three pictures of policemen. Show a different kind of policeman in each picture.
2. Oral directions: Draw a picture that shows who really pays the policeman.

For second-grade pupils studying about communication

1. Oral directions: Draw a picture of a person who must communicate because he has a problem. Draw the best machine that he can use to carry his words.
2. Oral directions: Suppose that you could not leave your house and you wanted to speak to your friend. He lives at the other end of the block. Your telephone does not work, and there is no one around to take a message to him. Draw a picture showing how you would communicate with him.

For third-grade pupils studying about the community

1. Draw a map of an imaginary city. Be sure to label all its parts. Show with red crayon the streets that have the heaviest traffic.
2. Draw a map showing two cities. Show how the two cities depend on each other.

For fourth-grade pupils studying about the state

1. Our state has grown very much during the last ten years in the number of people that it has. Suppose that another state would want to grow in the number of people that it has. What would you tell it to do?
2. Some people want us to have more state parks. Some do not. Answer the following questions: Why do some people want more state parks? Why do some people not want state parks? OR Draw two cartoons. Have one show why some people want more state parks. Have one show why some people do not want more state parks.

For fifth-grade pupils studying about the United States

1. Select an event, a person, or an invention that you think helped the most in the westward growth of the United States. Tell how it helped the most.
2. Pretend that you are a boy or girl in early Boonesborough. Write a paragraph or draw a picture that answers the following:

    What would be your chores?
    What would your dinner be like?
    What would you do during Indian attacks?
    What things would you do to have fun?

For sixth-grade pupils studying about Latin America

1. There are many poor people in Latin America. Here are several suggestions on how we can help them:

    a. Send money to the governments of Latin American countries.

   b. Send food and clothing and food directly to the people.

   c. Send teachers and advisors to help Latin Americans learn to use their resources better.

   d. Send nothing and let the Latin American people take care of their own problems.

Which of these suggestions do you think is best? Tell why. OR Select one of these as best and draw a cartoon showing it as best; then suggest one of the suggestions as worst and draw a cartoon showing it as worst, OR Select one of these: Write a list of reasons for its use; then write a list of reasons against it. OR Select one of these: Draw a cartoon in its favor, then draw another against it.

2. Using your desk outline map and crayons, show the trade relationships between Latin America and the other parts of the world. Show the kinds of products that are traded. On the back of your map, write a summary statement about the trade relationships between Latin America and other parts of the world.

For seventh-grade pupils studying about ancient Greece

1. Write a brief paragraph telling how an ancient Athenian felt about his rights as a citizen.

Write a brief paragraph telling how an ancient Spartan felt about his rights as a citizen.

Write a brief paragraph telling how you feel about your rights as compared to the feelings of the ancient Athenian or Spartan.

2. We know that Athens was conquered by Sparta. We have some ideas why this happened. Make a poster or write a newspaper editorial in which you warn the Athenians and suggest what they ought to do to prevent their downfall.

For eighth-grade pupils studying about government

1. Suppose that a strong group wants a law that will make it illegal for any person to criticize our government in a book, magazine, or newspaper. The group convinces a Representative to present a bill to the House. Trace its most likely path from this point. You may use a carefully labeled diagram in your answer or as your answer.

2. It is often said that there is a responsibility for every right. Choose five rights from our Bill of Rights. Describe each briefly. Then state a responsibility for each.

For ninth-grade pupils studying about world geography

1. Here are some facts about an imaginary country:

   a. Area: 156,356 sq. mi.

   b. Population: 3,746,202

   c. Location: Between 30° and 40° North latitude.

d. Topography: Two large valleys lying to the east and west of a range of mountains. Several large rivers angle out of the mountains and flow southward to a sea on the southern boundary of the country.

e. Resources: Rich soil, forests, coal deposits.

f. Transportation: Very poor.

g. Government: Generally democratic with a parliament and figurehead king.

From the facts given above, describe briefly the main industries of the country, its contributions to world trade, its political relationships with other nations, and its greatest problem as a nation in the world.

2. We know that most of the emerging nations of Africa are having difficulties as independent countries. They have several serious lacks. Make a list of these, and then for each lack suggest what the African people themselves can do about it.

You may use a carefully labeled diagram as a part of your answer or as the answer itself.

As may be noted above, subjective test items are as applicable in the early grades as they are in the later grades. In the early grades the medium of expression with which to respond to a subjective item is painted or drawn objects rather than language. It is to be noted also that certain items all through the grade require either a response to be made through a medium of expression other than formal language or give the pupil a choice in selecting between formal language and another medium. Such a practice encourages the pupil to organize facts and ideas in a way more suitable for him and without a penalty because of his lack of skill with formal language. In several instances the items are broken down into parts to which the pupil is to respond one at a time. This frees him to think about his response and discourages him from the "spray" response in which he writes down all that he can remember in a disorganized pattern of facts and ideas.

If the social-studies teacher decides to place heavy emphasis on the retention and application of facts and ideas in gathering data for evaluating his pupils, the least that he can do is to share his intentions with them. The pupils should be informed as to how much tests "count" as the teacher attempts to decide how much they have achieved. After so informing them, he follows the procedure of guiding them through a review before each test and patiently teaches them how to prepare for tests by themselves. If he does not do these things, his tests are little more than acts of vengeance.

To this point only the teacher-made devices are gathering data on how well children retain and apply (in a limited way) facts and ideas from social studies. As can be seen, the preparation of these devices requires time, care, and ingenuity. A somewhat simpler task is the preparation of teacher-made devices for gathering data on how well children use the various skills needed for acquiring facts and ideas in social studies.

Each of these skills by itself is of limited utility because each is a separate act in the skill of investigation. For example, if a child can analyze a statement of purpose such as a question or a topic and successfully determine the entry word or entry idea that he is to use in an index or a table of contents, and he can perform this act only, he is not going to go very far in his investigation. Other acts in sequence are required for him to complete his task. However, the teacher can gather data on how well a child investigates by preparing a device to measure each act. If he decides to do this, he must prepare devices for all the acts in various sequences such as the following:

Analyzing statements of purpose to determine entry words (index)
1. Finding the entry word in an index.
2. Interpreting the data after the entry word in the index.
3. Skimming the page or a series of pages to determine the best place at which to begin reading.
4. Note taking (or outlining).

Analyzing statements of purpose to determine entry ideas (table of contents)
1. Finding the entry idea in a table of contents.
2. Skimming a series of pages to determine the best place at which to begin reading.
3. Note taking (or outlining).

Analyzing statements of purpose to determine whether a globe or map is required
1. Location in an atlas. (Not always necessary in an elementary classroom).
2. Location on a map or globe, or both.
3. Interpreting the symbols on a map or globe.
4. Note taking.

Analyzing statements of purpose to determine what is the best source for information
1. Using various sources (including use of the table of contents or index).
2. Note taking (or outlining).

Tests for determining individual efficacy in the performance of such acts can be devised rather easily in some instances. An index or a table of contents in a basic textbook can often serve as the material with which the pupil works as he answers items on the test. A set of different reference books arranged on a table can be considered as the basic sources available in the classroom, and the pupil can indicate which he would use for the various purposes presented in the test. A page or a series of pages in a basic textbook can serve as a test artifact for skimming. In accord with the question on his tests, the child skims and writes as his response the first few words of the side heading. A carefully chosen page in a textbook makes an excellent artifact for testing note taking or outlining. A map in the basic textbook serves well as a test artifact for map reading. The overwhelming advantage of using classroom materials as test artifacts is that these materials are available to the child. The artificiality of the test is reduced.

Other tests may require a little more ingenuity in the preparation of the test artifact. An example of such a test:

Draw a line under the word in each of the following questions that will be a good entry word to look for in an index:
1. How is cotton harvested?
2. What are the uses of hemp?
3. Where is Savannah?
4. How much wheat is grown in Kansas each year?
5. Who was Henry Knox?
6. Why are sheep dipped?
7. What are the important products of Rumania?
8. How much steel is produced in Russia?
9. What is the population of China?
10. What causes soil erosion?

Such a test can be made more difficult by making the questions, or statements of purpose, more complicated.

One of the better devices for testing a child's ability in investigating is to link several of the acts together, as shown in the following example:

Do these things with the questions below:
1. Read each question carefully.
2. Draw a line under the word that you would use as an entry word.
3. Use the index in *Louisiana Today* to find the page where you would

begin to read. Write down the number of the page after the question.
1. How important is shrimp fishing in our state?
2. Where is Baton Rouge?
3. How much rice is grown in our state?
4. What is the population of our state?
5. What are the important industries of our state?

All the acts of a single sequence can be linked together, as in the following:

Use *American Transportation* as you work with the following question: Who invented the first successful steamboat?
1. Write the word you will use as an entry-word._____
2. On what page will you begin reading to find an answer to the question?
   _____
3. Where will you begin to read carefully to find the answer to your question? Write the first three words of the section here._____
   _____
4. What will your note be? Write it here._____
   _____

Developing devices for testing many skills offers few problems. Perhaps the greatest error in testing each act of a skill is that too much emphasis on a single act may lead the child toward a distorted idea of what the total skill is as a series of acts that must occur one after the other in rapid sequence or he may never achieve a total idea of the skill. Testing for a sequence of acts generally results in a better indication of how well the child performs a skill.

WORK SAMPLES

An excellent source for data on how well a child retains and applies ideas and how well he uses various skills is the work which he has performed. Careful examination of samples of his work from time to time reveals the growth that he has made over a period of time as well as a total picture of his ability. It is not unusual to find that children have lows and peaks of performance due to differences in commitment in the task, in feeling of healthy well-being, and other factors. Considered as a total, the work samples of a child provide, in full dimension of a child's ability, a series of closely interrelated skills or of a somewhat discrete skill.

Skills more or less discrete in nature include summarizing, note taking, outlining, and making an outline. There is no better indication of how well a child can use these skills than the products which he makes as a result of applying these skills. His summaries, sets of notes, and outlines are rich evidence of his competencies.

Interrelated skills are involved in preparing and presenting reports, preparing charts, diagrams, and maps, writing creative stories and poems, writing editorials, participating in play production and presentation, drawing cartoons and posters, and constructing models. These reflect what a child knows about a topic or issue, how well he organizes and presents facts, and how well he uses the supportive skills necessary to production. In a classroom in which there is much expressive activity at the close of study of parcels of facts and ideas, the teacher has readily available much evidence of children's achievement.

As the social-studies teacher examines work samples in which interrelated skills have been applied, his first concern is for the facts and ideas used and the organization and presentation of facts and ideas. He is concerned with spelling, handwriting, and aspects of draftsmanship, but only secondarily so.

All in all, work samples tend to be more valid and reliable than tests as sources for data on how well children retain and apply information. Work samples are excellent evidence to be presented to parents who are truly interested in how their children do. However, ours is a test-conscious society. The child's later years in the public schools will likely be fraught with tests which will often serve as the chief source for data on his progress. The elementary social-studies teacher has little choice but to present a testing program, if for no other reason than to teach children how to take tests.

EVALUATING THE CHILD AS A PERSON

Education, like other sciences, is a system of growing knowledge abstracted from a few relatively simple principles. In education these principles, which are themselves abstractions stated at a low level of sophistication, are about learning, children as children, and children as learners. The many ramifications of these principles form varied patterns of abstraction which branch out into vast, interwoven, ever-extending, ever-changing networks of ideas on how to instruct and educate children to become what they can become as measured on vague grids of cultural expectancies. One of the networks of ideas has to do with elementary social studies. With such a demanding array of ideas, the social-studies teacher often becomes so engrossed in guiding the child in developing as an inquirer, as a participant in group work, and as an informed person, that he forgets that the child is also a person. Of course, the basic principles, from which the pattern of abstraction stems and ramifies, reflect a concern for the child, but the emphasis is on the child as a learner whose choices are closely restricted. When the child is considered as a person, attention is focused on him as a being who chooses what is to be particularly his own from social studies.

Unfortunately, the child's exercise of free choice is often influenced negatively by the way in which his growth in social studies is reported to his parents. All too frequently teachers follow questionable practices such as downgrading pupils on the first report and upgrading them on the final report to show a fallacious increment of growth; downgrading active, challenging children and upgrading quiet, compliant ones; and emphasizing certain aspects of learning in the classroom but reporting only on others. When such practices are followed, the child's efforts are toward survival rather than seeking in social studies those things which he can claim as part of himself.

To encourage the exercise of the child's free choice in social studies, reporting practices should meet the following criteria:

1. The report should reflect the social-studies program in the class-room. If the program is predominantly one of inquiry, the child's growth as an inquirer will be reported both qualitatively and quantitatively. The weight given to inquiry in the over-all assessment of the child's growth in social studies will be clearly indicated.

2. The report should be based on an abundance of data gathered on the child's performance in the various areas of social studies. No area will be slighted for any other regardless of the weight given to any particular area.

3. The report should be expressed in terms understandable to both the child and his parents. Such reporting devices as the parent-teacher confer-ence, the parent-teacher-pupil conference, and a report form which includes a comprehensive breakdown of the areas of emphasis in social studies stated in terms of pupil-behaviors should be used.

Rigorous application of these criteria will result in an honest, straightforward report. To be sure, there will be difficulties. Parents may not understand the emphasis in the program, but the informed, sincere teacher should be able to help them understand. The gathering of abundant data on the child's performance requires an attention to detail not easily given in a busy classroom, but a judicious use of time makes the gathering of data possible. District reporting practices may not directly support comprehensive reporting, but few administrators will discourage teachers from using devices which richly supplement district policy. The greatest difficulty is that an honest, carefully prepared report occasionally may not be received well by the child and his parents. The usual reason for this is the inability of parents to accept the child as he is, which contributes to the child's inability to accept himself. However, the report must and should be given. If carefully presented, it may improve parent-child relationships.

In most instances, the carefully prepared report encourages the child to be a person in his own right. He has no burden of guilt or falsely based confidence. He is free to seek in social studies what is significant to him as an individual.

His freedom may be reflected in his overt, honest expression of enthusiasm for everything that occurs in social studies.

Or he may be more selective in using his freedom. Perhaps he will show a preference for going his way by seeking or developing and completing projects about topics or issues in social studies. He may find certain activities, such as gathering facts, so self-satisfying that he readily and happily commits himself to them each time that they occur.

His exercise of freedom may result in unpredictable behaviors, such as a deep fascination for maps, globes, and atlases, for an event such as the Civil War, for the discovery of Viking artifacts that challenge the credit given to Columbus for finding America, or for a distant people such as the Watusi of Africa or the Japanese. He may manifest a deep concern for some aspect of conservation or government or for a political, economic, or social issue. Most surprising of all, he may one day arrive at a significant generalization and turn to his teacher to ask, as much in wonder as in fun, "What if . . . ?"

Exercises for Further Understanding

1. Obtain a copy of several standardized tests that contain sections on social studies. Analyze each for the following:

(a) Types of items. Are they for the most part factual to determine retention of facts? If other kinds of items are included, what skills are being examined in the test? Are there items in which the pupil's ability to think critically is tested?

(b) Scope of the test. Are there samplings of learnings from all the social sciences, or are there only two or three from which samplings have been taken? Does the test include both subject matter and skills?

2. Develop an informal test for measuring ability at inquiry. If you are now teaching, or student teaching, develop the test for pupils in your classroom and apply it.

3. Devise an observation sheet to be used for gathering data on a child's behavior during group work in social studies. If you are now teaching, or student teaching, use the sheet as you observe several children. Or, if you have observation privileges at a nearby school, arrange to observe a child during group work in social studies. If possible, take a classmate with you to use the same observation sheet to observe the same child. Then compare your findings with your classmate's.

4. If you are teaching, or student teaching, make an anecdotal record of the behavior of a child whose behavior tends to be at the extreme range of normal expectancy. Or, if you have observation privileges at a nearby school, arrange to observe a child.

5. Use the unit which you have developed, or one of the units presented in the Appendix, as the basis for making an informal, objective test for the retention of facts and ideas. Develop the test for only one section of the unit. Then develop an informal, subjective (essay) test for the same section.

6. Develop a simple test for measuring children's ability to use reference books. If possible, try your test out on a group of children.

7. Develop a simple test for measuring children's ability to read maps. If possible, try it out on a group of children.

8. Suppose that a friend of yours who teaches grade five asserts that he has established a sound basis for evaluating his pupils in social studies. You discover that his sound basis for evaluating is a weekly test. What do you think about this? What further information will you need before you can really arrive at a sound opinion about this practice?

Selected References

Dunfee, Maxine, and Helen Sagl, *Social Studies through Problem Solving*, Chap. 12, "Evaluating Children's Progress toward Desirable Goals." New York: Holt, Rinehart and Winston, Inc., 1966.

Ebel, Robert L., "The Problem of Evaluation in Social Studies." *Social Education*, 24:6-10 (January 1960).

Gall, Morris, "Improving Competence in Judgment." *Social Education*, 30:88 (February 1966).

Hubin, Irene A., "The Evaluation of Citizenship." *Social Studies*, 49:96-99ff (March 1958).

Jarolimek, John, *Social Studies in Elementary Education*, 2d ed., Chap. 16, "Evaluation of Social Studies Learnings." New York: The Macmillan Company, 1963.

Michaelis, John U., *Social Studies for Children in a Democracy*, 3d ed., Chap. 18, "Evaluation." Englewood Cliffs, N.J.: Prentice-Hall, Inc., 1963.

National Council for the Social Studies, *Evaluation in Social Studies*, Harry D. Berg, ed., Thirty-fifth Yearbook of the N.C.S.S., Washington, D.C.: National Education Association, 1965.

Preston, Ralph C., *Teaching Social Studies in the Elementary Schools*, rev. ed., Chap. 14, "Evaluating Pupil Achievement." New York: Rinehart & Company, Inc., 1958.

Ragan, William B., and John D. McAulay, *Social Studies for Today's Children*, Chap. 14, "Evaluating and Reporting Pupil Progress;" and Chap. 15, "Evaluating the Social Studies Program." New York: Appleton-Century-Crofts, 1964.

Samford, Clarence D., "The Objectives of Social Living in Elementary Schools." *Social Studies*, 50:23-25 (January 1959).

Appendix

EXAMPLES OF UNITS IN SOCIAL STUDIES

Each unit included here follows a different strategy. In certain respects the units may differ from the units presented in Chapter 5, for each represents a different way of expressing instructional intent.

The units are offered as examples of strategic planning— *Farming as an Important Industry,* a thinking-emphasis unit for grade two; *Japan,* a fourth-grade unit reflecting the synthesized strategy; and *Economic Aspects of America's Beginnings,* an eighth-grade unit following the social-science strategy.

The grade for which each unit is prepared is of secondary concern. No assumption is made here that one strategy is better than the others at one grade level or another.

Unit: Farming as an Important Industry (Grade 2)

[As you examine this unit, take particular note of the provisions the teacher has made for placing in issue the supporting ideas as well as the "big idea."]

Social-Studies Generalization: Most of the people in our country are dependent in many ways upon farmers for a large number of the things they need and use every day.

SECTION I. BUILDING INTEREST IN THE UNIT

Teaching Purposes:
1. To guide the children toward an awareness of differences in land-use patterns in the city and the country.
2. To help them sense that there are different kinds of farmers.
3. To suggest to them the importance of farming as the beginning of an industrial change.
4. To guide them in organizing a structure of inquiry that lends direction to their study of the unit.

489

Content Related to Purpose:

Most of our people live in cities.

1. Most of the land in cities is used for dwellings, streets, stores, shops, and factories.
2. Most city people have little land to use for growing things.
3. Most city people have specialized jobs having little to do with farming.
4. Most city people know little about farming.

Materials

- Two pictures: an aerial view of a large city, an aerial view of farmland.
- A slice of bread, an empty sausage can with the label still on it, an empty corn-flakes box, and a spool of cotton thread.
- A series of pictures: Panel 1—a farmer hoeing; Panel 2—a farmer driving a tractor; Panel 3—a farmer at his desk; Panel 4—a rancher in a jeep.

Procedures

Using the aerial views, guide the pupils in a discussion which results in a basic understanding that land use in the city makes it impossible for city people to grow the things they eat.

Guiding the pupils' attention toward the slice of bread, the can, the box, and the cotton thread, have them react to these questions:

1. Does the farmer work in some way to help us have all of these things? How? In what way?
2. Thinking of the things that you are sure the farmer helps us have, do you believe that every farmer grows them, or that some farmers just grow special things? What makes you think so?

Presenting the pictures of the various farmers at work, ask this question: Do you think all of these men are farmers? Why?

Review the statements the pupils have made and indicate that from time to time they will again look at the pictures of the men (farmers) and at a slice of bread, the can, the box, and the spool of thread to see whether they have changed their minds.

SECTION II. WORKING IN THE UNIT TO ACQUIRE FACTS AND IDEAS

Facts and Ideas To Be Acquired (A)

A few of our people live away from the city on parcels of land which they use in various ways to produce foodstuffs and raw materials used in making useful things. The people who work the soil to grow things or who use the land to grow animals usually are called farmers.

1. Working the soil almost always includes these steps:
   a. Tearing up the soil (plowing)
   b. Breaking up the lumps of soil (harrowing, discing)
   c. Planting seeds or plants
   d. Sometimes keeping soil loose around plants (cultivating and weeding)
   e. Sometimes watering the plants (irrigating)
   f. Gathering the crop (cutting, pulling, picking, threshing)
2. Using the land to grow animals almost always includes these steps:
   a. Forming a flock or herd
   b. Caring for the flock or herd
   c. Separating the product from the herd or flock
      (1) Animals for meat
      (2) Animal products such as milk, wool, etc.

Materials (A)
- Film: *Growing Corn*
- Film: *The Poultry Farm*

Procedures (A)
Purpose setting: Guide the pupils into considering the kinds of things that a farmer who grows plants has to do, and the kinds of things that a farmer who raises animals or birds has to do. Record their responses on the chalkboard, then guide them into arranging the order of the things he does.

Investigation: Present the films.

Purpose checking: Show the pupils their recorded responses and guide them into checking the responses for omitted steps or steps out of order.

Expression: Have the pupils pantomime the acts of farmers who grow plants and of those who raise birds or animals.

Individual projects:
1. Plant a small garden at home, care for it, and report to the class about progress from time to time.
2. Write a story about a farmer.
3. Make a book about what the farmer does.

Facts and Ideas To Be Acquired (B)
Some farmers all over our country use their farms mainly as a means of growing things they can use themselves.
1. Such a farm is usually small: 30 to 80 acres.
2. Such a farm has a variety of small buildings:
   a. A small house for the family.

b. A barn, barnyard, a toolshed, a chickenhouse, a pigpen, and perhaps a silo.

3. Such a farm is laid out in small fields used for various purposes.

   a. A garden plot near the house used for growing vegetables such as tomatoes, lettuce, onions, radishes, beets, and the like.

   b. Small patches of land for potatoes and sweet corn.

   c. A pasture for cows to graze.

   d. Small fields for growing hay and grain for the animals to eat.

   e. Some fields for growing a crop or two to sell.

   f. Perhaps an orchard of fruit trees.

   g. Perhaps a berry patch.

4. The farmer on such a farm uses hand tools, animals, and some machinery to do his work.

   a. Hoes, spades, and cultivators.

   b. Mules or horses (sometimes a small tractor) for pulling loads.

   c. Plows, mowers, rakes, harrows, wagons, to be drawn across the fields in preparing them for planting, in planting crops, and in harvesting crops.

5. The whole family is often involved.

   a. The farmer does the heavy work in the fields.

   b. His wife and children do some of the lighter work.

      (1) Feeding the animals.

      (2) Care for the vegetable garden.

      (3) Milking the cows.

   c. His wife does much food preserving with the help of the children.

      (1) Canning meat, fruits, and vegetables.

      (2) Sometimes drying fruits.

6. The purpose of such a farm is to provide as directly as possible for the immediate needs of the farmer and his family.

   a. Vegetables and fruits to be eaten immediately and to be preserved for future use.

   b. Hogs, chickens, and cows to be used for meat.

   c. Chickens to produce eggs.

   d. Cows to produce milk.

   e. A specialty crop or two and other surpluses to be sold for money to buy foods, clothing, and tools that cannot be produced on the farm.

7. Although such farms as these are to be found everywhere in our country, there are many to be found in the South, East, and parts of the Middle West.

8. These farms have some importance to the rest of the people in our country.

a. They grow some surplus foodstuffs and raw materials used by others.

b. They provide steady work for some of our people.

Materials (B)

- A stylized sketch of a small farm on 28" x 22" tagboard, or a picture showing a panoramic view of a small farm.
- A stylized sketch of a huge farm on 28" x 22" tagboard, or a picture showing a panoramic view of a huge farm.
- Basic flannel-board figures: the farmer, Mr. McDonald; his wife, Mrs. McDonald; and his children, Jim and Mary.
- Sequence 1 to be used with basic figures: a house, a barn, a barnyard, a toolshed, a chickenhouse, a pigpen.
- Sequence 2, to be used with basic figures: a vegetable garden, a hay field, a pasture, a cornfield, an orchard.
- Sequence 3, to be used with basic figures: hoe, spade, and cultivator; team of horses, a wagon, a plow, mower, a hay rake.
- Sequence 4, to be used with basic figures: fresh fruits, fresh vegetables, canned fruits and vegetables, canned and smoked meat, dressed chicken and eggs, milk, sacks of dried foods.
- Sequence 5, a variety of articles of clothing, flour, sugar, coffee, books, tools.
- A large physiopolitical map of the United States.

Procedures (B)

Purpose setting: Presenting the two sketches of farms, have the pupils consider this problem: One farmer has a small farm (clarify what is meant by "small farm"). Another has a very large farm. Which of these two farmers do you think tries to grow and raise most of the things his family needs? Record the pupils hypothetical statements and guide them in analyzing which are the most reasonable.

Investigation: Using the basic flannel-board figures and sequences, conduct flannel-board "stories," in which the pupils respond to the various figures to the limits of their knowledge. Help children to correct and relate their knowledge through questioning and supplying information. Use the map to help the children gain some idea of where subsistence farming takes place.

Purpose checking: Guide the pupils in examining their original hypotheses. Help the pupils to understand that they have only those hypotheses relating to the self-sufficiency of one farmer. They must suspend judgment until the large farm has been studied.

Expression:

1. Dramatize a late summer day on a farm where the farmer and his family are involved in harvesting and preserving food.

2. Prepare illustrated charts showing what the farmer raises and what he has to buy.

Individual projects:

1. Make a small map of the farmer's farm showing the buildings and the uses of the various plots of ground.
2. Make a series of sketches showing the uses that the farmer may make of the things he raises. Example: Eggs for the family's use, such as for breakfast and baking, and eggs to be sold to obtain money for sugar, coffee, flour, and so on.
3. Make charts showing the work of the various members of the farmer's family.

Facts and ideas to be acquired (C)

Some farmers all over our country use small farms to raise a specialty crop or two to earn money.

1. Such a farm is usually small, 10 to 30 acres.
2. Such a farm usually has only a few buildings.
   a. Perhaps a home for the family, a tool shed.
   b. Sometimes no buildings at all (the farmer drives back and forth to his farm from his home in town).
3. Such a farm is laid out in a few large fields or may be on a big field.
4. The farmer uses hand tools and small machinery.
   a. Hoes, spades, and cultivating tools.
   b. A small tractor, a hand tractor, planting machines.
5. The farmer does most of the work himself.
   a. Sometimes members of his family help him.
   b. Sometimes he hires workers to help him to plant or harvest his crop.
6. The purpose of such a farm is to grow one or two crops at a time to be sold to stores and canneries.
   a. Tomato growing, from seed to fruit.
      (1) Growing the seedling.
      (2) Planting the seedling.
      (3) Protecting the plant from heat and cold.
      (4) Spraying the plant to prevent disease and harm from insects.
      (5) Cultivating and weeding the field.
      (6) Irrigating the field.
      (7) Picking the tomatoes.
   b. Orange growing.
      (1) Pruning the tree in late winter.
      (2) Disc-harrowing between the trees.
      (3) Building the irrigation ditches.

(4) Irrigating the trees.

(5) Spraying the trees to protect them from insects and disease.

(6) Picking the oranges.

7. Farms such as these produce fruits and vegetables for people all over the country.

Materials (C)

- The sketch of a small farm, listed in **Materials (B)**.
- A large sketch of a small farm used for growing a specialty. By comparison, it is somewhat smaller than the farm depicted in the sketch above and it is composed of one large field or two.
- A large chart of sketches showing Mr. Brown (the farmer), his wife, and three children of various ages from three to twelve: Billy, Ellen, and John.
- A large chart of sketches showing the buildings, tools, and machinery used on Mr. Brown's farm.
- A large chart of sketches showing workers helping with planting and harvesting.

*Basic social-studies book 2: *The Things We Need*, pp. 23-36, pp. 77-89.

Procedures (C)

Purpose setting: Present the sketch of the small farm (studied previously) and guide the pupils into reviewing the purposes of the subsistence farm. Then show the second sketch and present this problem: Here is another small farm even smaller than Mr. McDonald's farm. Do you see any other differences? A Mr. Brown owns this other farm. Of the two, Mr. McDonald and Mr. Brown, which do you think makes more money? What makes you think so?

Investigation:

1. Using the large charts, through discussion, guide the pupils toward basic understandings about Mr. Brown's work on his farm and the roles performed by his family and other workers.

2. Guide the pupils in the use of *The Things We Need* to learn how tomatoes and oranges are grown and processed, where such farms need to to be located, and why they must be located in such places.

Checking purposes:

1. Using the sketches, help the pupils to recall their original statements about which of the farmers made the more money and to reexamine their statements after learning about Mr. Brown and the truck and orange farm. Guide them toward a restatement of ideas in accord with their new knowledge.

2. Using the new farm sketch and the two sketches previously studied, present again the problems previously discussed. Again guide toward suspended judgment.

Expression:
1. Planning and painting two sets of wall panels, one showing tomato growing and the other showing orange growing.
2. Making a chart showing how Mr. Brown uses his product, whatever it may be, to provide for his family's needs.

Individual projects:
1. Using interview and research techniques, or both, find out about the growing of a fruit or vegetable and report findings to the class.
2. Find out from the produce man in the grocery store where his merchandise comes from.
3. Make an imaginary map of a small vegetable or fruit farm.

Facts and ideas to be acquired (D)

Some farmers all over our country use small farms to raise animals for what they produce or for meat.

1. Such a farm is usually small, 10 to 30 acres.
2. Such a farm usually has quite a few buildings.
   a. The farmer's home.
   b. Houses and pens with yards for the animals.
   c. Sheds for storing food for the animals.
3. Almost the whole farm is covered with buildings and animal yards.
4. The farmer may use many machines and small tools, or only a few, depending on what he raises.
5. The farmer does much work himself, but he may hire year-around workers to help him.
6. The purpose of such a farm is to produce meats and other foods used daily in the city.
   a. The poultry farm.
      (1) Obtaining baby chicks.
      (2) Caring for baby chicks.
      (3) Forming a laying flock.
      (4) Caring for the laying flock.
         (a) Feeding and watering.
         (b) Cleaning the houses.
         (c) Spraying the houses.
         (d) Helping the flock to lay.
      (5) Gathering eggs.
      (6) Sorting, cleaning, and packing the eggs for market.

(7) Farms such as these produce turkeys, chickens, and rabbits for meat.

b. The dairy farm.

(1) Bringing the cows from the feed lots to the milking barn.

(2) Milking the cows (in the morning and evening) by machine.

(3) Cooling the milk.

(4) Pasteurizing the milk.

(5) Bottling the milk.

(6) Delivering the milk.

(7) Caring for the farm.

    (a) Cleaning feed lots.

    (b) Cleaning the milking barns.

    (c) Keeping the buildings in good repair.

7. Small farms that raise specialty crops and produce poultry and dairy foods are near big cities or are near good transportation.

8. These farms are of great importance to the whole country.

a. They provide many fresh foods for people in the cities.

b. They also provide many foods to be canned and frozen to be used all through the year.

c. They provide steady work for some of our people.

Materials (D)

- The sketches or panoramic views of farms used in previous sections.
- A sketch or panoramic view of a farm showing many long, low buildings and fenced areas.
- Film: *The Poultry Farm.*
- *Basic social studies book 2: *The Things We Need,* pp. 107-114, pp. 120-125.
- Field trip: The dairy.

Procedures (D)

Purpose setting: Using the sketch of the farm with its long, low buildings, present this problem: This is Mr. Wong's small farm. Mr. Wong is a neighbor of Mr. Brown, and he makes about as much money as Mr. Brown, but he does not have to dig in the soil and he has a year-around worker to help him. This worker does not have to dig in the soil, but he is quite busy doing other things. Have you any idea how Mr. Wong farms and what he raises?

Investigation:

1. Show the film *The Poultry Farm* as a basic means of finding out about Mr. Wong's farm.

2. Compare the findings resulting from viewing the film with what is given in the text, *The Things We Need*.
3. For further verification of process and product on a small farm used to raise animals, guide the pupils into considering the dairy farm in terms of ways in which it is similar to and different from the poultry farm.
4. Check statements in *The Things We Need* and compare the findings with those resulting from a field trip.
5. Guide the pupils in relating their experience and in checking in *The Things We Need* to determine where the poultry farm and the dairy farm are located, and why such a location is important.

Checking purposes:
1. Using the sketch used for establishing purposes, have the pupils recall their original statements about Mr. Wong's farm and make restatements in keeping with their findings.
2. Guide the pupils in relating the poultry farm to the dairy farm and arriving at a generalization about the work on the small farm used for raising animals.
3. Using all the sketches of farms, introduce again the problem presented earlier. Again guide toward suspended judgment.

Expression:
1. Make two large flow charts showing the steps involved in producing eggs and milk.
2. Roleplay a three-way conversation among Mr. McDonald, Mr. Brown, and Mr. Wong as they discuss:
   a. Very hot weather.
   b. Very cold weather.
   c. A long period of rain.
   d. A rise in the cost of eggs.
   e. A drop in the price of tomatoes.
   f. The family vegetable garden.

Individual projects:
1. Make a diorama of a chicken farm.
2. Using interview or library research techniques, or both, find out about a turkey, duck, or rabbit farm and report findings to the class.

Facts and Ideas To Be Acquired (E)
Farmers in some part of our country use large farms to produce grains to be sold.
1. Such farms cover hundreds, sometimes thousands of acres.
2. Such a farm may have many buildings.

    a. A fine home for the family.

    b. A large barn for storing machinery.

3. Such a farm is laid out in huge fields for growing the main crop.

4. The farmer uses large machines.

    a. Big tractors.

    b. Gangplows.

    c. Large disc-harrows.

    d. Special planting machines.

    e. Special harvesting machines.

5. The farmer's important work is to direct the work of others, although he does much other work.

    a. Regularly hired workers.

    b. Seasonal workers.

    c. His family's help.

6. The purpose of such a farm is to grow a huge crop.

    a. The wheat farm

        (1) Preparing the soil: plowing, harrowing, fertilizing.

        (2) Planting the seed with huge drills, winter or spring.

        (3) Harvesting the wheat with combines.

    b. The corn farm

        (1) Preparing the soil: plowing, harrowing, fertilizing.

        (2) Planting the corn by machine.

        (3) Cultivating the corn.

        (4) Harvesting the corn with a corn picker.

    c. Similar kinds of farms are used for growing cotton and tobacco.

7. Such farms are located in certain parts of our country because only these places have the right kinds of growing conditions.

    a. The corn belt: generally from Iowa to Ohio.

    b. The wheat country: Western Washington to Minnesota as far south as Kansas.

    c. Cotton: California, Arizona, Texas, and the Southeast.

    d. Tobacco: the Southeast.

8. The large-crop farm is one of the most important parts of the farming industry.

    a. It provides raw foodstuffs and raw materials to be made into products needed or used by almost everyone in the country.

        (1) Wheat: bread

        (2) Corn to be fed to meat animals

        (3) Cotton for clothing

    b. It provides work for some of our people.

Materials (E)

- All the sketches of farms used previously.
- A large chart depicting the farmer's home and barn.
- A flannel-board sequence of the various machines used on the wheat farm.
- A large chart showing the farmer at work, doing some farming tasks himself, directing the work of others, and working at his desk.
- A large chart showing the various machines used on a corn farm.
- *Basic social studies book 2, *The Things We Need*, pp. 126-133, pp. 134-141.
- A physiopolitical map of the United States.
- A large chart showing articles basic to our culture which have their beginning with a farm product, grain, or vegetable fiber.

Procedures (E)

Purpose-setting: Using the sketches of farms, introduce again the basic problem: if there are two farms, and one is quite small and the other quite large, which of the two would be most likely used to raise things for a farm family? Through guided discussion based upon review of past learnings and examination of the sketches, help the pupils to see that smallness by itself is not the only factor to be considered. Land-use pattern is another important factor that must be considered. When this is clear to the pupils, have them treat the basic problem in terms of what they already know to determine what the land-use pattern on a large farm must be. Guide the pupils into considering the type of crop grown on such a farm.

Investigation:

1. Using the large charts dealing with the wheat farmer's home and barn, his machinery, and his tasks, clarify definitively what a wheat farmer is.
2. Guide the pupils in finding more precise facts about wheat farming in *The Things We Need*, pp. 126-133.
3. Verify the basic work of the farmer on the large grain farm by having the pupils compare wheat farming and corn farming. Guide the pupils in studying the chart showing the machinery used in corn farming and in using *The Things We Need* to learn about corn farming.
4. Through map study, help the pupils to see where corn and wheat is grown in their country and why they are grown in these places, with special emphasis on topography. Touch upon need for sun and rain.
5. Using the chart depicting useful articles made from grains or vegetable fiber, guide the pupils toward the realization that the farmer stands at the beginning of the industrial chain.

Checking purposes: Refer again to the basic problem treating of the subsistence use of a small farm or of a large farm. At this point, the pupils have a reasonable solution to the problem.

Expression:

1. Dramatize the basic roles of the wheat farmer and the corn farmer.
2. Write a report about the work of the wheat farmer or the work of the corn farmer, or illustrate the various phases of their work with sets of individual sketches.
3. Make charts identifying basic everyday articles used by almost everyone and indicate the farm raw material needed for its manufacture.

Individual projects:

1. Using interviewing or library research techniques, find out about other important basic crops such as rice, soybeans, tobacco, and sugar beets.
2. Using an outline map, color the wheat states.
3. Using an outline map, color the corn states.

Facts and Ideas To Be Acquired (F)

In some parts of our country farmers use big parcels of land to produce animals to be sold.

1. Such farms (in the west called ranches) often cover thousands of acres.
2. Such a farm may have a few buildings scattered over it.
   a. A home for the rancher.
   b. Small homes for year-around workers.
   c. Tool sheds.
   d. Feeding sheds.
   e. Corrals.
3. Such a farm is laid out in huge, fenced-off feeding areas where the animals eat grass (called ranges).
4. The farmer on such a farm uses several forms of transportation to help in his work, as well as hand tools.
   a. Riding horses.
   b. Small trucks.
   c. Occasionally his own small airplane.
   d. Small tools for mending fences and working with animals.
5. The farmer's important work is to direct other workers in the care of animals.
   a. Regularly hired workers.
   b. Seasonal workers.
6. The purpose of such a farm is to provide many animals to be sold or for products that the animals produce.
   a. The cattle rancher.

(1) Keeps a producing herd of cows and bulls.
   (a) Has them driven from one range to another.
   (b) Keeps the herd well by treating sick animals or removing them.
(2) Separates the meat animals from the producing herd.
   (a) Calves for veal—six weeks or a little older.
   (b) Yearlings—animals about a year old.
(3) Sends the yearlings to be fattened on other farms.

  b. The sheep rancher.

(1) Keeps a producing herd of ewes and rams.
   (a) Has them driven from one range to another.
   (b) Keeps the herd well.
     [1] By having the animals dipped in insecticides.
     [2] By treating sick animals or removing them from the herd.
   (c) Separates the meat animals from the herd (not always) when they are about six weeks old and sends them to market.
   (d) In spring, has his animals sheared of their wool.

7. Most of these farms or ranches are to be found throughout the West and Southwest.

8. The large animal farm or ranch is another one of the most important parts of the farming industry.

  a. It provides most of the meat for the people of our country.

  b. It provides raw materials for other things, such as:

(1) Leather for shoes.
(2) Fat for soap and other useful things.
(3) Fertilizers.

  c. It provides work for some of the people of our country.

Materials (F)

- A picture of a grazing range (without cattle or sheep) representing a high grassy area with rocky mountains in the background.
- A large chart showing the various buildings and structures on a cattle ranch.
- A large chart showing the animals and machines that a modern cattle rancher uses.
- A large chart showing the cattle rancher at work on the range and in his office.

*Basic social-studies book 2, *The Things We Need*, pp. 141-160.

• A physiopolitical map of the United States.

• A large chart showing animal products.

Procedures (F)

Purpose setting: Showing the picture, present this problem: From what you can see in this picture, in what ways do you think a farmer could use this land? What do you think a farmer would most likely use this land for? What makes you think so?

Investigation:

1. Using the large charts and guided discussion, help the pupils to understand generally the environment within which the cattle farmer, or rancher, works and lives.

2. Guide the pupils in the use of *The Things We Need* to find out about the details of the cattleman's work.

3. Verify the basic pattern of the farmer as the raiser of animals on a large plot of land by guiding the pupils in the study of the sheep farm. Similarities and differences should be noted.

4. Using the map, help the pupils to understand the location of large sheep and cattle ranches. Place emphasis on topography.

5. Using the chart of animal products, guide the pupils toward an understanding that animals as raw material provide more than just meat.

Checking purposes:

1. Using the picture as a focus for recall of earlier statements about the use of the land, guide the pupils in correcting and restating statements.

2. Make a chart showing the differences betwen the work of the wheat farmer and the cattle rancher.

Expression:

1. Prepare a series of dioramas showing the various kinds of work of the cattle and sheep rancher.

Individual projects:

1. Using library research techniques, find out about the different kinds of cattle raised for meat on big ranches. Report findings to the class.

2. Using library research techniques, find out about hog farming. Report findings to the class.

3. Interview the head of the meat department at a grocery store to find where the meat he sells comes from. Report findings to the class.

4. Make a map showing where cattle are raised in the United States.

SECTION III. TYING IDEAS TOGETHER

Teaching Purposes:

1. To guide the children in developing a summary of the ideas and facts studied.

2. To encourage them to integrate ideas through expressive activity.
3. To bring them to and through the point of generalization to arrive at the "big idea."
4. To guide them in verifying the "big idea."
5. To help them to explore and develop positive attitudes toward farmers.
6. To aid them in determining positive patterns of action.
7. To encourage them to extend their ideas about farmers.

Summary

A. Ideas to be Generalized
1. The farm and farming stands at the beginning of several industrial chains in the production of foods and other useful articles.
   a. Wheat, flour, bread.
   b. Cattle, meat.
      Cattle, leather, shoes.
      Cattle, fats, soap.
   c. Vegetables, canned or frozen vegetables.
   d. Cotton, cloth, clothing.
   e. Others.
2. City people depend on farmers
   a. For foodstuffs and other raw materials.
   b. For jobs in the industrial chain.
3. Farmers depend on other farmers.
   a. No farmer can produce all the goods he needs.
   b. Most farmers are specialists raising only a crop or two or one kind of animal.
4. Farmers depend on city people
   a. To manufacture the things they need.
   b. To buy their products.

B. Generalization about Attitudes. All individuals and families in a modern society must respect and appreciate other individuals and families who help to produce the things they need.
1. The farmer's work is often difficult.
   a. Long hours during certain times of the year.
   b. Often must work when it is very hot or very cold.
   c. Often requires strength and endurance.
2. Often his work is very dangerous.
   a. Dangerous machinery may get out of control.
   b. Animals sometimes dangerous.
3. A farmer has to be a responsible, intelligent person.

    a. He must plan well.

      (1) The right kind of crop or crops in terms of people's needs.

      (2) The right kind of crop or crops for his land.

    b. He must understand the effect that his crops may have on people everywhere.

      (1) He must take good care of his land.

      (2) He must think carefully about the rules the government suggests that he follow.

    c. He must use many skills to raise crops or animals—many young farmers go to college to learn more.

    d. He must be prepared to take losses.

      (1) Weather change or fire may cause him to lose his crop or animals.

      (2) He handles his money carefully.

      (3) He uses all his skills to make his farm produce again.

C. Generalizations about patterns of action: Each one of us must understand the farmer's problems and work in helping him to solve them.

    1. Farmers sometimes produce too much; we should work to find new ways to use his products.

    2. Farmers often feel that they do not get enough money for their crops; we should work to find new ways to process foodstuffs (the processing often costs much more than the raw material).

    3. Many farmers have water problems; we should be sympathetic to his problems and try to help him solve them.

    4. Many farmers live for long periods with little contact with the rest of the people; we should work to find ways to help him see that he is an important person and a real member of the country's group of people.

D. Extensions:

    1. Farmers working in different places do things differently.

      a. Many farmers in Japan grow rice.

        (1) They must work in water and mud.

        (2) They do much work by hand.

        (3) They wear different kinds of clothing.

      b. Some farmers in Africa raise cattle.

        (1) They work on foot.

        (2) They use long staffs to help them in their work.

        (3) Sometimes they must use spears to protect their cattle from wild animals.

    2. Farming has changed.

      a. Long ago most farmers worked to raise the things needed by their families.

b. Today most farmers in our country raise just one thing and sell it to earn money.
3. In other places around the world farming has not changed much.
4. New things are happening in farming.

Materials:
- The pupils' expressive products dealing with foodstuffs and raw materials having their origin on the farm.
- Various empty cans and other commercial food containers with labels intact.
- Vegetables and fruits in season.
- The various instructional charts and flannel-board cutouts dealing with tools and machinery used on various farms.
- The sketches showing the farmer at work in the field, directing others, at his desk, and in a jeep.
- Some of the pupils' large expressive products depicting the farmers' work (murals and wall panels).
- A series of simple sketches pointing up the farmer's problems: Sketch 1, an unhappy farmer with a big pile of wheat with a for sale sign on it; Sketch 2, an unhappy farmer looking at apples costing ten cents each, as he thinks of the penny he received for each apple; Sketch 3, an unhappy farmer looking for water; Sketch 4, an unhappy farmer walking away from his empty mailbox.
- A picture of a Japanese rice farmer.
- A picture of an African cattle herder.
- Several pictures of pioneers farming.

Procedures

Using the pupils' various expressive products dealing with foodstuffs and raw materials, the empty commercial food containers, examples of vegetables and fruits in season, and articles of dress being worn by the pupils, establish that the farmer and the farm stands at the beginning of various industrial chains that produce needed goods for everyone. Help the pupils to recall what they know and to relate facts and ideas together through discussion.

Using the same materials, guide the pupils to seeing their dependence on the farmer and the farm.

Using the flannel-board cutouts of Mr. McDonald and Mr. Brown, and referring to the other farmers studied, guide the pupils into an understanding that farmers are independent. Touch upon the relationship between the cattle farmer and the farmer who raises grain to feed animals to fatten them for market.

Using the various cutouts and charts showing the tools and machinery used by the farmers, establish the farmer's dependence on the many people who live in the city. Guide also toward the realization that the other people are the buyers on whom he must depend.

Using the pupils' expressive products showing the farmer at work, guide the pupils into roleplaying in situations reflecting the difficulties, dangers inherent in his work, his need for special training, and his need to be economically efficient.

Presenting the sketches depicting the farmers' problems, guide the pupils into considering each problem and attempting to solve them in terms of their own behavior now and in the future within their level of understanding.

Using the pictures of farmers in other places and times, guide the pupils toward an awareness of change in farming and an awareness of differences in farming in other places.

Alert the pupils to possibilities of the farmer and farming in the news as an area to explore during the current-affairs period.

Unit: Japan
(Grade 4)

[This unit, originally prepared by Mrs. Sally Collier of San Diego County Schools, has been adapted to follow a synthesized strategy. Particularly worthy of note are the previsions for children to investigate independently and for maintaining interest at a high level in each idea area.]

Social-Science Generalization: The Japanese people have developed a culture that preserves their ancestral influences yet helps Japan participate in a modern world of cooperating nations.

SECTION I. BUILDING INTEREST IN THE UNIT

Teaching Purposes:
1. To guide children in establishing points of interest in the study of Japan.
2. To help children to express their interests in the form of questions.

Working in the Unit to Acquire Facts and Ideas
1. Supporting ideas:
   a. Japan is a modern Asiatic nation consisting of a group of volcanic islands lying to the east of the Asian mainland.

    b. The Japanese people have developed unique ways of living because of the geographic location of their country, its size, its climate, its topography, the availability of resources, and their cultural history.

    c. Modern Japan accepts cultural, political, and economic interdependency with other nations.

2. Areas of interest to be explored:

    a. Japan as a geographical entity.

    b. Contrasts in ways of living in Japan as reflected in daily family life.

    c. Japanese as an Oriental language and the ways it influences study at school.

    d. Japanese products as a part of everyday life in America.

    e. Religion in Japanese life.

    f. Contrasts in the ways that Japanese people use for recreation.

Materials

- A globe, a world map (political), a physical-political map of Japan, and several pictures of Mount Fuji.
- Selected panels from the Fideler picture-series on Japan (showing family life at home).
- Three charts of Japanese phrases, each dealing with the same content but rendered in a different writing style (kanji and kata kana, kata kana, and romaji).
- A collection of Japanese products or product containers: a transistor radio, a can of smoked oysters, a can of tuna, a can of mandarin oranges, a variety of small toys and party favors.
- Two pictures: Buddhist temple and a Shinto shrine.
- A newspaper account of baseball exhibition games in Japan, a picture of people celebrating the cherry-blossom festival, and a picture of two kendo fencers.

Procedures

Conceal the above materials at or near the front of the classroom before the children enter the classroom.

Distribute small slips of paper to the children and ask them to write down the first thing that they think of when you say a certain word. Then say the word: *Japan*.

Have several children help in tabulating the results (be prepared for allusions to World War II). After the categories have been established, guide the children in examining the sets of materials listed above. Conduct a brief discussion of each.

After the children have made a brief, guided analysis of all the sets of the materials, encourage them to express what they would like to know more about by having them list their preferences individually on paper. With the assistance of several children, process these expressions of interest before the class. When this activity has been completed, encourage the children to examine the results to develop questions to serve as guides for further study.

SECTION II. WORKING IN THE UNIT TO ACQUIRE FACTS AND IDEAS

Content: Physical Aspects

Japan is an Asiatic nation.

1. Japan is located in the Pacific Ocean near the east coast of Asia.
2. Japan consists of four main islands and several hundred smaller islands.
3. The total land area of Japan is about the size of the state of California.
4. Over 95 million people live in Japan.
5. Japan has many mountains and volcanoes which are part of the Pacific Ring of Fire.
6. Japan's climate is influenced by latitude and longitude, ocean currents, monsoons.

Materials: Physical Aspects

• Outline map of Japan approximately 24″ by 36″ mounted on the bulletin board.
• World political map.
*Japan, Pitts, pp. 9-10.
*Japan, Minugh and Cory, pp. 10-30.
• Globe.

Procedures: Physical Aspects

Purpose setting:

1. Guide the children in examining their questions (developed during the initiation) related to the geography of Japan.
2. Heighten interest by having the children discuss what they would see and feel on an automobile trip down the length of the country in the middle of July and then in the middle of January. Use the outline map as a focal point for discussion.

Investigation:

1. Using the world map and outline map, guide the children in establishing the location of Japan.
2. Using the globe and the world map, guide the children in computing the distance from Tokyo to other cities in the world.

3. Using the maps presented in *Japan* (Pitts), help the children to understand the topography of the country and its relative size.
4. Have the children read in *Japan* (Minugh and Cory) to find out about volcanoes and the climate of Japan.

Purpose checking:
1. Have the children consider again what they would see and feel on a trip through Japan.
2. Guide the children in discussing the questions discussed earlier.

Expression: Distribute outline maps (desk size) and encourage the children to select one of the following to express: the topography of Japan, the climate of Japan during one of the seasons, or the distance of Japan from other countries or places across the seas or oceans.

Individual projects:
1. Make a relief map of Japan.
2. Make a list of other countries approximately the same size in area. List also the population figures for the various countries.

Content: Homes

The Japanese people have developed unique ways of living because of their particular location, size, climate, topography, and history. Japanese homes are built to adapt to the weather and the people's ways of living.
1. Most homes have wide roofs to protect the wooden walls and paper windows from rain and to keep out the glare of the sun.
2. A porch or veranda around the outside protects the house in heavy rains.
3. Wooden or plaster outside walls keep the winter cold out.
4. Homes are built high off the damp ground.
5. Screens, shutters, and shoji (paper windows) control the temperature of the homes.
6. Construction is loose so homes move but won't fall during earthquakes.
7. Japanese homes have sliding walls inside, and the number of rooms changes depending on the needs during the day.
   a. Furnishings are usually not seen when not in use.
   b. Japanese sleep on mats on the floor.
   c. People sit on the floor.
   d. Some homes have one room with Western-style furniture.
8. In each home is a place of honor or tokonoma where guests are seated and which holds special family treasures.
9. Beautiful but simple gardens are important to Japanese homes.
10. Most homes now have electricity and running water, though some country homes use oil lamps or candles for light.
11. Large modern apartment buildings have been built in large cities.

12. Large buildings in downtown areas reflect American and European influences.
13. Homes generally show excellent use of space because it is so limited.
14. Materials used in homes are those available from Japanese resources.

Materials: Homes

- Series of pictures of homes found in America (urban, suburban, rural), jungle area, Japan, Spain, Arctic (approx. 11″ x 18″).
- *Japan*, Dearmin and Peck, pp. 63-67.
- *Japan*, Minugh and Cory, pp. 196-197.

Procedures: Homes

Purpose setting:

1. Have the children analyze their question or questions (developed during the initiation) about Japanese homes for more complete meaning.
2. To build greater interest, present the pictures of homes in other parts of the world and have them decide which would be most suitable for the different parts of Japan.

Investigation: Guide the children in the use of books.

Purpose checking:

1. Again showing the pictures of homes, have the children discuss their suitability for use in Japan.
2. Guide the children in evaluating their findings as answers to the questions.
3. Encourage the children to develop reasons for Japanese homes being the way they are—guide them in considering such factors as climate, earthquake conditions, available materials, and customs.

Expression:

1. Using a corner of the classroom, have class plan and set up portion of Japanese home including tokonoma.
2. Encourage pupils to collect authentic items for the corner.
3. Draw pictures of Japanese homes.

Individual projects:

1. Sketch floor plan of typical Japanese farm home.
2. Library research on tokonoma.

Content: Clothing

Japanese clothing especially shows the change from an ancient to a modern nation.

1. Usually the old people dress as their ancestors did, while the younger people prefer Western-style clothing.

a. Kimonos are too long and loose to be practical in a modern industrial nation.

   (1) They get caught in machines easily.

   (2) It is hard to drive cars or ride bicycles.

b. Kimonos are still worn by old people, and on holidays by all.

   (1) Gay colors are worn by younger people, dark by the old.

   (2) An obi, or wide sash, holds the kimono in place.

   (3) Men often like to change into kimonos in the evening.

c. Japanese women do not wear hats with kimonos.

   (1) They use parasols to protect themselves from sun.

   (2) Fancy headdresses are worn for special occasions.

d. Japanese shoes worn with Japanese-style clothing are very different from our shoes.

   (1) Clogs (geta) or sandals (zori) are appropriate.

   (2) A special sock (tabi) reaches just above the foot.

2. Workers' clothing fits the jobs they are doing.

  a. Workmen wear a loose coat called a happi.

  b. Workmen wear hats which are usually large to protect them from the strong sun.

   (1) Some make their own hats of paper sacks, towels, straw.

   (2) Western-style hats are worn with western-style suits.

  a. Women working in the fields wear mompei, a kind of trousers.

3. School children wear western-style clothing.

4. Because there is much rain, Japanese need umbrellas and raincoats.

   (1) Umbrellas are heavy and called kasa.

   (2) Country people wear capes or raincoats made of straw.

5. In hot sticky weather, Japanese men and women carry fans of different shapes and designs.

6. Clothing shows both Chinese and Western influences.

Materials: Clothing

  *Japan, Minugh and Cory, pp. 28, 75, 198-205.

  *Japan, Dearmin and Peck, pp. 78-81.

  • A pair of geta.

Procedures: Clothing

Purpose setting:

1. Have the children study the questions about clothing that they had developed during the initiation. Enlarge upon what is meant by *clothing*, how its use and design is often influenced by weather conditions and social demands, and how custom is a factor.

2. Show the geta. Have one or two children try them to stimulate further interest in Japanese clothing.

Investigation:

1. Guide children in using their books to find out how people of Japan dress.
2. Encourage children to bring in samples of clothing they may have and to discuss them with the class.

Purpose checking: Have the children discuss the results of their reading to answer the questions.

Expression:

1. Design patterns suitable for kimono fabrics, using paints.
2. Make sketches illustrating Japanese in clothing appropriate for their activities.
3. Each child to make geta (bring simple materials from home).

Individual projects:

1. Research on Japanese clothing origins and symbolism.
2. Make a kimono or happi coat.
3. Make a folding fan with Japanese design.

Content: Food and Eating

The Japanese people like to eat simple foods in beautiful surroundings.

1. Sauces are used to give different flavors to simple foods.
2. Rice, the most important food, is served hot or cold, and usually with fish or vegetables.
3. Fish, a healthful food, is prepared many ways and served almost every day.
   a. Favorites include eel, mackerel, octopus, and sardines.
   b. Because Japan is surrounded by water, fish are plentiful.
4. Japanese people eat much less meat than we in the United States; they may enjoy fowl or meat once a week.
5. Vegetables are an important part of the Japanese diet.
   a. They are usually eaten when young and tender.
   b. Vegetables include beans, radishes, cabbages, onions, carrots, bamboo shoots, eggplant, sweet potatoes, seaweed.
6. Fresh fruits such as mandarin oranges, tangerines, and peaches are very popular.
7. Japanese beverages reflect the old world and the new.
   a. All Japanese drink tea, and serving it is considered an art.
   b. Sake is a wine made of rice and water.
   c. People like soft drinks too.
8. Meals are served on pretty dishes at low tables.
   a. Sometimes food is cooked next to the table on a hibachi.

b. Chopsticks are used for eating Japanese food, but knives and forks are used for eating American food.

c. Japanese people enjoy going to restaurants to eat too.

9. Foods reflect natural resources available in Japan.

10. American food preferences are being enjoyed in larger cities.

Materials: Food and Eating

- Resource person.
- *Japan,* Minugh and Cory, pp. 206-207.
- *Japan,* Dearmin and Peck, pp. 70-74, 202-206.

Procedures: Food and Eating

Purpose setting:

1. Guide the children in a brief discussion of the factors that influence Japanese clothing and homes. Have them consider whether these factors also influence Japanese food habits.

2. Have the children examine the questions they asked during the initiation. Help them to extend the questions in light of their recent discussion.

Investigation:

1. Invite a resource person to come and discuss life in Japanese homes. Pupils to prepare questions in advance.

2. Guide the pupils in reading of texts for information about eating habits and details of the tea ceremony.

Purpose checking:

1. Guide the children in analyzing their information with respect to the questions developed earlier.

2. Guide them in developing a list of American foods that would most likely be new to a Japanese person coming to this country.

Expression:

1. Pantomime dinner in a Japanese home.

2. Write a story: "If I were invited to a Japanese home for dinner . . ."

Individual projects:

1. Prepare menu for Japanese restaurant.

2. Visit and eat at a Japanese restaurant with family.

3. Research and report on history of tea ceremony.

Content: Language

Japanese is a language quite different from English in many ways.

1. There are three ways of writing Japanese:

a. Kanji was learned from the Chinese and includes about 30,000 signs, each standing for a different word.

b. Each of the 48 signs of kana is a syllable, and these are combined to form words.

c. Romaji is Japanese written with English letters, and the vowels always sound the same.

2. Magazines, newspapers, and books are usually printed in kanji or kana.

   a. The signs are in columns reading from top to bottom and left to right.

   b. The start of a Japanese book is where the ending of an English book would be.

3. Often Japanese symbols are written with a brush rather than with a pen.

4. People in different parts of Japan speak with different dialects, and not all Japanese people can understand each other.

5. Because the Japanese people have no sound for our letter "l," they sound this letter like "r" when pronouncing English words.

6. Japanese people are very polite and show respect for others by placing the letter "o" before the word meaning that person and use terms such as "your honored father."

7. The Japanese language reflects Chinese and English influences in vocabulary.

Materials: Language
• Chart showing "Japan" written in 3 different ways.
• Chart showing all the kata kana forms accompanied by romaji forms.
Japan, Dearmin and Peck, pp. 90-93.

Procedures: Language
Purpose setting:

1. Stimulate children's interest in the Japanese language by showing the chart showing "Japan" written three different ways. Relate the kanji form to the English translation of Nippon as "Land of the Rising Sun." Heighten interest in the language by presenting the kata kana chart. Recite the chart to have the children analyze the sounds for differences between Japanese and English.

2. Guide the children in reviewing their original questions about the language and extending them in accord with their interests.

Investigation:

1. Have the children try to use the kana forms to write these English words: mama, papa, daddy, tone, hen, piano, sofa, pen.

2. Encourage the children to develop a Japanese "spelling" for their own name.

3. Have the children write in kana the following names of persons and places: Osaka, Kobe, Yamamoto, Fujiwara, Hideki, Sho, Miyako.
4. Introduce the Japanese numbers to one hundred. Have the children examine them to discover how they differ in terms of notation.
5. Guide the children in the use of the text as it relates to the questions they have developed.

Purpose checking:
1. Have the children discuss their findings as answers to the questions.
2. Present these words borrowed from English: machi, koppu, handeru, takushi. Encourage the children to determine what they mean.

Expression:
1. Make a travel poster in which *Japan* is expressed in the picture itself and in Japanese writing.
2. Develop an illustrated calendar for next month.

Individual projects:
1. Research on courtesy and how it is reflected in everyday life of Japanese.
2. Prepare news sheet in Japanese style, reporting on classroom activities.

Content: Education

Education is very important to the Japanese and has changed a great deal in the last century.
1. One hundred years ago only children of the upper class went to school.
   a. There were no public schools.
   b. Other children helped at home, in business, or in the fields.
2. School laws were passed so all children attended for six years.
   a. They could go to junior high school after this.
   b. Only boys with the best marks went to high school or college, and few girls went to junior high school.
   c. Almost all Japanese learned to read and write, but they studied mostly about Japan and not the rest of the world.
3. After World War II, the Americans helped the Japanese learn to have a democratic government.
   a. Schools began teaching children how to live and work in a democracy.
   b. Americans made many suggestions to the Japanese for training good citizens.
4. Now the Japanese are teaching children to think for themselves and to learn more about the rest of the world.
5. New school laws have been passed.
   a. Boys and girls must go to school for nine years.

      b. Boys and girls may go to high school.

      c. To attend college, students must pass difficult tests; but many girls go to college and are becoming leaders.

6. Japan is building many new schools so classes will not be crowded.
   a. New classrooms are very much like ours, with windows, blackboards, maps, films, records, and the like.
   b. Children do not get their books free.
   c. Some schools have television lessons.
   d. Hot lunches are served in the classrooms.

7. Most children in Japan wear uniforms to school.

8. Japanese children go to school 5½ or 6 days each week.
   a. The school year is from April 1 until March 31.
   b. They have two weeks vacation at New Year's and one week vacation in spring and one month vacation in summer.

9. Japanese children still learn about Japan, but they also learn about other parts of the world and how nations must work together.
   a. They study the same subjects we do.
   b. Japanese children study other languages, too, including English.

10. Many Japanese ideas about education have been borrowed from the United States and European countries.

Materials: Education

- Film: "Schools in Japan"
- *Japan, Dearmin and Peck, pp. 217-223.
- *Japan, Minugh and Cory, pp. 105-129.

Procedures: Education

Purpose setting:

1. Guide the children in a review of the questions about Japanese education developed during the initiation of the unit. Have the children analyze the questions for completeness.

2. Stimulate greater interest by having the children discuss the most likely differences to be found between Japanese schools and American schools.

Investigation:

1. Present the film.

2. Guide the children in comparing the information offered in each book as well as that given in the film.

Purpose checking:

1. Have the children compare their sources of information for similarities and differences.

2. Guide the children in processing and organizing their information as related to the original questions.

3. Guide the children in developing a large chart showing how Japanese schools and American schools are alike and different.

Expression:

1. Roleplay the relationship between the Japanese teacher and his pupils.

2. Write a story about a Japanese boy or girl attending an American school on the first day.

Individual projects:

1. Make a clay model of a Japanese school child on his or her way to school.

2. Prepare an imaginary diary written by a Japanese boy or girl about a week at school.

3. Make a more extended study of Japanese education and report findings to the class.

Content: Employment and Industry

Many ways of earning a living are available to the people of modern Japan.

1. Although there is very little farm land, nearly one-half of the Japanese people are farmers.

   a. Because land is precious, most farmers live in tiny villages and go to their fields or rice paddies each day.

   b. Most farms are very small, approximately 2½ acres each.

   c. Each acre of farm land must provide food for five people because Japan is a crowded country with only one-fifth of its land available for farming.

     (1) Farmers use land carefully and raise crops on terraces on the sides of mountains.

     (2) In some places bays have been filled in or lakes drained to make more farm land.

   d. Most farmers own their land, but a few tenant farmers work for the owners.

   e. Farmers work mostly by hand but are starting to use small tractors and machinery.

   f. Rice, the most important and largest crop in Japan, needs a temperate climate and abundant rainfall.

     (1) Japan still must buy some rice from other places.

     (2) Rice farmers work hard in cold water to plan their rice, weed, fertilize, and protect it from insects.

     (3) Japanese people prefer white rice, though brown rice is more healthful.

(4) Rice straw that remains after the harvest is used for fuel and for making ropes, mats, baskets, and sacks.

g. Tea is also an important crop in Japan.

    (1) Tea grows on hillsides and takes little farm land.

    (2) Japan raises tea for its own use and to export.

h. Fruits and vegetables are grown on farms and in gardens to sell to people in small towns and cities.

i. Farms in southern and western Japan can raise a winter crop of wheat after they harvest their rice.

j. Japan has few farm animals.

    (1) Good grazing land is not available.

    (2) Small farms do not need expensive farm animals.

    (3) Recently some farmers started raising dairy cows, beef cattle, sheep, and pigs.

k. Most farmers cannot earn a living from their small lands, so they do other kinds of work also.

    (1) Some raise mulberry trees to feed silkworms.

    (2) Some fish while their families work the land.

    (3) Some prepare charcoal.

    (4) Some make toys to earn more money.

l. On Hokaido in the north there are larger farms with modern equipment and farm animals much like we have in the United States.

m. Farming in Japan follows traditional methods on the many small farms; Western methods are used on the large farms.

2. Fishing is so important to Japan that about one-third of the people earn their living this way.

a. Many farmers fish to earn extra money.

b. Some fishermen work for large companies and sail far away on large fishing ships.

c. Many fishermen own their own small boats that require extra care.

d. Women sometimes fish with hand nets or dive for oysters and abalone.

    (1) Oysters are sold to oyster farmers who force the oysters to form pearls.

    (2) The cultured pearl industry is an important part of Japan's fishing industry.

e. Women mend fishing nets and dig for clams also.

f. The Sea of Japan has excellent fishing.

    (1) The meeting of cold and warm water currents is very important to the fishing industry.

(2) When the water churns, it brings plankton to the top; the fish come to feed, and the fishermen catch them.

(3) Over half of the fish Japanese catch are within a few miles of shore.

g. Japan cans much of the fish and sells it to other countries, or trades it for goods the Japanese need.

h. The fishing industry is being modernized through the use of radar, helicopters, and modern equipment with large fleets.

i. The Japanese have made excellent use of Western ideas and have introduced innovations in developing their fishing industry.

3. In modern Japan many people earn their living working in manufacturing cities of Tokyo, Yokohama, Osaka, Nagasaki, Nagoya.

a. Japan buys most raw materials from other nations to make products she can sell back to them.

b. Japan builds more freighters and tankers than any other nation.

c. Japan builds automobiles and motorcycles for local use and export.

d. Japanese people have become skilled in making cameras, watches, clocks, television sets, transistor radios, computers, and x-ray machines.

e. The Japanese have always been known for toys and fireworks.

f. Japan sells more textiles than any other country.

(1) Japan does not raise cotton but buys raw wool and cotton from other countries to make into cloth.

(2) Japan also manufactures rayon and nylon.

(3) As other cloth becomes more popular, silk has become less important.

g. Japanese factories are modern, clean, heated, and use assembly-line procedures.

h. Some Japanese manufacturing is done in workshops and cottages by families who together make things of silk, clay, lacquer, bamboo or wood.

i. The import-export trade employs many Japanese at busy seaports.

j. Manufacturing is another Japanese industry in which they used Western ideas and built upon them.

4. Many Japanese earn their living by silk-making, although silk is no longer Japan's main export product.

a. Farmers and their families raise silkworms.

(1) They feed them mulberry leaves and keep the worms in warm, damp rooms.

(2) Full-grown worms are placed on straw or cardboard frames to spin their cocoons.

(3) When the cocoons are ready, the farmers take the frames with their cocoons to the silk factory to sell them.

b. The factories spin the silk into cloth.

(1) The cocoons are heated in ovens to kill the new moth inside.

(2) The cocoons are carried through steam and hot water to loosen their threads.

(3) The fine threads of the cocoons are wound on spools and spun into heavier threads.

(4) One cocoon makes about 1000 yards of strong thread.

(5) Finally the thread is woven into silk cloth by machines.

c. Silk cloth is dyed by hand and then baked in ovens to set the color.

d. Workmen wash the rolls of silk cloth in the river and spread them on the banks to dry.

e. Silk is used in clothing, stocking, gloves, and fishing lines.

f. Japan uses much silk and sells most of the rest to the United States.

g. Silk culture in Japan came as a result of interaction with the Chinese.

5. Some Japanese are miners.

a. Japan has many kinds of minerals but only in small amounts.

b. Soft coal, Japan's most valuable mineral, is used to make electric power.

c. Japan has only small amounts of iron and so must buy scrap iron and ore to make steel.

d. Japan has salt available from the sea water, and salt factories are found along the coast.

e. Japan has large amounts of limestone in all parts of the country; it is used for making cement.

f. The many volcanoes produce sulphur, which Japan uses for fertilizer, gun power, farm sprays, and to sell to others.

Materials: Employment and Industry

• Display of Japanese products used during the initiation.

*Japan, Dearmin and Peck, pp. 109-143.

*Japan, Minugh and Cory, pp. 52-90.

*Information Please Almanac

Procedures: Employment and Industry

Purpose setting:

1. Present the display of Japanese products and the questions developed during the initiation. Lead the children in relating previous learning

to both the display and the questions to pinpoint more precisely what is to be investigated.

2. Encourage the children to look around their homes for more Japanese products to make the display more complete.

3. Build interest in Japanese industry by having the children survey the occupations of their parents and consider whether a parallel might be found in Japan and, if so, where it would be located.

Investigation: Guide the children in the use of their textbooks and in comparing the information offered in each. Encourage them to check statistical specifics in the almanac.

Purpose checking:

1. Guide the children in examining the display of products and in rearranging the display to reflect the order of importance to Japanese industry.

2. Have the children reexamine the questions as an adequate frame of reference for investigating about industry. Guide them in making needed changes.

3. Direct the children's attention toward locating where the complex of parental occupations would most likely be duplicated in Japan.

4. Evaluate sources.

Expression:

1. Make an over-all map and a series of maps showing the location of industries in Japan. For the over-all map, develop a way of showing the importance of industries as depicted.

2. Paint mural showing main industries of Japan.

3. Suggested possibilities for group work:
   Farming: diorama of typical Japanese farm.
   Fishing: dramatize life of fisherman and his family.
   Silk-making: sketch and describe steps in the process.
   Mining: make graphs to demonstrate relative availability of minerals in Japan and require imports.

Individual projects:

1. Make a model of a Japanese fishing boat.

2. Research and report on rice, its nutritive value and methods of preparation.

3. Make chart showing Japanese-United States imports/exports.

Content: Religion

The Japanese have two main religions, Shinto and Buddhism.

1. Shinto, meaning "the way of the gods," dates back to the start of Japanese history.

    a. According to Shinto, there are gods or spirits in people, nature, and things.

      (1) The Sun Goddess is the greatest Shinto god.

      (2) The people used to believe that the emperor was a god to be worshipped as a descendant of the Sun Goddess.

      (3) Since World War II, the emperor has told the people he is not a god, but a man.

    b. Shinto families have shrines in their homes to honor family spirits.

    c. Shinto families also visit larger shrines frequently.

      (1) They ring a bell to get the attention of the gods, then say a prayer and leave a coin as an offering.

      (2) Babies are taken to the shrine and the gods asked to watch over them.

      (3) Boys are taken back at age 3 and girls at age 7.

      (4) Children of all ages go to a shrine on November 15, a special day when parents pray for health and happiness.

2. Buddhism is centered around Guatama Buddha, the founder in India 2500 years ago.

    a. Buddhist temples have statues of Buddha.

    b. People go to Buddhist temples to pray but leave their shoes at the door.

      (1) They toss coins into a wooden box.

      (2) They kneel and bow before the Buddha statue, burn incense, and strike a gong to tell Buddha their prayers.

    c. Buddhist families have small shrines at home for worship.

3. Japanese people may choose their own religion.

    a. A long time ago, everyone had to believe in Shinto.

    b. Many Japanese are both Shinto and Buddhist.

    c. Some Japanese are Christians.

4. The variety of religions in modern Japan is due to the interaction of the Japanese people with other peoples and to religious ways developed by the people over the centuries.

    a. Shintoism—developed in Japan.

    b. Buddhism—from the Chinese.

    c. Christianity—from European peoples.

Materials: Religion

• A picture of an official, taking the oath of office. His left hand rests on a Bible.

*_Japan_, Minugh and Cory, pp. 137-139.

*_Japan: Home of the Sun_, Dearmin and Peck, pp. 48-51.

Procedures: Religion

Purpose setting:

1. Using the flag as the point of reference, guide the children in discussing it as a symbol. Lead the discussion toward beliefs, feelings, and behaviors associated with it.

2. Using the picture, focus the children's attention on the Bible and its function in the ceremony—to symbolize the presence of God at the ceremony. Encourage the children to discuss other religious symbols that they have seen or used.

3. Guide the children in examining the questions developed during the initiation. Help them to clarify and extend their questions in the light of the previous discussion.

4. Encourage the children to think of religious symbols that might possibly be important in Japan and to discuss them.

Investigation: Help the children to use their textbooks to read for information as related to their questions.

Purpose checking:

1. Have the children discuss their findings about religious symbols used in Japan.

2. Guide the children in dealing with their questions. Have them consider also the questions that they might have asked.

3. Have the children compare ideas about freedom of religion in Japan and the United States.

Expression:

1. Make dioramas showing Japanese symbols of religion.

2. Write simple prayers that a Japanese child might possibly make at a shrine.

Individual projects:

1. Make a simple model of a Japanese religious symbol.

2. Prepare a brief report on Guatama Buddha.

3. Read some Shinto myths and report them.

Content: Recreation—Beauty and Fun

Like people everywhere, the Japanese like to have fun and to take time to enjoy beautiful things.

1. Japan has many special holidays and celebrations, or festivals, called matsuri.

   a. Children's Day on May 5 is very exciting.

      (1) Parents praise their children, and children thank their parents for their goodness and kindness.

(2) Girls bring their guests to see their dolls, while boys fly, from flagpoles, huge paper kites shaped like carp.

b. November 15 is a special holiday for taking children to visit the Shinto shrine.

c. Each month the Japanese celebrate something special from nature: a flower, a tree, snowflakes.

d. Japan celebrates a Star Festival and a Moon Festival.

e. There are many religious festivals each year.

f. New Year's celebrations last a whole month.

g. Most Japanese cities hold their own festival with parades, dancers, and huge crowds.

h. Japan's festivals and holidays have a basis in the unique traditions of the people.

2. Children enjoy story tellers and fortune tellers in the parks—a traditional form of entertainment.

3. Japanese people enjoy many games and toys.

a. Girls love dolls, and boys play with kites of all sizes and shapes.

b. Children like model airplanes.

c. The national game in Japan is called "Go".

d. Many Japanese children play battledore and shuttlecock, a game that has been played for many centuries with a paddle and a feathered cork and ball.

e. "One Hundred Poems" is a favorite Japanese card game.

f. Origami, or paper folding, is a popular activity.

g. Many toys, such as horses and other folk toys, are thought to have spirits to help sick children get well.

h. Games and toys show Western influences.

4. The Japanese enjoy sports.

a. Baseball is probably the favorite sport of all Japan.

b. Swimming is popular for there are many beaches.

c. Golf is well liked but too expensive for everyone.

d. Japan is noted for its wrestling, or sumo.

e. Judo is a sport taught in all Japanese high schools.

f. A kind of fencing called kendo is taught to boys in school.

g. The Japanese also like horseracing, tennis, volleyball, basketball, rowing, skating, skiing, mountain climbing.

h. Sports in Japan reflect a rich contrast between borrowed and traditional activities.

5. Art and beauty have a very important place in Japanese life.

a. Homes, dishes, furnishings, and clothing may all be works of art.

b. Japanese family gardens are especially beautiful.

(1) Most are small and planted with only a few flowers but many other plants and grasses.

(2) Trees such as the bonsai are grown in interesting sizes and shapes.

(3) Most gardens have stone lanterns or little bridges.

c. Japanese are skilled in flower arranging, and different arrangements have different meanings for certain occasions.

d. Japanese artists like to use water colors and try to show feelings or actions rather than exact likenesses.

e. The Japanese are known especially for their scrolls, painted screens, and block prints.

6. The Japanese people have their favorite musical instruments and music.

a. Most instruments were taken to Japan from China, India, and Korea.

(1) The koto is a stringed instrument placed flat on the floor.

(2) The biwa is a long, egg-shaped instrument with strings.

(3) Bamboo flutes are common and always played at New Year's.

(4) The favorite is an samisen, much like our banjo.

b. Western-style instruments and American music are becoming popular.

c. Japanese folk music started as poetry read in singsong fashion but today has tunes of its own.

d. Traditional Japanese music sounds strange to us because it is built on fewer notes than ours.

7. Plays in the Japanese theater are much like dances.

a. The Bugaku is a slow dance form over 1000 years old.

b. Elaborate and formal Noh plays were originally given outdoors but now are performed indoors with men actors wearing strange masks.

c. Kyogen plays are short and funny and are given in between the acts of the serious Noh plays.

d. The Bunraku or puppet play is presented in singsong voice with puppeteers in view behind large puppets.

e. In Kabuki plays, live actors move like puppets; they have exciting music, dancing, and acting.

8. Poetry is important to all Japanese people.

a. The emperor has an annual poetry-writing contest.

(1) The five best poems are chosen from many thousands to be printed in newspapers.

(2) The writers who win are invited to the emperor's palace to read their poems.

b. Most Japanese poetry is short, such as the favorite haiku.
  (1) Haiku is three lines long, contains seventeen syllables, and is about nature.
  (2) All Japanese children learn to write haiku.
c. All Japanese people know some poems by heart, and everyone makes up poetry.
9. Japanese traditions in the fine arts reflect an early Chinese influence as well as Japanese innovations.
10. Japanese ways of artistic expression have influenced people everywhere.

Materials: Recreation —Beauty and Fun
*_Japan,_ Dearmin and Peck, pp. 149-171.
*_Japan,_ Minugh and Cory, pp. 132-136, 140-150, 152-164, 208-219.
*Objects or pictorial representations of symbols associated with holidays and recreation: a cap pistol, a baseball bat, a football, an Easter egg, a menorah, a Christmas wreath or tree, a camp stove, and the like.

Procedures: Recreation—Beauty and Fun
Purpose setting:
1. To stimulate interest, present the objects and pictures and encourage the children to relate them to American recreational habits. Help to isolate the religious and cultural bases for these habits.
2. Guide the children in examining the questions developed during the initiation and in extending them for a more comprehensive research into Japanese recreation.

Investigation:
1. Guide the children in the use of their books to seek information.
2. Have the children compare the books for agreement and extensiveness of treatment of the topic.

Purpose checking:
1. Guide the children in considering the Japanese recreational practices in which they would feel at home and those which they would find new.
2. Encourage the children to arrive at an opinion about the comparative adequacy of their books.

Expression:
1. Make several murals: a general statement about Japanese recreational habits, a statement about Japanese recreation from a boy's point of view, and one from a girl's point of view.
2. Roleplay the various Japanese holidays.

Individual projects:

1. Write haiku or tanka and illustrate.

2. Using American artifacts, prepare a display for one of the children's festivals.

3. Prepare a chart of Japanese and American recreational practices showing both similarities and differences.

4. Research how judo or kendo found their place in Japanese culture and education.

Content: Transportation and Communication

Transportation and communication developments have helped make Japan a modern nation.

1. Communication among the islands that form the country is essential.
   a. The telegraph has been used in Japan since 1869.
      (1) People do not have to write well to send telegrams.
      (2) Telegrams are almost as popular in Japan as letters are in the United States.
   b. Ocean cables connect the islands to each other and to the rest of the world.
   c. Postal service is performed daily.
   d. Telephones have brought business people close together, but not many families have their own phones.
   e. Daily newspapers keep the Japanese people informed.
   f. Japanese people read many books and magazines.
   g. About half of all Japanese families own television sets.
   h. Almost every adult and child has a transistor radio.
   i. Moving pictures from Japan and America are very popular with the young people.

2. The people of such a crowded nation like to travel.
   a. There are few good roads because of the many mountains and the need to use land for farming.
   b. Japan has modern train service on all four major islands.
      (1) Honshu and Kyushu are connected by an underwater tunnel.
      (2) Subways and elevated trains of large cities are very crowded.
   c. City streets in Japan are so overcrowded that a traffic jam may last for many hours.
      (1) The Japanese use cars, bicycles, buses, streetcars, pushcarts, three-wheeled trucks, motorcycles, and taxis to travel in the city and country.
      (2) Because cars are expensive, not many families own them.

    d. Ships are needed between the islands and for transportation to other countries.

    e. Airplane travel to all parts of the world is available in Tokyo.

3. Based on Western adaptations and innovations in industry, Japan contributes richly to the world market in communication vehicles and is becoming increasingly important in the manufacture of transportation vehicles.

Materials: Transportation and Communication

- Expressive products from the study of the geography of Japan and its language.

Japan: Minugh and Cory, 178-189.

Japan: Dearmin and Peck: 88-89, 97-99, 103-105.

Procedures: Transportation and Communication

Purpose setting:

1. Using the expressive products, help the children to recall previous learning. Guide them in relating these facts and ideas to transportation and communication conditions in Japan.

2. Have the children examine their previously developed questions in light of the previous discussion.

Investigation: Guide the children in the use of their books to find out more about communication and transportation in Japan.

Purpose checking:

1. Guide the children in discussing their answers to the questions.

2. Have the children develop a rationale for transportation and communication in modern Japan.

Expression:

1. Dramatize a planned trip to Japan and its major cities and islands.

2. Develop descriptive charts comparing everyday utilization of transportation facilities by Japanese families and American families in urban and rural areas.

3. Roleplay the use of communication devices used in a Japanese home.

Individual projects:

1. Make a diorama of a Japanese street scene showing transportation.

2. Write a series of telegrams such as two Japanese people would be likely to write.

3. Develop charts or graphs comparing costs of communication and transportation in United States vs. Japan.

4. Chart commodities requiring transportation into and within Japan, and method.

SECTION III. CULMINATION

Content Related to Purposes

1. Japanese culture, a blend of old and new ways of living, makes it possible for the people to remain Japanese and to work with other nations at the same time.
    a. Japanese basic ways of living are in some ways determined by its geography.
    b. The basic ways of living reflect borrowings from East and West as well as Japanese innovations.
    c. Japanese culture has contributed to American culture.
    d. Japan contributes in an important way to the world market.
2. Ideas about attitudes: We respect the Japanese people for the ways of living they have developed and continue to develop as a nation and as a member of a world of nations.
    a. Many Japanese live and work and play as we do.
    b. Their Japanese ways of doing things show an outstanding use of resources.
    c. Japan is concerned with other nations of the world.
3. Ideas about patterns of action: We work to maintain and improve relations between the Japanese people and ourselves.
    a. We participate in community events honoring our relations with the Japanese.
    b. We try to establish a direct contact with the Japanese people.
    c. We continue to inform ourselves about Japan as a participant in the world market.
    d. We follow issues arising within Japan and between Japan and other nations.

Teaching Purposes:

1. To encourage the children to integrate facts and ideas through expressive activity.
2. To guide children toward a significant social-studies generalization.
3. To have the children verify the generalization historically.
4. To help the children to develop positive attitudes and patterns of action with regard to the Japanese people and their culture.
5. To encourage the children to apply their learning projectively.
6. To set the stage for children to extend their learning about Japan.

Materials:

• Examples of children's expressive products from each of the areas studied.

- Instructional model: a pair of geta, a Japanese-made transistor radio, and a hibachi.
- *Japan*, Pitts, pp. 136-146.

Procedures:

Guide the children in examining their expressive products to arrive at a summary of facts and ideas to be used for developing a large mural.

Help the children in planning and completing the mural.

Using the instructional model, guide the children toward generalization by asking, "Which of these objects most closely represents modern Japan?" Encourage the children to discuss the objects freely, to offer opinions and to support them with facts and ideas, and to arrive at a decision concerning the objects. (The hibachi most closely represents modern Japan because it is a traditional object manufactured by modern methods for world distribution. The statement reflecting this idea is the generalization).

Guiding the children's attention again toward the instructional model, invite the children to project themselves back two hundred years and ask which of the objects would have been most representative of Japan at that time. Make provisions for free discussion. The generalization will be found to be true in some aspects and untrue in others. Encourage the children to develop a new generalization suitable descriptively for both modern and old Japan.

Present the following problems to the children to guide them in exploring for attitudes about the Japanese people.

1. Suppose that a Japanese boy or girl recently arrived from Japan begins to go to your school. He or she is assigned to sit beside you. How do you feel about this?

2. Suppose that your father comes home one evening and announces excitedly that the whole family has won a trip to Japan. Six weeks will be spent there. How do you feel about this?

3. A Japanese visitor criticizes the ways that Americans live. He thinks their homes are too large and their ways of building are wasteful. How do you feel about this?

4. An American thinks that all Japanese goods should be barred from America. How do you feel about this?

Present the following problems to the children to guide them in exploring for patterns of action about the Japanese people and culture:

1. A Japanese trade fair is being held in your city. Several of your friends are going. What do you think you will do?

2. In your city there is a monument to the goodwill between a Japanese
   city and yours. How do you think you will act when you visit it?

Guide the children in roleplaying the preparations for receiving a Japanese
guest and the events that will transpire during the visit. Then reverse the
roleplaying—the preparation by a Japanese family for an American guest
and the events to transpire during the visit.

If possible, arrange for the children to establish a "pen-pal" relationship
with Japanese children.

Encourage the children to develop a bulletin board in anticipation of news
events about Japan.

Unit: Economic Aspects of America's Beginnings (Grade 8)

[At first glance, the content of this unit appears to be detailed and voluminous and the procedures somewhat sketchy and disjointed. The content is regarded as a tentative base for cognitive learnings which are implicit within the procedures. It may be the content experienced by the children, but chances are that it stands as something to work from, not at. Some of the facts and ideas may be omitted and others included.

As it stands, this unit could be followed only by the teacher who prepared it. His procedures serve as clues to what he plans to do, but his plans may be changed at any moment. Notice how he functions to keep inquiry open.]

Background for Cognitive Learning (A)
1. Economic welfare is a complex of conditions related to the satisfaction of an individual's or group's needs for goods and services at a commonly accepted level or range of levels.
    a. Needs for food, clothing, and shelter.
    b. Needs for personal protection.

    c. Needs for commercial intercourse.

    d. Needs for aesthetic and religious experience.

2. Various indices can be used to determine acceptable levels of economic welfare.

    a. Among individuals within a society:

      (1) Standard of dress for similar occasions.

      (2) Food consumption.

      (3) Quality and size of shelter.

    b. Among societal groups:

      (1) Standard of living.

      (2) Facilities for commercial intercourse.

Materials (A)

- Large magazine and newspaper pictures showing people in various socioeconomic settings.
- An opaque projector.

Procedures (A)

Discussion stimulators: The expression *standard of living* is a common part of our vocabulary. What do we mean when we use it? What do we mean when we say that so-and-so has a high standard of living? A low standard of living? How do we know?

Discussion pointers: I have here a series of pictures clipped from newspapers and magazines. They are pictures of people, some individuals and some in groups. Let's classify these people as having what we would call a high standard of living, an acceptable standard of living, or a low standard of living.

If we analyze and compare our classifications, we can find the factors which influenced our choices. What do you find?

Idea refiners: Do you think that these levels of standard of living that we have been talking about are subject to change? Were they different twenty years ago? Fifty years ago?

Do you think that these same levels of standard of living prevail in other countries?

The term *economic welfare* is frequently used to describe a set of conditions having to do with how people satisfy their needs and wants. Is standard of living in some way related to this?

Background for Cognitive Learning (B)

The economic welfare of a societal group is determined by the social forces which motivate the people, the availability of natural resources, the level of technological advancement developed by the people, the economic organization of the people for the production and consumption of goods, and opportunity for cultural exchange.

1. In the year 1000, the economic activity of most Western European peoples was directed toward a generally low level of subsistence.

    a. The dominant social force was the Christian religion, which

        (1) Formed a basis for social organization.

        (2) Controlled the life of almost every individual.

        (3) Provided an outlet for the human energy not needed for making a living.

        (4) Placed emphasis on other worldly values.

        (5) De-emphasized prosperity in this world.

    b. A strong social force was the need for protection from military raids by the Vikings, bands of outlaws, and noblemen asserting the right of might to establish property rights.

        (1) Many individuals denied themselves the right of freedom to serve an individual who could protect them.

        (2) Next to the religious leader was the military leader as the most prized individual.

    c. Education as a social force had little influence.

        (1) Education directed toward gross skills of fighting or tilling the soil.

        (2) Education in the use of abstract skills centered in the church to serve the church's needs.

    d. Natural resources were extensive, but relatively undeveloped.

        (1) The main resources were tillable land, forest, and stream for subsistence goods.

        (2) The ocean served as a resource to the people living near it, chiefly food.

        (3) A few mines for coal and metals easily converted to utility form.

    e. Technological advancement was at a low level.

        (1) The most advanced technological skills were those used to produce the tools of war.

        (2) Farming and animal husbandry were poorly developed as skills.

        (3) Weaving, dyeing, wood-, clay-, and metal-working were crudely developed skills.

        (4) Transportation innovations included stirrups and the horse-collar.

        (5) Navigation and sailing quite advanced in the north.

    f. The economic organization of the people reflected a structure developed for the support of the leaders of society (a class at the top of the social hierarchy).

   (1) The lower classes were to give as much of their produce as was demanded by the holder of the land (a nobleman).
   (2) The nobleman was often held to give a certain amount of the products of his land to a nobleman above him.
   (3) The lower classes were allowed whatever was left over for their own subsistence.
   (4) Churches frequently had holdings of their own.

 g. The economic organization of the people reflected little provision for commercial intercourse.

   (1) Few large population centers which would demand large amounts of goods and specialized labor.
   (2) Specialized labor, save for some crafts, not well-developed.
   (3) Trade within the community carried on by barter between individuals and families.
   (4) Little money in use.
   (5) Little trade between communities.
   (6) Occasional peddlers brought ornamental goods from distant lands.

 h. There was little positive contact between cultural groups.

   (1) Defense from the Vikings of the north.
   (2) Defense from the Tartars from the east.
   (3) Defense from the Moors from the south and east.

2. The comparatively low level of economic welfare accepted by the peoples of Western Europe was due in part to the lack of social motivation, the low level of technological development, an economic organization which promised, at best, survival for a majority of the population, and little opportunity for cultural exchange.

Materials (B)

*100,000 Years of Daily Life, Brosse, Chaland, and Ostier.
*The Medieval World, Heer.
• An opaque projector.

Procedures (B)

Discussion stimulators: Let us project ourselves back in time about a thousand years to take a look at the men who were our forebears. Where would we find these men? From what you've read and studied previously and from what you've viewed on television and motion-picture film, how would you describe these men in terms of their economic welfare? What would be a composite picture of these men and their ways of answering to their wants and needs?

Discussion pointers: For the moment, let's work within the limitations of a historian who has not the money to travel to Europe to visit old cities and great collections of objects from the past. The best that he can obtain is a set of photographs, or perhaps several sets. *(100,000 Years of Daily Life,* pp. 91-93; *The Medieval World,* illustrations 1-100). What interpretation can we make about the standards of living of medieval men?

At this point we have made the best interpretation that we can. Let's compare it with those made by others—another practice followed by historians. *(100,000 Years of Daily Life,* pp. 91-93; *The Medieval World,* pp. 41-44.) Which interpretation can we accept as most valid? How can we decide?

Idea refiners: Now that we have an idea about the economic welfare of medieval men in Europe, we can analyze it from another point of view. How do you think these men regarded their standard of living? How do you regard yours? What do you think were their most important beliefs? What kinds of things would they do to improve their way of life?

Background for Cognitive Learning (C)

1. In the year 1000, the economic activity of Middle Eastern peoples was directed toward a relatively advanced level of subsistence.
    a. There were several social forces which contributed toward this advanced level of subsistence.
        (1) Mohammedanism, a religion which was regulative of the individual's life, but did not deny him the right to prosperity.
        (2) A system of education which made abstractive skills available to a large segment of the population.
        (3) Relatively strong security from raids and pillage for a large segment of the population.
    b. Natural resources were not extensive but were relatively well developed.
        (1) Tillable land, often irrigated, for subsistence goods.
        (2) Untillable land used for animal husbandry.
        (3) Relatively few forests.
        (4) Seafoods available from seas.
        (5) Rich mines.
    c. Technological development was relatively well advanced.
        (1) Artisanry in metal, leather, clay, weaving, and dyeing well developed.
        (2) Horticulture and animal husbandry quite advanced.

    (3) Mathematics and medical science studied and in use.

    (4) Vehicles of transportation and communication relatively basic.

    (5) Navigation skills well developed.

  d. The economic organization of the people reflected a structure developed for the support of a large group of privileged people (on the basis of religion) so

    (1) Most menial tasks performed by slaves.

    (2) Many artisans manufactured goods for trade.

    (3) A wealthy class of noblemen controlled land and other resources.

    (4) Large population centers fostered the development of trade.

    (5) Location fostered the development of trade with other peoples.

    (6) Well-developed organization for commerce, including a stable money system.

  e. Because of location and the development of trade, Middle Eastern peoples had much contact with other leading cultures:

    (1) Byzantium to the west.

    (2) India and China to the east.

2. The relatively high level of economic welfare accepted by the peoples of the Middle East was due in part to positive social motivation toward individual prosperity, to good use of available natural resources, to a somewhat advanced level of technology, to an economic organization that encouraged the production of goods, and to continued opportunity for cultural exchange.

Materials (C)

*100,000 Years of Daily Life, Brosse, Chaland, and Ostier.

*The Rise of the West, McNeill.

• An opaque projector.

*The Cornerstone, Oldenbourg.

Procedures (C)

Discussion stimulators: Because so many of our forebears were Europeans, we frequently forget that there are other peoples. Let's take a look at the people who lived in the Middle East about a thousand years ago. What do we mean by *Middle East?* What are living conditions like there today? What do you think they were a thousand years ago?

Discussion pointers: Again working within the limitations of the historian, let's examine some photographs to see what we can find out about man living in the Middle East and his standard of living. (*100,000 Years of Daily Life*, pp. 88-90, 100-102.)

A modern historian gives us an idea about the technological development of these people. Listen carefully as I read this brief paragraph. *(The Rise of the West,* pp. 479-480.) If we compare the standard of living of medieval men with that of their contemporaries in the Middle East, what do we find?

Idea refiners: Suppose that there were such a thing as a time machine that could project us back into the past. Let us suppose further that we have a choice between medieval Europe and the Middle East of a thousand years ago. Which would you prefer? Why? Can you think of reasons for rejecting both? Why would neither be an acceptable choice for you?

Background for Cognitive Learnings (D)

1. There was contact, but a limited contact, between Western European and Middle Eastern peoples because of religious similarities and economic need.

   a. Similarities between Mohammedanism and Christianity.
      (1) Both held to the idea of one God.
      (2) They shared a common basis in Judaistic beliefs, but with different interpretations and emphasis.
      (3) The holy places for both were in the Middle East.

   b. Each year a few Christians visited the Holy Sepulchre in Jerusalem —a practice tolerated by the Mohammedans.

   c. The people of Italy, the most advanced of Western European peoples, had established trade with the people of the East and had built trade centers and colonies there.

2. Friction between the two cultures developed when the Seljuk Turks invaded the Middle East.

   a. The Seljuk Turks emphasized the need for Mohammedanism to be spread by force.

   b. Christians were persecuted.

   c. Italian holdings were threatened.

   d. Crusades, or great expeditions for reconquering the Holy Land, were organized and sent to the Middle East.
      (1) Nine Crusades in all.
      (2) Involved all the Western European peoples.
      (3) Were sent over a period of two centuries dating from 1095.

   e. There was so little food in Europe that little urging was needed to obtain men for armies; many regarded the Holy Land as the land of milk and honey.

3. The Crusades met generally with little success, but served to acquaint Western Europeans with a new standard of living.

    a. A new horticulture—new foods (spinach, peaches, and others) and new machines (the windmill and the water wheel).

    b. Varied and interesting cookery brought about by the use of spices.

    c. A use of fine fabrics of cotton and silk.

    d. An appreciation of artistic artifacts of metal, wood, leather, and wool for the home and personal use.

    e. A taste for travel.

    f. The uses of money.

4. This new standard of living brought about important changes in the economic organization of peoples in Western Europe.

    a. The need for fine products established manufacturing as an important industry.

    b. Cities developed as manufacturing centers.

    c. Men in the cities began gaining in independence through their control of production.

    d. Money replaced barter as a means of exchange.

    e. Many goods, particularly spices and fine fabrics, could not be produced; therefore, strong trade ties were built with the East.

Materials (D)

The Crusades, Lamb.

The Uses of the Past, Muller.

The Story of Mankind, van Loon (sufficient copies for class distribution).

A History of Business, Beard.

Procedures (D)

Discussion stimulators: By now you are acquainted with two different peoples who lived a thousand years ago. Do you think that these two peoples could come together to interact in some way? What possible forces could bring them together? What do you think would be the result of the interaction?

Discussion pointers (establish in a brief presentation that there were both economic and religious interaction between medieval men and their Middle Eastern contemporaries):

    Let's imagine what would happen if a group of devout Muslims who believed that Mohammedanism was to spread by force were to conquer Jerusalem. What do you think would most likely be the result as far as Europeans were concerned? What are your first feelings when you hear that the American flag has been dishonored in a foreign country? What do you feel like doing about it?

Discussion pointers: Writers of historical fiction are often able amateur historians. This brief excerpt from Zoe Oldenbourg's novel *The Corner-*

stone will tell you much about medieval man (pp. 11-15). From this excerpt, how would we describe medieval man?

Let's again try our hand at the work of the historian. This time we shall examine something that was a product of medieval times—something more intimate than a photograph. I am going to read you a speech that was actually given. Again we have some limitations. The speech was given in old French, a language similar to modern French, but different in some ways. It has been translated. Could translation make a difference in its validity as a source? How do you think medieval man in France would respond to this (*The Crusades,* pp. 37-40)?

How successful do you think this venture will be? Here are written accounts of what these Crusaders often suffered: *The Crusades,* pp. 89, 112. Analyze the following interpretations to determine which is the most valid: *The Uses of the Past,* p. 239; *The Crusades,* p. 5; *The Story of Mankind,* pp. 157-163.

Idea refiners: Which of the interpretations given tends to be mostly descriptive? The other two suggest a cause-effect relationship? Which of the two do you believe to be more accurate? How can you validate your belief?

Background for Cognitive Learning (E)

The various peoples of Western Europe were affected differently by the new changes in economic welfare.

1. The Vikings to the far north were influenced least.
   a. Not a part of the Christian community; therefore, not involved with the Crusades.
   b. Maintained such poor relations with other peoples that little was known of their exploratory activities in the North Atlantic.
   c. The need for arable land was an essential factor in prompting the Viking explorations, discoveries, and colonizations—once satisfied, there was no motivative power for further explorations.
2. The Italians in the south enjoyed a high level of economic welfare.
   a. Closest to the Middle East.
   b. Controlled ship traffic on the Mediterranean (Venice and Genoa, the city states, in particular, with well-developed merchant fleets and navies).
   c. Controlled money—Florence, the banking center of Europe.
   d. Most widely traveled of all Europeans—Marco Polo, the prime example, had traveled and lived in the Far East for twenty years and reported his findings.
   e. The level of economic welfare supported leisure-time activity—which, in turn, led to a high development of the arts.

3. The other peoples of Western Europe—notably the English, French, Spanish, Portuguese, Dutch, and those in the small Germanic kingdoms —became the "have-not" peoples in terms of spices and other goods from the East.
   a. The Italians controlled the Mediterranean routes.
   b. Overland routes were dangerous and hard to maintain because of robbers.
   c. Result: an upsurge of exploration supported by a new technology and the need for goods.
      (1) Better ships.
      (2) Better maps.
      (3) The compass.

Materials (E)

- Physical-political map of Eurasia.
- *The Story of Mankind,* van Loon (sufficient copies for classroom distribution).
- *The Rise of the West,* McNeill (pertinent excerpts duplicated for classroom distribution).

Procedures (E)

Discussion stimulators: Listen to this quote from Miriam Beard's A History of Business (p. 77) to see how she interprets the effect of the Crusades on medieval men. With whom does she agree, van Loon, Lamb, or Muller?

Project yourself into habits of life of the returning Crusader. How do you suppose that you would feel about your religion? Would you feel any different from the way you felt when you left on the Crusade? What kinds of things might be more important to you?

Let's add a few more conditions. Suppose that you return to find the land that was once yours has been given to another. Or suppose that you find that your land cannot produce the things that you want, or that its produce can bring you little money. How would you feel? How would you act?

Discussion pointers: On this map of Eurasia we can plot a series of conditions that existed in the thirteenth century at the close of the Crusades— the Middle East, that once served as a trading center for fine cloth, pottery, vases, spices, and the like, is closed to most of the countries of Europe; only the Italian merchants have contacts there and they jealously guard them. What choices are left to the people in central and western Europe? The people of northern Europe? How strongly were the latter committed to the Crusades? How did they procure luxury items?

Let's compare our interpretation with those made by others *(The Story of Mankind,* pp. 167-174, 139-144, 188-196; *The Rise of the West,* pp. 597, 598-599, 609, 624-625).

Idea refiners: As most of you have sensed by now, we have in part set the stage for the discovery and colonization of America. For the moment let us forget the facts that we remember from our previous studies of American history in earlier grades. Let's consider ourselves to be citizens of an European country in 1490. We shall pretend that we are well informed as to people and conditions all over Europe. If we were to make any predictions as to the future discovery of a huge mass of land across the ocean, what would be our best prediction?

Let's consider briefly what might have happened if medieval men and the people in the Middle East had been able to develop friendly relations. Would this have hastened or delayed the discovery of America?

Background for Cognitive Learnings (F)

The attempts to find new routes to the East financed by the "have-not" peoples of Western Europe led to the discovery, exploration, and colonization of America.

1. The Portuguese explored the Atlantic to the West and South.
    a. Prince Henry (Henry the Navigator) of Portugal made provisions for the exploration of northwestern Africa.
        (1) Began his preparations in 1415.
        (2) In 1419 established a school for navigators where careful records of findings were kept and maps were made.
        (3) Canary Islands discovered.
        (4) The Azores charted.
        (5) By about 1450 had explored the coast of northwestern Africa as far south as the Senegal River and the Atlantic Ocean as far west as the Cape Verde Islands.
        (6) Tried to seek the whereabouts of Prester John, supposedly the emperor of a great empire in the east.
        (7) Significance: much new knowledge about navigation.
    b. Bartholomew Dias, 1498, reached India to the east: significance—the Portuguese had a route of their own to the East.
2. Spain seeks a route to the East in a westerly direction.
    a. Christopher Columbus, financed by the king and queen of Spain, sets sail from Spain in 1492.
        (1) About as well informed as the best navigators of his day.
            (a) Aware of the Portuguese project and its findings to his time.
            (b) A student of maps and map-making, but,

(c) Ignorant of the size of the earth.
(2) On October 12, 1492, reached an island in what is now called the West Indies and assumed that he had reached India.
(3) Other voyages:
   (a) 1493, explored the West Indies.
   (b) 1498, reached the coast of South America.
   (c) 1502-1504, sailed along the coast of South America.
(4) Significance:
   (a) Although he did not know it, he had discovered a new land.
   (b) Bits of gold worn as ornaments by the Indians inspired hope in others for finding the sources of this gold and ultimate colonization.
   (c) Amerigo Vespucci, as a ship's navigator (first for Spain, then Portugal), named the lands he visited as "New World" because to his knowledge it was unknown to the ancients.
   (d) Others believed it to be a new land.
b. Ferdinand Magellan, a Portuguese navigator, sailing for Spain, led a sailing expedition around the world, 1520-1523.
(1) Discovery of Guam and the Philippines.
(2) Significance:
   (a) The existence of a new land proven.
   (b) A westerly, but unwieldy route found to the East.

3. England seeks a new route to the East.
a. John Cabot, an Italian sailing for England, finally convinced the King of England to finance a sailing expedition to the west to visit Japan.
(1) Voyages, 1497-1798, led to an exploration of the east coast of North America as far south as the Chesapeake Bay.
(2) Significance: established a claim for lands for England, but did not prompt further exploration.

4. France seeks a new route to the east.
a. Giovanni da Verrazano, an Italian sailing for France, was commissioned to find lands for settling and a westward passage through the new land to the East.
(1) Explored the east coast from what is the Carolinas to Labrador.
(2) Significance: established a claim for France in North America.
b. Jacques Cartier sought an all-water route to the East.
(1) 1534-35, found the mouth of the Saint Lawrence and sailed up it until stopped by rapids.

(2) Believed he had found the route, if only the rapids were cleared.

(3) Significance: heightened French interest in the New World.

5. Holland seeks a new route to the East.

   a. Henry Hudson, an Englishman sailing for Holland, sails in 1609 to seek a westward route to Asia.

     (1) Explores Hudson Bay and what is now the Hudson River.

     (2) Significance: established a claim for Holland to new lands.

6. Gradually interest in finding a westward passage to the East gave way to the interest in exploiting the new lands for profit.

   a. During the sixteenth century various Spanish expeditions set out to seek for gold and riches.

     (1) Many were unsuccessful.

       (a) 1528, Pánfilo de Narváez, expedition to Florida.

       (b) 1539-41, Hernando de Soto, expedition through the southeastern part of what is now the United States.

       (c) 1540-42, Francisco Coronado, the southwestern part of what is now the United States.

     (2) A few were remarkably successful

       (a) 1519-21, Hernando Cortés, conquered Mexico and wrestled gold and jewels as well as gold and silver mines.

       (b) 1531-33, Francisco Pizarro, conquered Peru and found vast quantities of gold and silver.

     (3) In seeking riches, the Spaniards also found excellent farmlands —leading to the colonization of the West Indies, Central America, and various parts of South America.

     (4) A share of the gold was set aside and sent to Spain for the King's treasury.

     (5) The land was held as the king's; he gave grants of it to leaders and his favorites.

     (6) Products from the land were to be sent to Spain.

     (7) Precious metals were of prime importance because it was believed that a nation's wealth was determined by the amount of gold and silver it had in its possession.

     (8) Spain's great wealth made it the most powerful of nations.

   b. During the sixteenth and seventeenth centuries, England, France, and Holland, aware of Spain's great wealth through colonization, sought also to exploit the new land.

     (1) English colonization.

       (a) Sir Walter Raleigh, 1587, organized and paid for an expedition to start a colony for seeking riches in Virginia; it failed.

(b) The London Company, 1607, a group of investors in England, financed an expedition for settling in America to seek riches and trade with the Indians—Jamestown.

[1] No riches found.

[2] Tobacco was found to be a profitable crop to raise and send to England.

[3] The colony succeeded.

[4] More and more settlers were wanted.

(c) The London Company gave permission to the English Pilgrims, a religious group, to settle in Virginia in 1620.

[1] Their ship blown off course.

[2] Settled in what is now Massachusetts.

[3] A successful colony.

(d) The Massachusetts Bay Company, formed by the Puritans, a religious group, settled in and around what is now Boston in 1630.

[1] A successful colony.

[2] Produced fish, farm products, fur, and lumber to be shipped to England.

(e) After these successful ventures, private individuals organized the settlement of colonies which became economic successes. The right to settle these lands was granted by the king—virtually a grant for a monopoly over the land.

[1] 1682, William Penn received lands in payment of a debt owed by the king to his father—Pennsylvania

[2] 1632, Lord Baltimore received lands from the king, but required to give the king one-fifth of all gold and silver found—Maryland.

[3] 1732, George Oglethorpe received lands to be developed as a barrier against the Spaniards to the south.

[4] 1670, a group of proprietors were granted the right to develop what is now the Carolinas.

(f) Such colonies as Delaware and Rhode Island were colonies split off other colonies for various reasons.

(2) Dutch colonization: by the Dutch West India Company was granted a charter by the government of the Netherlands—trade and settlement—1621.

(a) New Amsterdam (now New York)

(b) Fort Orange (now Albany)

(c) Economic organization

[1] Fur trade with the Indians

[2] Farm products

[3] Patroon system used to encourage farm production.

(3) French colonization:

    (a) Samuel de Champlain, 1608, explored the St. Lawrence River and Valley, established settlements at Quebec and Montreal.

    [1] Fur trade with the Indians

    [2] Feudal system of farm production established from parcels of land given by the king to his favorites.

    (b) 1718, New Orleans established after exploration of the Mississippi by Joliet, Marquette, and La Salle.

    (c) Other French settlements, for the most part trade settlements, in the Great Lakes and Ohio River valley areas.

c. As far as the United States area was concerned, Spanish settlement was more for political and religious reasons than for economic reasons.

    1) The richest production system was established in the Santa Fe area of New Mexico in 1609.

        (a) Pueblo skills exploited to produce precious metals and articles of gold and silver.

        (b) A feudal system prevailed.

    (2) In 1565, St. Augustine, Florida, founded by Pedro Menendez, to protect Spanish shipping.

    (3) In 1715, settlements made in southern Texas to strengthen Spanish claims there.

    (4) In 1769, Spanish missionaries under the leadership of Father Junípero Serra, established a series of missions from San Diego to the San Francisco area.

        (a) Basic purpose: to Christianize the Indians

        (b) Auxiliary purpose: to teach the Indians how to exploit available natural resources.

    (5) Compared to the easily acquired wealth from the mines of Mexico and Peru, the available wealth in the southwest area of the United States seemed quite poor.

Materials (F)

*Story of the American Nation, Casner, Gabriel, and Hartley (sufficient copies for classroom distribution).

*Encyclopedia of American History, Morris.

*American Historical Documents, Harvard Classics (excerpts duplicated for classroom distribution).

*The Rise of the West, McNeill.

American History Told by Contemporaries, Vol. 1, Hart (excerpts duplicated for classroom distribution).

Procedures (F)

Discussion stimulators: At this point of our study we have arrived at the idea that man's regard for his standard of living had something to do with the discovery and colonization of America. Do you think men felt that each was to be concerned about his standard of living and to do what he could to change it, or do you think men thought that concern for the standard of living of each person rested with the government?

Let's compare our idea with those of McNeill *(The Rise of The West,* p. 10). What could individual men do for themselves? Which individuals would most likely be able to follow their concern?

Discussion pointers: When you were in fifth grade you studied about the discovery, exploration, and colonization of America. Let's make a chart of the facts that you can recall. Which European countries were highly involved? Who were the men who made the discoveries and explorations? Do you think that these were the only countries and men involved? Could there have been others?

Usually a common era of history is repeated so many times that it becomes regarded as a complete parcel of knowledge. You have just indicated one expression of a complete parcel of knowledge in the chart that we have just made. Let's take a look at another such parcel as expressed in a textbook written for eighth-grade boys and girls *(Story of the American Nation,* pp. 14-66). Do we have a larger parcel now? Why? Do you think it is as complete as it can be? That it expresses all the important findings of American historians? Let's check in the *Encyclopedia of American History.* How can we account for the differences?

Let's adopt the role of historian for a short while. Again we must admit our limitations because of having to work with translations of documents, but let's see what we can find out about Columbus and his ideas about his discoveries *(American Historical Documents,* p. 22-46; *American History Told by Contemporaries,* pp. 44-48); how some of Cabot's contemporaries regarded his exploits *(American History Told by Contemporaries,* pp. 69-72); the strong feeling between England and Spain as seen in a pirate's account *(American History Told by Contemporaries,* pp. 75-81); the reactions of explorers and colonizers to the new land *(American History Told by Contemporaries,* pp. 89-132, 136-144); and conditions of colonization *(American Historical Documents,* pp. 51-61; *American History Told by Contemporaries,* 167-214).

Idea refiners: Remembering that we have looked only at excerpts of most of the documents, and accepting the fact that the collections represent only a small part of the documents produced during the period, we face the basic problem faced by many historians—just what statements of truth can we make on the basis of our findings? How true will any statement be? How can be validate them? Are our statements in agreement with what is offered in the *Story of the American Nation?* What general statement can we make about the events and conditions that led to the discovery, exploration, and colonization of America?

Do you agree with the diagram in *Visual History of the United States* (p. 11)?

Background for Cognitive and Affective Learnings

1. Spanish, French, and Dutch patterns of economic organization for exploitation of natural resources were successful for a time.

   a. The Spanish *encomienda* system.

      (1) A grant of land was given to a court favorite or to someone who had performed a valuable service.

      (2) So much of the products of the land to be given to the king.

      (3) Indians were used as the labor force.

      (4) Particularly successful in working the gold and silver mines.

      (5) Arable land well tilled provided for the subsistence needs of the settlers.

      (6) The *encomienda* was successful until ideas of individual freedom served to cause a revolt against it.

   b. The French: two patterns of economic exploitation.

      (1) Fur trade.

         (a) Establish friendly relations with the Indians.

         (b) Individual, adventurous traders trade with the Indians for furs.

         (c) Very successful.

      (2) Land-grant system.

         (a) The king gives a grant of land to a favorite.

         (b) The favorite arranged for tenants to come to the new land to farm for him.

         (c) The favorite was a landlord who took part of the crops from his tenants, charged them for basic services, and ruled them.

         (d) Largely a failure, because it was difficult to find men who wanted to leave France for such work.

   c. The Dutch: a commercial system built upon investment.

      (1) The Dutch West India Company chartered by the government

in 1621 to trade with the Indians and settle the new lands.

(2) Fur trade was successful.

(3) To settle the land, the company offered free land to individuals.

(a) To wealthy men who would bring fifty families to do the farming.

(b) Small farms to men who lacked wealth.

(4) Individual prosperity limited so much that the colonists allowed the colony to be taken by the English without a fight.

2. The types of economic organization for the exploitation of resources varied in the English colonies, and none was successful from a business point of view.

a. The company system (examples: the Virginia Company, the London Company, and the Massachusetts Bay Company). Operation:

(1) Investors buy shares in the company.

(2) Proceeds from the sale of shares finance settlers.

(3) Proceeds from the labor of the settlers to go to the investors over a period of years.

(4) At the close of a specified number of years, the settlers and shareholders to divide the land between them.

(5) A settler could also be a shareholder.

2. b. The proprietary system. Operation:

(1) A grant of land given to an individual by the king.

(2) A token fee given each year to the king.

(3) The proprietor exacted a fixed annual tax from the settler.

(4) The proprietor also sold land outright.

(5) Although the grant was free to him, the proprietor had sunk large sums of money into his colony.

c. Reasons for failure.

(1) No gold or silver available for an immediate return of profit.

(2) Land, the richest resource, required a long period of time before it could produce well.

(3) In many instances, what could be produced on the land could be produced just as well in England.

(4) Fur resources limited because of difficulties with the Indians.

(5) Fish resources required time for development.

3. Failure or success, the establishment of each colony brought a higher level of economic welfare to many Europeans.

a. In the Spanish colonies, many of the lesser nobility were far better off than if they had stayed in Spain.

b. In the French colonies, the numerous traders found a permanent home and greater freedom than they had known in France.

    c. In the Dutch colony, many individuals could own land, something all but impossible in the Netherlands.

    d. In the English colonies, large numbers of land-hungry people had established themselves and begun to prosper.

4. In the English colonies, greater provisions were made for individual prosperity as an important motivative force; therefore, when the investment schemes failed, the colonies continued to grow as an economic unit in the British Empire.

    a. Individual prosperity.

        (1) Supported by Colonialism in New England.

            (a) Prosperity as a sign of God's grace.

            (b) Dignity of labor.

            (c) Evil of idleness.

        (2) Notions of free enterprise in other colonies.

            (a) To develop trade and limited manufacturing in the Middle Atlantic colonies.

            (b) To develop the plantation system in the South for the production of tobacco, indigo, and rice.

    b. Abundance of resources and capital goods for an agrarian society.

        (1) Subsistence farming guaranteed a living.

        (2) Soil and climate in some places good for exotic crops—tobacco, indigo, and rice.

        (3) Most tools could be made locally.

    c. Transportation   lack and abundance of raw materials led to the development of a large shipping system.

4. d. An efficient, aggressive system of economic organization was developed.

        (1) A lively business of trade developed to bypass the limitations of the British Navigation and Trade acts which limited colonial economic intercourse to England.

            (a) Surpluses shipped to England as raw materials.

            (b) Manufactured goods shipped from England.

    c. Transportation lack and abundance of raw materials led to the (which was permitted) to buy English manufactured goods.

        (2) An efficient, although sometimes morally suspect by modern standards, labor force was maintained.

            (a) Efficient craftsmen.

            (b) Indentured servants.

            (c) Slaves.

(d) Apprenticeship.

(e) Tenant farmers.

(3) The merchant was considered one of the most respected persons in the community.

5. There was a place in the colonial economic structure, particularly in the English colonies, for every European, regardless of occupation or social status, plus the hope for improvement.

6. Many American traditional values about the individual and his responsibility to and for himself for his own economic welfare crystalized during the colonial period.

a. Extensive and varied use of natural resources to maintain and raise the level of economic welfare.

(1) In the face of limitations, ways are found to assure a continuing abundance of goods and services.

(a) In the colonial era

[1] The colonists, particularly the earlier ones, worked hard to make the wild land productive.

[2] The later colonists devised a trade system to bypass the English Navigation and Trade Acts.

[3] Throughout the colonial period, individuals were encouraged to settle new lands.

(b) In the modern era

[1] Modern industry seeks constantly to make better use of resources with the least amount of waste.

[2] Modern industry recognizes the need for government regulation, but competes within it to maintain production.

(2) New demand for goods and services are being continually created and met.

(a) In the colonial era

[1] The colonists worked to improve their living conditions in the early years.

[2] In later years, craftsmen set up shops and home factories.

[3] Apprenticeship periods were shortened from seven to three or four years.

[4] Merchants invested heavily in shipping ventures to provide desired goods.

[5] Advertising played a large part in selling and competing for sales.

[6] Traveling merchants and craftsmen carried goods and

services to the less thickly settled areas.

[7] There was always a demand for more workers, particularly in the crafts.

(b) In the modern era

[1] It is an American value that a man should strive throughout his lifetime to better his standard of living.

[2] Vast, new industrial complexes are being developed everywhere.

[3] The standard of living continues to rise.

[4] Well-trained, high-level craftsmen are in constant demand.

[5] Advertising creates demands competitively.

[6] Transportation and communication facilities serve to overcome the obstacles of time and space in production and distribution of goods.

(3) Individual enterprise in the beneficial exploitation of natural resources is always encouraged.

(a) In the colonial era

[1] Individuals were encouraged to settle new land.

[2] Social rank and occupation were no bar to developing a business within the available resources.

[3] Resourcefulness and ambition were highly prized virtues.

(b) In the modern era

[1] Items (2) and (3) above apply today .

[2] Free public education is pointed toward encouraging resourcefulness and requisite skills.

[3] Land reclamation and improvement as a governmental responsibility still serves to encourage individual enterprise.

[4] Monopoly is discouraged.

b. Although the interpretation of it has constantly changed, the basic idea of the dignity of labor is maintained.

(1) The efficiency of productive labor is maintained.

(a) In the colonial era

[1] In the early days, idleness was punished.

[2] Survival was impossible without a large expenditure of effort.

[3] A decent living was available for all who would work.

[4] Indenturing made it possible for a person to get to new land and opportunity by his own efforts.

[5] Apprenticing boys usually assured a basic education as well as a trade.

(b) In the modern era

[1] Modern public education supports preparation for entry into the labor force.

[2] Labor, through unionization, has become a force in its own right in the preservation of the dignity of labor.

(2) Predatory labor is discouraged.

(a) In the colonial era

[1] In the early days, any antisocial act involving stealing, swindling, and the like was harshly punished, sometimes without due process of law.

[2] In the later days, legal procedures were used to discourage swindling, cheating, and the like.

(b) In the modern era

[1] Legal provisions protect the investor and the consumer.

[2] In some instances, behavioral scientists seek to find ways to discover why some persons are predatory workers.

[3] Rehabilitation for honest labor is the aim of many penal institutions.

c. The need for capital goods to maintain production of goods and services is commonly recognized.

(1) In the colonial era

(a) Many colonial manufacturers recognized the need for capital goods—some had succeeded in smuggling plans for machinery from England.

(b) Ship building was well developed; transportation and trade were well developed.

(c) Craftsmen, such as blacksmiths, were in high demand, because of their ability to make tools.

(d) Ways of working with money as capital had been well developed.

(2) In the modern era

(a) Large areas in modern cities are given over to holding capital goods.

(b) Many industries produce capital goods of all kinds and provide maintenance services.

(c) Capital goods have come to mean such intangibles as good will and patent rights.

d. Managerial responsibility is highly respected.

(1) In the colonial era
  (a) In the earlier days, the merchants were suspect and not highly regarded.
  (b) In the later days, their ability, courage, and centrality for providing needed goods were recognized.
  (c) The independent craftsmen who sold his own products was a highly valued person in his community.
  (d) Manufacturing and trade endeavors were often supported by investments.
(2) In the modern era
  (a) The businessman is one of the most respected men in the community.
  (b) Trust in the managerial function has encouraged a wide structure of investment.
  (c) Modern public education supports preparation for the managerial function.
  e. Economic motivation has always been a force in the progress of man, but the Crusades and subsequent related events account at least in part for the level of economic welfare enjoyed in America today.

Materials

*Living Documents in American History, Scott (excerpts duplicated for classroom distribution).
*Basic History of American Business, Cochran.
*Visual History of the United States, Faulkner.
• A collection of newspaper editorial pages for classroom distribution.
*Information Please Almanac (sufficient copies for classroom distribution).
*World Book Encyclopedia.

Procedures:

Discussion stimulators: During the sixteen and seventeenth centuries Europeans came to colonize parts of what is now the United States. The reasons for their coming include the desire to enjoy a better standard of living. There are several choices open for an individual who wishes to do this. What do you think they are? Which of these choices would be the most preferred by men coming to an undeveloped area? Which would be the greater gamble? Which would be surer?

Discussion pointers: Here is one historian's interpretation (Visual History of the United States, p. 13) of how the early settlers chose to work at achieving a better standard of living. Let's analyze it to see what it really means. (Clarify encomienda, land-grant system, commercial system.)

Were these choices open to all individuals? Could there have been a labor problem? Have you any ideas on how this problem was solved?

Let's examine some early documents as historians would to see how the problem was solved (*Living Documents in American History,* pp. 70-89, 91-106; *Basic History of American Business,* pp. 101-103).

We know that eventually the French, Dutch, and Spanish lost their claims to the territory that now makes up the United States. We know that many of the early ventures to colonize failed. There is something in the documents that suggests why some ventures succeeded while others failed. What are your ideas about this?

It is true that business ventures—the profit motive—had much to do with getting settlers to America. Assuming that these ventures were successful, if only for a short time, could we say that only the investors profited? Could the workers have profited also?

If we analyze this interpretation of American history (*Visual History of the United States,* p. 15) as related to English motives for colonization, we may find some parallels with our own interpretation to this point.

Let's compare this interpretation with another (*Basic History of American Business,* pp. 9-28).

Idea refiners: Let us consider at this point one problem which most of you have. Most of you want things, some of them quite costly, such as your own private television or stereo, or perhaps a complete set of ski equipment or a motorbike. How do your parents react when you ask them to buy these things for you? What do they say—after the initial shock, that is? What do they often suggest as the means for obtaining the things that you want?

Now let us consider you for a moment. Can you think of reasons for wanting these things? Do you think that a French or German boy or girl of your age would be likely to make such requests of their parents? Can you think of a reason for your wanting these things that is not purely personal?

Where do you think that these ideas about wanting things that you think will make you happier and about working to obtain them came from?

Now let's explore some of the ideas that we cling to as being good. These ideas are about our ways of using our natural resources, the production and consumption of goods, how to regard businessmen and labor, and our preparing for future occupations? Let's analyze these editorial pages from the newspaper—almost everyone refers to at least a couple of these ideas.

What is the source of these ideas?

We have made a good case for the desire to have a standard of living as being a force in the beginning of America and for making the way it is today. Can you think of any other forces? The diagrams on pages 15 and 19 in *Visual History of the United States* will give you some hints. Which of these forces do you think is the strongest? Does time and prevailing conditions of various kinds make any difference?

How about the beginning of other nations during the past two hundred years? Canada? Australia? New Zealand? New African Countries? How shall we check on these quickly?

Suppose that we were to develop a history of our area that showed the development of industry from its beginning to date. How would we go about it?

INDEX